A Brontë Encyclopedia

A Brontë Encyclopedia

Robert Barnard and Louise Barnard

Blackwell
Publishing

© 2007 by Blackwell Publishing

BLACKWELL PUBLISHING
350 Main Street, Malden, MA 02148-5020, USA
9600 Garsington Road, Oxford OX4 2DQ, UK
550 Swanston Street, Carlton, Victoria 3053, Australia

The right of Robert Barnard and Louise Barnard to be identified as the Authors of this
Work has been asserted in accordance with the UK Copyright, Designs, and Patents Act 1988.

First published 2007 by Blackwell Publishing Ltd

1   2007

Library of Congress Cataloging-in-Publication Data

Barnard, Robert.
   A Brontë encyclopedia / Robert Barnard and Louise Barnard.
      p. cm.
   Includes bibliographical references.
   ISBN 978-1-4051-5119-1 (hardcover : alk. paper)   1. Brontë family—Encyclopedias.
2. Women and literature—England—History—19th century—Encyclopedias.   3. Novelists,
English—19th century—Biography—Encyclopedias.   4. Yorkshire (England)—Intellectual
life—Encyclopedias.   5. Women novelists, English—Biography—Encyclopedias.   6. Yorkshire
(England)—In literature—Encyclopedias.   7. English fiction—Women authors—Encyclopedias.
8. English fiction—19th century—Encyclopedias.   I. Barnard, Louise   II. Title.

PR4167.A3B76 2007
823′.809—dc22

                                                                    2006036993

A catalogue record for this title is available from the British Library.

Set in 10.5/13pt Minion
by Graphicraft Limited, Hong Kong
Printed and bound in Singapore
by Markono Print Media Pte Ltd

For further information on
Blackwell Publishing, visit our website:
www.blackwellpublishing.com

Contents

Illustrations

Abbreviations

Preface

This encyclopedia of the Brontës concerns itself with the family, their writings, and their lives. It tries to cover their own characters and experiences; the people they met, corresponded with, or were influenced by; the places they went to; and their works from the juvenile and adolescent sagas to the finished fiction and poetry. We took therefore, when conceiving it, the period between the dates 1777 (the birth of Patrick) and 1861 (his death) as our chosen focus of interest, though inevitably there is the occasional peek backward or forward.

This means that we have not dealt with ups and downs in the fortunes of the Brontës' writings after their deaths; the critical fashions which have promoted or demoted their literary status; the checkered fortunes of their manuscripts; the dramatic, musical, or film and television versions of their novels and even of their lives, and so on. These posthumous developments tell us more about the ages in which they occurred and the people that were involved in them than they do about the Brontës themselves, and their inclusion could only be justified if they were given a full social context – something out of the question in a work of comparatively modest size. It may well be, too, that early exposure to a television adaptation of *Wuthering Heights*, with Yvonne Mitchell doing her mature best as Catherine, and Richard Todd hilarious as Heathcliff, put me off adaptations for life.

We early on took the decision that the early writings could not be allowed to over-balance the book. We include summaries of all the novels, and brief or extensive entries on virtually all the characters, but that breadth of treatment could not be given to the tales and characters in the early works. The progress of the sagas, with treatment of the most important stories, is therefore mainly covered in the entry called for convenience "Juvenilia," and about 20 characters are given an entry to themselves. Fascinating though this writing is, and quite as extensive as the mature novels, we believe that the average reader will be mainly interested in the novels that the Brontës' reputation has been built on, and that can be read by an adult reader without the need to make allowances.

The last 20 years have seen "an abundant shower" of works of Brontë scholarship, and unlike the shower of curates in *Shirley* it has been scholarly, responsible, and wonderfully useful. Among many works I would name Juliet Barker's authoritative and (almost a first among biographies of the Brontës) scholarly life of the whole family, Christine Alexander's edition of Charlotte's early writings (1829–35), Victor Neufeldt's edition of Branwell's complete writings, Alexander and Sellars' *The Art of the Brontës*, Sue Lonoff's masterly edition of Charlotte and Emily's Brussels essays, Dudley Green's edition of Patrick's letters, and perhaps above all Margaret Smith's wonderful and nourishing edition of Charlotte's letters. Works such as these have undone the malign activities of Thomas J. Wise, the forger and literary con man, and his aide Clement Shorter. They have also made the writing of a book such as this immeasurably easier and more pleasant. We can only breathe fervent praise and thanks.

We are indebted to many people: three generations of curators and one of librarians (Ann Dinsdale, a constant help) at the Brontë Parsonage Museum, with special thanks to Linda Proctor-Mackley for help with the pictures; librarians and curatorial staff at the Bankside Museum in Halifax, the Keighley Public Library, the Brotherton Library at Leeds University, and the private Leeds Library, where one can still read the local papers of the first half of the nineteenth century in their original form, the National Portrait Gallery, and the Theatre Museum in (or once in) Covent Garden. Many individuals have been a great help and inspiration, including Dudley Green, Sarah Fermi, Ian and Catherine Emberson, Robin Greenwood, Steven Woods, and the late Chris Sumner. Our debts to Jenny Roberts, for pointing out errors, omissions, inconsistencies are legion. We are particularly indebted to Brian Wilks and to the Lambeth Palace Library for permission to quote from the recently discovered letter Patrick wrote to Bishop Longley shortly after Charlotte's death.

One of the strangest things about the Brontës (a reclusive family, apart from Branwell) is that objects associated with them keep appearing and new connections continue to be made. For example, in the last 30 years three new pictures of the Brontë women have surfaced, as well as an early photograph of the "Gun Group," which was later destroyed by Mr Nicholls, all but the portrait of Emily. After *The Art of the Brontës* was published many new pictures by them came to light. As I write, a hitherto unknown letter by Charlotte to W. S. Williams is coming up for sale at auction. All these discoveries feed the public interest in the family and their writings, and it has been a great joy during our years of connection with the Brontë Society to keep up with them and now to use some of them in this encyclopedia. We often wonder how many items of Brontëana remain hidden (deliberately or inadvertently) in Haworth.

The division of labor for this work has been as follows: Louise Barnard has trawled through years of local newspapers, particularly the Leeds ones, for items of interest about the Brontës and people known to them; she has kept an immense computer record of everything of interest about anyone whose life, however tangentially, touched the Brontës, and this record will be lodged in the Parsonage Library, where we hope it will be of use to scholars, genealogists, local historians, and so on. Robert Barnard is responsible for choosing which heads in her record would have an entry in the encyclopedia, and for writing all but one of those entries. We can therefore accept joint responsibility for any errors that have inevitably crept in.

Robert Barnard
Louise Barnard

Note on Spelling

We have avoided the insertion of "[sic]" in quotations from the original nineteenth-century sources, particularly Charlotte Brontë's letters. The reader can assume that spellings and punctuation that appear to be incorrect are reproduced as in the original manuscripts.

As Blackwell publications are marketed worldwide American spelling conventions have been followed.

Acknowledgments

The authors are grateful to the directors and staff at the following institutions for permission to use images in their collections:

The National Portrait Gallery, London for plates 16, 19, 34, 39 and colour plate 5.

The Brotherton Library, Leeds University for plates 25 and 28.

The Victoria and Albert Museum (Theatre Museum Collection) for plate 32.

Keighley Public Library for plate 21.

The Bankfield Museum, Calderdale MBC – Museums and Arts for colour plate 6.

The authors are also grateful to the following owners for permission to use material in their possession: Lord Shuttleworth for plate 20; Simon Warner, for colour plates 9 and 10; Monsieur Pechere for colour plate 7.

All other plates are from the Brontë Parsonage Museum, and our grateful thanks are due to the museum director for permission, and to the library staff, who were endlessly helpful.

A

A——: the "fashionable watering place" where the Greys set up their school in *Agnes Grey*. Anne mentions "the semi-circular barrier of craggy cliffs surmounted by green swelling hills" (ch. 24), and the town is almost certainly based on Scarborough.

A——: the river on which Millcote stands in *Jane Eyre* (v. 1, ch. 10). Millcote is probably Leeds, and A– therefore the river Aire, which may also have suggested Jane's surname.

A——, Monsieur: French academician before whom Ginevra Fanshawe displays her vanity and empty-headedness in *Villette*, pointing a contrast with Paulina de Bassompierre (see chs. 26 & 27).

Abbey, The: one of the *Lady's Magazine* novels that Charlotte ironically suggested she might have emulated if she had been writing 30 or 40 years earlier (to Hartley Coleridge, 10 Dec 1840). Margaret Smith tentatively identifies this as *Grasville Abbey* by G. M. (George Moore), published in the magazine in the 1790s.

Abbott, Joseph, Rev. (1789–1863): a man who knew Maria Branwell shortly before her marriage. He wrote to Charlotte in 1851 about Luddite activity in the Leeds area in 1812, and how frightened Maria was by his story of an encounter with a band of Luddites (Barker, 1994, pp. 53, 666). By then he was Registrar of McGill College in Montreal. He had heard the later story of the Brontë family from the loquacious Dr. Scoresby, and had been particularly delighted to read *Shirley*, covering as it did events in which he had played a small part.

See also Scoresby, Rev. William

Abbot, Martha: Mrs Reed's personal maid in *Jane Eyre*. A bitter, censorious self-server who dislikes Jane, though she is sharp enough to notice that she "always looked as if she were watching everybody" (v. 1 ch. 3).

Abbotsford: the home of Sir Walter Scott, near the town and abbey of Melrose, in the Borders area of southern Scotland. He bought the farmhouse in 1811, and greatly expanded it in a romantic baronial style. It was here that most of his major fiction was written. Charlotte visited the house during her brief Scottish holiday in July 1850. "[A]s to Melrose and Abbotsford the very names possess music and magic," she wrote to Laetitia Wheelwright (30 July 1850).

See also Melrose; Scott, Sir Walter

Abercromby, General Sir Ralph (1734–1801): Scottish soldier and MP. Served in Holland, the West Indies, and Ireland. In 1801 he was given command of the expedition to the Mediterranean. He led a successful expedition to effect a landing at Aboukir Bay (near Alexandria), but was mortally wounded there. Charlotte used his valor and death in her Brussels *devoir* "*La Prière du Soir dans un camp.*"

Adelaide: one of the parsonage geese, named after the Queen Consort of William IV, and mentioned in Emily's diary paper of 30 July 1841. In the next diary paper (30 July 1845) she records that the geese were "given away," presumably during her stay in Brussels.

Adrianopolis: the capital of Zamorna's newly bestowed kingdom of Angria, the building of which is described in sections of the juvenilia mainly dated 1834. The splendid (perhaps oversplendid) city attracts the new and would-be rich, and its combination of opulence and vulgarity is perhaps an image of its creator, Zamorna himself.

See also Juvenilia, 3. The rise of Angria

Adrienne Lecouvreur: play by Ernest Legouvé and Eugene Scribe which Charlotte saw in London (7 June 1851), with Rachel in the title role: "her acting was something apart from any other acting it has come in my way to witness – her soul was in it – and a strange soul she has" Charlotte wrote to Amelia Taylor (11 June 1851). Scribe's play was at the time only three years old. Scribe is best remembered today as the creator of the "well-made play" – beautifully carpentered, but essentially trivial dramas for a fashionable audience. He also wrote many opera libretti, but Cilea's opera on the subject dates from much later (1902).

See also Rachel; Vashti

"Advantages of Poverty in Religious Concerns, The": essay by Maria Branwell, the mother of the Brontës, and the only non-personal writing we have from her. It is well-meaning but clichéd in thought and expression. It attempts to prove that "a wretched extremity of poverty is seldom experienced in this land of general benevolence," and if it is, "the sufferers bring it on themselves." The arguments paraded are familiar ones, though when she talks of "the pride and prejudices of learning and philosophy" one feels that Patrick would have seen a less Austenish and more positive side to mental and moral education. The essay was probably written during her married life for possible insertion in the Christian magazines, to which Patrick also contributed. No contemporary published version has been found.

Aeschylus: Greek dramatist mentioned in Charlotte's early writings (e.g., "The Foundling"). Some fragmentary notes by Emily on his plays are in the Walpole Collection at The King's School, Canterbury.

Aesop: Greek writer of fables of the sixth century BC. Referred to in *The Professor* and in various letters from Charlotte to Ellen Nussey. One of the Brontës' earliest games, the play "Our Fellows," was directly inspired by him: "The people we took out of Aesops *Fables*" wrote Charlotte. ("The origin of the O'Deans," EW, v. 1, p. 6).

Agnes (no surname given): cantankerous old servant of Mme Walravens in *Villette*. She was formerly the servant of M. Paul's father and his family, and is when we meet her the recipient of his charity.

Agnes Grey (1847): possibly the work entitled *Passages in the Life of an Individual* which Anne's Diary Paper of July 1845 records herself as being engaged with. It is the archetypal "governess" novel as *Jane Eyre* is not, because it focuses mainly on the experience of teaching within a family unit. In its broad sweep the plan of the novel follows Anne's own experience: cosseted girlhood, followed by a short first situation, which provides her with a sharp shock, and then a second, much longer, one, in which her ideals and her moral standards are subjected to a slow disillusionment, and can be preserved only by strong personal tenacity.

Agnes begins her teaching life with the disadvantage of an almost total ignorance of the world and its values, brought about by the cloying determination of her family that she should remain their "baby." She explicitly ridicules in the first chapter her own illusion that a governessing career will be, in James Thomson's words, a "Delightful task!/ To teach the young idea how to shoot!" The Bloomfield family, her first employers, turn out to consist of children who are little short of monsters, and parents who have no idea of improving their behavior by any sensible system of learning, let alone by any inculcation of a moral framework.

Quite soon into her second situation, with the Murray family, Agnes sees the worldliness of the parents as the principal danger, and this time the danger threatens her as well as her pupils. The girls she teaches are much older than the Bloomfield children, and therefore already well on the way to corruption. Agnes fails to halt this, and the eldest daughter only begins to have a realization that Agnes's ideals might represent a better way than the one her family has shown her after she has fallen into a loveless marriage made for social and mercenary reasons.

It is significant that the last chapters of the book show Agnes not employed in a family environment, but running a small school with her mother. This, Anne seems to be saying, is the best form of education: one that can counteract the materialism and spiritual vacuity of the middle- and upper-class English family.

In the later chapters of the novel a rather pallid romance develops between Agnes and a clergyman, Mr Weston. Of more interest are the characters outside the Murray family, particularly Nancy Brown, a peasant woman, and Mr Hatfield, the local rector. The first displays a simple faith that contrasts with the Murrays' religion that is corrupted by their social values; the second shows how even a representative of religion can be tainted by worldliness and an obsession with personal and social advancement.

Discussion of the first novel of Anne, a much more even achievement than her second, has been twisted by a determination to turn it into a novelized autobiography. It is not that, and Anne's young life is followed in its trajectory, not in its details. It is a rich, amusing, sly work, and in its short compass tells one more about the life of a governess or teacher than any of the other Brontë novels.

See also Ingham family of Blake Hall; Robinson, Rev. Edmund; Robinson, Edmund; Robinson, Elizabeth; Robinson, Lydia (née Gisborne); Robinson, Lydia; Robinson, Mary

Aigredoux, Madame (no first name given): former schoolmistress of Paulina de Bassompierre. She asked Paulina to leave the school after her father came to see her every other day. See *Villette*, ch. 25.

Ainley, Miss Mary Anne: an ugly spinster in the parish of Briarfield in *Shirley*. Though ridiculed by the young, she is indefatigable in genuinely useful good work among the poor, and she is called in by Shirley when she determines on a comprehensive plan to relieve poverty. She is one of those whose lives are seen as exemplifying the possible fates of middle-class women by Caroline Helstone. Her life and character are analyzed in ch. 10: "Old Maids."

See also Mann, Miss

Aked, Robert: printer and bookseller of Low Street, Keighley. He printed Patrick's pamphlets "The Signs of the Times" (1835) and "A Brief Treatise on the Best Time and Mode of Baptism" (1836). He seems also to have run at some time a circulating library, though it is not known whether the Brontës patronized any such private establishment. Their father became a member of the Keighley Mechanics' Institute, which had a library, in the year 1832–3.

Akroyd, Revd. Thomas: a Wesleyan clergyman, native of the Halifax area, but ministering in South Liverpool. In 1857 he visited Haworth and met Patrick and Martha Brown. His account of the visit has been republished in BST 19 parts 1 & 2 (1986), and in Lemon (1996, pp. 35–40).

Alexander, Miss (first name unknown): an admirer of Charlotte from Wakefield, daughter of a Dr Alexander, living at Lupset Cottage. After her first letter, enquiring about the *Poems*, Charlotte wrote to Ellen Nussey (28 Jan 1850?) asking if she knew anything of her, but did not reply to her. After her second letter Charlotte replied (18 Mar 1850) but warned her that "it is scarcely worth your while to send for" the *Poems* – hardly fair on her sisters' contributions, or on her publishers who had taken over the volume, and inconsistent with what she had written of Emily's poetic gifts in the "Biographical Notice of Ellis and Acton Bell."

Allbutt, Mrs George (née Anna Maria Brooke) (b. 1818): wife of a Batley surgeon, and one of Ellen Nussey's circle. Charlotte occasionally sends conventional greetings to her, and expresses concern at her family's limited income, but it is presumably to this lady she refers when she writes, of Mme Heger, that "as to warmheartedness She has as much of that article as Mrs Allbutt" (to EN, late June 1843?).

Allbutt, Marianne (née Wooler) (1801–43): wife of the below-mentioned Thomas. She was in her mid-thirties when she married, but bore him at least two children (see below). Before marriage she had done some teaching at Roe Head School. Charlotte, years after her death, commented with approval that, though "tender and thoughtful" to her children, she "would not permit them to become tyrants" (to MW, 30 Aug 1853).

Allbutt, Rev. Thomas (1800–67): brother-in-law to Margaret Wooler, curate and later vicar of Dewsbury. It was when he succeeded John Buckworth as vicar that he was able to marry Marianne Wooler ("he did not shew himself mercenary in his first marriage" Charlotte wrote of him, 24 May 1848, when there seemed to be some question of his being interested in Ellen Nussey). He seems to have been a narrow evangelical: he advised Ellen against dancing, and he was shunned by Anne when she was going through a religious crisis in 1837.

Allbutt, Sir Thomas Clifford (1836–1925): son of the above two. He became a distinguished physician, claimed to have been the original of Lydgate in *Middlemarch* (G. S. Haight pours scorn on the claim in his *George Eliot*, 1968), and bequeathed Charlotte's letters to his aunt Margaret Wooler to the Fitzwilliam Museum, Cambridge. See H. Rolleston's *Life of Sir Clifford Allbutt* (1929) for his interesting and irreverent memories of the Brontë sisters.

allée défendue: a narrow, overgrown path in the gardens of the Pensionnat Heger, forbidden to the pupils because it bordered on a boys' school. Charlotte makes use of similar paths both in *The Professor* (see ch. 12) and *Villette* (ch. 12).

Allen, Anne: the gardener's wife at the Vicarage, Hathersage, who acted as servant and cook during Charlotte and Ellen Nussey's stay there in 1845.

Allison, William: coachman to the Robinson family, who later went to work for the man who was to become Mrs Robinson's second husband, Sir Edward Scott. It was almost certainly Allison who was sent to Haworth to break to Branwell the (untrue) story that by the will of her husband his widow would lose her inheritance if she saw Branwell again (letters of Branwell to J. B. Leyland, and Francis Henry Grundy, June 1846). The imprudence of Mrs Robinson in using her coachman to convey such intimate matters has been commented on, and he may have been privy to the affair throughout. He was paid, according to a Robinson account book, £3 "for journey" on 11 June 1846, shortly after the Rev. Edmund Robinson's funeral.

All Saints' Church, Cambridge: church where in 1806 Patrick's intention to be ordained was read out in the necessary *Si Quis*, and "no impediment was alleged," as Samuel Chilcote the curate certified.

All Saints' Church, Dewsbury: church where Patrick became curate in December 1809, remaining there until early 1811, some time after he had been appointed to the living of Hartshead. The church has been much altered since that time, notably in 1823, 1887, and most recently the early 1990s. The vicarage, where he lived with Rev. John Buckworth, was demolished in 1889.

All Saints' Church, Wellington, Shropshire: church where Patrick was curate from January 1809 to 4 December in the same year.

Allston, Washington (1779–1843): American artist, principally of landscapes, who trained in London and traveled extensively in Britain and Europe. Elected an Associate of the Royal Academy in 1818. Branwell made a version in oils from an engraving of one of his paintings, "Jacob's Dream." The *Penguin Dictionary of Art and Artists* notes Fuseli, Turner, and John Martin as among artists who influenced him – all artists to whom the Brontës were strongly attracted.

Ambleside: town in the Lake District where Harriet Martineau built her home The Knoll and tried to improve the educational standards and living conditions of the poor. Charlotte stayed there 16–23 Dec 1850.

American Review: periodical which contained a strongly hostile review of *Wuthering Heights* by G. W. Peck in its June 1848 issue. He was one of many Brontë reviewers who took them to task for "coarseness," repeating the word throughout his review. He also opined that "The whole tone of the style of the book smacks of lowness. It would indicate that the writer was not accustomed to the society of gentlemen" (in which he was certainly right). He also concedes "the rapid hold it has taken of the public," praises its "singularly effective and dramatic dialogue," and admits that "as a work of the imagination . . . it must take rank very high."

Anderson, John Wilson: Halifax-born artist, he was one of Branwell's artistic circle in Bradford in the late 1830s, but returned to Halifax to become keeper of the public baths. His life, and that of most of the circle, illustrates the precariousness of an artistic career in the area. His wife committed suicide by swallowing poison. "Reasons have been assigned for this dreadful act," said the *Leeds Intelligencer* darkly, "but whether correct or not we cannot vouch" (4 Nov 1837).

Anderton, Rev. William: a clergyman who took duties in Haworth both during the interregnum period before Patrick was accepted as perpetual curate, and again later (September 1821) at the time of Maria Brontë's final illness and death.

Andrew, Thomas: much-loved Haworth surgeon who probably died 3 May 1842. The monument to him was, thanks to Branwell, commissioned from J. B. Leyland, and was the subject of both meetings and correspondence, in which Branwell expressed some shame at the taste and manners of the Haworth worthies whom Leyland met. Andrew was, doubtless through extensive experience, an expert in treating typhus.

Andrews, Anna (later Mrs Hill): teacher, briefly superintendent, at Cowan Bridge School, said to be the original of Miss Scatcherd in *Jane Eyre*. Her name figured largely in the *Halifax Guardian* controversy over Cowan Bridge School, after the publication of Gaskell's *Life*, particularly in the exchanges between Arthur Nicholls and W. W. Carus Wilson, son of the school's founder. Later misunderstandings arose when this figure was confused with Miss Anne Evans, the original of Miss Temple. The fact seems to be that one of the defenders of the school in an American periodical, a woman married to the head of a college in Ohio called Hill, was taken to be the original of Miss Scatcherd. Sarah Fermi and Judith Smith have convincingly suggested that Miss Scatcherd was an amalgam of Anna Andrews Hill and an under-teacher at the school. They have unearthed fascinating evidence of Mrs Hill's activity in the Abolitionist cause in the US – evidence which casts her in a very different light from the sadistic figure we might assume from a simple identification with Miss Scatcherd (BST, v. 25, part 2, Oct 2000).

"And the Weary are at Rest": Branwell's last surviving attempt at fiction, probably written in 1845 if this is the "three volume *Novel* – one volume of which is completed" which he mentions to Leyland (10 Sep 1845?). The fragment begins in mid-sentence, and we do not know how much is lost that came before it, or indeed if anything more was written after what we have.

The fragment begins and ends with Alexander Percy's attempts to seduce Maria Thurston, whose husband is Percy's host at Darkwell Manor. Between these episodes is a long series of satiric scenes in which Percy and his usual associates, including Montmorency and Quashia, pass themselves off as enthusiastic dissenters. This section alone would in Victorian times render unpublishable any novel that contained it. As so often Branwell seemed to program himself for failure. The section long outstays its welcome, and even the seduction scenes lack force and focus. Though the setting is now England, with some very contemporary references (to the Duke of Devonshire's conservatory, for example, and Euston Square Station) the fictional techniques, and indeed the characters and situations, seem to have changed hardly a whit since the days of Angria. Branwell's fiction is still chronicle, something that goes on for as long as the author cares to continue it, but has no other shaping principle than that.

The missing first section was probably a reworking of the fragment Branwell wrote about the Thurstons in 1837 (see WPBB, v. 3, pp. 186–93), where Percy is launching a seduction while on a visit with his cronies to Darkwell Manor and its master, a man steeped in vice. The fact that the two fragments fit so easily together is an indication of the lack of development in Branwell's prose fiction compared to that of his sisters. In fact the two fragments are useful to show to people who believe Branwell could have written *Wuthering Heights.*

Angélique (no surname given): one of the troublesome pupils at Mme Beck's school in *Villette.* She tries to disrupt Lucy Snowe's first lesson (ch. 8), and is later seen at the concert (ch. 20).

Angria: Province and capital city in the Glasstown Federation, to the east of Glasstown itself. It is seldom referred to in the early juvenilia, seeming to be a personal fiefdom of Warner Howard Warner. It is a wild, remote area, sparsely populated, and modeled on Yorkshire. However, it is reluctantly awarded to Zamorna as his personal kingdom, a reward for his victories in the Wars of Encroachment, and it then becomes the center of interest for Charlotte, in particular in her writings after 1834. For a long time the name was used, misleadingly, as a generic term for the children's imaginary kingdom. From the start of its new status it is a brash, booming state, filled with the entrepreneurial spirit and ruled by someone who could be described as a cross between Henry V. and John F. Kennedy. The province is cruelly sacked and mismanaged during the civil wars, but its cities are rebuilt as fast as they were originally built, and they continue to prosper after the restoration of Zamorna, mellower and less hyperactive. His subjects are still seen as slightly vulgar and pushy, and contrasts are still drawn between its citizens and those of the more aristocratic cities of the Glasstown province.

See also Juvenilia, 3. The rise of Angria, 4. Angria redivivus; Zamorna

"Angria and the Angrians": Branwell's chronicle of events in Verdopolis and Angria subsequent to Zamorna's accession as king of the latter province. Enormously long (530 packed pages in WPBB), it was written between 1834 and 1839. The manuscript has been dispersed among many libraries, and sections are missing. We owe the whole to Neufeldt's reconstruction of many long and short fragments into a reasonably comprehensible whole. The work is treated in greater than usual detail here, because it is often our only source of information for events in the Glasstown civil war.

volume 1: This, the major section currently known, was written between May 1834 and January 1836. Angrian dates and British dates in this case coincide, as do some of the events: the period in Britain encompassed the dismissal by the king of Lord Melbourne's government, the minority government of Peel, and a bitterly fought general election. These events are mirrored, particularly in the later sections.

The first section (WPBB, v. 2, pp. 199–235) begins with the coronation of Zamorna and his Queen – a piece of pure 1930s Hollywood. The celebrations become riotous and ugly, but the real threat to the new kingdom comes from the East and from the black Africans. Richton, the narrator, travels to Adrianopolis as Verdopolis's Ambassador Plenipotentiary to the kingdom and sees the new, brash capital under construction. In Adrianopolis the two political heavyweights, Zamorna and Northangerland, are squaring up for a contest, both giving out enormously verbose addresses and proclamations. Then in sections 2 and 3 (WPBB, v. 2, pp. 236–77) Branwell indulges himself in lengthy parliamentary debates, lacking the point and vigor of earlier political brawls from him. Richton then hands over the narrator's role to Henry Hastings, who participated in the war with Quashia and the Ashantees.

This, Zamorna's second war, is precipitated by the Ashantees' slaughter of all the citizens of Dongola. Zamorna exhorts his men (in words that pre-echo Conrad's Kurtz) to "exterminate from the Earth the whole d–d race of Ashantees." His moral justification for this revenge is weakened by his claim that he had originally only come to the area "for the sole purpose of exterminating the Africans" (WPBB, v. 2, p. 303). The war is described in bloodthirsty detail and Hastings distinguishes himself, but Zamorna is (rather comically) diverted from his purpose by a by-election defeat in Adrianopolis. Hastings is sent to cover the events of peace as he already has covered those of the war.

The fourth and fifth sections (WPBB, v. 2, pp. 278–443) describe the victory of the "reform" party in general elections in Verdopolis, followed by attempts by the Verdopolitan government and the four kings to annul the grant of Angria to Zamorna as a fiefdom. As the volume ends Zamorna and Northangerland are, temporarily and uneasily, in alliance, and the whole country is on the verge of civil war.

volume 2: This part of Branwell's mammoth chronicle is more fragmentary than the first part, though Neufeldt believes that many fragments follow fairly closely on each other. The somewhat disordered impression may therefore be due more to Branwell's rambling style than to chicanery on the part of Thomas J. Wise, the vendor and dismemberer of Brontë manuscripts.

The first section (WPBB, v. 2, pp. 454–71) is narrated by Henry Hastings, who has been serving the Angrian army in a PR, tame historian position, and is now recalled to his company. However he is injured in battle, and the narrative becomes an omniscient, unattributed one.

The second section (WPBB, v. 2, pp. 272–8) is a scene between Northangerland, still nominally in the Angrian camp, and his old lover Louisa Vernon. Their daughter Caroline is present, and displays early signs of an obsession with Zamorna.

The third section is a tiny fragment, and the fourth (WPBB, v. 2, pp. 480–6) contains one of Branwell's growing number of drunken scenes, this one involving a raving Quashia and Northangerland.

The fifth section (WPBB, v. 2, pp. 496–9) reintroduces a recovered Henry Hastings as narrator. He is beginning to see the true natures of Northangerland and Zamorna: "Should our enemies even be annihilated, peace would not be gained. Mighty thoughts and immense ambition will only then develop themselves in a track of fiery light which all the world will behold as the path of Adrian and Alexander" (p. 497). The war for Angria as a semi-independent monarchy has begun, but not promisingly.

The sixth section (WPBB, v. 2, pp. 518–32) begins with one of Northangerland's mock-dissenter sermons, a new departure for Branwell, and continues with behind-the-front scenes from the war. It ends with a useful summary of the background to the war and the present belligerents.

The seventh section (WPBB, v. 2, pp. 533–60) returns to an omniscient narrator, and tells the story of Charles Wentworth, newly come into a fortune, who travels to Verdopolis to see the places and people of his adolescent dreams. Here he moons about listlessly for some time, until he is fired by the sight of Ellrington Hall and secures an interview with a skeptical and amused Northangerland, who involves him in his plots and projects for the developing war. Volume Two ends with an address by Northangerland to his supporters as the war reaches a crisis point.

Wentworth in Verdopolis is often taken, especially since Gerin's 1961 biography of Branwell, to be a fictionalized picture of that young man in London, unable to summon up the nerve to present himself at the Royal Academy. Even if, as is now believed, Branwell never went to London, the pages could be an imaginative projection of how he believed he would behave and feel. If so the picture of himself is far from flattering. Wentworth is an indecisive and spiritless creature for much of the time, with short-lasting bursts of action. He suffers from "aimless depression" and "a dissatisfied mind burdened with its mass of half-formed ideas" (WPBB, v. 2, pp. 537, 536). If this is a self-portrait it is one unusually lacking in self-promotion and self-deception.

volume 3: The first section (WPBB, v. 2, pp. 564–7) covers a visit to Northangerland from his mother. In a moving encounter she pleads with him not to disgrace himself by any further acts of treachery and treason. The next section (pp. 568–75) shows us Northangerland and his hangers-on planning to "throw this Metropolis into the utmost confusion" (p. 568). It continues with a cabinet meeting of the Marquis of Ardrah in Verdopolis, which is broken up by a rabble. The third section (pp. 576–9) begins with another summary of Northangerland's earlier career and ends with his oration to his victorious supporters, proclaiming one great Republic of Africa, with the abolition of all titles, the annihilation of the Church, the enactment of universal suffrage, with death for all who oppose the new regime. "We have undone everything but done nothing" he ominously proclaims (p. 578).

The fourth section (WPBB, v. 2, pp. 597–651) summarizes events in the early days of what appears to be Northangerland's absolute power. No whisper has made itself heard against his tyranny, and he has won a great victory over Zamorna at Edwardston, subsequently refusing to execute him, and instead exiling him to the Ascension Isle. Quashia drunkenly tells his fellow revolutionaries of the horrible death of Zamorna's eldest son, and we shift narration to Charles Wentworth, who gives a hideous account of the sufferings of Angria under the pitiless new regime. A scene between Northangerland and his mistress Georgiana Greville is interrupted by news of his daughter's approaching death. The death scene, which stretches Branwell to his limits, occupies the next 10 pages in Neufeldt. On his return to Verdopolis Northangerland hears of approaching mutiny in his army. He goes to the village of Northangerland where they are quartered, interrupts a drunken and quarrelsome meeting, and begins to assert his authority. We then switch to Warner addressing the motley collection of Zamorna-supporting militias, and this ends the very long section.

The fifth section (WPBB, v. 2, pp. 652–68) contains yet another recap on the history of Glasstown and Angria, the lives of Percy and his father, and also that of Zamorna. Why Branwell felt the need for another such summary is unclear.

volume 4: The work now degenerates, for the modern reader, into a series of fragments, mostly short. How much material is missing, how much never written, is unclear.

The first section (WPBB, v. 3, pp. 1–9) begins where Volume Three left off. Richton, the narrator, is sent with important strategic communications to Warner. All on the royalist side are anticipating the arrival of Zamorna, returned from exile. While talking to Warner, Richton learns that the Republicans, under Northangerland, are falling apart and fleeing. This section is followed by a piece of drunken knockabout comedy involving Quashia and black associates, ending in their flight.

The second section (WPBB, v. 3, pp. 10–13) takes place in Verdopolis, where Hector Montmorency has taken charge, but stares defeat and ruin in the face. The fragment ends with Zamorna and Fidena's army entering Verdopolis, and Montmorency and Quashia taking flight.

Section three is an interesting apologia by Branwell, in the person of Henry Hastings, the general tenor of which is that he is not as bad as rumor has painted him: "I take my glass of a night the same as another – well, I am in a continued and beastly state of intoxication," and so forth (WPBB, v. 3, p. 18). However, he then relates a drunken scene involving himself which fully justifies the rumors.

Neufeldt's fourth section is probably not part of this tale. Section five is an account (by a renegade, presumably Henry Hastings) of the retreating army of Republicans, who are having the worst of the fight with Zamorna and Fidena. Verdopolis and Angria are in the latter pair's hands, and reconstruction is taking place. Northangerland is nowhere to be seen or heard of. The sixth section (WPBB, v. 3, pp. 117–18) is another brief drunken piece, almost certainly by Henry Hastings, who talks of having forsaken "King, country and cause."

The seventh, a longer section, (WPBB, v. 3, pp. 132–43) starts as a conversation between Hastings, Wentworth, and Townsend, the last of whom tells unlikely stories of Zamorna and Northangerland. The scene descends into drunkenness, then to a prize fight between Hastings and one of Branwell's favorite characters, a muscular giant. In the tiny eighth fragment we seem to be concerned with Hastings proceeding on his way to his regiment, but making enquiries about his recent opponent.

The ninth section (WPBB, v. 3, pp. 145–56) takes place in a remote beer shop, and we soon realize that one of the drinkers is Henry Hastings, "broken from one military service and a fugitive in another." The familiar Branwell drunken jocularity leads into a fight with newcomers, then to recognition, when the newcomers turn out to be Montmorency, Quashia, and co. Officers of Zamorna's army surround the tavern and the Republicans and Revolutionaries are arrested.

The 10th segment (WPBB, v. 3, pp. 157–77) is told mainly by Richton, but has a substantial central section in which Northangerland returns home to his wife Zenobia, convinced he is about to die. Throughout the long period of war Zenobia had felt she had lost her identity, even her marital status, but she finally accepts her husband, and her position, back.

In the first part of this section Richton has gone to Percy Hall and meditated on Northangerland's second wife Henrietta Wharton, here called Harriet. In the last part Richton returns to Verdopolis where Parliament is about to reconvene and is appalled to find that Zamorna is contemplating a new war "for the destruction of blacks and the exploration of the interior" (p. 177).

Section 11 is a brief description of the opening of the new Parliament after years of revolution and repression. Section 12 is an early draft of "And the Weary are at Rest," an episode from Northangerland's early life.

volume 5: Angria and Verdopolis being for the moment in a state of "political sunshine," the last volume of Branwell's work begins with an attempt by Richton to write a biography of Angria's Prime Minister Warner Howard Warner (WPBB, v. 3, pp. 208–14). It is rather well done, but Warner is by Angrian standards something of a goody-goody and this means that Branwell loses interest and the biography ends when the subject is six. The second section (pp. 215–18) reverts to Henry Hastings, now "penniless and proscribed," waking with a terrible hangover in a squalid inn. He encounters his earlier drinking companion G. F. Ellen, but the fragment ends as Branwell starts to delve further into the latter's nefarious nature.

The third section (WPBB, v. 3, pp. 246–8) tells us that five years have elapsed since the civil war, and covers the changes: bankruptcies, stagnant economy, rubber-stamping legislature, heavy debts. But the king, along with Fidena and Warner, are named as popular and successful men.

The fourth section (WPBB, v. 3, pp. 249–70) begins with a savage attack on a remote farm by a mixed band of "Whites and Negroes" (p. 249) led by the deserter Henry Hastings. We next see him, a mysterious and desperate character, securing lodgings under the name of Wilson. He arouses attention at the lodgings by his compulsive drinking, and is fetched by a lord, who blasphemously bids him "take up thy glass and follow me." The scene shifts to Verdopolis, where Zamorna, as King Adrian, is attending the new Parliament. A daring attempt is made on his life, but it is unsuccessful. The reader, remembering Charlotte's "Henry Hastings," written at the same time as this, February–March 1839, assumes he is the would-be regicide.

The scene shifts to a great fête given by the Duke in Wellesley House, where the Earl and Countess of Northangerland make a surprise appearance. After a confrontation with Zamorna they are saved by his protection from a hostile crowd as they leave the party. This final confrontation between the two mutually admiring enemies would have provided a fitting end to Branwell's prose chronicles of Glasstown and

Angria. Instead we have a brief fifth section (WPBB, v. 3, pp. 271–2) dealing with the iniquitous nature of George Ellen. This is dated April 1839.

See also Fidena; Glasstown; "Henry Hastings"; Juvenilia; Northangerland; Quashia Quamina; Warner; Zamorna

Annabella: daughter of Lord Lowborough in *The Tenant of Wildfell Hall*, who reminds him painfully of his unfaithful wife.

"Anne Askew": essay written by Charlotte for M. Heger in June 1842, in imitation of Chateaubriand's "*Eudore/* Moeurs Chrétiennes/ IV Siècle" in *Les Martyrs* (1809). There are many important mistakes in this account of an English Protestant martyr, including which sovereign martyred her, but it contains a powerful description of preparations for torture, something which fascinated the Brontës, and a ringing ending "I am a Protestant," to echo Chateaubriand's climax "I am a Christian." Possibly Charlotte, in Brussels the embattled Protestant surrounded by people of a religion she hated and feared, made the historical changes deliberately: her climax rings more challengingly if Anne Askew is being martyred by the Catholic Mary rather than by her father Henry VIII. Perhaps, too, the final cry is aimed defiantly at M. Heger, the only Catholic who represented any kind of temptation to change her religion.

Antwerp: Belgian port from which Charlotte and Emily embarked when they returned to England in November 1842 after the death of their aunt. On all other journeys to and from Belgium they went via Ostend. Notwithstanding this, Charlotte made Antwerp the familial home of the Moore family in *Shirley* – a place where they were once "known rich" (v. 1, ch. 5).

Apostolical succession: the subject of a "noble, eloquent high-Church" sermon by William Weightman on 26 Mar 1840, during the dispute in Haworth concerning Church rates, in which he "banged the Dissenters most fearlessly and unflinchingly" (CB to EN, 7 Apr 1840?). Anne was at that point at home, between her positions at Blake Hall and Thorp Green, but it can surely only be coincidence that in *Agnes Grey* her repulsive and ridiculous cleric Mr Hatfield has as his favorite subjects for sermons "apostolical succession" and "the atrocious criminality of dissent" (ch. 10).

Appleby, Westmorland: home of William Weightman, where he attended the Grammar School. His reputed favorite girlfriend, Agnes Walton, lived nearby.

Armitage (no first name given): presumably a mill-owner, described in ch. 1 of *Shirley* as shot on the moor.

Armitage, Miss (no first name given): a young lady with red hair spoken of as a possible wife for Robert Moore in *Shirley*, and one of the attenders at the Sunday School feast in ch. 17. She is, apparently, one of five (see ch. 19).

Arnold, Mary (née Penrose) (1791–1873): widow of Thomas Arnold. Though Charlotte, after meeting her several times, came to like her, her initial impression was of a woman whose manner lacked "genuineness and simplicity" (letter to James Taylor, 15 Jan 1851). In the same letter she criticized both the mother and her daughters for implied shallowness: when the talk turned to literature or anything else of an intellectual nature, their opinions were "rather imitative than original, rather sentimental than sound." The eldest of Mrs Arnold's daughters she knew as the wife of W. E. Forster.

See also Forster, William Edward and Jane

Arnold, Matthew (1822–88): poet, critic, eldest son of Thomas and Mary Arnold. Charlotte and he were fellow-guests for dinner at the home of Edward Quillinan, widower of Wordsworth's daughter Dora. As with his mother, Charlotte's first impressions were unfavorable, centering on his "seeming foppery" and "assumed conceit," but she later in the evening perceived "real modesty" and "genuine intellectual aspirations" (letter to James Taylor, 15 Jan 1851) in the man who was to become one of the great critics and thinkers of the age. He described her on the same occasion as "past thirty and plain, with expressive gray eyes though" (letter to his future wife Frances Lucy Wightman, 21 Dec 1850). He later took an intense dislike to *Villette*, describing it as a "hideous, undelightful, convulsed constricted novel," and "one of the most utterly disagreeable books I ever read." Remembering his meeting with Charlotte he then described her as "a fire without aliment – one of the most distressing barren sights one can witness." In his exaggerated, almost hysterical reaction both to the woman and her novels he seems to be responding to only one side of Charlotte, the angry feminist, and he seems to be terrified that she may represent the woman of the future. Arnold made handsome amends for this, and for his finding only "hunger, rebellion, and rage" (letter to Mrs Forster, 14 Apr 1853) in her novels (as if they were somehow illegitimate subjects for fiction), by his handsome tribute to Emily in "Haworth Churchyard," written within two months of Charlotte's death. This early praise of her powers as a poet anticipates much later comment when her fame grew.

Arnold, Dr Thomas (1795–1842): Charlotte wrote extensively to James Taylor and William Smith Williams about Dr Arnold after reading his *Life* by A. P. Stanley. She responded, as she always did with such men, to the force and pedagogical power of the man, though her response contains some fear as well as much admiration. She comments on his "justice, firmness, independence, earnestness," though she sees faults too, finding him "a little severe – almost a little hard." She is also struck, probably in contrast to herself, by "the almost unbroken happiness of his life" (letter to James Taylor, 6 Nov 1850). When she was obsessed by what she saw as the Roman Catholic threat to the Established Church she cried "Oh! I wish Dr. Arnold were yet living or that a second Dr. Arnold could be found" (letter to WSW, 9 Nov 1850).

Ashby, Lady (no first name given): mother of Sir Thomas Ashby in *Agnes Grey*, and a woman with a "haughty, sour spirit of reserve" (ch. 17). Rosalie Murray finds after marriage that she is not mistress in her own house, due to the continual residence of her mother-in-law.

Ashby, Lady Rosalie: *see* Murray, Rosalie

Ashby, Sir Thomas: suitor and later husband of Rosalie Murray in *Agnes Grey*. He is young and rich, with a dissolute life in the past. The marriage is without love, and produces a daughter rather than the heir Sir Thomas expects. The only time we see him directly is in ch. 23, a quietly dramatic encounter.

"Ashworth": The first of Charlotte's unfinished attempts at a novel, written probably in late 1840. She transposes the Earl of Northangerland to an English background, with many of his characteristics intact (e.g., hostility to his sons, musical genius) but successfully integrated into a raffish, semi-criminal circle, first in the south of England, then in Yorkshire where he was notable for "his great triple character of demagogue, cow-jobber, and horse jockey" ("Ashworth," Monahan, ed., 1983, p. 93). Later sections of the novel deal with young women at a boarding school and Yorkshire society – they lack the energy and sweep of the earlier chapters, but they are meaty and could have been productive of a rich stew. Among other foreshadowings of the mature novels we find: the hostile brothers theme, the brothers in question being the unacknowledged sons of Ashworth, inevitably called Edward and William; the poor young woman in a betwixt-and-between situation among her "betters," in Ellen Hall's case as a half-boarder at school, forced to do menial tasks for the better-off girls and destined to be a governess; and the elderly gentlemen, part gentry part tradesmen, who rail against the modern world in accents that recall Mr Yorke in *Shirley* and York Hunsden in *The Professor*.

Charlotte probably sent a draft of the early chapters to Hartley Coleridge, from whom she seems to have received a polite but dampening reply. Her flippant letter of thanks for this exists in draft form. See Melodie Monahan's edition of the fragment in *Studies in Philology* (1983).

See also Coleridge, Hartley; Hall, Ellen; "The Moores"; "Willie Ellin"; "Emma"

Athenaeum: weekly periodical, whose literary editor Charlotte met at dinner at the Smiths, and which gave mixed notices to the Bells' publications. One of the few journals to review *Poems*, it picked out Emily as the poet of the family, and talked of her "fine quaint spirit" and "an evident power of wing" (4 July 1846). H. F. Chorley, later a bête noire of Charlotte's, wrote of the "reality" in *Jane Eyre*, but pre-echoed many later critics in finding that, after Jane's flight from Thornfield, "we think the heroine too outrageously tried, and too romantically assisted in her difficulties" (23 Oct 1847). *Wuthering Heights* was found "[i]n spite of much power and cleverness" to be "a disagreeable story" (25 Dec 1847), but *The Tenant* was described as "the most interesting novel which we have read for a month past" (8 July 1848) – perhaps not the most whole-hearted of recommendations. Their unfavorable review of *Shirley* was made up for by a balanced review of *Villette*, which found the opening chapters an out-of-key beginning, but was full of praise for the body of the book, which it described as "a book which will please much those whom it pleases at all." Its much-quoted sentence "Her talk is of duty, – her predilections lie with passion" was not intended as praise, but is acute. As late as 1857, though, faced with both Gaskell's *Life* and *The Professor*, it commented that the "over-tragic life-drama of Charlotte Brontë so much amazed the world, that it feels disposed . . . to err on the side of gentleness" – and to prove it was of sterner stuff it produced yet again the portmanteau word "coarse" in its review of the posthumous novel (13 June 1857).

See also Chorley

Athénée Royale: a prestigious boys' school in Brussels, under the patronage of King Leopold, where M. Heger taught. His situation, teaching in a boys' school and his wife's girls' school, and the proximity of the two establishments, one overlooking the other, surely suggested Crimsworth's similar experience in *The Professor*. A correspondent of E. C. Gaskell's told her that at some point Heger gave up teaching at the Athénée because he was unable to introduce religious education there. However, the diploma he gave Charlotte was sealed with its seal.

"*Athènes Sauvée par la Poésie*" ("Athens Saved by Poetry"): an ambitious and subtle *devoir* written in Charlotte's last months in Brussels. Athens has been conquered by Sparta. At a drunken victory banquet the Spartan generals are entertained by Lysander. The brutal conquerors and their cooler, scheming leader have a Greek poet brought in to celebrate their triumph: the approaching destruction of Athens and the enslavement of its people. He sings instead of one of the tragedies of the Greek past: the killing of Agamemnon on his return from Troy. He takes in all the human actors in the drama: Agamemnon himself, Electra, Clytemnestra, Iphigenia. As his long poem draws to an end he realizes his audience are not rapt but drunkenly sleeping. The downbeat and ironic ending was disapproved of by M. Heger, but Charlotte leaves us with the possibility that the names of Agamemnon and Electra, "continually ringing in his ears" during his drunken sleep, was what changed Lysander's mind so that instead of destroying Athens he negotiated a treaty with it.

Sue Lonoff's analysis of this essay (BE, 1996, pp. 334–57) is notably sensitive and informative.

Atkinson, Mr: dentist of 14 East Parade, Leeds, who was consulted by Charlotte in October 1849 and treated her in April 1850, perhaps the John Atkinson who was a member of the Royal College of Surgeons and had a practice in East Parade, Leeds, in the 1820s and 30s, or his son. Charlotte wanted to "ask him if he can do anything for my teeth" (to EN, 20 Oct 1849?) – a perennial problem for her.

Atkinson, Henry George (?1815–84): collaborator with Harriet Martineau on the *Letters on the Laws of Man's Social Nature*, a work which caused great controversy by its agnostic (or, in Charlotte's view, atheistic) viewpoint.

Atkinson, Mary: wife of Rev. Thomas Atkinson of Liversedge, subject of several letters from Charlotte to Ellen Nussey in 1849–50, and presumably a member of Ellen's Birstall/Gomersal circle. She was diagnosed as consumptive in 1849, but though she was "wasted" when Charlotte and Ellen saw her in July 1850, she shortly after became a mother. She died almost immediately afterwards, and Charlotte commented to Ellen that her child "could only be reared to die" (2 Sep 1850). The baby died in October.

Atkinson, Rev. Thomas (1780–1870): Patrick's Cambridge-educated predecessor as perpetual curate of Thornton. He suggested the exchange whereby Patrick took the position at Thornton, and he Patrick's at Hartshead. This was to facilitate his courtship of Frances Walker, of Lascelles Hall, near Huddersfield, whom he later married. The swap with Patrick took place in May 1815. He and his wife later became godparents to Charlotte, and may have paid or contributed to her fees at Roe Head. He was a nephew of Hammond Roberson, and both he and his wife had private incomes.

See also Green House; Roberson, Rev. Hammond

Atlas: newspaper whose literary editor Charlotte met at George Smith's. Its review of *Wuthering Heights*, found in Emily's writing desk, testifies to the shock the novel produced on its early readers, but it has several insights that acknowledge its power: it calls it a "natural unnatural" story, and concludes that, whereas *Jane Eyre* was a "great performance; that of Ellis Bell is only a promise, but it is a colossal one" (22 Jan 1848). Earlier it had said that Charlotte's novel made "the pulses gallop and the heart beat" (23 Oct 1847), though it found Helen Burns untrue to life. Its review of *Shirley* was disapproving, but Charlotte returned to its favor with *Villette*. The newspaper represented well the combination of enthrallment and disapproval which was the initial public reaction to the Bells in their lifetime.

Audubon, John James (1785–1851): American ornithologist whom Charlotte recommended to Ellen Nussey, along with Bewick and White of Selborne, for reading in Natural History. Part creole, part French, Audubon studied with David, and worked at various disparate enterprises, in some of which (including investment in a steamboat at the bottom of the Mississippi) he involved George Keats, John's brother, to the latter's great financial loss. Audubon also tried portrait painting, but all this was undertaken to enable him to research and finance his magnificent (and expensive) *The Birds of America* (1827–8). Audubon's *Ornithological Biography*, published in five volumes during the 1830s, was probably the work of his that the Brontës knew best. Patrick wrote with some pride in his copy: "There are 5 volumes of this work – price £1.4.0 each – amounting together to £6.0.0. All these have I procured – P.B. 1852."

The work mixes natural history with biographical and philosophical matter, making it "one of the great autobiographical documents of the Romantic movement" and its author "a kind of culture hero" (R. Berman, "Charlotte Brontë's Natural History," BST, v. 18, pt 94, 1984).

See also Bewick, Thomas

Austen, Jane (1775–1817): Charlotte's antipathy to Jane Austen's novels when she encountered them at the prompting of G. H. Lewes is well known, as are the terms in which she describes them: "the Passions are perfectly unknown to her . . . even to the Feelings she vouchsafes no more than an occasional graceful but distant recognition . . . what throbs fast and full, though hidden, what the blood rushes through . . . *this* Miss Austen ignores" (to WSW, 12 Apr 1850). *Pride and Prejudice* she describes to Lewes as "a carefully-fenced, highly cultivated garden with neat borders and delicate flowers – but . . . no open country – no fresh air – no blue hill – no bonny beck" (12 Jan 1848). She presumably gave no weight to Elizabeth's cross-country walk to Netherfield to visit the sick Jane, involving dirty stockings. The two women saw the world, and our place in it, from entirely different standpoints, though Jane's interest in the Gothic suggests that she might have approached an understanding of Charlotte's cast of mind, whereas Charlotte could never have approached an appreciation of Jane's. One wonders whether, when Caroline in *Shirley* says "Helstone is also proud and prejudiced," Charlotte may be sending a message to Lewes: this is pride as I understand it, this is prejudice as it operates in the real world, not the pale reflections of them in Miss Austen's polite society.

See also Bigger, Miss

Austin, Henry: secretary to the General Board of Health, with whom Patrick corresponded in 1850–51, in an attempt to improve Haworth's water supply. Patrick protested over and over at the "long and tedious delay" (10 July 1851), even after he had called a meeting of Haworth residents and got their agreement to his plans.

Austin, J. I.: author of a work called *Manhood – the cause of its premature decline*, which Branwell presciently noted down, perhaps with an intention of purchasing it, in his Luddenden Foot notebook. The price was 3/6d, and it was obtainable from 4 St Ann's Street, Manchester.

Aykroyd, Tabitha (Tabby), née Wood (ca 1770–1855): the Brontës' cook and general servant from 1824. She soon became a center of warmth, story-telling and fun (often as their butt) for the Brontë children, supplying qualities that Aunt Branwell, for all her good intentions, lacked. Her place in the household, and the young Brontës' affections, is evidenced in the early juvenilia, and in the Diary Papers of Emily and Anne, which also bear witness to the inspiration her broad Yorkshire dialect was to them. It is clear that in those early years she nagged them, nourished their imaginations, and treated them (as they treated her) as equals. They repaid her in 1836 by going on hunger strike when, she having broken a leg, Aunt Branwell wanted her out of the Parsonage. They won on that occasion, but Tabby did leave in 1839 to live with her sister, Susannah Wood. She returned to the Parsonage, probably in 1843 (though references in Charlotte's letters of 29 May and 2 June 1843? suggest she had been living there for some time). She may have come back in part as company for Emily, but her lameness did allow her to do some of her old duties (probably including boiling the potatoes "to a sort of vegetable glue!", CB to EJB, 1 Oct 1843); these she clung to tenaciously, and vigorously supervised Martha Brown in the work she herself could no longer manage. Her strong, simple mind, nourished on Methodism, meant she fulfilled her responsibilities with a sense of duty, refusing to gossip about the family she served, or pry into their affairs, but interested in everything they did. Charlotte's later letters contain accounts of various illnesses of Tabby, and also her strong opinions (such as that George Smith's gift of a portrait of the Duke of Wellington was in fact of "the Master"). She is fictionalized, or at least aspects of her are, as Hannah, the Moor House servant in *Jane Eyre*, and she plays a part on the last page of *Shirley* as Martha. She was buried by Arthur Nicholls in Haworth Churchyard, just outside the Parsonage wall – one of the few people prominent in the Brontë story to be buried there.

See also Wood family

Aylott and Jones: publishers and booksellers of Paternoster Row. Charlotte wrote to them 28 Jan 1846 to see if they would publish a short collection of poetry, if necessary "on the Author's account." They agreed to publish it if the author covered the cost of paper and printing. On 6 Feb 1846 Charlotte revealed that the poems "are the work of three persons – relatives." Thereafter the printing and publication went smoothly, Charlotte paying £31.10.0 in March and a further £5 in May, with some extra payment for advertising. Of this they received back £24.0.6 when Smith Elder bought and reissued the remaining sheets of the volume in 1848. There was in March "a little mistake" (to Aylott and Jones, 28 Mar 1846) which was possibly Branwell opening a letter or package, so Charlotte asked for post to be addressed to Miss Brontë instead of C. Brontë Esqre. By May Charlotte was sending the names of journals she wished to be sent review copies, and the early reviews were favorable enough for her to authorize in July the spending of a further £10 on advertisements, with a quote from *The Critic*, though these were later deferred or cancelled.

Charlotte seems to have been very satisfied with her dealings with the firm, in spite of the meager sales of the volume. She enquired (6 Apr 1846) whether they would be interested in publishing "three distinct and unconnected tales," this time not at the authors' expense. However, the firm published mostly theology and classical works, and Aylott had, according to his daughter, "very narrow views regarding light literature." Thus the novels began their travels around the more important publishing houses of London.

B

Baines, Edward: name of the father (1774–1848) and son (later Sir Edward, 1800–1890) who were respectively proprietor and editor of the *Leeds Mercury*. This is recorded in Charlotte's "History of the Year" as one of the two newspapers the Parsonage household took. The *Mercury* was the Whig paper, and its editor was therefore regarded with suspicion and loathing by the young Charlotte ("if there is any one I thoroughly abhor, it is that man" – to EN, 13 Mar 1835). The three sons of the elder Baines, Matthew Talbot, Edward, and Thomas appear in the juvenilia ("Tales of the Islanders," v. 3, ch. 3) as Toltol, Nedned (also known as Raton), and Tomtom. The *Mercury* regularly indulged in slanging matches with the *Leeds Intelligencer*, its Tory rival, recalling the verbal battles in *Pickwick Papers* between the *Eatanswill Gazette* and the *Independent*.

Baldwin, Cradock, & Joy: the Paternoster Row publishers of Patrick's *The Maid of Killarney* (1818).

Baldwin, Sarah (née Crowther): wife of the incumbent of Mytholmroyd, who in 1857 entered into a furious controversy with Arthur Bell Nicholls in the *Halifax Guardian* concerning the Clergy Daughters' School. As she had not entered the school until 1830, five years after the Brontës left, more heat than light was generated by her side of the correspondence. One suspects personal animus was involved, as well as a desire to defend her old school.

Ball, Mrs Thomas: landlady of the house in 83 Boundary Street, Manchester, in which Charlotte and Patrick rented rooms while he was recovering from his cataract operation in 1846. Thomas Ball was an "agent," while Mrs Ball, who was ill and away from home, was a former servant of the surgeon who operated, Dr Wilson.

Ballynaskeagh: small town in County Down to which Patrick's family moved in the early 1790s. The house was a more substantial affair than the ones which are believed to have housed the family earlier, and it remained in the family until the latter half of the nineteenth century.

Balzac, Honoré De (1799–1850): French novelist to whom Charlotte was sometimes compared. When she came to read him she forced herself to see his good points ("is it [his force] not in the analysis of motive, and in a subtle perception of the most obscure and secret workings of the mind?" – to G. H. Lewes, 17 Oct 1850), but felt an instinctive dislike of his work.

Banagher: small town in present-day County Offaly, where Arthur Bell Nicholls lived with his uncle the Rev. Alan Bell and his family from the age of seven. Charlotte went there on her honeymoon and was impressed by Cuba House, which had served as the family home, with nearby the school of which the Rev. Bell was head. Charlotte was openly surprised at the state in which the family lived ("like a gentleman's country-seat" – to MW, 10 July 1854). Banagher was hardly more than a main street (in which Arthur was photographed in old age): it contains the church of St Paul's, where Arthur was buried, and Hill House, where he lived with his second wife Mary Anna, née Bell. In the early 1840s Trollope lived here, working as a surveyor's clerk in the Post Office.

Bangor: town in north Wales visited by Charlotte and Arthur Bell Nicholls during the first stage of their honeymoon in June 1845.

Barbara (no surname given): servant at Lowood school in *Jane Eyre*.

Barber, Rev. John: Vicar of Bierley. Wrongly identified by many writers, including Wise and Symington, as the vulgar and intrusive visitor to the Parsonage in February 1850. This was in fact the Rev. Andrew Cassels.

Barber of Seville: *see* Rossini, Gioacchino

Barbier, Henri Auguste (1805–82): French poet and dramatist, whose poem "L'Idole" was translated by Charlotte in March 1843 as "Napoleon." Barbier was a strongly political poet with a command of invective in support of social causes, described by Charlotte in *Shirley* as "rude vigour" (footnote to ch. 27 in World Classics edn.)

Bardsley, Rev. James: a young clergyman whom Patrick nearly had as his first curate in 1833. The Archbishop of York refused to sanction the appointment, and he became curate in Keighley and later in Bierley. He resigned during a dispute with the Vicar of Bradford, Dr. Scoresby. He was on friendly and visiting terms with the Brontë family. After leaving Brierley he was senior curate in Burnley Parish Church and incumbent of St Philip's, Manchester.

Barraclough, James: tradesman of Haworth, who took some notable photographs of Patrick at the end of his life (1860).

Barraclough, Rev. Moses: drunken and hypocritical Methodist preacher, with a wooden leg which proves a drawback when he tries to court Robert Moore's servant Sarah in *Shirley*. He leads the deputation to Moore in ch. 8, and is later described as praying by the roadside "in an advanced stage of inebriation" (ch. 13). This is all very much in the tradition of the depiction of dissenters in Charlotte and Branwell's Angria writings.

Barrett, Mrs (no first name given): Lucy Snowe's old nurse in *Villette* who comforts Lucy after the death of Miss Marchmont and tells her of opportunities for British women in families on the Continent. She later is the means by which Lucy receives the (somewhat unlikely) gift of conscience money from Miss Marchmont's cousin (ch. 42).

Bartolommeo Della Porta, Fra (ca 1472–1517): one of the painters "whose works I wish to see" (ms. by Charlotte dated 1829). In her early story *The Swiss Artist* (EW, 1826–32, pp. 92–4, 115–17) the young artist Alexandre and the Comte de Lausanne visit the Louvre, where they are struck by "the sacred sublimity" of this artist. Though this sounds like mere vague generalization, Bartolommeo was admired for the simplicity and decorum of his style, and his introduction of drapery rather than contemporary costume for his sacred figures. He was active mainly in Florence, influenced Raphael, and may have been intimidated by the latter's greater mastery.

Bassompierre, Louise De: a pupil at the Pensionnat Heger in 1842 who was taught the piano by Emily, who also gave her a picture of a tree. She found Emily "*plus sympathique*" than her sister, though "*moins brilliante.*" The name is taken by Mr Home and his daughter Paulina in the later parts of *Villette*.

Bates, Mr (no first name given): surgeon or doctor used by Lowood school in *Jane Eyre*. He is summoned when Helen Burns's illness is in its terminal phase.

Batley: Yorkshire town near Dewsbury, birthplace of Margaret Wooler.

"Battell Book": earliest known writing of Branwell (12 Mar 1827). The book contains five small pictures, also the earliest known by Branwell (see AOTB, pp. 284–5).

Batty, Dr. W.: physician to Cowan Bridge school, probably the brother-in-law of Carus Wilson. In an incident mentioned by Mrs Gaskell, he spat out food prepared for the children, and later recommended moving the school from its unhealthy location.

See also Bates

Beale, Dorothea (1831–1906): pioneer of women's education and founder of Cheltenham Ladies' College. She taught at the "reformed" Clergy Daughters' School at Casterton in 1857–8, the year when the spotlight was on it, due to Gaskell's *Life*. Beale wrote of it as "an institution in which the government is entirely by punishments"; her biographer, Elizabeth Raikes, may be echoing her when she says that hearts "were turned to stone, or depressed into hopeless terror," and that "religious forms, phraseology, even emotions were assumed by those who were prone to self-deception, or over-anxious to please." Miss Beale herself also mentions some examples of the contrary reaction: "great girls constantly professing not to care about religion."

Beaver, John (d. 1843): one of the Haworth Church trustees, and one of the nominators of Patrick to the living in 1820. His will became the subject of a scandalous forgery case at York Assizes in 1843, at which Patrick, one of the will's witnesses, gave evidence. See article by S. Fermi and D. Kinghorn (BST, v. 21, pts 1 & 2, 1993).

Beck, Désirée: eldest daughter of Mme Beck in *Villette*. She is described (ch. 10) as a "vicious child" – dishonest, destructive and provoking.

Beck, Fifine: the most attractive of Mme Beck's daughters in *Villette* – a "passionate, warm-tempered, bustling creature" whose illness (ch. 10) is the means of bringing "Dr John" to the Pensionnat.

Beck, Georgette: youngest daughter of Mme Beck in *Villette*, whose nature is not analyzed, though we see her plaintive and demanding when she is ill with a fever (ch. 11).

Beck, Mme Modeste Maria (née Kint): the proprietress of the Pensionnat de Demoiselles in *Villette*, and employer of Lucy Snowe. Her character is analyzed in ch. 8, but the whole book provides an amplification of Lucy's early impressions. The adverse side of her character is dwelt on and dramatized at greater length than her undoubted capability as the director of a girls' school. Lucy is revolted by her cunning, her lack of principle, her devotion to expedience. She is seen as a spy and an intriguer, one who rules in her small world by gaining knowledge of the affairs of all those in it – often by illegitimate means. She is the perfect politician, and her unscrupulousness is frequently put down to, or allied with, her religion. She is only comprehensively defeated at the climax of the book, when Lucy's "My heart will break!" foils her attempts to separate her from M. Paul – the victory of true feeling over Jesuitical cunning.

Against all this the woman's calm competence, cool judgment, and occasional daring unorthodoxy (seen both when she uses Lucy as a teacher and Dr John as the school's physician) count for little in the total picture the reader gets of her. There is one oddity in the presentation of this character: though she must be fairly recently widowed, no mention is made of her husband or his fate.

It is generally accepted that the character is based on Mme Heger, though it is likely to be a partial and slanted picture, granted the awkward relationship in which Charlotte stood to her.

See also Heger, Claire Zoë; Reuter, Zoraïde

Beckwith, Dr Stephen (d. 1843): benefactor of York Minster, of whom Joseph Leyland made a recumbent figure for his monument there. Du Maurier records that he was paid £250 and had to find his own material – "an impossible task at the price" (IWBB, 1972 edn., p. 176).

Beddgelert: North Wales village visited by Charlotte on her honeymoon. The drive from Llanberis to Beddgelert "surpassed anything I remember of the English Lakes" (to Catherine Wooler, 18 July 1854).

Bedford, Mr and Mrs: Patrick's landlords at Lousy Thorn Farm, Hartshead; former servants at Kirklees Hall. Mentioned several times in the "courtship" letters of Maria to Patrick – they tried to call on the Fennells, and helped with an order of blankets for the boys of Woodhouse Grove School.

Beethoven, Ludwig van (1770–1827): Emily played piano arrangements of several of his works, including movements from the Fourth, Sixth, and Seventh Symphonies. See Wallace (1986, ch. 4), for music Emily played at home and music she could have heard while she was in Brussels.

Belcombe, Dr Henry Stephen (1790–1856): physician who specialized in the humane care of the mentally sick and ran the private Clifton House asylum in York. It was here that Ellen's brother George Nussey was cared for 1845–53. Charlotte did not care for Dr Belcombe's style of reporting on the case ("so cold, so formal – so little explanatory" she wrote in a letter to Ellen (August 1845?) but undoubtedly the Nusseys got the best treatment available for George.

Belgium: the kingdom that Charlotte knew was formed after a revolt against the Dutch masters of the region in 1830. The Belgians chose Leopold of Saxe-Coburg, widower of George IV's daughter Charlotte, as their king. He and his second family are glimpsed in *Villette* ch. 20. In the Middle Ages the area was prosperous and rich in artists, but decline had set in by the eighteenth century. Charlotte disliked the people intensely, concentrating her spleen on their Catholicism, phlegm, and supposed provinciality (odd from a provincial who habitually distrusted London people and manners). "I count the Belgians as nothing," she wrote to Ellen Nussey in June 1843. The Belgians were believed in Britain to have behaved in a cowardly fashion at Waterloo (in *Vanity Fair* ch. 32, the lover of Pauline, Amelia's cook, "was too good a soldier to disobey his Colonel's orders to run away," and Thackeray comments that Belgian troops "signalised themselves in this war for anything but courage"). At that date, of course, they had no country of their own to fight for. Their reputation may have predisposed Charlotte against the native Belgians, and her contempt was fierce. Interestingly the Papal Nuncio to Brussels in 1843, later to become Pope Leo XIII, was rumored to have gained great influence over the Protestant King Leopold.

See also Brussels; Labassecour; Leopold; Pensionnat Heger

Bell, Acton, Currer, and Ellis: the pseudonyms adopted by the Brontë sisters
for the 1846 *Poems*, and retained for all the novels. There has been considerable speculation about possible sources of both first names and surnames (see e.g., Barker, 1994, p. 480), the inconclusiveness of which suggests that the Brontës' first concern was not to provide any obvious clues to their identities. The main point is that none of the first names are male forenames: they are (like Shirley, which did not become a popular female first name until after the publication of Charlotte's novel) family names used as first names, a common procedure at the time (witness Branwell).

Bell, Rev. Dr Alan (1789–1839): maternal uncle of Arthur Bell Nicholls, who
virtually adopted the boy and his brother from the large farming family into which they had been born. He was headmaster of the Royal School at Banagher, and sent Arthur to Trinity College, Dublin. He and his home, Cuba House, are mentioned in a letter of Charlotte to Margaret Wooler (10 July 1854) written during the honeymoon tour, when she and Arthur stayed with his widow and her family.

Bell, Harriette Lucinda, née Adamson (1801–1902): wife of Dr Alan Bell
above, who with him brought up Arthur Bell Nicholls. She was born in Dublin, and she and her children were hosts in Banagher to Charlotte and her husband on their honeymoon tour of 1854. Charlotte describes her (to MW, 10 July 1854) as "like an English or Scotch Matron quiet, kind and well-bred," adding that she had apparently been brought up in London (she seems in fact, to have been there only briefly). After being refused the living at Haworth, Nicholls returned to Banagher to live with his aunt at Hill House, to which they had moved, and in 1864 he married his cousin Mary Anna Bell.

Bell, Harriet Lucinda (1833–1911): younger sister of Mary Anna. She and
her sister were both at Cuba House when Charlotte and Arthur stayed a week there on their honeymoon tour.

Bell, Rev James Adamson (1826–91): son of Dr Alan Bell, cousin of Arthur
Bell Nicholls. Charlotte met him on the honeymoon tour, and he visited the couple at Haworth in 1855. He is the subject of unusually warm praise in some of the last letters Charlotte wrote. She described him to Ellen Nussey as "a true gentleman by nature and cultivation" (19 Jan 1855) and to Amelia Taylor, Joe's wife, as having "a mind stored with information gathered from books and travel" whose visit was "a real treat" (21 Jan 1855?). He was headmaster of the school in Cuba House from 1849 until

he closed it down in 1865, resulting in an unseemly dispute with the Royal Commission on Endowed Schools, since he continued to draw his stipend.

Bell, Joseph Samuel (1831–91): son of Dr Alan Bell. He met Charlotte and Arthur in Dublin during the honeymoon tour. He was a student of Trinity College, as Arthur had been, and at the time had "just gained 3 premiums" (to MW, 10 July 1854).

Bell, Mary Anna (1830–1915): daughter of Dr Alan Bell, cousin of Arthur Bell Nicholls, whom she married in 1864. She had met Charlotte in 1854 and was especially solicitous about her memory. She had her husband's coffin placed under the Richmond portrait, but was forced to sell Brontë memorabilia in 1907 and 1914. She and her sister Harriet were described by Charlotte as "strikingly pretty in appearance – and their manners are very amiable and pleasing" (to MW, 10 July 1854). She and her husband declined into genteel poverty, partly due to Arthur's refusal to seek further positions in the church after his bitter experience in Haworth.

Bellerby, Henry: York bookseller, with a shop (which still stands) at 13 Stonegate. He also ran a lending library and a newspaper, the *Yorkshire Gazette*, as well as magazines with a Church of England slant. The Robinsons had an account with him, and Branwell was able to borrow books from his library: in June 1845 he requested *Blackwood's*, *Quarterly Review*, Freycinet's *Voyage Autour du Monde*. Among the poems of his that Bellerby printed in the *Gazette* were "The Shepherd's Chief Mourner" and "The Emigrant."

Bell's Life in London **and** *Bell's Sporting Life*: sporting periodicals to which Branwell had access, and which fed his obsession with pugilism. The former, according to Leyland (1886), was taken by "an innkeeper at Haworth," the latter was borrowed from the Shake Hands public house, fetched for Branwell by Benjamin Binns, the Haworth tailor's son. He mentions *Life in London* in "And the Weary are at Rest."

Bendigo *see* Thompson, William

Bennett, Edward Turner: author of *The Gardens and Menagerie of the Zoological Society Delineated*, a volume purchased by Patrick in 1831. Charlotte copied a drawing of the palm squirrel from the first volume, *Quadrupeds* – the original by William Harvey, based on an engraving by Bewick.

Bennock, Francis (1812–90): a persistent admirer of Charlotte's who claimed to be a "patron of Authors and literature" (ECG to John Forster, September 1853), and who in spite of discouragement intruded on Charlotte and Mrs Gaskell during the first day of the latter's stay in Haworth in 1853. Somewhat surprisingly, Charlotte agreed to stay with him and his wife in London, May 1854, but her engagement intervened.

Benson: butler at Grassdale Manor in *The Tenant of Wildfell Hall*. Abused and sworn at by Arthur Huntingdon in a vivid scene (ch. 30), he is later chosen to help Helen and Rachel escape from the house. Later still we are told that "every decent servant had left" the house (ch. 47), among them Benson.

Benson, Dr Edward White (1829–1896): cousin of Charlotte's Sidgwick charges at Stonegappe, who visited Patrick in 1858 and recorded that he was "too old and too composed to mind" Mrs Gaskell's inaccuracies about himself. Benson later became headmaster of Wellington College. Here his flagellomania seems not to have counted against him, and it certainly did not prevent him, in 1882, from becoming Archbishop of Canterbury. The Brontë connection continued into the next generation, with his two sons, A. C. and E. F. Benson, writing on the family.

Bentinck, Lord George (1802–1848) and Lord William (1774–1839): Lord George was possibly the politician chosen by Anne as her "chief man" for the communal play "The Islanders." He was at that date (1829) more famous for his interest in the turf and the hunting field than as a politician. A Canningite Tory, he veered towards the Whigs at the time of the Reform Bill, then back to supporting Peel, breaking with him over the repeal of the Corn Laws. He is described by Robert Blake as "a man of violent temper and extreme prejudice" who "pursued his enemies with unrelenting virulence" (*Disraeli*, 1967, p. 229). A very un-Anne choice. Possibly it was his support for Catholic Emancipation that attracted her. However, it is also possible that Anne's "Bentinck" was Lord William, who had fought in the Peninsular campaign and in 1827 was made governor-general of Bengal. In 1829 he abolished (so far as possible) suttee, a fact that was mentioned in Charlotte's first essay for M. Heger, "Sacrifice of an Indian Widow."

Bentley, Joseph Clayton (1809–1851): one of Branwell's circle of artists in Bradford, specializing in landscape paintings and engravings.

Berry, Abraham: Baptist minister in Haworth. A supporter of Patrick's campaign to improve the village's water supply.

Berry, John: a Haworth "factory boy" who emigrated to Massachusetts, and in 1850, when speculation as to the identity of Currer Bell was beginning to spread, wrote to his local paper, the *Boston Weekly Museum*, with some memories of the Brontë family, mainly Patrick and Keeper.

Bethlehem Hospital: one of the sights of London, better known as Bedlam, visited by Charlotte during her last London visit in 1853, when she chose to see "rather the *real* than the *decorative* side of Life" (to EN, 19 Jan 1853).

Betty (no surname given): nurse to the Bloomfield children in *Agnes Grey*, who loses her place for "whipping" the children (ch. 4).

Bewick, Thomas (1753–1828): Newcastle wood-engraver who revolutionized the techniques of his craft. Patrick owned his best-known work, *The History of British Birds* (1797, 1804), and all the Brontë children copied pictures from it. Emily in particular seems to have learnt from it the art of capturing the spirit of birds and animals in pictures. The opening pages of *Jane Eyre* embody the appeal of the book for Jane/Charlotte: the pictures of bleak foreign shores which seem to mirror her situation and fate, and the glimpses of everyday life going on in the backgrounds. "Each picture told a story" says Jane; "mysterious often to my undeveloped understanding and imperfect feelings, yet ever profoundly interesting." On Jane's return to Gateshead as an adult the volumes are among the first things she notices, along with *Gulliver's Travels* and the *Arabian Nights*. Charlotte wrote "Lines on Bewick" in 1832, four years after his death, and two years before her letter that advised Ellen Nussey "For Natural History read Bewick" (4 July 1834) along with Audubon, Goldsmith, and White of Selborne. The influence of Bewick extends beyond the Brontës' own pictures: his spirit informs the treatment of nature and all animate things in their novels. Branwell wrote an appreciation of him for the *Halifax Guardian*, and his mingling of natural creatures with grotesque or vaguely threatening settings informs many of his pictures, as it does too Jane Eyre's pictures described in ch. 13.

Bicker, Hannah and Sarah: fellow pupils of the Brontës at Cowan Bridge School. Sarah died at the school in 1826, Hannah after being withdrawn, in 1827.

Bigger, Miss: author of *The Fair Carew*, about which Charlotte wrote with unusual enthusiasm to W. S. Williams and George Smith in several letters of November 1851: "This writer is [as] shrewd as Miss Austen and not so shrewish. . . . I was reminded of Thackeray's wit and wisdom but never of his vinegar and gall" (to WSW, 10 Nov 1851). The idea that Charlotte had discovered a fictional masterpiece does not survive a reading of the work.

"Biographical Notice of Ellis and Acton Bell": Charlotte's account of her two dead sisters, prefixed to the second edition of *Wuthering Heights* and *Agnes Grey*, published by Smith Elder in 1850. Her intention, she wrote (to WSW, 20 Sep 1850) was "to give a just idea of their identity, not to write any narrative of their simple, uneventful lives." The fullest account of this essay is in Nicola Diane Thompson's *Reviewing Sex* (1996) which sees Charlotte as exaggerating the critics' hostility to *Wuthering Heights* on its first publication in order to distance Emily's novel from her own.

Birstall: town near Dewsbury, where Ridings, Ellen Nussey's home when she first met Charlotte, is situated. The town remained her place of residence for most of her life. Birstall and its inhabitants feature in many of Charlotte's letters as a consequence. Ellen is buried in the churchyard of St Peter's.

Birstwhistle, Miss (no first name given): one of the attenders at the Sunday School feast in *Shirley* (ch. 17).

Black Bull Inn: the Haworth public house close by St Michael's church and the Parsonage that by tradition was Branwell's favorite place of resort. The proprietor in the 1820s and 30s was Abraham Wilkinson, and he was succeeded in 1841 by Enoch Thomas, who died in 1848. By the time of the 1851 Census William Sugden was the landlord (see note by Ann Dinsdale in BST, v. 21, pt 7). Certainly the pub seems to have been the best eating place in Haworth at the time, and it had a "large room" where musical concerts were held. It was here that Branwell was said to suffer some kind of seizure after hearing the supposed terms of Mr Robinson's will. Here too Francis Grundy met him for the last time in September 1848, when he "described himself as anxiously waiting for death" – which in fact came within days.

Blackwood's Magazine: high Tory periodical originating in Edinburgh as a rival to the Whig *Edinburgh Review* and having J. G. Lockhart, James Hogg, and "Christopher North" (John Wilson) among its editorial team and contributors. The Brontë family were lent the periodical by Mr Driver until 1831, and were still reading it in 1841 ("Aunt . . . has just been reading Blackwood's Magazine to papa" – EJB's diary paper, 30 July 1841). Charlotte called it "the most able periodical there is" ("History of the Year," 1829), and Branwell launched a brash attempt to become one of its contributors in the 1830s, which was ignored. Its tone in criticism was hard and satirical, notably in their attacks on the "Cockney school" of poetry (Keats, Leigh Hunt, etc), and the young Brontës often caught its vitriolic tone in their juvenilia. The bibulous "Noctes Ambrosianae" were particularly appreciated by the young readers in the Parsonage, and the fact that, unusually, the magazine included fiction added to its appeal.

See also Fraser's Magazine

"Blackwood's Young Men's Magazine": successor to "Branwell's Blackwood's Magazine," taken over by Charlotte in August 1829 and rechristened. Six numbers appeared monthly, December's being a double number. The little books are a miscellany, including poems, reviews, stories, and advertisements. When it resumed in August 1830 Charlotte dropped the "Blackwood's" from the title, but all three series are a testimony to the appeal the magazine had to their young imaginations.

Blake Hall: home of the Ingham family, where Anne became a governess in April 1839. It was a large, handsome eighteenth-century house, the extensive grounds of which may have afforded Anne some consolation during a trying time. They included a "vinery, peach houses, stable, coach houses, barn and sheds" (Chitham, 1991, pp. 58–61, which has the fullest account of the house). It was demolished in 1954.

Blakeway, Elizabeth: the daughter of a London wine merchant who George Smith married in 1854. Mrs Gaskell described her (to EN, 9 July 1856) as George's "very pretty, Paulina-like little wife." Charlotte's letter of congratulation to Smith on his engagement (10 Dec 1853) was distinctly unfulsome.

Blanche, Mlle (surname unknown): teacher at the Pensionnat Heger, particularly disliked by Charlotte. She mentions her "white passions" when her lips disappear (to EJB, 29 May 1843) and says that her character "is so false and so contemptible I can't force myself to associate with her" (to EJB, 2 Sep 1843). Probably the original of Zélie St Pierre in *Villette*.

Bland, Susan: the "oldest and best" of Charlotte's Sunday School pupils, who in 1840 was thought to be dying. William Weightman's visit to her and his generosity in sending the port wine the doctor had recommended, along with a jar of preserves, caused Charlotte to revise her opinion of him: "he is not all selfishness and vanity. . . . God bless him!" (to EN, 29 Sep 1840?). Margaret Smith notes that no Susan Bland was buried in Haworth at this time, and conjectures she may be the "Susey" written to on 13 June 1848. She seems to have been the daughter of John Bland of 83 Main Street.

Blémont, Caroline de: pupil of noble family at Mlle Reuter's in *The Professor*. Beautiful, sensual, and "scarcely purer than Lucrèce de Borgia," she is one of the three trouble-makers described in detail in ch. 10.

Blessington, Marguerite, Countess of (1789–1849): society hostess of mildly scandalous life, who lived in a ménage à trois with her husband the Earl and Count D'Orsay. She was beautiful, graceful, and much admired by Byron (her most successful book was *Conversations with Lord Byron*, 1834) and Dickens. Her novels (including *The Governess*, 1839) are mostly society confections of a vapid kind but she was a notably successful editor of annuals. Charlotte's picture "Zenobia Marchioness Ellrington" (15 Oct 1833) seems to be loosely based on a portrait or portraits of the Countess.

Bligh, Mr (no first name given): former curate of Horton in *Agnes Grey*, a "seedy" man, as negligent in visiting the poor as Mr Hatfield.

Bloomfield Family: the first names of the senior members of the family in *Agnes Grey* are significantly not mentioned. They are newly rich and keep their distance from servants. Mr Bloomfield, Agnes's first employer, is a retired tradesman, who "could not be prevailed upon to give a greater salary than twenty-five pounds to the instructress of his children" (ch. 1). A vulgar, querulous, discontented man, with poor manners and judgment, he is addicted to gin and water, to which Agnes attributes his dingy complexion. Mrs Bloomfield, wife of the above, is an overfond mother and a poor employer. She is inconsiderate to Agnes, and does not give her the authority necessary to keep the children in order. The household, it is implied, is ill-run, and there is little love between husband and wife. Mrs Bloomfield senior, mother of Mr Bloomfield, is insincere and a trouble-maker, with a much-vaunted veneer of religion. She can be won by flattery, which Agnes scorns to apply (see ch. 4). Mary Ann, the eldest daughter of the Bloomfields, is a backward, sly, and obstinate child of nearly six. Fanny, the second daughter, is a pretty child, but mischievous and untruthful (she is only four). Harriet, the youngest daughter, is a "fat, merry, playful" child, not yet old enough for the schoolroom. Tom is the only son of the Bloomfields. A boy of seven, he is headstrong, imperious, and cruel. His mother dotes on him and insists he be "led, but not driven." Like many in the Brontë novels he is judged by his treatment of animals: the scene in ch. 5 with the nestlings is one of the most painful in the novels.

Boanerges: nickname for Branwell used in a letter from Charlotte to Ellen Nussey (29 Sep 1840?), and possibly an established family joke. Brontë is Greek for "thunder" and in Mark 3 verse 17 they could read of the brother disciples James and John, and that Jesus "surnamed them Boanerges, which is, The sons of thunder." This is the sort of biblical joke or flippant citation that caused raised eyebrows from some readers of Charlotte's and Emily's novels.

Boarham, Mr (no first name given): suitor to Helen Lawrence (later Huntingdon) in *The Tenant of Wildfell Hall*, a droning, tedious, narrow-minded man whose character is analyzed in ch. 16.

Boissec, M. (no first name given): one of the "dandy professors," a colleague of M. Paul Emanuel, before whom Lucy has to display her talents, or lack of them, in ch. 35 of *Villette*.

Bolton Abbey: located in present-day North Yorkshire, this was the destination of an excursion made by the Brontë children and a party of Nusseys in August/September 1833. The Brontës and Ellen went in a humble gig from Haworth and were much condescended to by the attendants at the Devonshire Arms until the handsome carriage-and-pair carrying the Nussey party arrived (so, at any rate, Ellen tells us). The ruined Abbey was very much to the Brontës' taste, raised as they were on Scott. Ellen records that Branwell was "in a phrensy of pleasure, his eyes flashed with excitement, and he talked fast and brilliantly" ("Reminiscences," *Scribner's Monthly*, May 1871). In the next year (1834) Charlotte exhibited a drawing of the Abbey at the Royal Northern Society for the Encouragement of the Fine Arts's exhibition in Leeds, but this was a copy of an engraving by Edward Finden, which was itself a version of a Turner drawing of 1809 (see AOTB, p. 228).

The Brontës and Ellen may have made another excursion to the area in June 44 (see Barker, 1994, pp. 438, 920).

Booth, Ann: lodging-house keeper in Garrison Street, Bridlington, with whom Charlotte and Ellen stayed for one week at the end of their East Coast holiday in Sep/Oct 1839.

Booth, James: the gardener at Fieldhead in *Shirley*.

Borrow, George Henry (1803–81): writer of autobiographical and travel books, much appreciated by Patrick and Charlotte: "In George Borrow's works I found a wild fascination, a vivid graphic power of description, a fresh originality, an athletic simplicity (so to speak) – which give them a stamp of their own" (to WSW, 4 Feb 1849). Borrow's veracity has been questioned, and his romanticization of gypsy life mocked, but there is no doubting the vigor and vividness of his best work.

Boultby, Mrs: wife of the vicar of Whinbury in *Shirley*. A solicitous, foolish woman. Grace Boultby (ch. 16) may be Mrs Boultby or a daughter.

Boultby, Dr Thomas: vicar of Whinbury in *Shirley*. A large, complacent gentleman, much ministered to by the ladies.

Bowles, Caroline (1786–1854): poet and second wife of Robert Southey. She apparently gave "advice and encouragement" to Branwell when he sent her his poem "Sir Henry Tunstall" (letter from Branwell to *Blackwood's*, 6 Sep 1842). Southey married her after his first wife went mad and died in an asylum, but he himself had a mental breakdown a few weeks after the second marriage, and for the last four years of his life (he died in 1843) he was nursed by his new wife.

Bradford: the nearest large town to Haworth and, thanks to the Industrial Revolution, a thriving, expanding, polluted place. The younger Brontë children were born nearby at Thornton. Branwell tried to make a living there as a portrait painter between summer 1838 and February 1839, but declining demand and lack of talent defeated him. He lodged with the Kirbys at 2 Fountain Street. Though the Vicar of Bradford was Patrick's superior in the Church, the town generally does not loom large in the Brontës' lives. Very little is left of the Bradford Branwell would have known.

Bradford Herald: a new Tory newspaper to which Branwell submitted a sheaf of poems in 1842. Many of the poems appeared simultaneously in this paper and in the *Halifax Guardian*, and also later in the *Yorkshire Gazette*.

Bradford Post Office: Charlotte's letters contain constant complaints of delays, dishonesty, and so on at the Bradford Post Office, and requests that mail be addressed to "Haworth near *Keighley* instead of *Bradford*" (to WSW, 27 Nov 1847). The *Leeds Intelligencer* for 12 November 1836 has a long report on embezzlement at this office.

Bradford School of Industry: charity school, to which Patrick applied for a suitable nursemaid in 1816. Nancy Garrs, who was chosen, and Sarah Garrs who followed her into the household, went through this institution.

Bradley, Rev. James Chesterton (1818–1913): curate of Oakworth 1844?–47 and the original of David Sweeting in *Shirley*. He had left the area by the time *Shirley* was published and the rest of his long life was spent in Paddington and the West Country. While curate in Keighley he had conducted the funeral service for Aunt Branwell. He was instantly recognized as Sweeting, in the Haworth area, not least by his flute-playing.

Bradley, John (1787–1844): housepainter, artist, and occasional architect from Keighley. Gave art lessons to the Brontë children probably 1829–30. He is said to be the painter of one of the surviving portraits of Patrick, and was certainly the recipient of at least two of Charlotte's early artistic efforts. The *Leeds Intelligencer* (4 Dec 1828) records him as having lost four sons within the previous 18 months.

Branderham, Rev. Jabes: the author of a printed sermon entitled *Seventy Times Seven*, over which Lockwood nods during his enforced night stay at Wuthering Heights, who subsequently appears in his dream delivering a sermon of comic tediousness and a Nonconformist obsession with the minutiae of sin. Satire on the Methodists and other Protestant sects is common in the Brontë novels, and goes back to their early writings. The satire here is of a verve and comic vigor that marks it off from Branwell's heavy-handed philippic in "And the Weary are at Rest."

See also Bunting, Rev. Jabez

Branwell, Maria *see* Brontë, Maria

Branwell, Elizabeth (1776–1842): the sister of Maria Brontë, and the least known and written-about member of the Parsonage household. This may be because Charlotte felt little affection for her. The references to her in letters are respectful but quite lacking in warmth.

Her first visit to the Brontës (June 1815–July 1816) was to Thornton. Her doings there are chronicled in Elizabeth Firth's diary. Among other things she stood godmother to Elizabeth Brontë. She probably returned to Yorkshire in the Spring of 1821 to help nurse her dying sister and to supervise the children of the household. She seems to have stayed on until her own death, though she never ceased to regret the climate and gaieties of her native Penzance. The enormous sacrifice she made, presumably from a sense of duty, has been insufficiently appreciated.

She seems to have kept to her room a great deal of the time, adding to the young Brontës' freedom downstairs. She taught the girls sewing and probably the early stages of reading and writing. She seems to have been set in her ways by the time she arrived, and she organized things to accommodate her preferences and convenience, naturally enough. The servants found her "near" (stingy), and her insensitivity to the children's love of Tabitha Aykroyd led to a successful "strike" against her being removed from the household after an accident (Christmas 1836). She was in conflict too with the children about their over-inclusive love of animals. Emily's Diary Note of 1845 includes a catalogue of animals, and there seems animus against her dead aunt in her mention of Nero and the geese who were all given away. There is the irritation of one who wants to see more of the world than Haworth and Keighley in Charlotte's references to her aunt's supposed plans for a trip to Liverpool: "Aunt – like many other elderly people – likes to *talk* of such things but when it comes to putting them into actual practise she rather falls off" (to EN, 4 Aug 1839).

Nevertheless Aunt Branwell came good at crucial moments of her nieces' lives: she was generous in financing their Brussels trip, and her legacy would have been the basis of their school at the Parsonage if pupils could have been found. Her generosity in the former case apparently surprised Charlotte, and Branwell's grief at her death seems sincere ("I have now lost the [guide] and director of all the happy days connected with my childhood," letter to F. H. Grundy, 29 Oct 1842), but this is always difficult to estimate with Branwell. Nothing any of the children wrote about her brings her to life as Ellen Nussey's sketch does:

> Miss Branwell was a very small antiquated little lady, she wore caps large enough for half a dozen of the present fashion, and a front of light auburn curls over her forehead . . . She took snuff out of a very pretty little gold snuff box, which she sometimes presented with a little laugh as if she enjoyed the slight shock and astonishment visible in your countenance . . . when we all met for tea, she would be very lively and intelligent in her talk, and tilted argument without fear against Mr. Brontë.
>
> ("Reminiscences," *Scribner's Monthly*, May 1871.
> See also text from ms. in CBL, v. 1, pp. 589–610)

The idea that Aunt Branwell brought into the family an obsession with damnation and the gloomier doctrines of Calvinism does not hold water. Winifred Gerin's over-the-top exposition of this notion is well refuted by Juliet Barker (1994, pp. 281–3). She does, however, seem to have been a "stickler," who ran the family by imposing discipline, a routine, and strict and conventional standards of behavior. This was probably necessary and for the good with a family of such original children.

See also Penzance; Kingston, Elizabeth Jane

Branwell family: Maria Brontë and Elizabeth Branwell were the daughters of Thomas Branwell, a successful property owner and merchant of Penzance, and his wife Anne, née Carne. The marriage of 1768 seems to have produced eight daughters and three sons, though four of these children died in infancy. Thomas died in 1809, Anne the next year. Among the sisters of Maria and Elizabeth were Anne, Charlotte (who married a Branwell cousin in Penzance on the same day as Maria married Patrick, and who CB was said to resemble), and Jane, who married unhappily a prominent but peccant Methodist preacher, John Kingston. Among the brothers was Benjamin, who became Mayor of Penzance in 1809.

Branwell visitors stayed with the Brontës on at least two occasions. In 1840 they were visited by John Branwell Williams and his family, cousins of their aunt, and Charlotte as usual preferred the male to the female – "Mr Williams himself was much less assuming than the womanites" (to EN, 14 Aug 1840?). Thomas Brontë Branwell, son of Charlotte Branwell, visited in September 1851, and Charlotte's "the coast is now clear" (in a letter to MW, 22 Sep 1851?, proposing a visit) suggests that he wasn't someone she was anxious her friend should meet.

"Branwell's Blackwood's Magazine": tiny magazine conducted by Branwell in the first six months of 1829, which mirrored the real periodical in its mixture of travel, fiction, poetry, reviews, and so forth. He handed the magazine over to Charlotte in the summer of 1829, "tho I shall write now and then for it." She renamed it "Blackwood's Young Men's Magazine" but ran it on similar principles.

Braun, Fräulein Anna: German tutor of Lucy Snowe and Paulina de Bassompierre in *Villette*. She is an emotional, hearty-eating woman who finds her students' English reserve puzzling and depressing.

Brearley Hall: seventeenth-century house near Luddenden Foot where Branwell lodged while working at the station there (1841–2). His landlords were the farmer James Clayton and his wife Rachel.

Bremer, Frederika (1801–65): Swedish novelist, pioneer feminist, many of whose novels were translated into English by Mary Howitt. Anne at least read her, and Charlotte "laughed out" (to ECG, 6 Nov 1851) at Mrs Gaskell's description of her. This may well have concerned the Swede's habit of spitting in all possible locations (ECG to Maria James, 29 Oct 1851).

Bretton, Dr John Graham: the object of Lucy Snowe's affections in the first half of *Villette*. He is first seen as a schoolboy in the opening section of the novel – healthy, hearty, generous, and the object of the child Paulina's interest and love. He reappears lightly disguised as Dr John, first to help Lucy when she arrives in Villette (though he apparently does not recognize her or her name), then as a medical visitor to the Pensionnat. His character is analyzed throughout the novel, often with a sort of wonderment that any man could be so good, so beautiful, so clearly destined for happiness. The effect of those such as Dr John and his mother on those around them is best expressed in ch. 19. This is not to say he is an impossible hero: the chaffing relationship between him and his mother, mentions of his mental limitations, his infatuation with Ginevra Fanshawe, all prevent this. Nevertheless he seems to exist in a glow of warmth that easily explains Lucy Snowe's hunger for the contact with him that his letters provide (chs. 21–2). Her feeling for him is that of a silently nurtured love that comes close to worship. With the reappearance of Paulina, however, any hopes she may have cherished evaporate.

Graham Bretton is generally agreed to be a portrait of George Smith, Charlotte Brontë's publisher. Many biographers believe she was in love with him, and some that they came close to getting engaged.

Bretton, Louisa Lucy: Lucy Snowe's godmother in *Villette*. She is a kindly, matronly woman with a strong sense of humor and an overwhelming love for and pride in her son. The center of the presentation of her is the humorous duels with her son, but Lucy often emphasizes that she shares with him the faculty of imparting happiness to less fortunate people: "the means to give pleasure rose spontaneously in their minds" (ch. 19). In the case of Mrs Bretton there is perhaps some slight undertow of doubt left in the reader's mind, partly by her long separation from Lucy and her affairs just at the time when she would have been most useful, partly by the fact that her interest and favors seem to alternate with forgetfulness and unconscious neglect. This may correspond with some doubt or suspicion on Charlotte's part of the nature and actions of George Smith's mother, almost certainly the character's model. Shortly after sending the completed manuscript to her publisher she wrote to Ellen Nussey about a "very kind" note from Mrs Smith: "I almost wish I could still look on that kindness just as I used to do: it was very pleasant to me once" (9 Dec 1852?). It is possible that she regarded Mrs Smith as hostile to any engagement between herself and George.

Brewster, Sir David (1781–1868): eminent Scottish physicist, inventor of the kaleidoscope, one-time editor of the *Edinburgh Review* and the *Edinburgh Encyclopaedia*, to which Mrs Gaskell's father contributed. He showed Charlotte round the Great Exhibition of 1851, an honor she greatly appreciated: "he gave information in the kindest and simplest manner," she told Ellen Nussey (24 June 1851?), but she confessed to Margaret Wooler that "he looked on objects with other eyes than mine" (14 July 1851).

Briarmains: home of the Yorke family in *Shirley*. The family is based on the Taylors of Gomersal, the house on their home, the Red House. The description of the house is very exact, and tribute was paid to this by Mary Taylor in a letter of 13 August 1850 to Charlotte. Charlotte's attitude to the family, particularly Joe ("Martin Yorke") fluctuated, but her attitude to the house was constant: she loved it for its evidences of culture and thought, for the excitement of the disputes that took place within it, and for the chances it gave her to inspect good pictures.

See also Red House; Taylor, Anne; Taylor, John; Taylor, Joseph, Taylor, Joshua II; Taylor, Joshua III; Taylor, Martha; Taylor, Mary; Taylor, William Waring.

Bridlington (alternatively Burlington) and Bridlington Quay: seaside towns in East Yorkshire, Bridlington being a mile inland from the Quay. After their month at Easton Farm in August/September 1839, Charlotte and Ellen had a week in lodgings in Garrison Street, in the Quay. Charlotte's great joy was her first sight of the sea, "its glorious changes – its ebb and flow – the sound of its restless waves" (to HN, 28 Oct 1839) which made infinitely more impression on her than the fact that part of the journey to the East Coast was her first experience of railway travel. Ellen Nussey in her "Reminiscences" mentions Charlotte's amusement at the conventionality of most of the visitors to the Quay, the evening Parade of visitors on the pier striking her as "the greatest absurdity." Charlotte and Ellen stayed there again in June 1849 after Anne's death, again at Easton Farm.

"Brief Treatise on the Best Time and Mode of Baptism, A": tract by Patrick printed by R. Aked of Keighley in 1836, and part of a local tract war. The pamphlet defends infant baptism and contains some knockabout humor on the superiority of the Irish.

Briery Close: house rented by the Kay-Shuttleworths above Windermere, the present building being a replacement. In the old, chalet-style building Charlotte met Mrs Gaskell while both were staying there in August 1850, which was the beginning of their friendship. Ironically the house is just above Lowood, the name of which Charlotte had used for her school in *Jane Eyre*.

Briggs, Mr (no first name given): a London solicitor with an "official, nasal voice" who stops the marriage of Jane Eyre and Mr Rochester (v. 2, ch. 11). He also brings Jane news of her dying uncle, and informs St John Rivers of the events which led to Jane's flight from Thornfield (v. 3, ch. 7).

Britannia: weekly newspaper. It reviewed *Wuthering Heights* not imperceptively, calling it (15 Jan 1848) "a fragment . . . of colossal proportion," one which proceeds from a mind "of limited experience, but original energy and of a singular and distinctive cast." The same paper criticized *Jane Eyre*'s "total want of . . . construction" but praised its "deep insight into character" (6 Nov 1847).

British Museum: there is no record of any of the Brontës visiting the great museum, but it was something Branwell longed to see. However, he wrote somewhat Micawberishly in his last years that though he had once longed for a week to range through it, "now . . . my eyes would roam over the Elgin marbles, the Egyptian saloon and the most treasured volumes like the eyes of a dead cod fish" (to J. B. Leyland, 24 Jan 1847).

Broad, The: home of Mary Burder near Wethersfield in Essex.

Broadbent, Dr (no first name given): a speaker at a Bible Society Meeting in *Shirley*, commented on by the Misses Sykes – a beautiful speaker, but "like a butcher in appearance" (ch. 7).

Brock, Marie: the imbecile pupil in *Villette* with whom Lucy is left almost alone at the Pensionnat during the long vacation. She is described as "lethargic," but with "an aimless malevolence" (ch. 15), and later Lucy tells M. Paul that it was terrible to be alone with her.

Brocklehurst family: family of Robert Brocklehurst in *Jane Eyre*. Apart from Robert, the family consists of: Mrs Brocklehurst, wife of Robert, who makes an appearance before the girls at Lowood with her daughters, and is characterized by a costly cloak and a false front of hair; Miss Brocklehurst, eldest daughter of Robert; Augusta, second daughter of Robert, whom he quotes as commenting on the "quiet and plain" look of the girls at Lowood School, making them look "almost like poor people's children" – a quote he brings out for Aunt Reed's benefit, calculating – rightly – that it will appeal to her as a fate for Jane. The elaborately curled hair of the sisters, and their rich, elegant attire, expose the double standards of Mr Brocklehurst in v. 1, ch. 7. Master Broughton and Theodore, presumably sons of Robert, are mentioned by Mrs Reed. Naomi, mother of Robert, was the foundress of Lowood Institution – the significance of the word "Institution" is something that much puzzles the child Jane Eyre.

Brocklehurst, Robert:
the ruling power at Lowood School, where Jane is sent by Mrs Reed, and the son of the foundress. In a long line of stern and hypocritical evangelical clergymen in fiction, he is presented as a man of double standards who encourages luxury and social pretension in his own womenfolk, but enforces an anti-natural state of abstemiousness and ugliness in the girls at Lowood. He is depicted as totally out of touch with the realities of childhood, and a harsh and inefficient manager of the school, who is responsible for the spread of the typhus epidemic among the girls weakened by privation. This "black marble" clergyman is described in terms which sometimes suggest a kinship with St John Rivers. The original is assumed to be Rev. Carus Wilson.

Brontë, Anne (1820−49):
Anne Brontë was born at Thornton on 17 Jan 1820, and was christened on 25 March, her godparents being Elizabeth Firth and Fanny Outhwaite (a legacy from whom eased the last months of Anne's life). She grew up in Haworth, the loved and pampered youngest child of a large family and the favorite of Aunt Branwell. She seems to have felt the disadvantages of that position more keenly than she appreciated the conveniences. Charlotte's first story began "There was once a little girl and her name was Ane," but later she put into the mouth of Branwell's fictional alter-ego, Patrick Benjamin Wiggins, the view that Anne was "nothing": the danger was that as baby of the family she would be both cosseted and despised.

The family was reluctant to let Anne shake off the protection of home, and she first left Haworth for any length of time when she was nearly 16, after Emily had failed the test of leaving home to go to Roe Head school. Anne took her place in Autumn 1835, and the next decade saw her away from home more than any of her sisters. Though she was often unhappy, these experiences gave her a certain independence which being at home would have denied her, and this is no doubt the reason for her persistence in seeking situations as a governess and in retaining them even when she disliked the people she was forced to live among.

We have little record of Anne's stay at Roe Head, for Charlotte was preoccupied during the two years Anne spent there by her own spiritual and emotional problems. We do know that towards the end of her time there she was ill, and asked to see the Moravian minister of the area, James la Trobe, who left an account of their discussions of religion. The episode suggests that Anne did not feel at home with the conventional Anglican clerics of the vicinity, or their views. Anne seems to have left the school at the end of 1837, and then to have been at home in Haworth for over a year. The only traces we have of her in this year, 1838, are a few poems, all written in or around the school holiday period (January and July–August), suggesting the company of Charlotte acted as a stimulus.

In April 1839 she became a governess to the Ingham family of Blake Hall, a house of some pretensions. Though we cannot regard the account of Agnes Grey's first situation as a literal record, or even a very close one, of Anne's at Blake Hall, Charlotte records that the children there were "excessively indulged" (to EN, 15 Apr 1839) and it is likely they taxed all the powers of a fledgling governess. She seems to have left the post, or been dismissed, around Christmas 1839.

Her next post, at Thorp Green, near Little Ouseburn, lasted much longer. Chitham (1991) puts the date of her taking up the position in May 1840, which would mean she stayed for five years. In two successive diary papers she expressed her dislike of the situation, and the Robinsons do seem to have been worldly and untrustworthy. However, she gained the affection and trust of her girl pupils, and the parents seemed to have allowed or encouraged her to introduce Branwell into the household as tutor to the young son of the family, Edmund. On the other hand it is possible that Branwell, enthusiastic walker and railway-man, visited Anne at Thorp Green and was recognized by Mrs Robinson as ideal tutor material. From the time of the affair – real, imagined, or invented – between Branwell and Mrs Robinson, Anne's uneasiness and dissatisfaction increased. Mrs Gaskell mentions "expressions of agonising suspicion in Anne's letters home," but she was anxious to attribute Charlotte's depression at this time to worry about Branwell, rather than its real cause, her impossible love for M. Heger.

Anne had herself, in all probability, fallen in love in the early 1840s with William Weightman. Chitham (1991), who examines the evidence most closely, concludes this is likely to be the case, and that several poems refer to him, before and after his early death. The only external evidence is Charlotte's picture of Weightman "sighing softly" at Anne in church, and she looking "so quiet, her look so downcast – they are a picture" (to EN, 20 Jan 1842).

Anne left her situation in June 1845, and Branwell was dismissed soon afterwards. Branwell's course was thereafter downhill, and Anne may have felt partially responsible for this, adding to a didactic strain in her as a writer. Her first novel is low-key, beautifully judged, and can be seen as a criticism of or counterbalance to her sisters' more heightened and romantic productions. *Agnes Grey* has always had admirers, but her second, *The Tenant of Wildfell Hall*, though it sold reasonably well, was disliked by Charlotte and most of its early readers. In this and the previous century its picture, unsparingly detailed, of an unhappy and ill-matched marriage, has gained it many admirers.

After her release from governesshood Anne went on two expeditions, to York with Emily in 1845 and to London with Charlotte, to reveal the facts about the Bells' authorship, in 1848. Otherwise she seems to have remained at Haworth, writing poetry and fiction. One poem "The Three Guides," was published in *Fraser's Magazine*. She had always been of weak health, suffering particularly from asthma. That she was tubercular began to be clear during Emily's last sickness, and was confirmed by "Mr Teale, Surgeon, Leeds" as Mr Brontë called him, early in the New Year, 1849. She succeeded eventually in getting away to try the efficacy of sea air in one of her favorite places, Scarborough, where she had gone each year with the Robinson family. She died there on 28 May 1849.

The character of "dear, gentle Anne," as Ellen Nussey called her, has led to her being overshadowed and counted as inferior not just in literary interest but in biographical importance to her sisters – a situation which has only been remedied in recent years. Her quietness hid a great strength of character, a spiritual tenaciousness and sense of quest, particularly in her holding to and proclaiming her belief in universal salvation. It is worth remarking that Charlotte's word to describe her is not "shy" but "taciturn," which seems to link her with Emily, her friend and ally in the family, at least until the last years, when she seems to have judged harshly of Emily's character and spiritual state. Charlotte's remark that "it is with difficulty one can prevail on her to take a walk or induce her to converse" (to EN, 7 Oct 1847) raises the question of whether her picture of the three sisters discussing and reading aloud the novels they were writing was something of a cozification.

Anne seems to have spent much of her life, like Agnes Grey, in escaping from the limitations imposed on a youngest child by a loving but underestimating family. For the reader and critic of today she makes her own mark as person, thinker and writer: at last she has escaped from the shadow.

See also Ingham family; Robinson, Elizabeth; Robinson, Lydia (née Gisborne); Robinson, Lydia; Robinson, Mary

Brontë, Charlotte (1816–55):

Charlotte was the first of the Brontë children to be born at Thornton, on 21 April 1816. Her godparents are believed to have been Frances Walker and Thomas Atkinson. Charlotte, alone of the children who survived to adulthood, spoke of a memory of her mother, playing with the infant Branwell, and she was very touched when her father, in 1850, showed her the bunch of letters Maria had written to him during their courtship months. The crucial events of her early years were the death of her mother in 1821 and the year at Cowan Bridge School (1824–5) which left her with feelings of loss, deprivation, and anger which found memorable vent in the early chapters of *Jane Eyre*. The greatest loss, that of her two elder sisters, meant she assumed the leadership of the children, acting as substitute mother in areas where Aunt Branwell proved deficient. The leadership was shared with Branwell in the childhood games, which gradually developed and coalesced into what we inaccurately call "Angria."

It was Charlotte who was sent away to a good school, Roe Head, for a concentrated period of 18 months (1831–2). The presumption was that she would pass on what she had learnt to the younger girls – a logical and useful expedient for a poor family. There she made friends, Ellen Nussey and Mary Taylor, who were to last a lifetime and were to be the only strong links to the outside world which all the children shared and valued. The education she received was broader in scope than many boys in British public schools received, and her distinction as a pupil was acknowledged when she was invited to return as a teacher in 1835. The relationship with the headmistress Margaret Wooler, involving some choppy patches, nevertheless survived, and culminated in her giving Charlotte away at her wedding in 1854.

By the time of her teaching years at Roe Head the childhood games had become more intense and all-consuming, with the Byronic figure of Zamorna (or Douro) and his loves occupying much of Charlotte's emotional life. It was the inevitable weakening of this preoccupation that led to a lot of the unhappiness Charlotte experienced during her years of teaching at Roe Head and its successor Dewsbury Moor (1835–8). Another factor was her temporary preoccupation with religion of an unhealthy Calvinistic brand. Perhaps most important of all was that Charlotte found she disliked teaching, yet had to face the likelihood that teaching would be her fate in life if she did not marry.

This aversion was strengthened by two periods of governessing, in particular the brief one with the Sidgwick family at Stonegappe and Swarcliffe (May to mid-July 1839), a time she looked back on later in life with an intense loathing. The year with the Whites (Mar–Dec 1841) was less stressful, but she felt demeaned by the position and (what she perceived as) the commonness of her employers. In both posts a pattern was established: she liked the male of the household much more than she liked the female.

Her home life was much happier, with visits from friends, the arrival in Haworth of William Weightman, and continued creativity through poetry and the Angrian saga. Later contributions to this steamy narrative veer between the old chronicle form, where several narratives are kept in the air in the manner of a modern soap opera, and stories in which the narrative tends more towards the novella, with concentration on one single topic, usually the love-life of Zamorna. Gradually and reluctantly she realized she had to break free of "that burning clime where we have sojourned too long" ("The Farewell to Angria") and try to write saleable prose of one kind or another. While at the Whites she began organizing a period in a Continental school for herself and one of her sisters, to fit them to run a school of their own, but also perhaps to give them a range of experience and a depth of knowledge that they might draw on if they managed to become writers in their own right. Significantly, perhaps, Emily was chosen to accompany her – she was never likely to become a willing or successful teacher, but Charlotte clearly saw her as the more stimulating companion and the more likely writer. Anne she still saw as the baby. She had already had two proposals of marriage, rejected without regret or second thoughts. Now she was preparing for the possibility of life as a writer.

The first year (1842) at the Pensionnat Heger in Brussels was marked by their teacher, Monsieur Heger's, awareness that he had acquired two outstanding pupils, and by Charlotte's realization (and perhaps eventually Emily's too) that chance had sent them to sit at the feet of a brilliant natural teacher. (No other teachers at the school made any impression on them, apparently). Gradually Charlotte's admiration developed into love. That she was aware of this even during the first year is evidenced by her later confession to Ellen Nussey (14 Oct 1846) that she returned to Brussels "against my conscience – prompted by what then seemed an irresistible impulse."

After Aunt Branwell's death in October 1842 Charlotte returned alone for a second year in Brussels. Why did she go back? What could she hope for? What could be more demeaning than sitting round hoping for Mme Heger somehow or other to be removed? Charlotte was rewarded by a year of hopelessness, loneliness, and depression, as Heger and his wife kept her increasingly at arm's length. She returned to Haworth at New Year 1844.

By now the sisters had received small legacies on the death of Aunt Branwell. Since Emily had decided to remain at home, we have a few letters from Brussels from Charlotte

to Emily, emphasizing her homesickness and loneliness – these are among the few letters of the young Brontës to each other that have survived. Her first year back at home
saw her struggling with despair and unrequited love, and writing the desperate, rather
shameful letters to Heger. Eventually she survived by reigniting her wish to become a
published author. Her discovery of Emily's poetry, her recognition of the distinction
of the verse her sister was then (1844–5) writing, led to the project of a volume of
poetry by the sisters, and to the commencement of three novels, then as now the most
likely bringers of a reasonable financial return. The three novels were *The Professor*,
Wuthering Heights, and *Agnes Grey*. And when these novels started their wearisome
round of publishers, Charlotte began *Jane Eyre*.

Though Charlotte was one of three equals in the creative process of writing (she
often emphasized that each took her own way, and was seldom swayed by criticism)
it seems likely that she played a leading part in the marketing of the products. She
was the first Brontë to sell a novel to a publisher, Smith, Elder, willing to take all the
financial risks, and she was rightly bitter about Thomas Newby, who procrastinated
about publishing her sisters' works and supplied a shoddy end-product even as he pock-
eted the subsidy he demanded from them. Charlotte was eventually rather sore at the
£500 George Smith gave her for *Villette*, but she seems to have felt, illogically, that
payment should be in accord with the pains taken in the writing of a work, rather
than its likely sales.

The coming of George Smith and his editor W. S. Williams into her life marked
a turning point. Now she had regular contact with the outside world, with a lively
social and intellectual circle which she enjoyed experiencing vicariously rather than
in person. Parcels of books came from Smith, Elder to Haworth. Perhaps even more
stimulating, letters from London dealt with current events, literary gossip, moral questions, even religious topics. She became a literary person talking on an equality with
other literary persons. She was a sad and frustrated person transformed.

Naturally she wanted her sisters to enjoy a similar success, both financially and
intellectually. This was an extension of the "mother" role that had been part of their
relationship since childhood. There were also less attractive aspects to the role, such
as her tendency to diminish Anne's writing and personality, ignoring her persistence
and integrity to concentrate on her shyness and muteness. (Emily's impossibility as a
social animal was not similarly criticized, presumably because she felt it was justified
by her intellectual strength and daring). In the matter of her advocating a change of
publisher she met with a blank wall of refusal. Probably because they objected to being
towed in her wake, they stuck with their "scamp" publisher Newby.

The success of *Jane Eyre* in Autumn 1847 brought joy and transformation to
Charlotte, but it also reinforced her instinct for anonymity. This was threatened by
Newby's determination to muddy the waters first as to which Bell "brother" had written which novel, then on whether there were really three of them or only one. This
forced Charlotte and Anne to go to London (Emily characteristically refused) to prove
that there were more than one, they were female (though she made a bad error in
lumping Emily with them under that denomination), and they were not responsible
for the self-serving confusion spread about by Newby. This was the first of Charlotte's

visits to London as a successful author – visits which gave her mixed pleasure and pain and helped to weaken the effectiveness of the pseudonymous cover the women had devised for themselves.

The success and also the writing of *Shirley* were interrupted by a terrible series of illnesses and deaths. Charlotte's strength as a leader and mother-figure was never more threatened or exercised with more pain and stress. Emily died three months after Branwell, Anne five months after Emily. The concentration of mental and physical anguish was nearly unbearable. Emily's death was the most devastating, since she declined to be seen or advised by a doctor. Knowing tuberculosis because she knew Haworth, she was certain what her fate would be. But declining false hope for herself, she also denied it to others. Anne, hoping against hope for more time, took medical advice and made the experience of loss for Charlotte a little more tolerable. By the summer of 1849 she was home again, after Anne's death in Scarborough, pacing round the dining room alone, clinging to her father as her only link with the past, and now and then making excursions into the outside world – either to London and the hospitality of the Smiths, or to such hosts as Harriet Martineau, the Kay-Shuttleworths (reluctantly), or Mrs Gaskell.

Romantic interests entered her largely solitary life. James Taylor was a character who interested and yet repelled her by his assertiveness and his dogmatism. George Smith could not fail to attract: young, handsome, successful. Perhaps before long she attained the same conviction that Lucy Snowe had concerning John Bretton – that he was a creature from another world altogether, too fortunate and sunny-natured ever to consider a more introverted and unhappy creature such as herself in a romantic light. But if Charlotte attained such a conviction it was a precarious one, as witnessed by her letter of "congratulations" on Smith's engagement (10 Dec 1853) which was graceless and ungrateful.

The romantic interest, when it came, was unexpected. Charlotte's contempt for the ecclesiastical breed loosely characterized as "curates" had been made obvious both on social occasions and in *Shirley*. But her assessment of Arthur Bell Nicholls in that novel (ch. 37) as Mr Macarthey, though shaded with humor and satire, was by and large admiring. He had clearly cherished a lonely love for her for years. When he eventually made his declaration in December 1852 it was not altogether unforeseen by Charlotte, but still a shock. Her father's determined opposition was another. Her refusal left a tiny area for hope, and she was certainly interested and flattered by the obvious power of his attachment to her. Eventually, and partly because Nicholls's replacement as curate was such a disaster, Patrick and Charlotte both accepted that a marriage was going to take place, which it quietly did on 29 June 1854.

Her modest expectations of happiness were greatly exceeded, and it is clear that both sides worked hard to forge a genuine partnership. There is obvious sincerity in her references to him during their brief marriage: "he *is* 'my dear boy' certainly – dearer now than he was six months ago" (to EN, 26 Dec 1854). But by early 1855 Mr Brontë's worst fears were realized and Charlotte was pregnant. To Joe Taylor's wife Amelia she wrote in late February: "my sufferings are very great – my nights indescribable – sickness with scarce a reprieve." So many clergymen's wives of her acquaintance had suffered or died through their late first pregnancies that both she and those around her in the Parsonage seem to have realized what would be the likely outcome. She died early on 31 March 1855.

Charlotte's character was complex, contradictory, not always likeable. She *was* the slave to duty that Ellen Nussey always tried to portray her as, but this tells only a small part of the story. She could be ruthless in decision making, and also in her judgments of others (which were often hasty, based on hearsay, and needing to be revised). She was by nature a straight dealer with others, with a preference for honesty and direct-ness, but she could fall from this ideal, as when she hid her authorship from her friend Ellen Nussey, or sneered at her fiancé's qualities of mind during her engagement. Her discarding of Branwell when he failed (admittedly spectacularly) to live up to the family's expectations was near-total and unattractive.

On the other hand, those who got to know her well honored as well as loved her, not only for what she had suffered, but for the moral standards she took as her watch-word. In appearance she was tiny, provincially dressed, with a large forehead and bad teeth. Many people commented on the beauty of her eyes, and with a sympathetic audience her shyness and silence could alternate with eloquence when her imagina-tion was seized by a subject. The disastrous dinner party with Thackeray's lady friends both social and literary (when his chaste mistress Mrs Brookfield noticed her false hair-piece) was more a comment on the inadequacies of the company she was expected to mingle with than of Charlotte herself.

See also Heger, Constantin; Nicholls, Rev. Arthur Bell; Nussey, Ellen; Smith, George; Taylor, Mary; Williams, William Smith

Brontë, Elizabeth (1815–25): the least-known of the Brontë children, perhaps

because she came in age between two exceptional girls, Maria and Charlotte. She was born in Hartshead but christened in Thornton, after the family's move there. She is sometimes described as the home-maker of the young ones. This may be because Patrick, in the game of the mask (see entry for Patrick Branwell Brontë), asked about "the best mode of education for a woman," and she replied "that which would make her rule her house well" (to ECG, 30 July 1855). Patrick also said that his second daugh-ter had "good solid sense" (to ECG, 20 June 1855). Surprisingly she was the only Brontë girl whom "Miss Temple" (Ann Evans) had any vivid memory of in the 1850s when Mrs Gaskell consulted her. Elizabeth, she told Charlotte's biographer, had slept in the school superintendent's room for some time, after injuring herself, and "she bore all the consequent suffering with exemplary patience" – a stoical patience she had no doubt learnt from her elder sister. The reports of Elizabeth when she arrived at the school were scathing ("Works very badly. Knows nothing of Grammar, Geography, History or Accomplishments") though this may have been part of a school policy of denigrating the standard of the pupils when they arrived: Elizabeth had had some time at Richmal Mangnal's old school in Wakefield, and her sewing ("work") was good enough for her to complete the obligatory Brontë sampler when she was seven. She left Cowan Bridge School "in ill-health" on 31 May 1825, and died "in decline" on 15 June, the second of two deaths of the older sisters in the family that left painful and long-lasting memories for Branwell in particular.

Brontë, Emily Jane (1818–48):
Emily Brontë was born at Thornton on 30 July 1818, and was christened on 20 August. In April 1820 the family moved to Haworth, and this was to be Emily's home, with only four periods away, all of months only, for the rest of her life.

The first of the periods was at the Clergy Daughters School at Cowan Bridge, which she attended from November 1824 to June 1825. She was described in the register as reading "very prettily and works a little." Miss Evans, the school superintendent, remembered her for Mrs Gaskell's benefit as "a darling child . . . quite the pet nursling of the school" (ECG *Life*, v. 1, ch. 4).

The years succeeding this tragic experience were probably crucial to Emily's artistic and personal development. In the late 1820s she participated in the collective family imaginative life: in the Glasstown saga, its creation and development, but also in more private "bed plays" with her bed partner Charlotte, who wrote in 1829: "Bed plays mean secret plays; they are very nice ones." The connection with Charlotte was broken when the latter went to Miss Wooler's school in 1831, and by the time she returned Emily's strongest relationship was with Anne. Probably discontented with their inferior role in the Glasstown/Angria story, they had created Gondal, which occupied them intermittently for the rest of their lives. By the time Ellen Nussey paid her first visit to Haworth in the summer of 1833 she noted that the two were "like twins – inseparable companions." She said that Emily "talked very little," but tells of her moralizing over tadpoles and says that "No serious care or sorrow had so far cast its gloom on nature's youth and buoyancy," without suggesting what the care or sorrow was which, by implication, later did just that.

The next period away from Haworth was when Emily went with Charlotte to Roe Head School as a pupil, while Charlotte taught. Her stay there was short, from July to October 1835 (it could be still shorter: Anne, most biographers believe, was established in her place by 27 October). When, 15 years later, Charlotte gave reasons for Emily's failure to endure Roe Head she stressed Emily's love of the moors and liberty, but she may have been influenced by a desire not to offend Margaret Wooler. It may have been that at 17 she was unable to endure any sort of discipline. It may have been the fact that most of the other pupils were much younger than herself. In any case contemporary evidence is lacking, there being no letters that deal with the matter.

The years that follow show Emily beginning to write poetry (usually dating it, as her older siblings often dated their Angrian pieces, most usefully for future biographers). This poetic activity ran concurrently, apparently, with prose tales of Gondal which have not survived. In one of the diary papers which Emily and Anne wrote in imitation of Lord Byron, that of 1837, they record the activities both of Angrian characters and of Gondal ones ("the Emperors and Empresses of Gondal and Gaaldine preparing to depart from Gaaldine to Gondal to prepare for the coronation . . . Northangerland in Monkey's Isle – Zamorna at Evesham"), suggesting that both the juvenile sagas were at this stage open and shared.

In spite of her meager formal education Emily secured a post as teacher at Law Hill School at Southowram, near Halifax. Charlotte's letter recording her "slavery" at the school was printed in Gaskell and so offended the school proprietress Miss Patchett that she would never thereafter talk about her teacher. One pupil later told Ellis Chadwick that Emily told her pupils that the house dog was dearer to her than they were. That she sustained this removal from Haworth better than that to Roe Head is attested by her poetic activity, which survived intermittently but intensely in spite of the "slavery," and by her receptiveness to the houses and stories in the vicinity of Law Hill. High Sunderland Hall contributed at least one feature to Wuthering Heights, as did the story of Jack Sharp, the man for whom Law Hill had been built. Thus Emily certainly made good artistic use of her time at Law Hill, which was probably from Autumn to Spring 1838–9.

We have no evidence that Emily considered taking further posts in the years that followed, years in which she consolidated her powers as a poet. However, when the idea was mooted of going to the Continent to widen their horizons and improve their command of modern languages, preparatory to opening a school, it was Emily who was Charlotte's chosen companion. This is in some ways odd, since by 1844 Charlotte was telling M. Heger that, in their plans for a school, "Emily is not very fond of teaching but she would nevertheless take care of the housekeeping" (24 July 1844). Either the preference of Emily over Anne for Brussels represented a mere personal preference on Charlotte's part, or the discovery of her inaptitude for teaching was only made when they were already there. Or, perhaps most likely, Charlotte recognized the power of Emily's mind, its need for the stimulus of further education.

The Brussels months (February to November 1842) left little obvious imprint on Emily's imaginative life, though we do have her often ambitious essays for M. Heger to add to our meager store of her prose writings. She and he did not "draw well together at all" (to EN, May 1842). This may be further evidence of Emily's inability to accept any authority other than her own, since M. Heger was probably the most remarkable man she ever met. She at least initially disliked his system, and was in turn disliked by most of the little girls she taught, especially the Wheelwright sisters, to whom she taught the piano. On the other hand Louise de Bassompierre found Emily more "*sympathique*" than Charlotte, and a friendly relationship between the two young women is attested by Emily's having given her a drawing. Most contemporary evidence from these months seems to agree in finding Emily increasingly odd, remote, silent, and willful.

After her return from Brussels she stayed at Haworth until her death, apart from brief trips to York and Manchester. She took little part in parish life, neither teaching in the Sunday School nor, apparently, attending church. To John Greenwood, the crippled stationer who supplied the family with paper, she was an interesting and intensely attractive character. To others she seemed withdrawn, impossible. After her return from Thorp Green Anne seems to have begun to draw apart from her, apparently disapproving of her views and her increasingly arrogant character. What is undeniable is that Emily played a full part in the creative ferment that produced from the sisters five novels in three years – years that were the most productive, and perhaps the happiest, of her life, especially as these years saw some remarkable poetry as well. Charlotte's reports of her reluctance to publish her poetry may testify only to Emily's habitual opposition to other people's ideas. She was after all, the only one of the sisters whose published work was all put before the public under a form of vanity publishing. Charlotte testified to the pain that hostile reviews brought her. In those years of hope and trouble Emily seems to have been the one who least condemned Branwell in his decline, and perhaps even sought to involve him in her own creative life.

Emily is often said to have caught a cold at Branwell's funeral, though two weeks after his death Charlotte reported that her father and "dear sisters" had "stood the storm well." By the end of October and from then on the progress to her death was inexorable, made worse for her sisters and father by her refusal to accept any help from doctors, whom she regarded as "quacks." She died, reportedly on the parlor sofa, on 19 December 1848.

Emily's character, about which we have little and contradictory testimony, will always be a matter of controversy. On the one hand we have M. Heger's feeling that she should have been "a great navigator," and Charlotte's rather odd view that "Ellis will not be seen in his full strength till he is seen as an essayist" (to WSW, 15 Feb 1848). On the other hand, Charlotte's statement that when discussing with Emily any course of action it was best "not to advocate the side you wish her to favour; if you do she is sure to lean in the opposite direction" (to WSW, 22 Nov 1848) suggests obstinacy veering toward an unintelligent contrariness or cussedness. She seems to have enjoyed putting her sisters in the position of suitors, pleading for a course of action: this happened on the publication of the poems, the sale of railway shares, the calling of a doctor as she sickened. On her staggering artistic development in her short life there can be no two views. One thinks, to take just one aspect, of how the Byronic dwelling on dungeons, crude tyranny, pathetic captives, and so on in the weaker Gondal poems is transmuted and domesticated in *Wuthering Heights*, where the cruelties become isolated blows, the dungeons a remote farmhouse, the tyranny a purely domestic use of chicanery and brute force. The immense gain in power by concentration and intense use of language can be paralleled in the best poems, where the vocabulary is gradually refined and concentrated, so that she uses only those words she can endow with immense force. Her nurture of her own creative life was possibly her substitute for an emotional one. It may be that her consciousness of her own potential greatness led her to destroy her second novel as unworthy to follow her one masterpiece.

See also Law Hill; Pensionnat Heger

Brontë, Maria (née Branwell) (1783–1821): the mother of the Brontës spent her early life in Penzance, part of a family group with a respected and central position in the town. Whether, like her sister later on, she regretted the climate and gaieties of her native town when she moved to Yorkshire we can only guess. She had a family of her own to occupy, and more than occupy, her time.

The immediate cause of her long and difficult journey to Yorkshire was her aunt Jane Fennell's need for help with the domestic arrangements at Woodhouse Grove School, of which her husband had recently become head. It was a new foundation for the sons of Methodist preachers, and arrangements were still extempore bordering on the chaotic. There was a strong Methodist strain in the Branwells' religion, and it may be that Yorkshire as an evangelical mecca was a strong part of its attraction for her, as it had been, since his ordination, for Patrick.

Patrick was serving as a visiting examiner in the Classics at the school when they met and were attracted in mid-1812. Quite soon after, an engagement became an agreed thing, and during this time Maria wrote nine charming but strong-minded letters which give us our best idea of her humor, her faith, and her ability to marshal ideas. She was torn between a natural pride that she had been for some years "perfectly my own mistress, subject to no control whatever," consulted and even deferred to by her mother and elder sisters, and on the other hand her feeling deeply "the want of a guide and instructor." These contrary impulses were ones that her daughter Charlotte was to struggle with, in life and fiction.

The couple were married (along with Jane Fennell, Maria's cousin, and Patrick's loquacious friend William Morgan) at Guiseley Church on 29 December 1812, and the pair went to live at Hartshead, where their first two children, Maria and Elizabeth, were born. They transferred by means of a "swap" to Thornton in 1815, and found there a ready-made circle of friends that was very much to their taste. Baby followed baby, and by the end of the decade doubts were beginning to be felt about Maria's health. When the controversial move to Haworth finally took place in April 1820 Maria had only eight months left to her in which she could fulfill the duties of incumbent's wife. She fell critically ill in January 1821, probably with cancer, and from then on she and her family could only wait for the end. Patrick spoke of her "more agonising pain than I ever saw anyone endure" (to John Buckworth, 27 Nov 1821), and about her hardly seeming to notice what went on around her. Death, when it came in September, was certainly a relief.

Charlotte alone retained a memory of her mother, and this, oddly, was of her playing with Branwell, rather than with one of the younger girls. She was moved when Patrick showed her the letters written to him during their courtship year, and concluded her account to Ellen simply: "I wish She had lived and that I had known her" (16 Feb 1850?). Patrick, who knew her best, should be allowed the last word: he wrote to Mrs Gaskell of his wife's "sound sense, her affectionate disposition, and delicate tact and taste" (3 Nov 1856).

See also "Advantages of Poverty"; Branwell family

Brontë, Maria (1813/14–25):

Brontë, Maria (1813/14–25): eldest child of Patrick and Maria, the only one both born and christened in Hartshead. She made a very strong impression on those around her and others outside the family circle. The picture of her as Helen Burns is not much to modern taste, as she seems a child without a childhood, something that also struck Mrs Gaskell very forcibly. Patrick, even at the end of his life, was still full of admiration at her precocious talents: "Maria had a powerfully intellectual mind" he wrote to Mrs Gaskell (20 June 1855), as if she was one of his contemporaries at Cambridge, not a girl who only just reached double figures in age. Charlotte was equally bowled over by her sister: "She described Maria as a little mother among the rest, superhuman in goodness and cleverness" (EN, "Reminiscences," CBL v. 1, p. 593). Lock and Dixon (1979) claim that Patrick taught Maria Latin and Politics: if this is so, Cowan Bridge School had no measuring-rod for their girls in Politics, and nothing is said of either subject in the register of admissions. The most vivid impression of Maria, one that maintains an element of childishness, is in Mary Robinson's *Emily Brontë* (chs. 2 & 3), but unfortunately it is unclear whether this is based on recollections of people who knew her, or is a piece of pure imaginative writing.

The last few years of Maria's life were spent being a mother to her younger siblings, providing the sort of warm and tolerant love that her mother could no longer give them, and her aunt was apparently temperamentally averse to giving them. For a few months (late 1823) she and Elizabeth were pupils at Crofton Hall School in Wakefield, but the fees proved too high. It would have been infinitely preferable if Maria had been sent there alone for a longer course of concentrated education, and had then come home, as Charlotte later did from Roe Head, to pass this on to her sisters and brother. Instead in 1824 she and Elizabeth were sent to the Clergy Daughters' School at Cowan Bridge, to be followed by Charlotte and Emily. This job lot of Brontë girls cost Patrick half his annual income, as Juliet Barker points out, but the human cost was infinitely greater. It seems likely that communication with home was discouraged by the school authorities, or at least censored. At any rate it seems to have come as a terrible surprise to Patrick to hear of Maria's suspected tuberculosis. He immediately went to North Lancashire and took Maria back home. Mary Robinson (1889) at least shows instinctive insight into the girl when she talks about her at Cowan Bridge: "her careless ways, ready opinions, gentle loving incapacity to become a machine" (p. 35). Being back in Haworth put her among people whose evangelicalism was loving and hopeful, enabling her to face her inevitable death without the threats, blackmail, and hell-fire prophecies that might have been her lot at the Clergy Daughters' School. She died on 6 May, after nearly three months of terrible suffering. The pathos of the little body in the coffin never left Branwell, but it is the fierce anger of Charlotte at the treatment of her she had witnessed at school which means she has lived in minds and hearts to this day.

Brontë, Rev. Patrick (1777–1861):

the father of the Brontës was probably born in a tiny peasant cottage in Emdale, Co. Down, in the north of Ireland. The meager remains of this cottage are today shown to tourists, and give a vivid picture of the humble nature of Patrick's antecedents. It is almost incredible that 25 years later he was to become an undergraduate at St John's College, Cambridge. The family, however, were upwardly mobile, however gentle the slope, and before long they were living in a farmhouse in Ballynaskeah, and Patrick, the eldest child, was receiving an education, probably supplemented by intensive self-education. By the age of 16 he had established his own school, and around 1798 he became tutor to the sons of the Rev. Thomas Tighe. This was at a time of great national unrest (Wolfe Tone's Irish Rebellion), and by accepting this employment Patrick probably threw in his lot with the ruling caste in Ulster. Crucially Tighe was a graduate of St John's College. It seems certain that Tighe not only predisposed Patrick to an association with the Wesleyan party in the Anglican church, but also encouraged him to try for an English education, and perhaps an English career. In 1802 he entered St John's as a sizar – a college-subsidized student – his name being entered in the register as "Branty," which was also the form it first took in the residence register. Patrick had it changed to Bronte, Nelson's dukedom bestowed by the King of the Two Sicilies. The dieresis came later, and was only used occasionally by Patrick himself.

Patrick kept himself at college by means of exhibitions (a form of scholarship), subsidies from wealthy evangelicals, and above all by living frugally, which he continued to do throughout his life. He associated with Methodists and distinguished himself as a classical scholar – to such an extent that he may have expected more rapid promotion in the Church than actually occurred. It seems likely that he was held back by his humble background. He graduated in 1806, was ordained in August of the same year, and became curate to an absentee vicar at Wethersfield in Essex. Here he learnt his trade, but became involved with Mary Burder, more than 10 years younger than himself. The details of this unsuccessful relationship, including an unofficial engagement, were bitterly disputed later when he tried to resume contact with her, and it is clear that, with justice or without it, Mary was bitterly hurt by Patrick's actions.

In 1809 he transferred first to Wellington in Shropshire, then to Dewsbury in Yorkshire; in both promotions the evangelical connection was important and strengthened. His first position where he might call himself his own master was the perpetual curacy at Hartshead, a parish sorely tried and divided by the industrial unrest known as the Luddite movement, which features in *Shirley*. Patrick seems to have distinguished himself for firmness, but also for his compassion in dealing with the machine-breakers. It was while he was at Hartshead that he met, courted, and married Maria Branwell, who was helping her relatives the Fennells at the recently founded Methodist school for boys at Woodhouse Grove, Appleby Bridge, between Leeds and Bradford. He took his bride to Clough House, in Hightown, and there his first two daughters, Maria and Elizabeth, were born.

In 1815 he moved to Thornton, near Bradford, the first parish where he and his family left a strong mark. It was a poor parish, as all of his parishes were, but he formed enduring links with the "gentry" of the place, particularly the Firths and the Outhwaites. Elizabeth Firth's diary tells us of births and christenings, tea-drinkings, and the long and prophetic visit of Elizabeth Branwell, Patrick's sister-in-law. As one by one the family increased to its destined six we get a sense of a happy and well-integrated unit, with strong friendships and loyalties. These were to be stretched in later years by the widower Patrick's proposal to Elizabeth Firth and Dr Outhwaite's anger at something unspecified that led to an unusually trenchant reply from Patrick (20 Sep 1844), with the Jane-Eyreish declaration that "that God to whom you refer, will judge You and [me], on the day of Doom, when we shall be more on a Level than we now are."

Happy though they were at Thornton, the growing family cried out for a parish that would provide a larger stipend. Haworth called, not least because it had a strong evangelical tradition. Its position was peculiar, however, in that all appointments to the perpetual curacy were claimed by the church trustees to be in the gift of them-selves alone. They also held the purse-strings and paid the incumbent. The various nominations by the vicar of Bradford and the riotous opposition to them by the Haworth inhabitants brought the parish into considerable disrepute, and led to Patrick's withdrawal of his name for consideration. By the time he reconsidered and accepted the living in Haworth he can have been in no doubt that he had a formidable con-gregation and a massive task.

The course of Patrick's life over the next few years was determined by death – first that of his wife Maria, then of the two eldest children, Maria (his favorite) and Elizabeth. Patrick tried to find a second wife, and he appears at his least sympathetic in his trans-actions with Mary Burder (again), Elizabeth Firth, and Isabella Dury – possibly because he in truth wanted a mother for his children rather than a wife. In the end he settled down with his wife's sister as a substitute mother for the four remaining children, with Patrick as the firm but loving head of the household. Speculation on the relations between the two elders has been largely absent in biographies, though a prominent naming of Deuteronomy 25 on the fly-leaf of one of Patrick's bibles might give one cause for thought. In parish matters Patrick was sympathetic but somewhat remote: he found in Haworth no gentry figures to mix with on equal terms as he had in Thornton, and perhaps the circumstances of his appointment taught him that the people there were not accustomed to be lorded over.

By now he was a published author, with four volumes to his credit – volumes which were doubtless on the Parsonage shelves, along with Byron and Cowper, accustoming his children to the possibility of authorship. At Haworth Patrick published some of his sermons, for example on the Crow Hill bog burst and the early death of William Weightman. He also greatly enjoyed writing to newspapers on topics such as the bog burst, capital punishment, infant baptism, and Church rates. He educated his own son, passing on his love of the classics but not much else. He watched as Branwell slipped from his influence and fell under that of the local macho men – superior man-ual workers such as John Brown the sexton. He shows at his least sure and decisive in the matter of finding paid employment for Branwell, veering from bank clerk to portrait painter within a matter of months. Eventually Branwell found his own jobs, with hardly happier outcomes.

Patrick was justly proud of his mastery of the more theatrical sides of his clerical activities, particularly of his impromptu-style sermons. In more private moments with parishioners he could show great sympathy and understanding, as in the letter to Eliza Brown (10 June 1859) informing her indirectly and gradually of the death of her baby. Since, due to the lack of local gentry, the Brontë family occupied an almost royal posi-tion in the village, leaders in manners, morals, and style, he and the children attracted iconoclasts, in particular those who circulated gleefully the rumors that he was an imbiber. Patrick called these foes' gossip "the groundless, yet pernicious censures of the weak – wicked – and wily" (to Mr Milligan, 9 Oct 1838), and variously attributed the tales to the remedies he had taken for dyspepsia and weak eyesight.

If his relations with his parishioners were mostly distant, with his family he was close, tender, and far-sighted. There is a strong tradition that his favorite child was

Emily, whom he believed was the most talented of them all. Certainly he taught her Latin and shooting, both usually male prerogatives. Perhaps he saw her as the reverse side of Branwell's showy and shallow brilliance. His tenderness towards Anne and their closeness is movingly shown in his "My *dear* little Anne" when the visiting specialist in 1849 virtually pronounced a death sentence on her. His only written comment on his dreadful year of loss, after two deaths and in sight of the third, was to Mr Rand, the former teacher at Haworth: "For these things we may weep, since Christ himself wept over his dead friend" (26 Feb 1849). For the modern reader Mr Brontë invokes his God and Savior rather too readily, but we have lost the certainty and knowledge of the Scriptures that produces that kind of familiarity.

The two crusades of Patrick's later life were education and health, in particular the provision of a pure water supply. His constant concern (understandable, considering his background) with providing a basic education for the children of Haworth and the surrounding villages has been well treated by Brian Wilks (BST, v. 18 no. 5, 1985), and can be traced from aspiration to reality in a series of letters from him and his curate Arthur Bell Nicholls to the National Society asking for financial assistance – not eloquent, but dogged, persistent ones, with an eye fixed on the practical and attainable. The quest for untainted water went slowly, with aid and advice from London proving difficult to get, in spite of the appalling death-rates in Haworth. His campaign was belatedly crowned with success when the new reservoir above Hall Green was inaugurated.

His behavior at the time of Charlotte's courtship by Nicholls has been much criticized. Old people do not as a rule behave better than their younger selves: they are worried about the comfort and security of their last years. No doubt Patrick would have preferred to end his life in the familiar Parsonage alone with his last daughter. No doubt too he was worried about a pregnancy at her age. However, he suffered one of his rare defeats. His relationship with Arthur was never warm, but it became respectful, and he honored him for keeping his commitment to Charlotte, to care for her father if she died. There is a strong sense during her final illness and death of the two men clinging together first in anxiety, then in grief.

Patrick's concern to have a fitting monument for his famous daughter in the form of a memoir by a fellow writer (one doubts whether he imagined anything as ambitious as the biography that his commission actually produced) is a natural clutching at straws to alleviate the totality of his bereavement. Nicholls's contrary instinct for privacy and dignity is doubtless to be respected, but without Gaskell's *Life* our knowledge of the Brontës would be scanty indeed.

The two men passed Patrick's last years mostly in peace, he getting by through his natural stoicism, Arthur through hard work. Patrick, in the occasional disputes between them, doubtless enjoyed the victories he gained through the privileges of his position and age. He certainly behaved splendidly throughout the controversy about the inaccuracies and exaggerations about him in the *Life*, proving that what really interested him was a fitting memorial to Charlotte. He tried, unless circumvented by his son-in-law, to meet visitors attracted by Charlotte's fame, and greatly enjoyed such grand visitors as the Duke of Devonshire. Throughout 1861 he drifted towards death, which came on 7 June.

Patrick, in spite of his exceptional background, was very much a man of his time. He was more flexible in his opinions than most people today, being conservative by instinct but always willing to consider the case put by opponents. A generosity of mind meant that he understood the desperation of the Luddites, and his campaign against the horror and mean-mindedness of the Poor Law regime for paupers was as whole-hearted as Dickens's. He was in many ways an eighteenth-century parent, involving his children in his own activities and preoccupations (as in the glimpse we have in the juvenilia of a family reading of a big debate on Catholic emancipation, or another snapshot of Charlotte helping with the proof-reading of one of his published sermons). He wrote to Bishop Longley, 10 days after Charlotte's death, "I have lived long enough, to bury a beloved wife, and six children – all that I had – I greatly enjoyed their conversation and company, and many of them, were well fitted for being companions to the wisest and best. Now they are all gone – their image and memory remain, and meet me at every turn" (unpublished letter of 10 April 1855). On the other hand, some of his opinions now seem impossibly dated and ridiculous, for example his conviction that a woman could have no use for money. Charlotte herself impressed upon his friends that he could be formidable, even frightening. "I only wish you were here to see Papa in his present mood: you would know something of him. He just treats him [Nicholls] with a hardness not to be bent – and a contempt not to be propitiated" (to EN, 18 Dec 1852).

He himself seems to have been conscious that he was by contemporary standards an exceptional man, and he was not averse to claiming his own part in the making and upbringing of his exceptional brood of children: "I do not deny that I am, somewhat exccentrick. Had I been numbered amongst the calm, sedate, *concentric* men of the world, I should not have been as I now am, and I should, in all probability, never have had such children as mine have been." (to ECG, 30 July 1857). Branwell's friend Francis Grundy provides us with a good visual likeness in *Pictures of the Past*: "upright, handsome, distantly courteous, white-haired, tall; knowing me as his son's friend, he would treat me in the Grandisonian fashion."

See also Burder, Mary; Firth, Elizabeth; Morgan, William

Brontë, Patrick Branwell (1817–48): the fourth child and only son of

Patrick and Maria, born on 26 June, at Thornton. No doubt he was welcome as the first boy, but it was also important to have the greater potential earning power of a male as a future support when necessary for his sisters, since their father was already middle-aged. Branwell's precocity meant that he and Charlotte in early life were on an equality, and participated as such in their childish games. Though Charlotte said at his death that "My poor Father naturally thought more of his *only* son than of his daughters" (to WSW, 2 Oct 1848), the evidence does not altogether bear this out, even the evidence of the childhood years. When Patrick asked his children questions to which they were to reply from behind a mask most of the topics proposed were general or abstract (e.g., "what was the best mode of education for a woman"). But the only personal question asked, of Emily his junior, was what he should do with Branwell "who was sometimes a naughty boy" (ECG, *Life*, ch. 3). Already one senses worry or uncertainty about him.

The joy of creativity and the ebullience of Branwell's inventiveness probably meant that doubts about him were slow to invade his sisters' minds. Charlotte's only memory of her mother was of her playing with Branwell, so the two were probably intertwined tenderly in her mind. Branwell's most vivid and continuing memories from early days were of the deaths of his two sisters, and they haunt his poetry. His companionship was at this stage entirely female, for if he went to school at all it was for a short time, at the rather inadequate Haworth Grammar School. His father was for most of his childhood his teacher for "male" subjects, and otherwise he seems to have joined his sisters. The longing for male company must have been strong, and there are indications in the juvenilia that he exulted to his sisters about the greater freedom and possibilities he would enjoy through being male, as well as boasts about his precocious ability to hold his drink (boasts which were roundly ridiculed by Charlotte in "My Angria and the Angrians").

That he profited by his father's classical training is evident from the translation he did as a young man of Horace's *Odes*, Book I. Evidence of his talents as a writer is more mixed when we look at his contribution to the Glasstown/Angrian saga. In the early writings one is dazzled by the virtuosity which takes aspects of *Blackwoods* and other contemporary journalism and converts them into a varied, kaleidoscopic chronicle of their childish kingdoms. Later one is still impressed by the scope and extent of these writings, but there is abundant repetition and a certain sameness about the doings of Northangerland which one is not conscious of in Charlotte's development of Zamorna. Already, it seems, Branwell was reaching his peak, and one wonders whether he was conscious of this, and realized that his sisters were outstripping him intellectually and artistically. If so, it would have been a bitter blow.

While his sisters were being prepared fairly systematically for what was almost the only profession open to them, teaching, no such preparation was being made in the case of Branwell. Probably Patrick thought his mercurial son should sample and range widely before choosing a career. Almost certainly he would have preferred a safe and lucrative career for him, but equally he must have realized how far he himself had strayed from safe paths for his class, and as an author how important it was to find an outlet for creative impulses. Branwell's only real attempt to find work was his series of letters to *Blackwoods*, proposing himself as one of their stable of writers. The tone of hectoring braggadocio he adopted in the letters doomed what was already a pretty hopeless enterprise: he was 18.

He may have been usher in a Halifax school as a first job – Leyland says so (v. 1, p. 154) and he was in a position to know – but the first paid work we know of for certain was his time as a portrait painter in Bradford (1838–9), for which he had prepared himself by lessons with William Robinson, the Leeds artist. Whether he ever believed in his talent as a painter may be doubted. His portrait of his landlady Mrs Kirby is his masterpiece in the comic mode, just as his portrait of Emily from the Gun Group is his masterpiece in the serious mode: Mrs Kirby could be an illustration by Phiz of Tony Weller's second wife, oozing propriety, disapproval, and narrowness of views. But his other portraits, both of friends and of customers, have as much life as a monarch's image on a postage stamp.

So his career thereafter was teaching, the new world of the railways, then teaching again. All these positions tore him away from the macho men of Haworth, who had welcomed him to the all-male delights of pubs and the Masonic Lodge of the Three Graces, which he had joined before the set lowest age. This separation had the advantage of Branwell starting a correspondence with them, usually via John Brown. These letters, best read in the unexpurgated extracts in Juliet Barker, should be treated warily with regard to facts, but they give a vivid picture of Branwell's scabrous humor, his boastfulness, and his need to be accepted in a man's world.

The first post, teaching the sons of Mr Postlethwaite of Broughton-in-Furness, lasted for the first half of 1840 and began, if we believe Branwell himself, with a riotous alcoholic debauch at Kendal. Before long he settled into his job, emphasizing to John Brown that, though he sits "drinking tea and talking scandal with old ladies" (13 Mar 1840), the young ones are a different matter, and they "little think the devil is so near" them. Barker posits an illegitimate child as a result of his time in Broughton, but the evidence (a note of Lord Houghton's in the late 1850s, probably based on gossip from William Brown, John's brother) is very slight, and could very likely be Branwellian boasting. The highlight of Branwell's stay in Broughton was his visit to Hartley Coleridge, when the two hopeless beings seem to have got on well. By summer he had been dismissed from Mr Postlethwaite's employment.

He was not to remain idle for long, however. In August 1840 he began work as clerk on the Leeds and Manchester Railway, first at Sowerby Bridge, then at Luddenden Foot, both within easy reach of Halifax and its notably vigorous artistic life. The new railways presented him with plenty of opportunities for new friendships with congenial souls – young, adventurous free spirits such as Francis Grundy, who was to remain a friend for the rest of his life, as did the Leylands, prominent in Halifax literary and fine-arts circles. Luddenden Foot, however, seems to have seen him regress to a life of "malignant yet cold debauchery," according to a letter to Grundy, in which he declares he would "rather give my hand than undergo again" such a life (22 May 1842). Juliet Barker doubts this claim, but it has a ring of truth to it that the boasts of drinking bouts and the breast-beating in letters to John Brown lack. He certainly was a negligent "clerk-in-charge" at Luddenden Foot, for he allowed one of his underlings to steal a little over £11, and for this he was dismissed in March 1842. He had been employed for over 18 months, a record for him.

After nine months at home Branwell was rescued by his sister Anne who presumably procured him the post of tutor to the one boy in the Robinson family of Thorp Green, where she had been governessing since May 1840. As usual with Branwell, early auguries were favorable. Charlotte reported after he had been there almost a year that Anne and Branwell were "both wonderously valued in their situation" (to EN, 23 Jan 1844), hardly bothering to disguise her surprise. But it was in May of the previous year that Branwell had written to John Brown that "my mistress is DAMNABLY TOO FOND OF ME," and in November 1843 that he sent Brown the tasteless present of a lock of her hair.

There is a plethora of explanations for Branwell's dismissal from Thorp Green in June 1845, other than his own: one suggests he was amorously involved with the Robinsons' eldest daughter, another that he seduced their son, yet another that he had been caught passing forged checks. Juliet Barker's discovery of a transcript of parts of his letters from Thorp Green does not really settle the matter: what Branwell said of himself to John Brown is not the best of evidence. But on the whole the sequence of events (Mrs Robinson sending him money regularly, his own spectacular collapse, and so on) fits best with an affair which Branwell hoped and believed would end in marriage when the lady's increasingly sick husband died. Crucially, Anne was in the best position to know the truth, or at least she had the most evidence to base an opinion on, and the clearness of mind to weigh it. Yet she never to our knowledge suggested to her sisters that the affair with Mrs Robinson might be a delusion of Branwell's or even a downright lie.

It has been pointed out with increasing emphasis that Branwell did not go hopelessly to the bad after his dismissal (something he should have got used to over his checkered career). He wrote poetry, notably "Penmaenmawr," made attempts to find another job, tried to rewrite Angrian material as a straight novel ("And the Weary are at Rest"). A slide needs to start from some way above ground level. When Mr Robinson died and Mrs Robinson manufactured lies to rob him of all hope he began to decline so rapidly that the sisters despaired of him: ". . . while he is at home I will invite no one to come and share our discomfort" Charlotte wrote to Ellen early on in his dissolution (8 Sep 1845), and her hardness only increased with time. Perhaps she gave him no sympathy because she suspected that this was not a grand passion such as her own recent and hopeless love. His letters mention his hopes of living "in more than competence . . . to try to make myself a name in the world of posterity, without being pestered by the small but countless botherments" (to Leyland, 24 Jan 1847), a pretty clear indication that Branwell aimed at an easy existence which he had done nothing to deserve.

He now declined into a shambling wreck and a constant embarrassment to the rest of the Parsonage inhabitants. After he set his bed alight Patrick was forced to sleep with him for his own and the rest of the family's safety, and by the end he was writing pleading notes to John Brown for "Five pence worth of Gin" because "I know the good it will do me" (undated). Emily called him a "hopeless being," and whether she meant "without hope" or "inspiring no hope in others" she was right. He had the grace to say "Amen" to his father's last prayer for him, displaying a belated consideration for his family and perhaps a final rediscovery of the faith of his childhood. He died on 24 September 1848, the first of the tragic trio of deaths.

Branwell is first and foremost, in the popular mind, that drug-bewildered ruin of his last years. Some will also be conscious of his years of childhood promise, the voluminous writings, the fun with his sisters, his place as popular entertainer to the village from the warmth of the Black Bull. Often he is seen as the spoilt child, too egotistical and undisciplined to fulfill his early promise. But it is at least as likely that his downward path started with his realization, around the mid-1830s, that he was far from the most talented member of the family, a humiliating realization to the only boy. Anyone might think from reading the early juvenilia that he was the most talented fiction writer of them all, but that realization fades as he becomes more and more determined to chronicle at inordinate length the doings of his camp, Northangerland's, in the Angrian wars. By the end the spark had gone out, and he was no fun at all.

See also Brown, John; Grundy, Francis; Leyland, Francis; Leyland, Joseph; Robinson, William

Brooke, Leah Sophia (1815–55): fellow pupil of Charlotte at Roe Head, daughter of John Brooke, partner in the wool firm of Halliley, Brooke and Hallileys, which went bankrupt in 1834. Her sister, the "little prattling amiable Maria" (to EN, 21 July 1832) was also a pupil at the school, but see entry for Mrs George Allbutt for Charlotte's opinion of her as an adult.

Brooke, Mrs Thomas: Huddersfield woman (probably Ann, née Ingham, married to Thomas Brooke of Northgate House) who considered Charlotte as a governess to her children "but she wants music and singing" so "the negotiation is null and void" (to EN, 12 Nov 1840).

Brookfield, Mrs Jane (1821–96): the love of Thackeray's mature years, who was invited to meet Charlotte in June 1850 at his home – an evening which was conspicuously unsuccessful in its aim of introducing her to a more sophisticated female circle. Mrs Brookfield ascribed its dullness to Charlotte's "inability to fall in with the easy badinage of the well-bred people with whom she found herself surrounded" (Charles and Frances Brookfield, *Mrs Brookfield and her Circle*, cited Delafield, 1935, p. 181).

Brookroyd House: home of Ellen Nussey from August 1836 till 1858. It was smaller but more comfortable than Rydings. Charlotte stayed there many times, most notably when she was correcting the proofs of *Jane Eyre*, of which Ellen supposedly knew nothing. It is still standing, and in private hands (see picture Whitehead, 1993, p. 71).

Brougham, Henry, First Baron (1778–1868): Whig politician, active in the reformist administrations of 1830–4. He had ably defended Queen Caroline in the divorce action of 1820, but his oddities and extremism lost him friends, and he was dropped from Lord Melbourne's later ministries. He was a bête noire of the young Brontës, and Charlotte was complaining as late as 1850 about his "outrageous impertinence in the House of Lords" (to EN, 26 Aug 1850).

Broughton House: home in Broughton-in-Furness of Mr Postlethwaite, to whose sons Branwell served as tutor 1839–40. A Georgian house on the corner of the main street of the town and opposite the King's Head, it is still standing. Branwell lodged a short way up the hill.

Broughton-in-Furness: town nine miles from Ulverston, where Branwell lived while tutor to the Postlethwaite boys. He described it as "a little retired town by the sea-shore, among wild, woody hills" (to John Brown, 13 Mar 1840). There is a possibility he fathered an illegitimate child during his stay there but nothing like proof has been adduced.

Brown (no first name given): acquaintance of William Crimsworth in the town of X –, possibly workmate or fellow lodger. Mentioned but not described in ch. 5 of *The Professor*.

Brown (no first name given): servant at the Murrays' in *Agnes Grey*, ch. 7.

Brown, Misses: according to Mrs Gaskell the names adopted by Charlotte and Anne during their visit to London to right the confusion about the identities of Currer, Ellis, and Acton Bell.

Brown, Mr (no first name given): elderly friend of Hunsden who finds Crimsworth a post at M. Pelet's school in *The Professor*. He is lightly characterized as grave and businesslike, but Crimsworth later complains that he is "an old gossip" (see chs. 7 and 22).

Brown, Bill: son of Nancy Brown in *Agnes Grey*.

Brown, Eliza: daughter of John Brown and sister of Martha. She worked at the Parsonage in 1855 (when she witnessed Patrick's will) and again in 1861 when Martha was occupied in nursing Patrick, acting as one of the chief mourners at his funeral. She inherited Brontë memorabilia from her sister, but she and her daughter Mary Popplewell gradually sold them off.

Brown, John (1804–55): stonemason and sexton of Haworth parish church, and a particular friend of Branwell's. He was a manly and competent figure, and seems to have taught Branwell boxing, as well as initiating him (illegally early) into the Three Graces Masonic lodge, of which he was Master. The Parsonage trusted him to take charge of Branwell in his years of decline (e.g., on his trip to Liverpool in 1845), but it may be doubted whether this was wise. Branwell's letters to him are filled with boasting about his sexual dangerousness and his drinking prowess – constant themes which he clearly expected to be well received. These letters seem to have been shown around the males of the village, and their boastful tone casts doubts about how far we can believe the recently discovered copied fragments of letters about his affair with Mrs Robinson (Barker, 1994, pp. 459–61). Brown died soon after Charlotte in 1855 of "dust on his lungs."

Brown, Martha (1828–80): servant at the Parsonage from 1841 until Patrick's death in 1861, first as assistant to Tabitha Aykroyd, later taking on more and more of her duties. Daughter of John Brown, she thus came from a family the Brontës trusted and knew well, and soon fitted into the Parsonage. Her health was uncertain: she had several periods of severe illness, and Charlotte often expressed concern that she should spare herself heavy cleaning duties (this was a concern that spilled over into *Shirley*, ch. 11). Charlotte's letters to her are letters to a servant who is also something of a friend, and she had a part to play in all the main events of Charlotte's last years, and of Patrick's, in whose will she was left £30, more than three years' wages. Meta Gaskell described her as a "blooming, bright, clean young woman" (letter to E. Shaen, 6 Nov 1860 in W & S, v. 4, p. 239) – she was then in her early thirties.

Though Martha was bitterly opposed to Arthur Bell Nicholls at the time of his proposal to Charlotte, it is to both of their credit that they later became very close. According to Juliet Barker Martha went with him to Ireland in 1861, and largely remained with him until her death on a visit to Haworth. A different account is given in Cochrane (1999) and in Palmer (2004). Both believe that Martha came to Banagher on visits, often lengthy ones, but was mainly resident in Yorkshire.

Martha's large collection of Brontëana, acquired either from the sisters directly or from Nicholls, was a boon to collectors when sold by her sisters after her death.

Brown, Mary (d. 1866): wife of John Brown, mother of Martha and landlady

of Arthur Bell Nicholls who convinced her he had gone mad when she heard him "giving vent to roars of laughter as he sat alone – clapping his hands and stamping on the floor" (to EN, 28 Jan 1850?) when he read *Shirley*. She was one of the chief mourners at Patrick's funeral.

Brown, Nancy: a poor widow in *Agnes Grey*, sick and troubled in her mind about

religious matters. She acts as a touchstone in the novel, as many of the characters in the second half are judged by their treatment of her, and her cat.

Brown, William (1781–1835): father of John, sexton at Haworth, 1807–35.

He was a witness to Aunt Branwell's will.

Brown, William (1808–75): brother of John, he succeeded him as sexton 1855–75.

With his father he witnessed Aunt Branwell's will in 1833. He described Patrick and Arthur Bell Nicholls after Charlotte's death as "still *ever near* but *ever separate*" (Meta Gaskell to Emily Shaen, 6 Nov 1860 in W & S, v. 4, p. 241), possibly a phrase he had prepared for the many visitors who sought him out in Haworth. The allegation that Branwell had an illegitimate child in Broughton-in-Furness emanates from him, and he showed Lord Houghton Branwell's letters to John Brown from Thorp Green concerning his love for Mrs Robinson (see Barker, 1994, pp. 459–61).

Browne, Dr J. P.: phrenologist whom Charlotte and George Smith visited in

June 1851. His assessments are in the Brontë Parsonage Museum. Charlotte thought that of Smith was "<u>like-like-like</u> as the very life itself" (to GS, 2 July 1851) but implies that that of her lacked "shadow" (to GS, 8 July 1851). On phrenology see Sally Shuttleworth: *Charlotte Brontë and Victorian Psychology* (1996).

Browning, Elizabeth Barrett (1806–61) and Robert (1812–1889):
both poets Charlotte did not admire. She wrote to Margaret Wooler (14 Feb 1850) of the former writing in a "wordy, intricate, obscure style of poetry," and damned them both by preferring Sydney Dobell's *The Roman* to "all the Brownings and Barrett Brownings and Lytton Bulwers in the world" (to WSW, 25 Oct 1850). The coupling of their names with Bulwer's would have been particularly wounding. Elizabeth Barrett Browning wrote to Miss Mitford of the "half savage and half free-thinking" qualities of *Jane Eyre* – a more perceptive remark.

See also Bulwer-Lytton

Brunty/Brontë family:
the primary evidence that Patrick maintained friendly connections with his family in the North of Ireland consists of a series of letters or notes to his siblings Hugh, James, and Mary. These letters have their oddities. The letter of 1843 is a piece of patriotic exhortation to Hugh urging Protestants to stick together and arm themselves against their "insidious, And Malignant enemies" (20 Nov 1843), though insisting that prudence, justice, and due precaution must be allied with courage. That of 1853, also to Hugh, is a note on the single-volume edition of *Jane Eyre* which is more a mini-bibliography than a family communication. None of the letters mentions visits by any of his siblings to Haworth, but since it is probable that only the occasional letter has survived there is no particular reason why the ones we have should mention such visits.

The family of Patrick's parents, Hugh Brunty and Eleanor/Alice, née McClory, was large and could have been an eighteenth-century designer family: five boys being succeeded by five girls. Their names were Patrick, William, Hugh, James, and Walsh/Welsh, all born between 1777 and 1786, and Jane, Mary, Rose, Sarah, and Alice, born between 1789 and 1795/6. Some of the stories of the Brunty connection with the Haworth family bear the stamp of untruth. Here is Hugh swearing vengeance on the *Quarterly* reviewer of *Jane Eyre*: "White with passion, the words hissing from his lips, he vowed to take vengeance on the traducer of his niece. The language of malediction rushed from him, hot and pestiferous, as if it had come from the bottomless pit, reeking with sulphur and brimstone" (Wright, 1893, p. 282).

But one should not assume that one unlikely story told in the language of a penny dreadful throws doubt on all stories that are part of the oral history of the family. The problem is the difficulty of threading a path between William Wright, Rose Heslip, the daughter of Patrick's sister Sarah who spoke much of the family in the late nineteenth century, and all sorts of other local traditions. One piece of more concrete evidence, however, is the fact that Patrick left in his will £40 to his brother Hugh to be divided equally between his various brothers and sisters "to whom I gave considerable sums in times past." This may explain a feeling one gets from the letters that he prefers to approach them on other than personal matters.

Brussels: capital of Belgium, where Charlotte lived for two years (1842–4), Emily for one (1842). The country had become independent of the Netherlands in 1830 after a revolution, and they had chosen Queen Victoria's favorite uncle, Prince Leopold of Saxe-Coburg and Gotha, as king. The Brontës, therefore, were visiting an infant among nations, and one which, if you believe Mrs Trollope (*Belgium and Western Germany in 1833*), almost immediately regretted its revolution. Though Charlotte sometimes characterizes Brussels as "brilliant," "cosmopolitan," or "elegant," these adjectives usually have derogatory undertones, and there can be no doubt she thought it provincial and disliked its inhabitants. We know nothing of Emily's reaction to the city, and she never used it in her writing. Charlotte, on the contrary, used the old city, later largely destroyed by Leopold II, as the main setting of *The Professor* and *Villette*, and used details for the background of Robert and Hortense Moore in *Shirley*. The Pensionnat Heger was in the Rue d'Isabelle. Other places of interest that the Brontës knew include the Chapel Royal and the church of Sainte Gudule, where Charlotte went to confession. A close study of the Pensionnat in the context of Brussels and its history is to be found in Ruijssenaars (2000, 2003).

Buckworth, Rev. John (1779–1835): curate and vicar of Dewsbury for the whole of his clerical career. Patrick served as his curate 1809–11, and remained on friendly terms with him for the rest of his life. An evangelical and a hymn-writer, Buckworth was a strong supporter of the missionary movement. His "energetic and appropriate" addresses were praised in the *Leeds Intelligencer* (1823), but his usefulness as a minister was for long periods marred by ill health. He was married to Rachel Halliley, daughter of John Halliley, a rich manufacturer and partner of Halliley and Carter. The failure of this firm was a matter of concern to Charlotte (letter to EN, 10 Nov 1834), and both husband and wife are mentioned several times in letters from her and Patrick.

Bull, Rev. George Stringer: vicar of Bierley, where his patron was Miss Currer of Eshton Hall. He was a determined campaigner for the rights and welfare of factory children, a campaign that Patrick warmly supported. He resigned his post in 1840, in the course of a fierce disagreement with Dr Scoresby, the vicar of Bradford.

Bull's Head Inn: coaching inn in Bradford, where an umbrella of Charlotte's and a letter from Ellen Nussey remained for over a month in 1835 (letter to EN, 8 May 1835). Gerin conjectured that Branwell enjoyed the musical ambience of the inn while he lived in Bradford.

Bulwer-Lytton, E. G. E. L. (1803–73): novelist, playwright, and poet. Branwell was reading his *Eugene Aram* to Charlotte when Emily and Anne wrote their 1837 diary paper. Later Charlotte's mentions of him are tinged with contempt, and posterity has agreed. His fiction was various, including novels of fashionable life, Newgate novels (of which *Aram* was one), historical novels, and futuristic novels. By the end of the century his fiction was beginning to seem stale: the fustian of his dialogue, the empty gesturing of his philosophizing, had dated him irredeemably. Today he has no readership beyond the student of fictional fashions in Victorian times. His life, however, including the scandalous history of his marriage to Rosina Wheeler and her determined hounding of him for 40 years after their separation in 1834, is full of interest of a rather gruesome but piquant kind.

Bunsen, Robert Wilhelm (1811–99): German physicist, inventor of the Bunsen burner. His father was Prussian ambassador to London 1842–54. Charlotte met Robert with his new wife when she visited the Arnolds at Fox-How, Ambleside, in August 1850.

Bunting, Rev. Jabez (1779–1858): Methodist leader whose sermon delivered at Woodhouse Grove School's dedication of a new chapel was said by Lock and Dixon (on no evidence) to have inspired the Jabes Branderham sermon in *Wuthering Heights*. There were reasons why Bunting may not have been popular in Haworth Parsonage however: he was one of the leaders that brought the Methodists out of the Anglican communion, resulting in John Fennell leaving Woodhouse Grove, and he refused to bury Luddite rioters shot in the attack on Cartwright's mill (1812). However, there is probably no more than the coincidence of their initials and first names to suggest this identification.

Bunyan, John (1628–88): author of *Pilgrim's Progress*, a book the Brontës possessed, and quoted from frequently both in the early writings and the novels. Great-Heart, the Slough of Despond, and the Giant Despair are among the features of the book they refer to, and imagery drawn from it is strong in Anne's poetry.

Burder, Mary (?1789–1866): niece of Patrick's landlady in Wethersfield when he was curate there, 1806–9. She was, as he wrote when he tried to renew the relationship after his wife's death, "the *first* whose hand I solicited" (PB to Mary Burder, 28 July 1823), but she was only 18, much wealthier than him, and a Congregationalist. Whether any one of these elements, or a combination of them, was decisive in preventing the marriage is uncertain. There was definitely an understanding between them, if not an openly acknowledged engagement, for the above quotation continues: "and no doubt I was the *first* to whom *you promised to give that hand*." Mary Burder's daughter Mrs Lowe ascribes the villain's role to Mary's uncle, who acted as a *de facto* guardian after the recent death of her father John Burder. However, her story that he intercepted Patrick's letters to his niece is contradicted, as Barker (1994) notes, by Mary's letter of 8 August 1823, when she talks of "a recent perusal of many letters of yours bearing dates eighteen hundred and eight and nine and ten addressed to myself and my dear departed Aunt." In the end we have to make our own judgment or conjecture of what happened and who if anyone was to blame. It is clear that Mary Burder felt a deep sense of grievance against Patrick. It is obvious too that Patrick, in his replies, shows less than his usual confidence. His explanation of the breach at the time (to Rev. John Campbell, 12 Nov 1808) is allusive and muddled: he quotes Paul's "Be not unequally yoked," then sets against it quotes from Virgil, Solomon, and St. Matthew. In any case it is unclear whether the inequality is of wealth and social status, or lies in differing religious affiliations.

Soon after the resumed correspondence Mary Burder married the local Congregationalist minister, with whom she had four daughters.

Burnett, Rev. Dr. John (?1801–70): successor to Dr Scoresby as Vicar of Bradford, and a much less controversial figure. He visited Haworth to preach during Charlotte's brief married life, and pleased her by saying Patrick was looking no older. Seven years later he helped conduct Patrick's funeral and preached his funeral sermon.

Burns, Helen: Jane Eyre's best friend at Lowood, and one who softens the harshness of her first weeks there. She contrasts strongly with Jane, being pious, studious, bent on self-improvement, and willing to accept criticism and discipline. She dies a holy death, from consumption, and the characterization was criticized from the time of *Jane Eyre*'s publication as too good to be true. Charlotte Brontë denied this. She had based the character on her memories of her eldest sister Maria.

Burns, Robert (1759–96): poet with whom Branwell felt a particular affinity, and whose poetry and the songs derived from it figure prominently in the early writings and novels. It was at Luddenden Foot, his time of "malignant yet cold debauchery," that Branwell thought most of Burns, entering his name in his notebooks as a suitable subject for a poem, and as an example of the triumph of the soul over adversity. His short poem "Robert Burns" was written at this period.

Burton Agnes: village near Bridlington visited by Charlotte and Ellen Nussey in 1839. It was a former parish of Ellen's brother Henry.

Busfeild, Rev. William: Rector of Keighley in succession to Theodore Dury. He was a strong-minded, energetic minister, unafraid of controversy and fond of getting his own way. His wife was approached when the Brontës were thinking of setting up a school, even though "she knows us only very slightly" (to EN, 10 Aug 1844?).

Butler, William Archer (?1814–48): reviewed *Poems* in the *Dublin University Magazine*, finding in the volume "a sort of Cowperian amiability and sweetness." He was Professor of Moral Philosophy at Trinity College, Dublin.

Butterfield, Richard Shackleton (1806–69): radical laissez-faire mill-owner of Keighley and Haworth who fought Patrick over his attempts to improve the village's water supply and unsuccessfully took his workers to court when they staged a walkout. Charlotte was torn in her sympathies, "enjoying Mr. Butterfield's defeat," yet feeling it was "calculated to make working-people both discontented and insubordinate" (to PB, 2 June 1852).

Byron, George Gordon, 6th Baron (1788–1824):

no literary or political figure in early nineteenth-century Britain, not even the Duke of Wellington, had more influence on the Brontës' writing than Lord Byron. They were saturated in his poems, his life, his "image." In the famous letter to Ellen Nussey (4 July 1834) where Charlotte tries to direct her reading she not only recommends the whole of his work (as, too, Shakespeare's) on the ground that "the bad are invariably revolting you will never wish to read them over twice," but she also puts Moore's *Life* of the poet among recommended biographies. The man and his works were inextricably intertwined by this time, as the Brontës' lives and works were to be after the Gaskell biography.

The Byronic image infiltrates the juvenilia gradually, changing the Marquis of Douro from an all-round paragon to a wholesale and sadistic seducer, with strong Satanic overtones. But where the Byronic hero is an outsider, at least apparently, forced into a life of piracy or revolt of one kind or another, Douro has had any number of silver spoons in his mouth from birth, and takes over Angria/Zamorna from inside. The provenance of Douro is underlined by his being one of Glasstown's greatest poets ("Byron Himself . . . must fail before him" – "The Politics of Verdopolis," WPBB, v. 1, p. 351), though he has to share the comparison with Patrick Benjamin Wiggins, at least in that modest character's own estimation ("My Angria and the Angrians," EW, v. 2, pt 2, p. 250). The Byronic hero did not, on the whole grow old, so one aspect that was unique to the Brontës was Zamorna in late middle age, still sniffing interestedly at possible female prey, yet on the whole tired, the hell-fire dampened, with a new ability to look at himself and his former activities with irony. Charlotte's picture of him in her later novellas, however, could owe something to Byron's weary, amused self-analysis in *Don Juan*: "No more – no more – Oh! never more on me/ The freshness of the heart can fall like dew" (1 ccxiv and passim) was one of the Brontës' favorite quotes, appearing appropriately in a late letter (24 Jan 1847) from Branwell to Leyland.

The debt to Byron in the early writings does not end there. The erratic career of Northangerland, always happiest when a rebel, is clearly based on the Eastern tales, and the emotional basis of much of Emily's early Gondal poetry, with its love of personification, its emphasis on prisons, especially dungeons and chains, springs not just from "The Prisoner of Chillon," but from such adolescent Byron works as the "Elegy on Newstead Abbey," printed in *Hours of Idleness* (1807). The notion of satiric contests between rival poets could spring from his *English Bards and Scotch Reviewers*.

The effects of the Byronic hero on the characterization of men in the mature Brontë novels are difficult to treat briefly, particularly in isolation from other possible influences such as Richardson, Fielding, and the Gothic novel. Anne seems most determinedly to turn the coin of Byronism to its reverse side in Arthur Huntingdon, revealing the drunkenness, turpitude, and amoral pleasure-seeking that were one part of Byron's nature. Heathcliff and Mr Rochester are more typical in that they are both to some degree outcasts, both lawless beings who seek to flout convention and the established order. Both have strong male allure (which the repellent Huntingdon lacks), but even Rochester's glamour does not, for Blanche Ingram, survive the "gypsy" revelation that his estate is worth less than she imagines. Though Heathcliff still more determinedly puts himself outside accepted moral codes, he still plays the gentry at their own games and therefore turns eventually into a mirror image of them.

Other aspects of the Byron story played their part in shaping the novels. His incestuous love for Augusta Leigh, his half sister, may have influenced *Wuthering Heights*. Technically Heathcliff and Cathy's love is no more incestuous than David Copperfield marrying Agnes Wickfield, but Emily's pair have the feel of being brother and sister through their closeness during their upbringing. Rumors of the Byron/Augusta affair could have been brought to Haworth by William Weightman from the Durham area, where Byron's wife's family had their seat, or divined from hints in Byron's works, particularly *The Bride of Abydos*. Byron's overhearing of Mary Chaworth's remark to her maid "What! Me care for that lame boy!" is a convincing source for Cathy's overheard "It would degrade me to marry Heathcliff, now." His 1816 poem "The Dream," with its brother/sister love theme, one of the lovers ending in madness, the other in misery, convincingly foreshadows the development of *Wuthering Heights*. All in all the shaping role played by Byron in the Brontës' writings is much easier to demonstrate than any similar role for Walter Scott.

In 1841, when she was writing her diary paper in Scarborough, where she was staying with the Robinsons, Anne misquoted Byron: "How little know we what we are/ How less what we may be!" Byron's words come at the end of the 15th canto of *Don Juan*, where Juan is involved with the Lady Adeline Amundeville, an English lady "of the purest vintage" who soon "'gan to ponder how to save his [Juan's] soul." We do not know for certain that Anne read any of *Don Juan*, and she could have come across Byron's words in any book of truisms. But we remember the situation in *The Tenant of Wildfell Hall*, how closely it resembled Byron's marriage, and we feel convinced that Anne took advantage of the uncensored reading permitted in the Parsonage and read the whole of that great poem. Charlotte later seemed to repent of her permissive advice to Ellen to read everything, declaring that "Had I a brother yet living – I should tremble to let him read Thackeray's lecture on Fielding" (to GS, 26 Mar 1853). But we may doubt whether Branwell's sins were the result of his reading and rejoice that Byron sowed such splendid seeds in the minds of his sisters. This is only one of many calls Mr Brontë has on our gratitude.

Byron, Harriet: heroine of Richardson's *Sir Charles Grandison* (1753–4). The novel was admired in the late eighteenth century, and Jane Austen dramatized scenes from it. By the time of the Brontës it had slipped into disrepute and ridicule, mainly due to the irredeemable virtuousness of its hero and other central characters. Charlotte shared the general skepticism, as can be seen in her draft and fair-copy versions of her letter to Hartley Coleridge (Dec 1840), as well as references in "Ashworth" and *The Professor*.

C

Cairnes, John Elliot (1823–75): Professor of Political Economy at Trinity College, Dublin. He visited Haworth in 1858, and his description of it in a letter to a friend includes accounts of the Greenwoods' shop, the church and sexton, and Martha and the Parsonage. Martha's ignorance of the incident leads him to cast doubt on Mrs Gaskell's account of Emily's vicious pummeling of Keeper for sleeping on the Parsonage beds. See Lemon (1996).

Calverley Church *see* St Wilfrid's

Campbell, Rev. John Barnwell: curate of Glenfield in Leicestershire, whose successor Patrick considered becoming in 1808, at the height of his involvement with Mary Burder. He had been at Cambridge with Patrick. A letter to him from Patrick (12 Nov 1808) casts some, but not much, light on the breaking of the engagement between him and Mary Burder.

Campbell, Thomas (1777–1844): Scottish-born poet who later settled in London. His narrative poems and ballads were immensely popular, not least with the Brontës. Charlotte included him in a list of poets recommended to Ellen Nussey (4 July 1834), and quoted him both in her early writings and her novels. She was especially enthusiastic about John Martin's picture, now in the Walker Gallery, Liverpool, based on Campbell's poem "The Last Man." Campbell was one of the few poets approved of by Byron in his scathing *English Bards and Scotch Reviewers*.

Cannan, William: Haworth surgeon briefly in 1842, successor to Thomas Andrew. He died of DTs in October 1842, and Patrick wrote on the same day to inform his estranged wife and enquire about funeral arrangements. Sarah Fermi's article "A Religious Family Disgraced" (BST, v. 20, p. 5, 1992) suggests that his wife was the

Greenwood daughter who had an illegitimate child by her brother-in-law (ECG, *Life*, ch. 3).

Captain: referred to as "Captain Somebody," a military fop on a visit to the Greens at Horton (*Agnes Grey*, ch. 13).

"Captain Henry Hastings" *see* "Henry Hastings"

Carlisle, George William Frederick Howard, 7th Earl of (1802–64):
Before succeeding to the title he was, under the courtesy title of Viscount Morpeth, MP for the West Riding from 1832 to 1841, and again from 1846 until he became Earl of Carlisle in 1848. He shared a platform with Patrick during election meetings in 1835, and again in 1837, though, being a Whig, his presence probably did not impress Charlotte. However, when he introduced himself to her in May 1851 at Thackeray's lecture on Congreve and Addison – as "a Yorkshireman," which doubtless pleased her – she found him courteous and kind (to PB, 31 May 1851). Himself an author, Lord Carlisle was later Viceroy of Ireland.

Carlyle, Thomas (1795–1881): historian, essayist, and thinker. Charlotte
probably met him at Thackeray's on 12 June 1850, the melancholy evening chronicled by Thackeray's daughter Lady Ritchie and by his friend Mrs Brookfield. If so, Charlotte's silence on the subject is odd, because her interest in him comes out in several references to him in letters to William Smith Williams. She dislikes his style and is skeptical of his hero-worship, but talks of his "manly love of truth" and his recognition of intrinsic greatness "considered apart from birth, rank or wealth" which she admired (letter of 16 Apr 1849).

Caroline (no surname given): only sister of Mrs Pryor and aunt of Caroline
Helstone in *Shirley*. Mentioned in ch. 25.

"Caroline Vernon": Charlotte's last substantial contribution to the Angrian Saga
(1839). The title is Fanny Ratchford's (Ratchford, 1941). Caroline is Northangerland's natural daughter by Louisa Dance, and she has been brought up by her vain and ridiculous mother to retain the clothes and appearance of childhood into her teens. When Quashia writes a drunken letter suggesting himself as her mate, this prompts Northangerland to take a belated interest in her. Zamorna has been acting as her guardian, and in her simplicity she has, as he later tells her, "sported many a time . . . on the brink of an abyss you never thought of" (FN, p. 352). Northangerland takes over guardianship of her, escorting her to Paris. When they return to Verdopolis he has to keep his child from Zenobia, and sends her to a remote cottage, Eden. From there she escapes to throw herself on Zamorna's protection, and falls into the abyss that he has often seen waiting for her. The story ends with a furious row between Northangerland and Zamorna, now her "protector" rather than her guardian.

The story is notable for its pre-echoes of the later novels, with Caroline falling into the trap which Jane Eyre runs away from, mentions of Zamorna's "alternations of frost & fire" (FN, p. 357) which was to become one of the image patterns of that novel, and the early Caroline being Charlotte's first fully achieved charming young girl. With minor changes the tale as we have it could have been part of a novel about the English landed aristocracy, though it would probably have been classified by critics as one of the "silver fork" novels satirized by Dickens in ch. 28 of *Nicholas Nickleby*. It certainly shows Charlotte disciplining herself to present a fully thought-through and potentially tragic central story, with the adolescent Caroline as its central figure and the Duke of Zamorna seen for what he is, an ageing roué. In Caroline's overheated and undisciplined fixation on her guardian, what Charlotte calls "the crudities of her over-stretched fancy" (FN, p. 313), we can imagine Charlotte facing up for the first time to her own immaturities so evident in earlier episodes in the Angrian saga.

The story was written in the summer and late autumn of 1839.

See also Juvenilia, 4. Angria Redivivus

Carr, Charles (d. 1832): solicitor of Gomersal. He was professionally involved in matters connected with Joshua Taylor's bankruptcy in the 1820s. His family remained close to the Taylor and Nussey families, with whom they had connections, and Charles's widow Grace was known to Mary and Ellen until the time of her death aged 88 in 1863 (see letter of MT to EN in Stevens, 1972, p. 138).

Carr, Charles (1807–80): son of the above, who married Eleanor Walker, sister of Mary, wife of John Nussey, the Royal Apothecary and Ellen's brother. Charles Carr was the solicitor who drew up Charlotte's marriage settlement (see Juliet Barker, "Subdued Expectations," in BST, v. 19, pts. 1 & 2).

Carter, Mr (no first name given): surgeon in the Thornfield district in *Jane Eyre*, called to Mr Rochester after his riding accident and to Richard Mason after he has been attacked by Bertha Rochester.

Carter, Rev. Edward Nicholl (1800–72): brother-in-law of Margaret Wooler, having married her sister Susan, 30 December 1830. He was curate at Mirfield Parish Church, and probably prepared Charlotte for confirmation in 1831/2. He or his wife may have been instrumental in getting Anne and Charlotte their posts at Blake Hall and Stonegappe. It was while she was at Lothersdale that Charlotte became closest to the family, though she declared "At home I should not care for them" (letter to EJB, 8 June 1839). The Carters were parents of Ellen, Edward, and Susan, about whom Charlotte wrote frequently to Miss Wooler later on, having a special interest in Susan, who was a baby when she was at Stonegappe. It was in this period that she referred to the Rev. Carter as "a friend who having temporarily been lost is again found" (to MW, 7 Dec 1852). Two of the Carters' daughters later set up a school at Oakwell Hall, Birstal.

Cartman, Rev. Dr William: English master and later headmaster of Skipton Grammar School. He preached frequently at Haworth in the 1850s, including at Charlotte's funeral, on the text "And all wept, and bewailed her: but he said, Weep not; she is not dead, but sleepeth" (Luke 8: 52). He procured spiked devices to help the aged Patrick get around in icy conditions, and came to comfort him in his last years. He officiated at his funeral in June 1861.

Cartwright, William (1775–1839): cloth-merchant, who had leased from William Horsfall Rawfold's Mill in Liversedge, which was attacked by Luddites on the night of 11/12 April 1812. He was shot at one week later, but was unscathed. These incidents were the basis for the attack on Hollow's Mill and the attempt on Robert Moore's life in *Shirley*. Like Moore, Cartwright, according to Gaskell, had "foreign blood in him . . . and spoke French well, of itself a suspicious circumstance to the bigoted nationality of those days" (ECG, *Life*, ch. 6).

Cassels, Rev. Andrew (1806–74): vicar of Batley from 1839, and formerly of Morley. He visited the Parsonage February 1850, and caused something of a stir with his loud voice, vulgarity, and his pressing Patrick to dine with him at the Black Bull and share a bottle or three with him. Even Patrick had to admit he was "rather shabby-looking" (CB to EN, 16 Feb 1850?). He did not want "the trouble of a wife" (ibid), but after his marriage in 1857 his wife presented him with a frequent series of blessings. He was a graduate of Patrick's own college, but Charlotte was right when she doubted his claim to be 37. He was clearly pushy and insensitive and the *Leeds Mercury*'s claim (13 Mar 1841) that he secured some unpaid tithes by a mixture of "friendship and intimidation" seems to capture the essence of the man.

Casterton: site, a few miles from Cowan Bridge, of the Clergy Daughters' School after 1833 and to the present day under its new name of Casterton School.

Castle Tavern, Holborn: prompted by the account in Leyland (1886), Winifred Gerin devotes several pages to this sporting tavern, kept by Tom Spring, a former prize-fighter, which Branwell would have read about in the sporting magazines he devoured as a boy. However, Branwell's visit to London in the mid-1830s is now generally discounted, so Leyland's narrative of the striking impression Branwell made by his "unusual flow of language and strength of memory" (Leyland, 1886, v. 1, p. 145) must be classed as probably among Brontë myths. However, see entry for Woolven.

Castleton: famous caverns in Derbyshire visited by Charlotte and Ellen from Hathersage in 1845.

Catherine, Lady (no surname given): Irish baroness, pupil at Frances Crimsworth's school, and much loved for her enthusiasm and generosity. See *The Professor*, ch. 25.

Cato: a dog. See Plato

Cator, Rev. Thomas (1790–1864): Rector of Kirk-Smeaton, whom Arthur Bell Nicholls served briefly as curate in 1854, during his period of separation from Charlotte. He was apparently a wealthy pluralist and well-connected.

Catton, Thomas (1760–1838): astronomer, fellow and tutor of St John's College, Cambridge and curator of the college observatory. He became Patrick's tutor there in 1804 and may have passed on to him a love of observing the heavens.

Caunt, Benjamin (1815–61): celebrated prize-fighter, son of a servant of Lord Byron, a noted aficionado of the sport, at Newstead Abbey. He won the Boxing Championship from Bendigo in 1838, but lost a return match on 9 September 1845. The day after this contest Branwell sent a sketch of the contest to J. B. Leyland. Bendigo was awarded this contest in the 93rd round, giving point to F. Leyland's comment about prize-fighting in general, that the two fighters "pounded each other till they were unlike anything human" (v. 1, p. 117).
See also Castle Tavern

Cave, Mary (later Mrs Matthewson Helstone): the woman whom Hiram Yorke in *Shirley* loved, a girl of "living marble; stillness personified" (ch. 4), who after a couple of years' neglect by her husband went into a decline and died.

Cave, Mrs (first name unknown): wife of Rev. Wilmot Cave Brown Cave, vicar of Hope. Visited Ellen and Charlotte while they were staying at Hathersage. She announced that she and her husband intended to call on Henry Nussey and his bride when they returned from their honeymoon, which reassured Ellen that some past unpleasantness between them and her brother was now forgotten. It seems likely Rev. Cave was one of the list of people Henry offended.

Cavendish, William George Spencer *see* Devonshire, Sixth Duke of

Chambers, Messrs: publishers of *Chambers's Edinburgh Journal*, whom Charlotte consulted about suitable publishers for new poetry. Their "brief and businesslike but civil and sensible reply" led to the sisters contacting Aylott and Jones, who published the volume in 1846. See "Biographical Notice of Ellis and Acton Bell."

Chambers's Edinburgh Journal: a journal of the arts and sciences, founded in 1832 and aimed at a popular audience. Mary Taylor tried her hand at writing for them in 1849, but her piece was not published. In *Shirley* Charlotte noted that Caroline Helstone and William Farren would have loved it if it had existed in 1812 for its "marvellous anecdotes of animal sagacity" (ch. 25). Later called *Chambers's Journal*, it existed until 1938.

Chapelle, M.: brother-in-law to M. Heger's first wife, Marie-Josephine Noyer. Charlotte gave English lessons to him and Heger, and tried to make them "pronounce like Englishmen" (letter to EN, 6 Mar 1843), by no means always part of language teaching at that time. He was said by Winifred Gerin (1971, p. 133) to be a music teacher at the Brussels Conservatoire under whom Emily studied music, but Robert K. Wallace ("Emily Brontë and Music," BST, v. 18, pt 92, 1982) was assured by the librarian of the Conservatoire Royale that he was never connected to that institution. M. Heger's letter to Patrick when Emily returned to Haworth said that she "allait apprendre le piano; recevoir les leçons du meilleur professeur que nous ayons en Belgique" (5 Nov 1842) – that is, that she was *about to have* lessons from the best teacher in Belgium. Whether this was M. Chapelle, or whether she was about to go from him to an even better teacher, is unclear.

Chapel Royal: in the Place du Musée, Brussels, it forms part of a rococo palace built for Charles of Lorraine. Emily and Charlotte attended Sunday service there, and it is one of the places where William Crimsworth looks for Frances after her disappearance (*The Professor*, ch. 19).

Chapel Street, Penzance: Number 25 was the birthplace and early home of Maria and Elizabeth Branwell. The house is a substantial one, as befits the family's standing in the community, and it retains today its prominent position in one of the town's busiest streets. The interior has recently been extensively remodeled.

Chapter Coffee House: the respectable but dingy inn in London which was patronized by Patrick as a young man; then by him, Charlotte, and Emily on the way to Brussels; then by Charlotte and Anne in 1848 on their visit to assure George Smith that there was more than one Bell author. It had a bookish past and a male air, and it provided materials for description in *The Professor* (ch. 7) and *Villette* (ch. 5), as well as in Trollope's *The Warden* (chs. 16–19). In her later visits to London Charlotte stayed with the Smiths.

Charles (no surname given): Etonian school-fellow of William Crimsworth in *The Professor* to whom he addresses the letter that comprises ch. 1. He is characterized as sarcastic and cold-blooded, a type for which Crimsworth seems to feel an affinity.

Charles Thunder: either the first or both names were used by Charlotte in letters, and generally in the Nussey family. The first name springs from her own, the surname from the fact that Brontë is the Greek for "thunder."

Charlotte (no surname given): younger sister of the stewardess on "The Vivid." She is apparently about to marry imprudently (see ch. 6 of *Villette*).

Charnock, Elizabeth (?1808–55): daughter of John Charnock of Leeds, she seems to have become engaged to Ellen's brother Richard Nussey in 1834 (CB to EN,

4 July 1834), but not to have married him until 1846, by which time she was 43. Her health was a topic in several letters from Charlotte to Ellen in 1854, after she had had a stroke. An early description has her as "clever, and aimiable" (to EN, 4 July 1834) but later accounts of her and her husband find them "*very* vulgar" (to EN, 20 Sep 1851?).

See also Nussey, Richard

Charnock, Rev. James (?1761–1819): Patrick's predecessor as perpetual curate of Haworth. He had had the position since 1791, and died, aged 57 and "after a lingering illness" (*Leeds Intelligencer*, 31 May 1819).

Charnock, Rev. Thomas Brooksbank (1800–47): son of the above. He had no parish of his own, and was thus available to officiate when asked by Patrick to do so. He married a Cullingworth lady, Mary Waddington, and lived there himself. He took his own life in 1847, for reasons unknown though the *Leeds Intelligencer* talked of "frequent depression of spirits so as to incapacitate him for duty" (30 Oct 1847).

Chartists: Chartism was the most important working-class activity in the first half of the nineteenth century, and almost all of its aims, involving universal suffrage, secret ballots, and payment of MPs, were eventually achieved. Charlotte wrote sympathetically about the movement to William Smith Williams ("their grievances should not indeed be neglected, nor . . . their sufferings ignored," 20 Apr 1848), perhaps because she was at the time researching an earlier democratic movement, Luddism. In those months too there was a large Chartist demonstration near Haworth, and others in West Yorkshire.

"*Chat, Le*": essay written by Emily for M. Heger, and dated 15 May 1842. The essay is misanthropic, though with tongue in cheek. Humans cannot be compared with dogs, who are far too good, but they can be compared to cats because they share the same vices – guile, hypocrisy, cupboard love and so on.

Chateaubriand, François René, Vicomte de (1768–1848): French statesman and author, and one of the masters of French style that M. Heger encouraged Charlotte and Emily to imitate. The essays that resulted are Charlotte's "*La Prière de Soir*" and "Anne Askew," the first based on his *Génie du Christianisme*, the second on *Les Martyrs*.

Chateau De Koekelberg: expensive finishing school in Brussels attended in 1841–2 by Martha Taylor, and in 1842 by Mary Taylor as well. It was run by Mme Goussaert (née Catherine Phelps, of Devon), on whose death certificate the school was described as a "Pensionnat des dames anglaises." It seems to have attracted mostly English and German girls, and was thus much less suitable than the Pensionnat Heger for pupils who wished to learn fluent French. The school was badly affected by Martha Taylor's death there in 1842.

See also Taylor, Martha

Chenier, André Marie de (1762–94): French poet. The fact that he perished on the guillotine during Robespierre's Reign of Terror greatly added to his romantic appeal. Charlotte used his poem "La Jeune Captive," written in prison shortly before his death, as one of her models for her *devoir* "La Jeune Fille," among the earliest she wrote in Brussels. Caroline Helstone in *Shirley* is said by Hortense to prefer that poem to all Racine and Corneille, but in a rather supercilious note to Caroline's reading of the poem in ch. 6 Charlotte says that there is at least one poem superior to Chenier's, one that is "inartificial, genuine, impressive," and she adds – perhaps at last shrugging off M. Heger's tastes – "To how many other samples of French verse can the same epithets be applied with truth?" (*Shirley*, World's Classics edn, ed. M. Smith and H. Rosengarten, 1979, p. 657). The poem she refers to is Millevoye's "*La Chute des Feuilles*" (see entry below).

"Chenille, La" (The Caterpillar): Charlotte's companion-piece to Emily's better known essay "*Le Papillon*" (The Butterfly). Both were written 11 August 1842.

***Children's Friend, The*:** a monthly magazine for children compiled by the Rev. Carus Wilson, and published in Kirkby Lonsdale. The magazine often contains death scenes, and in general seems to do little to justify its title. It is the inspiration for the *Child's Guide* which Mr Brocklehurst gives to Jane Eyre (ch. 4).

Cholmondeley, Mrs (no first name given): chaperone to Ginevra Fanshawe in *Villette*. Ginevra is in her last months at school, and is allowed a great deal into society, where Mrs Cholmondeley takes somewhat imperfect care of her. She at first responds to Ginevra's demands for gifts of clothes, but soon finds her so shamelessly importunate that she has to call a halt (see ch. 9).

Chorley, Henry Fothergill (1808–72): music critic of *The Athenaeum*. His judgments were widely respected and feared, but as he was hostile to and contemptuous of the two greatest opera composers of his time, Verdi and Wagner, his reputation has not worn well. Charlotte met him in London in December 1849, and was repelled and suspicious. In a letter to William Smith Williams after her return home (19 Dec 1849) she speaks of her uncertainty whether her reaction to him should be "utter contempt and aversion," or whether there was some latent good there to modify that judgment. She speaks of his "unpleasant features, his strange voice . . . his very foppery and grimace," and called him "a peculiar specimen," though she does admit that he "tantalized me." He was no doubt included in Charlotte's wry comment that the critics she met "seemed infinitely grander, more pompous, dashing, shewy" than the authors (to MW, 14 Feb 1850). It may have been awareness on his part of having aroused Charlotte's hostility that led him to warn Mrs Gaskell of the perils of quoting from her letters without her executors' permission.

Christ Church, Scarborough: church close to Wood's lodgings where Anne's funeral service was held. She was then buried in the churchyard of St Mary's (the church itself was unavailable for the service, as it was undergoing renovation and rebuilding). The service was attended by Charlotte, Ellen, and a third woman who was probably Margaret Wooler.

Christian Remembrancer: one of the "principal organs," according to Charlotte, "of the High Church Party" (to MW, 13 Apr 1853), which published wounding reviews of both *Jane Eyre* and *Villette*. Anne Mozley, who wrote the *Villette* review, was a strong supporter of the Oxford Movement, and her family (which included the editor of the *Remembrancer*) was allied to the Newmans. Lady Eastlake's description of the author of *Jane Eyre* as one who has "long forfeited the society of her own sex" is perhaps remembered by Mozley and transmuted into "an alien . . . from society" (*Christian Remembrancer*, Apr 1853). This monstrous resort to personalities drew from Charlotte a dignified reply to the editor in which she explained briefly, and with no attempts to elicit sympathy, the reasons for her "seclusion." The letter was printed, with a grudging commentary, when the journal reviewed Mrs Gaskell's *Life* in October 1857. The two reviews of her novels were acknowledged by Charlotte to be able, and more satisfying than certain sorts of enthusiasm.

Church Missionary Society: an evangelical group that educated young men for ordination and missionary activity. It was supported by Patrick's vicar at Dewsbury, and by Patrick in sermons at Keighley in 1819. Missionary activity abroad, however, does not figure as one of his main concerns in his letters.

Church of England Journal: published a constructive and enthusiastic review of *Jane Eyre* which Charlotte said "gratified me much, and chiefly because it *was* the *Church* of *England* Journal" (to WSW, 23 Dec 1847).

Church of England Quarterly Review: published unfavorable reviews of both *Jane Eyre* and *Shirley* which Charlotte did not resent: "it is a *conscientious* notice . . . this is the critics' real opinion" (to WSW, 29 Mar 1848).

Church Pastoral Aid Society: an organization dedicated to providing assistance for overworked clergymen, usually in the form of a curate. "Their conditions . . . are somewhat strict" Patrick said (letter to J. C. Franks, 10 Jan 1839), meaning that they insisted on the appointee being from the Church's evangelical wing. They supported William Weightman and, perhaps more surprisingly, Arthur Bell Nicholls.

"Chute des Feuilles, La": *devoir* written by Charlotte for M. Heger early in her second period in Brussels. It takes as its starting-point the elegy of the same name by Millevoye, and becomes an analysis of the poem and its inspiration and a meditation on poetry generally. Charlotte's standpoint is essentially Romantic (e.g., she talks about genius not pausing to reflect, about a poem being produced "without work and as if in a single effort" – the sort of misleading claim Coleridge often made about his own poetry), and it received both approbation and some skepticism from M. Heger.

The poem, renamed "Jeune Malade" is praised in a note Charlotte wrote to ch. 6 of *Shirley*.

Clapham, Henry (d. 1855): son of a Keighley manufacturing family, he married Mary Robinson, youngest daughter of the Thorp Green family. There seems to have been no love on either side, and Charlotte claimed that all the girls were pressured to marry by their mother, to get them off her hands before she became Lady Scott. Clapham was a much-admired local musician, with a fine bass voice, and when he died in 1855 the bell-ringers of Keighley parish church rang with muffled bells a peal containing 1855 changes. The *Leeds Intelligencer* claimed he had never been known to use an offensive expression to anyone. After his death Mary married a Derbyshire clergyman.

Clapham, Robert (?1788–1855): land agent, from 1849 husband of Ann Nussey, Ellen's sister. His first wife, Susanna, had died in November 1848. His new wife expressed some distaste at his ungenteel habits, but Charlotte's impatience with her ("Ann wants shaking" – letter to EN, 23 Aug 1849?) is indicative of her liking for the man, as is her constant concern for his health and her sending of friendly messages. She wanted to bring him and her husband together, but by the end of March 1855 both Clapham and Charlotte were dead.

Clara (no surname given): one of the mistresses who succeeded Céline Varens in Rochester's life. She is a German woman, characterized as honest but mindless.

Clayton family: of Brearley Hall, with whom Branwell lodged while working on the railway at Luddenden Foot. The family consisted of James and Rachel, and their sons Henry and Jonas.

Clementi, Muzio (1752–1832): Italian-born composer, brought to England in his early teens, where he lived, aside from concert tours on the Continent, for the rest of his life. His piano music was and is used by innumerable aspiring pianists, including Emily Brontë. She marked for performance two of his sonatas in her volumes of the *Musical Library*.

Clergy Daughters' School, The: at Cowan Bridge, near Tunstall, attended by four of Patrick's daughters in 1824–5: Maria and Elizabeth from July 1824, Charlotte from August, and Emily from November. Maria was removed, mortally sick, in February 1825, Elizabeth likewise in May, Charlotte and Emily in June, though there is some dispute about this last date.

There can be no doubt that the situation of the school was unhealthy, and that this was exacerbated by food that was basic and disgustingly cooked. The amount of time devoted to sermons and religious instruction was clearly excessive, especially for the smaller children, and the tone, taken from Rev. Carus Wilson, with his strong preoccupation with death and damnation, made for an atmosphere that was gloomy and destructive of security. The comments of Miss Beale on the Casterton School 30 years later make one shudder at the sort of atmosphere and discipline likely in the earlier years, when Carus Wilson had more unchecked sway.

It may be suggested that this was a school not very different from others of similar aims, for example Woodhouse Grove School, with whose teaching and domestic arrangements both the Brontë parents had been associated. But a child at school knows only his or her own miseries, and is in no position to make comparisons. All the linkage of the two suggests is that an authority that cares too insistently for a child's soul is likely to be too neglectful of bodily, intellectual, and human needs.

The ill health which was a feature of the early years of the school remained so even after the removal to Casterton. The *Leeds Intelligencer* in 1840 reported a typhoid epidemic there, with 70 children suffering from it, of whom three had died. Of the 53 pupils there in the Brontës' time, at least seven either died there or went home to die, others left for reasons of ill health.

The syllabus was basic, and included "womanly" concerns such as "all kinds of Needlework, and the nicer kinds of housework," but extras were available, and all the Brontë children except Elizabeth had one or more special "accomplishments" paid for. Even in such a place of sparse nourishment, bodily and mental, there were some rays of hope. The superintendent, Ann Evans, was regarded by Charlotte as an angel of light and a paragon of wisdom and right behavior.

Patrick's selection of this school for four of his children is understandable: it was aimed at parents precisely in his situation, and it was cheap; he knew something of Carus Wilson, had probably met him, and agreed with his evangelical sympathies if not the perverted form they too often took; the school was highly recommended, and had patrons whom he approved of – men such as Charles Simeon and William Wilberforce. If he investigated it too superficially, accepted too much on trust, he was horribly punished by the deaths of two daughters, one his especial favorite.

Charlotte always insisted that her picture of the school as Lowood if anything downplayed the deprivation and horror: "Had I told *all* the truth, I might indeed have made it far more exquisitely painful" (letter to Smith, Elder, 12 Sep 1847). One of her great joys in the early days of *Jane Eyre*'s success was hearing an elderly clergyman, reading it, exclaim that it was a picture of Cowan Bridge, with Brocklehurst standing for Carus Wilson and Miss Temple for Miss Evans: "he pronounced them faithful and just – he said too that Mr – [Brocklehurst] 'deserved the chastisement he had got'" (to WSW, 4 Jan 1848).

The literal truth to life of Charlotte's picture of the school was also a feature of the acrimonious dispute in the *Halifax Guardian* between her husband and Sara Baldwin, wife of the vicar of Mytholmroyd, whose memories of the school were from a period five and more years subsequent to the Brontë girls' time there.

See also Andrews, Miss A; Beale, Dorothea; Cowan Bridge; Evans, Ann; Wilson, Rev. William Carus

Cliff, The: Scarborough street, also known as St Nicholas Cliff, where Anne lodged on several occasions with the Robinsons, and where she came to die. All these stays

were in lodgings owned by William Wood in the upper town, with fine views out to sea. Anne enjoyed, according to Ellen Nussey, "the most glorious sunset ever witnessed" (ECG, *Life*, v. 2, ch. 3) on the evening before she died.

Cliff House, Filey: lodging house where Charlotte and Ellen stayed in June 1849, after the death of Anne. Charlotte returned in May 1852, when Mrs Smith the landlady "seemed glad to see me" (letter to EN, 6 June 1852), and stayed nearly a month. The house still stands.

Clifton: village which was joined to Hartshead to make Patrick's first independent parish. This was the more populous part, with some substantial farmhouses.

Clough House: the residence in Hightown to which Patrick took his bride Maria Branwell. It was a good-sized house with three living rooms and five bedrooms. Their daughters Maria and Elizabeth were born there. The house still stands, and is privately owned.

Cobbett, William (1763–1835): journalist who rose from rural poverty to considerable position and acclaim. He ran the *Weekly Political Register* which, starting as a Tory periodical, later became a powerful organ for the Radicals, which is doubtless why the young Charlotte described Cobbett and his principles as "no great favourites of mine" (to EN, 13 Jan 1832).

Cockill sisters: Elizabeth (1813–54), Hannah (1810/11–93) and Sarah (1812–96), all daughters of Mrs Hannah Cockill (1784–1856). They kept a school at Oakwell Hall from the late 1830s to 1852, and were related to the Nussey family. Charlotte commented when Elizabeth died that it was "difficult to realise the entrance of Death. They seemed so cheerful, active, sanguine" (to EN, 7 Nov 1854).

Colburn, Henry (d. 1855): one of the foremost fiction publishers of the first half of the nineteenth century. He had a reputation for sharp practice and puffery of his own publications, which were mainly aimed at circulating libraries, but his authors included many solid names of the second rank, including Bulwer-Lytton, Frances Trollope, Surtees, Disraeli, and Mrs Gore, whose "silver fork" style of novel he made a specialty of. He missed the chance of publishing three writers of a higher rank when in 1846 he refused the three tales offered to him by Currer, Ellis, and Acton Bell.

Colchester: Britain's oldest town, founded by the Romans. Patrick was curate at St Peter's for three weeks in the summer of 1807. The church had strong evangelical connections.

Coleridge, Hartley (1796–1849): eldest son of Samuel Taylor Coleridge, he was one of the few men of letters known personally to any of the Brontës before Charlotte's years of fame. Points of resemblance between him and Branwell have often been noted. He was a spoilt and indulged child, who invented, wrote about, and enacted scenes from an imaginary state called Ejuxria. He never really grew up, having only tangential connections with the real world, and his drinking bouts were part of a pattern of escape from responsibility and self-loathing. He genuinely had many of the traits assumed by Dickens's Harold Skimpole in *Bleak House* (see entry Hunt, James Henry Leigh): his waif-like air, his child's irresponsibility, a lovable eccentricity of manner. His reply when asked whether he paid rent to the Richardsons, who cared for him for the last 15 years of his life in Nab Cottage, near Grasmere, was pure Skimpole: "Rent – I never thought of that." Wordsworth's forecast, when he was six, that Nature would preserve for him "A young lamb's heart among the full-grown flocks" proved remarkably accurate.

Branwell is said by both Leyland and Gerin to have met Hartley Coleridge during his time in Bradford, but that seems unlikely. Coleridge had left the area when the Leeds publisher of his 1833 *Poems* and his *Worthies of Yorkshire and Lancashire* went bankrupt. He lived the last 16 years of his life in Westmorland (see E. L. Griggs: *Hartley Coleridge*, 1929), writing a great deal, finishing little, publishing almost nothing. It was during this happy but unsatisfactory phase of his life that Branwell wrote to him from Broughton-in-Furness.

Branwell enclosed with his letter of 20 April 1840 a translation of two of Horace's *Odes*, and his own poem "At dead of midnight – drearily." He must have been delighted and astonished by the response, because as well as praise he seems to have received an invitation to visit the poet at Nab Cottage. Though we do not know any details of the talk, it resulted in Branwell's translation of Book I of Horace's *Odes*, which he sent to Coleridge in June, with an accompanying letter speaking of the "delightful day" they had spent, and talking of "my first conversation with a man of real intellect." Nothing came of this, perhaps because Branwell's letter seemed to confer on Coleridge a responsibility and status he always fled from. However, at the end of November Coleridge was drafting a reply which spoke of Branwell's "masterly" versification and "racy English."

This attempt to at last put together an answer may have been prompted by an approach from Charlotte towards the end of that year, which he must have replied to in late November, possibly making connections with the other young literary aspirant from Yorkshire. She sent him the manuscript we now call "Ashworth," her first attempt at a novel proper. We do not have his letter, but we have both her draft of her reply and the letter itself, and we can conjecture that he was not very enthusiastic about the piece, conjectured about her sex and her politics, and generally displayed "candour and civility" (letter, 10 Dec 1840). His wish to know how she had heard of him and his place of residence may have been genuine puzzlement, or possibly a bit of fishing to have a guess confirmed.

The sisters later sent him a copy of their poems, as they did to several other men of letters, when they despaired of further sales.

Collins, Rev. and Mrs John: curate of Rev. T. Dury and later Rev. W. Busfeild in Keighley. Though Charlotte greatly admired his fiery oratory at a meeting in the

school-room on Church rates and talked of his "noble integrity" (to EN, 7 Apr 1840?), she later confessed to an aversion to him "in an uncontrollable degree" (letter to EN, 12 Nov 1840). By then his wife had visited the Parsonage and told Patrick of her husband's "drunken, extravagant, profligate habits," and the fact that he "treated her and her child savagely." Patrick advised her to leave him, and she promised to do this. However, she seems to have had a second child by him, and she returned to the Parsonage in April 1847 to tell them of "her undeserved sufferings, agonies and physical degradation," and the "hideous disease" her constitution had triumphed over (letter to EN, 4 Apr 1847?). She had regained a respectable position in society, and kept a lodging-house in Manchester. Her story, and her husband's character, may have contributed to *The Tenant of Wildfell Hall*.

Juliet Barker's suggestion (1994, p. 901) that Mrs Collins's husband did not leave her until 1847 seems unlikely, since the April 1847 letter seems to imply a long and slow fight to regain health and social position.

Commercial Inn: pub near the Northgate, Halifax, where in January 1848 Branwell had what he described as a "fainting fit" (letter to Leyland, ca 9 Jan 1848). The landlord was a Mr Crowther.

Conway: port in North Wales, where in a comfortable inn, probably the Castle Hotel, Charlotte spent the first night of her honeymoon.

Cook, Ann (1825–40): friend of Anne Brontë at Roe Head School, daughter of Thomas Cook of Dewsbury. Charlotte describes her affectionately as "warm-hearted – affectionate – prejudiced – handsome" (to EN, 24 Aug 1838), and was clearly shocked by her death in January 1840. Ann's sister Ellen was also at the school. On Ellen Nussey's suggestion Charlotte's reactions to her death were inserted into the *Life* to please her surviving relatives.

Cooper, Sir Astley (1768–1841): surgeon to George IV, who was chosen by Branwell as the chief of his Islanders ("Tales of the Islanders," v. 1, ch. 2). He was a surgeon at Guy's Hospital and Professor at the College of Surgeons, and he raised the prestige of surgery as a profession and advanced the study of anatomy. He is still mentioned in the early writings as late as "Mina Laury."

Corneille, Pierre (1606–84): neo-classical French dramatist, especially famed for his tragedies. Judging by references in *Shirley* and *Villette* Charlotte found his plays distasteful when introduced to them by M. Heger, but she was horribly impressed by Rachel's performance as Camilla in *Horace*: "she will come to me in sleepless nights again and yet again" (letter to Sydney Dobell, 28 June 1851).

Cornhill: street in the City of London, close to the Bank of England, where Smith, Elder had their premises at no. 65, with a bookseller's on the street, offices behind and above. In the course of Charlotte's long correspondence with George Smith,

W. S. Williams, and James Taylor the word "Cornhill" became a synonym for her friends there, their actions and opinions, for example, "Are you satisfied at Cornhill, or the contrary?" (to WSW, 15 Nov 1849); "Cornhill and London have receded a long way from me" (to GS, 25 Apr 1854).

See also Smith, Elder & Co.

Cornhill Magazine: published by Smith, Elder from 1860, and edited by Thackeray. It was fantastically successful in its early years, with plentiful advertising and high sales. It published Charlotte's last fictional fragment "Emma" with the agreement of A. B. Nicholls, who also provided it with hitherto unpublished poems by Emily and Charlotte.

Cottage in the Wood, The see poetry and miscellaneous writings of Patrick Brontë

Cottage Magazine: a publication for working-class Christians edited by the Rev. John Buckworth, Patrick's friend and superior in Dewsbury. He published or republished both prose and verse by Patrick, including his letter of 27 November 1821 about his wife's death, and the Crow Hill bog sermon. According to Ellen Nussey, Maria Brontë his wife also contributed (see CBL, v. 1, p. 609).

Courtney, John: dramatist whose adaptation of *Jane Eyre*, entitled *Jane Eyre or The Secrets of Thornfield Manor*, was staged at the Victoria Theatre in London only a few months after the novel's first publication. William Smith Williams went, and reported adversely to Charlotte, making it clear that this was a travesty of her novel (see CBL, v. 2, pp. 25–8).

See also Victoria Theatre

Cove, The: seaside home of Rev. Carus Wilson at Silverdale, where Charlotte and Emily probably spent a night (31 May–1 June 1825) before returning home from Cowan Bridge.

Covent Garden: the opera house was attended by Charlotte and Anne 8 July 1848 on their first visit to London to clarify the question of the Bells' authorship. They saw *The Barber of Seville* which Charlotte thought "very brilliant" (to MT, 4 Sep 1848), though she thought, probably rightly, there were operas she would have enjoyed more. She went again in early June 1850. Among operas she could have seen was *Les Huguenots* by Meyerbeer.

Cowan Bridge: hamlet two and a half miles from Kirby Lonsdale, on the main road between Leeds and Kendal, where Carus Wilson first established the Clergy Daughters' School. Some of the buildings still stand. The situation was generally judged unhealthy.

Cowper, William (1731–1800): poet much loved by all the Brontës for his gentleness and the troubled melancholy of his life. There is a long discussion of him in *Shirley* (ch. 12), Anne wrote a poem to him which talks of "The long long years of dark despair/ That crushed and tortured thee" (AB, *Poems*, ed. Chitham, p. 84) and Branwell speaks of Cowper's life "Led through a rayless vale of tears" (BB, *Poems*, ed. Winnifrith, p. 136). Their favorite poem was "The Castaway," which Charlotte, through Shirley, as usual imagines as written under an irresistible impulse which "would not suffer him to stop to add ornament to a single stanza" (*Shirley*, ch. 12). The appeal to Anne of a mind convinced of its own damnation (the poem ends "But I beneath a rougher sea,/ And whelmed in deeper gulfs than he") is obvious, and may have strengthened the attraction for her of the doctrine of universal salvation.

Cox, Robert: friend of Patrick at Cambridge, who suggested to him that he take the curacy of Glenfield, within Cox's parish of St Mary's, Broughton Astley. Patrick traveled there, wrote to John Campbell that Mrs Cox was "just such a wife, as I wish both you & I to get" (12 Nov 1808), but decided against accepting the post.

Crimean War (1853–6): war in which Britain and France allied to thwart what they saw as Russian aggressive designs on the ailing Turkish empire. Patrick was recorded by Charlotte (to L. Wheelwright, 8 Mar 1854) as throwing himself "heart and soul" into the matter, and later she and her husband helped him in his endeavors to solicit money for the Patriotic Fund for the wounded and for the families of the dead. This work may have disillusioned her with the war. By the end of that year she wrote to Margaret Wooler (6 Dec 1854) her view that "no glory to be gained can compensate for the sufferings," and that "as we advance towards middle age – nobleness and patriotism bear a different signification to us to that which we accept while young."

Crimsworth (no first name given): father of William and Edward Crimsworth, a —shire manufacturer who lost a large fortune and died a bankrupt. See *The Professor*, ch. 1.

Crimsworth (no first name given): uncle of William and Edward Crimsworth. An astute mercantile man who brought up the two brothers until the younger, William, was nine, but then forced their maternal relatives to take on the responsibility of William's education. See *The Professor*, ch. 1.

Crimsworth, Edward: elder brother of William. Physically powerful, with a taste for exercising power tyrannically, he is a manufacturer in the town of X—, where he employs his brother William for a time, until his brutality brings about an end to the relationship. He is later said to have lost both money and wife, but he recoups his fortunes and his wife returns to him. Finally he is said to have become even richer through railway speculations. The nature of this cold, hard man is analyzed at length in *The Professor*, chs. 1 and 2. The relations between the two brothers is prefigured in those between Edward and William Percy in the early writings. In neither case is the extreme animosity between the brothers given a rational explanation.

Crimsworth, Frances *see* Henri, Frances Evans

Crimsworth, Mrs (no first name given, probably née Seacombe):
mother of Edward and William. Of aristocratic birth, she was thought by her relatives to have married beneath her, and died six months after her husband, giving birth to William. Her nature is analyzed through her portrait in ch. 3 of *The Professor*, and is thought by Hunsden to be sensitive but lacking in force and character. William sees her as a more refined likeness of himself, and later prizes the picture, which is acquired for him by Hunsden (ch. 22).

Crimsworth, Mrs (no first name given): wife of Edward Crimsworth.
She is flirtatious, slightly childish, with a coquettish vanity and "good animal spirits." She is described most fully in ch. 1 of *The Professor*; later she is said to have been misused by her husband when he was in financial difficulties, so that she returned to her father's. She was, however, coaxed back when Edward restored his fortunes.

Crimsworth, Victor: son of William Crimsworth and Frances Henri. His
temperament and education are the subject of a lengthy exposition at the end of *The Professor* (ch. 25). He is loving, sensitive, but also with an "electrical ardour and power" which needs to be disciplined. Gerin (1961, ch. 3), following Leyland, suggests convincingly that the whole analysis is a reflection on the lessons of Branwell Brontë's upbringing.

Crimsworth, William: central figure and narrator of *The Professor*. The archetypal Brontë orphan, his father died before, his mother at, his birth. He was brought up first by his father's manufacturing family, later by his mother's aristocratic one, who had to be blackmailed into accepting responsibility for his education. At the beginning of the novel he rejects the (highly conditional) aristocratic patronage of the Seacombe family, and after three months working in an industrial town for his tyrannical brother he goes to Brussels. Most of the rest of the novel concerns his experiences as a teacher there.

Crimsworth's character can be seen as partly a consequence of a lonely and loveless childhood. He is withdrawn, quietly sardonic, and finds it difficult to give himself unreservedly in friendship or love. Even in the first chapter he remarks to his correspondent that, though they were friends at Eton, yet "I never experienced anything of the Pylades and Orestes sentiment for you." He is thus initially happiest in the sort of sardonic, joshing relationship he has with Hunsden. It is possible too that his inexperience of close relationships makes him misjudge other people: his first estimates of both M. Pelet and Mlle Reuter are wide of the mark. It is only with his slowly developing love for Frances Henri that he becomes more complete as a human being, and finds he can both love and be loved.

The character of Crimsworth, like the character of Lucy Snowe, does not call for unmixed admiration from the reader. He is cold, priggish, censorious. Yet though his explicit concern with his own integrity may grate, this is the one thing he has as a defense; only this can save him from a series of bad decisions – social, moral, and amorous.

The characterization of Crimsworth is often criticized as being too "feminine," and containing too much of Charlotte Brontë herself. Since her creation of a totally "male" figure, Mr. Rochester, is often dismissed as an absurd wish-fulfillment fantasy, it would seem that Charlotte cannot win with some critics. In fact Crimsworth is very much an individual, and a convincing product of his childhood and background. It is notable that many elements in the analysis above could also apply to Jane Eyre and Lucy Snowe, products of similarly loveless childhoods, though, lacking their tempestuous love conflicts, Crimsworth never engages the reader emotionally to the degree they do.

Critic, The: periodical which was among the few to notice the 1846 *Poems*: "this small book . . . has come like a ray of sunshine" it said, because it consisted of "original thoughts, expressed in the true language of poetry" (4 July 1846). It later gave unstinted commendation to all of Charlotte's novels, praising for example her "fertile invention, great power of description, and a happy faculty for conceiving and sketching character" (30 Oct 1847). Charlotte referred to it as "our old friend 'the Critic'" (to WSW, 10 Feb 1849?).

Crofton Hall: school in Wakefield formerly owned and run by Richmal Mangnall. It is generally assumed that this was the "good school in Wakefield" to which Patrick said (letter to ECG, 20 June 1855) his elder daughter first went. The identification springs from the fact that the school was attended by both Fanny Outhwaite and Elizabeth Firth, whose diary for her period there still exists. When it was advertised to let in 1844 ("Seven bedrooms, stabling for five horses . . . also two excellent gardens well stocked with Fruit Trees") the house was said to have been used as a girls' school for "upwards of 80 years" (*Leeds Intelligencer*, 29 June 1844).

Croly, Rev. Dr George (1780–1860): preacher whose reputation drew Charlotte and Anne, escorted by William Smith Williams, to his church of St Stephen's Walbrook during their London visit of 1848, only to find he was not preaching that day. He was something of a literary Jack-of-all-trades, publishing volumes of poetry (e.g., *Paris in 1815*), a play (*Catiline*), and novels (e.g., *Salathiel*, a version of the Wandering Jew legend, and *Marston*). The judgment quoted in the *Leeds Intelligencer* (7 Mar 1835) that he was "one of the most distinguished poets of our generation" was overgenerous.

Crosby, Dr John: physician to the Robinson family of Thorp Green, resident in Great Ouseburn. Branwell regarded him as a friend and ally, and was in communication with him after his dismissal until his death. He also apparently received money from him, possibly as Mrs Robinson's intermediary, possibly as a member of the Masonic

Lodge, aiding a fellow Mason in distress. Mrs Gaskell's assertion that Mrs Robinson sent Branwell "twenty pounds at a time" (*Life*, v. 1, ch. 13) is in some degree borne out by Branwell's references in letters to money expected from Crosby, and his use of the word "advance" (to J. B. Leyland, 17 June 1848?) may suggest a regular subsidy. But caution always needs to be exercised about his veracity.

Crosse, Rev. John (1739–1816):

vicar of Bradford from 1784 who shortly before his death appointed Patrick to the curacy of Thornton. He was highly respected and nearly blind. William Morgan wrote a memoir of him. He was succeeded by Henry Heap.

Cross Roads Inn:

at Crossroads, between Haworth and Keighley. Branwell and William Dearden met here to have literary contests. Here Branwell, it was claimed, read from the manuscript of *Wuthering Heights*, giving rise to the belief that he was the novel's author. This claim resurfaces regularly, but has never been given credence by any Brontë expert. The inn still stands.

Cross Stone:

small hamlet near Todmorden where John Fennell became minister in 1817. The Brontë children and Aunt Branwell stayed at the Parsonage, which still exists, in September 1829, from where Charlotte wrote the first surviving letter from any of the four siblings (23 Sep 1829).

Crowe, Catherine (1790–1876):

author of novels, first of a sensational nature, mainly concerned with crime, later of supernatural stories. She attended Thackeray's dinner (12 June 1850) to meet Charlotte, but though they had an interest in phrenology in common, conversation did not flourish on this occasion.

Crow Hill bog:

the bursting of this bog occurred in September 1824 when only the three youngest children were at home in Haworth, the three eldest being at the Clergy Daughters' School. The phenomenon was caused by a thunderstorm, coming after days of rain, and the bursting sent a great wall of mud and stones toward Ponden, where the children were sheltering with their nurse Sarah Garrs. The eruption poisoned rivers and stopped mills working for several days. Patrick's sermon on the subject was published, as was a simplified version for children. He believed the phenomenon was an "earthquake," and defended this view in the Leeds newspapers, but few were convinced then or later. His account in the sermon of his anxiety for his children is a good example of his preaching style at its most vivid.

Crowther, Rev. Thomas:

vicar of St. John's in the Wilderness, near Halifax. Preached regularly at Haworth, particularly in aid of the Sunday School. He was known as a friend to the cause of child factory workers. He helped Patrick in Haworth while Arthur Bell Nicholls was away on his honeymoon.

Crystal Palace *see* Great Exhibition

Cuba House: a Georgian mansion in Banaghar, attached to the Royal School, where Arthur Bell Nicholls was brought up by his uncle and aunt, the Rev. and Mrs Alan Bell. He brought Charlotte there on their honeymoon in July 1854, and Charlotte commented, impressed, that it "looks externally like a gentleman's country-seat" (to MW, 10 July 1854) and commented on the "English order and repose" in the running of it (to Catherine Wooler, 18 July 1854).

Currer, Miss Frances Mary Richardson (1785–1861): rich book-collector, heiress to the Richardson family, whose charities and generosity to her tenants were well known. Her library was famous, and in 1830 she loaned paintings to the Northern Society for the Encouragement of the Fine Arts Exhibition, in Leeds, including Veronese, Rembrandt, and Poussin. She may be the "benevolent individual, a wealthy lady" (PB to John Buckworth, 27 Nov 1821) who helped Patrick financially after the death of his wife. She was Patron of Bierley Chapel, where William Morgan was ordained minister in 1811. She is one of the most likely candidates to have inspired Currer Bell's first name.

D

D, Mrs: directress of the "first English school at Brussels," who employs Frances Henri as a teacher (*The Professor*, ch. 21).

Daily News: founded as a Liberal newspaper in 1846, with Dickens briefly as its first editor. Its reviews of Charlotte's novels habitually gave her pain. She described the notice of *Shirley* as "unutterably false," and even its praise she regarded as "silly and nauseous – and I scorn it" (to WSW, 1 Nov 1849). Harriet Martineau's review of *Villette*, criticizing Charlotte for centering women's lives exclusively on love, was the cause of Charlotte's breach with her. On the other hand, the *News* printed a notable tribute to her, by Martineau, after her death.

D'Aubigné, Jean Henri Merle (1794–1872): French/Swiss Protestant minister, author of *The History of the Reformation* (1835–53). Charlotte, who had earlier read his letter to the Bishop of Chester, published in *The Record*, heard him preach (1 June 1851) in French, and she commented especially on hearing the language again: "it was pleasant – half sweet – half sad – and strangely suggestive to hear the French language once more" (to EN, 2 June 1851?). The children, rather oddly, gave his name to a hotel in Angria (Branwell's "Angria and the Angrians," WPBB, v. 2, p. 543).

Davenport, Mrs Caroline (d. 1897): cousin of Lady Kay-Shuttleworth, whom Charlotte met twice in her social round in London in June 1851, describing her to Patrick as "a very beautiful and fashionable woman" (26 June 1851) after they were fellow-guests at one of Samuel Rogers's breakfasts. She was a widow when Charlotte met her, but in February 1852 she married Lord Hatherton.

Davies, Mr (no first name given): the husband of Ginevra Fanshawe's sister Augusta in *Villette*. He is much older than she, and has had yellow fever, but the Fanshawe family all feel she has "done perfectly well" (ch. 6).

Davy, Mildred: spinster aunt of Mary Burder, with whom Patrick lodged at Wethersfield (1806–09) in a house conveniently opposite the church.

Dean, Ellen (Nelly): housekeeper at both Thrushcross Grange and Wuthering Heights. Her mother had been Hindley's nurse, and she seems to have attached herself to the Heights even as a child, before she had a regular place there. She goes to Thrushcross Grange with Catherine Earnshaw on her marriage, and is kept on by Heathcliff after he has acquired the property. She therefore is Lockwood's housekeeper when he rents the house, and it is she who tells him the story of Heathcliff, Catherine, and the younger Catherine. She is a comfortable, homely body who only partly understands the significance of the terrible actions she is narrating. However, she tells us that she has educated herself through the library at the Grange, and her reflections, though sometimes platitudinous, can also sometimes surprise us by their acuteness, for example: "we *must* be for ourselves in the long run; the mild and generous are only more justly selfish than the domineering" (v. 1, ch. 10) – an odd judgment from one who seems to be a Christian; or "you'll not want to hear my moralising, Mr. Lockwood: you'll judge as well as I can, all these things; at least, you'll think you will, and that's the same" (v. 2, ch. 3).

Dearden, William (1803–89): schoolmaster of Keighley, Huddersfield, and Bradford. He was born in what W. C. Newsam called "the once romantic village of Hebden Bridge" (*The Poets of Yorkshire*, 1845, which also numbered Patrick among its subjects). He had some reputation as a poet ("The Bard of Caldene"), and it was on the occasion of what was meant to be a poetic contest with him at the Cross Roads Inn that Branwell, he claimed, read stray leaves of *Wuthering Heights*, leading to the legends of Branwell's authorship of the book. On the publication of Gaskell's *Life* he began vigorously defending Patrick in the *Bradford Observer*, and his intemperate and inaccurate words were taken up by national organs. He very soon became the sort of champion whom everyone wishes would pack up his lance and keep quiet. Patrick wrote to him specifically to say he wished "nothing more should be written against Mrs. Gaskell" (letter of 31 Aug 1857), but to no avail.

Dearden was the author of "Star Seer," "The Maid of Caldene," and "The Death of Leyland's African Bloodhound."

Deb (no surname given): servant to the Yorkes in *Shirley* (see ch. 4).

De Capell family: Yorkshire group living at De Capell Hall in Charlotte's unfinished novel "Ashworth." The most important figure in the fragment is the father of the family, with a background in "Mills and Warehouses" but with "a hidden fund of family pride that might have suited a Lord" (ch. 3). He is clearly one of the ancestors of Yorke Hunsden in *The Professor* and Hiram Yorke in *Shirley*. His children include a spoilt daughter, Amelia, and the usual heavily contrasted two sons. The daughter makes a vivid preliminary appearance, but the boys are not sufficiently established to show whether they are to turn out to be new versions of the Percy brothers in the juvenilia.

Delavigne, Casimir (1793–1843): French dramatist and poet. M. Heger read to Charlotte and Emily Delavigne's "Death of Joan of Arc," and perhaps his "Life of Joan of Arc." According to Gaskell this was the inspiration behind Charlotte's devoir "*La Mort de Moïse*," though Sue Lonoff (BE) suggests some more relevant inspirations, such as de Vigny's poem "Moïse." If he read them the "Death" early enough, it could have been a source for Charlotte's "Sacrifice d'une Veuve Indienne," though the circumstances of the burning women are very different. The tone of both Delavigne's poems is hotly French-nationalistic, and it may have amused Heger to read and discuss them with his hotly English-nationalistic pupils.

Dent, Colonel: a "fine, soldierly man," and one of the guests at Rochester's house party in *Jane Eyre* (v. 2, ch. 2).

Dent, Mrs: wife of the above. Less showy and worldly than most of the guests, she shows signs of good sense and compassion.

De Quincy, Thomas (1785–1859): literary critic, essayist, and confessed opium addict. Branwell sent him his poem "Sir Henry Tunstall" in 1840, and he was one of the literary men to whom Charlotte sent unsold copies of the Bells' *Poems* in 1847. There is no record of any reply to either initiative.

Derby, Stanley Edward George Geoffrey Smith, 14th Earl of (1799–1869): leader of a section of the riven Conservative Party 1846–68 and three times briefly Prime Minister. It was in the year after his first ministry that Charlotte wrote scornfully that "Lord Derby's 'christian tone and spirit' is worth 3 halfpence 1/4" (to EN, 23 Mar 1852).

De Renzy, George (b. 1827): a troublesome young clergyman who served as Patrick's curate 1853–4, during the row with Arthur Bell Nicholls over his wish to marry Charlotte. When Patrick reluctantly agreed to the proposed marriage, de Renzy seems to have resented the consequent termination of his curacy. He complained to John Brown and others, and insisted on a long holiday at the end of his term, so that Patrick would be without a curate during the honeymoon. He was "perfectly smooth and fair-spoken to Papa," Charlotte said, but he continued to "give what trouble he can" to Patrick whose nature, Charlotte said, was against "harsh decided" measures (to EN, 14 May and 7 June 1854). He left Haworth four days before the wedding.

Description of London, A: William Darton's 1824 book was acquired by Branwell "aged 10 years and 9 months," and it was one of the sources for his prodigious knowledge of London. The engravings of buildings brought judgments from Branwell – "capital," "tolerable," "execrable" (the Haymarket Theatre), and so on.

Deutsches Leserbuch: a German reader acquired by Anne in 1844, a German dictionary having been bought the previous year. These were possibly for use with her

Thorp Green pupils, or perhaps to enable Anne to match Emily's accomplishments in the language.

devoirs: these exercises, done in Brussels for M. Heger by Charlotte and Emily are usually translated, if at all, as "essays." However, though some of them are recognizable as essays, most of them are not: they are imaginative descriptions of incidents from history, analyses of moral dilemmas, letters of a social nature, natural descriptions. The historical ones, which clearly the sisters enjoyed greatly, deal with such times as the Hundred Years' War, the night before the battle of Hastings, Old Testament times and so on, and they are lightly dramatized, so as almost to become short stories.

See also "*Athènes Sauvée par la Poésie*"; "*Chute des Feuilles*"; "*Immensité de Dieu*"; "*Justice Humaine*"; "*Mort de Moïse*"; "*Mort de Napoléon*"

Devonshire, William George Spencer Cavendish, 6th Duke of (1790–1858): bibliophile and diplomat, a gregarious and democratic man, with an especial fondness for literary figures. He confessed to his diary that he "worshipped" Dickens, and he admired *Jane Eyre*, which pleased Charlotte "especially if he be – as I suppose he is – an intelligent man as well as a Duke" (to WSW, 13 Jan 1848). He had met Patrick while at Cambridge, according to Lock and Dixon (1979), and visited him in August 1857, a year before his own death, when he was very deaf and Patrick was nearly blind. Patrick was distressed when his parishioners appealed to him for financial help toward the heating system for the church and schools, especially as he had received from the Duke a generous gift of game after his visit. There is an amusing account in a letter of Mrs Gaskell (13/14 Sep 1857) of a visit to the Duke at Chatsworth around this time.

See also Paxton, Sir Joseph

Devonshire Arms: coaching-inn in Church Street, Keighley, now known as the Korner Bar, after many years as the Grinning Rat, and one of the few Keighley buildings that the Brontës knew which still survives. Ellen was sometimes met there on her visits to Haworth, or took a conveyance from there.

Devonshire Arms Hotel: hotel at Bolton Bridge, still surviving, where the Brontës met the Nussey party in September 1833, on the way to see the ruined Bolton Abbey.

Dewsbury: town in West Yorkshire. Christianity came here early, it being one of several places in the North of England to be converted as a result of the monk Paulinus's missionary zeal. When Patrick Brontë went to the town in 1809 evangelical Christianity was once again a hallmark of the area, and here and in nearby Hartshead he fitted in well and aroused admiration for his principles and his humane instincts. The town at the time was at a turning-point in its development: the vicarage in which Patrick initially lodged was a fourteenth-century dwelling, but in the town

as a whole the old hand-loom weaving culture was giving way to the modern world of factories and mills. Heavy duty cloth was being manufactured – blankets, uniforms, and so forth – and the discarded material was being reprocessed as "shoddy" (the modern usage of the word for anything second-rate dates back to the mid-nineteenth century).

Charlotte Brontë's association with the district began in the 1830s with her two periods as pupil and mistress at Roe Head School. By then the new machinery had won its inevitable victory, and the Luddite riots of Patrick's time had become part of the local legends. Many buildings still standing within the Dewsbury district have strong associations with Charlotte: Roe Head itself, Dewsbury Moor (to which the school transferred in 1838), the Red House, Oakwell Hall, Rydings, and Brookroyd. Though close to the town for several years of her life, Charlotte seldom mentions it in her letters, and often speaks of its prominent families with something like contempt. Nevertheless it was nearby Birstall and Gomersall that provided her with Ellen Nussey and Mary Taylor, the two best friends of her life, while the Taylor family as a whole provided her with a succession of fascinating character studies.

Dewsbury Moor: Margaret Wooler moved her school in early 1838 to Heald's House, at Dewsbury Moor, just above the town of Dewsbury itself. Charlotte was intensely depressed at this point in her life ("I could have been no better company for you than a stalking ghost," she later wrote to Miss Wooler, letter, Nov/Dec 1846?), but after a period of recuperation over the summer she returned to teach at the school until Christmas of that year. The house still stands.

"diary papers": these were written by Emily and Anne at intervals of first three and later four years, with the later ones on or around Emily's birthday. They were kept in a tin box, and the previous ones were read, hopes and prophecies compared with reality, then new ones were written. They were probably private to the two, and conventional orthography was of little account – a fact that John Malham-Dembleby used in his book *The Confessions of Charlotte Brontë* (1954) to "prove" that Charlotte must have been the author of *Wuthering Heights* because the barely literate Emily could not have written it.

The diary papers consisted of:

1834: paper dated 24 November, written jointly. It includes the much-quoted sentences: "The Gondals are discovering the interior of Gaaldine Sally mosley is washing in the back Kitchin."

1837: paper dated 26 June, Branwell's birthday, written jointly. Includes a picture of the two girls seated at the parlor table, with papers and the tin box scattered around.

1841: two papers, both dated 30 July, Anne's written in Scarborough, where she was with the Robinsons, Emily's in Haworth. Anne's paper expressed her dislike of her situation and her wish to change it. Emily's has two tiny pictures of herself. Both papers are, or were once, in the Law Collection, whereabouts unknown.

1845: two papers dated 31 July (Anne's) and 30 July (Emily's). Their contrary views of the Gondal saga, Emily still delighting in it, Anne somewhat bored with it, is sometimes taken to indicate the beginning of a rift between them.

Dick: pet canary at the Parsonage who in Anne's diary paper of 1845 was "hopping in his cage."

Dickens, Charles (1812–70): whether Charlotte Brontë and Dickens ever met is uncertain. It was claimed that they did by a visitor to Haworth, John Stores Smith, who said that Charlotte disliked what she saw as his "ostentatious extravagance." George Smith, remembering at the end of his life, also said that they had met. If so the meeting was not recorded in any of the extant letters of the two voluminous letter-writers, so they clearly made little impression on each other. Though Charlotte was emotionally more drawn to Thackeray's style and subject matter, she admired Dickens. She was impressed by *David Copperfield* and by the Chancery sections of *Bleak House*. However, after reading the first number she decided, like most readers then and since, that Esther Summerson as part narrator was a mistake, calling her sections "weak and twaddling," and talking of the picture of her as a caricature of an amiable nature (to GS, 11 Mar 1852). On the back of "Farewell to Angria" (late 1839) Charlotte noted "Boy destroyer/ Mr Squeers/ Dotheboys-Hall Greta Bridge/ Yorkshire/ Favoured by Chas Dickens Esqre." No doubt the powerful scenes at the Yorkshire school in *Nicholas Nickleby* spoke to Charlotte of her own experience at Cowan Bridge, and in this note, written while *Nickleby* was still being published in parts, we see the first glimmerings of Lowood School. When she made this note Dickens was 27, and the author of *Pickwick Papers* and *Oliver Twist* as well as *Nickleby*. The romance of his instant success as a novelist in his early twenties must have appealed strongly to the ambitious 23-year-old in Haworth. Dickens wrote sympathetically about Charlotte at the time of her death, turning down an article on her on the grounds that it might be "saddening and painful to her husband" and that, as far as an "account of her trials" went, "such as she wanted given, she has given herself," no doubt referring to the Biographical Notice of her sisters (letter from Dickens to Frank Smedley, 5 May 1855). Dickens, sadly, was recorded by an unknown friend in the last years of his life, in reply to Georgina Hogarth's calling *Jane Eyre* an unhealthy book, as replying that "he had not read *Jane Eyre* and said he never would as he disapproved of the whole school. He had not read *Wuthering Heights*." This Podsnappian dismissal makes one regret less that some scratched-out lines in the record of this conversation may have recorded further views on the (unread) Brontës. See Jerome Meckier, "Some Household Words," *The Dickensian*, v. 71, pt 1, 1975.

See also Thackeray

Digby, Dr (no first name given): the young Graham Bretton's headmaster in *Villette*, mentioned in ch. 3.

Dindonneau, Duc de: son of the King and Queen of Labassecour. The name means "young turkey," and is consistent with the derisive farmyard imagery applied to Belgium throughout *Villette*. The sound of the name is also trivial and childish. He is doubtless a memory of Charlotte's view of the future Leopold II, then Prince Royal, later one of the most notorious monarchs in Europe, at a concert on 10 December 1843 at the Salle de la Grande Harmonie in Brussels (see Gerin, 1969, pp. 248–52).

Dixon, Abraham (1779–1850):

husband of Mary Taylor's aunt Laetitia, and head of a family that Charlotte and Emily met and visited in Brussels. Formerly of Leeds, he was making a living as an "inventor" in Brussels. Earlier a son, Abram, had described him as "stumbling from scheme to scheme & disappointment to disappointment" (CBL, v. 1, p. 297). He lost two daughters in 1836, and his wife in 1842, after which his Leeds home, 35 Springfield Place, was sold by auction. A letter from Mary Taylor to Ellen Nussey (1 Nov 1842) suggests that he was a taciturn man: he is equated with Emily. Hay Hall in Birmingham later became the family home. Charlotte was invited to spend Christmas with them and the Taylors in 1849, but declined.

Dixon, George (1820–98):

son of Abraham. Described by Charlotte as "a pretty-looking & pretty behaved young man – apparently constructed without a back-bone" (to EN, 13 Oct 1843?). Like many of Charlotte's thumbnail dismissals of people this seems wide of the mark. He became MP for Birmingham (1867–76) and Edgbaston (85–98) and a prominent educational reformer. He was the first president of the National Education League. In the early 1840s he traveled between Birmingham and Brussels for the firm of exporters who were then his employers.

Dixon, Mary (?1809–97):

daughter of Abraham. Charlotte describes her as "very elegant & ladylike" (to EN, 30 Jan 1843?), and they became fairly close friends during the Brussels years, so that when Mary went to travel in Germany for her health Charlotte lamented that "since Mary Dixon left I have had no friend" (to EN, 13 Oct 1843?). Her health remained a problem, Charlotte commenting on her as "a piteous case" (to EN, 10 May 1851) and saying that "It is grievous to think of her" (to Amelia Ringrose, 7 June 1851). Like many a Victorian invalid, she lived to a great age. A chalk profile portrait of Charlotte, acquired by the Brontë Parsonage Museum in 2004, is attributed to Mary Dixon, presumably made during the years in Brussels. See Rachel Terry, "New acquisitions at the Brontë Parsonage Museum" (BS, v. 27, pt 3, Nov 2002).

Dixon, Thomas (1821–65):

son of Abraham. Charlotte's description of William Smith Williams as "a pale, mild, stooping man of fifty – very much like a faded Tom Dixon" (to MT, 4 Sep 1848) gives us some idea of how she saw him. Like his brother he traveled backwards and forwards to Brussels, studying German at one time with King Leopold's librarian. He took first class honors at mathematics at Cambridge in 1844 and won a Fellowship at Jesus College.

Doad o'Bill's:

a repentant sinner in the Wesleyan chapel episode in *Shirley* (ch. 9).

Dobell, Sydney (1824–74): poet of the "Spasmodic" school, subjects of much ridicule when their poems were first published, today almost forgotten. Charlotte read his major poems *The Roman* and *Balder*. Her reactions to them may be tinged with gratitude: Dobell had recognized the potential of the Bells from the first. His anonymous notice of the *Poems* in the *Athenaeum* reserved the word "inspiration" for Emily's contribution but was generally favorable. He later became convinced that all the Bell novels were from one hand, and wrote his well-known notice of *Wuthering Heights* under the delusion that it was a first attempt at fiction by Currer Bell. This notice in *Palladium* was one of the novel's earliest intelligent appreciations, however, and its description of it as "the 'large utterance' of a baby god" has been much quoted. He pointed to many notable passages in the novel which have since become central to our understanding and appreciation of it. His description of Catherine as "so wonderfully fresh, so fearfully natural" hits the mark exactly, as does that of Joseph as "a museum case" specimen of an old family servant. From the time of this review of "Currer Bell's" novels, Charlotte entered into a long and interesting correspondence with him, unoffended by his description of *Shirley* as "labouring on an exhausted soil." The exchanges cover his work as well as her own and her sisters', and Dobell never forfeited the good will engendered by his early reviews. He was crippled by a fall in 1866, and was an invalid for the last years of his life.

dogs: the Brontë dogs are well-known – Keeper, Flossy, and Grasper, the last known mainly from his portrait by Emily. The fictional dogs are legion, not always individualized except by names, which range from the heroic to the downright threatening. They include Apollyon ("High Life in Verdopolis"), Bijon (renamed Clumsy; see "Les Deux Chiens," BE, p. 60), Blood ("Tales of the Islanders"), Gnasher (*Wuthering Heights*), Hector ("Henry Hastings"), Juno (*Wuthering Heights, Agnes Grey*, "Henry Hastings," and "Caroline Vernon"), Moloch ("High Life in Verdopolis"), Pilot (*Jane Eyre*), Prince (*Agnes Grey*), Roland ("Ashworth"), Skulker (*Wuthering Heights*), Surgeon ("Poetaster"), Tartar (*Shirley*), Throttler (*Wuthering Heights*), Wolf (*Wuthering Heights*).

See also Flossy; Flossy Junior; Grasper; Keeper; pets of the Brontës

Dolores (no surname given): rebellious pupil in Lucy Snowe's first lesson at Mme Beck's Pensionnat (*Villette*, ch. 8). She has a "dark, mutinous, sinister eye" and is "dreaded and hated by all her associates." Lucy shuts this Catalonian student in a closet, and from then on experiences no major discipline problems.

Donne, Rev. Joseph: the curate of Whinbury in *Shirley*. He is the most objectionable of the trio of curates: self-important, rude, with a grating manner and a determination to look down on all things Yorkshire. His darkest hour comes in ch. 15 when he is terrorized by Tartar and ejected from Fieldhead by Shirley for intolerable rudeness. His marriage to a "sensible, quiet, lady-like little woman" was the making of him, we are told at the end of the book. He was based, with the light disguise of a Frenchification of his surname, on the Rev. Joseph Brett Grant, head of the Grammar School in Haworth in 1844, later vicar of Oxenhope.

Dorlodot (no first name given): young girl, pupil at Mlle Reuter's school in *The Professor*. Mentioned, but not characterized, in ch. 17. In *Villette* (see ch. 14), Alfred de Hamal's aunt is Madame la Baronne de Dorlodot – *à dorloter* is to pamper or fondle.

***Douglas Jerrold's Weekly Newspaper*:** started by the author of *Black-ey'd Susan* and *Mrs Caudle's Curtain Lectures*. It reviewed *Jane Eyre* very favorably, describing it as "original, vigorous, edifying, and absorbingly interesting" (20 Nov 1847). Though its reviewer of *Wuthering Heights* was "disgusted, almost sickened" by its cruelty, he was convinced the author wanted only "the practised skill to make a great artist; perhaps a great dramatic artist" (15 Jan 1848).

Douro, Marquis of *see* Zamorna

Driver, James (d. 1840): grocer of Haworth. Possibly the "Mr Driver" of Charlotte's "History of the Year" who lent the Brontë family *John Bull* and *Blackwood's Magazine* (but see Driver, Rev. Jonas). He was very likely the "Mr Driver" of Emily and Anne's 1834 diary paper – it was at his shop that Branwell heard the erroneous gossip that Sir Robert Peel was to be invited to stand for Leeds in the forthcoming election.

Driver, John: son of the above. Wine and spirits merchant of Liverpool, presumably the "John Driver of Liverpool, youngest son of Mr James Driver of Haworth" who married Sarah Carter of Foxholes near Lancaster" (*Leeds Intelligencer*, 31 Jan 1835). Patrick wrote to him in 1838 to request help in finding Branwell a position in a bank in Liverpool "since, I think it would be to his advantage to go farther from home" (letter of 23 Feb 1838; see BST, v. 21, pt 7, 1996), not a judgment later experience would bear our. He also procured tickets for Charlotte to sit in the Ladies Gallery for the Royal Literary Fund Dinner of 1850, but though she was eager to go, she was in the event unable to make the visit to London.

Driver, Rev. Jonas (d. 1831): clergyman, incumbent of Shireshead near Lancaster, but apparently resident in Haworth. Barker (1994) conjectures he was the man who lent the Brontës *Blackwood's* (but see James Driver). His death date would explain Charlotte's complaint (letter to BB, 17 May 1832) about seeing no periodical.

Dronsart, Adèle: pupil at Mlle Reuter's in *The Professor*, and characterized in ch. 12. Stout and blooming to look at, she is described as suspicious, sullen, envious, and deceitful – shunned by the other pupils because "bad as many of them were, few were as bad as she."

Drumballyroney, Co. Down: parish where Patrick was born, taught in his own school, and was tutor to the Rev. Thomas Tighe's children. He left in 1802. Local tradition has it he returned to preach in the church there after his ordination. The parish is rural, and at the time was poverty-stricken.

Dublin: Charlotte and Arthur Bell Nicholls stayed two days in Dublin at the start of the Irish section of their honeymoon, being met by his brother and two other relatives, all of whom impressed Charlotte. They were also there briefly on their way home (July 1854).

Dublin Review: periodical that in 1850 contained a review that dealt with both *Shirley* and *Jane Eyre*, and included what reads like an attack on Lady Eastlake's piece in the *Quarterly* as well as on others who thought *Jane Eyre* "not strictly proper." Charlotte relished the boldness of their defense of the book, calling it "discriminating" and "very able" (to WSW, 3 Apr 1850).

Dublin University Magazine: favorably but not very perceptively reviewed *Poems*, so that Charlotte was anxious for review copies of the novels to be sent to them. However, she found the critic of *Jane Eyre* to be "not . . . too bright" (to WSW, 1 May 1848). The notice of *Shirley* used words that were common in the treatment of the book: "the coarse, the vulgar and the eccentric have no charms for us" (see Winnifrith, 1973, p. 124). Margaret Smith (CBL, v. 1, p. 471) suggests that Arthur Bell Nicholls may have been a subscriber, and this may have been why it was on a list, with better-known journals, that Charlotte sent to Aylott and Jones (7 May 1846) telling them to send review copies.

Dubois, Victoire: pupil at the Pensionnat Heger who sent Charlotte, some months after her leaving Brussels, a packet of letters from her pupils in the first class. In her reply Charlotte said, not quite truthfully, "I knew I loved my pupils – but I did not know that they had for me the affection those letters express" (18 May 1844).

Duncan, George: Clerk in Charge at Sowerby Bridge station. Branwell sketched him while he was his assistant there in 1840–1.

Dury, Caroline (b. 1820): one of the many young ladies William Weightman was reported as paying court to. She was the daughter of the Rev. Theodore Dury by his first wife.

Dury, Isabella: sister of the Rev. Theodore Dury. She wrote to a friend in 1823 indignantly denying that she had quarreled with her brother over Patrick, and that she had ever had "the most distant idea" of marrying him. His lack of fortune "and six children into the bargain" were the reasons given.

Dury, Rev. Theodore (1788–1850): rector of the Keighley parish church, St Andrew's, from 1814 to 1840, having been presented with the living by the sixth Duke of Devonshire, his contemporary at Harrow. His first wife, Caroline Bourchier, died in November 1820, and his second, whom he married in 1822, was Anne Greenwood, sister of Charlotte's employer Sarah Hannah Sidgwick of Stonegappe – both daughters of a wealthy Keighley manufacturer. Dury was active in founding the Keighley

Mechanics' Institute, and in the Keighley Auxiliary Bible Society, to which the Rev. Carus Wilson was a regular visitor. He entertained each year hundreds of Sunday School pupils ("the scene was lively beyond description" said the *Leeds Intelligencer* of the 1827 gathering, when 600 were entertained). He retired to the probably less demanding living of West Mill, in Hertfordshire.

Plate 1: Blake Hall, home of the Ingham family, near Mirfield, a Georgian house of some pretension. The children Anne was governess to were, however, "desperate little dunces."

Plate 2: Bolton Abbey. This drawing by Charlotte is a copy of an engraving by Edward Finden, but by the time she made it Charlotte had probably seen the Abbey in the company of the younger Nusseys.

Plate 3: John Brown, sexton of Haworth, painted by Branwell in the late 1830s.

Plate 4: Landscape with trees and a river. This drawing, done by Anne in December 1943 at Thorp Green, is possibly from nature.

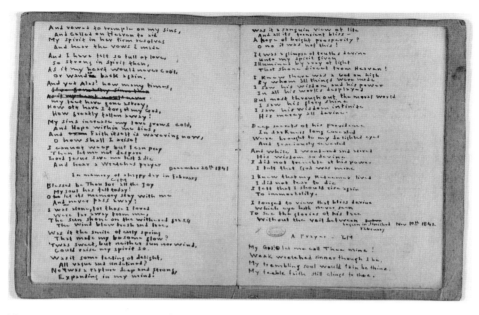

Plate 5: Anne Brontë: manuscript of the poem "In memory of a happy day in February" written in February and November 1842, together with the last verses of the poem "Despondency" and the first verses of the poem "A Prayer."

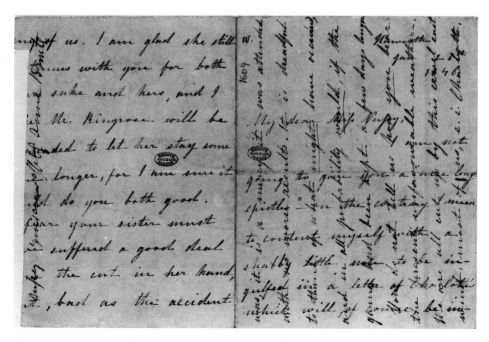

Plate 6: Part of a letter from Anne to Ellen Nussey, dated 26 January 1848. In imperfect condition.

Plate 7: Patrick Branwell Brontë: part of the first version of the unfinished poem "Sleep Mourner Sleep!" written 13 January 1837.

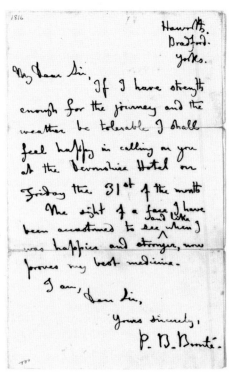

Plate 8: Letter to Francis Grundy from Branwell, probably written in late October 1845.

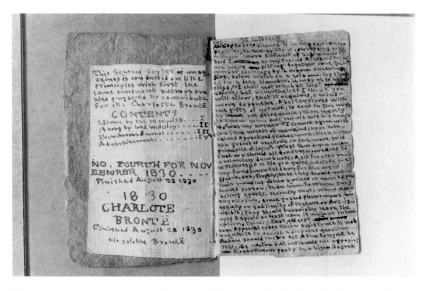

Plate 9: Charlotte Brontë: verso title page to *The Young Men's Magazine*, Second Series, Number four, finished on 28 August 1830.

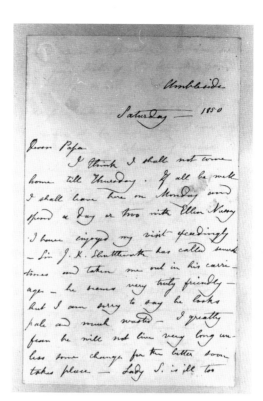

Plate 10: Letter to Patrick Brontë from Charlotte written 21 December 1850, from Harriet Martineau's house, The Knoll, in Ambleside.

Plate 11: Emily with her animals. Sketch by Emily on her 1845 diary paper. Keeper is shown in the foreground with Emily, Flossy and a cat on the bed. Aunt Branwell, now dead, had felt very strongly about animals on beds.

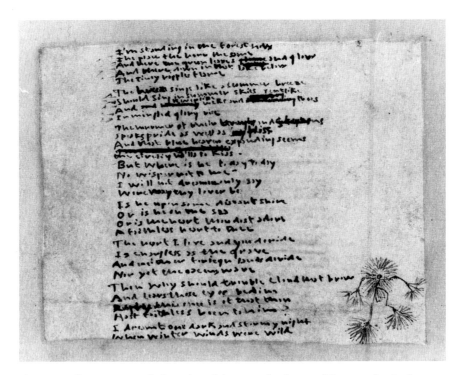

Plate 12: Emily Jane Brontë: draft version of the poem that became "Thou standest in the greenwood now."

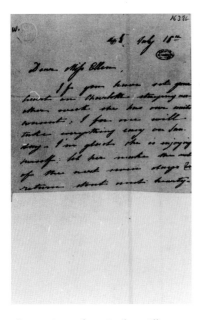

Plate 13: Letter from Emily to Ellen Nussey, written probably 16 July 1845 to the vicarage in Hathersage, Derbyshire, where Charlotte and Ellen were staying.

Plate 14: The Reverend Patrick Brontë, photographed towards the end of his long life.

Plate 15: The Clergy Daughters' School at Cowan Bridge was attended by all the Brontë daughters except Anne. Maria and Elizabeth left the school only to die at home.

Plate 16: Elizabeth Gaskell was Charlotte's friend in the years after the deaths of Emily and Anne and her biographer after her death.

Plate 17: Gawthorpe Hall, the Lancashire home of the Kay-Shuttleworth family, which Charlotte visited in March 1850, when the seventeenth century house was being renovated. She was greatly impressed by it.

Plate 18: The Reverend J. B. Grant, curate in Haworth and Oxenhope, portrayed by Charlotte as Mr Donne in *Shirley*.

Plate 19: Haworth Main Street in the later nineteenth century.

Plate 20: Sir James Kay-Shuttleworth was one of the creators of state education in England. He pressed his hospitality rather too vigorously on Charlotte in her later years.

Plate 21: Keighley hovels by John Bradley. Sketches of the poorer parts of Keighley by the artist who probably first taught the Brontës art.

Plate 22: Emily taught at Law Hill, a school for girls, probably from September 1838 to March 1839, a productive period for her.

Plate 23: G. H. Lewes was prominent in London literary life and one of its most acute critics of fiction. Charlotte was fascinated by but suspicious of him.

Plate 24: J. B. Leyland, sculptor of Halifax, one of Branwell's closest friends.

Plate 25: Patrick Reid "turned off." Drawing on a letter from Branwell to J. B. Leyland. The lower picture depicts a drunken scene Branwell presumably took part in. The upper one is a self-portrait of Branwell and refers to a local man hanged in January 1848 for murdering an elderly couple and their servant girl.

Plate 26: Reverend William Morgan was perhaps Patrick's best friend, but to the younger members of the family he was a bore to be avoided.

Plate 27: The Reverend Arthur Bell Nicholls, Charlotte's husband, around the time of their marriage.

Plate 28: Northangerland by Branwell. Ink drawing of the artist's chosen alter-ego, from about 1835.

Plate 29: Northangerland, by Charlotte. Portrait of the Angrian anti-hero as a young man, painted by Charlotte about 1833.

Plate 30: Ellen Nussey, Charlotte's best friend, is here seen in later life.

Plate 31: Pensionnat Heger by Wimperis. Wimperis's illustrations to the collected edition of the Brontë novels (1889–95) concentrated on the actual buildings which had inspired the fictional ones rather than on characters.

Plate 32: The great actress Rachel, seen here in *Phèdre* three years before her death.

Plate 33: Red House, home of the Taylor family in Gomersal, not far from Roe Head. It was described in detail as Briarmains in *Shirley*.

Plate 34: Elizabeth Rigby, later Lady Eastlake, the sternest of the early critics of *Jane Eyre*.

LYDIA·LADY·SCOTT

Plate 35: Lydia Robinson, wife of Branwell's employer at Thorp Green, and probably his mistress.

E

"Earl of Liverpool": steam packet which Charlotte took back to Brussels in January 1843, insisting on occupying her berth overnight while the ship was at anchor in the Thames (see ECG, *Life*, ch. 12). Named after the second Earl, Prime Minister 1812–27.

Earlsheaton: village near Dewsbury. It was during a Sunday School walk thither that Patrick threw a drunken man into a ditch – an incident that was fictionalized in *Shirley* ch. 17. The story originates in W. W. Yates: *Father of the Brontës* (Leeds, 1897).

Earnshaw, Catherine: sister of Hindley Earnshaw and heroine of *Wuthering Heights*. When Mr Earnshaw brings home the foreign-looking child he calls Heathcliff her first reaction, like her brother's, is to reject the interloper. This soon changes, and the two form a relationship which is not brother-and-sister, nor that of lovers, but something stronger and more enduring than either. By nature Catherine is headstrong, conscious of her ability to charm, capable of pettishness and deceit. When she is bitten by the dogs at Thrushcross Grange she is forced to stay there, and so begins a process of double seduction in which she is seduced to the more artificial and social values of the Lintons, while they, especially Edgar, are seduced by her vitality and beauty. When she returns to the Heights the wayward ranger of the moorlands has become a young lady who believes marriage with Heathcliff would "degrade" her (v. 1, ch. 9).

Her marriage to Edgar Linton is initially happy if unequal: all the giving seems to be on his side. With Heathcliff's return the situation changes catastrophically, because Catherine can never see any further than her own desires or imagine anyone having legitimate expectations that run counter to her own. Her willfulness leads to a series of rows that destroy her mental and her physical health. She dies giving birth to her namesake, Catherine Linton.

In Emily Brontë's scheme of things death is not the end. Catherine's spirit hovers over the last chapters of the book (Lockwood's second visit to Yorkshire) and, by its absence, and Heathcliff's desperate longing for it, over the intervening chapters as well. By one of the many parallels in the book, just as in childhood she had stopped Heathcliff setting traps over lapwings' nests, so her spirit prevents Heathcliff's long-meditated plans for revenge on the younger generation from coming to fruition. When Lockwood talks at the end of the book of the young lovers leaving the Heights "For the use of such ghosts as choose to inhabit it" we are in no doubt as to whose ghosts they will be.

Sanger (1926) estimates her dates as 1765–1784.

Earnshaw, Frances: wife of Hindley, and briefly mistress of the Heights. A superficial, rather silly woman, but with little malice. She is ill at the time of her arrival at the Heights, but the nature of her illness is kept from her. She dies shortly after the birth of Hareton, which according to Sanger (1926) is 1778.

Earnshaw, Hareton: only child of Hindley Earnshaw in *Wuthering Heights*. His mother dies while he is still a baby, and as his father declines into an alcoholic shambles it is Heathcliff who directs his upbringing and, by design, reduces him to the level of an uncouth farmhand, as Hindley had done to him. It is thus that we see him first, through Catherine Linton's eyes, though there are always suggestions of something better hidden beneath. After the death of Catherine's husband this other aspect emerges – manly, tender, eager for knowledge. In the final pages of the book he and Catherine seem destined for a comparatively normal romantic union and life as country landowners.

See also Heaton family

Earnshaw, Hindley: elder brother of Catherine Earnshaw in *Wuthering Heights*. His choice of a violin as his present from Liverpool from his father suggests other directions for his life than actually happen. When his father returns home with the child Heathcliff he feels resentful and displaced in his father's affections, and his mistreatment of the boy alienates the two still further. When he returns to the Heights after his father's death he enjoys robustly (and not a little sadistically) his new position of authority over Heathcliff. In other respects he has a brief period of happiness with his wife Frances, a child-like woman, but on her death he slides further and further into drunkenness, gambling away his own future and his son Hareton's. There is a certain sodden dignity about him in Isabella's accounts of his attempts at revenge on Heathcliff, but inevitably they come to nothing. There are distinct questions to be asked about his death, according to Joseph, who clearly believes Heathcliff has hastened it. His dates, in Sanger's (1926) estimation, are 1757–84.

Earnshaw, Mr (no first name given): owner of Wuthering Heights and father to Hindley and Catherine. A somewhat stern, authoritarian figure, but with a quixotic good nature. As he fails in health he becomes querulous and senses challenges to his authority. His "adoption" of Heathcliff has been much commented on by critics (see entry for Heathcliff).

Earnshaw, Mrs (no first name given): wife of the above. Her character is barely sketched in, though we learn of her dislike of Heathcliff when he first arrives at the Heights. She dies when he has been there about two years (spring 1773, according to Sanger 1926).

Eastlake, Lady *see* Rigby, Elizabeth (Lady Eastlake)

Easton House: farmhouse two miles inland from Bridlington. Charlotte and Ellen Nussey stayed there in September 1839, and soon after their arrival walked to the coast so that Charlotte could have her first view of the sea – "dark blue and green and foam-white" (to EN, 24 Oct 1839). According to Ellen they stayed with the Hudsons, most unwillingly, for a month, but were then allowed a week on their own in lodgings in Bridlington. Charlotte referred to this later as "one of the pleasant recollections of my life" (to EN, 4 Mar 1845?), and painted at the time a watercolor of the house and gardens, with the Hudsons in the foreground – a picture rather uncharacteristic of Charlotte's usual productions, and now only known from a photograph. She and Ellen stayed with the Hudsons again in June 1849, after the death of Anne. The house, in the tiny hamlet of Easton, was built in 1810 and demolished around the 1970s.

Eccles (no first name given): acquaintance of William Crimsworth in X—, possibly a workmate or fellow lodger. Mentioned but not described in ch. 5 of *The Professor*.

Eclectic Review: periodical that reviewed *Villette* unenthusiastically in March 1853. Taking Horace's view that poetry should aim to charm and please as its starting point, the *Review* claimed that *Villette* failed on both counts, with its "insipid" characters, its lack of "one instance of attractive virtue" and its dwelling on "all the vapid details of a girls' school-room" (see Allott, 1973, pp. 90–2). Charlotte pleaded with William Smith Williams (9 Mar 1853) not to withhold such reviews from her: "I *must* see such as are *un*satisfactory and hostile." Earlier, the *Review* had been repelled by *Wuthering Heights* in its reprint of 1850, though it had used the Biographical Notice to sentimentalize the three sisters and their lives.

Economist, The: periodical founded in 1843. It reviewed *Jane Eyre* favorably, even finding "a certain raciness decidedly agreeable," and calling it the most "striking" novel it had read for years. Charlotte later complained "The literary critic of that paper praised the book if written by a man – and pronounced it 'odious' if the work of a woman" (to WSW, 16 Aug 1849). She was, however, misremembering. Its review of *Shirley* was much less enthusiastic.

Edinburgh: Charlotte spent two full days in the Scottish capital (3–6 July 1850) in the company of George Smith and his sister, who had made the journey to fetch home their younger brother. Charlotte was prepared to love the city ("I always liked Scotland as an idea" she wrote to WSW, 20 July 1850), and in the event it proved to be a sort of ideal for her: she quoted Scott's "mine own romantic town" in the same letter to express her enthusiasm. The party visited Abbotsford, the abbey at Melrose, and climbed up to Arthur's Seat. The company no doubt contributed to the enchantment, but the same company had never made London remotely as attractive. After her return home the comparison to London recurs in her letters, always to the larger city's disadvantage, for example, "Edinburgh compared to London is like a vivid page of history compared to a huge dull treatise on Political Economy" (to L. Wheelwright, 30 July 1850). Mrs Gaskell surely gets it right: "Scotland was a land which had its roots deep down in her imaginative affections" (*Life*, ch. 27).

Edinburgh Review, The: Whig periodical founded in 1802 by Francis Jeffrey, Sydney Smith, and Charlotte's bête noire Henry Brougham. It reviewed *Jane Eyre* and *Villette* favorably, but G. H. Lewes's review of *Shirley* caused Charlotte such an attack of rage that she felt "cold and sick" (to WSW, 10 Jan 1850). Lewes's examples of "coarseness" do seem particularly perverse or twaddling, and his use of his knowledge of her sex ungentlemanly.

Egan, Pierce, the elder (1772–1849): sporting journalist and author of comic tales. Branwell read his *Bell's Sporting Life* and probably his *Boxiana*, subtitled "Sketches of Ancient and Modern Pugilism." He may have learnt from Egan about the Castle Tavern in Holborn.

Eliot, George (Mary Ann Evans) (1819–80): novelist, a great admirer of Charlotte Brontë, though she protested that the self-sacrifice of Jane Eyre ought to be "in a somewhat nobler cause than that of a diabolical law which chains a man body and soul to a putrefying carcase," and she also complained, rather oddly, that the characters talked "like the heroes and heroines of police reports" (to Charles Bray, 11 June 1848). Her enthusiasm for *Villette*, however was unbounded: "What passion, what fire in her," she wrote in 1853, and "There is something almost preternatural in its power" (to Mrs Charles Bray, 15 Feb 1853).

Eliza (no surname given): cook at the Briarfield Rectory in *Shirley*.

Ellesmere, Earl of (1800–57): Francis Egerton, 1st Earl, was a statesman and man of letters, a translator from German (*Faust*) and Italian. He sent Charlotte an order to view his picture collection during her visit to London in June 1851, which she "enjoyed very much" (letter to PB, 26 June 1851).

Elliotson, John (1791–1868): physician. Quoted by Patrick in his copy of Graham's *Modern Domestic Medicine* on the subject of hydrophobia (rabies). The quote, dated

1848, possibly apropos of Emily and the dog in Church Lane, is to the effect that "all things have been tried to cure this disease, and all have failed." Elliotson's reputation suffered when he took up the cause of Mesmerism. He was the first physician to use the stethoscope.

Elliott, Ebenezer (1781–1849): lyric poet and "Corn-Law Rhymer," from his fierce opposition to the "tax on bread." Charlotte sent the Sheffield poet a copy of *Poems* of 1846 when disposing of the many unsold copies.

Ellis, Mrs Sarah Stickney (1799–1872): writer for and about women, with strong views on proper behavior. She found the "coarseness" of *Jane Eyre* and *Shirley* hard to stomach, but when she called on Charlotte (Jan 1850) the latter felt she had in fact been "influenced and stirred" by the novels (to WSW, 10 Jan 1850). Her background was Quaker, and she tried to make a living from art before turning to authorship, usually of an improving kind. H. S. Twycroft-Martin, in the *Oxford Dictionary of National Biography*, suggests that "Her graphic presentation of alcoholism," in her volume of stories called *Family Secrets* (1842) "is without parallel in the early 1840s, and may have influenced . . . Ann [sic] Brontë's *The Tenant of Wildfell Hall*." She was the author of *The Daughters of England*, followed by *The Wives* and *The Women* of the same country.

Elrington/Ellrington *see* Northangerland

Emanuel, Josef: half brother to Paul Emanuel in *Villette*. He lacks his brother's force of character and is "as much under his control as were the girls themselves" (ch. 20). He is most fully described in ch. 38.

Emanuel, Paul Carl (or Carlos) David: cousin of Mme Beck and teacher at her Pensionnat de Demoiselles in *Villette*. A fiery-hearted, dramatic, fearsome man, with a tender heart and an intensely honorable and charitable nature. His vanity and hunger for praise is touched on many times in the novel, as are his choleric outbursts at anything that touches a nerve or offends his aesthetic or moral senses. Equally, his penitence is readily forthcoming, as is a tender care for those who need it. His subservience to the Catholic Church and to his confessor Père Silas is perhaps the most surprising aspect of his character, but that character is so rounded, and so beautifully observed, that small surprises abound. The switch of interest in the final third of the book from Graham Bretton to him has been often criticized, yet M. Paul has been hovering in the background, waiting for the prominence he deserves, from Lucy's first night in Villette, when he recommends her engagement as nursery-maid.

M. Paul's fate at the end of the book is left slightly ambiguous, after reproaches from Mr Brontë, yet no reader will miss the obvious intention of the author that he should die. No plot line can ever be said to *demand* a perfectly arbitrary accidental death such as M. Paul's in a storm at sea, but Charlotte obviously felt the pattern of the novel and of Lucy's life, one of deprivation enlivened by occasional bursts of warm sunshine, ruled out a happy ending. The mutual love was itself perhaps sufficient wish-fulfillment in her eyes: a fulfilling marriage would have been excessive.

There has been little doubt, especially since the publication in 1914 of Charlotte's letters to him, that the picture of M. Paul Emanuel was based on Constantin Heger, her teacher in Brussels.

Emdale (also spelt Imdel): birthplace of Patrick, in the parish of Drumballyroney.

Emerson, Ralph Waldo (1803–82): American poet and essayist of the "Transcendental" school. Charlotte found his essays "of mixed gold and clay – deep and invigorating truth – dreary and depressing fallacy" (to WSW, 4 Feb 1849). She read one of them to Emily on the evening before she died.

"Emma": Charlotte's last attempt at fiction, possibly a reworking of the unfinished "Willie Ellin." It was started in late 1853, and was read to her husband in late 1854. Thackeray published it, with a personal tribute to the author, in *Cornhill Magazine*, March 1860. The story concerns a young girl, not in herself attractive in person or manner, who is left at a struggling girls' school by a dashing and plausible father or male protector. As long as the delusion of a wealthy background persists she is treated by the teachers as the darling of the school. When payment fails to arrive their attitude changes, and they call in a local bachelor, William Ellin, who discovers that the name and address of the father are fiction. When they confront the child she faints, and there the fragment ends.

See also "Willie Ellin"; "Ashworth"

English Churchman: organ of the High Church party in the Church of England. It deplored Charlotte's tirades against Catholicism in *Villette*.

Enoch, Frederick (b. ca 1827): one of two purchasers of the 1846 *Poems*. He wrote requesting the Bells' autographs, and received the card with them on which is now in the Brontë Parsonage Museum. He lived in Corn Market, Warwick, worked as a printer and stationer, and later wrote lyrics for a number of songs.

Epps, John (1805–69) and George Napoleon (1815–74): brothers, homeopathic doctors. It was to one of them, probably John, that Charlotte wrote an account of Emily's condition and symptoms on 9 December 1848, 10 days before she died. Epps sent medicine Emily refused to take and an opinion "expressed too obscurely to be of use" (to EN, 19 Dec 1848). Charlotte's memorandum, printed in Wise and Symington (v. 2, p. 292), was lost for many years, but was rediscovered in 1997 in an autograph book in the British Library collection.

Era: periodical that published an extremely enthusiastic review of *Jane Eyre* (28 Nov 1847), saying it surpassed "all the serious novel writers of the day" (unfortunately specifying Bulwer-Lytton, G. P. R. James, and Disraeli), compared it to the cartoons of Raphael, and drew from it the moral that "the practice of simple propriety, founded on strict morality and religious principles, is the sure road to ultimate bliss."

Eshton family: Mr Eshton is an acquaintance of Mr Rochester, who attends a house party at their home, the Leas, and afterwards brings most of the guests back to an unscheduled party at Thornfield (*Jane Eyre*, v. 2, ch. 1). Eshton's appearance is striking, even theatrical, and he proposes to Lady Ingram, unsuccessfully of course, that Jane Eyre should be invited to join the charades. His wife is a handsome and kindly disposed woman, who contrasts sharply with the Ingrams. Their daughter Amy is small, child-like, and lively, and she treats the visit of the "fortune teller" to Thornfield as a great joke. She has a sister, Louisa, who is taller and more elegant.

Esther *see* Lee, Esther

Eugene Aram: novel written in 1832 by Edward Bulwer, later Bulwer-Lytton, later 1st Baron Lytton. Usually classed with the "Newgate" novels of, for example, Ainsworth and Dickens, it has little of the sensationalism of *Jack Shepherd* or *Oliver Twist*. For much of its length it is a picaresque novel, tracing the journeys of Walter Lester as he attempts to find, or discover the fate of, his father. His trail leads to a sordid murder, apparently for gain, many years before in Knaresborough. The murderer is found to be Eugene Aram, about to be married to Walter's cousin Madeline. The book ends with Aram's trial at York, his condemnation to death, his confession to Walter, and his death on the gallows.

The author is interested in the gentle scholar-murderer, emphasizing over and over that this is the man who would step aside to avoid treading on a worm or snail, yet is one who can philosophically convince himself of the rightness of murder in certain circumstances. In spite of any amount of heightened declamation by the central character, this paradox is not handled very interestingly. But for the modern reader the fatal barrier to any currency for Bulwer-Lytton's novels today is the absurdly orotund and melodramatic style, where windows become "admittants of the celestial beam," and so forth. It may be that such a style had some appeal to the adolescent Brontës, and Patrick's letters are not free of similar affectations.

It was this book that Branwell was reading to Charlotte in Aunt Branwell's room when Emily and Anne wrote their diary paper of June 1837. There was a copy of the novel in the Keighley Mechanics' Institute Library.

Eulalie (no surname given): one of three trouble-makers among the pupils at Mlle Reuter's school, characterized in ch. 10 of *The Professor*. She is large, beautiful, and lethargic, and seems on the surface like a "figure, moulded in wax." When chided over slovenly work she resembles an "incensed turkey."

Euston Square Station: the station in London for the trains from Leeds. In 1843 Charlotte left Leeds at 9.00, and should have arrived at Euston at 8.00, but was two hours late. In 1852 she wrote to Mrs Smith that she would leave Leeds at 10.25, and should arrive at Euston Square at 4.15.

Evans, Ann (1795–1857): the original of Miss Temple in *Jane Eyre*. She was appointed superintendent at the Clergy Daughters' School, succeeding Miss Andrews (probably one of the originals of Miss Scatcherd), whose appointment had been temporary. Charlotte clearly loved and admired her, and no criticism of her has been made, beyond her inability to change an inherently bad system. She left in 1826 to marry the Rev. James Connor, later Rector of Knossington, near Melton Mowbray. They had no children. See Brett Harrison, "The Real 'Miss Temple'" (BST, 16, 85, 1975) for an explanation of the frequent confusion between Ann Evans and Mrs Hill (née Andrews) who later, from America, sprang to the defense of Carus Wilson. It was Ann Evans who referred to Emily as "a darling child . . . quite the pet nursling of the school" (ECG, *Life*, ch. 4), a description borne out when, in a letter of condolence to Patrick on his loss of his daughters in 1825, she sent her love to "little petted Em" (Barker, 1994, p. 141).

Evans, William: MP for North Derbyshire, married to Lydia Robinson's sister Mary, and appointed by Edmund Robinson one of the executors of his will dated 2 January 1846. He was one of the trustees who, according to Branwell, "detest me" (letter to J. B. Leyland, June 1846), and the man who ordered Mrs Robinson "to return me, unopened, a letter which I addressed to Thorp Green and which the Lady was not permitted to see" (to J. B. Leyland, 24 Jan 1847). Caution must be exercised whenever Branwell is dealing with this matter.

Examiner, The: periodical founded in 1808 by Leigh and John Hunt. The former's description in the journal of the Prince Regent in 1813 as "a libertine over head and ears in debt and disgrace, a despiser of domestic ties, the companion of gamblers and demireps. . . ." brought him a fine and two years' imprisonment. The journal's championship of Shelley and Keats brought it ridicule from older-established organs. The editor from 1830–49 was Albany Fonblanque, who wrote a review of *Jane Eyre* which gratified Charlotte. Her opinion of this radical journal was always high, and she always mentally excepted it from animadversions on critics in general. Charlotte had dinner with London critics, including that of *The Examiner*, at the Smiths' in December 1849. Its review of *Wuthering Heights* was one of five in Emily's writing desk at her death: it spoke of "considerable power," but used the inevitable word "coarseness." However, Mrs Gaskell's tribute to their "genial and generous appreciation of merit" (*Life*, v. 2, ch. 2) clearly applies to the reception of Charlotte's novels in the journal.

Eyre, Jane: heroine of the book that bears her name. The facts of her birth and background (orphan, born of a disapproved marriage) and the details of her story (flight from a suitor after he attempts to marry her bigamously) might suggest staple fictional fare. In fact she is a brilliantly original as well as a subtle creation. The young Jane, both at Gateshead Hall and Lowood School, is a rebel and truth-teller: she stands up against tyranny, unfair discrimination, perverted principle. The young woman who goes to Thornfield has a concern for her own integrity as a person, thinks deeply about the roles and possibilities open to a woman, and speaks with her employer as a social and intellectual equal. At the same time, as she falls deeper and deeper in love, she seems to worship him both on the physical and intellectual level. The tension between desire for independence and the desire to submit is brilliantly conveyed. Jane is also a woman of strong, and somewhat traditional, religious and moral beliefs (this is sometimes missed by modern commentators). Thus there is no question in her mind of living as Rochester's mistress, though the struggle to break away from him is palpable. Thus too, she admires unequivocally St John Rivers' vocation as a missionary, though undercutting the picture of him is resistance to his authoritarian and almost inhuman temperament.

The picture of Jane is one of the most complete in British fiction, and the depth of understanding (or of intuition) of her character springs partly from the variety of the means Charlotte Brontë uses to convey it: dreams, pictures, books, extreme mental states and images contribute. The images of fire and ice that dominate the book do not only or mainly sum up the two men in Jane's life: they represent extremes in her own temperament she must reconcile, as she reconciles the passionate love she feels with the ironic humor which is its natural form of expression to her. While various generations since the book's creation have expressed doubts about Rochester and Rivers, the creation of Jane has never seemed less than a triumph of psychological insight and sympathetic understanding.

Eyre, Mr John: uncle of Jane Eyre. He never appears directly in the story, but acts throughout as a potential and actual *deus ex machina*, preventing her bigamous marriage to Rochester and providing her, by his death, with a competency. The machinery of the plot creaks somewhat, but since he is first mentioned by Bessie (v. 1, ch. 10) and later by Mrs Reed on her deathbed (v. 2, ch. 6), his interventions in Jane's life are not surprising.

Eyre, Mrs Mary: resident, with her son, of North Lees Hall, near Hathersage. Ellen and Charlotte borrowed their pony to go up into Covedale. Charlotte may have borrowed her name and aspects of her house for her best-known heroine and Thornfield.

Eyton, John (d. 1823): vicar of Wellington and Eyton, in Shropshire. Patrick was his curate in 1809, and his fellow curate was William Morgan, who became his friend for life.

F

F—, Lady: one of Huntingdon's early mistresses, whom his wife blames for contributing to his corruption (*The Tenant of Wildfell Hall*, ch. 24). The account of this affair corresponds closely to the version accepted in the Brontë family of the Branwell/Lydia Robinson affair.

F—, Lord: guest at Rosalie's coming-out ball in *Agnes Grey*, a man who hates his "nasty, cross" wife (ch. 9).

Fairfax, Mrs Alice: housekeeper at Thornfield, and a distant relative of Mr Rochester. Mild, kindly, and conventional in views and conduct, she has notions of social propriety which are sorely tested by the proposed marriage of Jane Eyre and Rochester. Though a benign presence in the Thornfield section, she has none of the strong mind or independent judgment of that other Brontë housekeeper Nellie Dean.

Fanny (no surname given): servant at the Briarfield Rectory in *Shirley*, and devoted friend and ally to Caroline Helstone. She usually escorts Caroline home when she has been visiting, for example at Hollow's Cottage.

Fanshawe, Augusta: sister of Ginevra, and one who has made a worldly, prudent marriage. Mentioned in *Villette*, ch. 6.

Fanshawe, Captain (no first name given): father of Ginevra in *Villette*. He is a half-pay officer, but said by Ginevra to be "well-descended" (ch. 6).

Fanshawe de Bassompierre de Hamal, Alfred: son of Ginevra Fanshawe and Alfred de Hamal mentioned in ch. 40. Ginevra's maternal feelings and fussiness about her adored son seem somewhat out of character. The picture may be based on

Joe Taylor's wife, the former Amelia Ringrose, whose fussiness as a mother (actually justified by her child's poor health) aroused Charlotte's amused exasperation.

Fanshawe, Ginevra: English pupil at Mme Beck's Pensionnat in *Villette*, and the unwitting cause of Lucy Snowe's seeking employment there. She is vain, superficial, and selfish, and regards the rest of the world as put there for her own purposes, if it be only to flatter her or set her off well by contrast. This may be one reason why she attaches herself to Lucy, even when explicitly despising her for having to work and for having no pretensions to "birth." Lucy sees through her pretensions and glitter, yet retains a grimly amused affection for her. Indeed, during the dreadful long vacation she has fantasies in which Ginevra "became with me a sort of heroine" (ch. 15). Elsewhere she dreams of her.

Her treatment of Dr John ("Isidore"), however, Lucy finds deplorable and heartless, and her behavior over gifts from her chaperone and suitors grasping and dishonest. She finally elopes with de Hamal, but as usual with Ginevra things are arranged, debts paid, and Ginevra lives out her life "suffering as little as any human being I have ever known" (ch. 40).

The portrait is said by Clement Shorter to be based on a Miss Maria Miller, a pupil at the Pensionnat Heger. The evidence for this is slight, but Charlotte's opinion of this lady is obvious from a letter of about 23 June 1852 to Laetitia Wheelwright. An alternative original for Ginevra was proposed by Charles Lemon, "The origins of Ginevra Fanshawe" (BST, v. 16, pt 81, 1971). This was Susannah Rodway Mills, later Mme Baudry, who, like Ginevra, eloped from the Pensionnat Heger.

"Farewell to Angria": Charlotte's 1839 considered (but slightly premature) farewell to the romantic fantasy world which had occupied her for the previous decade. She emphasizes that she has seen its landscapes in all seasons, its characters from every angle, and she underlines the difficulty of quitting "my friends and my intimate acquaintances." The farewell is less than wholehearted, and she promises only to quit for "awhile" (*sic*) that land where the "skies flame, the glow of sunset is always upon it" (Frances Beer, ed., *The Juvenilia of Jane Austen and Charlotte Brontë*, 1986, p. 367). In spite of the "Farewell" (not Charlotte's title for the short note) Angrian characters and themes loom large in the earliest extant attempt at a proper novel by Charlotte, "Ashworth."

Farren family: family of William Farren in *Shirley*, consisting of Grace, his wife, a clean, orderly, managing woman, though very poor, and several children, of whom Ben and Michael are named.

Farren, William: one of the workers rendered unemployed by the new machinery in *Shirley*. A thinking, hard-working, and adaptable man, he is described as "hard-favoured, but modest, and manly-looking" (ch. 8). He is regarded by Charlotte Brontë as typifying the most independent and reflective side of the Yorkshire working man, and he puts the case for such as himself simply but strongly through various conversations in the novel.

Feather, James: young man for whom Patrick wrote a recommendation to the National Society in 1844. He was particularly solicitous to mention that Feather's "abashed" manner should not lead them to undervalue his "intrinsic worth."

Fénelon, François de Salignac de la Mothe (1651–1715): French writer and cleric who displeased the Pope with his *Maximes des Saints sur la Vie Intérieure*, and King Louis XIV with his romance *Télémaque*, which was regarded as a satire on the court and a critique of the government's aggressive policies. His acquiescence in the judgment of the religious and civil powers which he served was widely admired. He may be the "certain French nobleman who attained a purer and higher degree of sanctity than has been known since the days of the early Martyrs" referred to in Charlotte's letter to Ellen Nussey (20 Feb 1837?). He is certainly referred to at length in ch. 5 of Branwell's "The Politics of Verdopolis" (WPBB, v. 1, pp. 353–4) and in the "Long Vacation" chapter in *Villette*. *Télémaque* is referred to in *Shirley* (ch. 27).

Fennell, Rev. John (1762–1841): born in Shropshire, he was a teacher at a Methodist school in Penzance when he met and married in 1790 Jane Branwell, aunt of Mrs Brontë. He was subsequently headmaster of a school in Wellington, where he met Patrick Brontë, and at Woodhouse Grove School at Rawdon, near Leeds. His appointment of Patrick, by now at Hartshead, as visiting examiner in classics led to Patrick's meeting with Maria Branwell, who had come to help her aunt in the domestic arrangements at the new school.

Fennell's time at Woodhouse Grove was brief, because the split between the Methodists and the established Church was widening, and he chose to remain an Anglican. He took holy orders, and became first a curate at Christ Church in Bradford, later, in April 1819, being nominated to the perpetual curacy of Cross Stone, in Todmorden. His wife died, aged 76, in May 1829, and the young Brontës visited him in September of that year (Charlotte's earliest letter is dated from the Parsonage House).

He married again in July 1830, the bride being Elizabeth Lister, daughter of a Leeds merchant. Though some skepticism has been voiced about the size of the old man's second family, it seems in fact to have been six children (the sixth being Thomas Edward born 19 Dec 1840), and there are records of the marriages of three of his daughters (*Leeds Intelligencer*, 9 May 1857, 24 July 1858, and 23 July 1859). By 1839 he was advertising for a curate – hoping for "a decidedly pious and active young man who, if requisite may have a title" (*Leeds Intelligencer*, 6 June; n.b., a title is a certificate required for ordination). The curate he got was Sutcliffe Sowden. Two years later Charlotte told Ellen Nussey he was "very ill" (3 July 1841?), and he died in October of that year.

Patrick sent regards to Mrs Fennell when he wrote to John White of Rawdon on 22 September 1842. If this was John's widow, this may be a clue as to how Charlotte got her position as the Whites' governess.

See also Sowden, Rev. Sutcliffe; Woodhouse Grove School

Ferndean Manor: the blind Rochester's refuge after the fire at Thornfield. It is described as "retired and hidden" in an unhealthy situation (*Jane Eyre*, v. 3, ch. 1) and as an old building but a manor house of "no architectural pretensions" (v. 3, ch. 11). It aptly mirrors Rochester's mental and physical condition when Jane comes to find him at the end of the novel.

Ferrand, Mrs Busfeild: wife of William Busfeild Ferrand. She visited Charlotte and Patrick at Haworth in August 1850, with a party of her guests, including Lord John Manners. Charlotte found her "very gentle and unassuming," and said she preferred her to Lady Shuttleworth (to EN, 26 Aug 1850).

Ferrand, William Busfeild (1809–89): local landowner and Conservative politician, of Harden Grange, near Bingley. Charlotte declined an invitation to the Grange, which brought on her a visit from his wife (see above). He was the eldest son of Currer Fothergill Busfeild, and took the additional name of Ferrand in 1839 (see *Leeds Intelligencer*, 10 Dec 1839). A man of intemperate language and "Young England" views (i.e., a conservative and romantic nostalgia for a hierarchic and religion-based society), he was very active politically in the area, doubtless with the support of Patrick, who in 1853 wrote a fulsome letter of thanks for a present of game, one of which weighed 26 ounces, "the greatest weight, I ever knew" (23 Aug 1853).

Fidena, Duke of (Prince John Augustus Sneaky): in the Angrian stories, son of the King of Sneaky's Land. The King's opposition to his son's marriage to Lily Hart takes a great while to overcome. The Duke becomes politically involved as an ally of Zamorna, whose friend he is but whose personal life he strongly disapproves of. His honorable conduct eventually means he is one of the most trusted men in Verdopolis, and he becomes the Federation's Prime Minister. His devotion to the principles of "justice and Religion" (WPBB, v. 2, p. 528) mark him out from most of the other politicians except Warner.

Fieldhead: the home of Shirley Keeldar in *Shirley*. It is picturesque and irregular, and thus romantic in its appeal. When Shirley returns to the area it has been empty for 10 years, apart from a gardener and his wife, but it has been kept in good repair, and the estate brings in good rents for Shirley: a substantial one from Hollow's Mill, but "a larger share comes from the landed estate around it" (ch. 18). This enables Shirley to take a position as one of the gentry, but also to involve herself in the burning question of the new machines.

Charlotte's description is based almost certainly on Oakwell Hall in Birstal, and the name comes from a hamlet and manor house close to it. At one time Charlotte considered using Fieldhead as the title of the novel.

See also Oakwell Hall

Fielding, Henry (1707–54): English novelist admired by Branwell, but deplored as an immoral influence by Charlotte. Her presence at Thackeray's lecture on him in June 1851, and her reading of its printed version, provoked the longest summary of

her objections to his work, in a letter to George Smith in March 1853. In it she reveal-
ingly says "Had I a brother yet living – I should tremble to let him read" it, which
reinforces her comparison in the Preface to *Jane Eyre* of Fielding to a vulture who "could
stoop on carrion."

Filey: Yorkshire seaside resort south of Scarborough. Charlotte stayed there with
Ellen Nussey after the death of Anne, and again for about a month in May–June 1852.
On the second occasion she emphasized to correspondents that she was *"quite alone"*
(to MW, 23 June 1852), and though she was unwell for part of the time, she seems to
have relished the opportunity for solitary contemplation of the sea. She described to
Patrick standing for an hour on the cliffs, "watching the tumbling in of great tawny
turbid waves – that made the whole shore white with foam and filled the air with a
sound hollower and deeper than thunder" (letter of 2 June 1852). In 1849 she and
Ellen walked to Filey Brigg, but in 1852, on her own, she was "frightened back by two
cows" (to EN, 6 June 1852), animals that habitually terrified her.

Finchingfield Park: near Braintree, in Essex. Where Mary Burder was living in
1823 when Patrick, by then a widower, proposed to renew acquaintanceship with
her.

Finden, William (1787–1852): English engraver. Charlotte copied many of
his works, particularly from his *Illustrations to the Life and Works of Lord Byron*. Among
the more ambitious are her versions of "The Maid of Saragoza" and her picture "English
Lady," which is a version of Finden's engraving from E. T. Parris's portrait of Lady
Jersey. Emily was still copying his engravings as late as 1842, when she gave her version of his "Ianthe" the title "The North Wind." Charlotte also copied some engravings by his brother Edward (1791–1857).

Firth, Elizabeth (1797–1837): of Kipping House, a close friend of the Brontë
family in Thornton. She had lost her mother in a gig accident the year before they
arrived, and was acting as her father's housekeeper and hostess. She called on the Brontë
family first on 7 June 1815, and thus began a growing intimacy which is recorded
in her diary (now in the Sheffield University Library). Already by August of that year
Elizabeth was standing godmother to Elizabeth Brontë, as later she was also to do for
Anne. The diary becomes a series of records (unfortunately not elaborated on) of social
occasions involving the Firths (including Elizabeth's new stepmother), and the
Brontës and their visitors, most notably Elizabeth Branwell.

The connection did not cease after the Brontës' move to Haworth. When Maria Brontë
became terminally ill Elizabeth Firth visited her and the family, and at least once took
the eldest children back on a long visit to Kipping House. Three months after Maria's
death Patrick stayed with Elizabeth in Thornton, and on his return home wrote her
a proposal of marriage. She seems to have given him a decided rejection, which her
diary referred to as "my last letter to Mr Brontë" (14 Dec 1821). Such anger could not
have been caused simply by a lack of love for him. She may have felt the proposal

came much too soon after his wife's death, or that he was very much beneath her socially and in wealth. She was in any case 24 to his 44.

The acquaintance was in fact renewed in 1823, when Patrick visited her. She was shortly after to marry Rev. J. C. Franks, Vicar of Huddersfield, and her connection thereafter was mainly with the Brontë children. She visited the eldest three at Cowan Bridge in 1824, and Charlotte at Roe Head in 1831. Anne and Charlotte were invited to the Franks's vicarage in the summer holidays of 1836 from Roe Head, a visit they very much resented having to pay. Elizabeth Franks died at the home of her friends the Outhwaites in Bradford, where she was perhaps consulting Dr Outhwaite professionally, since the *Leeds Intelligencer* (16 Sep 1837) refers to "a protracted indisposition." She and her husband had five children.

Firth, John Scholefield (1757–1820): father of Elizabeth, doctor of Thornton.
He had been widowed in 1814, but he was remarried in 1815 to Anne Greame, and the three Firths formed the basis of the Brontës' circle during their time at Thornton. John and his daughter were godparents to Elizabeth and Anne, John and his second wife godparents to Branwell. In September 1820 he and his daughter dined at Haworth Parsonage, and he died, visited by Patrick, shortly after Christmas the same year. Winifred Gerin's idea (1961, pp. 96–7) that his widow helped finance Branwell's projected trip to London (which never, in all likelihood, took place) is based on a misreading of Patrick's letter (6 July 1835) to Elizabeth Franks, née Firth: when he refers to Elizabeth's father and stepmother as Branwell's "sponsors" he is surely only reminding her that they were Branwell's godparents.

Fish family: Dr Edward Fish was the surgeon of Broughton-in-Furness, with
whom Branwell lodged January–June 1840. His house, High Sykes House, was just up the hill from the Postlethwaites' in the square and is still standing. Branwell described him as "a respectable surgeon, two days out of seven is as drunk as a lord!" and his wife Ann as "a bustling, chattering, kind-hearted soul" (letter to John Brown, 13 Mar 1840). Their daughter Margaret was described as "fair-faced, blue-eyed, dark-haired, sweet eighteen," and with his usual boasting about women he added: "she little thinks the devil is so near her!"

Fletcher, Rev. John (1729–85): Swiss-born cleric of Wesleyan sympathies. His
name is an anglicization of de la Flechère. He was ordained priest in 1757 and in 1760 accepted the living of Madeley in Shropshire, an industrial community where he became a revered figure. Patrick met his widow Mary when he became curate at Wellington, and he was attracted by her evangelical sympathies, as well as by the clerical group she had gathered around her. This included William Morgan and John Fennell.

Flossy: King Charles spaniel, reputedly a gift to Anne from the Robinsons, who joined
the Parsonage menagerie around 1843. Flossy is often referred to as female – by Gerin, Alexander, and others – probably due to a mistranscription by Mrs Gaskell of a letter of Charlotte's of 1854. "Did I tell you that our poor little Flossy is dead? She

[for He] drooped for a single day . . ." (to EN, 7 Dec 1854). In fact he was male, and was referred to as such in Anne's 1845 diary paper. The fact that Ellen took one of his puppies (mother unknown) may have added to the confusion. He was much drawn and painted by the Brontës, especially by Emily in her picture of him chasing birds, and in a group with Keeper and Tiger. Anne also painted an unfinished watercolor of him on a window sill. Anne wrote to Ellen in the year of her death about Flossy's relish for a sheep hunt, and Charlotte wrote movingly after her return home alone in the summer of 1849 of Flossy and Keeper's reception of her, and their expectation of her sisters following. On Flossy's death at the end of 1854 she wrote "no dog ever had a happier life or an easier death" (to EN, 7 Dec 1854).

Flossy Junior: offspring of the above, who has also been endowed with a sexual ambiguity as deep and mysterious as that of her first owners, the Bells. The puppy was given to Ellen ("gift of Mr B" her note says on a letter of Charlotte's) in July 1844, and in a letter of 10 August 1844 (?) Charlotte writes "I fear by what you say Flossy Junr behaves discreditably & gets his Mistress into scrapes." However, this was a slip, perhaps attributable to the sex of Flossy Senior. Ellen, in a letter to Mary Gorham (22 July 1845), refers to her throughout as female. Charlotte later in the same year relays the opinion of Emily and Anne that Flossy Junior should not be expected to rear all of her large litter of puppies: "they will pull their poor little mother to pieces" (4 Nov 1845). She died in 1851, a mysteriously awful death, which Charlotte could not "[screw] up nerve to tell Papa about" (to EN, 10 May 1851).

Follett, Miss: Margaret Smith's reading of the name of a woman who was engaged to Henry Nussey in 1840 (Wise and Symington read "Halkett"). Ann Nussey considered her "bold," and possibly attempted to break the engagement. However, Charlotte wrote to Henry Nussey a month after commenting to Ellen on Ann's hostile attitude and she mentions his "future partner," though in guarded terms (26 May 1840). No marriage took place.

Fonblanque, Albany (1793–1872): editor of The Examiner 1830–47, and probably author of the discriminating review of Jane Eyre which gratified Charlotte. He probably also wrote the review of Shirley which, though appreciative, commented on her undue tenderness toward those of a Tory turn of mind and her harshness toward radicals and industrialists. Whatever Charlotte's politics at this point in her life, probably unpindownable, he certainly was right that the cast of her mind had a Tory slant enduring from childhood partialities, and she admired his acuteness. He was succeeded as editor by John Forster.

Forbes, Dr John (1787–1861): expert on consumptive diseases who was consulted by post on Anne's consumption in 1849 and backed the advice of Dr Teale. He was a friend of George Smith's, and extremely distinguished and in advance of his time. He made Charlotte's acquaintance after one of Thackeray's lectures on the English humorists, and on one of her later visits to London (Jan 1853) took her round the Bethlehem Hospital. No doubt it was on this occasion that he told Charlotte of the successful use of chloroform in operations, a remark that Patrick noted in his copy of Graham's *Modern Domestic Medicine*. He was also a pioneer in the use of the stethoscope.

Forçade, Eugène: French critic whose review of *Shirley* in the *Revue des Deux Mondes* aroused Charlotte to unusual enthusiasm. In letters to William Smith Williams and Ellen Nussey in November 1849 she shows how completely she feels he has understood the novel. She calls him "the subtle-thoughted, keen-eyed, quick-feeling Frenchman" and says he "follows Currer Bell through every winding, discerns every point, discriminates every shade" (22 Nov 1849). Earlier, his review of a translation of *Jane Eyre* in the same journal aroused equal enthusiasm in Charlotte, and lightened the dark days of Emily's last illness.

Forget Me Not: a Christmas annual published by Ackerman in the 1820s and 1830s, containing stories, poems, and engravings, several of which were copied by the Brontë family. For example, Charlotte copied Chevalier's engraving of "Woman with Lyre," while Branwell copied a print of John Martin's "Queen Esther," both executed in December 1830 and from the 1831 issue of the annual, published early, no doubt for the Christmas market. An earlier issue, in addition to the expected contents, contained "a Chronicle of remarkable Events during the past Years, a Genealogy of the Reigning Sovereigns of Europe and their families, a list of the Ambassadors resident at the different Courts, and a Variety of other useful references to Persons of all Classes" (*Leeds Intelligencer*, 18 Dec 1822).

Forster, John (1812–76): editor of *The Examiner* from 1847, whom Charlotte met at the Smiths' house in December 1849. He was the friend and later biographer of Dickens. Like all who met him Charlotte was struck by his "loud swagger"; like most who met him she seems to have liked him.

Forster, William Edward (1819–86) and Jane: the former was a wool trader from the Bradford area, later a prominent politician and the architect of the 1870 Education Act. He was married to Thomas Arnold's eldest daughter Jane, and together they made several unexpected and unwelcome descents on Charlotte and her father, pressing invitations on her very much in the manner of that other educational pioneer Sir James Kay-Shuttleworth. In his case the invitations were resisted and Forster's comment "she will not, I expect cannot, leave him" (to R. M. Milnes, Jan 1852) was wide of the mark – she could, but would not. However, Jane Forster's description of Charlotte as like her own Jane Eyre, adding that she "moved so quietly and noiselessly, just like a little bird . . . barring that all birds are joyous," was much more perceptive. It is Juliet Barker (1994) who convincingly identifies the "neighbour" quoted in Gaskell (*Life*, v. 2, ch. 22) as Jane Forster.

Foster, Henry (1804–54): mill-owner of Denholme, near Haworth. A portrait of him reputed to be by Branwell remained in the family until 1970, and when the family home, White Shaw, was sold it was given to the Brontë Parsonage Museum. Though Alexander and Sellars (AOTB) note several distinct departures from Branwell's usual techniques and procedures, they accept the picture as genuine.

"Foundling, The": a Glasstown story, written in the spring of 1833. With "Something About Arthur" it is one of the earliest surviving contributions to the saga written after Charlotte's return from Roe Head. It concerns the discovery of the foundling Edward Sydney by an old peasant couple in England, his emigration to Glasstown where he becomes involved in politics on the side of the Marquis of Douro, his love for Lady Julia Wellesley, and the discovery that he is the son of Frederick, Duke of York and King. The material is not very different from Charlotte's pre-Roe Head stories. There are strong magical and supernatural elements; the Genii make a last appearance; Douro, Rogue, and Montmorency die and are restored to life, and so on. There are strong folk-story and fairy-story elements, and the wedding scene with the bride's resounding "I will – not" is the stuff of television soaps. It is all done, however, with great brio and freshness, and the new confidence of a Charlotte who has been away from home, made new friends outside the family, and participated in a communal experience of education is very evident. As sometimes happens in Charlotte's juvenilia, the whole story is dismissed a year later by Charles Wellesley in "Corner Dishes" as "one wild farrago of bombast, fustian and lies" perpetrated by his rival Captain Tree. By spring 1834, when that was written, magic was no longer a welcome ingredient in the Glasstown stew.

Foundling Hospital: the brainchild of Thomas Coram, merchant of London, the hospital received its charter in 1739 and opened in 1745. It was for the illegitimate children and orphans of the poor, and it quickly became a popular charity, especially through the regular performances of Handel's *Messiah* from 1750 on. Tattycoram in *Little Dorrit* illustrates some of the ambiguities and frustrations of the position of these children when taken into well-off households. Charlotte in her quest for the realities of London life visited the hospital on her last visit there in January 1853.

Fountain Street, Bradford: where Branwell rented lodgings and a studio from Isaac Kirby, at number 2.

Fox How: Lakeside retreat of the Arnold family, which Charlotte made a twilight visit to in August 1850, while she was staying at Briery Close. She described the house as "like a nest half-buried in flowers and creepers" (to James Taylor, 6 Nov 1850). On her visit to Harriet Martineau at Ambleside in December 1850 she saw much more of the place and the family, described at length in a letter to James Taylor of 15 January 1851.

Fra Bartolommeo *see* Bartolommeo Della Porta, Fra

Frank (no surname given): fiancé to Miss Marchmont, whose story is told in *Villette*, ch. 4. He was killed by a fall from a horse very soon before they were due to be married.

Franks, Rev. James Clarke: son of Rev. James Franks, incumbent of Sowerby Bridge, and his wife Sarah, née Clarke; husband of Elizabeth Firth, whom he married in 1824. The pair visited the young Brontës at Cowan Bridge during their wedding tour, and had the reluctant Charlotte and Anne to stay for a week in 1836. Franks was clearly an active clergyman and a high-flyer. After his wife's death he returned to Cambridge, where he had been a star student. Charlotte mentions in a letter to their mother a daughter Elizabeth and a son Henry James. The eldest son, John Firth, later claimed that Charlotte during her week's stay with the family, never said a word to him.

Fraser, Miss: assumed name under which Charlotte visited Dr Browne, a phrenologist, George Smith taking the name Mr Fraser.

***Fraser's Magazine*:** Tory magazine, founded in 1830, which Aunt Branwell apparently subscribed to from 1832 onwards. It was founded by the Irishman William Maginn, with Hugh Fraser. It boasted an extremely distinguished list of contributors in its early years, and its independence of general publishing houses gave its reviews a particular authority. When the Bells became authors it repaid their interest. In 1848 it printed Anne's long poem "The Three Guides," and also "The Narrow Way" (i.e., "Believe not those who say"). Its reviews of Charlotte's novels, usually by G. H. Lewes, were enthusiastic and authoritative, though they sometimes annoyed Charlotte. Charles Kingsley's review of *Tenant* was a muddled affair, and the magazine does not seem to have noticed *Wuthering Heights*. Charlotte's youthful opinion that the magazine would be "rather uninteresting" (to BB, 17 May 1832) compared to *Blackwood's* was a typical piece of adolescent partisanship. Its interest in the Bells was sympathetic and intelligent, right up to its review of *The Professor*, with its reference to "the lone woman sitting by the desolate hearthstone" and to "all that she had lost and suffered" (v. 16, May 1857). Two years earlier they had published Matthew Arnold's tribute to the whole family, his poem "Haworth Churchyard."

Frédéric, Madame: mentioned only as a poor Frenchwoman who, with her husband, briefly cared for Adèle after the death of Céline Varens (*Jane Eyre*, v. 1, ch. 11).

Freemasons: The Masonic Lodge at Haworth, known as the Three Graces, underwent something of a revival in the 1830s. Kenneth Emsley wrote (BST, v. 20, pt 5, 1992) that the lodge contained "a wide cross-section of members from the local community," especially skilled artisans. Branwell was initiated, probably through the instigation of John Brown, while still under age, in February 1836. The society no doubt ministered to the love of secret organizations which is seen in the juvenilia and is part of the underbelly of Romanticism. Branwell was a regular attendant in 1836–7, thereafter an occasional one – one of many examples in his life of an early enthusiasm which exhausted itself. The fact that Branwell was willing to act for a time as secretary (probably one of few in Haworth capable of doing so) and that Patrick was willing to preach a special sermon for them, illustrates the loss of that revolutionary impulse in the move-ment that had attracted men such as Mozart. The Lodge met first in the Black Bull, then in the King's Arms, and later had a permanent home in what is now Lodge Street, then known as Newell Hill. This tiny cul-de-sac was also home to the Haworth Mechanics' Institute, and to William Wood, the Parsonage's carpenter and cabinet-maker.

"French and English": a game played at Roe Head School, which Ellen Nussey tells us in her "Reminiscences" Charlotte could never be induced to join in. Ellen con-jectures that she associated the "merry voices" of the players with her early, homesick days at the school.

French Theatre: theatre in King Street, London (otherwise known as the St James's) where Rachel performed in 1851. Charlotte saw her twice in June, first as Adrienne Lecouvreur, then in Corneille's *Horace*, playing Camille.

Friendship's Offering: one of the fashionable annuals that proliferated in the early nineteenth century. The Brontës seem to have owned or had ready access to the 1829 volume. In 1830 Charlotte copied a figure from Landseer's "Hours of Innocence," which appeared in engraved form there, and on 30 September of the same year she wrote accomplished critiques of three other pictures in the annual: Campbell Castle, The Will, and The Minstrel Boy.

Frobisher, John: prominent figure in the musical life of Halifax. He was the organ-ist to the Parish Church, and conductor of the Choral Society. Branwell, knowing him from his Halifax days, wrote to him in March 1846 and sent him his poem "An Echo from Indian Cannon," a patriotic piece inspired by an incident in the First Anglo-Sikh War, with the suggestion that he publish it to the tune of Gluck's "mater divinae gratiae," or in an arrangement of his own.

Frost, Lucy: Lucy Snowe, heroine of *Villette*, was first Snowe, then had her sur-name changed to Frost, a change that was regretted in a letter to William Smith Williams of 6 November 1852. It was subsequently changed back to Snowe.

Froude, J. A. (1818–94): historian, biographer, and in his earlier years novelist and religious controversialist. Charlotte found his *The Nemesis of Faith* (1848) "morbid," but with "sprinklings of truth" (to James Taylor, 19 Dec 1849?).

"Funeral Sermon for the Late William Weightman, M. A.": Patrick's sermon, taking as its text St Paul's First Epistle to the Corinthians 15: 56–8, was printed by J. U. Walker of Halifax, and profits went to the Sunday School. The *Leeds Intel-ligencer*, noticing the pamphlet, spoke of the dead man's "sterling piety, his amiability, and cheerfulness", and described the sermon as "plain and touching in its language, simple yet expressive" (29 Oct 1842).

Fuseli, Henry (1741–1825): real name Johann Heinrich Füssli or Fuessli, which is the form preferred by Juliet Barker. Swiss-born artist and former clergyman, who was encouraged in his artistic aspirations by Reynolds, and learnt his technique, like the Brontës, by copying other people's pictures – in his case by going to Italy and copying Michelangelo's "Last Judgment." His paintings were grand, often horrific or phantasmagoric. One of Charlotte's notable pictures is "Lycidas," a version of Fuseli's "Solitude at Dawn," one of his illustrations of Milton.

G

G—, Georgiana: daughter of a baronet, she is a pupil at Frances Henri's school. Mentioned in ch. 25 of *The Professor*, she is not characterized further.

G—, Julia: sister of the above, also mentioned but not characterized.

G—, Lord: guest at Rosalie's coming-out ball in *Agnes Grey* (ch. 9).

Gale, Mrs (no first name given): wife of John. Her reactions to the curates, their noisiness and rudeness, mirrors the reader's own, and her character is briefly suggested by the "spark of the hot kitchen fire" in her eye (*Shirley*, ch. 1).

Gale, Abraham: a boy of six, son of John and his wife in *Shirley*.

Gale, John: a "small clothier" and landlord of Mr Donne in *Shirley*. It is in his house that the first chapter takes place.

Gap of Dunloe: celebrated beauty spot near Killarney, Co. Kerry, Ireland. It was here, during her honeymoon tour, that Charlotte's horse, frightened by the crumbling and perilous path, reared and threw her. The horse was released, and Charlotte uninjured.

Garnett, William: Haworth parishioner prominent in the attempt in 1826–7 to suppress the so-called whist shops, which were drinking dens selling illicit alcohol. This was presumably the William Garnett who was landlord of the White Lion, and therefore a far from disinterested participant in the campaign.

Garrett, Mary: mentioned only as a pupil at Jane Eyre's Morton school (v. 3, ch. 7).

Garrs, Nancy (1803–86) and Sarah (?1806–99): sisters, trained at the Bradford School of Industry, who became servants to the Brontë family in July 1816 and August 1818 respectively. They were warm-hearted girls, and good nursemaids for the children, participating in their games and walks. After Mrs Gaskell described them as "rough affectionate warm-hearted, wasteful sisters" Patrick wrote them a testimonial (17 Aug 1857) describing them as "kind to my children, and honest, and not wasteful." It was Sarah who was walking with the younger children at the time of the bursting of the Crow Hill bog, and sought shelter with them in a porch. The sisters kept up their interest in the family, and Nancy attended Patrick's funeral. Sarah, now married to William Newsome, had settled in America, living in Ohio and Iowa. Both sisters, due to their longevity, became sources for the second generation of Brontë biographers, giving them reminiscences of the famous authors when very young, and information about the household routines at Thornton and Haworth.

Gaskell, Elizabeth Cleghorn, née Stevenson (1810–65): English novelist, friend and biographer of Charlotte. She was already a literary figure of some note when the two first made contact, having published *Mary Barton* in 1848. When Charlotte received a note from her in November 1849, probably to thank her for a copy of *Shirley*, she wrote to William Smith Williams (17 Nov 1849?) that in her nature "it mournfully pleases me to fancy a remote affinity to my Sister Emily." But since she fancied the same about others, including Harriet Martineau and Sidney Dobell, this tells us more about Charlotte's need for an intellectual companion on her own level than it does about Emily. She was clearly intent on liking Gaskell before they ever met, and when they did the accord was mutual. The meeting took place at the lakeland house Briery Close, rented by the Kay-Shuttleworths. Both women could clearly have done without the company of their host, who pressured them into doing what he wanted them to do, rather than what they wanted to do, and irritated them with his generalizations about the nature and abilities of women. Charlotte confided her history to her new friend, whose letters then became full of the sad story, often with inaccurate details. The details were mostly corrected for the *Life*, but the general impression of poverty, repression, and gloom remained, and has colored the popular view of the Brontës' lives ever since.

Charlotte corresponded with Gaskell for the rest of her life, and seemed struck and heartened that a woman could be so happy both in her family and her artistic life. She visited the Gaskells in Manchester three times in subsequent years: in late June 1851, late April 1853, and early May 1854. A proposed visit by Gaskell to Haworth in June 1853 had to be put off due to Charlotte's influenza, but it took place in September of that year. The dispute between father and daughter was rumbling on at this time, and Gaskell "caught a glare of his stern eyes over his spectacles at Miss Brontë once or twice which made me know my man" (ECG to John Forster, Sep 1853) – thus reinforcing the view she already had of him (probably an unfair one, but in line with remarks about him by Mary Taylor and Ellen Nussey). After the first of her visits to Manchester Charlotte described Mrs Gaskell as "kind, clever, animated and unaffected" (to GS, 1 July 1851), and she never had reason to revise her opinion. Acutely conscious of her own lack of animal spirits and social graces, she seems to have regarded Mrs Gaskell as a being of ineffable grace and good fortune, in particular in being able to combine a happy and bustling family and social life with a literary career.

The request to her to write Charlotte's biography came as a result of Ellen Nussey's complaint to the Parsonage about an article in *Sharpe's London Magazine*, itself based partly on a letter of Mrs Gaskell's written after her first meeting with Charlotte. Arthur Nicholls first dismissed the article as "harmless" (letter to EN, 11 June 1855) and unworthy of reply. However, Ellen's suggestion of Gaskell as a suitable biographer took root in Patrick's mind, and he wrote to her on 16 June suggesting she write "a brief account" – later modified in the same letter to "a long or short account of her life and works." She accepted the task immediately, and began applying to the people who knew Charlotte best.

She immediately saw that Ellen, with her store of hundreds of letters, was her best authority. Comment has been made on her reluctance to apply to Patrick concerning family matters, but his memory was soon shown to be unreliable, and the letters to Ellen had much more authority. She may have been reluctant to let him know that what she was planning was much more than a simple memoir, and that it would deal with painful family matters such as Branwell's decline. She worked with incredible speed, and the *Life* was published in March 1857, to immediate critical acclaim, which was soon succeeded by doubts.

The book was open to attack on three fronts. The first was the supposed eccentricities (some of them bordering on madness) of Patrick. He made light of these, except for the allegation that he denied his children meat. He did eventually inform her of the errors, and made a dignified defense of his supposed eccentricities: "Had I been numbered amongst the calm, sedate, *concentric* men of the world, I should not have been as I now am, and I should, in all probability, never have had such children as mine have been" (to ECG, 30 July 1857). Mrs Gaskell said he had "acted like a 'brick'" (letter to GS, 23 Aug 1857).

The second attack concerned Cowan Bridge School, which attracted many defenders, few of whom had been there in its early days as the Brontës were. Here Mrs Gaskell's doughtiest supporter was Charlotte's widower, and on the whole they won the argument.

The most important attack was on behalf of Lady Scott (Lydia Robinson). In this connection it must be said that Mrs Gaskell knew what she was doing ("I have three people I want to libel – Lady Scott (that bad woman who corrupted Branwell Brontë," letter to GS, 2 Oct 1856) and was allowed by her publisher to do it. Without proof beyond family tales it was inevitable she (or her husband acting for her) should be forced to apologize, and her publisher withdrew the libelous passages. The balance of opinion 150 years later would probably be that her remarks about Lady Scott were unwise but true.

Though the controversies certainly weakened readers' faith in Mrs Gaskell as a biographer, the merits of the *Life* won through, and it is today accepted as one of the great biographies in English. Though the pervading dreariness of her account would be challenged, on the whole, and unlike most biographies written shortly after their subject's death, it justifies Gaskell's despairing wail: "I *did so try* to *tell the truth*" (letter to EN, 16 June 1857).

See also Nicholls, Arthur Bell; Nussey, Ellen; Taylor, Mary

Gaskell, Florence Elizabeth (1842–81): one of the "four little girls – all more or less pretty and intelligent" who, "scattered through the rooms of a somewhat spacious house – seem to fill it with liveliness and gaiety" (letter to Mrs Smith, 1 July 1851) in Charlotte's account of her visit to the Gaskells in 1851. She is often mentioned affectionately in Charlotte's letters, usually coupled with her sister Julia.

Gaskell, Julia Bradford (1846–1908): the youngest Gaskell daughter, who stole Charlotte's heart on her visit to Manchester and is often mentioned with something like awe in the letters. She is "that dear but dangerous little person" (to ECG, 6 Aug 1851) and "that small sprite" (to ECG, 20 Sep 1851). More seriously she said that "I think hers a fine little nature – frank and of genuine promise" (to ECG, 9 July 1853). She may well have influenced the portrait of Paulina Home in *Villette*.

Gaskell, Margaret Emily (1837–1913): second daughter of the Gaskells. Charlotte often coupled her name with her mother's in writing to the latter, and suggested that "Meta [her nickname] has inherited Mamma's gift" (to ECG, 22 May 1852). Meta wrote a long account to Emily Shaen, a family friend, of the visit she and her mother paid to Patrick Brontë in 1860, where she described the "gentle, quiet, sweet, half-pitiful expression on his mouth" (6 Nov 1860).

Gaskell, Marianne (1834–1920): the eldest Gaskell daughter. In spite of Charlotte's reference to "four little girls" in the Gaskell house during her visit in 1851, Marianne was in fact away at school at the time. Since Marianne did not make herself known when they both attended one of Thackeray's lectures, Charlotte probably met her during her April 1853 visit to Plymouth Grove, because later in that year she refers to Marianne and Meta as "dear, happy girls" (to ECG, 9 July 1853).

Gaskell, Rev. William (1805–84): Mrs Gaskell's husband, and a Unitarian minister at Cross St. Chapel in Manchester. Apart from a description of him as "a good and kind man" he seems to have made little impression on Charlotte. He was, however, a notable figure in Manchester life, with charitable and far-sighted initiatives in education, in bettering the working and living conditions of the poor, and in religious life. He had a lifelong interest in dialect study, and he taught both at Manchester New College (where he was Professor of English History and Literature) and at Owens College, which was to develop into Manchester University. He was a humane, scholarly man whose influence in the Lancashire area was immense.

Gateshead Hall: home of Aunt Reed and her three children in *Jane Eyre*. Mr Lloyd describes it as "a very beautiful house" (ch. 3), and it is certainly a fine one. Apart from the normal rooms we are told of a breakfast room, a nursery, a conservatory, a housemaids' apartment, and a housekeeper's room. In the grounds there are a grove, a shrubbery, a plantation and a porter's lodge. A great many different kinds and degrees of servant are mentioned. However, every prospect does not necessarily please here. The red-room is a place of terror and ghosts, and the curtained window seat in the breakfast room is not only a place of peace but a refuge for Jane from cruelty both physical and mental. This double face to the house lends credence to E. H. Chadwick's (1914) claim that it is based on Stonegappe. When Jane returns to the house it has lost most of its terrors and has become a house for the disappointed and discontented, where petulance and frustration are seen as the results of Aunt Reed's spoiling of her own children.

See also Stonegappe

Gawthorpe Hall: near Burnley, home of Sir James and Lady Kay-Shuttleworth, visited by Charlotte in March 1850 and with her husband in January 1855, the last time she left home. Though her description of the family and their relationships to Ellen Nussey (19 Mar 1850) was in many ways imperceptive, her description of the house was accurate and atmospheric. It was indeed "250 years old," having been begun in August 1600, and the general effect was and is "grey, antique, castellated and stately." In a letter to W. S. Williams (16 Mar 1850) she talked of listening to Sir James's monologues "by the fireside in his antique oak-panelled drawing-room." The room still exists, largely as she knew it. Work, however, was just beginning, under Sir Charles Barry, to mirror more fitly Sir James's sense of his wife's family's importance. The house today is largely as it was when these alterations and improvements were complete. It was transferred to the National Trust in 1970, and is very popular with visitors.

Geefs, Fanny (1805–83): painter whose triptych "La Vie d'Une Femme" was exhibited in the Brussels "Salon" of 1842. As first noted by Winifred Gerin, this became the four panels which Charlotte describes in chapter 19, "The Cleopatra," in *Villette*, where the painting is described as "flat, dead, pale and formal," and the women depicted as "insincere, ill-humoured, bloodless, brainless nonentities!". In spite of her name, she was an Irish woman, married to the sculptor of the General Belliard statue in Brussels (Ruijssenaars, 2000, ch. 6).

Geller, William Overend: acquaintance of Branwell in Bradford. A painter and engraver, he was an admirer of John Martin, and seems to have copied his luridly lit grandiosity. Of his "Daniel's Accusers Cast into the Den of Lions," exhibited at the Northern Society exhibition of 1830, the *Leeds Intelligencer* complained that "Mr Geller's notions of a lion's den are of a very peculiar kind" and "We do not much admire his violet-coloured light."

General Board of Health: the Whitehall body with whom Patrick corresponded in an attempt to get an adequate water supply for Haworth. His campaign began in 1849, and lasted nearly 10 years. Not surprisingly he complained bitterly about the "long, and tedious delay" (to Secretary of General Board, 10 July 1851).

Genii: supernatural beings in the juvenilia, who allow Charlotte, Branwell, Emily, and Anne to appear in their own stories, creating dangers and difficulties, rescuing characters from them and if necessary resurrecting them from the dead. Their names are Tallii (Charlotte, perhaps based on a childish pronunciation of her name), Brannii, Emmii, and Annii. They gradually fade out as the supernatural becomes something associated with early childhood.

George Hotel, Bradford: public house in Market Street, where Branwell met up with his artistic friends. The landlady, Miss Rennie (also spelt Renney and Reaney), "greatly prided herself on seeing at her house, in their hours of leisure, the artistic and literary celebrities of the neighbourhood" (Leyland, 1886, v. 1, p. 203).

George Hotel, York: a coaching inn, where Anne, Charlotte, and Ellen Nussey stayed the night of 24 May 1849, on the trip to Scarborough where Anne was to die. A pillar and first floor window in Coney Street are all that remain of it (see picture in Whitehead, 1993, p. 147).

George IV (1762–1830): as Regent he makes a brief appearance in Branwell's "History of the Young Men," and in *Shirley* he is described as "an unprincipled debauchee" (ch. 4), "the fat 'Adonis of fifty'" (ch. 23) and "the royal profligate" (ch. 37). He is one monarch about whom even conservatives and royalists seem happy to be rude. The Brontë children chose Frederick, Duke of York, his brother and at the time heir to the throne, rather than him, for a prominent role in the founding of Glasstown.

Gérard, Constantine: grandfather of Robert Moore in *Shirley*, a merchant of Antwerp ruined by trade uncertainties and unwise speculations (see ch. 2).

Gérard, Hortense: daughter of the above and mother of Robert, Louis, and Hortense Moore.

"Ghaist's Warning, The": ballad of Danish origin that Scott notes in *The Lady of the Lake*. Emily misquotes it slightly in ch. 9 of *Wuthering Heights*, where Nelly sings it while rocking the baby Hareton.

Giacinta (no surname given): one of the successors to Céline Varens as Rochester's mistress. An Italian, "unprincipled and violent" (*Jane Eyre*, v. 3, ch. 1).

Gibson, Mr (no first name given): brother of Mrs Reed in *Jane Eyre*. It was presumably at his London house that Georgiana Reed enjoyed a London season where she was "much admired for her beauty" (v. 2, ch. 6), and it is there that she goes after the death of her mother. He is mentioned only.

Gibson, Mrs (no first name given): wife of the above, mentioned by Georgiana Reed.

Gibson, Mary Alice: second wife of Rev. William Morgan, whom he married in Calverley church in 1836. She bore him a son, dying in 1852.

Gill, Mrs (no first name given): Shirley Keeldar's housekeeper in *Shirley*. She is a woman who has "wronged" (i.e., cheated) Shirley again and again and been forgiven. An interview between her and Shirley is described at length in ch. 14, which makes clear the nature of the cheating. Subsequently she is devoted to her and trusted by her, particularly in emergencies such as the bite of the "mad" dog.

Gimmerton: village nearest to Wuthering Heights and the Grange. It is never described and is not necessarily based on Haworth or anywhere else, but like most substantial villages at this time it has a doctor, a clergyman, and a lawyer, who all play small parts in the action. It also has a fair and a church band of the kind that Hardy loved. Emily seems to have changed her mind about the spelling, because Jabes Branderham preaches his monstrous dream-sermon in the Chapel of Gimmer*den* Sough, and Lockwood recalls that he had passed it in his walks and that it "lies in a hollow, between two hills" (ch. 3) – near a swamp – the "sough" – which virtually embalms the corpses buried there. This turns out to have relevance in the story, when Catherine is buried in a corner of the churchyard almost indistinguishable from moorland, to have her coffin opened up years later ("I saw her face again – it is hers yet") by Heathcliff at the time of Edgar's death. The novel ends there, by the three graves.

Gisborne, Thomas (1758–1846): father of Lydia Robinson. He lived the life of a squire-clergyman, though more involved in the religious side than his son-in-law Edmund Robinson. He lived at Yoxall Lodge, Yoxall, in Staffordshire. He was a Prebendary of Durham Cathedral and he had published a volume of sermons and a book on moral philosophy. He was a friend of Wilberforce, which led Gaskell in the first edition of the *Life* into the overexcited statement that in Lydia's early home had "sat those whose names are held saintlike for their good deeds" (ch. 13). On the other hand Edmund Robinson's sister Jane is supposed to have referred to "pious, canting Gisborne." He frequently holidayed in Scarborough, perhaps to be with his daughter and her family. He died in 1846, in his eighties. His children and grandchildren seem to have married into the religion-orientated gentry and aristocracy.

Glascar: township in agricultural land in Aghaderg parish, where Patrick either taught in the local Presbyterian school or perhaps as he himself claimed (to ECG, 20 June 1855) "opened a public school."

Glasgow Examiner: among the earliest and most enthusiastic reviewers of *Jane Eyre*, declaring it "of surpassing power and interest" and predicting even better work in future from the author's pen.

Glasstown: Great Glasstown (variously spelt) is the most important province in the Glasstown Federation, with Glasstown itself (later called Verreopolis and Verdopolis) the capital city. Originally a place of fantasy and fairy-tale, it soon assumes the character of a real nineteenth-century city, with thriving commerce, a merchant fleet, factories and mills, and a semi-criminal underclass ready to rob and riot. There is also, very important for Charlotte, an established aristocracy, whose doings are the stuff of rumor and gossip. As a political center Glasstown is also a place of constant intrigue. It has a varied and changing series of political groupings, and the parliamentary debates are one of Branwell's major interests, leaving Charlotte to concentrate on love, lust, and family intrigues. As interest shifts from Glasstown to Angria, with its creation as a semi-independent kingdom, Glasstown becomes endowed with the aura of an ancient, conservative, but serenely beautiful city, slightly left behind in the race for power, wealth, and prestige.

See also Angria; "Angria and the Angrians"; Juvenilia

Gloucester Terrace, London: no. 76, later renumbered as no. 112, was the home of George Smith and his family from March 1850, and it was there that Charlotte stayed on all her subsequent trips to London. The house was situated to the North of Hyde Park, not far from Paddington Station. Charlotte often used the address as shorthand for the Smith family, as she used Cornhill as shorthand for the publishing firm of Smith, Elder and all who worked there.

Goethe, Johann Wolfgang von (1749–1832): German poet and dramatist. Charlotte was interested in him, but denied his greatness, calling him "clear, deep, but very cold" (to WSW, 15 Sep 1849?). She criticized him for egotism, and said "he thought no more of swallowing up poor Eckermann's existence in his own than the Whale thought of swallowing Jonah" (to WSW, 13 Sep 1849). Eckermann was the author of *Conversations with Goethe* (1837), which Charlotte had read. Goethe is on Hunsden's bookshelves in *The Professor* (ch. 4), and his motto "*ohne Hast aber ohne Rast*" is quoted in *Shirley* (ch. 10) and *Villette* (ch. 13), where it is rendered as "unhasting yet unresting."

Goldsmith, Dr J.: pseudonym of Sir Richard Phillips, writer and publisher (1767–1840). His *Grammar of General Geography* (1823 edn) was heavily used by the Brontë children, both in their studies, and to provide names and apparent geographical legitimacy for their imaginary kingdoms. Anne or Emily has entered Gondal names in Goldsmith's "Vocabulary of Proper Names" – for example Gondal itself ("a large island in the north Pacific") is entered between Gomera, one of the Canaries, and Gondar, capital of Abyssinia.

Goldsmith, Oliver (1728–74): poet, novelist, and playwright. His poetry prefigured some of the preoccupations of Romanticism, and his *Vicar of Wakefield* was admired by Romantic writers, including Goethe, for its handling of pathos and simple sentiment. Charlotte noted that the novel was much used in Continental schoolrooms (see *Professor*, ch. 7; *Villette*, ch. 20). Charlotte's recommendation of him "For Natural History" (to EN, 4 July 1834) was more eccentric, but the young Brontës enjoyed *The Deserted Village*, *She Stoops to Conquer*, and the abridged *History of England*. Jane Eyre refers to his *History of Rome* in ch. 1, particularly its account of the early monstrous emperors, and later she quotes from *The Traveller*. He was, in other words, an important part of the Brontës' imaginative landscape, particularly in their early years.

Gomersal: home of the Taylor family, who lived in the Red House, to the west of Birstall, where Rydings, home of the Nusseys, was situated. Charlotte Brontë was well acquainted with both villages, and used them in *Shirley*. Mary Taylor and Ellen Nussey, by then far from friendly, both died here in the 1890s, Mary at High Royd, which she rented from her brother, Ellen at Moorlane House.

Gomersal Bank: private bank, established by Joshua Taylor, situated near the Red House stables. Many manufacturers established banks in the early nineteenth century. The bank collapsed at the time of Taylor's bankruptcy in 1826. See H. Ashwell Cadman's *Gomersal Past and Present* (1930).

Gondal: Whereas the setting of Charlotte's and Branwell's early writings is fully known through the mountain of material they left, that of Emily and Anne's is sketchy, due to the disappearance of the prose chronicles. Several attempts have been made to trace Gondal's history, through the poems of Emily and Anne, through the mentions in their diary papers, and through the odd scrappy list of names and characteristics which they drew up as *aides mémoires*. Fanny Ratchford (1941) was the first to try, but though she had many inspired pieces of guesswork she has generally been accused of muddying the waters by assuming for no good reason that Rosina, A. G. A., and Geraldine Sidonia are one person. (Of course characters continually change names in the Glasstown and Angria saga, but that is as they ascend the greasy pole of aristocratic promotion, and mirrors real life. They always retain their forenames.) W. D. Paden (*An Investigation of Gondal*, 1958) gives a very detailed chronology, but one is not always convinced that his sources justify his assumptions. Laura Hinkley (*The Brontës: Charlotte and Emily*, 1945), whose account is largely accepted by Philip Henderson (in his introduction to the Folio Society edition of Emily's *Complete Poems*), is probably the one that is most convincing, and seems to tie in with many of Emily's poems. It is notable that Anne deals almost entirely with characters who play no part in Emily's narrative, and they and their fortunes have proved to be largely irretrievable.

Hinkley sees the early part of Gondal's history as dominated by Julius Brenzaida, Prince of Angora, a figure in the Zamorna mode. The loves of his life are Rosina and Geraldine Sidonia: the first becomes his queen, the second bears his child, who is A. G. A. Julius is warlike and treacherous, and after sharing a coronation with Gerald, King of Exina (one of many subsidiary kingdoms in Gondal and Gaaldine) he imprisons and then executes Gerald. Julius is then involved in civil war (possibly known as the First War), and is assassinated.

His daughter, A. G. A., grows up as a female equivalent, beautiful, changeable, and ruthless. Among her lovers are Alexander of Elbë, Fernando De Samara, and Alfred Sidonia of Aspin Castle. All die. A. G. A. becomes queen, but republicanism is rampant and civil war breaks out, during which A. G. A. is murdered. Emily's last poem concerns this war.

Whether this conjectured framework adds to an appreciation of the Gondal poems is doubtful. One or two things may be said in addition. Emily's Gondal poems often slot in neatly to this summary, but not in chronological order. It seems likely that in its early stages the main outlines were laid down (perhaps in discussion, dramatization, or in written versions of some parts). Probably subsidiary characters and minor plot developments were sometimes fixed on early too. The poems and prose pieces could then be written to give an account of whatever in the saga it took their fancy to cover at any time. Retrospective pieces could also be written; for example, Emily's writings on the First War are mentioned in her 1845 diary paper.

This working pattern could explain the rather surprising remark in the same diary paper that on her and Anne's visit to York they "were" a variety of Gondal characters including Juliet Augusteen and Cordelia Fitzaphnold "escaping from the palaces of instruction." This seems too reminiscent of the Palace School (with convenient dungeon) of the early years of the Glasstown saga still to be part of Emily and Anne's imaginary kingdoms when they were in their mid-twenties. It should be emphasized that, though over many of the events described and over much of the nomenclature there hangs an air of tushery, many of the poems the saga gives rise to transcend their source magnificently.

The settings of the Gondal saga comprise two islands in the South Pacific of which Gondal is a Yorkshire-based country of moorlands and snow, and Gaaldine is a more tropical land, but subject to the other. This, we remember, was conceived in the early days of the nineteenth-century expansion that led to Empire. Contrasts between climates, too, always interested Emily and Anne. There were bound to be similarities between Gondal and the world of *Wuthering Heights*, since they are the work of the same mind. But too much has been made of these resemblances: when Emily's poems relate crucial Gondal events (e.g., "The Death of A. G. A." or "Gleneden's Dream") we are awkwardly conscious of the synthetic nature of the inspiration, the omnipresence of melodrama, and hysterically heightened emotions. In *Wuthering Heights* Emily puts such childishness triumphantly and totally behind her.

See also poetry, Emily's

Gooch, George: a railway engineer, and acquaintance of Branwell Brontë and Francis Grundy. Branwell seems to have given him an account of Mrs Robinson's supposed state of mind after her husband's death, which he was to pass on to Grundy, for in a letter dated by M. Smith around July/August 1846 he brings Grundy further up to date with her "declining health."

Due to Grundy's cavalier way with letters, some biographers have taken this to be the name of the Robinsons' coachman (in fact William Allison). Gooch could be a son or relative of Thomas L. Gooch, frequently cited in the *Leeds Intelligencer* as the engineer, with George Stephenson, of the Manchester and Leeds Railway Company.

Gore, Mrs Catherine Grace Frances (née Moody) (1799–1861):

novelist of upper-class life. She is often classed with the "silver fork" novelists, but her books, sharp, observant, and witty, have nothing in common with the novels of the fashionable life satirized by Dickens in *Nicholas Nickleby* (ch. 28) and by Thackeray in *Lords and Liveries*. George IV admired her novels, as he had Jane Austen's, and Mrs Gore claimed artistic kinship with the earlier writer.

Mrs Gore and Charlotte nearly met in 1851, after she had inherited property and returned to live in England after 18 years in France. Earlier, in 1850, she had left a parcel, probably at Cornhill, containing one of her best novels, *The Hamiltons*. "I knew nothing of the circles you describe before I read 'The Hamiltons' but I feel I do know something of them now" Charlotte wrote to her (27 Aug 1850).

Gorham, Mary (later Mrs Thomas Swinton Hewitt):

Ellen Nussey's second-best friend. They remained on close and visiting terms right up to Ellen's death. They met while Ellen was on a visit to her brother Henry, at Earnley, near Chichester. Charlotte and Mary both visited Ellen in Hathersage, in her brother's new vicarage, but the visits did not overlap. Though they never met subsequently, Charlotte strongly approved of the letters from Mary that Ellen sent her, citing her "serene, trusting strength" but noting "while happy in herself, how thoughtful she is for others!" (to EN, 10 Mar 1852?). She also approved of her attitude to motherhood, often comparing it to Mrs Joe Taylor's.

Goton (no first name given):

cook at Mme Beck's school in *Villette*. Lucy is left alone with the "cretin" and Goton during the long vacation. She is barely characterized, but her baked apples are given M. Paul's seal of approval (ch. 30).

Governesses' Benevolent Institution:

a body founded in 1843, usually referred to by Charlotte as the "Governess Institution." It attempted to raise the status of governesses by the provision of lectures at Queen's College, London, leading to oral examinations and a certificate of competence. Charlotte's reactions were mixed. On the one hand she felt it was "absurd and cruel" to raise standards, when not a half or a quarter of governesses' attainments are required in the teaching and are not reflected in their salaries (to WSW, 12 May 1848). Later, when his daughter was hoping to embark on a Queen's College course, she told the same correspondent that "an education secured is an advantage gained . . . a step towards independency" (to WSW, 3 July 1849). Kathryn Hughes records in *The Victorian Governess* (1993) that no woman sat on the governing body of the GBI, or taught at Queen's College above assistant level.

Graham, Arthur (real name Arthur Huntingdon):

son of Helen and Arthur Huntingdon in *The Tenant of Wildfell Hall*. He is the cause of the first and many subsequent meetings of Helen and Gilbert Markham, and concern for his welfare is one of the mainsprings for Helen's actions during her marriage to Arthur. A charming, lively child, devoted to animals.

Graham, Helen (a.k.a. Helen Lawrence and Helen Huntingdon): the assumed name of the mysterious tenant of Wildfell Hall (Graham was her mother's surname). She is strong-minded, devout, and loving. When her loving nature leads her into a marriage that soon goes wrong and eventually becomes a disaster, her strong sense of principle engages her in a moral dilemma which makes this novel one of the most important analyses of an unhappy marriage in Victorian fiction. The decision to leave Arthur Huntingdon is taken for her child's sake rather than her own, but it has resonances concerning women's rights in the most important relationship of her life. The framing story of the novel shows her first repelling the attentions of neighbors, then falling in love with the narrator of the book, Gilbert Markham, whom she finally marries after the death of her husband.

Graham, Thomas John: physician, whose *Modern Domestic Medicine* was published in 1826, with second and third editions in 1827 and 1829. Patrick possessed the first edition, and testifies to his high opinion of it on the flyleaf, and in the numerous annotations with which he supplemented it. He clearly used the book for illnesses and disorders in the family and the parish generally. His commentary and addition of remedies and symptoms of which he has heard or which he has observed cover the whole range of complaints, including asthma, cancer, cholera, and toothache. He is particularly interested in the stomach and bowels, and cures for indigestion and flatulence. His long account of his own cataract operation is of particular interest. The book and Patrick's commentary both suggest medicine poised between, on the one hand folk remedies and cures based on intelligent observation, and on the other a science.

Grame, Mr (no first name given): Sir Philip Nunnely's steward who gave a job to the "mad" and out of work Antinomian weaver Mike Hartley. It was while he was working for him that Mike had a "vision" of soldiers (*Shirley*, ch. 1).

Granby, Mr (no first name given): mentioned only (v. 3, ch. 8) as the husband-to-be of Rosamond Oliver in *Jane Eyre*. He is grandson and heir of Sir Frederick Granby, also only mentioned.

Grant, Rev. Joseph Brett (?1820–79): Arthur Bell Nicholls's predecessor as Patrick's curate at Haworth, taking up the position in late 1844, and performing his last duties in May 1845. He became curate and later perpetual curate in nearby Oxenhope, and was a close ally of Nicholls during his dispute with Patrick over his suit for Charlotte's hand; when they finally married he and his wife were asked "to the breakfast – *not* the ceremony" as Charlotte told Ellen Nussey firmly (letter of 16 June 1854). He was a pall-bearer at Patrick's funeral.

Judging by Charlotte's portrait of him as Mr Donne in *Shirley* she disliked him intensely, finding him conceited, intrusive, and insensitive. She acknowledged the portrait was of him, and remarked wonderingly that "It is a curious fact that since he read 'Shirley' he has come to the house oftener than ever and been remarkably meek and assiduous to please" (to WSW, 3 Apr 1850). He married Sarah Anne Turner, of Woodford in Essex, and if *Shirley* and Mr Donne are any guide she was "a most sensible, quiet, lady-like little woman" and "the making of him" (ch. 37). The man had much to endure, including Mr Brontë sometimes addressing him as Mr Donne (W & S, v. 4, p. 258), but it seems likely his self-esteem pulled him through. One would certainly not have wished to be among the audience at the Haworth Mechanics' Institute being addressed by him "on the advantages of knowledge" (*Leeds Mercury*, 6 Apr 1850).

Grasper (ca 1830–ca 1838): Keeper's predecessor as Parsonage dog, which cost Patrick eight shillings in tax – no mean sum at the time. Emily's drawing of him (Jan 1834) suggests he was an Irish terrier. Judging by the number of similar dogs to be seen all year round in Haworth, he lives on in his descendants.

Grassdale Manor: the house which sees most of the vital incidents which mark the rapid deterioration of the marriage of Helen and Arthur Huntingdon. It is an old manor that makes no impression as a building, consonant with Anne's lack of interest in houses as such, only in what happens in them.

Graves, Mr (no first name given), also spelt Greaves: the "stony" assistant of the elder and younger MacTurks in *Shirley*, all doctors in the Nunnely district whom Shirley, when she fears death, wants to have kept away from her (ch. 28), and who attend on Robert Moore.

Great Exhibition of 1851: Charlotte visited it five times in June, usually with a degree of skepticism or exhaustion. Her most enjoyable visit was in the company of Sir David Brewster, and her most vivid and positive account of it is in a letter to Patrick (7 June 1851) when she describes it as "vast – strange new and impossible to describe" and evokes the "living tide" of silent people going through it. Her comment to Mrs Gaskell (14 June 1851?) that it was "not much in my way," and that to Margaret Wooler (14 July 1851) that she "never was able to get up any raptures on the subject" probably sum up her reactions most honestly. Donald Hopewell noted in that other Exhibition year of 1951 that "Four or five times she went to the House of Glass (did she remember that 'Glasstown' was the capital of the Angrian kingdom of her girlhood's romantic writings?)" (*The Enduring Brontës*, Brontë Society, p. 8) – a pertinent question, but there is no evidence that she made any connection. Her main reaction was boredom, and her principal objection, apart from the exhaustion its vast size induced in her, was that "its wonders appeal too exclusively to the eye and rarely touch the heart or head" (to MW, 14 July 1851).

See also Brewster, Sir David

Greaves, Mrs (no first name given): housekeeper to the Huntingdons at Grassdale Manor in *The Tenant of Wildfell Hall* (see ch. 40).

Green (no first name given): Edgar Linton's lawyer, but in fact a creature of Heathcliff's, as is shown at the time of Edgar's death (*Wuthering Heights*, v. 2, ch. 14).

Green House: the Mirfield home of the Atkinsons visited by Charlotte during her 18 months as a Roe Head pupil. It was described in the *Leeds Intelligencer* (10 May 1834) as "situated on an eminence, commanding a view of Kirklees park and vale of the river Calder."

See also Atkinson, Rev. Thomas

Greenhow, Rev. Edward: a "worthy and indefatigable clergyman" (*Leeds Intelligencer*, 31 Aug 1839), apparently curate at Great Ouseburn, who was preferred to the living of Nun Monkton in November 1844. An entry in Mr Robinson's account book ("Mr G. for Governess 25/0/0") suggests to Edward Chitham that Anne, in her last months at Thorp Green, when she only had one Robinson pupil, also taught the Greenhow daughters, who were much younger, and had part of her salary paid by their father (see Chitham, 1991, p. 116).

Green, Jane: one of the Murrays' neighbors at Horton in *Agnes Grey*. Several times mentioned, but not characterized.

Green, John: clerk at the church where Rochester hoped to marry Jane Eyre (*Jane Eyre*, v. 2, ch. 2).

Green, Mr (no first name given): an admirer of and potential suitor for Rosalie Murray in *Agnes Grey*. A neighbor, also called Squire Green in ch. 16, he is described as "rich enough, but of no family, and a great stupid fellow, a mere country booby" by Rosalie herself (ch. 9).

Green, Susan: one of the Murrays' neighbors at Horton in *Agnes Grey*.

Greenwood, Brontë (b. 1859): son of John Greenwood, the stationer. Mr Nicholls refused to christen him with this name, possibly because he resented Greenwood's role as informant on the Brontë family's affairs to Mrs Gaskell and others. He was a sickly child, and Patrick eventually christened him to save Nicholls from censure if the baby died unbaptized. A very full account by Meta Gaskell appears in Lock and Dixon (1979, pp. 519–22) and the same authorities claim the boy "thrived and flourished" in the USA.

Greenwood family of Bridgehouse: The Greenwoods of Bridgehouse, the oldest mill in Haworth, were the foremost manufacturing family in the village until the mill's failure in 1848, when they were superseded by the Merralls. The older generation consisted of James Greenwood (1763–1824) and his wife Martha (1766–1833). Even before his father's death the middle son of the family, Joseph, had taken over another mill owned by the Greenwoods, Springhead (see next entry). That left the eldest and youngest sons John (1784–1833) and James Jr (1793–1857) operating Bridgehouse mill, James continuing on his own after John's death. James Jr built himself a substantial residence, Woodlands in Stubbing Lane. This branch of the family were Particular Baptists, worshiping at the Hall Green Chapel, and they were prominent in the rows in the late 1830s over the obligation on Nonconformists to pay Church rates.

The Brontë children seem to have visited the older generation of Greenwoods, first with their mother, then with their aunt. There was a story in the Greenwood family of Charlotte being rebuked by Martha Greenwood for cheekiness to her aunt, and being told not to come visiting again until she had apologized to her. Relations with the younger generation do not seem to have been close, perhaps because the Brontës took the side of the Springhead branch of what seems to have been a divided family. When James Jr failed, Charlotte wrote to Ellen Nussey (18 Aug 1848) of the "great and unexpected reverse of fortune" and the "great distress in the village" caused by the consequent unemployment, but there seems to be no personal feeling involved.

It was James Jr's sister Elizabeth who was (probably) seduced by her brother-in-law William Sugden, husband of her sister Mary Anne, and bore his child. She later married William Cannan, but seems to have separated from him. The story was told, under a somewhat inadequate veil of anonymity, by Mrs Gaskell, who laid particular emphasis on the family ostracizing their own daughter but continuing normal relations with her wealthy seducer. The affair is well covered by Sarah Fermi, "A 'religious' family disgraced" (BST v. 20, pt 5, 1992).

Greenwood family of Springhead:
effectively the family of Joseph Greenwood (1786–1856), second son of James Greenwood Sr of Bridgehouse, who acquired, or perhaps was given, Springhead Mill when quite young. Though he did not remain in the cotton trade long, letting the mill from 1822 onwards, he remained a strong force in Haworth until the early 1850s, and one that usually worked contrary to the interests of his own brothers. He became an Anglican, a church land trustee, and a Tory, and was thus a natural supporter of Patrick Brontë on most, but not all, issues (he supported Richard Butterfield's petition to annul elections to the local Board of Health, a move that was a grievous set-back to the cause of sanitary reform). Patrick went to great lengths in the mid-1830s to have him made a magistrate, eventually succeeding in June 1836. The basis of Joseph Greenwood's local power was land and presumably rent from his mill, which was let to the Merralls. In 1853 he and his sons went bankrupt, and he moved to Utley, near Keighley.

Branwell mentioned the elder son disrespectfully in a letter to John Brown in 1840, calling William Greenwood "Prince William at Springhead" (described as "fat") and ridiculing his "godly" friend Parson Winterbottom, minister of the West Lane (not the Hall Green of the other Greenwoods) Baptist Church at that time, suggesting William may have reverted to a branch of the family's old faith. He was certainly a mason of the Three Graces Lodge. He and his brother James around this time seem to have been woolstaplers, in association with their father. The fate of these two men after the family collapse is uncertain.

The daughters of Joseph Greenwood were certainly ill-fated. They were contemporaries of the Brontë girls, and a note from Charlotte to Ann in 1836 accepting an invitation to tea suggests relations were friendly, if not particularly close. The eldest, Sarah, of whom a watercolor exists, possibly by Charlotte, in the Brontë Parsonage Museum, died in 1833, aged around 17. Her sister Ann, Anne Brontë's contemporary, died in 1838 aged around 18. The last sister, Martha (1818–76), went mad around 1840, and was confined in an upper-floor room in the family home until they were forced to leave Haworth. She thus joins the many possible originals for Bertha Rochester – the numerousness of these is not altogether surprising, since care and confinement at home was more compassionate than incarceration in an institution and cheaper than the sort of private care George Nussey and Thackeray's wife enjoyed.

With the failure of Joseph Greenwood the influence of the Bridgehouse Greenwoods ended in Haworth. Robin Greenwood's unpublished *Haworth's Landowners, Mills and Millowners and Other Principal Families During the Brontë Era 1820–61* (1999) has a great deal of information about these and other Haworth notables.

Greenwood, John (?1807–63):

the Haworth stationer from whom the Brontës bought paper after he established his modest stationer's business (ca 1843). He wrote to Mrs Gaskell "I did so like them to come when I had anything for them; they were so much different to anyone else; so gentle, and kind, and so very quiet. They never talked much" (quoted in ECG to GS, 4 June 1855). He added, however, of Charlotte: "I could talk with her" (ECG, *Life*, ch. 14) He collected his store of Brontë memories, particularly of Emily, into a notebook whence come many familiar stories: Emily when Branwell set fire to his bed, Emily separating fighting dogs in Church Lane, Emily learning to shoot. He clearly regarded the whole family with a misty-eyed adoration.

Charlotte in her turn liked him and admired his dogged spirit in adversity. She arranged favorable terms for him to sell the cheap edition of *Jane Eyre*, and when in London wrote asking Martha how he prospered. She hoped he could give up his wool-combing work which he had combined with his small business. When she died he was the first to inform Mrs Gaskell, and she begged him for every detail he could procure of the sad event: "I want to know EVERY particular . . . You would oblige me *extremely* if you would, at your earliest leisure, send me every detail . . . *Any*thing else you can ever remember to tell me about her will be most valuable" (letters of 4 Apr 1855 and 12 Apr 1855). Clearly the idea of some kind of memoir or article was already in her head.

Mrs Gaskell gives us our fullest account of him:

> The writer, poor fellow, is a kind of genius in his way; & I know that Miss Brontë was a little afraid of his being too much of a Jack-of-all-trades to succeed in any. He is part mason, part gardener, plaisterer painter and what not, besides having a little stationer's shop . . . He is a little deformed man, upwards of 50 years of age.
>
> (to GS, 4 June 1855)

Juliet Barker takes a jaundiced view of Greenwood, as she does of many people Charlotte liked and admired such as Ellen Nussey and Mrs Gaskell. She calls him a "self-important busybody" (1994, p. 774) and portrays him hawking round news of Charlotte's death before she was even decently buried. Certainly the brevity of Mrs Gaskell's later letters to him suggest she got more than she bargained for in the way of correspondence. She had, nevertheless, begged him for every detail, and he presumably had taken her request at face value. He had, in his own words "never had any school education" (ECG, *Life*, ch. 14), so his acquaintance with the niceties of polite behavior and usage was limited. This seems an inadequate reason to bring down on him the posthumous scorn of Juliet Barker.

Greenwood, John: father of Sarah Hannah Sidgwick, Charlotte's employer, with whom the Sidgwicks and their governess stayed in June–July 1839 at his summer residence Swarcliffe House, near Harrogate. He was by then old (he had in 1836 declined to qualify as a magistrate "on account of his great age," *Leeds Intelligencer*, 2 July) and sick, though he lived until 1846. John Greenwood, a Keighley industrialist, was also father to Anne Dury, wife of the rector of Keighley, and cousin of the Greenwoods of Bridgehouse. He lived at the Knowle, Keighley, one of its finest houses.

See also Sidgwick, Sarah Hannah

Greenwood, John (1795–1837): organist at Keighley, Leeds, and Halifax churches and composer of religious music, chiefly psalm settings. His hasty departure from Leeds was apparently due to business failures ("particularly in the sale of Pianofortes, never being able to make the price they cost me," *Leeds Intelligencer*, 14 Aug 1838) rather than his private life (his earlier Gretna Green marriage in 1823 was repeated in the parish church). His two visits to Haworth in 1834, one to inaugurate the new organ in St Michael's Church, had a great effect on Charlotte and Branwell, who gave him cameo roles in the former's "My Angria and the Angrians" (EW, v. 2, pt 2, pp. 251–3) and the latter's "Angria and the Angrians", where Branwell characterizes him as "the most wandering and easy minded being extant" (WPBB, v. 2, p. 217). He died of consumption.

Grey, Aunt (no first name given): the "kind, prim" woman who recommends Agnes Grey to Mrs Bloomfield whom she asserts, mistakenly, to be a "very nice woman" (ch. 1).

Grey, Mrs (no first name given): mentioned only as one of the much-put-upon governesses to the Ingram girls (*Jane Eyre*, v. 2, ch. 2). This seems to be a surname that the Brontës associated with governessing.

Grey, Agnes: central character in the novel that bears her name. She has always been cosseted by her mother and sister as the baby of the family, and has to fight their protectiveness in order to go out into the world and earn her own way. Her inexperience means that she can make little headway against the indiscipline and ignorance of the Bloomfield children in her first post, though she manages to retain the integrity which is a central concern with her (as it is with William Crimsworth). The worldly Murray family assault that integrity constantly, but gradually Agnes's moral standards are recognized by the girls, even though they seldom change their conduct because of them. Agnes becomes a sort of touchstone and, during Agnes's visit to her, Rosalie recognizes the desolate nature of the married life she has chosen. Though Agnes is, throughout the book, rigid in her standards and quick to judge others, she grows in confidence and maturity until her marriage to Mr Weston, making this a genuine if small-scale *bildungsroman*.

Agnes Grey was the name of a nursemaid of the young Byron. However, her first name is not given in Moore's *Life*, only that of her sister May who succeeded her.

Grey, Agnes *see* Pryor, Mrs Agnes

Grey, Alice: mother of Agnes and Mary. The daughter of a squire, she was considered by her family to have married beneath her. A capable manager, she is clearly the bedrock of the family, both before and after the financial disaster which overtakes them, but her very efficiency means that Agnes has difficulty in asserting herself and claiming independent status as a woman. After her clergyman husband's death she receives an offer from her father to "make a lady" of her again (ch. 19), but this she indignantly refuses. She and Agnes start a small school in A——, which she continues with an assistant teacher after Agnes's marriage.

Grey, Mary: elder sister of Agnes Grey, she combines with her mother in treating Agnes as a child. She marries (see ch. 8) a Mr Richardson, the vicar of a neighboring parish.

Grey, Richard: father of Agnes Grey, and a clergyman in the North of England. It is his financial imprudence which brings about the wreck of the family's fortunes in ch. 1. Loved and cherished, it is clear that he is "babied" by the family, and protected from the worst consequences of his own incompetence. He dies in ch. 18.

Grimsby, Mr (no first name given): hard-drinking and swearing friend of Arthur Huntingdon in *The Tenant of Wildfell Hall* – one of those regularly invited to the autumn shooting-party at Grassdale manor, and unlike some of the others an unredeemed ruffian.

Grimshaw, Rev. William (1708–63): incumbent of Haworth from 1742 until his death. He became strongly imbued with Wesleyan principles, even building a chapel for Methodists in West Lane, precursor of the present church. Both Charles and John Wesley preached in Haworth, the former claiming to have had a congregation of three to four thousand in the churchyard in the morning, and more than double that in the afternoon. Grimshaw himself became a local legend, and since he was high in the Methodist hierarchy he made the name of Haworth known in evangelical circles. Stories were circulated of his whipping reluctant townsfolk into church, praying outside the cottage of a recalcitrant sinner so that "he will die with the word of God in his lungs," and publicly shaming adulterers and other sinners. To the modern sensibility he sounds unbearable: a bigot and a bully. His methods and mentality, however, may have been the only things that could establish religion as a force to be reckoned with in such a rough congregation.

His body was taken across the moors to be buried beside his wife's in Luddenden churchyard, where it must have been a powerful reminder to Branwell in 1841 of home and the righteous paths from which he was straying. This was particularly so because Johnny Grimshaw, Rev. Grimshaw's drunken reprobate of a son, had gone to the bad at Ewood, the farm he had inherited in the parish of Midgley, further up the hill from Luddenden. Stories of him, both in Haworth and Luddenden, must have furnished Branwell with a powerful, if negative, role model.

Grundy, Francis Henry (b. 1822?): friend of Branwell from his Luddenden Foot days. He was himself a railway engineer, lodging at the time in Halifax with a nephew of George Stephenson. He was also the son of a minister, in his case a Unitarian, and was joyously kicking over the traces of his background and upbringing. He participated in Branwell's excesses of the time, but he remained faithful to the friendship: it was he to whom Branwell appealed when he hoped for re-employment on the railways, and apparently it was he through whom Branwell approached the Martineau family and Leigh Hunt. He kept in touch during Branwell's long decline, asking him to Skipton to meet him in the summer of 1846, and going to Haworth to see him, shockingly altered, in his last days.

His book *Pictures of the Past* (1879) was in part an attempt to put the record straight, as he saw it, about Branwell. Marred by muddled memory and the misdating of Branwell's letters, it nevertheless gives a lively and vivid picture of the younger man, with a strong pathos and sense of wasted talents in the account of their later contacts. Grundy was a very fallible human being, but on the whole a good friend. His claim that Branwell told him he had himself written "a great portion of *Wuthering Heights*" is possible but extremely unlikely: the secret of the Bells' identities was still jealously guarded at the time of Branwell's death, and the book itself had made no great splash.

Gryce, Miss (no first name given): a heavy, snoring Welshwoman, fellow teacher of Jane Eyre in her later years at Lowood (*Jane Eyre*, v. 1, ch. 10).

Guardian, The: High Anglican periodical, which was enthusiastic about *Jane Eyre* but later joined the crowd of those sneering at the unladylike nature of the author's heroines, especially Lucy Snowe.

Guizot, François (1787–1874): chief minister of Louis Philippe at the time of the 1848 revolution – both men being characterized by Charlotte as "men of dishonest hearts" (to WSW, 25 Feb 1848). A conservative Protestant and a distinguished writer with a good record of promoting education, he is the sort of figure that Charlotte in her earlier years would have heartily approved of. Her politics in later years were more ambiguous.

Gulstone, Josepha: author, under the pseudonym "Talbot Gwynne," of *The School for Fathers*, which is given one of Charlotte's longest pieces of fictional criticism in a letter to W. S. Williams of 3 April 1852. Her praise is loaded with implied reservations, and gives a strong impression of her tastes and literary ideals. She notices "a graphic rendering of situation, and a lively talent for describing whatever is visible and tangible – what the eye meets on the *surface* of things." She clearly dislikes the female characters, calling one "a pretty little actress, prettily dressed, gracefully appearing and disappearing and re-appearing in a genteel comedy . . . and – that is all." There are pointers in the whole critique for some of the reasons why Charlotte elevated Thackeray at the expense of Dickens.

Gun Group: portrait painted by Branwell ca 1834 of himself holding a gun, and his three sisters, of which only the side view of Emily remains, torn from the rest by Arthur Bell Nicholls and kept as the only good likeness. The rest of the picture he destroyed. It was seen by John Elliot Cairnes in 1858, and described as "a shocking daub, not up to the rudest sign board style." About the same time it was photographed, and John Greenwood the stationer gained access to it and took tracings of the sisters' heads. Martha Brown had a copy of the photograph, a very poor one, and from it a crude drawing was made to illustrate Horsfall Turner's *Haworth, Past and Present* (1879). Today we have all these things as clues from which to reconstruct the complete picture. The figures are woodenly grouped, seated round a table, with the physically small Branwell somehow towering over the lanky Emily. On the table in front of them are dead game birds, and near Emily's hand some books. Without justifying Nicholls's destruction of the rest of the picture, it would be generally agreed today that the portrait of Emily is Branwell's masterpiece.

Gustave (no surname given): nephew of Alfred de Hamal and a pupil at the boys' school which (as in *The Professor*, though there it assumes more importance) is situated next to Mme Beck's school in *Villette*. It is through the sick Gustave that his uncle Alfred de Hamal gets to see what was going on in the garden of the school, and eventually gains admission to it.

H

Habergham: part of Padiham, near Burnley, Lancashire. In November 1854 Arthur Bell Nicholls was offered the living of All Saints, Habergham by Sir James Kay-Shuttleworth. The church had been recently built by the Shuttleworth and Dugdale families, adjacent to Gawthorpe Hall, Lady Kay-Shuttleworth's family home. Such proximity to a man who irritated her greatly would certainly not have pleased Charlotte, though the £200 a year the living was worth would have been welcome security for Arthur. Luckily, Arthur's promise to remain at Haworth as long as Patrick lived could be given as the reason for their refusal of the offer.

Haigh, Ann and Hannah: subjects of a waspish letter from Charlotte (to EN, 20 June 1833) in which she asks "Do you not think Mrs Bradbury has made an excellent choice of a partner for life?" and notes that Hannah Haigh "has been elevated to the office of house-keeper at Colne Bridge" and comments "doubtless she will fulfil its duties with great self-complacency." Ann Haigh was second daughter of Thomas Haigh of Colne Bridge House, who married "Mr Bradbury, surgeon" in May 1833 (*Leeds Intelligencer*, 11 June). Perhaps as a consequence of this, her sister or some other relative took her place as the housekeeper at Colne Bridge. Hannah had been a pupil at Roe Head, and is mentioned by Martha Taylor in a letter to Ellen Nussey of 17 May 1832.

Halford, Sir Henry (1766–1844): physician to three kings (George III and IV and William IV) and friend to the Duke of Wellington. He was sometimes used on non-medical matters – for example, he was the Prince Regent's emissary when he was trying to persuade his daughter to marry the Prince of Orange, and he informed William IV of his accession. According to Charlotte's note "The origin of the Islanders" (12 Mar 1829) he was one of Anne's choices for "who should live in our Islands."

Halford, Jack: friend and brother-in-law of Gilbert Markham, to whom the whole narrative of *The Tenant of Wildfell Hall* is addressed. Married to Rose Markham, but does not figure in the story.

Halifax: town in West Yorkshire (formerly West Riding of Yorkshire). It is noted for its position, surrounded by hills "steep enough," as Pevsner observed, "to make car driving an adventure" (*Yorkshire: the West Riding*, 1959). The difficulties of access made it an individual and independent part of Yorkshire, but the coming of the railway, in which Branwell played his part, was a great boon. Defoe in the early eighteenth century depicts an idyllic social order and a beneficent economic system based on peasant weavers contributing to the town's main industry, the clothing trade:

> We saw the houses full of lusty fellows, some at the dye vat, some at the loom, others dressing the cloths, the women and the children cording and spinning . . . Not a beggar to be seen, nor an idle person . . . The people in general live long, they enjoy a good air, and under such circumstances hard labour is naturally attended with the blessing of health.
> (Defoe, *Tour Through the Whole Island of Great Britain*, 1724–6)

By the Brontës' time the town was in the early stages of the industrialized cloth industry, with near-slavery for many, especially the children, and the radicals of the time supporting total freedom of operation for the mill-owners.

There is no reason to think that Branwell or Emily, who both worked close to the town, wished to investigate working conditions, or would have been allowed to had they tried. Emily worked as a teacher at Law Hill School (1838–9), Branwell probably as a school usher (ca. 1837) and on the railway at Sowerby Bridge and Luddenden Foot (1840–2). Branwell, however, certainly took part in the town's vigorous artistic and intellectual life, attended concerts by the Choral Society, and began his association with the *Halifax Guardian*. Emily may well have been taken with the schoolgirls in her charge to the local museums and cultural events.

Among the still surviving buildings in the town that Branwell at least knew are the handsome parish church, dating from the fifteenth century, the Piece Hall, built in 1775 as a cloth market, and the Old Cock Inn (now, perhaps fortunately, called the Old Cock Hotel).

Halifax Guardian: the foremost Halifax newspaper. It had been edited in the early 1830s by George Hogarth, who shortly afterwards joined the London *Morning Chronicle*, where he encouraged his young colleague Charles Dickens to write what became *Sketches by Boz*. Dickens married Hogarth's daughter Catherine in 1836. The *Guardian* retained a strong interest in the arts, published 12 poems and one article by Branwell between 1841 and 1846, and gave good coverage to all the musical and artistic happenings in the town.

Hall, Cyril: the vicar of Nunnely in *Shirley*, and the clergyman most sympathetically treated in that book. He is scholarly, kindly, and charitable in the most practical way. He is a great favorite of Caroline Helstone and a benefactor of the Farren family (ch. 8).

The original of the character is said to be the vicar of Birstall, William Margetson Heald, who put in his claim in an amusing letter to Ellen Nussey (CBL, v. 2, p. 324).

See also Heald, Rev. William

Hall, E. S.: surgeon of Haworth. He was active with Patrick in his attempts to secure a better supply of water to the town, and was one of the promoters of a railway line from Manchester to Keighley, which would have passed through Haworth (*Leeds Intelligencer*, 11 Oct 1845).

Hall, Ellen: the "drudge-like half boarder" in "Ashworth" (Monahan ed., 1983, p. 55), whose treatment by Miss De Capell, arrogant and contemptuous, is contrasted by the sympathetic concern for her shown by Miss Ashworth.

Hall Green Baptist Chapel, Haworth: built in 1824 by a group of the Particular Baptist Church who later, in the 1880s, split off to become a Strict Baptist Church (the Haworth Baptists remain divided to this day). Inside it is a surprising and beautiful building in the Italian renaissance style. The Hall Green Baptists were active in the movement to abolish Church rates. Patrick attended a meeting there on the subject in February 1837, at which he and his companion "prudently contented themselves with holding up their hands against the resolution" (*Bradford Observer*, 2 Mar 1837).

Hall, Margaret: The sister to the Rev Cyril Hall, and in many ways his double. Charlotte told W. S. Williams that the original of the character had called *Jane Eyre* a "'wicked book', on the authority of the 'Quarterly'" (21 Sep 1849), a remark which troubled Charlotte.

See also Heald, Harriet

Hall, Misses: acquaintances of Ellen Nussey, who accompanied her and Charlotte to the caverns at Castleton, and annoyed Charlotte by being "lively and noisy" (letter from EN to Mary Gorham, 22 July 1845).

Hall, Pearson: a relation of Cyril and Margaret, and a solicitor in Stilbro', consulted by Shirley when she fears she may die.

Halliley family: leading manufacturers of Dewsbury, and members of the firm of Halliley, Brooke and Halliley. The family impinged on the Brontës' lives in a number of ways.

John Halliley Senior, of Grove House and Aldams Mill, was a strong supporter of Patrick in his endeavors to prove the innocence of William Nowell of Dewsbury, charged with desertion from the army in 1810. John died in 1828. He was the father-in-law of

John Buckworth, whose wife Rachel, along with all her sisters, was left the handsome sum of £4,000 by her father.

John Halliley Junior, also active in the Nowell case, became head of the firm in 1828, and was therefore badly affected when the firm went bankrupt in 1834. Charlotte wrote agitatedly about this to Ellen Nussey (10 Nov 1834). However, the bankruptcy, caused by a "stoppage" of the London firm Halliley and Carter, was not the end of the family business.

Edward Halliley, brother of John Halliley Jr, also went bankrupt in 1834, presumably from the same family-related cause, but he also seems to have continued in business, which was as a cloth merchant in Leeds. He married Susanna Hirst of Gomersal, and it was with her that Charlotte corresponded in 1840 about her advertisement for a governess. The tone of Charlotte's announcement that "I have given Mrs Edward Halliley her coup de grace" (to EN, 24 Jan 1840) suggests that she was by now reluctant to involve herself with the family.

Hamal, Colonel Alfred de: the favored admirer of Ginevra Fanshawe in *Villette* and eventually, after elopement, her husband. He is a military dandy, always described in doll-like terms, perhaps to emphasize his inferiority to the physically impressive Graham Bretton. He is "pretty and smooth" and "so nicely dressed, so nicely curled" (ch. 14). The implication throughout is that his charm is vapid, he is as selfish and trivial as Ginevra, and they deserve each other. It is he who is the supposed ghostly nun who appears at intervals in the school and its grounds – an aspect of the book many have found rather silly.

Handel, Georg Friedrich (1685–1759): German-born composer who settled in England. His oratorios aroused great enthusiasm in Branwell, who mentions them in his juvenilia, and his music was used by Emily and Anne in their piano studies. The new church organ in St Michael's, Haworth was inaugurated with *Messiah* (or more probably parts of it), in March 1834, and Branwell persuaded a friend "Mr M—" (almost certainly one of the Merralls, Hartley or Michael) to buy a copy of *Samson* he saw in a shop window, later repaying the gift by painting M—'s portrait with the names of Bach, Handel, Haydn, and Mozart in the four corners (Leyland, v. 1, pp. 239–40).

Hannah (surname unknown): servant, probably for rough work, at the Parsonage, who left around May 1843, leaving Emily "burdened with the charge of the little girl, her sister" (CB to EJB, 29 May 1843, see also her letter of 2 June 1843? to PB). Margaret Smith (CBL, v. 1, p. 321) suggests possible identification with Hannah Dawson, an old servant, who according to the *Halifax Courier* of 8 December 1908 was present at Charlotte's deathbed.

Hannah (no surname given): the sole servant of the Rivers, and a strong, opinionated country woman. Initially suspicious of Jane Eyre, seeing her, understandably, as a beggar, she is soon won over. After Jane's access of inherited wealth she goes back

as servant to Moor House. Probably derived from Tabitha Aykroyd, the Brontës' old servant.

Harcourt, Edward (1757–1847): Archbishop of York from 1807 until his death. Visited Haworth in 1824 to consecrate a further extension to the churchyard, taking tea at the Parsonage afterwards.

Hardacre, Mrs: employee of the Clergy Daughters School who accompanied Elizabeth Brontë back to Haworth to die, at the end of May 1825.

Hardaker, Elizabeth (d. 1888): kept the drugstore at the top of Main Street in Haworth, patronized by Branwell, and where Tabby was taken when she dislocated her leg in 1836. She it was who told Mrs Gaskell of Aunt Branwell's eagerness to pension Tabby off, how it went against Patrick's "liberal nature," and how the children "'struck' eating" until Tabby was allowed to remain with the charges she had helped to bring up. Gaskell describes her as "a clever, intelligent Yorkshire woman" who functioned in Haworth as "village doctress and nurse."

Harden, Mrs (no first name given): the housekeeper at Lowood school, one "after Mr Brocklehurst's own heart", apparently a scrimping, domineering woman "made up of equal parts whalebone and iron" (*Jane Eyre*, v. 1, ch. 8).

Harden Grange: the home of Busfeild Ferrand, MP for Knaresborough, to which Charlotte was invited in 1850, but declined to go. It was near Bingley, with a fine garden and a vinery, pinery, and a peach house.

Hardman, Mrs and Miss (no first names given): Mrs Pryor's previous employer and pupil in *Shirley*. Their attitude to their governess is discussed in detail in ch. 21, and Charlotte Brontë takes the opportunity of hitting back at Lady Eastlake's review of *Jane Eyre*: some of her more absurd and unpleasant reflections on the governess and her position in upper-class families are put into the mouth of Mrs Hardman. The obvious allegory of the name, and the strained way the sentiments of mother and daughter are introduced makes this one of the weaker sections of the novel, and allies this pair rather too obviously with Blanche Ingram and her mother in *Jane Eyre*.

Hardy, R. Spence: author of *William Grimshaw, Incumbent of Haworth* (1860), who visited Patrick in the late 1850s and described him as "hoary and roseate as the mountain-snow when crimsoned by the setting sun."

Hare Exhibition: founded by Sir Ralph Hare for "thirty of the poorest and best-disposed scholars" of St John's College, Cambridge, and worth around £5 a year. Patrick was awarded this Exhibition for four years from 1803.

Hare, Julius (1795–1855) and Augustus (1792–1834): authors of *Guesses at Truth*, which Charlotte was sent by Smith, Elder in 1849. This popular work by two Anglican clergymen, first published in 1827, had recently been published in a new edition. Charlotte was reminded of Pascal's *Pensées*, but "it is as the light of the sun recalls that of the Moon" (to WSW, 13 Sep 1849).

Hargrave, Mrs (no first name given): a hard, worldly woman in *The Tenant of Wildfell Hall*, whose devotion to outward show hides a penny-pinching nature in private. She is mainly interested in making "good" marriages for her daughters, and her influence with them is opposed by Helen Huntingdon.

Hargrave, Esther: younger daughter of the above. She is urged and tutored by Helen Huntingdon only to make a marriage for love, in which good principles are valued higher than worldly goods. She is a high-spirited, happy girl, though hard-pressed by her mother. At the end of the book she marries Frederick Lawrence and becomes Helen's sister-in-law.

Hargrave, Milicent: elder sister of the above. She has less spirit than her younger sister, and is pressured by her mother into a marriage with Ralph Hattersley, one of Huntingdon's hard-drinking and gaming set, a man for whom she initially feels great aversion. Her lack of spirit brings out the sadist and the exhibitionist in him, but eventually she uncovers the small sparks of goodness and nurtures them into a full-scale reformation.

Hargrave, Walter: brother of the above. One of Huntingdon's set, but somewhat apart from them, he is in love with, or perhaps merely interested in seducing, Helen Huntingdon. His courtship of her is punctuated by a good deal of melodrama, including many unconvincing "asides," and his motivation is unclear. He is, however, an obviously worldly man, whose subsequent career revolves around the pursuit of rich women to recoup his fortunes.

Harold (ca 1022–66): King of England January–October 1066, defeated at the Battle of Hastings. He is the subject of one of Emily's most striking essays for M. Heger ("Portrait: *Le Roi Harold avant la Bataille de Hastings*"). She contrasts his life in a palace, surrounded by fawning courtiers, with his transfiguration on the battlefield: it is there that he becomes not just a king, but a hero. Harold's situation is probably similar to others she had imagined in the Gondal saga.

Harper and Brothers: American publishers of most of the Brontë novels, who negotiated with their British publishers to receive the first sheets of new Bell novels. When Thomas Newby offered them *The Tenant of Wildfell Hall* with the claim that the Bell works were "all the production of one writer" (CB to MT, 4 Sep 1848) Harper and Brothers were naturally annoyed with Smith, Elder, who had promised them first sheets of Currer Bell's next novel, *Shirley*. They had already published *Wuthering Heights* as "By the author of 'Jane Eyre'."

They were the victims of, rather than collaborators in, Newby's chicanery, but nevertheless, if they could not get first sheets, they were as shameless at pirating work as other American publishers. On meeting a daughter of one of the brothers on his first visit to New York Thackeray genially enquired: "So this is a pirate's daughter, is it?" (D. J. Taylor: *Thackeray*, 1999, p. 333).

Harris, Alexander (1805–74): author of *Testimony to the Truth*, a work which Charlotte admired, calling it "a book after my own heart.... When I could read no other book, I read his and derived comfort from it" (to WSW, 1 Feb 1849). He claimed to have heard through a friend that Charlotte had said "it is the only book which in some states of mind I can bear to read, EXCEPT THE BIBLE," which squares with her remarks to Williams. Like other Christian writers she admired he plays down the importance of priesthood and authority, and emphasizes the individual's personal understanding of the Scriptures. See Marion J. Phillips, "Charlotte Brontë and the Priesthood of all Believers" (BST, v. 20, pt 3, 1991).

Charlotte admired much less his *The Emigrant Family*, saying "he scarcely possesses the creative faculty in sufficient vigour to excel as a writer of fiction. He *creates* nothing – he only copies" (to WSW, 5 Apr 1849). He seems to have been one of many Victorian writers who aimed to use the novel for propagandist purposes, without any talent for fiction.

Hartley: the name of several Haworth families. Hartleys were postmasters over several generations, and one holder of the office was told categorically by Patrick that there was "no such person" as Currer Bell in the parish. A Joseph Hartley owned a butcher's shop in the immediate vicinity of the church which was "an intolerable nuisance" according to the parish clerk. The same man fought Patrick over his sanitary plans for Haworth. The name is common in the Haworth area to this day.

Hartley, Margaret: niece of the Kirbys of Fountain Street, Bradford, with whom Branwell lodged when he tried to make his way as a portrait painter. She was clearly taken with him, as most people were, and came to his defense after his death: "He was a very steady young gentleman," she said, "his conduct was exemplary, and we liked him very much." She became a Mrs Ingham. The three portraits of the family, donated to the Parsonage Museum in 1952 by the Ingham family, are among Branwell's better efforts.

Hartley, Michael: the Antinomian weaver in *Shirley*. Mad with religion, drink, and "levelling" politics, he is not the cunning hypocrite that Moses Barraclough is, and Robert Moore finds a "wild interest in his ravings" (ch. 13). Hartley respects Moore as the mill-owner with the most brains in Yorkshire, and *therefore* chooses him as a "sacrifice" (ch. 1). It is he who attempts to murder him, but he is never caught or even pursued, and he dies of delirium tremens (ch. 37).

Hartshead-Cum-Clifton: the parish which Patrick Brontë served as perpetual curate from 1811 to 1815. It consisted of two villages, of which Hartshead had the church (St Peter's, still standing) and Clifton had the larger population: at over a thousand it was more than twice that of Hartshead. Though he was licensed by John Buckworth in July 1810, following the death of William Lucas, his predecessor, he seems not to have taken up the post actively until March 1811, his duties being taken by David Jenkins, whose brother was later to figure in the Brontës' Brussels years. He discovered soon after taking up the position that he had not arranged for announcements of his appointment on successive Sundays in the church, so the process had to be gone through a second time. According to Patrick himself the living was worth only £62 a year. During his time at Hartshead Patrick married, became a father, and had to cope with the sort of Luddite violence that is the background material for *Shirley*. He lived first at Lousy Thorn Farm, and on his marriage or soon after at Clough House, Hightown. He left Hartshead when he swapped livings with Thomas Atkinson who occupied a similar but better endowed curacy at Thornton.

See also Dewsbury; Thornton

Hasler, John: printer of Crane Court, Fleet Street, London, who printed the *Poems* in 1846. Charlotte claimed that she and her sisters could correct the proofs from memory, but four errors were allowed to stand, and an errata slip had to be inserted.

Hatfield, Mr (no first name given): Rector of Horton, and one of Rosalie Murray's suitors in *Agnes Grey*. He is a worldly toady, bent on self-betterment, whose religion lies mainly in show and insistence on the privileges of the clergy, but this is oddly combined with gloomy views that seem closer to Calvinism than Puseyism. He is judged by his attitude to the poor and his treatment of animals (Nancy Brown's cat, Matilda Murray's dog). He is perhaps the most unpleasant, most unredeemable character in the book.

Hathersage: village of stone houses in the Derbyshire Peak District, ten miles from Sheffield, believed to be the original of Morton in *Jane Eyre*. Charlotte stayed there for three weeks in July 1845, lodging with Ellen Nussey at the vicarage, which Ellen was getting ready for her brother Henry and his bride. While there Charlotte visited North Lees Hall, and the caverns at Castleton. The parsonage was an eighteenth-century stone house, and in the church (whose paintings and eccentric arrangements were ridiculed in a letter from EN to Mary Gorham of 21 May 1844) the name Eyre is prominent, as it was too at North Lees Hall, their onetime home, which may have provided hints for Thornfield.

Hattersley, Helen: the young daughter of Milicent Hattersley, née Hargrave, in *The Tenant of Wildfell Hall*.

Hattersley, Ralph: one of Arthur Huntingdon's hard-drinking and swearing set. He marries the reluctant Milicent Hargrave, and for some time mistreats and misuses her. As Huntingdon's outrageous and licentious conduct reaches its height he begins to have doubts about his own behavior and finally repents. He eventually (ch. 50) becomes a country gentleman with a happy family life.

Hattersley, Ralph: son of the above, one of the "fine family of stalwart sons and blooming daughters" mentioned in ch. 50.

Haussé, Mlle (first name possibly Marie or Justine): one of the teachers at the Pensionnat Heger. She fought with Mlle. Blanche ("They hate each other like two cats," CB to EJB, 29 May 1843), and Charlotte declined to make an intimate friend of her. The Wheelwright girls claimed to have recognized her as Hortense Moore when they read *Shirley*.

Haworth: The village that the Brontës made famous only began to acquire an identity of its own in the seventeenth century. In Richard II's reign it had 40 tax-payers, so some kind of township existed, probably consisting of workers in the wool trade and subsistence farmers. The church was built as a chapel-of-ease to cater for the needs of far-flung farmers and cottagers, and of passing travelers. Of the last-named there were many, as Haworth was on the principal thoroughfare that linked East to West in the Northern counties. Such travelers were still common in the Brontës' day, and often Branwell was called on to entertain them. The incumbent of this chapel-of-ease, St Michael's and All Angels, was a perpetual curate, and remained so until 1864.

In the seventeenth century the Presbyterian divine Oliver Heywood, whose parish was Halifax, thundered against "immorality, corruption, and profanity" in Haworth (Leyland, v. 1, ch. 1), so Mrs Gaskell's picture of the place and its inhabitants was not just an idiosyncratic reaction but part of a long tradition of demonizing. In the next century William Grimshaw expressed the conviction that "the majority of the people were going to hell with their eyes open" (ibid). But it was Grimshaw who first put Haworth on the national map. He was high in the Wesleyan hierarchy, could invite John Wesley to preach in Haworth (which he did to massive crowds), and built a Wesleyan chapel as part of rather than a competitor with the Anglican establishment in the village. Staunchly supported by the local church trustees (an important point, since they paid the incumbent's stipend), he made Haworth a beacon of light in the pervading air of eighteenth-century laxity. "Haworth" wrote his biographer John Newton, "would scarcely be known at a distance, were it not connected with the name of Grimshaw." He believed this proved that it was one of the places which "owe all their celebrity to the gospel" – the gospel and some brilliant PR by Grimshaw himself, one might argue.

Grimshaw's Haworth was a village of handloom weavers and agricultural workers. The coming of the industrial revolution changed all that. The mills, mostly small or medium-sized, were situated at the bottom of the hills to take advantage of water power, so they did not greatly affect the appearance of the village around the Parsonage. Most of the villagers, however, including the children, became mill-workers, slaving for long hours but earning a pittance. The combination of terrible working conditions and primitive sanitary arrangements meant that life for the average citizen of the village was nasty, brutish, and short. Life expectancy was 26 years, an age that all the Brontës who reached adulthood exceeded. Charlotte often records illness, epidemics, and discontent among the villagers and death among her Sunday School pupils. How much she actually knew about conditions in the mills we do not know because she never mentions in letters having been inside one. In *Shirley* it is perhaps significant that when at Hollow's Mill the children are released from work for half an hour at eight o'clock for breakfast Charlotte expresses a feeble hope that they have enough to eat. Significant too is that we never enter the working area of the mills in the novel. We get a fuller picture of working conditions for children in the mills from Mrs Trollope, who made a special expedition to the North to see for herself before writing *Michael Armstrong*, than we do from Charlotte who lived all her life among mills and their workers.

The principal social concerns of Haworth during Patrick's long curacy were sanitary conditions and education. He played a leading part in both struggles, as he did in the fruitless campaign against the new Poor Laws. He was the sort of Tory who could see the evils brought in the train of new inventions and a rigid and soulless economic theory. Both the establishment of the National School and the provision of a clean water supply were carried through against determined opposition from the mill-owners and rate-payers of the district. It is a pleasant thought that Sir James Roberts, the man who bought Haworth Parsonage for the Brontë Society, was himself a product of the school Patrick brought into being.

In the Haworth of the Brontës' time mill-owners, professional men, and tradesmen replaced the gentry. This left the family both lonely and rather special in the village. On the one hand Patrick did not have a little circle of friends, as he and Maria had had in Thornton. Often we have the feeling in his and his children's letters of their being cut off from all but superficial intercourse with those living around them. On the other hand, when we read John Greenwood's diary, with its breathlessly admiring stories about Emily in particular, we see that the family must have served as a gentry-substitute, acting as models for the village particularly in manners and tastes.

The shape of Haworth is still roughly that of the Brontës' time, particularly West Lane, Main Street, and Bridghouse Lane. However, between the present-day Rawdon Road and Main Street there was in Victorian times a slum popularly known as Brandy Row. The village today ends somewhat further along West Lane than in the mid-nineteenth century, but it is still possible to go straight from the Parsonage on to the moors, as the Brontës so often did. Like all such places, particularly those popular as retirement areas (a popularity quite incomprehensible in Haworth's case), a certain amount of unsuitable building has taken place, though not enough to spoil the Brontëan ambience. More serious is the transformation of the village into a tourist mecca, a process that began around the time of *Shirley*, when true rumors about the authorship and false rumors about the book's setting began to circulate in the North. In the nineteenth century, tourism provided a nice sideline for the villagers, particularly the old, and one suspects that stories were invented at the flash of a sixpence. In more recent times, with the collapse of the mills, tourism has become one of the main earners for the area, much trumpeted (though inadequately supported with facilities) by Bradford, the local authority. But with all the changes, with the many incomers and outgoers and the changing tastes and requirements of the visitors, the people of Haworth retain some of the "strange eccentricity" and "wild strength of will" which Mrs Gaskell, with a wealth of anecdotage, attributed to them (*Life*, ch. 2). The wonder is that no significant use of their home village was made by the Brontës in their novels.

See also Parsonage, Haworth

Haydn, Franz Joseph (1732–1809): a favorite composer of the Brontës.
Branwell, Leyland records, was a particular admirer of the Masses, and in the Luddenden Foot notebook wrote of his intention of attending *The Creation* at Halifax. His name, along with Handel, Bach, and Mozart, went into the corners of Branwell's now lost portrait of Hartley or Michael Merrall. Emily marked music by him for special attention in her copy of *The Musical Library*. Haworth heard a selection from *The Seasons* in 1834, and other music by him in March 1845. In a late addition to Gaskell's *Life* (3rd edition), a "Yorkshire gentleman" described Haworth as "the abode of musical taste and acquirement," and recorded being met there by an orchestra "filled with local performers . . . to whom the best works of Handel, Haydn, Mozart, Marcello etc. etc., were familiar as household words" (see ECG, *Life*, pp. 433–4).

Hayne or Hane, Mellany (both names are variously spelt): a
schoolfellow of Charlotte's at Cowan Bridge School, who according to Mr Brontë was "a hungry, good-natured, ordinary girl" who protected Charlotte from petty tyrannies (ECG, *Life*, ch. 4). She was about 17, and her sister was the oldest "girl" at the school, aged 22. Their fees were paid by their clergyman brother. Research by Sarah Fermi suggests Mellany married John Storrs in Nova Scotia in 1844. The information that she was "a West Indian" was omitted from the third edition of Gaskell's *Life*, and, following Sarah Fermi's research on her, this was probably right. However, there were family connections with the West Indies, as also with other figures interesting to the Brontës (Byron, Parry, etc). See Fermi, "Mellaney Hayne: Charlotte Brontë's School Friend" (BST, v. 27, pt 3, 2002).

Heald, Harriet (d. 1854): unmarried sister of the Rev. William Heald.
Charlotte expressed concern about her health to Ellen Nussey during the period 1848–9, when she was writing *Shirley* and possibly using her as the original of Margaret Hall in that novel. She had, on the authority of the *Quarterly Review*, declared *Jane Eyre* to be "a wicked book," a judgment which Charlotte said "coming from her – I will here confess – struck somewhat deep" (to WSW, 21 Sept 1849). Miss Heald was later, however, curious for information about the originals of characters in *Shirley*.

Heald, Rev. William Margetson (1803–75): vicar of Birstall, who succeeded
his father of the same name in that position in 1836. He married in 1844 Mary Carr of Gomersal, but Charlotte's knowledge of him would mostly have been from when

he was a bachelor, looked after by his sister Harriet. It is thus he is depicted as the Rev. Cyril Hall in *Shirley*. He seems to have been one of the few clergymen Charlotte genuinely admired, and this is reflected in her picture of him in *Shirley*, where he has to counterbalance a great deal of satire and scorn directed at the other clerical figures.

Heald's Hall: a handsome house in Liversedge, owned by the Rev. Hammond Roberson, in which he ran a successful school from 1795. The house was put up for sale in 1823, but it seems likely it was only let, again as a school, to the Rev. Hugh Hughes. It was put on the market again in 1830 and 1848, when it was said to be in the occupation of Henry Roberson Esq. (*Leeds Intelligencer*, 20 May 1848). It is now a hotel and restaurant.

See also Helstone, Rev. Matthewson; Roberson, Rev. Hammond

Heald's House: building on a hill above Dewsbury, birthplace of the Rev. William Heald, to which Margaret Wooler moved her school in the first part of 1838. Charlotte taught there until the end of the year, but the situation displeased her, and she later described it in a letter to Ellen as "an obscure & dreary place – not adapted for a school" (2 Nov 1841). This was after she had finally rejected an offer to take over the school, which had been run briefly and unsuccessfully by Miss Wooler's sister Eliza. The house still stands, in the vicinity of Dewsbury Hospital.

Heap, Rev. Henry (1789–1839): vicar of Bradford from 1816. In 1819 there began the acrimonious battle between him and the trustees of St Michael and All Angels, Haworth, about the appointment of a successor to James Charnock as perpetual curate. Heap claimed he had a right to nominate the successor; the church trustees, correctly, that they had the right to choose their own minister. Heap nominated first Patrick Brontë, then, after unpleasant squabbling, Samuel Redhead, who was subjected to the worst violence and indignities that Haworth could devise. Eventually, early in 1820, agreement was reached that the trustees and Heap would join together in nominating Patrick.

Heap's comparative youth may account for his inept handling of this dispute. He was notably intolerant of dissent, and this, combined perhaps with some bitterness about the circumstances of his nomination of Patrick to Haworth, may have led to his playing little part in the first 20 years of Patrick's Haworth ministry. He is seldom mentioned in his correspondence. However, he did have his portrait, now lost, painted by Branwell.

Heathcliff: the central character of *Wuthering Heights*. Heathcliff is his only given name, the name of a brother of Catherine and Hindley Earnshaw who died in childhood. He is brought to the Heights by Mr Earnshaw from a trip to Liverpool. This has caused some comment from critics, who have conjectured *inter alia* that he is Earnshaw's illegitimate son. But Emily Brontë does not go into the whys any more than the hows of the matter (how does a gentleman traveling on foot get an unwilling and aggressive seven-year-old from Liverpool to Yorkshire?). The fact is merely stated, to give it the simplicity of an event in myth or folklore: thus was the cuckoo introduced into the nest. His "cuckoo" status is further underlined by his skin color: "He is a dark-skinned gypsy in aspect, in dress and manners a gentleman" (ch. 1).

Any suggestion that Heathcliff's later deeds were the result of and revenge for his social degradation by Hindley Earnshaw is negated by the text. The incident of the horse (v. 1, ch. 4) shows him to be acquisitive and cunning from the start. To a degree the strong relationship with Catherine, in which the two come to regard themselves as in some way identical, keeps such qualities in check, even during the period when Hindley brutalizes him and reduces him to an outdoor laborer. He suffers this treatment to stay near Catherine, and it is only when she has been "gentrified" and starts noticing his degradation that he leaves. How he makes his fortune we are not told, but we do not doubt him capable of it.

His return shatters whatever order there is at the Heights and destroys the apparent calm of the Linton marriage. The drunken gambler Hindley is easily enmeshed, so that on his death there is no way his heir can claim the estate. Heathcliff makes no attempt to hide his scorn for the marriage Catherine has made nor his contempt for her husband. But Catherine's power over him is lessened now by what he regards as her treachery, and she cannot prevent his eloping with Isabella Linton for reasons that are purely mercenary and dynastic. This acquisitiveness in the man does not prevent him having two scenes with Catherine on her deathbed that can only be compared to Shakespeare in their power and passion.

After Catherine's death Heathcliff devotes himself to his dynastic schemes, degrading Hareton, gaining control of Linton Heathcliff, his son, on his wife's death, and taking advantage of the young Catherine's infatuation with Linton to marry them. Thus when Edgar Linton dies Heathcliff is in control of both estates, and we see him through Lockwood's eyes in the opening chapters of the book as the despot of his small kingdom.

It is essentially the burgeoning love of the younger Catherine and Hareton that robs his magnificently successful revenge of its savor, and he begins to see her face in them, and in everything around him. He dies in a sort of magnificent yet terrible consummation with her spirit.

To some nineteenth-century commentators he was unquestionably a villain. "Heathcliff, indeed, stands unredeemed; never once swerving in his arrow-straight course to perdition," said Charlotte Brontë in her "Editor's Preface" to the 1850 edition, and a writer in *Cornhill* (1873) compared him to Iago and Goethe's Mephistopheles. The twentieth century has changed course: "Emily Brontë's vision of life does away with the ordinary antithesis between good and evil," said Lord David Cecil in 1934; "it is an essential trait of Emily Brontë's attitude that it accepts all experience" (*Early Victorian Novelists*, Collins/Fontana reprint, 1964, pp. 122–3). Thus what strikes the modern reader is the astonishingly non-judgmental nature of the novel, and in particular the treatment of Heathcliff and his actions.

Sanger (1926) estimates his dates as 1764–1802.

Heathcliff, Linton: the son of Heathcliff and Isabella Linton in *Wuthering Heights*. Reared until early adolescence by his mother, he is weak, self-pitying, sadistic – an amalgam of the worst qualities of both parents. His nature is repellent throughout, which may explain why we accept Heathcliff's leaving him to die without medical aid. He is Edgar Linton's heir due to an entail on the property, and thus is an important part of Heathcliff's territorial ambitions. According to Sanger (1926) his dates are 1784–1801.

Heaton family of Ponden Hall, Stanbury: an influential though far from prosperous family in the Haworth area during the Brontës' time. The large family included the elder Robert and his wife Alice, née Midgley and among their children the younger Robert (b. 1822), William, and John. The younger Robert has been linked romantically with Emily through a tenuous family tradition, and it has been noted that Hareton is an anagram of R. Heaton. The elder Robert was a church trustee at the time of the row over Patrick's appointment to Haworth. Gerin (1971, p. 32) claims that the younger Brontës had access to the library at Ponden, but this has not been proved. During Ellen's visit to Haworth in July 1844 she seems to record in her diary "fun and fatigue" with the Heaton family, but the entry is ambiguous. The Heatons' fortune and position declined steadily in the later nineteenth century. Eddie Flintoff (*In the Steps of the Brontës*, 1993) suggests a general coolness between the Brontës and the Heatons, based on the formal tone of all existing letters between them.

Heaton, William: minor poet, a handloom weaver by trade, and author of *Flowers of Caldervale*. Leyland (ch. 17) quotes from a letter in which he pays tribute to Branwell's knowledge of poetry and conversational powers which impressed him when he knew him at Luddenden Foot. The description is somewhat flowery ("I have often heard him dilate on the sweet strains of the nightingale . . .") and is not altogether consonant with our impression of Branwell's activities at Luddenden Foot. Branwell lent him books and charmed him: "I shall never forget his love for the sublime and beautiful works of Nature" (Leyland, v. 1, ch. 17).

Hebden Bridge: a small town across the moors in the direction of Lancashire, a popular area for picnics and scenic excursions. Leyland records visits by Charlotte to the home of her husband's friend Sutcliffe Sowden, and Gerin (1961) records The White Horse as one of Branwell's favored pubs in the area, but we have not been able to verify either of these statements.

Heger, Claire Zoë (née Parent) (1804–90): superintendent or *directrice* of the school at the Pensionnat Heger in Brussels attended by Charlotte and Emily in 1842, and Charlotte alone in 1843. She was the daughter of an emigré from France, and the origins of the school seem to have been in one run by an aunt of hers, a nun. She it was, however, who acquired the Pensionnat in the Rue d'Isabelle in 1830. Her marriage to Constantin Heger was happy, and Charlotte's references to her during her first stay are all respectful and grateful, though less than affectionate. It is only some months into her second stay that the tone of the references changes – first, significantly, in letters to Emily, who knew her ("You are not to suppose . . . that I am under the influence of *warm* affection for Mde Heger. I am convinced she does not like me," to EJB, 29 May 1843), and then, more circumspectly to Ellen: "She is not colder to me than she is to the other teachers – but they are less dependant on her than I am" (to EN, late June 1843).

Later comments show Charlotte beginning to turn Mme. Heger into a fictional character: "Madame Heger is a politic – plausible and interested person – I no longer trust her" (to EN, 13 Oct 1843). In a note on a geography book dated the next day Charlotte tells of someone who "seems a rosy sugar-plum but I know her to be coloured chalk." It may be that the rare letters of this year from her to Emily survive because she intended to use these strong reactions to the woman for fictional purposes in the future.

Mme Heger was naturally anxious to neutralize Charlotte's undisguisable adoration for her husband. It was a situation anyone in charge of a school would know well, and would have had to deal with. Getting at her real character is difficult. The long and happy marriage with Constantin is significant, as are the tributes of former pupils, but many people found "something cold and formal in her make-up" (ECG, *Life*, ch. 11). Gaskell's attempt to attribute the rift between Charlotte and her to Mme Heger's formalistic Catholicism was of course a cover-up.

See also Pensionnat Heger; Rue d'Isabelle

Heger, Constantin Georges Romain (1809–96): husband of Claire Zoë, a professor (i.e., a teacher of boys) at the Athénée Royal, and an occasional teacher at his wife's school, where he taught the senior classes French and gave individual tuition to especially bright pupils.

He was the son of a prosperous Brussels jeweler, but an unwise loan ruined the family's fortunes when he was barely of school age. He lived briefly in Paris, attracted by a career in law, but when he returned to Brussels in 1829 he began teaching, for which he had a vocation. He participated in the 1830 Revolution (largely fought by the French-speaking population) against Dutch rule. He married Marie Joséphine Noyer in that year, but she and their only child died in 1833. He began giving lessons at Zoë Parent's school about this time, and married her in 1836 – a situation which (except its outcome) is mirrored closely in that of William Crimsworth in *The Professor*, including the propinquity of the boys' and girls' schools. In the next 10 years they had six children.

Charlotte's picture of the man with whom she fell in love was from the start of a piece with the picture she drew of him as M. Paul Emanuel in *Villette*: "a little, black, ugly being. . . . sometimes he borrows the lineaments of an insane Tom-cat – sometimes those of a delirious Hyena" (to EN, May 1842). She insisted throughout the first year that the only persons she cared for in Brussels were both the Hegers. When she went back alone, she began to give English lessons to Heger and his brother-in-law M. Chappelle, and this clearly gave her great pleasure and amusement. Soon, however, she is complaining of a lack of contact with him: "I rarely speak to

Mr now for not being a pupil I have little or nothing to do with him" (to BB, 1 May 1843). This is difficult to square with the six mostly lengthy and ambitious *devoirs* that have survived from her second Brussels year.

Though she had wrestled with her conscience before returning to Brussels, Charlotte began to face up to the truth of her situation in the summer, and even then she could not admit it to friends or even herself: "I fancy I begin to perceive the reason of this mighty distance & reserve it sometimes makes me laugh & at other times nearly cry," she writes, referring to Mme Heger's behavior (to EN, late June 1843?). In the latter part of the year she struggled with her feelings. In the autumn she went to Mme Heger to give her notice, but Heger, perhaps unwisely, "pronounced with vehemence his decision that I should not leave" (to EN, 13 Oct 1843). She finally summoned the determination to leave at the end of the year, confessing "I think however long I live I shall not forget what the parting with Monsr Heger cost me" (to EN, 23 Jan 1844). By this stage her feelings could have been no secret from her friend.

The love played out its course in the series of passionate, pathetic, and abject letters she wrote him in French over the next two years. It is sometimes said that he never replied, but hers of 18 November 1845 clearly states "Your last letter has sustained me." The matter and manner of these letters are extremely painful. "Monsieur," she writes on 8 January 1845, "the poor do not need a great deal to live on – they ask only the crumbs of bread which fall from the rich men's table – but if they are refused these crumbs – they die of hunger." "Oh it is certain that <u>I shall see you again one day</u>" she writes on 24 July 1844 "– it really has to be – for <u>as soon as I have earned enough money to go to Brussels I shall go – and I shall see you again if it is only for a moment</u>." But she never did.

Heger probably could be criticized for his handling of this strong emotional situation. Mme's action in retrieving Charlotte's torn-up letters from his waste-paper basket and sewing them together was unattractive but wise. Speculation about the extent of the affair would probably still be rife if she had not done so. A schoolteacher's absolute probity was at that time, and until recently, of paramount concern. Heger showed Mrs Gaskell these letters when she visited Brussels, but she concealed their nature from the readers of the *Life*.

Heger had a long marriage and a long life, and was prominent in Brussels's scholastic and academic activities. *Villette* was a cause of great embarrassment to himself and his wife (and probably did them harm with parents of potential pupils). Though he informs, in one way or another, all of Charlotte's novels, she never dealt with the core (and most interesting aspect) of the situation: an unmarried woman's love for a man she knows from the beginning to be married.

Heger family: the children of Constantin and Claire Heger consisted of Marie (b. 1837), Louise (b. 1839), Claire (b. 1840), Prospère (b. 1842), Julie (b. 1843), and Paul (b. 1846). Charlotte wrote (24 July 1844) that she was afraid the three eldest would have forgotten her. She recorded later that "your [Heger's] forehead never had a severe look when Louise and Claire and Prospère were near you" (18 Nov 1845). It was Paul who presented Charlotte's letters to Constantin to the British Museum.

Helstone, Caroline: the more passive of the two heroines in *Shirley*. Though her part in the action consists largely of being acted upon rather than herself acting, she is the reflective center of the book, and her meditations on, for example, women's role in the world, and particularly the position of single women, highlight one of the central themes. She is shy, sweet, but able to hold her own in debates with Shirley, if not with her uncle. Characteristically her illness provides one of the turning-points of the novel, and it is then, when she is most passive, that her mother, Mrs Pryor, reveals her real identity to her. She is in love with Robert Moore throughout the book, but it is a half-hidden love, very different from Jane Eyre's. It is perhaps a disappointing conclusion that, after all her thoughts on wider opportunities for women, Robert promises her at the end only a Sunday school and a day school to manage, but perhaps that is the most likely future for her in view of her character and her probable relationship with her husband.

Caroline is often said to be a portrait of Ellen Nussey, and Ellen seems to have believed this herself. Anne Brontë is another possible model for many of her characteristics, and her views are often Charlotte's own.

Helstone, James: the drunken and dissolute father of Caroline Helstone in *Shirley*. She has some recollections of a time spent in his charge (see ch. 7), when she was mistreated and neglected. When this was is unclear, since her mother, Mrs Pryor, later says that she "resolved to leave you in your uncle's hands" (ch. 24). Critics and readers have generally found Caroline's background and parentage vague and unsatisfactory.

Helstone, Matthewson: uncle of Caroline Helstone and Rector of Briarfield in *Shirley*. He is a stern, unbending man, though one of firm principles. He is unsuited to the company of women, whom he despises, though he reacts unusually positively to Shirley. In politics a Tory, he is totally unsympathetic to the starving workmen of the district, and his only answer to the unrest is unrelenting harshness. His supposed mistreatment of his wife (mainly neglect, due to an entire failure to understand a woman's needs or viewpoint) has resulted in outright hostility between him and Mr Yorke. His appearance and character are analyzed in chs. 1 and 3.

The character has been recognized, since Mrs Gaskell's *Life*, as based on that of the Rev. Hammond Roberson, a clergyman and schoolmaster in Liversedge.

Henri, Frances Evans: teacher of needlework in Mlle Reuter's school in *The Professor*, first introduced in ch. 12. The book charts the growing love between her and William Crimsworth. She has great problems with discipline, but when she starts learning English in Crimsworth's classes she immediately is seen as someone with imagination and judgment. Her person is described in ch. 14, and in ch. 17 we learn more about her background. She is the daughter of a Swiss pastor and an English mother, both dead. She lives with her aunt and makes her living by lace mending and teaching. The book charts her growing independence and the blossoming of her character. The scene in which she describes her dismissal by Mlle Reuter, who has realized she is a rival, is both richly comic and revealing. It is notable that after her marriage she insists on having a life independent of her husband's. She starts a school which she successfully directs until they have earned a competency sufficient to retire to England. She is a heroine of great charm and growing wisdom, and has long been recognized as one of the successes of the book.

Henri, Julienne: aunt of Frances, above. Her father's sister, she had taken charge of Frances when her parents died. We learn most about her in ch. 17 of *The Professor*. It is while she is sick that Frances is relieved of her teaching post at Mlle Reuter's, and at her grave in the Protestant cemetery in Brussels that Crimsworth finds Frances again after Mlle Reuter has done her best to separate them.

"Henry Hastings": untitled manuscript which Charlotte wrote in early 1839. It takes up characters and events which Branwell had been dealing with for several years. The manuscript is defective, and between the first and second parts that we have there must have been a section which shows Hastings escaping from his captors, sinking further into treason and debauchery, making an attempt on Zamorna's life, and finally being recaptured. By the beginning of the second section he is about to be tried by a military court. The tale as we have it is told partly by Charles Townshend in his usual flippant style, partly through quotation from Sir William Percy's diary, and partly by Townshend posing as an omniscient narrator of events in which he played no part. This multiple-narrators scheme could have suggested that of *Wuthering Heights* but here the effect is far from satisfactory, and it adds to the disjointedness of the narrative which contains material whose connection to the main plots is not always made clear.

The two major elements in the tale are Elizabeth Hastings's relationship with her brother, who from a brave and talented soldier-poet ("Angria and the Angrians") has degenerated into a drunken and brutal criminal, and her love for Sir William Percy, who has been involved in her attempts to help her brother. Elizabeth herself is proud and independent, though not always wise in her judgments. She instinctively knows she must help her fugitive brother when he turns up at the house she is looking after, but she deceives herself into thinking he is more sinned against than sinning, and could still have a noble future. She also seems to the modern reader to view Sir William through rose-tinted spectacles. She is, however, a free-spirited and attractive woman, and a real precursor of Jane Eyre.

We should not make too much, however, of connections with Charlotte's life or with her first published novel. Henry Hastings is not Branwell: a young man who is not living up to earlier promise is a very different figure from a drunken murderer and attempted regicide. One had only a failing portrait-painting business to his discredit, the other was a national hate-figure in Angria. It is worth mentioning that when, six years later, Branwell did spectacularly betray the hopes in him, Charlotte took a very different line from Elizabeth, who "did not think a pin the worse of [her brother] for all his Dishonour" (FN, p. 242).

And though Elizabeth Hastings may often recall Jane Eyre in her reasons for re-buffing Sir William Percy, the situation is very different. Percy is a figure less formidable, less passionate, and less basically honest than Rochester. He wants Elizabeth only for a mistress, and that for worldly reasons. He is essentially a flawed, hollow man, and the whole episode is on a much lower emotional plane.

Other Angrian themes intrude on the story, as Charlotte keeps topics alive for later use. These include Zamorna winning over his suspicious wife yet again, in spite of her vast experience of his unfaithfulness, and also his determination to wage a war that will leave "not a black piccaninny . . . to cheep between this and Tunis" (FN, p. 260). What is regrettably unclear is Charlotte's attitude to these aims.

Herschel, Sir John Frederick William (1792–1871): astronomer. He admired *Jane Eyre* and seems to have written to Charlotte to tell her this. She wrote (to WSW, 11 Dec 1847) that she could "hardly credit that anything I have done" could give pleasure to such a man.

Heslip, Rose Anne (1821–1915): daughter of Sarah Brontë or Brunty, Patrick's sister. She married David Heslip and came to live in Yorkshire, dying in Heckmondwike. Whether her time in the North of England overlapped with the lives of the Brontës, and whether there was any contact between them, is uncertain. She rejected in a newspaper interview most of William Wright's (1893) stories about Patrick's forebears.

See also Brunty family

Higgins, George: parishioner of Horton in *Agnes Grey*, whom the rector Mr Hatfield hopes he has frightened out of his sin of "Sabbath evening walks" (ch. 10).

High Royd: house owned by Mary Taylor's brothers, where she settled on her return to England from New Zealand in 1859. It is still standing.

High Sunderland Hall: large, battlemented building, its stone walls dating from shortly before the Civil War, high above Halifax and visible from Law Hill. Though clearly a much grander building than Wuthering Heights, and very differently positioned (close to a major town), it seems established as one of the inspirations for Emily's moorland farmhouse. It was in her time inhabited by tenant farmers and laborers, but it bore clear signs of its grander past in a splendid gateway, including large carved figures, and a similarly elaborate doorway. These features were probably re-imagined as the "grotesque carving lavished over the front, and especially about the principal door" in ch. 1 of *Wuthering Heights*. There were other farmhouses Emily could have seen with pretensions signifying a notable past history, but none with signs of grandeur and lineage comparable to High Sunderland Hall's.

High Sykes House: where Branwell lodged in Broughton-in-Furness. His landlord was Edward Fish, a surgeon of the town, and he lived with the family. It is still standing.

High Town: suburb of Liversedge, then part of the Hartshead-cum-Clifton parish. Patrick and Maria lived there in Clough House for the first years of their married life.

Hill House: the house, close to the church in Banagher, where Arthur Bell Nicholls lived after his return to Ireland. It was his married home for over 40 years, and became something of a shrine to his famous first wife. It is still standing.

Hirst, Mrs Abraham: servant of the Atkinsons, sent to fetch Charlotte on her reluctant visits to them at Green House, Mirfield. Described Charlotte, perceptively, as "spare of speech and nice in manners, though somewhat awkward, and evidently observant" (Barker, 1994, p. 177).

Hodgson, Rev. William (?1809–74): Patrick's curate 1835–7. A strong supporter of the established Church, he backed Patrick on the matter of Church rates, and in his opposition to the Poor Law. His time as curate went unnoticed in Brontë letters, and his only appearance in the Brontë story was when he later brought his curate David Pryce over from Colne on a wife-hunt in 1839. Pryce's proposal of marriage to Charlotte was firmly rejected.

Hoffmann, E. T. A. (1776–1822): German Romantic writer and composer, whose tales are often thought to have influenced Emily. The connection was noted by her first biographer Mary Robinson (1889), and connections between *Wuthering Heights* and tales by Hoffmann, especially "Das Majorat" have often been pointed out. Such arguments seem frail today, so superficial and sensational does the supposed inspiration seem beside Emily's great novel.

Hogg, James (1770–1835): poet, novelist, and contributor to *Blackwood's Magazine*, known as the Ettrick Shepherd. He was one of those (with Lockhart and Wilson) whose combative and amusing articles and reviews enraptured the young Brontës. On his death Branwell wrote one of his vainglorious and tactless letters to *Blackwood's* offering himself as Hogg's natural successor: the letter began "Sir, Read what I write," and ended "You have lost an able writer in James Hogg, and God grant you may gain one in Patrick Branwell Brontë" (7 Dec 1835). This was unwise, and not only because it was indecently hasty: the man was barely a fortnight dead. Hogg's position in the *Blackwood's* hierarchy was more uncertain than the young Brontës knew. Though welcomed at first, his humble rural background and poor education made him fit in badly with the obsessive cult of "gentlemanliness" which *Blackwood's* pursued. He found himself the butt of jokes in Wilson's *Noctes Ambrosianae*, where he began to be depicted as a drunken clown. His articles were rejected, and – worse – his name was put to pieces that he did not write or agree with, for example pieces forwarding the magazine's campaign against the similarly low-born Keats and the "Cockney school" of poets in general. The editorial standards of *Blackwood's* clearly anticipated those of the modern tabloid, and both Hogg and his wife felt bitterly betrayed by the writers whom he had imagined were his friends.

See also Blackwood's Magazine; Lockhart, John Gibson; Wilson, John

Hogg, Mrs (no first name given): landlady of Mr Malone mentioned in ch. 1 of *Shirley*.

Holden's Dollar Magazine: American literary periodical that gave a long and enthusiastic review to *Wuthering Heights* in June 1848. It was under the impression the book was by Charlotte, as claimed on the title page of the American edition, and drew comparisons between it and *Jane Eyre*; but its appreciation of the power of the novel was rare at the time, especially in the States. See A. J. Frank, "An American Defence of Wuthering Heights, 1848" (BST, v. 16, pt 84, 1974).

Hollow's Cottage and Mill: In *Shirley* Hollow's Cottage, adjacent to the mill, is a domestic refuge for Robert Moore and for Caroline Helstone, who takes lessons there and learns the Belgian-style domestic arts from Hortense Moore. Though it is described at one point as "snug" it has its uninviting side, particularly in view of the aggressive discontent of Hortense, and her inbuilt grievance that anyone should do or think anything other than as a Belgian would do. The mill itself features prominently in the first volume of the novel, and Charlotte thought of *Hollow's Mill* as a possible title: her publishers objected to this, we do not know on what grounds, and by the time she was finishing the novel Charlotte herself no longer found it "appropriate" (to WSW, 21 Aug 1849). This was probably an acknowledgement on her part that the interest of the novel had shifted from the mill to her two young heroines. It is perhaps significant that we see a lot of the mill's yard and counting house but never go on to the factory floor; we get no picture anywhere in the book of a working mill. We have interesting and thrilling scenes set within the mill's boundaries, we get insights into its management and financial problems, yet we see its work force mainly *en masse*. As early as chapter 5 Charlotte makes, and communicates to the reader, a resolution not to investigate conditions there: "Let us hope," she says of the working children, "they have enough to eat; it would be a pity were it otherwise." We thus get no sense of the hunger and terrible tiredness of this pitifully young section of the workforce, and interest turns away from the mill. It may be that Charlotte felt she knew too little of manual labor, and in particular of manual labor 35 years before the time of writing. We even know nothing of any experience she may have had of working conditions inside Haworth or Hunsworth mills.

See also Haworth; Luddite riots; Moore, Robert

Holmes, Betty: parishioner of Horton in *Agnes Grey*, whom the rector hopes to have cured of the "sinful indulgence of her pipe" (ch. 10).

Home, Mr (no first name given), afterwards Count de Bassompierre: father of Paulina in *Villette*. He is to the outside world a stern, sensible man with a scientific bent. To his daughter he is intensely loving and indulgent, and thus reluctant to let her grow up. He has an active conscience, which accuses him of overseverity when his wife dies: the fact that his health suffered from this led to Paulina's stay with the Brettons. In all Home is the kind of intensely masculine yet tender figure that Charlotte always found attractive.

Home, Ginevra: the "giddy, careless" woman married by Mr Home in *Villette*. The marriage was unhappy, she neglected her child, and there was a separation. She was also aunt of Ginevra Fanshawe. See chs. 1 and 24.

Home, Paulina Mary, afterwards Pauline Mary Home de Bassompierre: the attractive child who dominates the early chapters of *Villette* and who, when grown up, marries Graham Bretton. She is independent yet affectionate, childish yet adult in many of her aspirations, down-to-earth yet fey. The portrait is done with such individuality that the moment she re-enters the novel as a young woman (ch. 23) one recognizes the speech of the child. This portrait, one of the greatest child-pictures in British fiction, is done admiringly and lovingly, yet Lucy Snowe recognizes ruefully that such a person, whose life may be said to "anticipate the happiness of Heaven" (ch. 37), is cut off by her destiny from the lot of more ordinary mortals such as herself.

Various originals have been proposed for the character, including Fanny Whipp, a relation of the Hudsons of Easton, with whom Charlotte and Ellen stayed in 1839, and Mrs Gaskell's daughter Julia.

homeopathy: system by which an illness is treated by small quantities of a drug which would produce in a healthy person the same symptoms as the sufferer has. It was urged on Charlotte by W. S. Williams as a treatment for the dying Emily, but the sick woman dismissed it as "only another form of Quackery" (CB to WSW, 22 Nov 1848), though she later admitted "it cannot do much harm" (ibid., 9 Dec 1848).

Hoppin, Professor James M. (1820–1901): Yale professor who visited Haworth in the late 1850s, after Gaskell's biography and before Patrick ceased preaching. He attended service at St Michael's, and in "the intermission" was invited to call on Mr Brontë. Even in those last years he found him "naturally a social man, with a mind fond of discussion, and feeding eagerly on new ideas." In the afternoon he heard Patrick preach on the text that had attracted his son, Job 3.17: "There the wicked cease from troubling; and then the weary be at rest." See Lemon (1996, 62–5).

Horne, Richard Hengist (1802–84): poet and dramatist, notable in his time for his epic poem *Orion*, published defiantly at one farthing a copy, *A New Spirit of the Age* (with the then Elizabeth Barrett), and the tragedy *The Death of Marlowe*, which reminded Charlotte of the best of Dumas. She was also enthusiastic about *Orion*, which she found "Very real, very sweet" with "passages instinct both with power and beauty" (to R. H. Horne, 15 Dec 1847).

Hornsea: coastal town in present-day Humberside, then in Yorkshire where Charlotte visited Margaret Wooler in early October 1853 – "a happy and a pleasant week" (to MW, 18 Oct 1853).

Horsfall, Mrs Zillah: the nurse who is appointed to tend Robert Moore after he has been shot in *Shirley*. She is a perfect terror who worsts Mrs Yorke and Hortense Moore by her breadth, height, bone, and brawn (ch. 32). Like Sarah Gamp she is a "dram-drinker," and Moore hates the sight of her. It takes Martin Yorke to seduce her away from the sick-room with gin so that Caroline and Robert can talk.

Hortense (no surname given): pupil at Mlle Reuter's, one of the three trouble-makers characterized in ch. 10 of *The Professor*. Stout and ungraceful, she is mischievous and a giggler.

Hotel Cluysenaar: in the Rue Royale, Brussels, and said to be the original of the Hotel Crécy in *Villette*.

Hotel d'Hollande: hotel in the Rue de la Putterie, near the coach terminus, where Patrick and his daughters spent their first night in Brussels in 1842.

Houses of Parliament: Charlotte was taken to see Sir Charles Barry's impressive new building by W. S. Williams in December 1849 and again by George Smith in June 1850, when he left her in the Ladies Gallery and Charlotte became so absorbed by the debate that she never signaled to him any desire to be taken away.

Howard, George William Frederick *see* Carlisle, George William Frederick Howard, 7th Earl of

Howitt, Mary and William: authors and journalists, editors of *Howitt's Journal of Literature and Popular Progress*. The journal called *Jane Eyre* "One of the freshest and most genuine books which we have read for a long time," and Mary Howitt tried to get contributions from Charlotte, which she refused. The fact that William Howitt was "a quaker!" (to EN, 16 Nov 1849) probably didn't help.

Huddersfield: The town, though extremely important in the region, does not figure prominently in the Brontës' lives, except for a week-long visit Charlotte and Anne paid to Elizabeth Franks (née Firth) and her husband, the Vicar of Huddersfield, in 1836 – a most reluctant visit on the girls' part. Charlotte also stayed in the area in January 1839, when she visited Amelia Walker at Lascelles Hall.

Hudson, John and Sophia: substantial farmers who bore Charlotte and Ellen off from Bridlington to Easton House for the first part of their seaside holiday in autumn 1839. Charlotte and Ellen again stayed with the Hudsons, not too happily, in June 1849, after the death of Anne. Three years later, staying at Filey, Charlotte heard that the

Hudsons were in "quite reduced circumstances: I was very sorry to hear this" (to EN, 6 June 1852). Charlotte's references to the Hudsons in letters are always affectionate, expressing gratitude for their kindness to a stranger.

See also Easton House

Hudson, Thomas Duckett: chemist and bookseller of Keighley, who ran a circulating library in the High Street which the Brontës are believed to have used.

Hugo, Victor (1802–85): French poet, dramatist, and novelist, probably the greatest of the French Romantics. Heger used a small part of his "Mirabeau" in dictation lessons, and as stylistic exemplars for his Brontë pupils to follow. The influence (much transformed by different situations, but easily observable) may be seen in Emily's "Le Roi Harold avant la Bataille de Hastings" and in Charlotte's "Pierre l'Ermite."

Hume, David (1711–76): philosopher, also author of one of the first scholarly histories of England, starting with the reign of James I. This was recommended by Charlotte to Ellen in a letter of 4 July 1834.

Hunsden, Hunsden Yorke: manufacturer of X—. Friend of William Crimsworth in *The Professor*, who aids him after his rebellion against his brother's despotism. He is radical, highly cultivated, proud of his usefulness as a wealth-creator, contemptuous of the uselessness of the aristocracy. He is naturally satirical – much of his speech consists of a "flaying" of William – but this hides a warm heart and disinterested fellow-feeling. However, we hear at the end of the book of his love for Lucia, an Italian, and we infer that his inability to transcend national and class barriers and marry her makes him an incomplete person, one who takes refuge in irony and sarcasm. In this he is contrasted with William Crimsworth, who is able to ignore those same barriers. His name, a sort of Yorkshire parody of an aristocratic name, is perhaps meant to suggest that the millocracy have a class structure of their own as rigid as the aristocratic one. The character is clearly derived from Charlotte Brontë's connections with the Taylor family and their circle, in particular Mary Taylor's father Joshua. For this reason there are clear resemblances to Mr Yorke in *Shirley*, and to Mr de Capell in "Ashworth." His character is analyzed most fully in ch. 4.

Hunsworth: name of a mill owned by the Taylors, with an accompanying house and village. Charlotte stayed there on occasion, but she found the "abominable smell of gas" (to EN, 29 Sep 1846) nauseating, complaining of "headache, sickliness, and flatness of spirits" (to EN, 20 Feb 1845?). It was the home of Mary Taylor sporadically after the death of her father in 1841, and also of John and Joe Taylor.

Hunt, James Henry Leigh (1784–1859): poet, belle-lettrist and journalist. Though his talent was slight, it was cleverly used, and the charm of his personality gained him numerous patrons, whose generosity was usually stretched to its limits by his financial demands. Charlotte was pleased with his praise of *Jane Eyre*, and in her turn enjoyed his *A Jar of Honey* and *The Town*, with its "pleasant, graceful, easy style, varied knowledge, just views and kindly spirit" (to WSW, 16 Apr 1849). The picture of him as Harold Skimpole in *Bleak House* was, Dickens always insisted, confined to his mannerisms and turns of speech. However, Hunt had Skimpole's financial irresponsibility and eagerness to solicit and accept financial help from any source. Skimpole's published diary, accusing his benefactor Jarndyce of being "the Incarnation of Selfishness" is not unlike Hunt's relationship with and subsequent published account of Lord Byron. He lives today only in his "Rondeau" ("Jenny kissed me") and in his description of the Prince Regent ("This Adonis in Loveliness was a corpulent gentleman of fifty!") in the article which led to his imprisonment, and which is telescoped into "the fat 'Adonis of fifty'" in *Shirley*, ch. 23.

See also Examiner

Hunt, Thornton Leigh (1810–73): son of the above, one of the "little Yahoos" of whom Byron complained when they lived with him in Pisa. He offered Charlotte what she called "a place in your band" when recruiting writers for *The Leader*, founded by him and G. H. Lewes (CB to Thornton Hunt, 16 Mar 1850). The first *Leader* appeared at the end of that same month, and in April the first of his children by Lewes's wife Agnes was born. The un-Victorian code of the group was notorious in literary circles, but if Hunt detected a sympathizer in the author of *Jane Eyre* he was mistaken.

Hunts and Hall's: milliners of Commercial Street, Leeds where Charlotte bought a seemingly "grave and quiet" bonnet, which later seemed "too gay with its pink lining" (to EN, 10 May 1851).

Huntingdon, Mr Arthur: husband of Helen Huntingdon ("Helen Graham") in *The Tenant of Wildfell Hall*. He is initially a man of great charm, but the reader immediately suspects a lack of principle and deeply ingrained habits of self-indulgence. The marriage is almost from the first troubled, and Helen later analyzes that he is "a man without self-restraint or lofty aspirations" (ch. 29). Devoted as he is to animal pleasures at best, to gambling and debauchery at worst, he has no checks of religion or firm principles to stop him satisfying every impulse to indulge in trivial or sensual pleasures. Eventually tiring of his staid wife and her strict principles, he has an affair with Lady Lowborough, sinks further into drunkenness, and brings into the house a paramour as governess to his son, whom he tries to bring up to conform to his own "manly" standards. Helen is forced to flee to protect her son. When she returns to nurse her husband in his last illness she finally wrings from him a sort of repentance, though this is not sentimentalized, and it seems hardly more than the penitence of a shallow mind faced with death.

Traits of Huntingdon's character and details of his behavior may have come from Branwell, but the idea that he is a character study of Branwell seems wide of the mark: it is difficult to imagine a Branwell without talent, which Huntingdon is, though in the early sections he has a certain charm.

Hurst, Harriet: nursemaid to Paulina Home in *Villette*. She brings her to the Brettons' home in ch. 1. She is later (ch. 23) reintroduced as one of the servants of the de Bassompierres.

hypochondria: mentioned in all Charlotte's novels as a terrible affliction. It is analyzed at some length in *The Professor*, ch. 23; it afflicts Northangerland in the juvenilia; and Lucy Snowe attributes it to the King of Labassecour (Leopold I of the Belgians) in ch. 20 of *Villette*. Charlotte uses the word in its original sense: nervous depression for which there is no ascertainable cause.

I

Ignatius, St (?35–?107): Bishop of Antioch in the first century AD, who wrote seven letters to Roman Christians, one on his way to martyrdom. One of those, in translation, was recommended by M. Heger to Emily and Charlotte for stylistic analysis and imitation. Charlotte, according to Mrs Gaskell, felt that some of the English missionaries in Africa displayed similar heroism, and her version of Ignatius was her "Lettre d'un Missionaire, Sierra Leone, Afrique." This manuscript cannot at present be located.

Ilkley: a small, smart town 16 miles from Leeds and 15 miles from Harrogate. It was a favorite place of Margaret Wooler's. Charlotte stayed there in August 1853, on the way back from her abortive trip to Scotland with Joe and Amelia Taylor. She remained only three days, because she had lost her box "and without clothes, I could not stay" (to MW, 30 Aug 1853). She liked the place greatly, however, and went to stay with Miss Wooler there in the first part of September. It was also considered (rather unadventurously) by Emily and Anne for their expedition in June 1845, before they opted for York.

"*Immensité de Dieu, L'*" (The Immensity of God): *devoir* written by Charlotte for M. Heger probably (according to Lonoff, BE) in Spring 1842. It takes as its springboard the fourth poem in Lamartine's *Harmonies poétiques et religieuses*, second series ("*L'Infini dans les cieux*").

Ingham, Dr Amos (1827–89): Haworth surgeon from 1852. Mrs Chadwick quotes him as confirming the story of Branwell setting his bed alight. Charlotte in her last months sent twice to him for medicine for Tabby, and he attended Charlotte in her last illness, giving on her death certificate "Phthisis" as the cause.

Ingham family of Blake Hall: Anne's employers from April 1839 until probably the Christmas holidays. Joshua (1802–66), the father, was of a puritan, stern, and unsympathetic nature, sharing an antipathy for female vanity and ostentation with the Rev. Carus Wilson. He was of a family of business people, and was prominent in the Mirfield area as a magistrate and colliery owner. Twelve years after Anne's stay he was prosecuted for manslaughter over the death of a child of four run over by one of the colliery wagons, but eventually no evidence was offered and he was found not guilty. His wife Mary (1812–99) was the daughter of Ellis Cunliffe-Lister, MP for Bradford. She was described by Charlotte on Anne's authority as "extremely kind" and "mild" (to EN, 15 Apr 1839 and 24 Jan 1840). However, she gave her no authority to exact discipline, with the result that the children, already spoilt, became still worse in their behavior. The two eldest children Joshua Cunliffe, aged six, and Mary, aged five, were Anne's pupils. Still in the nursery were Martha, Emily, and Henrietta (Harriet) who died aged one year about the time Anne left (*Leeds Intelligencer*, 7 Dec 1839). In succeeding years Mary Ingham produced further children with dismal regularity, though several died in infancy. Susan Brooke gives further information about the later fates of the Ingham children in "Anne Brontë at Blake Hall" (BST, v. 13, pt 68, 1958), as does John Nussey (*Yorkshire Archaeological Journal*, v. 55, 1983). Some of the stories of Anne's difficulties recall *Agnes Grey*, though Mrs Ingham was in no doubt the fault was Anne's: she was a "very unsuitable governess" (Chitham, 1991, p. 60).

Ingham, Maria: daughter of Stephen Taylor of Stanbury, whose portrait was painted by Branwell in about 1838–9 (see AOTB, p. 330). She married in November 1839 James Ingham, a wool-stapler of Bradford. Charlotte wrote to her (4 or 11 Sep 1839) to cancel an engagement to make a call. Other letters are believed to have been destroyed.

Ingram, Dowager Lady (no first name given): one of the principal guests at Rochester's house party in *Jane Eyre*. A snobbish, rude, domineering woman. The depiction of this woman has been widely condemned as crude caricature, and the dialogue of her and her daughters ridiculed as impossibly arch and heavy.

Ingram, Hon. Blanche: guest at Mr Rochester's house party, and the supposed object of his amorous attentions. See above for common criticism of her depiction by Charlotte Brontë. Her interest in Rochester springs almost entirely from her own growing maturity (she has been disappointed in marital speculations already) and her ideas of Rochester's wealth. The supposed "fortune teller" considerably dampens her ardor and both she and her mother become cold towards him. The leaden sprightliness of her conversation is not convincing, and it may be that Charlotte Brontë betrays her ignorance of upper-class society in this caricatured picture, as Lord David Cecil suggests (*Early Victorian Novelists*, Collins/Fontana reprint, 1964, pp. 96–7).

Ingram, Hon. Mary: sister to the above. Milder, less haughty, she is also "deficient in life" (v. 2, ch. 2), and plays little part in the action.

Ingram, Theodore, Lord: brother to Blanche and Mary. Described as "tall and phlegmatic" (v. 2, ch. 2), he has only a walk-on role in the novel.

Inkersley, Thomas: printer and bookseller of Bradford. He printed Patrick's *The Maid of Killarney*, and his sermon on the Crow Hill bog eruption. He later became Postmaster of Bradford and gave up bookselling, dying in 1844.

Isabelle (no surname given): one of Mme Beck's school pupils in *Villette*, a well-meaning but unintelligent girl, who believes Lucy will burn in Hell because she is a Protestant, and who makes a brief appearance in ch. 38 showing a "wistful stupidity."

Isles of Arran, Jersey, Man, and Wight: chosen respectively by Emily, Anne, Branwell and Charlotte as their "Island of our own," as recorded in Charlotte's "The origin of the Islanders" in 1829. This list is repeated in "First Volume of Tales of the Islanders" (30 June 1829) but there Anne is said to have chosen Guernsey.

J

Jackson, John (1801–48): apprentice to Thomas Bewick, and born in the same village. Branwell, in his *Halifax Guardian* article of 1 October 1842, compares the more elaborate and ambitious productions of Jackson and Robert Allen Branston (1778–1827), apparently so much more sophisticated than Bewick's, with their "cross hatching, and rich black inking," but concludes that though they are good for "a half hour's wonder," the "unpretending vignette" of Bewick is preferable – a good example of the Brontës' tendency to remain faithful to the enthusiasms of childhood. See BST (v. 24, pt 1, April 1999) and Neufeldt (WPBB, v. 3, pp. 397–400).

Jackson, Thomas: parishioner of Horton in *Agnes Grey*. A "queerish old body" (ch. 11), but one whose "certain hope of a joyful resurrection" (ch. 10) the Rector perversely hopes to shake.

Jacob (no surname given): casual passer-by (ch. 51) during the scene in which Eliza Millward tells Gilbert Markham that Helen Huntingdon is to be married, in *The Tenant of Wildfell Hall*.

"Jacob's Dream": picture by Branwell, copied from a print of the same name, which in its turn was taken from a picture by the American artist Washington Allston, who trained in England and was an admirer of Turner and John Martin, as the Brontës were. This picture was acquired when a museum devoted to the Brontës was first mooted, and remains in the Brontë Parsonage Museum collection.

James, G. P. R. (1799–1860): historical novelist who churned out works of a pretty standard nature from the late 1820s (starting with *Richelieu*) to the late 1840s when his bubble burst and he became generally ridiculed. He became a consul in America and later in the Adriatic, and in his last years published little. Charlotte's remark that he was "a miracle of productiveness" (to WSW, 1 May 1848) was probably satiric in intention, though she may have been attracted by his highly colored narratives and Tory politics.

James, John: one of Branwell's drinking companions during his months in Bradford, 1838–9. He later published *The History of Bradford and its Parish* (1866).

Jane Eyre (1847): the novel begins in the middle of a typical day for the child Jane, one in which she hides away to escape through her imagination from the tyranny of life with her relations the Reeds. Aunt Reed is the austere law-maker of the household, with her pampered son John as its bully and torturer, intent on keeping down rebels and outsiders. After a sort of fit when she is imprisoned in the red-room, Jane wins a silent victory over the clergyman Mr Brocklehurst, and a more exuberantly vocal one over Aunt Reed. She is sent away to school.

Lowood School is run on gloomy and repressive lines, with a Calvinistic religion that poisons lives and relationships. The girls are prepared for a life of deprivation and servitude, and only the strong survive with their individuality intact. Poor food, insistence on mortifying the flesh, and sheer ignorance of childish needs ensure that the guiding force at the school, Mr Brocklehurst, becomes the second authority figure to be hated by Jane, along with the sadistic Miss Scatcherd. But after an epidemic illness which kills Jane's saintly friend Helen Burns, things improve. Jane succeeds in getting an education, and is eventually ready to leave the school and take her place in the world as (almost the only position open to her) a governess.

Jane's first employer, Mr Rochester of Thornfield Hall, is far from typical or representative of the species. He is handsome (to modern, though not to nineteenth-century, taste, as Jane repeatedly insists), intelligent, and willing to treat Jane as an equal. He is also, apparently, unmarried. He in fact bears psychological scars from a loveless upbringing and a marriage engineered by his materialistic family. A bond between him and Jane is cemented when she rescues him from death at the hands of a woman who is (though Jane does not realize it) his demented wife. After a house party at which Jane is tormented by jealousy of the haughty beauty Blanche Ingram, Rochester proposes, and preparations for the wedding proceed, though they are accompanied by all sorts of ill omens. At the altar the marriage is prevented by the revelation that Rochester has a wife, the part-Creole Bertha Mason, who lives with a keeper in Thornfield's attic. After prolonged pressure from Rochester to live with him as his wife, for as such he regards her, Jane escapes from Thornfield.

There follows a journey of fairy-tale hardships for Jane, before she lands up on the doorstep of St John Rivers and his sisters. She is nursed back to health and becomes a teacher at the village school. Here too she is pressurized to make a marriage, by Rivers. It would be a union loveless on both sides, entered into because he thinks a missionary needs a wife and he sees Jane as ideal for the purpose. This dilemma poisons Jane's discovery that the Rivers family are her cousins. She is saved from making a disastrous decision when she hears by supernatural agency the voice of Rochester calling for her. When she goes in search of him she finds Thornfield burnt down and

Rochester, blind, being cared for by servants at the remote Ferndean. He has been injured trying vainly to rescue his wife from a fire she started. The book climaxes with its famous line: "Reader, I married him."

The novel, with its combination of Gothic elements and realistic characterization, its powerful plea for women to be able to lead more interesting and varied lives, was an instant success, though a backlash started after some months with accusations of coarseness and irreligion. The book has remained a cornerstone in the struggles of successive generations of feminists.

Jem: consumptive villager of Horton (*Agnes Grey*, ch. 11).

Jenkins, Rev. David (d. 1854): Patrick's successor as curate at Dewsbury, who also stood in for him at Hartshead-cum-Clifton in the early months when he was still taking duties in Dewsbury (1810–11). He became curate in Pudsey in 1816, and remained there for many years. It was presumably through him that Charlotte made contact with his brother Evan in Brussels in 1841, when looking for a suitable school on the Continent. His daughter Harriet (d. 1834) was a fellow-pupil of the Brontës at Cowan Bridge School, qualifying because her mother had died in April 1824.

Jenkins, Rev. Evan (?1797–1856): chaplain at the British Embassy in Brussels and Chaplain to King Leopold I, a Protestant with strong ties to Britain. Jenkins's wife was active in finding out about the most suitable schools in Brussels for Charlotte and Emily to attend, and both husband and wife were most hospitable to the pair, until they found out that their invitations to spend Sundays with the family gave their guests "more pain than pleasure" (ECG, *Life*, ch. 11). The job of escorting the silent sisters from the Rue d'Isabelle to their parents' home in the Chaussée d'Ixelles was very much disliked by the couple's two sons John and Edward. The Brontës attended Anglican service at the Chapelle Royal taken by the Rev. Jenkins, though during a period of absence or illness his place seems to have been taken by "that unclerical little Welsh pony" his nephew Joseph Walker Jenkins, son of David and curate of Batley (to EN, 6 Aug 1843). The couple were unstintingly friendly to the Brontës, inviting Charlotte, with other English people, to Christmas dinner in 1843, just before she left the Belgian capital for home.

Jenny (no surname given): servant to the Linton family at Thrushcross Grange (see *Wuthering Heights*, v. 1, ch. 6).

Jerrold, Douglas William (1803–57): dramatist, critic, novelist, and humorous writer. His novels were not successful, but *Black-Eyed Susan* was a great success in the theatre, and *Mrs Caudle's Curtain Lectures* were much-loved humorous pieces. Passionate and irascible, he won the friendship of Dickens, but Thackeray regarded him and his brand of radicalism with suspicion. When, after the revolution against Louis Philippe, literary men were prominent in the new government of France, Charlotte suggested, tongue-in-cheek, that Thackeray and Jerrold and other literary men might be "selected to manufacture a new constitution for England" (to WSW, 28 Feb 1848). Elsewhere (CB to GS, 15 Jan 1850) she names Jerrold as among "the whining small fry of quill-drivers" whom Thackeray "towers above." *Douglas Jerrold's Shilling Magazine* was enthusiastic about the Brontës, but it was a short-lived periodical.

Jersey, Frances, Countess of (1753–1821): mistress of George IV when Prince of Wales, friend of Lord Byron. Charlotte copied a picture of her by E. T. Parris, from Finden's engraving of it. She called the picture "English Lady," and dated it 15 October 1834.

Jew's basket *see* London Society for Promoting Christianity Amongst the Jews

Jewsbury, Geraldine (1812–80): novelist and journalist. She was an admirer of Carlyle and a friend of him and his wife, but her major energies in fiction and journalism were in pressing for more opportunities and freedom for women – her views were very close to, and may have influenced, Mary Taylor's. Charlotte met her in London, probably in the summer of 1850, and wrote to John Stores Smith (25 July 1850) that she regarded "as an honour any expression of interest" from her or Mrs Gaskell.

John (no surname given): coachman at Thornfield. He drives Jane (very slowly) there on her taking up the post as governess to Adèle. He and his wife Mary look after the blind Mr Rochester at Ferndean, and it is his phlegmatic but happy comment ("She'll happen do better for him nor ony o' t' grand ladies" (v. 3, ch. 12) which is the only reaction we are given to the marriage of Rochester and Jane.

John (no surname given): servant to the Linton family at Thrushcross Grange (see *Wuthering Heights*, v. 1, ch. 6).

John (no surname given): servant at Fieldhead who assists Shirley during the discomfiture of Mr Donne (ch. 15), and is later (ch. 28) described as her "foreman."

John (no surname given): one of the servants of the Huntingdons in Grassdale Manor in *The Tenant of Wildfell Hall*.

"John Henry": alternative title for "The Moores."

John-of-Mally's-of-Hannah's-of-Deb's: one of the supposed suitors of the Moore's maid Sarah, mentioned by Martin Yorke to get Hortense Moore out of the way and allow a visit for Caroline Helstone to Robert (*Shirley*, ch. 33). Wroot (1935) says this custom of inventing names that embody pedigrees "even unto the third and fourth generations" was mainly a Lancashire one, though it was not uncommon in the Huddersfield district or in Haworth.

Johnson, Samuel (1709–84): Charlotte recommended him to Ellen: "For Biography, read Johnson's lives of the Poets, Boswell's life of Johnson," along with several other standard works (4 July 1834). Johnson was not a figure likely to be of any lively interest to Charlotte, however, and it is no surprise to find Jane Eyre, attracted by the title *Rasselas*, discovering the book itself to be "dull to my trifling taste" (ch. 5), though Helen Burns's more mature mind finds it congenial. Mary Taylor reports Charlotte's view that "Johnson hadn't a spark of cleverality in him" (MT to ECG, 18 Jan 1856). Branwell, however, was impressed by "The wisdom deep, the courage strong" ("The desolate earth – the wintery sky," 15 Dec 1841) of the man, and thought a great deal about him while at Luddenden Foot.

Johnstone, Agnes and Catherine: pupils at Lowood School whose "two clean tuckers" (ch. 7) in a week annoyed Mr Brocklehurst. Mentioned only.

Jones, Mr (no first name given): bookseller in Paternoster Row in ch. 6 of *Villette*.

Joseph (no surname given): servant and farm laborer at Wuthering Heights. A canting Nonconformist, his speech is a long whine of condemnation and a calling down of divine retribution on those around him. This speech, in broad Yorkshire dialect, is so vivid as to make him almost likable, and he takes a foremost place in a long line of fictional studies of English (and Scottish) hypocrisy. The concept of Joseph owes a lot to such figures as Caleb Balderstone, Edgar's servant in *The Bride of Lammermoor*.

Joseph (no surname given): worker in the stables at Horton Lodge whose company is agreeable to the horsy Matilda Murray (*Agnes* Grey, ch. 18).

Joubert, Madame (no first name given): governess to the Ingram girls. Plagued as all their governesses were, she reacted with "raging passions." Mentioned only (*Jane Eyre*, v. 2, ch. 2).

Jowett, Dr Joseph (1752–1813): Regius Professor of Civil Law at Cambridge. He was the non-resident incumbent of Wethersfield, and Patrick in his time there acted as his curate.

"*Justice Humaine, La*": *devoir* written by Charlotte on 6 October 1842. The essay deals with topics familiar in popular discussions of penal matters even today – remand prisoners kept in jail with the lowest of criminals, finding the finest legal brains pitted against them in court, having to bear a stigma if found not guilty. These may well have been matters that Patrick, interested and experienced in legal matters, had discussed with his children.

Justine Marie (no surname given): once fiancée of M. Paul Emanuel in *Villette*. Due to the business failure of M. Paul's father their marriage was forbidden by Justine

Marie's family. She had not the strength of mind to go against her family's wishes, and entered a convent where she shortly afterwards died. Though she is worshiped as a saint by her family, her fiancé, and Père Silas, Lucy also sees in her portrait "a weak frame, inactive passions, acquiescent habits" (ch. 34).

Juvenilia: The Brontë children's "plays" and their imaginary kingdoms probably go back to their early childhood, and the period when the children's leader was the eldest child, Maria. In his letter to Mrs Gaskell of 30 July 1855 Patrick records Maria and Elizabeth as participating in the "little plays." No other record of these early imaginative games survives.

1. The "Young Men's" play and the founding of the Glasstown: Charlotte records in March 1829 the names of the three main "plays" that occupied the surviving children in the late 1820s (recording their activities and creative lives was very important to the young Brontës, and became regularized in Emily and Anne's diary papers). The main play was the "Young Men," which grew into the Glasstown and Angrian saga. "Our Fellows" was influenced by Aesop's *Fables*, featured "people 6 miles high," but left only fragmentary traces. "Islanders" overlaps in characters with the "Young Men" play, centers on a school with the Duke of Wellington as its nominal head, and brings in the children themselves as "Little King and Queens."

The story of Mr Brontë's present of a set of 12 soldiers to Branwell has often been told because it is the beginning of the main strand in the children's juvenilia. The soldiers were all given names and became the literary property, if not the actual property, of one or other of the children. Charlotte's choice of the Duke of Wellington remained a preoccupation of hers for life; Branwell chose the Emperor Napoleon; Emily and Anne had soldiers who later grew into the explorers Parry and Ross. Over the years the characters developed and changed. The central characters became not Wellington but his son, not Napoleon but Northangerland, who developed many of the characteristics of that great military leader. The box of soldiers, in short, was the seed-bed of juvenile fantasies, and the flowers from these seeds were often predictable, but sometimes very surprising.

In the early period of composition their "plays" did not feature in their writings to the exclusion of all else: Charlotte in particular wrote stories with no, or only tangential, connection with the three "plays." These stories are sometimes long (e.g., "The Adventures of Ernest Alembert"), often so short and inconsequential as to be almost pointless (e.g., "The Keep of the Bridge," 13 July 1829 or "A Scene in my Inn," 8 Sep 1829). Sometimes real life intrudes into an imaginary setting, as in the relation of how the Commons debate on Catholic emancipation was received at the Parsonage ("Tales of the Islanders," v. 2, 6 Oct 1829), or Branwell's account of an argument on the nature and purpose of poetry between him and his sisters (WPBB, v. 2, p. 149). Branwell himself cuts a comic figure in Charlotte's juvenilia as Patrick Benjamin Wiggins – boastful, mendacious, full of his own imagined importance.

In the written pieces of the Young Men saga that we have (an important proviso, since much vital material may have gone missing), Branwell's main concern seems to be to provide a believable and lively background against which the main events can take place. Glasstown (Verdopolis) and Angria are states on the west coast of Africa settled by British exiles who set up independent governments. Branwell creates inns and publishing houses, he invents his own Glasstown version of *Blackwood's Magazine* ("Blackwood's Young Men's Magazine") in which Glasstown and other matters can be discussed. This early Branwell reveals his love of controversy, and of lively and very personal discussions – things he found in, for example, the local Leeds newspapers, the *Intelligencer* and the *Mercury*, and which he could provide an African equivalent to, where political differences could degenerate into slanging matches. The rivalry between Captains Bud and Tree, both journalists, mirrors a burgeoning rivalry higher up the social scale between Wellington's two sons, the Marquis of Douro and Lord Charles Wellesley. These rivalries enable Branwell and Charlotte sometimes to present us with two alternative versions of the same events, with widely differing interpretations depending on the character of the teller.

If Branwell's natural habitats are newspaper offices and taverns, Charlotte's are palaces and extensive grounds. In her various stories at this date she includes a brief account of the building of the Glasstown ("A Romantic Tale," ch. 3, 15 Apr 1829), as well as later revelings in its wealth and architectural glories ("The Adventures of Mon Edouard de Crack," 22 Feb 1830): "The king's palaces were of radiant white marble, richly ornamented with massive silver imagery and the architecture was the soul of nobleness, grandeur, magnificence and elegance combined." It is she too who first presents the contrasting characters of the two Wellesley boys ("A True Story," August 1829 in BYMM), to be taken up by Branwell (e.g., in "The Liar Detected" of 19 June 1830, by which time he or Charlotte had had the brilliant idea of turning Lord Charles into a journalist).

In general, however, it seems as if important events were covered in physical and verbal "plays," but were avoided in the written records, perhaps because the children sensed the events were too tremendous or too adult to be convincingly rendered by their literary abilities as they were at that point developed.

The children's own appearance in the "Young Men's" play is as the four Genii (Brannii, Tallii, Emmii, and Annii), and this role is rather more controversial than the little king and queens. The Genii have at their command all manner of magic, including that of bringing characters back from the dead – a great tension-destroyer this. Though it might be assumed that they function as beneficent presences in the early affairs of the Glasstown, in fact they are often resented as all-powerful beings unsuitable in a democracy (unfavorable comparisons are drawn between Glasstown and Great Britain in this respect). It seems as if Branwell led the way in resentment of the Genii's omnipotence, thus foreshadowing his self-identification with the rabble-rousing Northangerland.

The question of the four Genii leads one to wonder about Emily and Anne's participation in the saga dominated by their elder siblings. If they wrote any pieces to contribute to it they presumably were destroyed at the same time as the prose parts of the Gondal saga. That they remained privy to the events in Angria is proved by Emily's 1837 birthday note ("Queen Vittoria ascended the throne this month.

Northangerland in Monkey's Isle – Zamorna at Eversham"). Apart from as Genii, where they act as part of the group, they figure in Charlotte's "A Day at Parry's Palace" (EW, v. 3, pp. 229–33), which satirizes them for their near-moronic silence and comments on the Haworth-like homeliness of Parry's land and its inhabitants ("No proud castle or splendid palace . . . No high-born noble . . . Nasty factories, with their tall black chimneys" – very different from the pair's later imaginings of Gondal and its inhabitants). This is about the full extent of their appearances in the early writings. One wonders whether the younger pair put up a nominal participation but were already – in the inseparable companionship of which Ellen Nussey wrote – beginning to sow the seeds of what was to become their Pacific kingdom of Gondal.

As the new decade begins, and as Charlotte and Branwell reach adolescence, a change begins to come over the juvenilia. This is gradual and partial. Charlotte has not yet lost her taste for stories in which a solitary figure is taken on a supernatural journey by a stranger. However, she is beginning to individualize her characters with a more confident touch, often through dramatized conversations. Relationships are becoming more interesting, with Douro and Charles Wellesley beginning to grow apart, and Douro embarking on his first love affair, with Marian Hume (copying the love of the actual Marquis of Douro, Wellington's eldest son, for the daughter of his father's doctor), an affair already complicated by the voracious interest shown in Douro by the Lady Zenobia. There are at this date signs that the form of the later Angrian "tales" – juggling several sets of characters and plots in one loose structure – is forming in Charlotte's mind. And as the supernatural element begins to fade, new characters, often sources of later conflicts, begin to appear: we note the name Quamina (for a "good Ashantee," ancestor of Quashia) and also that of Rogue.

The future, as it turns out, belongs to Rogue, as the instigator of many of the important plot developments in the next phase of the juvenilia. In December 1830 Branwell begins his "History of the Young Men," which he was not to finish until five months later (WPBB, v. 1, pp. 137–69). He begins with his version of the story of his soldiers, and then goes on to narrate what he and his sisters "realy pretended did happen" (to use his delightful and accurate phrase) to the 12 young men, carrying them through the founding of Twelvestown (precursor of the Glasstown), through wars with the Ashantees, including various massacres of them which Branwell takes very coolly in his stride, and through the reign of Frederick I, terminated by the death of the real Duke of York, on whom he was based, and the crowning of his successor, Stumps, as Frederick II.

This long summary of events which had presumably evolved in their play was the first of several such retraversals of earlier material by Branwell, and was in the nature of a step backwards to make a more ambitious stride forwards. For while it was being written Charlotte had gone away to school at Roe Head, leaving Branwell in effective control.

2. War and peace (1831–3): The second phase of Charlotte and Branwell's childhood creation of the Glasstown is transitional in forms, subject matter, and approach. For example, the magical elements become less and less important, but the Duke of

Wellington remains, albeit usually in the background or as a secondary figure, to solve problems, lead armies, or get his sons out of scrapes. In this period Branwell largely forsakes the daring and clever narrative experiments of the first phase for a fairly straightforward chronicle style. Charlotte, on her return from Roe Head, where she considered putting an end to the Glasstown saga, in fact re-enters the imaginary world with enthusiasm and brio. Sometimes her contributions consist of a miscellany of short pieces, for example "Arthuriana, or Odds and Ends." More often she prefers the simple romantic short story, for example "The Foundling," which introduces Edward Sydney, whose love for the Lady Julia is rewarded with a marriage which in later narratives quickly turns sour. In a similar style of story, "Lily Hart," an orphaned girl, reduced to poverty after the death of her mother, is reunited with the man whom earlier she had nursed back to health. At that earlier period this man, "cold and distant" (EW, v. 2, pt 1, p. 303) was thawed by her feminine attractions, sang to her accompaniment, and had a friend who formed the other part in the trio, one who had "a certain lofty imperiousness in his manner" (ibid, p. 310) and who aided the romance. This triangle, though different in details of plot and relationships, nevertheless has some of the seeds that made the central situation of *Jane Eyre* so gripping. The men in the story turn out to be the Marquis of Fidena and the Marquis of Douro.

In the writings of these years the events of the early history of the Glasstown are followed much more closely, and in more detail, than in the earlier pieces, though chronology is often forsaken for backward glances at the main characters' pasts. Rogue (usually spelt Rouge or Rougue) becomes by marriage Lord Elrington (or Ellrington), and blossoms during these years into Branwell's anti-hero: a swaggering, hard-drinking, conspiring man, single-mindedly possessed by the pursuit of his own enrichment and advance. Branwell chronicles the Great Rebellion, led by Rogue (in "Letters from an Englishman") and his life as a pirate, during which he encounters and marries Zenobia, Lady Elrington ("The Pirate"). During the Great Rebellion Rogue becomes captain of misrule: even within his own armies dissension reigns, and helps to bring about his defeat and (temporary) death ("Letters from an Englishman," v. 6; WPBB, v. 1, pp. 230–8). In the same narrative Douro progresses from being a tailor's dummy to a military leader, though one with strong comic-book connotations ("with one mighty effort he broke his bonds," ibid, WPBB, v. 1, p. 237).

In later wars Rogue and Douro are sometimes on the same side (e.g., in "Historical Narrative of the 'War of Encroachment'" in which the French invade Africa), but in general their relationship is one of rivalry, treachery, and suspicion. Branwell's accounts of wars are almost always tedious catalogues of troop movements, maneuvers, and battles involving enormous casualty figures (he was apparently convinced that excitement is increased if the number of dead is put at 20 thousand rather than two thousand). In politics, however, he can create convincing and exciting debates in the Glasstown legislative assemblies, where the Aristocratic party (effete and defeatist) is opposed by the Rationals, with the Duke of Wellington at their head. The debates in the "Historical Narrative of the War of Aggression," with their rhetoric, their phony passion hiding egotism and greed, their occasionally genuine involvement with the predicament of the army, mirror in tone, though not in subjects, the debates on parliamentary reform going on in those years in the two chambers of the British Parliament.

Charlotte's contributions take very different subjects, almost as if war and peace in the Glasstown or Verdopolis, as it is starting to be called, exist simultaneously. She chronicles loves, and by the end of the period is preparing to chronicle the loss of love. Her settings are either magnificent palaces or rural retreats (not too humble: Lily Hart and her mother live in a "quiet and modest mansion, situated in one of the remote suburbs of Verdopolis," EW, v. 2, pt 1, p. 301). The main change is in the nature of Douro, possibly springing from Charlotte's deeper understanding of the full complexity of the Byronic heroes on which the mature Douro is modeled. After playing a rather silly trick on an aspiring author, we are told that he has on his face "a smile of . . . cold, triumphant, deep and devilish meaning" ("Arthuriana," EW, v. 2, pt 1, p. 243). Though later in the same piece becoming a father brings "some touch of human feeling" to Douro (ibid, p. 248), his brother fears for the baby the same upbringing, the same companionship, and therefore the same "fatal seeds of that pride and those bad passions" which will make him a replica of that "vast and baleful Upas-tree" that is his father (p. 249). Though "The Secret" tells of the Douro marriage surviving a crisis, the time is not far away when Douro will withdraw himself from the erstwhile Marian Hume, and she will die. The stage is also set for that fruitful animosity between brothers which eventually will find a place in the Brontës' mature fiction. It is arguable that the event which began the change in the chronicles to what Christine Alexander calls "early writings" was the return of Charlotte from Roe Head. While Charlotte was writing "The Foundling" and "The Green Dwarf" Branwell was mired in "Real Life of Verdopolis," a constipated and muddled account of conspiracies and war. But the first manuscript he began after absorbing Charlotte's pieces was "The Politics of Verdopolis," which is much more sharp, shapely, and involving and above all very much better told. Branwell could learn, though he certainly also could slip back to bad old ways.

3. The rise of Angria (1834–5):

The new prominence of Angria in the remaining juvenilia is a consequence of the Wars of Encroachment, in which Douro and Rogue, or Zamorna and Northangerland as they can henceforth be called, unite to defeat a force of black native warriors and French invaders. In "The Wool is Rising," Zamorna, by now married to Northangerland's daughter Mary Percy, tells the Verdopolis Parliament his demands in return for his triumphs in the war: "I demand my fields of battle, I demand the provinces of Angria, Calabar and Zamorna to be yielded up to me in uncontrolled sovereignty . . ." (WPBB, v. 2, p. 34). From being a province of Verdopolis worth no more than an occasional mention, Angria now becomes the center of interest of all the later juvenile writings.

The great advantage of this for the two writers, now in their later teens, was that all the childish baggage of Glasstown could be cast off. Affairs in the new province were adult, sometimes sophisticated, with the excitements and emotional conflicts of a regular novel. In atmosphere they most resemble a historical novel of the period such as Bulwer-Lytton's (one is not suggesting influences so much as common impulses). One can sense the exhilaration and anticipation of this new beginning in Branwell's description of the building of Adrianopolis:

> On one wide ready-cleared space I was told that a Noble Cathedral is about directly to be erected. On another the stones are even now piled up for the raising of a vast Hall of Commerce. We passed under the framework of a great brick Hotel and turned by a large church where we saw men bearing in great metal pipes and heard the random notes of an organ diapason . . .
>
> ("Angria and the Angrians," WPBB, v. 2, p. 215)

The energy of the description of this instant city is paralleled by Charlotte's rough sketch of the future of her imaginary kingdoms in "A Leaf from an Unopened Volume" (17 Jan 1834, EW, v. 2, pt 1) – a sort of ground plan for the saga in which the burgeoning grandeur is coupled with moral and social decline. She makes a start in chronicling this decline in "High Life in Verdopolis" (Feb–Mar 1834) in which we clearly see the decline in the character of Zamorna, now displaying all the more negative sides of the Byronic hero: arrogance, sadism of an emotional kind, and incorrigible adultery. In this story his new queen, only three months married, feels the full force of his tyrannical and changeable nature.

Branwell, on the other hand, uses the first year of his new kingdom's creation to trace the career of Northangerland – the character whom he now unequivocally adopts as his *alter ego*, embracing his sins and treacheries with little of the moral thimblerigging that is necessary for Charlotte when she traces the career of her own increasingly diabolic hero Zamorna. Branwell's "Life of Alexander Percy" is perhaps the pinnacle of his achievement in the juvenilia: we wonder at the exuberance and vigor of this 17-year-old writer as we do not feel inclined to when he reaches 18, 19, and beyond, and becomes bemired in rather than intoxicated by his own facility of invention.

Needless to say, Angria does not have a peaceful birth. Zamorna's arrogance and the jealousy of rival Verdopolitan politicians ensure that. The coronation of the new King and Queen of Angria is the opening event in Branwell's enormous (but now fragmentary) chronicle called by Victor Neufeldt, following the use of this title three times in the text, "Angria and the Angrians" (v. 2, pp. 200–6). The inspiration for this richly melodramatic scene is presumably not the cut-price coronation of William IV (1831), but the magnificently stage-managed one of George IV (1821) with perhaps some hints from that of Napoleon, as when Zamorna scorns the crown which the Primate of Verdopolis is preparing to set on his head and instead "crowns" himself with a helmet, with a sword for a scepter. Thereafter the chronicles of both authors are concerned partly with details of the new kingdom – a bustling, commercial, *arriviste* community, compared with the more aristocratic if equally quarrelsome Verdopolis – and with the deteriorating political situation. Zamorna and Northangerland are made by similar temperaments to be bitter enemies, but are drawn together from time to time both by political convenience and a reluctant admiration for each other. Northangerland withdraws to Stumps's Land, ostensibly sick, but returns for a tremendous parliamentary clash with Zamorna, chronicled by Charlotte in her "Scrap Book" (EW, v. 2, pt 2, pp. 304–9, 369–77). As political events push the new province ineluctably towards war, first against the Ashantees, then shading off into civil strife, the events fall once again into Branwell's hands as Charlotte goes off to be a teacher at Roe Head. On his own Branwell marks an important change of direction by putting his narrative into the hands of the young soldier-poet Henry Hastings. In doing so he provides a source of rich interest for Charlotte in one of the most ambitious of her later narratives.

4. Angria redivivus (1836–40): The emerging civil conflict in Angria soon takes on a comprehensible, though fluid, aspect. For detailed coverage of these wars see "Angria and the Angrians." On the one hand is the government in Verdopolis, with allies such as Quashia and his Ashantees, and the French. On the other side are the Angrians, led by Zamorna, Fidena, and Warner. Northangerland stands poised to defect to either side. The point of dispute is the position of Angria, whose state of near-independence from the Confederacy is bitterly resented in Verdopolis and rescinded by its parliament.

Branwell's partiality for endless battles, with detailed accounts of the maneuvers and casualty lists, is well known, but they seem at this point to be losing some of their appeal. Though "Angria and the Angrians" is fragmentary, the fact that he is switching his attention away from the theatre of war is attested by his decision to summarize political developments, which he does at least twice (WPBB, v. 2, pp. 529–32, 601–2). Character clashes come more to the fore now, with a notably effective scene between Northangerland and his mother, and another with two of his mistresses, Louisa Dance and Lady Greville. There are also effective scenes with Charles Wentworth, a new character whose introduction into Verdopolis has often been thought, since Gerin's (1961) biography of Branwell, to mirror Branwell's own disastrous visit to London (if, of course, it ever took place).

Most effective of all is Northangerland's scene with his dying daughter, Zamorna's queen, Mary Percy. Branwell trumpeted this scene to Charlotte extensively in advance, like a modern soap opera publicist, but on the whole it lives up to its billing. In its melodramatic and sentimental way it hits the spot, with Mary even putting across a grain of Branwellian free-thinking ("Oh father, they have talked to me about heaven: they have been either trying to fit me for it, or to pacify me with it. But they know nothing . . . ," WPBB, v. 2, p. 618). The narrator also manages a thumbnail sketch of the problems of a young Charlottian heroine: "there never was a being more entirely of feeling and more utterly destitute of the sterner qualities of the mind" (WPBB, v. 2, p. 617). Charlotte has her revenge when she returns to Haworth for Christmas 1836 and reverses the death, something the young Brontës were experienced in doing for their characters.

Much less engaging are the drinking scenes, which seem to go on for ever, and give the impression that the Verdopolitan coalition were in a permanent state of inebriation. At year's turn 1836–7 Northangerland is Lord President of the Verdopolitan Confederacy, in charge of a crumbling coalition of treacherous bullies who are wreaking murderous havoc through Angria and beyond.

Zamorna, however, is on his way back. The armed struggle by which he regains control of his kingdom is not well documented in the extant juvenilia, and Charlotte as usual tends to avoid military detail, concentrating on the situation after his return, and the controversy caused by his continued association, in a love–hate relationship, with his father-in-law Northangerland. Much is made of the latter's extreme unpopularity in Angria, where he cannot come without hostile demonstrations.

Charlotte's manuscripts of these last years of Verdopolis and Angria are of several different kinds. Some of them are recapitulations of earlier events with the changed perspective of later maturity (e.g., "Four Years Ago" and "The Duke of Zamorna," which is a mélange of past and present events). Others are jumbles of events with no central character or continuous interest – they resemble episodes of a soap opera that aim at an update on happenings all over the spectrum of its subject matter (e.g., "Stancliffe's Hotel"). The manuscripts of most interest to the modern reader are those where she seems to be moving towards the novel proper, with greater concentration on a few characters and their emotional preoccupations. Those manuscripts, notably "Henry Hastings," "Caroline Vernon," and the "Return of Zamorna" are much closer than earlier ones to being stories or even novellas. Charlotte is still conscious of the need to keep events going on around the main characters, but the central concern is the emotional predicaments of the main actors, and these are kept constantly in mind. Thus Elizabeth Hastings' love and support for her brother through his time of degradation and vilification are both dramatized and analyzed. Caroline Vernon grows up from being a neglected child of enormous but dangerously unprincipled charm (a foretaste, but only superficially, of Adèle Varens and Paulina Home) to a sophisticated young woman bent on getting what she wants: the illicit love of the married Zamorna. It is worth noting that "Henry Hastings" has a largely new subject for the juvenilia, whereas "Caroline Vernon" reproduces the outline of an earlier triangle (Northangerland + one of his daughters + Zamorna, with Quashia representing a serio-comic threat from outside): the shape of the plot-line is the same, though the characters of Mary Percy and Caroline make the atmosphere of the narrative very different.

After this story, apart from an early attempt at "Ashworth," Charlotte said goodbye to Angria and began to gather material that would enable her to grapple fictionally with the real world. Branwell did not manage a clean break, but (if the surviving manuscripts are a fair sample) continued toying with material from which all vitality had been drained. He really had "sojourned too long" and too wholeheartedly to "quit for awhile that burning clime" (CB, "Farewell to Angria," in Francis Beer, ed., *The Juvenilia of Jane Austen and Charlotte Brontë*, 1986, pp. 366–7).

K

Kavanagh, Julia (1824–77): novelist and social commentator. Charlotte heard of her when she reviewed *Jane Eyre*, and she judged from W. S. William's account of her life and character that she belonged "to a class I peculiarly esteem . . . where genius is found unmarred by extravagance, self-reliance unalloyed by self-complacency" (to WSW, 22 Jan 1848). Her letters are henceforth peppered with enquiries about Kavanagh's welfare, probably prompted by the fact that she supported herself and her mother by her writing, since they had both been deserted by her father M. P. Kavanagh, a fringe literary figure. When Charlotte met her in her "poor but clean and neat little lodging" she found a figure even tinier than herself, with "a large head and (at first sight) a strange face," and she found her a "poor little feeble, intelligent, cordial thing" who "wastes her brain to gain a living" (to EN, 12 June 1850). Of Kavanagh's novels, Charlotte seems most to have admired the first she read, *Madeleine* (1848). *Nathalie* is sometimes said to have influenced *Villette*, begun in the year Charlotte read it (1851), but *Daisy Burns* (1853) seemed to her full of "tawdry deformities" (to WSW, 9 Mar 1853). Of Kavanagh's non-fiction, she read *The Women of Christianity*. Kavanagh's fiction was moderately popular and profitable, though Mrs Oliphant in 1855 complained that she did "little else than repeat" a pattern in which conflict between a man and a woman leads to love – a pattern which she finds too in Charlotte Brontë and Mrs Gaskell, where "love itself, always in a fury, often [looks] exceedingly like hatred" ("Modern Novelists – Great and Small" in *Blackwood's Magazine*, May 1855). After the death of her mother Kavanagh lived in France, dying in Nice. She was the victim of one of Newby's usual tricks when her father's novel *The Hobbies* (1857) was described on the title page as "edited" by his daughter Julia.

Kaye, Jack (d. 1848): astrologer, known according to the *Leeds Intelligencer* as "The Wise Man of Haworth" (30 Jan 1848). Leyland records that Branwell and Grundy, on visits to Haworth, would "pay curious visits to the old fortune-teller, with the curates" (v. 1, ch. 17).

Kay-Shuttleworth, Sir James Phillips, 1st Baronet (1804–77):

physician, educationalist, and author. Born James Phillips Kay in Rochdale, he studied medicine at Edinburgh University, and practiced for a time as a doctor. He later found his métier as an administrator, first of the Poor Law in East Anglia, later as secretary to the Privy Council's Committee on Education. For this work, which laid the foundations for a national system of free education, and for his founding of a training college for teachers in Battersea, he is regarded as one of the pioneering fathers of state education. The demanding nature of the work, however, led to a breakdown in health in 1848–9, which resulted in his retirement, and the award of a baronetcy.

It was in the next year, 1850, that he became one of the first tourists to Brontë country – one of those who "are beginning to come boring to Haworth," as Charlotte put it. In the same letter (to EN, 11 Mar 1850?) she described her first reactions to him: "Sir James is very courtly, fine-looking; I wish he may be as sincere as he is polished. He shows his white teeth with too frequent a smile; but I will not prejudge him." This initial reaction set the tone for later descriptions of him: she conceded his public good works and general benevolence, but she found him intrusive and insensitive, unable to understand her shyness, and the limits it imposed on what she could do. That same year, and reluctantly, she visited him twice, first at Gawthorpe Hall, near Burnley, later at Briery Close, by Lake Windermere, where she met Elizabeth Gaskell for the first time. The fact that neither woman greatly liked her host must have speeded their intimacy. In her account of the visit (in an unpublished letter to W. S. Williams 27 Aug 1850), Charlotte sighed, "If I could only have dropped unseen out of the carriage and gone away by myself," and confessed that during Sir James's lectures on the faults of the artist class, "all the while vagrant artist instincts were busy in the mind of his listener."

She visited him again only once, briefly, with her husband in January 1855, but he paid frequent and not always welcome attentions to her when she was in London. Whether she was aware of his domestic situation (see next entry) is unclear. He visited her and the Rev. Arthur Bell Nicholls in Haworth (letter to EN, 14 Nov 1854) to offer the latter the living of Padiham, near Gawthorpe, but Mr Brontë's health prevented Nicholls accepting it. After Charlotte's death Sir James was partly instrumental in securing the publication of *The Professor*.

In later life he was High Sheriff of Lancashire, and was active during the cotton famine of 1861–5. He also published two novels of Lancashire life, *Scarsdale* and *Ribblesdale*, which John Sutherland (1988) describes as "rich in local colour and topography."

To the biography of him by Frank Smith (*The Life of Sir James Kay-Shuttleworth*, 1923), his son contributed a memoir of his private character which is of great interest. Some details seem to the modern reader to give grounds for Charlotte Brontë's and Mrs Gaskell's less than reverent attitude to him. There is an excellent modern biography by R. J. K. Selleck (1994).

Kay-Shuttleworth, Janet, Lady (1817–72):

Only daughter of Robert Shuttleworth of Gawthorpe Hall, who died in 1818. She married James Kay (see preceding entry) in 1842, when he added her name to his. She accompanied Sir James on his first visit to Haworth, and was Charlotte Brontë's hostess first at Gawthorpe, then at Briery Close later in the same year, 1850. Charlotte describes her as one who had "frankness, good-humour and activity" (to EN, 19 Mar 1850), though she was in fact ill during most of the second visit.

In 1853 she left England for the Continent, where she spent much of her later life, apparently in search of health, but also due to the increasing influence of the German-Polish governess, Miss Poplawska, whom Charlotte Brontë met on her visit to Gawthorpe. This lady, whom Charlotte found "quiet, well-instructed, interesting," and whom she liked "better than anything else in the house" (to EN, 19 Mar 1850), exerted an "almost hypnotic" influence on Lady Shuttleworth, according to her son, the first Lord Shuttleworth, and was determined to keep her away from her husband, whom Miss Poplawska hated. No awareness of this interesting situation is to be found in the letters of Charlotte Brontë, or indeed in those of Elizabeth Gaskell. The son implies that there was some kind of reconciliation, presumably epistolary or verbal, shortly before his mother's death in 1872.

See also Gawthorpe Hall; Poplawska, Rosa

Keble, John (1792–1866): poet, clergyman, and scholar, pillar of the Puseyite wing of the Church of England. Ellen Nussey records that Charlotte came to admire his *The Christian Year*, and "could not endure to hear any one recite" the poems in it "who did not feel their beauty & meaning" (see CBL, v. 1, p. 609).

Keeldar, Charles Cave: apparently the name of Shirley Keeldar's father (see ch. 21 of *Shirley*).

Keeldar, Shirley: the mistress of Fieldhead, and one of the two heroines of *Shirley*. Her first name was at that time a family name, not a girl's first name – it was that novel and its heroine that made it popular.

Shirley is the active, opinionated, decisive heroine, and it is her independent state that allows her to be so. She takes a position in the local society that would normally be a man's, and she rejoices in her ability to argue with the men, take steps to alleviate poverty, make decisions for herself. She is an attractive character, never more so than in her tussle, physical and intellectual, with Mr Donne (in ch. 15). She does not, however, exert any great influence on the social areas of the story, in particular the struggle between the mill-owners and workers. The account of the love between her and Louis Moore, which takes over the last section of the novel, has generally been found to be weak.

Mrs Gaskell reported that Shirley was a picture of Emily Brontë "had she been placed in health and prosperity." Most critics and commentators, including Mrs Gaskell herself, have been dissatisfied with this attribution, and feel it is a sentimentalized portrait, in which much of what made Emily Brontë individual has been left out.

Keeper (ca 1837–51): dog officially owned by Patrick, but unofficially Emily's. He was probably acquired between June 1837 (not mentioned in Emily and Anne's

diary note) and April 1838, when he was painted by Emily. Variously described as a "tawny bull-dog" (ECG, *Life*, v. 1, ch. 12), "half mastiff, half bull-dog" (ECG to an unknown correspondent, late September 1853) and a "conglomerate, combining every species of English caninity from the turnspit to the sheepdog, with a strain of Haworth originality superadded" (John Stores Smith in *Freelance*, 14 Mar 1868). Alexander and Sellars's guess of "labrador and mastiff cross-breed" seems to hit the mark (AOTB, p. 380). Charlotte described him as "grim as ever" (to EN, 1 July 1841), and as a "devouring flame" when food was in question (to EJB, 1 Oct 1843). As Shirley's Tartar he is described as stretched beside his mistress, her hand resting on him "because if she takes it away he groans and is discontented" (ch. 22).

Many of the stories about Emily also include Keeper: the story of her separating Keeper and another powerful dog fighting in Church Lane by scattering pepper over their noses while the male population of Haworth ("other animals, who thought themselves men," as John Greenwood described them) stood by watching; the story of her pummeling Keeper's head and eyes to teach him not to lie on the Parsonage beds (uncharacteristic of the Brontës' treatment of animals, but well-attested). The dog attended Emily's funeral, and howled for many days afterwards outside her little bedroom. Mrs Gaskell records him as "falling into old age after her death" (ECG, *Life*, v. 2, ch. 10), and Charlotte was terribly touched when she returned to the Parsonage after Anne's death that the dogs should welcome her, the least animal-orientated of the Brontës, in a "strange, heart-touching way – I am certain they thought that, as I was returned, my Sisters were not far behind" (to WSW, 25 June 1849). Keeper "went gently to sleep" in December 1851, and Charlotte was glad, because "people kept hinting that he ought to be put away which neither Papa nor I liked to think of" (to EN, 8 Dec 1851). Emily painted him in the well-known "Keeper – from life," and in "Keeper, Flossy and Tiger," which has disappeared.

Keighley:
"Keighley is a small town four miles from here" recorded Charlotte in almost the earliest of her surviving childhood writings ("The History of the Year"), while Branwell in December 1830, noting down the history of his sets of soldiers, wrote that "I got from Keighley another set," after his first set from Bradford and before the famous set his father brought back from Leeds for him. These early references point to Keighley's place in the Brontës' lives: it was the nearest town of any importance, and they walked there for things that could not be procured in Haworth, whether it was newspapers, books, toys, or items of clothing. Later they would go there to lectures (but this seems to have been a special treat), and after the arrival of the railway to the town Charlotte's letters are peppered with train times, journey times, and arrangements for transporting visitors those last four miles to Haworth.

Doubtless there were social contacts – with the vicar's family, the Durys, and other clergy, and perhaps also with the Keighley Greenwoods. The most feeling reference to the place in Charlotte's letters is her complaint that "the gossiping inquisitiveness of small towns is rife in Keighley," which is why the people there were "sadly puzzled to guess why I never visit" (to WSW, 1 Oct 1849?), suggesting that what past visiting there was had ceased as rumors of her authorship had spread.

Useful though Keighley was to the Brontës, particularly its libraries (the Mechanics' Institute one, and at least one circulating library), there is no feeling of any affection for the place in any of the Brontës' letters or personal documents, and perhaps for this reason it has never become a place for sentimental exploration by Brontë lovers. Very little, indeed, exists that they would have known. The Devonshire Arms was until recently a disco-pub called The Grinning Rat, now changed to the Korner Bar, and the present parish church was built in the 1840s.

Keighley Mechanics' Institute: the movement to found mechanics' institutes was an early nineteenth-century phenomenon that quite soon became predominantly middle-class. Keighley's was founded in 1825, and Patrick joined in 1833. The library was strong on theology and science, but the young Brontës could also find there history, biography, and poetry, which would be more to their taste, as well as fiction, including the novels of Walter Scott and the eighteenth-century novelists for whom Charlotte conceived such an aversion. Lectures were also part of the education program of the institutes: an early speaker at Keighley was Edward Baines Jr, whose 1830 lecture on "The Moral Effects of Unrestricted Commerce" was listened to by 700 people "with almost breathless silence" (*Leeds Intelligencer*, 4 Mar 1830). Later lectures included William Weightman defending the study of the classics and Patrick Brontë on "The Influence of Circumstances," which must have given him plenty of scope.

Kelly (first name unknown): a "very intelligent man," probably a servant of the Nusseys, who drove Charlotte back to Haworth after her stay at Rydings in February 1835. He lightened Charlotte's melancholy with tales of his life as a sailor, and she commented on his excellent "flow of language" (to EN, 13 Mar 1835).

Kendal: town in Westmoreland (now Cumbria) where Branwell took "a half-year's farewell of old friend whisky" with "a party of gentlemen at the Royal Hotel" (BB to John Brown, 15 Mar 1840). He was on his way to his tutoring post in Broughton-in-Furness. As no trace has been found of a Royal Hotel in Kendal, it has been suggested that Branwell's memory was whiskey-hazed, and he in fact spent the night at Kirkby Lonsdale, where there was and is a Royal Hotel.

Kennedy, Rev. W. J.: secretary to the National Society, to whom Patrick addressed more than 20 letters, many of them long and detailed, between November 1843 and April 1845. Arthur Bell Nicholls, who arrived in Haworth in May of that year, then took over the correspondence from the now near-blind Patrick.

Kenneth, Mr (no first name given): the Gimmerton doctor who is called in from time to time throughout the time-span covered by the action of *Wuthering Heights*. Though he makes frequent appearances, Emily does not bother to endow him with any character to speak of.

Kilkee: town in Co. Clare visited by Charlotte and her husband on their honeymoon tour. Though Charlotte had her first experience of "Irish negligence" here, the natural compensations were enormous: "a wild, iron-bound coast – with such an ocean-view as I had not yet seen – and such battling of waves with rocks as I had never imagined" (letters to Catherine Wooler and Catherine Winkworth, 18 July and 27 July 1854).

Killiner, Henry: porter at Luddenden Foot. A drinking companion of Branwell's, it was his carelessness or dishonesty with the account books which led to Branwell's sacking in 1842, since they were his responsibility.

King, Mrs (no first name given): William Crimsworth's landlady in *The Professor* (see ch. 3), who finds him (a typical Charlotte touch) quieter and steadier than any of the curates she has had as lodgers.

King of Labassecour: seen by Lucy Snowe at the concert in ch. 20 of *Villette*. Lucy Snowe conjectures him to be a "nervous, melancholy man," and a prey to hypochondria. He is based on Leopold I, cousin by marriage, uncle, and confidant of Queen Victoria, who had briefly been married to Princess Charlotte, daughter of the Prince Regent. He was elected King of the Belgians in 1830. The chapter is based on a concert which Charlotte presumably herself attended on 10 December 1843.

King's Arms: pub in Haworth which on occasion served as a mortuary for bodies on which inquests were held, and for the Court Baron (a manorial court attended by tenants of the lord of the manor for the regulation of local affairs) presided over by Mrs Ferrand. The pub also owned the barn opposite the Parsonage seen in many early photographs.

Kingsley, Charles (1819–75): novelist, clergyman, and early Christian Socialist. He wrote one of the most interesting and balanced reviews of *Tenant*, but conceived a notion, from the opening of *Shirley*, that Charlotte was "a person who liked coarseness." When he had read, and been greatly moved by, the *Life*, he wrote to Mrs Gaskell how thankful he was he had never expressed this misconception in print (14 May 1857). Charlotte for her part greatly admired his *The Saint's Tragedy*, and wrote a long critique of it to Mrs Gaskell (6 Aug 1851).

Kingston, Elizabeth Jane (1808–78): niece of Maria and Elizabeth Branwell, daughter of their sister Jane and her scapegrace Methodist husband John Kingston, whom she left when Elizabeth Jane was a baby. She was bequeathed one-fourth of Elizabeth Branwell's money, as were all three of the Brontë sisters, the sum amounting to around £300 each. Charlotte wrote their co-heiress friendly and concerned letters in 1846, and Patrick apparently wrote to her as late as 1859. She died in poverty.

Kint (no first name given): one of two ushers at M. Pelet's school in *The Professor*, despised and tyrannized over by him (see ch. 11).

Kint, Madame (no first name given): mother of Mme Beck in *Villette*, mentioned in ch. 22.

Kint, Victor: brother of Mme Beck in *Villette*, who helps Lucy Snowe look for her lost letter in ch. 22, and reappears in the fête scene (ch. 38).

Kipping House: fine Restoration house in Thornton, owned by the Firth family. It and the attached farm had 23 acres of land "in a high state of cultivation" (*Leeds Intelligencer*, 30 Oct 1823), and fine gardens between the house and the river. The growing young Brontë family were entertained here by the Firths often during their Thornton years, and for this reason Patrick's later visit there, after Elizabeth Firth's marriage, was a melancholy one – he "could not feel comfortable, and I s[oo]n departed, intending, never to call again" (to Elizabeth Franks, 28 Apr 1831). The house still stands.

Kirby, Isaac: dealer in ales, living at 2 Fountain Street, Bradford. Branwell lodged with him and his wife from summer 1838 to about February 1839, while trying to make a career as a portrait painter. He was particularly fond of one of the two Kirby children, whose prattle enchanted him. He was less fond of Mrs Kirby, and when he painted her he produced one of his most vivid works, verging on caricature, and suggesting that if he had any artistic future it would have been in the Gilray or Cruikshank tradition. After he left Bradford he became involved in a dispute with Mrs Kirby about his failure to varnish the picture: "Mrs Kirby's name is an eyesore to me," he wrote in exasperation to J. H. Thompson (24 Aug 1839).

Kirkcudbright: Scottish town where Charlotte stayed one night in August 1853 on her abortive trip to Scotland with Joe and Amelia Taylor and their troublesome baby. She was particularly struck by the scenery between it and Dumfries – "richly cultivated, and well-wooded" (to MW, 30 Aug 1853).

Kirklees Hall: an old, rambling country mansion, in the Brontës' time owned by the Armytage family, not far from Hartshead church. In its grounds were the remains of a convent, and legends of Robin Hood attached themselves to the place. Ellen Nussey identified this as the Nunnely Priory of *Shirley*.

Kirk Smeaton: near Pontefract. Arthur Bell Nicholls was curate here for nine months (August 53–June 54) during the dispute with Patrick about his desire to marry Charlotte.

Kirkstall Abbey, Leeds: at the time one of the most famous of ruined medieval monasteries. It was certainly visited by Patrick and Maria during their courtship, though there is no evidence they got engaged there, as is often stated. An oil painting of the

Abbey is listed in the bill of sale for the Parsonage effects after Patrick's death. Charlotte's three pictures of the place may all have been versions of this or of some hitherto-unidentified engraving, rather than from life. One was exhibited at the Royal Northern Society for the Encouragement of the Fine Arts exhibition in Leeds in 1834.

Knoll, The: home in Ambleside of Harriet Martineau, where Charlotte stayed in December 1850. Her bedroom was apparently the one over the dining room, and she described the house as "arranged at all points with admirable neatness and comfort" (to EN, 18 Dec 1850).

Knowles, James Sheridan (1784–1862): prolific dramatist, novelist, and lecturer on drama, described overenthusiastically by the *Leeds Intelligencer* as "The Shakespeare of our times" (27 Apr 1844). He sent Charlotte a copy of his *George Lovel*, one of two novels he wrote after undergoing a religious conversion. Charlotte wrote to W. S. Williams asking for personal details: "do you know anything about him as a man?" (22 Feb 1850).

Knox, Mary: wife of Mary Taylor's brother Waring, who married her in New Zealand. She was the daughter of a doctor – "an idle fool" according to Ellen Taylor (to CB, Aug 1850) – and niece to Robert Knox (1791–1862), author of *The Races of Men*, a Scottish anatomist who was involved in the trials of Burke and Hare. Mary Taylor was pessimistic about the marriage of Mary and Waring.

Koslow, Aurelia: a pupil at Mlle Reuter's school in *The Professor*, analyzed in ch. 12. She is described as "a half-breed," that is, she is part-German, part-Russian. She is slovenly and ignorant, with a battery of devices to get attention for herself.

K. T.: an admirer of Charlotte's novels, who corresponded with her under his initials only. She was pleased with his critique of *Shirley*, and told him he had "truer feelings and more delicate perceptions than ordinary" (6 Dec 1850), and she was probably correct when she guessed him to be an artist and an Irishman (the clue for the latter guess perhaps being his address at "Miss Kelly's, 153, Fleet St.").

L

Labassecour: the name by which Charlotte characterizes, and ridicules, Belgium in *Villette*. It ("the farmyard") is a name singularly inappropriate for a country predominantly urban, of which Charlotte knew well only its capital city. All other names are reductive or sneering (Villette: little town, Duc de Dindonneau: turkeycock) and she joins Thackeray, but not Mrs Trollope, in condescending to the country for being small and for having no glorious history behind it. Still more objectionably, she endows the inhabitants with characteristics that are uniformly mean or degraded. When Lucy goes to an art exhibition it is to a modern exhibition that could be sniggered at, rather than pictures in the great Flemish tradition which could not. That this "little town" had also a vigorous social and artistic life she cannot entirely conceal, since she sets chapters at a concert and at the performance of the actress Rachel, though even there she seizes on every opportunity to mock. It is a typical and sad performance, one such as made English travelers notorious on the Continent. By the time she came to write *Villette* her identity was pretty widely known, and there must have been many to wonder what qualifications this reclusive woman from Haworth had to indulge in such unremitting denigration of a country and people she had lived among for two years.
See also Belgium; Heger; *Villette*

Lady's Magazine: copies of this periodical probably came with Maria Branwell from Penzance, suffering shipwreck in the process. Charlotte told Hartley Coleridge that these treasures, "discoloured with brine" were read "as a treat on holiday afternoons or by stealth when I should have been minding my lessons" (10 Dec 1840). She also recorded that Aunt Branwell preferred the fiction in it to the "trash" that was modern literature, but also that her father burnt them because they "contained foolish love-stories." This apparently uncharacteristic action of Patrick's is understandable to Tom Winnifrith, since *Ethelinde*, which Charlotte mentions, concerns a woman who bears two children by a man whose wife has gone mad, suggesting that Patrick's incendiarism came too late (Winnifrith, 1973, pp. 85–6). The magazine began publication in 1770, specialized in Gothic fiction published serially, and was subtitled "Entertaining Companion for the Fair Sex."

La Malle (no first name given): pupil at Mme Beck's school in *Villette* (ch. 28).

Lamartine, Alphonse De (1790–1869): French poet whose "*L'infini*" (the fourth of his *Harmonies Poétiques et Religieuses*) was recommended reading for Charlotte in Brussels, and used by her in her *devoir* "*L'immensité de Dieu.*" She was greatly interested in his political involvement after the 1848 revolution, but concluded that there were "too few" Lamartines in France for him to be an effective politician (to WSW, 29 Mar 1848).

Lamb, Charles (1775–1834) and Mary (1764–1847): essayist, critic, and poet, and his sister, with whom he collaborated on *Tales from Shakespeare* and also *Mrs Leicester's School*, a favorite book of Margaret Wooler's. Charlotte wrote about the "touching" history of their devotion to each other to Miss Wooler and W. S. Williams in 1848. The story of Mary's periodic fits of murderous madness (in one of which she killed her mother by stabbing her through the heart) seems to have been new to her then, so it could not have contributed to her very different maniac in *Jane Eyre*.

Landseer, Sir Edwin Henry (1802–73): immensely popular artist, the subject of a poem by Branwell: "On Landseer's Painting 'The Shepherd's Chief Mourner.'" Charlotte copied his "Hours of Innocence" in one of her earliest watercolors. His intensely human animals were calculated to appeal to the Brontës. Charlotte was also naturally much taken with his picture of Wellington on the field of Waterloo, which she saw at the Royal Academy in 1850.

Langweilig, Mr (no first name given): German Moravian minister, with a name suggestive of long-windedness, whose talk at the Bible Society Meeting sends Mr Sykes to sleep (see *Shirley* ch. 7).

Lannoy, Hortense: pupil in the first class at the Pensionnat Heger of whom Charlotte gives a particularly unpleasant account: her ears are "red as raw beef," her face was "black as a 'blue-piled thunder-loft'" (a quotation she later uses in *Jane Eyre*) and she feels she needs the services of "a person qualified to cast out a devil" (to EJB, 29 May 1843).

Lascelles, Rev. Edward: vicar of Little Ouseburn, and apparently a high-handed and erratic pastor. He may have been the original of Mr Hatfield in *Agnes Grey*, though with Anne's fiction such identifications have to be treated with caution. Early in Anne's stay with the Robinsons he married the eldest daughter of his predecessor the Rev.

Anthony Watson (Dec 1841) – possibly suggesting the "elderly spinster" Mr Hatfield married, "weighing her heavy purse against her faded charms" (*Agnes Grey*, ch. 22).

Lascelles Hall: home of Amelia Walker, about two miles from Huddersfield. Charlotte and Anne spent a day there during their week-long 1836 stay with Mrs Franks, and Charlotte paid a longer visit in January 1839 – "O dear! I wish the visit were well over" she wrote to Ellen Nussey (20 Jan 1839). The Old Hall, home of the Walkers, was sixteenth century, with Georgian additions. The *Leeds Intelligencer*, advertising it for letting in 1846, mentioned "Lofty bed rooms, water closets . . . and excellent cellars" (30 May 1846). It is still standing.

"Last Sketch, The": title given to what is now usually called "Emma," Charlotte's last sketch for the opening of a novel, when it was published with a fine introduction by Thackeray in his periodical *Cornhill Magazine*. Charlotte's widower said that Thackeray's remarks "are greatly admired in this neighbourhood" (to GS, 11 Apr 1860).

La Trobe, James (1802–97): a pastor, later Bishop, of the Moravian Church, who was summoned to visit Anne when she lay ill at Roe Head School in 1837. Unlike Margaret Wooler, La Trobe had no doubts about the seriousness of Anne's illness ("her life hung on a slender thread" he later wrote to William Scruton), and he paid her several visits, reading the Gospels with her ("The words of Jesus opened her ear to my words"), and discussing her religious doubts and fears. It is generally agreed that a version of Calvinism was rife in the Dewsbury and Mirfield parishes, and La Trobe's doctrines, pointing the way to, if not actually embracing, a belief in universal salvation, was to be influential on Anne for the rest of her life, and in her writings. See Margaret Connor, "The Rescue: James La Trobe and Anne Brontë" (BST, v. 24, pt 1, 1999).

Laury, Mina *see* "Mina Laury"

Law Hill: house with adjacent farm, built high up to the east of Halifax in Southowram. Jack Sharp, whose story contributed to *Wuthering Heights*, built this house for himself, and came here to continue his inglorious career after being forced out of Waterclough Hall. Emily came here in 1838, to teach in a school run by Miss Elizabeth Patchett. The school, much larger than Roe Head, had about 40 pupils, of whom 20 were boarders. These were aged between 11 and 15, but it may be there were younger children among the day girls, and these may have been the ones Emily taught. Miss Patchett had turned an old warehouse in the adjacent court into the schoolroom, apparently with a bedroom overhead for the boarding pupils. Whether Emily slept with them or in the main house is unclear.

Ellis Chadwick (1914) has the fullest account of Emily's time there, including many stories familiar from later biographies, for example, the story of her preference for the house-dog over her pupils. It was Chadwick who first insisted, apparently against much of the evidence, that Emily must have been there in the winter of 1838–9, relying on the evidence of one of her pupils. This dating has now been confirmed by Edward Chitham, and it is generally accepted that Emily taught here September 1838 to March/April 1839 (Chitham and Winnifrith, 1983, pp. 22–9).

See also High Sunderland Hall; Sharp, Jack

Lawrence, Frederick: brother of Helen Huntingdon in *The Tenant of Wildfell Hall*. His family had formerly lived in Wildfell Hall, but they moved some time before the action starts, and he is, when the story opens, squire of Woodford Hall. He is a gentlemanly, cautious man, but somewhat shy and reserved, perhaps because he was brought up by a drunken father. His character is analyzed in ch. 4. Towards the end of the book he marries Esther Hargrave.

Leader, The: journal conducted by G. H. Lewes and Thornton Hunt, established in 1850, when Charlotte declined an invitation to be one of its team of writers. Charlotte wrote surprisingly favorably of the journal, particularly of the "spirit of fairness and courtesy in which it is on the whole conducted" (to James Taylor, 15 Jan 1851), but rejected some of its principles, doubtless as being too radical and unorthodox. In one heavily satirical letter to Lewes she affected to detect an inclination towards Catholicism in it "which will kindle the glow of holy expectation in the heart of Cardinal Archbishop Wiseman" (23 Nov 1850). *The Leader* was at one with more conservative journals in condemning in *Wuthering Heights* and *Tenant* "the coarseness apparently of violent and uncultivated men," but it admired *Villette* enormously, Lewes's review exclaiming: "In Passion and Power – those noble twins of Genius – Currer Bell has no living rival, except George Sand" (12 Feb 1853).

"Leaf from an Unopened Volume, A": futuristic Glasstown story, written in early 1834. Though the events are set in 1858 they are written from a perspective of much later, when the "overgrown dominion" of Adrian's empire has been overtaken by "desolation," and the splendor of Northangerland House has been reduced to "roofless desolate decay," part of the "wide waste of ruins that now remain to tell us what Adrianopolis once was" (EW, v. 2, pt 1, pp. 326, 336). The matter of the story is a familiar mix of festering hatreds, concealed paternities, and indescribable splendor, but the splendor is already undercut by the ferocious mutual ill-will of Adrian's unpromising sons. Douro himself is middle-aged in this story, but still magnificent, brilliant, and terrifying. He is also near-invincible in war, having just achieved his lifelong ambition of wiping out the Ashantees and executing Quashia, who is treated by the narrator as a noble savage. The combination of the disunity of the younger generation and Adrian's unqualified autocracy are underlined by peeps into the future, where the royal family of Angria are to meet the fate of the Bourbons in France.

Leah (no surname given): servant at Thornfield, and an intimate of Grace Poole (*Jane Eyre*, v. 1, ch. 11 etc).

Leaven, Jane: sister of Bobby, presumably named after Jane Eyre.

Leaven, Robert (Bobby): son of Bessie and Robert. He is "a little fellow of three years old" (ch. 10) at the time Jane Eyre leaves Lowood, and is seen playing quietly with his sister when Jane returned to Gateshead.

Leaven, Robert: coachman at Gateshead. He marries Bessie Lee while Jane Eyre is at Lowood, and takes Jane back to Gateshead to Mrs Reed's deathbed. Not otherwise characterized.

Lebel, Joachim-Joseph: director of the boys' boarding section of the Athénée Royal. French-born, and a refugee from the July Revolution of 1830, he is believed to be the original of M. Pelet in *The Professor*, also a Frenchman.

Ledru, Léonie: pupil at Mlle Reuter's school in *The Professor*. A sharp, quick-witted creature, unlike most of the other pupils. Crimsworth suggests that if she had been a boy she would have been the archetype of the unprincipled attorney. Analyzed in ch. 14.

Ledru, Monsieur (no first name given): music teacher at Mlle Reuter's school in *The Professor*, mentioned in ch. 9. It is implied he is not to be trusted with young girls.

Lee, Bessie, later Leaven: nursemaid at Mrs Reed's home, Gateshead. Jane prefers her to anyone else at Gateshead, though she has a hasty temper and "indifferent ideas of principle and justice" (ch. 4). She seems a woman of impulse, and constricted by the family situation at Gateshead, but she is as often pleasant and gay as sharp, and she can tell a story well, a trait Jane appreciates. Her later appearances in the story confirm her sturdy regard for Jane.

Lee, Esther (?1785–1848): the Buckworths' housekeeper in Dewsbury mentioned in Patrick's letter-poem "The Dog Tweed's Letter to his Mistress."

Leeds: the city was a fairly frequent place of resort for the Brontës, though nothing remains that we know they visited. Patrick was in the town during his courtship and "on June the 5th AD 1826" he bought Branwell a replacement set of soldiers there ("History of the Young Men," WPBB, v. 1, p. 138). Charlotte exhibited her pictures of Bolton and Kirkstall Abbeys at the Fine Arts exhibition of 1834, and very possibly visited it (Leyland implies that she and Branwell did, probably with their father). Branwell probably visited Leeds to take painting lessons from William Robinson, and with the coming of the railways it was much more accessible, as well as a place of waiting in transit to elsewhere. Anne and Charlotte took the night train to London from there, and all Charlotte's later journeys started from Leeds. Here she came to visit her dentist, being very conscious of her poor teeth, and special purchases were made here,

Colour plate 1: Anne Brontë by Charlotte. Watercolor picture of the 14-year-old Anne, one of two portraits painted of her youngest sister in girlhood by Charlotte.

Colour plate 2: Hermit, by Branwell. Watercolor by Branwell, dated 1830. Probably based on pictures of saints he had seen, but giving a strong impression, as does his writing of the period, of why he was considered at that time the most gifted of the family.

Colour plate 3: Image of Charlotte, about 1843. This newly discovered chalk drawing of Charlotte may be the portrait painted by Mary Dixon in Brussels during Charlotte's second stay at the Pensionnat Heger.

Colour plate 4: Woman in Leopard Fur, by Charlotte. Watercolor of a typical Charlotte woman, painted around the time she was writing "Caroline Vernon" (October 1839).

Colour plate 5: Emily, from the Gun Group. This picture of Emily, torn by Mr Nicholls from a group portrait known as the Gun Group (Branwell carries a gun), is generally agreed to be one of Branwell's most sensitive paintings.

Colour plate 6: H. Warren, Halifax from Beacon Hill. Picture of the town, painted about 1860, showing the rapid inroads of industrialism during the Brontës' lifetime.

Colour plate 7: M. and Mme Heger and their family, probably painted about three years after Charlotte's return to England.

Colour plate 8: Nero, by Emily. One of Emily's pictures from life. This watercolor was painted while Nero was a resident at the Parsonage as mentioned in the diary note of 1841. By the next diary note he had been "given away," probably by Aunt Branwell, while Emily was in Brussels.

Colour plate 9: The Parsonage, the home of the Brontës, including the Wade extension to the right, built in the 1870s. On the right of the picture is the Sunday School.

Colour plate 10: Moorland scene, including Top Withens, one of the possible models for Wuthering Heights, at least in its situation.

including items for her trousseau. The city that Dickens found "a beastly place" and pronounced "Except Preston it is one of the nastiest places I know" (to Mary Dickens, 1 Feb 1867), was for the Brontës useful, if not particularly pleasant.

Leeds Intelligencer: the "most excellent Tory newspaper" (CB, "History of the Year," EW, v. 1, p. 4) which the Brontës read as children, and which Patrick still had read to him at the end of his life (Wemyss Reid, 1877, ch. 12). It was edited for a time (1822–5) by the poet Alaric Watts, but the driving force behind it was the proprietor John Hernaman. It published many letters from Patrick, including those on the Crow Hill bog eruption, and others on the reform of the criminal code, Catholic Emancipation, and the new Poor Law. Branwell probably got his job with Mr Postlethwaite through its advertisement pages, and it published (lifting it from *Fraser's*) Anne's poem "The Narrow Way." It praised *Jane Eyre*'s "faculty of psychological analysis" and its "force and originality." The editors conducted a weekly sparring match with the *Leeds Mercury* not unlike that between the Eatanswill *Independent* and *Gazette* in *Pickwick Papers*.

Leeds Mercury: like the *Intelligencer* a weekly paper, but, unlike its rival, of strong Whig sympathies. Patrick conducted his campaign to free William Nowell (1810) in its columns, and later his letters to the *Intelligencer* also appeared in the *Mercury*. Charlotte was supplied by its editor with back numbers when she was researching the Luddite riots for *Shirley* – perhaps she felt it would take a more sympathetic line than its Tory rival.

See also Baines, Edward

Leeds Railway Companies *see* York and North Midland Railway Company

Leigh, Charles: son of the house where Mrs Barrett is housekeeper in *Villette* (ch. 5).

Leigh, Mrs (no first name given): mother of Charles, a woman who had been "good-looking, but dull" (ch. 5) at school with Lucy Snowe, who now had become, after marriage and motherhood "beautiful and kind-looking." She is one of several characters in *Villette* who achieve a fulfilled life which Lucy feels she cannot hope for.

Leighton, Mr (no first name given): rector of the church near Staningley attended by the Maxwells and Helen in *The Tenant of Wildfell Hall*. He is referred to as "Mr Blatant" (ch. 20) by Huntingdon when he affects to repent and become evangelical during his courtship of Helen.

Leopold I, King of the Belgians (1796–1865): a prince of Saxe-Coburg and Gotha, he was married briefly to Princess Charlotte, the Prince Regent's only child, and he remained in England until elected to the throne of Belgium in 1831, when he modeled his title on that of Louis Philippe, King of the French, whose daughter he married in 1832. He had previously, and uncharacteristically, married an actress, morganatically and briefly. He advised Princess and Queen Victoria for many years on the duties of a constitutional monarch, and brought about her marriage to his nephew Albert. Charlotte saw Queen Victoria on a visit to her uncle, when she "enlivened the sombre court . . . which is usually as gloomy as a conventicle" (to EJB, 1 Oct 1843). She probably saw the royal family at a concert in December 1843, later using the experience to transform them into the ruling family of Labassecour in ch. 20 of *Villette*, in which she endowed the king with her own characteristic hypochondria. Earlier he had appeared in the juvenilia as "a very mean sort of personage, with an appearance of cunning . . . that is very disagreeable" (EW, v. 1, p. 29).

See also Belgium; Brussels; King of Labassecour

Lewes, George Henry (1817–78): critic, biographer, and man of letters.

He greatly admired *Jane Eyre* and *Villette*, but was disappointed by *Shirley*. His review of the last emphasized his personal knowledge of the author, and the fact that she was a woman, which Charlotte resented. The review left Charlotte feeling "cold and sick" (to WSW, 10 Jan 1850), and her feelings about him were always ambiguous. After reading his first novel *Ranthorpe* she wrote to him that "It fills the mind with fresh knowledge. Your experience and your convictions are made the [reader's]" (22 Nov 1847). However, writing to W. S. Williams she wonders why, when he teaches his readers, he makes "his hearers feel as if their business was, not quietly to receive the doctrines propounded, but to combat them?" (26 Apr 1848). She concludes that he has "a touch too much of dogmatism, a dash extra of confidence," and though she was moved by what she fancied as his resemblance to Emily (he was considered a notably ugly man, so this was no compliment) she always felt his treatment of her to be ungentlemanly and self-serving. By the time he and George Eliot began their relationship Charlotte's correspondence with the literary world was effectively over, so we have no comment on the matter.

They met only once, in June 1850, when a foolish remark about their both having written "naughty novels" brought Charlotte's wrath on his head, though the meeting ended in guarded cordiality. It was perhaps to even the score that two months later she described him to W. S. Williams as "a very vexatious and rather naughty little man" (unpublished letter, 27 August 1850). When he reviewed *Villette* he marveled at its "astonishing power and passion" which triumphed over its unconventional story-telling, though again he hinted at Charlotte's personal history when he talked of "a strong mind nurtured in solitude" (*Westminster Review*, April 53). The novel came to have a very special place in his and George Eliot's affections.

Leyland, Francis (1813–94): brother of Branwell's friend Joseph Leyland, and

himself an acquaintance and admirer of the young Brontë. He went into the family's bookselling and printing business, but also had artistic interests of his own, designing the corporate seal for Halifax, and submitting for the approval of the Queen and Prince Albert an elaborate example of his bookbinding, embodying Etruscan motifs.

He married Ann Highley in 1845, but she died young in 1849 (*Leeds Intelligencer*, 3 Nov 1849). When he read Mrs Gaskell's account of Branwell in the *Life* he visited the Parsonage with the store of Branwell's letters and poems he had inherited from his brother, with some idea of publishing them as a corrective to the overdarkened account in the *Life*. Not surprisingly Nicholls and Mr Brontë were against this. The intention of doing justice to his friend's talents remained (he had in the early 1840s probably helped him to get poems published in the *Halifax Guardian*), and he nursed the idea of a biography. When Mary Robinson further blackened Branwell's memory in her slightly hysterical biography of Emily he finally brought the project to fruition in *The Brontë Family, with special reference to Patrick Branwell Brontë*. Since many contemporaries of the Brontës were still living, and Leyland tried to be a conscientious recorder, many familiar stories have their origin here. Ellen Nussey, writing to Mary Robinson about Leyland's review of her book, calls him "most unfair and uninformed in what he says, and illogical in the assumptions he makes," but this is unjust, as is Robinson's claim that he had "absolutely no first-hand knowledge of Branwell" (EN to Mary Robinson, 14 July 1883, Mary Robinson to EN, July 1883). He made good use of his personal knowledge, the close friendship of Branwell and his brother, and his connections with other members of Branwell's artistic circle.

Leyland, Joseph Bentley (1811–51):

noted sculptor and friend of Branwell Brontë. He began his career young, and was exhibiting powerful work in the early 1830s in the North and London. It may be that the young Brontës attended the 1834 exhibition of the Northern Society for the Encouragement of the Fine Arts, where Leyland exhibited his much-admired bust of Satan. He later had success in London, especially with his group of African bloodhounds, before returning to his native Halifax, where his commissions were mainly of an ecclesiastical nature, though he was working on a large group when he died, of dropsy, imprisoned for debt in Manor Gaol, Halifax.

His artistic vision seems to have been impaired by a sort of gigantism: the word "colossal" is used ominously often in accounts of his completed works in newspaper reports, as well as in his brother's account of him in *The Brontë Family*. Even the African bloodhounds group was larger than life-size, though the report of the group in the *Leeds Intelligencer* (17 Dec 1836), with its description of the animals being depicted "as just roused up from sleep . . . and their momentarily suspended actions and eager expression are represented with the animation of Life" suggests a delicacy not entirely subordinated to size. Whether this was a feature of the enormous Satan bust, his Spartacus, and his Thracian falconers is open to question. His use of inferior materials may be a consequence of his devotion to size, but it meant that even in his lifetime many of his works were smashed in transit or were subject to decay. His memorial to Stephen Beckwith, a beautiful work, may still be seen in York Minster, but his journeyman work on church memorials is of no great distinction.

Branwell was instrumental in getting him work of this kind in Haworth, frequently embarrassed by the "gothic ignorance and ill-breeding" (to Joseph Leyland, 29 June 1842) of those commissioning his work. Leyland was also an aspiring poet, and Branwell set great store by his judgment, sending him work in progress. Leyland was strong, handsome, and worldly wise (though a prey for scroungers), and Branwell was always drawn to this type. Art, poetry, and binge drinking drew them together, and made this the strongest and most lasting friendship in Branwell's short life. His distinguished medallion of Branwell may be seen in the Brontë Parsonage Museum.

Lieutenant (other names not given): referred to as Lieutenant Somebody-else, he is a visitor to the Greens at Horton (*Agnes* Grey, ch. 13).

"Life of Alexander Percy, The": a long retrospective narrative of the early events of Northangerland's life, written by Branwell in 1834–5, and incomplete. Born to a father as brutal and untrustworthy as himself, Percy's early promise and talents (including transcendent genius as a pianist) are soon corrupted. When he marries Augusta di Segovia against his father's wishes he is kidnapped away on his orders to the Philosopher's Island, where he founds an atheistical society and through intensive study becomes Senior Wrangler. Back in Wellington's Town he resumes his marriage and his war with his father, and conspires with his wife (in terms reminiscent of *Macbeth*) to kill his father. When not only his father but also his wife are murdered by his creditors, using the malevolent hit-man Robert Sdeath, he is desolate for a time, but is briefly rescued by a marriage to the saintly Mary Henrietta Wharton. Here the manuscript becomes fragmentary.

The chronicle seems an attempt to rid Glasstown of the fanciful and supernatural elements which it had had in its early years. Percy's history becomes a political and social *exemplum* which, in spite of longueurs, is lively, entertaining, and a considerable achievement for an 18-year-old. It is one of the rare longer manuscripts of the juvenilia to concentrate on one figure and his history. Victor Neufeldt's edition of this and the rest of Branwell's literary production is exemplary, but difficult to obtain. A reader's version with a stimulating introduction was published by Robert Collins (1993) as *The Hand of the Arch-Sinner* (it includes "Real Life in Verdopolis").

See also Juvenilia; "Angria and the Angrians"

Life of Charlotte Brontë: the first full-scale Brontë biography, written by Elizabeth Cleghorn Gaskell and published two years after Charlotte's death in 1857. The immediate impulse behind the commissioning of the *Life* was an article in *Sharpe's London Magazine*, which was partly based on letters Mrs Gaskell had written after her first meeting with Charlotte, when she still had in her head inaccurate gossip deriving from the Burnley woman, Martha Wright, who had nursed the Brontës' mother in her last illness. Ellen Nussey pressed on Charlotte's father and widower the need for a corrective account and suggested Mrs Gaskell as the ideal author. After first dismissing the article with laughter, Patrick changed his mind and approached Charlotte's friend, who already had the idea of writing a memoir of Charlotte for her daughters to read.

Once the project was agreed, Mrs Gaskell worked with great speed. She saw over 300 letters from Charlotte to Ellen, and some to Emily and her father. She began to visit people and places Charlotte had known, beginning with her second visit to Haworth, which produced the memorable picture in Chapter 2 of a village apparently on the very edge of civilization. Later she made contact with London friends, with M. Heger (though not Madame) in Brussels, as well as Yorkshire people Charlotte was educated with or counted as friends. Mary Taylor contributed from New Zealand, and some comments of hers on the first edition of the biography were included in the third edition.

It is often alleged against Mrs Gaskell (e.g., by Juliet Barker in BST, v. 21, pt 4, 1994) that she relied too heavily on Ellen and not enough on Patrick and Nicholls who were "the most obvious and most knowledgeable sources for her book." But were they? Nicholls was close to Charlotte only in the last two years of her life, and her father was nearly 80, with a distinctly fallible memory. Surely any biographer would prefer a friend of the subject's own age with a cache of written evidence. Mrs Gaskell may also have realized that the work she was engaged on was very much more ambitious than the simple memoir that had been suggested, though in the event Patrick (but not Nicholls) hailed the scope of the work with surprise and delight when it was published.

The acclaim that greeted the work was soon marred by controversy over her account of the Branwell/Mrs Robinson affair. Mrs Gaskell had warned George Smith, her publisher, of the libelous potential, but he had not demurred at publishing her allegations. When she was forced to withdraw those passages dealing with this matter many people's faith in the veracity of the book was shaken, though before long the passion and affection of her assessment of Charlotte won the day. Undoubtedly, and influenced by her own instinct as well as Ellen's, she highlighted Charlotte's long-suffering and the miseries of her life, elevating her to near sainthood. In the process she blackened the picture and the reputations of Patrick, Branwell, even Emily, as well as Haworth itself. On the other hand she created an unforgettable picture of a woman struggling to realize her creative vision, trying to reconcile the duties she owed to others with those she owed to herself, and striving to find satisfying ways for women in the mid-nineteenth century to use their talents and their ideals.

See also Brontë, Charlotte; Brontë, Patrick; Nussey, Ellen; Taylor, Mary

Lille: city in northern France. Charlotte and Emily for a time changed their plan to attend a school in Brussels to one in Lille. Charlotte, however, regretted the change, perhaps feeling that Brussels would be less provincial, and eventually the Pensionnat Heger in the Belgian capital was chosen. Patrick visited the town on his way home from accompanying them to Brussels.

Linton, Catherine: only child of Edgar Linton and Catherine Earnshaw in *Wuthering Heights*. Motherless from her birth, she grows up charming and willful, using all her childish arts to get her way. Her fascination with Linton Heathcliff is easily explained, since he is the only male of her education and class she has ever known. Her marriage to him (there is no description of how or by whom they were married) puts her and any property she might have claimed entirely in Heathcliff's power, which accounts for the petulant, shrewish creature she has become when Lockwood first meets her. As her relationship with Hareton grows warmer and closer it provides the catalyst for Heathcliff's end, since he sees in them so many reminders of himself and Catherine Earnshaw that he loses his hold on life and his long-meditated revenge. At the end of the novel her marriage to Hareton and removal to Thrushcross Grange are happily anticipated by Nelly. Sanger (1926) puts her birth date at 20 March 1784.

Linton, Edgar: husband of Catherine Earnshaw, father of Catherine Linton and master of Thrushcross Grange in *Wuthering Heights*. As a child he is depicted as spoilt, pettish, and feeble, but Nelly's picture of him as an adult is almost wholly admirable: a loving, tender husband, a good master, a loving, if too indulgent father. In many ways his qualities are "eighteenth century" (he is cool, rational, with a sense of what is proper and what is due to him in a stable social order), as opposed to the more "romantic" qualities of Heathcliff (passionate, rebellious, self-assertive). He dies unable to prevent his entailed estate passing to Linton Heathcliff or (due to his lawyer being bribed by Heathcliff) to secure any personal property for his daughter. Sanger (1926) gives his dates as 1762–1801.

Linton, Isabella: sister of Edgar Linton in *Wuthering Heights*. In her early appearances she is, like him, spoilt and childish. She never matures into the admirable adult he becomes, but her marriage to Heathcliff, a romantic whim based on ignorance of his character and aims, does give her a certain strength and individuality springing from the need to oppose his neglect and mistreatment. When she escapes from the Heights she is pregnant, and she brings up her son – unwisely it would seem by the result – somewhere near London. Sanger (1926) gives her dates as 1765–97.

Linton, Mr (no first name given): father of Edgar and Isabella. It is his dogs who savage Catherine, and we have the impression of one who prides himself on his position as landowner and magistrate, and who disapproves of one such as Hindley who lets the status of himself and his family degenerate. The scene of Cathy's reception at the Grange, and Heathcliff's rejection from it (v. 1, ch. 6) marks the beginning of Catherine's "seduction" from the ways of the Heights to the ways of the Grange.

Linton, Mrs Mary: mother of Edgar and Isabella. She is a conventional woman, shocked at the condition and language of Heathcliff and Catherine under Hindley's rule. Like her husband she dies before the marriage of Edgar and Catherine, from a fever they contract from the latter.

Lisnacreevy, County Down: where Hugh Brunty or Prunty rented a house when Patrick was one year old. The family stayed in the area throughout Patrick's childhood and young manhood.

Lister, Miss: a pupil at Roe Head, much hated by Charlotte, who singled her out for her inability or disinclination to understand what she was taught. Possibly

Harriette Cunliffe Lister, who married W. Clement Drake Esdaile, a barrister, in August 1846.

Little Ouseburn: village close to Thorp Green, where Anne was governess 1840–5. Anne attended the village church and left a pencil drawing of it.

Liverpool: a city much talked about as a holiday venue for all the Brontës in 1839, but for most of them it remained "a sort of castle in the air" (CB to EN, 4 Aug 1839). Branwell, however, took himself off there with some friends, including Hartley Merrall, whom he persuaded to buy the score of Handel's *Samson* and other religious music. He seems to have been there before, in Spring 1835, and went again after the Robinson debacle in July 1845, when he also visited North Wales, in the company of John Brown. It is perhaps as a consequence of Branwell's stories of the city, including the poverty-stricken immigrants who came to its docks, that it became Heathcliff's city of origin, whence he was carried by Mr Earnshaw the 60 miles back to Wuthering Heights.

Lloyd, Mr (no first name given): an apothecary, called in by Mrs Reed for the servants, but also for Jane Eyre, making a distinction with her own children, who were seen by a physician. He is a kindly, probing man who understands Jane's situation at Gateshead and is instrumental in getting her sent away to school.

Lockhart, John Gibson (1794–1854): one of the moving spirits behind *Blackwood's Magazine* in its early days, and later editor of the *Quarterly Review* (1825–53). The savagery of his attacks on Keats and others in what he termed the "Cockney School" of poets raised questions about his judgment. His quarrel with the London editor John Scott culminated in a duel which Lockhart left to his second to fight. Scott was killed, leaving Lockhart with a reputation for opportunism and downright cowardice. He married Sir Walter Scott's daughter Sophia, and later wrote a great biography of him. Scott wrote his *Tales of a Grandfather* for the Lockharts' invalid son Johnny, who died young. Emily chose both father and son as inhabitants of "her" island of Arran in 1825 (CB, "The origin of the Islanders," 12 Mar 1829). Lockhart would not have agreed with his contributor Elizabeth Rigby's notorious review of *Jane Eyre* in the *Quarterly*. Lockhart thought Charlotte "far the cleverest that has written since Austen and Edgeworth were in their prime," though he also thought her, or possibly her creation Jane, "rather a brazen Miss" (letter to Mr and Mrs Hope, 29 Dec 1847). His nickname was "The Scorpion," and it was well earned.

See also Blackwood's Magazine; Hogg, James; *Quarterly Review*; Scott, Walter; Wilson, John

Lockwood, Mr (no first name given): the tenant of Thrushcross Grange, who gives us our first glimpse of Wuthering Heights, and hears the story of the inhabitants of both houses from Nelly Dean. A superficial observer, the fact that he gets so many things wrong on his first two visits to the Heights emphasizes his status as outsider and gives a kind of comedy to his observations. He claims with some pride an unhappy love affair in the past, but his view of himself as a misanthropist is as wide of the mark as his judgment of Heathcliff ("His reserve springs from an aversion to showy displays of feeling" (ch. 10) etc). In the course of the book he imagines an increasingly tender relationship with the younger Catherine, but the reader is never in doubt that this is a further piece of self-deception. In narrative theory he provides a superb example of the "unreliable narrator."

London: London for the young Brontës represented a cornucopia of art and a vibrant center of literary and political activity. When they came to create Verdopolis and Adrianopolis the principal buildings were splendid, and touched by fairy-tale and the architectural imaginings of John Martin. But alongside the unimaginably grand palaces and public buildings was a warren of inns, publishing houses, offices, and booksellers which was far closer to the realities of London life. Branwell made himself the local expert on the capital by means of maps, engravings, and guide books, but his knowledge was a mixture of reality and dream, and he probably never saw the city itself (perhaps funking the chance to see it, knowing it could never live up to its existence in his imagination).

When Charlotte and Emily first saw it, as tourists, they indulged in an orgy of culture-vulturing, as Mary Taylor described to Mrs Gaskell: "she seemed to think our business was . . . to see all the pictures and statues we could. She knew the artists, and knew where other productions of theirs were to be found" (EGG, *Life*, 3rd ed., ch. 11). It seems likely that similar impulses drove them when in Brussels to sample whatever they could afford to of the cultural life of that city too.

The next visit to London that was more than a mere passing through was that taken by Charlotte and Anne in July 1848 to correct the rumors put around by Newby that all the Bell novels were the product of one man. The impulse was typically honest, but seems not to have been shared by Emily. It may be, too, that Charlotte rebelled at having novels she basically disliked attributed to her. The visit clearly exhausted both women, and they were not helped by George Smith's generous impulse to show as much of London life as he could to these two country mice. It would be hard to imagine an opera less likely to appeal to them than *The Barber of Seville*, but the *Barber* was on, and the *Barber* it was.

The other visits to London were by Charlotte alone, after the year of deaths. Her activities there mingled seeing sights with being seen. Her greatest pleasure seems to have sprung from seeing pictures, including ones in private collections, and, at least in the early visits, from being mothered by Mrs Smith. The first visit of her bereavement (November/December 1849) was notable for her meeting with Thackeray and a dinner for critics, whom she did not admire. The second (May/June 1850) was marked by her portrait being painted by Richmond, the excruciating party at Thackeray's, and the sight of her childhood and adult hero, the Duke of Wellington. The visit of the next year (May/June 1851) was dominated in a less than pleasant way by the Great Exhibition, but it also saw her enjoying, without altogether approving of, Thackeray's lectures on the English humorists, and a visit to a phrenologist. The last visit, in January 1853, occurred when she was becoming alienated from the Smiths, and saw her concentrating on "rather the *real* than the *decorative* side of Life" (to EN, 19 Jan 1853), perhaps as a sort of silent criticism of some of the Smiths' arrangements for the earlier visits (she records Mrs Smith's amazement at her tastes in the same letter, but says she took no notice).

It would be wrong to say that Charlotte was unimpressed by London on her visits, but she does meticulously record her embarrassments and disillusions along with the pleasures of the visits. To set against the intended kindnesses of the Smiths, Thackeray, and W. S. Williams there were the constant attempts of the Kay-Shuttleworths to pay her attention and introduce her to people – attentions she emphatically did not think of as kind. She was by then a lion, but one who would infinitely prefer to be a mouse.

London Society for Promoting Christianity Amongst the Jews: a society with a cause very close to many clergymen's hearts in the nineteenth century, but not to Charlotte's. She liked contributing neither to the charity nor to their fund-raising wheeze of a "Jew's basket": in *Shirley* (ch. 7) she clearly classes herself among those who "would rather see the prince of darkness himself at their door . . . than that phantom basket." Whether she objected to the aims of the society or to the objects of their concern is not clear.

London Zoo: visited by Charlotte in June 1850, and the subject of a long, descriptive passage of particular verve and vividness in a letter from her to her father (4 June 1850). She goes at length into the animals and birds she saw, the noises they make, and the especial curiosities: the "great Ceylon toads not much smaller than Flossy" and the "cobra di capello" with the "eyes and face of a fiend." The care and creative flair that go into this account tell us a lot about her relationship to her father as well as about the zoo, then in its early years.

Longley, Dr Charles Thomas (1794–1868): Bishop of Ripon (1836–56), then quickly upwardly mobile to the bishopric of Durham (1856–60) and the archbishoprics of York (1860–2) and Canterbury (1862–8). He visited Haworth in 1853, staying overnight at the Parsonage and earning a humorous tribute from Charlotte: "the most benignant little gentleman that ever put on lawn sleeves" (to EN, 4 Mar 1853). He came to Charlotte's rescue when she was teased by the "curates" for putting them in a book, and he noted A. B. Nicholls's dejection and guessed at its cause. He returned in 1860, when Nicholls acted as his host. That Patrick found in him much more than a "benignant little gentleman" may be surmised by the tone and matter of the recently discovered letter to him which Patrick wrote 10 days after Charlotte's death (see entry on Patrick Brontë).

Lord Nelson: inn at Luddenden frequented by Branwell and his artistic friends in the Halifax area. It was a seventeenth-century building, formerly known as the

White Swan, and it housed on the first floor a large library to which Branwell may have wheedled access for himself, though he is not recorded as a member. Still standing and serving.

Lothersdale: the village around Stonegappe, where Charlotte was governess to the Sidgwick children. Mr Sidgwick was one of the prime movers in the building of its church, Christ Church, and he gave "an elegant déjeuné" (*Leeds Intelligencer*, 3 Nov 1838) on the occasion of its consecration in November 1838, six months before Charlotte arrived there.

Louise-Marie, Queen of the Belgians (1812–50): daughter of King Louis-Philippe and third wife of Leopold I, whom Charlotte probably saw at the concert in Brussels she used for ch. 20 of *Villette*, where the Queen of Labassecour is described as "mild, thoughtful, graceful."

Louison (no surname given): one of the servants of the de Bassompierres in *Villette* – one who cannot understand a word Paulina says (ch. 23).

Louis-Philippe, King of the French (1773–1850, reigned 1830–48): eldest son of the Duc d'Orléans, he became king, under a new and more democratic title, following the revolution against the reactionary Charles X. The subject of much comment from Charlotte as his fall heralded the beginning of the year of revolutions, 1848: "unhappy and sordid old man!" she called him, and wondered "What sort of spell has withered [his] strength?" (letters to WSW, 25 and 28 Feb 1848).

Lowborough, Lord (no first name given): friend of Arthur Huntingdon and member of his set in *The Tenant of Wildfell Hall*. He is the most complex of the set, and depicted in greatest depth. He is a man of compulsions and black moods, and he is marked off from the rest by his sense of sin, as well as his sense of the waste and triviality of their sensual pleasures. His marriage to Annabella Wilmot is based on love as well as his need for money, and for a long time he is too devoted a husband to see through her or to guess at her adultery with Huntingdon. His disillusion is powerfully depicted in ch. 38. He is rewarded, after Annabella's death, with a happy marriage (see ch. 50). Anne's depiction of his complex, morose, strong-passioned character is a considerable achievement.

Lowood School: boarding school for girls in *Jane Eyre* (officially Lowood Institution, and also referred to in ch. 9 as "the Orphan Asylum"), one of the many notable schools in Victorian fiction. Life at the school is spartan, discipline harsh, the philosophy behind it class-bound, Calvinistic, and hostile to all independence of thought and action. Jane refers to the "chilly harborage of Lowood" (v. 2, ch. 6), which sums up the physical and emotional atmosphere of the school. The son of the founder, Mr Brocklehurst, sets the tone, and he is obsessed by the damnation of wicked children. He also controls the regime of punishment which amounts to sadism, and he is followed in this by the worst of the teachers (Miss Scatcherd) and silently opposed by the best (Miss Evans).

The school depicted, seen through the eyes of a passionate and imaginative child, was immediately recognized as being the Clergy Daughters' School (Cowan Bridge). Even more tellingly, it was taken by many reviewers to be not just a study of one bad school, but to describe a typical charitable institution for girls. "How many similar establishments are there at this moment in 'merry England'?" asked the *Observer*, clearly expecting the answer "many."

See also Clergy Daughters' School; Wilson, Rev. William Carus

Lucas, Rev. William: incumbent of Hartshead. He suffered from ill-health, and Patrick first stood in for him, and then in 1811 succeeded him.

Lucia (no surname given): the love of Yorke Hunsden's life, whose portrait he carries. She is only mentioned at the end of *The Professor* (see ch. 25), and then it is suggested that his not marrying her is the cause of his odd, bitter character. Frances Henri suggests that she was independent, broke away from conventional constraints, perhaps was on the stage, and this was why Hunsden could not break free of his own social constraints and marry her (unlike William Crimsworth and Frances Henri). These conjectures are not confirmed, but no contrary explanation is given.

Luddenden Foot: village between Halifax and Hebden Bridge, where Branwell became "clerk in charge" of the new railway station in April 1841, remaining until March 1842, when he was dismissed due to money having gone missing. Branwell seems to have left one of his subordinates in charge once too often. The village contained several inns, and up the hill in Luddenden itself was the Lord Nelson. Luddenden also was the site of the grave of William Grimshaw and nearby Midgley was the scene of his son Johnny's drunken decline. Juliet Barker doubts the truth of Branwell's description of his own debauched year here, but – even remembering his tendency to self-dramatization – it has the ring of truth: he talks of "the malignant yet cold debauchery, the determination to find how far mind could carry body without both being chucked into hell" (to Francis Grundy, 22 May 1842).

Luddite riots: the often violent protests of skilled textile workers against the introduction of machinery in the Northern counties (1811–16). Charlotte heard of these times from her father, and perhaps also while she was at Roe Head or with the Nusseys and Taylors. When she came to write *Shirley* she used back numbers of the *Leeds Mercury*.

Lupton, Mrs (no first name given): complacent mother at Edward Crimsworth's birthday party in ch. 3 of *The Professor*. She contemplates with pleasure the attentions Hunsden pays her daughter.

Lupton, Sarah Martha: the dashing and well-formed daughter of the above, to whom Hunsden pays not-very-serious attentions, mainly to prove a point to Crimsworth.

Lutwidge, Rev. Charles Henry: vicar at Burton Agnes, to whom Henry Nussey acted as curate in 1838. Nussey was asked to resign, as his ability to fulfill his pastoral duties had been impaired by a head injury after a fall from a horse. He rather optimistically proposed to Lutwidge's sister Mary Anne Lutwidge but was rejected. Charles and Mary Ann Lutwidge were Lewis Carroll's uncle and aunt.

Lynn, Eliza, later known as Eliza Lynn Linton (1822–98): novelist and journalist. Leaving her motherless and unloving home she made a career for herself in London, in journalism on the *Morning Chronicle* and *Household Words*, and as a novelist. Charlotte wrote that she had not read either *Amymone* or *Azeth* (historical novels of ancient Greece and Egypt, the latter published by Newby on the author paying him £50), but "I have seen extracts from them which I found it literally impossible to digest" (to WSW, 22 Nov 1848). Earlier that year (18 Jan) she had written to Lewes that she preferred even Jane Austen to the "windy wordiness" of Eliza Lynn, whose novel *The Priest of Isis* she found "both turgid and feeble." Lynn was a perceptive friend to both Dickens and Thackeray, and sold the former his longed-for home, Gad's Hill. After an unsuccessful marriage she returned to fiction with a series of hard-hitting novels which had much more success, though her dislike of the "new woman" and her general opposition in later life to the feminist movement probably limits her appeal today.

Lynn family: in *Jane Eyre*, family of Sir George Lynn, who attended Rochester's house party. Lady Lynn is haughty and richly dressed, and the sons Frederick and Henry are described as "dashing sparks."

M

Macarthey, Mr (no first name given): the "good Irishman" who succeeds Mr Malone as curate of Briarfield. He is "decent, decorous, and conscientious," though he is narrow, convention-bound, and has a horror of dissenters. He is only introduced at the end of *Shirley* (ch. 37) to balance the portrait of Malone.

Macarthey is always identified with Arthur Nicholls, and this is all but confirmed by Charlotte's letter to Ellen Nussey (28 Jan 1850?) in which she records his riotous enjoyment of the curates' scenes, and says he "triumphed in his own character." Some of his behavior in Haworth after Charlotte's death seems to confirm the accuracy of the picture. Charlotte's marriage to him must be one of the few instances of a novelist subsequently marrying the model for one of her characters.

Macaulay, Thomas Babbington (1800–59): essayist and historian, who became in the 1840s and 1850s one of the great panjandrums of the British literary scene. His essays for the *Edinburgh Review* made his name, but he published them in volume form only reluctantly, after a pirate version had appeared in America, probably conscious that the combination of dogmatism and superficiality was best left within the covers of a periodical. He was an incessant and voracious reader, multi-lingual, and, as Lord Melbourne feelingly remarked, "cocksure . . . of everything." Charlotte begged from George Smith a copy of the first two volumes of his *History of England* which her father wanted to read. Branwell sent him specimens of his writing, perhaps because Macaulay had distant family and Clapham Sect connections with the Robinson family. He received back "a complimentary letter" which he claimed, improbably, gave his employer Edmund Robinson "a day's sickness" (BB to Joseph Leyland, 25 Nov 1845?). He also claimed in an October 1845 letter to Grundy that though "at the kind request of Mr Macaulay" he had "striven to rouse my mind by writing something that I ought to make deserving of being read, I find I really cannot yet do so."

McClory, Eleanor, Elinor, Alice, or Ayles (d. ca 1822):
mother of Patrick Brontë. She married Hugh Brunty about 1776. Among traditions originating with William Wright in *The Brontës in Ireland* (1893) are that she was "a young woman of dazzling beauty" (p. 80), that she was a Catholic (p. 81), and that Patrick forwarded the sum of £20 to his mother every year once he got to England. This last would have been a formidable slice out of his tiny income as a clergyman. The other statements have been questioned too. According to many commentators she converted to Protestantism on her marriage, but Edward Chitham (1987, p. 9) believes that "She remained loyal to Catholic religion even after marrying the apparently religionless Hugh Brunty." Juliet Barker (1994) on the other hand believes that "there is no first-hand evidence that Eleanor McClory was ever a Catholic" (p. 835). It is perhaps best to admit that we know next to nothing about the lady, and leave her in the Celtic twilight where she seems most at home.

McNeile, Rev. Hugh (1795–1879):
strong evangelical and anti-Catholic cleric heard by Branwell at St Jude's, Liverpool in 1839, when according to Leyland (v. 1, ch. 15) he made a "stenographic report" of McNeile's sermon. Later a Canon of Chester and Dean of Ripon.

Macpherson, James (1736–96):
poet who claimed to be the translator but was in fact largely the author of epic tales by "Ossian" or Oisin, a Gaelic figure of historical-mythological significance. Controversy over the authenticity of these works exercised Dr Johnson and others in the latter part of the eighteenth century. A copy of *The Poems of Ossian* (1819 edition) was in the Parsonage library, and the children were obviously excited by the controversy it had aroused. It figures largely in "Branwell's Blackwoods Magazine" of June and July 1829.

Macready, William Charles (1793–1873):
generally accounted one of the great nineteenth-century actors, though he entered the theatre reluctantly, and left it early. Dickens was an admirer, and one of his closest friends. He pioneered greater fidelity to Shakespeare's texts, but this did not redeem his tragic assumptions in Charlotte's eyes: "anything more false and artificial – less genuinely impressive than his whole style I could scarcely have imagined" she wrote to Margaret Wooler (14 Feb 1850) after seeing him as Macbeth and Othello.

Macturk, father and son (no first names given):
name of two doctors in the Briarfield area in *Shirley*. The father is described as "less of a humbug" (ch. 24) than Dr Rile, but Shirley will have nothing to do with either of them when she fears death from hydrophobia. His character is elaborated during Robert Moore's illness: he is described as "dangerous to vex: abrupt in his best moods; in his worst, savage" (ch. 32). It is he who procures the formidable Mrs Horsfall as nurse for Moore. His son is not individualized.

Macturk, Dr William:
physician of Bradford, who was summoned by Mr Nicholls in Charlotte's last illness, when he pronounced that the illness "would be of

some duration, – but that there was no immediate danger" (ABN to EN, 1 Feb 1855). Oddly enough he, by name and profession, had already put in an appearance in *Shirley*, presiding over Robert Moore's serious illness (see above).

Magherally Church, County Down: scene of the wedding of Hugh Brunty and Eleanor McClory, father and mother of Patrick Brontë.

Maid of Killarney, The: *see* poetry and miscellaneous writings of Patrick Brontë

Malone, Peter Augustus: curate of Briarfield in *Shirley*. A tall, stalwart man, arrogant, bellicose, and insensitive. This coarse, greedy, overloud man is also genuinely brave, or at least careless of danger. With ladies he is awkward, but his love of money makes him pay court in clumsy fashion to several women in the novel, including Shirley, but with no success. He is said at the end to have left the area for a reason which it is implied was a disgraceful one; however, Charlotte teases the reader by withholding any details.

The portrait is based on James William Smith, one of her father's curates (1843–44).

Manchester: Charlotte paid three visits to Mrs Gaskell in Manchester: a brief one at the end of her long London stay in late June 1851; a longer one in April 1853, which she described as "the very brightest and healthiest [week] I have known for these five years past" (to ECG, Apr 1853); and a last, pre-nuptial visit at the beginning of May 1854. Earlier, in 1846, she had made a reconnaissance visit with Emily to find an eye surgeon to operate on her father's cataract, and then a lengthy stay for the operation in August of that year, during which she began *Jane Eyre*. Branwell, according to Leyland, visited Manchester while working on the railway at Luddenden Foot.

"Manchester" was often used by Charlotte as shorthand for the ordinary industrial worker ("The smutty, intelligent mechanics of Manchester," "Ashworth" ch. 2), their employers the mill-owners and industrialists, and the political economists of the age ("men of Birmingham or Manchester – hard men, seemingly knit up in one thought, whose talk is of free trade," *The Professor*, ch. 25).

Manchester and Hebden Bridge and Keighley and Carlisle Junction Railway: proposed branch line beginning from Hebden Bridge, on the Manchester–Leeds line, and proceeding via Haworth and Keighley, where it would join the line from Leeds and Bradford up to Carlisle. Branwell applied in 1845 for a job as secretary to the railway's committee, but he did not get the job, and the branch line was never constructed.

Mangnall, Richmal (1769–1820): founder and headmistress of Crofton Hall School, near Wakefield, which was probably the "good school" Patrick mentioned to Mrs Gaskell (letter of 20 June 1855) which his two eldest daughters attended for a time after the death of their mother. Miss Mangnall was by that time dead, "after a

severe illness, which was borne with the utmost christian resignation" (*Leeds Intelligencer*, 8 May 1820), but her influence lingered on in the younger girls' education in her widely used *Historical and Miscellaneous Questions*, taught at Roe Head.

Mann, Miss (no first name given): one of the two "old maids" in *Shirley*, in whose fates Caroline Helstone sees prefigurings of her own fate. She is on the surface forbidding and censorious, but she is straight and honest, and she has behind her a lifetime of attending to sick relatives (a fate which did indeed await Ellen Nussey, often said to be the original of Caroline Helstone).

Manners, Lord John (1818–1906) later 7th Duke of Rutland: an associate of Disraeli in the Young England party in the early 1840s, he was a minor poet and a member of several Conservative administrations in the second half of the century. He visited Haworth with a group from Mrs Busfeild Ferrand's house party in the summer of 1850, Charlotte describing him as "tall, stately – black-haired and whiskered," but her father appreciated the "well-timed present" of two brace of grouse (to EN, 26 Aug 1850). Toward the end of his long life he was one of the pall-bearers at Gladstone's funeral.

Manon (no surname given): servant of the de Bassompierres in *Villette* – one who cannot understand a word Paulina says.

Marchmont, Maria: Lucy Snowe's first employer in *Villette*. Chapter 4, concerned with unspecified family disasters for Lucy, then proceeds to analyze the unamiable but honest woman who offers her a home and paid duties. The description is heavy with adjectives and eventually explains the contradictions of her character by recounting the early death in a riding accident of her fiancé – thus rather clumsily anticipating Charlotte's preferred ending for Lucy Snowe's love for M. Paul Emanuel.

Marchmont, Mr (no first name given): Miss Marchmont's second cousin and heir – "an avaricious-looking man" who turns out "a thorough miser" (ch. 5), but who, somewhat surprisingly, sends Lucy £100 as conscience money in the last chapter of *Villette*.

Marie, Mlle (surname unknown): teacher at the Pensionnat Heger, whom Charlotte described as "talented & original," but one whose "repulsive & arbitrary manners" made for her enemies of the whole school except for the two Brontës (to EN, May 1842).

Market Street, Thornton: where the second home of Patrick and Maria Brontë was situated from 1815–20. After years as a butcher's shop and then a restaurant, it is now again in private hands but open to the public in the summer months. The fullest account is given by Ellis Chadwick (1914). The room in which the younger Brontës were born is to the right of the hallway, the family dining room to the left.

The family had two servants, so the bedrooms upstairs had to sleep up to 10 persons. The house was then known as the Parsonage, and the brass tablet with the birthdates of the Brontës who were born there was affixed by the Brontë Society in 1902.

Markham, Fergus: younger brother to Gilbert in *The Tenant of Wildfell Hall*. A high spirited, facetious, boisterous, rather tiresome figure. On the last page he somewhat surprisingly marries a vicar's daughter.

Markham, Gilbert: a young farmer, and a central character and narrator in *The Tenant of Wildfell Hall*. In the early sections of the book his affections switch easily from Eliza Millward to "Helen Graham," the mysterious tenant, and the first section depicts the halting progress of their relationship. He is not a very complex figure but the violence of some of his behavior (particularly the attack on Mr Lawrence) is surprising and not altogether convincing. In the last section of the novel he acts the conventional role in a common romantic scenario, being unwilling to force himself on Helen once she is widowed because she is too wealthy for him. Of course at the end of the novel they marry. Anne, unfortunately, does not succeed in animating this off-the-peg fictional device.

Markham, Mrs (no first name given): mother of Gilbert Markham in *The Tenant of Wildfell Hall*. A conventional fictional mother-figure, doting, anxious to prevent her son making an unsuitable marriage.

Markham, Rose (later Halford): sister of Gilbert. A lively, sweet, gossipy girl, married to the man who is the recipient of Gilbert's supposed "letter," the narrative device of the novel.

marriage settlement: such settlements were one of the ways by which a woman could control all or part of her independent fortune or income after marriage in the years before the Married Women's Property acts. Charlotte's, drawn up in May 1854, stipulated that the income from her independent fortune of £1,678 was to remain in her control and would revert to Patrick if she died childless before her husband-to-be. However, these provisions were negated by the will made six weeks before she died, in which she left everything "absolutely and entirely" to her husband.

Marsh, Mrs Anne (1791–1874): novelist, also known as Anne Caldwell and Mrs Marsh-Caldwell. Daughter of James Caldwell, a JP and one-time MP, she married a banker who, soon after, was swindled out of his money. Encouraged to write by Harriet Martineau, Mrs Marsh managed to support her family of seven children until her fortunes changed. Her best-known books were *Two Old Men's Tales* (which according to Mrs Gaskell Charlotte read only after she had written *Jane Eyre*) and *Emilia Wyndham*. Charlotte's interest in her was aroused during the speculation about the authorship of *Jane Eyre*. The *Weekly Chronicle* said that it had been tempted, while reading the book, to believe it was written by Mrs Marsh under a pseudonym, until the writer came to the conclusion that "a man's more vigorous hand is, we think, perceptible," thus managing to be doubly wrong.

Marshall, Ann (?1802–47): confidante and maid to Lydia Robinson. If Branwell is to be believed, she corresponded with him regularly, giving mendacious accounts of her mistress's health, with such melodramatic touches as the vow she was supposedly forced to make to her husband on his deathbed to sever all connections with the family's former tutor. The fact that Edmund Robinson signed promissory notes to her to the value of £520 has given rise to much contradictory comment: was the money loaned to him by Ann for safe-keeping? If so, how did a maid earning £12 a year come to command such sums? Was it payment for spying on her mistress and the tutor? A very large sum for such a service, particularly as Mr Robinson seems always to have believed in the innocence of his wife. Some form of pension arrangement, as Juliet Barker suggests? Were the Robinsons as employers so far ahead of their time? The mystery does not currently admit of any certain solution. What seems certain is that she was privy to part at least of what transpired between Branwell and Lydia Robinson. Or, as Branwell put it in his stagy and exaggerated way, Marshall "saw him do enough to hang him" (see Barker, 1994, p. 461).

Martha (no surname given): servant of the Brettons in *Villette*, who nurses Lucy Snowe after she has been taken to their home unconscious in ch. 16.

Martha (no surname given): the old housekeeper of the narrator in *Shirley*, who ends the book with her stories of "fairishes" in Fieldhead Hollow. No doubt Charlotte is thinking of Tabitha Aykroyd, the Parsonage servant.

Martin, John (1789–1854): English painter whose grand works on literary and biblical themes became part of the young Brontës' mental landscape. He was born near Hexham, Northumberland, and the vast panoramas of that county may have contributed to the "immeasurable spaces" of his most characteristic paintings. His first great success was with *Joshua Commands the Sun to Stand Still*, followed by *Belshazzar's Feast* – prints of both of which were in Haworth Parsonage. He lodged for a time with Prince Leopold of Saxe-Coburg, who became godfather to one of his sons and patronized him when he became the Prince Regent's son-in-law, a patronage continued later when he was King of the Belgians.

Martin sent many of his enormous biblical pictures to be exhibited (admission one shilling) in suitable locations around the country, a proceeding which may have been thought ungentlemanly by his fellow artists. Certainly he and the Royal Academy waged vigorous war with each other for a time, and a certain sniffiness persists to this day among some critics ("Merely Hollywood" is the *Penguin Dictionary of Art and Artists'* description of his large canvasses). However, his last works, including *The Great Day of His Wrath* and *The Plains of Heaven* are immensely popular with today's Tate Britain visitors. In 1850 Charlotte admired his *The Last Man* (based on lines by Thomas Campbell) at the Royal Academy – "a grand, wonderful picture" she called it (to PB,

4 June 1850). His third son, Charles, became a portrait painter, specializing in literary figures such as Dickens, Longfellow, and Washington Irving. His deranged brother Jonathan attempted to burn down York Minster in 1829.

Martineau, Harriet (1802–76): novelist, journalist, and pioneer popularizer of the doctrines of the political economists. Born into the talented family of a textile manufacturer, she was deaf from an early age, and turned to writing when the family lost its fortune in 1829. She lost her early faith, moving gradually towards atheism, and her health was always (at least by her own account) precarious. Like Dickens she had a firm belief in mesmerism, and claimed it had cured her of a tumor in 1845. Her only novel to gain any popularity was *Deerbrook* (1839), though the short fictionalized *Illustrations of Political Economy* (1832–4) were her first major success. She built her own house in Ambleside, where she tried with some success to live by her own social ideals. Her *Autobiography* was published posthumously.

Charlotte's admiration for Miss Martineau was first expressed in the year of *Deerbrook*, through the naive but enthusiastic Caroline Vernon: she says she "must have been the cleverest woman that ever lived" (FN, p. 309). Charlotte initiated the connection when she asked George Smith to send Martineau a copy of *Shirley* with a dedication and an accompanying note. Their first meeting took place in London in December 1849, and it seemed that their very different religious and social beliefs would not get in the way of an immediate and warm human understanding which established itself in the two hours they spent together over tea. Thereafter Martineau pressed Charlotte to visit her at Ambleside, and when the week-long visit was finally paid it cemented the relationship. Though all the time stressing her disagreements with this controversial figure, especially when writing to her more conventional friends such as Ellen Nussey, Charlotte stressed too the personal qualities that she found so attractive: "Without being able to share all her opinions philosophical, political, or religious . . . I yet find a worth and greatness in herself, and a consistency, benevolence, perseverance in her practice such as wins the sincerest esteem and affection" (to James Taylor, 1 Jan 1851?). She was amused by the despotism such a radical thinker exercised over the Ambleside locals, but found her "a very noble and genial being" and confessed, most unusually for her, "I *did* enjoy my visit to Miss Martineau very much" (to GS, 7 Jan 1851).

Thereafter things went less well, with her attempts to interest George Smith in publishing *Oliver Weld*. Though she had described Martineau to Smith as "a greater writer" than Mrs Gaskell, she was suppressing her own misgivings about the likely quality of the book. She had to admit, having read it, that "The interest is not very enchaining" (to GS, 19 Dec 1851). George Smith refused the novel, and it was a year after this that Charlotte, perhaps unwisely, asked Martineau to "give me your thoughts upon my book [*Villette*] – as frankly as if you spoke to some near relative" (21 Jan 1853). Martineau protested in her review of the novel that all the female characters were possessed by one thought only – love: "There are substantial, heartfelt interests for women of all ages, and under ordinary circumstances, quite apart from love" (*Daily News*, 3 Feb 1853). And in a private letter to Charlotte she persisted: "I do deeply regret the reason given to suppose your mind full of one passion – love – I think there is unconscionably too much of it (giving an untrue picture of life) and, speaking with the frankness you desire, I do not like its kind" (Barker, 1994, p. 719).

This was a frankness Charlotte definitely did not desire. Martineau not only seemed to cast doubt on a central tenet of Charlotte's existence: she also seemed to denigrate the most important emotional event of her life. The relationship ended suddenly and swiftly, and she wrote to George Smith "my wish indeed is that she should quietly forget me" (26 Mar 1853).

On the publication of the *Life* Martineau got into lengthy and bitter controversies with Patrick and Arthur Bell Nicholls, and into more genteelly conducted ones with Mrs Gaskell. It is difficult to reconcile the cantankerous and pettifogging character of these controversies with the determined but sensitive figure we see in the letters Charlotte wrote during and after her stay at Ambleside, and it may be that the place, and a new friendship, blinded her to Martineau's inability to brook disagreements or to understand doubts about her views and practices.

See also Atkinson, Henry George

Martineau, Rev. James (1805–1900): theologian and scholar, younger

brother of Harriet. He was professor of Mental and Moral Philosophy at Manchester New College when Francis Grundy submitted to him Branwell's "Triumph of Mind over Body." Martineau had taught Grundy for a while, and was a colleague of his father. He sent Branwell "kindly and truthful criticism." Mrs Gaskell admired him, though she was less enthusiastic, when he and his family visited her at her holiday home, at having to talk "sense by the yard" (ECG to Marianne Gaskell, 5 July 1853). Charlotte commented on some sentences of his that Gaskell seems to have quoted in a previous letter that they are "some of them gems most pure and genuine; ideas deeply conceived – finely expressed" (to ECG, 20 Sep 1851). He remained in Manchester until 1857, when he transferred with the college to London. He was its principal from 1869–85.

Martyn, Henry (1781–1812): tutor at St John's College, Cambridge. He suc-

cessfully organized an approach in 1804 to William Wilberforce to get help for the poor Irish college-subsidized student Patrick Brontë. In 1805 he went to India as a missionary, his preferred helpmeet Lydia Grenfell refusing to accompany or join him. He learned Hindustani, Hindi, and Persian, and made various translations of the New Testament, Psalms, and the Prayer Book. He went into Persia as a missionary and died of fever in Tokat (in present-day Turkey). It was plausibly suggested by Clement Shorter that he could have been one of the models for St John Rivers in *Jane Eyre*.

Mary (no surname given): wife of John, and a servant of Mr Rochester in *Jane*

Eyre. The pair look after Mr Rochester at Ferndean, and she receives the news of the marriage of her master with Jane with a phlegmatic calm that contrasts with her husband's pleasure.

Mary (no surname given): servant at Thrushcross Grange who announces the elopement of Isabella Linton.

Marzials, Mme: the lady who, early in 1842, was supposed to accompany Charlotte and Emily to school in Lille, a plan which was abandoned when the Pensionnat Heger in Brussels was recommended to them. Probably Mary Anne, née Jackson, daughter of the editor of the *Methodist Magazine*, who married the pastor of the Protestant Established Church in Lille, Antoine Théophile Marzials in 1834 (*Leeds Intelligencer*, 27 Sep 1834).

Mason, Antoinetta: mother of Bertha. The fact that she was mad and in an asylum was kept from Rochester until after his marriage.

Mason, Hester: one of the principal characters in G. H. Lewes's *Rose, Blanche and Violet* (1848), which was the subject of two letters of critical appraisal from Charlotte to W. S. Williams (26 Apr and 1 May 1848). In the second, in an odd confusion of life and fiction, Charlotte says she never doubted that the picture of her was from life, but that if, on the contrary, she was a fictional creation, "I wish him better and higher and truer taste next time he writes a novel."

Mason, Jonas: father of Bertha. He is a man of "vast" possessions but he schemes to entrap Rochester into a marriage with his daughter, allowing him no opportunity to find out her true nature. In this he is helped by Rochester's father, who is keen for his second son to marry money.

Mason, Richard: elder son of Jonas, brother of Bertha. He is clearly the best of the family, and held in a sort of contemptuous affection by Rochester who he has admired in the West Indies. His concern for his sister brings him more than once to Thornfield, though for his pains he is savagely attacked by her. It is Richard Mason, urged on by Jane's dying uncle, who comes to Thornfield to stop the marriage of Jane and Rochester.

Massey, Gerald (1828–1907): poet and early Christian Socialist. John Greenwood in his notebook adapted the lines he wrote on the poet Thomas Hood to apply to the death of Emily: "The world may never know the wealth it lost,/ When she went dashing to her Tearful Tomb,/ So mighty in her undeveloped Force." He lectured in Bradford and elsewhere in the late 1850s on Charlotte, first accepting unreservedly Mrs Gaskell's highly colored stories of Patrick, later retracting the charges and trying to give his audience a fairer picture of the Brontës' father.

Master, The: the original manuscript title of *The Professor*.

Mathew, Theobald (1790–1856): Catholic priest and apostle of temperance, whose mass meetings of pledge-signers aroused wonder and admiration in the 1840s in England, Ireland, and the United States (where he declined to attend an anti-slavery meeting, on the grounds that he was "not sure there was any prohibition of slavery in Scripture" – *Leeds Intelligencer*, 8 Sep 1849). Branwell refers to him in a letter to J. B. Leyland (29 June 1842) saying "his conversation" (presumably meaning quotes from him) "is too cold and freezing for comfort among the moors of Yorkshire."

Mathilde (surname unknown): pupil of Charlotte's at the Pensionnat Heger who wrote to her affectionately after her return to England, saying how much she valued Charlotte's expression of "esteem" for her.

Mathilde (no surname given): pupil at Mme Beck's, later an ex-pupil who attends the concert in ch. 20 of *Villette*.

Mathilde, de — (surname otherwise not given): pupil at Frances Crimsworth's school in *The Professor*, mentioned in ch. 25. Daughter of a Belgian count, but otherwise uncharacterized.

Matou, Rosine: the portress at Mme Beck's in *Villette*. She is outspoken, bright, vain, and has a particular fondness for money and a willingness to do anything to earn it. She is a typical "soubrette," but the vividness of the sketch, together with some similarities to the character "Rosalie" in *The Professor*, suggest it may have been based on the portress at the Hegers' establishment.

Matthieu (no surname given): servant of the de Bassompierres mentioned in ch. 37 of *Villette*.

Maurice, Frederick Denison John (1805–72): theologian of Unitarian upbringing, later converting to the Church of England. He was a pioneer Christian Socialist, proponent of higher education for women and of adult education generally. Charlotte found him the "most in earnest" of those preachers she heard in London in 1851, and said if she had the choice "it is Maurice whose ministry I should frequent" (to James Taylor, 15 Nov 1851). When, following the publication of his *Theological Essays*, he lost his professorship of theology at King's College, London, Charlotte protested strongly in a letter to Mrs Gaskell at his ousting (see Marion J. Phillips, "Charlotte Brontë's Favourite Preacher," BST, v. 20, pt 2, 1990).

Maxwell, Mr (no first name given): uncle to Helen Huntingdon in *The Tenant of Wildfell Hall*. One's impression (mainly from ch. 20) is of a relaxed, easy-living old gentleman of no great principles or intellectual grasp.

Maxwell, Mrs: aunt to Helen Huntingdon in *The Tenant of Wildfell Hall*, and wife of the above. Addressed as "Peggy" in ch. 16. She is a religious, somewhat joyless woman of good heart but narrow mind. It may be conjectured that her own marriage prefigures in milder form what she fears, rightly, will be Helen's marriage with

Arthur Huntingdon. She ends the novel living with Helen and Gilbert Markham at Staningley.

Mayne, Rev. William: incumbent of St John's, Ingrow, between Keighley and Haworth, who was one of the coffin-bearers at Patrick's funeral. Earlier he had been one of Arthur Bell Nicholls's referees when he was seeking missionary appointments in Australia. His second wife was the eldest daughter of John Fennell's second marriage.

Medallion portrait of Branwell: according to Francis Leyland (v. 2, chs. 7 & 8) this was the result of a pact between Branwell and Joseph Leyland, whereby Branwell would complete his poem "Morley Hall" in return for Leyland making a medallion sculpture of his friend. Branwell never, so far as we know, fulfilled his side of the bargain. There are references to the medallion in letters between the two in the first half of 1846, for example, "I could wish that my head was as cold and stupid as the medallion which lies in your studio" (June 1846). Eventually he requests, if there is a duplicate, to have it, protesting rather unconvincingly that he doesn't care a fig for it himself, but his sisters would like it for the family (2 July 1846). The fine, if idealized, medallion is our best source of knowledge of Branwell's appearance. It has hung for many years in the Parsonage dining room.

Melcy, Blanche de: a pupil at Mme Beck's school, and one of the ringleaders of the disruption when Lucy Snowe takes her first class there. She is described as "the eldest, tallest, handsomest, and most vicious" of the trouble-makers in *Villette* (ch. 8).

Melcy, Madame de (no first name given): sister of Alfred de Hamal in *Villette*, and mother of the above. Her sons are the means by which de Hamal gains access to the school (see ch. 40).

Melrose: town and ruined abbey near Sir Walter Scott's home Abbotsford, used by him in the novel *The Monastery*. Charlotte saw it on her visit to Scotland with George and Eliza Smith, and said it was one of the places that stirred feelings of "deep interest and admiration" (to James Taylor, 5 Sep 1850).

Meltham, Harry: one of the possible husbands for Rosalie Murray. He is referred to frequently in *Agnes Grey*, but not characterized further than being a younger son, "rather good-looking, and a pleasant fellow to flirt with" (ch. 9).

Meltham, Sir Hugh: father of Harry and Miss Meltham, husband of Lady Meltham; neighbor of the Murrays in *Agnes Grey*. He is characterized only as an "old codger" (ch. 9). His wife and daughter are merely mentioned.

Melvill, Henry (1798–1871): popular preacher, heard by Charlotte in the summer of 1851. It was probably one of his Tuesday sermons at St Margaret's, Lothbury, that she attended and admired.

Merrall, Hartley (1819–95) and Michael (1811–81): the two youngest sons of a prominent mill-owning family in Haworth, whose heyday was in the latter part of the nineteenth century. Several stories have clustered round Hartley: there is the story of the young Branwell attending Keighley Feast with him, where his excitement knew no bounds – "he screamed out at the top of his voice, 'Oh! my nerves! my nerves! Oh! my nerves!'" and on the way back home lost his spectacles in a wrestling match with Hartley; another story concerns a visit the two made to Liverpool, when Hartley was persuaded to buy Branwell a copy of Handel's oratorio *Samson*, and was later rewarded by a portrait of him, now lost, in which the names of great composers were painted into each corner of the picture (Leyland, v. 1, pp. 88–9, 239–40). These stories were reattributed by Juliet Barker (1994) to the elder brother Michael, but we prefer the traditional identification, since Leyland, writing in 1886, says he has the Keighley Feast story from "The survivor of these two friends," and he thanks "Mr H. Merrall" but not "Mr M." in his Preface. A copy of Leyland's book, inscribed by him to "Mr Merrall," and containing terse marginal comments on Branwell and Emily, recently surfaced in America and was bought by Mr Kent Bicknell (see my *Emily Brontë*, 2000, p. 58). Michael Merrall was the most effective mill-owner of the family, and was prominent in the Haworth Mechanics' Institute, where he paid tribute to Charlotte on her death. Earlier he had made a presentation to Arthur Bell Nicholls on his (temporarily) quitting Haworth during the row with Patrick. Which of the two brothers was the talented organist is unsure – possibly both were. It was "E. Merrall," the eldest son, Edwin, who was sent wedding cards on the occasion of Charlotte's marriage to Nicholls.

mesmerism: the belief that an influence, once called "animal magnetism," can be exerted over a subject in which the person's normal senses are in abeyance, and his or her will and actions can be controlled by the mesmerist, often with beneficial effects on the physical and mental health of the subject. Dickens was a great believer in and practitioner of it, as was Harriet Martineau. According to the latter, Charlotte was "strangely pertinacious" in urging her to mesmerize her, which, though reluctant, Martineau eventually attempted, stopping "the moment she called out that she was under the influence" (ECG, *Life*, 3rd. edn, v. 2, ch. 9). This account should be treated with caution. Charlotte herself said that "though the result was not absolutely clear – it was inferred that in time I should prove an excellent subject" (to James Taylor, 15 Jan 1851).

Metcalfe, Richard: solicitor in Keighley. He went to London to arrange the transfer of stocks owned by Charlotte from George Smith, who had been acting for her in financial matters, to Joe Taylor, who was to act as trustee for her money after marriage. This was accomplished by her marriage settlement, drawn up by Metcalfe, and shows Charlotte's initial determination to keep control of what she had earned by her writing.

Methodist Magazine: founded by John Wesley, this included in its contents poetry, sermons, narratives of an improving or didactic nature, and so forth. Aunt

Branwell had a set, and it seems as if the Brontë children reacted against the magazines' shrill and tendentious tone. In *Shirley*, Caroline Helstone, in a period of loneliness, reads "mad Methodist Magazines" which had belonged to her Aunt Mary, with their "preternatural warnings, ominous dreams, and frenzied fanaticism" (*Shirley*, ch. 22).

Michael (no surname given): groom at Thrushcross Grange who is bribed by the younger Catherine with books and pictures to facilitate her visits to the Heights during Nelly's illness (v. 2, ch. 10).

Miles, Mr (no first name given): John Reed's schoolmaster, mentioned in the first chapter of *Jane Eyre*.

Mill, Harriet (née Hardy): formerly wife of John Taylor; author of the article "Emancipation of Women" in the *Westminster Review* (July 1851) commented on by Charlotte in a letter to Mrs Gaskell (20 Sep 1851). She had first thought, rightly, it was the work of a woman – but one of "hard jealous heart, muscles of iron and nerves of bend leather." When she learned, or thought she did, that it was the work of John Stuart Mill, long-term partner and recent husband of Harriet, she felt "disposed to scorn his heart," though admiring his head. She particularly praised the article's arguments on maternity and on the logic of opening all positions for women: "if there be a natural unfitness in women for men's employment – there is no need to make laws on the subject." There was a heated exchange of letters between John Stuart Mill and Mrs Gaskell after the *Life* had included this letter.

Miller, Maria: one of the few other English pupils at the Pensionnat Heger. She was a friend of the Wheelwrights, but Charlotte is said to have taken her for a model when creating Ginevra Fanshawe in *Villette*. She reappears in the Brontë story as Mrs W. P. Robertson, when she writes an apparently affectionate letter to Laetitia Wheelwright, concealing until the postscript the real reason for resuming contact – soliciting a subscription towards the publication of a book of some kind, whether her own or her husband's is unclear. Charlotte, writing to Laetitia (23 June 1852?), is scathing both about the person ("selfish . . . worldly . . . impudent") and her current place of residence: "Boulogne is the asylum of a not very respectable class." One would guess the Wheelwrights knew this quite as well as Charlotte.

Miller, Miss (no first name given): under-teacher at Lowood School in *Jane Eyre* – overworked, careworn, and victim of a bad system.

Millevoye, Charles-Hubert (1784–1816): early Romantic French poet, much in favor in the first decade of the nineteenth century, on whose poem "*La Chute des Feuilles*" Charlotte wrote an essay during her second stay in Brussels. She also made an English translation, and praised the poet highly in a footnote to *Shirley* (see World's Classics edn, ed. M. Smith and H. Rosengarten, 1979, p. 657). In a notebook of Ellen Nussey's, after copying some verses of this poem, she wrote: "in my opinion the French language does not possess anything more truly poetical than this effusion" (CBL, v. 1, pp. 414, 609).

Milligan, John (1812–76): surgeon of Keighley. It was a prescription of his ("nothing received from the hands of any Medical Gentleman, has ever done me, more good" – PB to Milligan, 9 Oct 1838), which seems to have contained alcohol, that gave rise to rumors in Haworth that Patrick had taken to the bottle. Patrick had particularly asked for Milligan's signed prescription "to counteract . . . the groundless, yet pernicious censures of the weak – wicked – and wily."

Mills, Susanna (later Mme Baudry): fellow student with the Brontë girls at the Pensionnat Heger. She wrote to the *South Wales Echo* in 1901, mentioning a recent meeting with the Hegers' daughter Louise, and claiming to "remember perfectly well" Charlotte and Emily. The letter is quoted in Wise and Symington (v. 1, p. 255), where her name is given as Susanna Bandy. Descendants of hers have claimed that she was the original of Ginevra Fanshawe in *Villette*, citing as evidence that she also eloped, in her case with a captain of the French navy, Edouard Baudry. She thus vies with Maria Miller for the doubtful honor of inspiring that shallow if enticing young lady.

Millward, Eliza: younger daughter of the Rev. Michael Millward in *The Tenant of Wildfell Hall*. In the early stages of the novel Gilbert Markham thinks himself in love with her, much to his mother's displeasure. When he transfers his affections to Helen Huntingdon she comes out in her true colors: her sprightliness becomes mischief-making, and she shows herself jealous and bent on petty revenge. As is so often the case with the less attractive young ladies in nineteenth-century fiction, she is later said to have married into trade (ch. 48).

Millward, Mary: elder sister to the above. A plain, thoughtful young woman, undervalued by her family and most of their acquaintance, who does a great deal of good in the parish and is eventually rewarded with the hand of the scholarly Richard Wilson.

Millward, Rev. Michael: father of the above, and incumbent of Lindenhope, the parish where most of the characters of *The Tenant of Wildfell Hall* reside. A gregarious but sententious man, with strict but unintelligent notions and a strong concern for his own comfort and convenience. One of many unfavorable sketches of clerics in the Brontës' works.

Milnes, Richard Monckton, later Lord Houghton (1809–85): English politician, occasional poet, and literary bigwig. He was MP for Pontefract 1837–63, first in the Tory, later in the Liberal interest. He was a figure of enormous energy, who knew and brokered with everyone who mattered, and did everything that might provide him with a new and delectable sensation. He had a magnificent collection of pornography, and he championed the poet Swinburne, many of whose unorthodox tastes he shared. His pioneering life of Keats was for many years the standard work.

He introduced himself to Charlotte at one of Thackeray's lectures, and shortly afterwards dined with her at the Kay-Shuttleworths', but was unimpressed by her. However, during the troubled period when Patrick was opposing his daughter's connection with Arthur Bell Nicholls he met him (his family seat was close to Kirk Smeaton, whither Nicholls had "exiled" himself) and dangled in front of him two chances of possible Church preferment, which Nicholls refused. At Mrs Gaskell's instigation he attempted to get him a pension, but he was – unusually for him – unsuccessful. He was, in gratitude for his interest, sent a wedding card when all the difficulties were overcome. After Charlotte's death he visited Haworth, displaying a special and characteristic interest in the scapegrace of the family, Branwell. He talked to William Brown, and transcribed letters to John Brown, by then dead, in which Branwell talked of his affair with Lydia Robinson – at first in tones of apprehension at her interest in him, later as the *grande affaire* of his life. Milnes also recorded the talk of an illegitimate child in Broughton-in-Furness. Later still he was consulted by Wemyss Reid on behalf of Ellen Nussey, concerning the disposal of Charlotte's letters to the British Museum. Milnes was unenthusiastic at the prospect of the Museum paying Ellen for them – a decision that had enormous and unfortunate consequences when they were acquired by the literary forger and con-man T. J. Wise. He was caricatured as Mr Vavasour in Disraeli's novel *Tancred*.

See also Swinburne

Milton, John (1608–74): a favorite poet of the Brontës, and the source of many quotations and more oblique references. Several such can be found in the juvenilia, for example to those school-room regulars "L'Allegro" and "Il Penseroso," but references to *Paradise Lost* start as early as Branwell's 1830 "Letter from an Englishman." The children could by then not only have read (parts of, probably) the great poem, but perhaps also seen John Martin's mezzotint illustrations to it. By 1834 Charlotte was telling Ellen Nussey: "If you like poetry let it be first rate, Milton . . ." (4 July 1834). The year before had seen put forward in "The Foundling" a claim for "the greatest British poet, philosopher, statesman and historian viz: – Milton" (EW, v. 2, pt 1, p. 57). Quotations from this rich source, including from less well-known poems, continued through the years of juvenile writing into the novels. *Shirley* is particularly rich in Miltonic quotes, and several in *Jane Eyre* include, along with many from *Paradise Lost*, references to *Samson Agonistes* and "Lines at a Vacation Exercise." Branwell at Luddenden Foot meditated a poem on Milton's life, and in general it seems that the admiration for him and his work was genuine and enthusiastic among the Brontës.

"Mina Laury": story written by Charlotte in her Christmas vacation from Roe Head, 1837–8. Mina Laury, a soldier's daughter, had featured, usually in a minor role, in earlier writings, most notably in "Something About Arthur," where she puts herself in the young Arthur's debt by saving him from a lion. Later she had acted as maid or housekeeper to the Duchess of Wellington, to Zamorna's second wife Marion, and to Zamorna himself. She had also tried, desperately but to no avail, to save his son from Quashia's troops during the civil war.

The story concerns the love which Lord Hartford has conceived for Mina. Desperately, and knowing her entire subservience to Zamorna, he decides to propose to her. He receives not only a refusal but also a full statement of her entire devotion to Zamorna: "he superseded all things – all affections, all interests, all fears or hopes or principles – Unconnected with him my mind would be a blank – cold, dead, susceptible only of a sense of despair" (FN, p. 147). Zamorna and Hartford fight a duel in which the latter is seriously wounded. Mina, at the lodge where she is housekeeper, receives a visit from a mysterious lady who turns out to be Zamorna's third wife. Zamorna, who comes on a visit, satisfies himself that Mina feels nothing for Hartford, placates his wife, and takes her away. Mina, as always, is perfectly happy however badly she is treated.

The tale is a study of emotional masochism, and the reader feels that Charlotte recognizes this trait in herself, finds it unhealthy and even ludicrous, yet cannot be entirely unsympathetic to it. In this story Mina admits her "infatuation" (FN, p. 148), regards opposition to Zamorna as "impious and blasphemous" (p. 147), and Charlotte comments: "she lost her identity – her very way of life was swallowed up in that of another" (p. 165). Charlotte declines to be moralistic about Zamorna ("I will merely relate his conduct without note or comment," p. 164) but is clear that he is an egotist, an emotional cannibal who cannot allow anyone else "to look at anything which belongs to him." She did not find much more to do with Mina in later episodes.

As with most such stories other Angrian matters are covered as well as the main plot: Zamorna and Northangerland, Angrian anger at their continued apparent closeness, and Zamorna's neglect and deception of his wife.

Minnie (no surname given): servant of William and Frances Crimsworth. Mentioned but not characterized. Also known as Mimie.

Mirabeau, Honoré-Gabriel Victor Riqueti, Comte de (1749–91): scion

of a French noble family who in his early years pursued a career of dissipation and reckless defiance of all authority. With the coming of the French Revolution he found his metier as orator and leader, though his aim was to unite the revolution behind the king, producing a democratic monarchy on the English model. This was a notion Louis XVI was incapable of accepting or even understanding, and when Mirabeau died (of natural causes) the Revolution was already being taken over by more extreme figures.

Charlotte wrote at length about Mirabeau in a letter to W. S. Williams (22 June 1848) after reading his *Life* by the 20-year-old John Stores Smith, who she was later to entertain at Haworth. She felt that the young author minimized Mirabeau's "errors" (as she later accused Thackeray of making light of Fielding's). She found Mirabeau a mixture of "divinity and dirt", and she thought the latter predominated: it was "a miserable and degraded life," and he died "a dog's death, for want of self-control – for want of morality – for lack of religion." It is notable that Branwell, then nearing the end of his life, could be described in similar terms, and Charlotte may have been influenced in her judgment by Branwell's earlier admiration for, or identification with, the French politician. He described his career in the words of Northangerland at some length in "Angria and the Angrians" (WPBB, v. 2, p. 548): he dwells on "the most dissipated of lives" which yet culminated in a funeral which "was Rather an Apotheosis than a human Entombment." Charlotte also encountered the contradictions of the man in the "*dictée*" that M. Heger drew from Victor Hugo's "*Sur Mirabeau*" (see BE, pp. 108–17).

Miret, Demoiselles: M. Miret's three daughters in *Villette*, ch. 41.

Miret, M. (no first name given): the "short-tempered and kind-hearted" bookseller who is Lucy Snowe's landlord when she starts her own school at the end of *Villette*.

Mirror of Literature, Amusement and Instruction, The: this periodical, which according to Leyland had been read by the young Brontës, gave *Jane Eyre* a hostile review in December 1847 – at a time when most of the notices were enthusiastic. The reviewer, George Searle Philips, who much later wrote an article on Branwell, whom he seems to have known, claimed that "Religion is stabbed in the dark – our social distinctions attempted to be levelled, and all absurdly moral notions done away with." He was in no doubt that the writer was an "authoress," but his claim that she had written "another production quite as bold . . . quite as much distinguished for its insidious tendency, as the present volume" suggests that he had hit on the wrong authoress as his candidate: Charlotte's contributions to the *Poems* hardly answer this description. Charlotte herself dismissed the review as "the result of a feeble sort of spite" (to WSW, 29 Mar 1848).

"Misses Brontë's Establishment, the": the school projected by the three sisters, which eventually, because of Patrick's increasing blindness in 1844–5, was modified into taking pupils at the Parsonage in Haworth – probably always a hopeless proposition. Friends were written to, cards with terms were distributed (£35 per annum was the sum quoted), and some of those approached, such as the Whites at Rawdon, seemed genuinely regretful that they could not send a child to the proposed school. In the two months from August to October 1844 the Brontës were forced to face the fact that "there are no pupils to be had" (to EN, 2 Oct 1844?). In the scheme Emily was to be responsible for the housekeeping, since she was "not very fond of teaching" (to M. Heger, 24 July 1844?), but since languages, drawing, and music were the extras mentioned in the prospectus, it may be she would have had a role in teaching some or all of these. "Now I dont desire a school at all" she wrote in her diary paper of 1845, which was probably an understatement.

Mitchell, Walter: a man mentioned in a long letter from Charlotte to Ellen Nussey (20 Nov 1840), mostly on love matters. She advises her to "coquette with him a trifle if you were so disposed" because there was no danger of breaking his heart.

In view of a reference to Hippocrates later in the letter, it seems likely that this was the Birstall surgeon who in 1842 married Catherine Parkinson of Halifax, and who died suddenly in 1847.

Mitton Hall: visited by Charlotte on her first visit to the Kay-Shuttleworths at Gawthorpe Hall, along with the Sherburn Chapel in Mitton Church – among the "pictures pleasant to contemplate" mentioned in Charlotte's thank-you letter to Lady Kay-Shuttleworth (22 Mar 1850).

Monastery, The: novel by Sir Walter Scott published in 1820, a possible source for the theme of hostile brothers that runs through Brontë writings, from Branwell's "The Wool is Rising" (Edward and William Percy), through Charlotte's "Ashworth," *The Professor* (Edward and William Crimsworth), to the late fragment "Willie Ellin," and *Wuthering Heights*. The brothers are described (e.g., ch. 11) in terms very similar to the Brontës' characters, but Halbert and Edward Glendinning have a loving relationship until they become rivals for the affection of Mary Avenel. The hostility in the Brontë figures seems always to be ingrained rather than explicable by rational causes. The novel would in any case appeal to the Brontës by its mixture of the historical and the supernatural, and its setting in wild and lawless border country.

Monk's Hall: farm in the grounds of Thorp Green, where Branwell lodged during his time as tutor to Edmund Robinson, and which he sketched on 25 August 1844. The farm still stands, in the grounds of the Queen Ethelberga School.

Montgomery, James (1771–1854): poet of Scottish birth, educated at the Moravian School in Fulneck, near Leeds (his father was a pastor in that church), and later settling in Sheffield, where he edited the *Sheffield Register*, renamed when he became its owner the *Sheffield Iris*. His politics shifted from left to right: he was imprisoned for seditious writings in 1795, but accepted a pension from Peel in 1835. Apart from some popular hymns, his best-known work was *The World Before the Flood*. Montgomery had given a series of six lectures on "The Principal British Poets" in Bradford in 1841, while Branwell was not far away in Sowerby Bridge. In the next year Branwell reported that Montgomery had been sent or shown some of his "head work," and along with "plenty of puff and praise" had recommended him "to turn my attention to literature" (to Francis Grundy, 9 June 1842).

Moore, Hortense: sister of Robert and Louis, and housekeeper for Robert in *Shirley*. She is not unkindly, but she is blinkered, and can see no value in any custom she was not brought up to, nor virtue in any code or opinion other than her own. She is stately, conservative, and has a great sense of dignity and position. Her character is analyzed fully in ch. 5.

Moore, Louis Gérard: brother of Robert and Hortense in *Shirley*. He is tutor in the Sympson family, and in that capacity has in the past taught Shirley. He is quiet yet persistent, perceptive yet commonsensical, and in the end he wins the hand of Shirley. He has generally been thought a disappointing lover for her, and certainly his character (perhaps hobbled by the fact that he first appears two-thirds of the way through the book) seems pallid, as if the mere fact of his being in a teacher–pupil relationship with Shirley was enough for Charlotte.

Moore, Robert: father of Robert, Louis, and Hortense Moore in *Shirley*. Mentioned in ch. 2.

Moore, Robert Gérard: mill-owner and one of the three central figures in *Shirley*. His determination to repair his family's fortunes by introducing the new machinery is the motive force behind the social themes of the novel which dominate the first third of the book, but thereafter become of more secondary and occasional interest. He is an intelligent, sensitive, and compassionate man, but these qualities get pushed to one side by his family and business concerns, and his determination and single-mindedness means he is picked out by the working men as their principal enemy. His determination even leads him at one point to contemplate a mercenary marriage to Shirley Keeldar, but his affection, though it is often pushed to one side, is all for Caroline Helstone, whom he is to marry at the end of the book.

He is perhaps the most complex character in *Shirley*, though he certainly does not have the vivid presence of Mr Rochester, or engage the reader's interest so passionately. His character is analyzed in ch. 2.

Moore, Thomas (1779–1852): Irish poet. His lyrics were great favorites with Charlotte, as testified by Ellen Nussey (see CBL, v. 1, Appendix, p. 609), and there are references to or quotations from a great many of his works in the juvenilia or later works: to the enormously popular *Lalla Rookh* and *Irish Melodies*, and to the much less well-known *Fudge Family in Paris* (in "Angria and the Angrians"), and even his life of the eighteenth-century Irish patriot and rebel Lord Edward Fitzgerald (in "Caroline Vernon"). The favorite work, however, was the life of Byron, which Charlotte recommended to Ellen in the well-known letter telling her what she should read (4 July 1834). Apart from the less documentable influence that his picture of the poet had on such figures as Mr Rochester and Heathcliff, Finden's illustrations greatly attracted Charlotte and Emily, who produced versions of the engravings. It may even be that Emily and Anne's tradition of writing diary papers springs from Moore's account of Byron's habit of writing detailed memoranda while he was at Harrow as if "he had a sort of vague presentiment that everything relating to him would one day be an object of curiosity and interest" (ch. 3), something one feels in the Brontës' case as well.

"Moores, The" or "John Henry": alternative titles, both of them given by later editors, to an untitled manuscript of Charlotte's. This fragment of a novel was probably written between Smith Elder's rejection of *The Professor* and the commencement of *Shirley*. Essentially it is a rewriting of the early section of *The Professor*, with some details that were later to find a more congenial home in *Shirley*. The novel begins with a marital dialogue between the newly married John Henry Moore and his wife Sarah Julia. The dialogue lacks conviction, as does the rambling and detailed letter from John Henry's younger brother William which follows. The second chapter has more of reality about it, with the arrival of William and of a friend of Sarah Julia called Alicia Wynne. We have a brief beginning to a third chapter, but by this stage Charlotte had decided either that it was no improvement on her original novel, or that Smith Elder were immovably set against any version of *The Professor* as the follow-up to *Jane Eyre*.

Moor House, also called Marsh End: home of the Rivers family since the seventeenth century, three miles from the village of Morton. It is here that Jane Eyre comes to rest at the end of her flight from Thornfield. Through the kitchen window she sees the Rivers girls, Diana and Mary, learning German together, a vignette surely based on Emily and Anne, and though her plea for shelter is rejected by the servant Hannah she is taken in by St John Rivers. It is here that her journey back to health and to integration into society is begun. It is here, too, that she plans to live with Diana and Mary before the voice of Mr Rochester summons her back to Yorkshire.

Moravian Church: a Protestant sect that could trace its ancestry back to the fifteenth century Bohemian Brethren, and had communities in various parts of Britain, where they pursued their pietistic lifestyle. Fulneck (part of Pudsey, near Leeds, and only four miles from Birstall) was one such community, still active today, and there was a Moravian Chapel in Gomersal which two of Ellen Nussey's sisters were involved in. The piety and inclusiveness of the sect was looked on kindly by Anne, and one of its pastors played an important role during her crisis of faith at Roe Head. Charlotte, we may suspect, looked on the sect less kindly, since she had Mrs Yorke in *Shirley* approve of it, and names one of its ministers, a German, Mr. Langweilig (or long-winded).

See also La Trobe

Morgan, Jane (née Fennell) (1791–1827): cousin of Maria Brontë, daughter of John Fennell and his wife Jane, née Branwell. During the courtship of Patrick and Maria there are numerous affectionate references to Jane in the letters Maria writes to her fiancé, and this period culminated in the joint marriage of Patrick and Maria, William Morgan and Jane, each man officiating at the other's wedding, in Guiseley Church 29 December 1812. Subsequently she was probably godmother to the Brontës' eldest daughter Maria, and to Emily Jane. She was buried in her father's parish of Todmorden. Her husband subsequently gave Patrick her Greek prayer book as a memorial of her.

Morgan, William (1782–1858): Welsh-born clergyman of Methodistical sympathies who became a friend of Patrick's during their time at Wellington, and remained one for the rest of his life. He was probably responsible for Patrick's engagement as examiner at Woodhouse Grove School, and he and Patrick each conducted the other's marriage ceremony at the joint wedding in Guiseley Church, where they became cousins-in-law through Morgan's marriage to Jane Fennell. Thereafter the friendship was kept up, Morgan being in demand to officiate at christenings, and later at funerals. He became a figure of fun to the younger generation: Charlotte commented in 1840 on the patience with which William Weightman endured "that fat Welchman's prosing" (to EN, 17 Mar 1840), and much later, when a visit was threatened, she wrote to Ellen (6 Apr 1853) "I trust in goodness he will not stay long" and refers to the visit as "the infliction." However, she was surprised by his enthusiastic reception of *Jane Eyre* and *Shirley*, and perhaps revised some of her opinions about his character and attitudes. He called on George Smith in 1853 and suggested that the French phrases in *Villette* be translated in footnotes (something generations of students would applaud), but this was never done.

His first wife died in 1827, and in 1836 he married Mary Alice Gibson of Bradford in Calverley Church. She died in 1852, and he published a memorial to her: "Simplicity and Godly Sincerity." He was married again shortly afterwards. He edited *The Pastoral Visitor* "to assist the Devotion of the CHURCH, the FAMILY and the CLOSET" (*Leeds Intelligencer*, 3 Dec 1821). He was clearly indefatigable, enthusiastic, and opinionated, and probably quite hard to bear. One report of him at a meeting on the Factory Act in 1836 said simply "Rev. William Morgan spoke at considerable length" (*Leeds Intelligencer*, 12 Mar 1836).

"Morley Hall": poem by Branwell concerning a house once believed to have belonged to an ancestor of the Halifax Leylands. It was a project undertaken as a return for Leyland's medallion bust of Branwell. He wrote in April 1846 asking for details of the elopement of a sixteenth-century woman of the family, which was to be at the heart of the poem of "several cantos" (Leyland, v. 2, p. 242), and in October of that year, in an unusually exuberant letter, he said that the poem was "in the eighth month of her pregnancy and expects ere long to be delivered of a fine thumping boy" (to J. B. Leyland, early Oct 1846). All we have is a pedestrian 90 lines of introductory matter. Juliet Barker (1994) conjectures that the rest was lost. On the other hand this could be another example of what Hartley Merrall said of his onetime friend in a marginal note on his copy of Leyland's book: "he was untruthful, and did nothing he talked of."

***Morning Chronicle*:** as well as reviewing Charlotte's novels favorably, the newspaper mentioned her in an article on the governess question, along with Harriet Martineau, Maria Edgeworth, and (somewhat puzzlingly) Jane Austen. Charlotte was pleased with this unusual kind of notice, and wrote to W. S. Williams (12 May 1848) that "an allusion of that sort seems to say more than a regular notice."

"*Mort de Moise, La*": one of the longest and most ambitious of Charlotte's *devoirs* for M. Heger, almost certainly written in July 1843. Heger told Mrs Gaskell that this followed on from his reading to her one of Delavigne's poems on Joan of Arc. However, it has been suggested that he misremembered, and that the *devoir* shows the inspiration of a similarly named poet, Alfred de Vigny, and his poem "Moïse." The essay begins with Moses summoning the tribes of Israel to receive his blessing ("a vast crowd, a whole nation reunited, five hundred thousand persons, not counting women and children," BE, p. 312) as Charlotte, following her Old and New Testaments, rather surprisingly puts it); then there is a diversion into the question of whether the biblical account should be taken literally or allegorically; then there is a last section which narrates Moses' journey to the summit of Mount Nebo, as described in *Deuteronomy*, and tacked on to the moment of his death, after a survey of the various fortunes of the Jewish people in the years after it, is a vision of a woman holding a child: "His soul has recognised the Messiah" (BE, p. 322).

"*Mort de Napoléon, La*": long *devoir* almost certainly written in May 1843, extensively corrected and later almost rewritten by Heger. The *devoir* begins with a meditation on whether the ordinary person, or mediocrity, can judge the greatness of such a man as Napoleon; it goes on to contrast his beginning and his end; it distinguishes his genius as "his power to be wholly self-sufficient" (BE, p. 274), and it then slides into an encomium of his conqueror – Wellington being characterized as "of another species" (BE, p. 278). Lonoff rightly calls this the "most political of her devoirs" (p. 309), but also draws attention to personal undercurrents following on from Charlotte's lonely situation at the Pensionnat, with little contact with the man she felt such a passion for.

Morton: village which has St John Rivers, for the time being, as its vicar. Here Jane Eyre teaches the village girls, awarding them by the end of her stay an encomium rather like a Sunday School prize, and gets to know, and to be loved by, their parents, mainly farmers. In the vicinity live the nouveaux riche Oliver family, of which the daughter, Rosamund is in love with and loved by St John Rivers. Oliver owns the village industry, which is needle manufacture, as in Hathersage, and the village's vicarage is immediately next to the church and churchyard, as in Hathersage.

See also Hathersage

Mosley, Sally: presumably a heavy-duty occasional servant at the Parsonage, immortalized in Emily and Anne's 1834 diary paper as "washing in the back Kitchin."

Mount Pleasant, No 83, Boundary Street, Manchester: where Charlotte took lodgings in 1846 to nurse her father after his cataract operation. The lodgings were kept by a former servant of the eye surgeon Mr W. J. Wilson, and cost one pound and five shillings a week.

Moxon, Edward (1801–58): English publisher specializing in poetry who at one time or another issued works by Wordsworth, Tennyson, Southey, Rogers, Patmore, and Browning. Charlotte recommended his most recent edition of Wordsworth to her publishers as a model for the Bells' *Poems*, but this idea was abandoned.

Mozart, Wolfgang Amadeus (1756–91): one of the Brontës' most admired composers. Leyland records Branwell as particularly enthusiastic about his masses, and Emily played arrangements of his best-known operatic overtures and other major works (see Wallace, 1986). Mozart's was one of the names Branwell painted into the corners of his portrait of Hartley Merrall.

Mozley, Anne (1809–91): author of two reviews of Charlotte's novels in the *Christian Remembrancer*, which was published by her brother. That of *Jane Eyre* (probably by her) pre-echoed many later criticisms of the novel (e.g., Mr Rochester is "the vision of a woman's fancy," Helen Burns is the "feeblest character in the book . . . a simple seraph," and the house party scenes are "the fashionable world seen through the area railings"). That of *Villette* called the earlier Currer Bell "soured, coarse, and grumbling" and admitted that she had "gained both in amiability and propriety" in the intervening years. She shows some appreciation of aspects of the novel, but she insists that characters such as Lucy Snowe (and by implication Currer Bell) "do not know the power of home over the heart . . . We want a woman at our hearth." This review prompted a reply from Charlotte which revealed something of her own life and circumstances (something she could not have done if Emily had still been alive), and this in turn elicited an apology from the editor of the *Remembrancer*.

Mühler, Heinrich: one of Mme Walraven's party at the fête in *Villette*. He is a "young fair-haired foreigner" (ch. 39) who gets uneasy at the attentions M. Paul pays to his ward Justine Marie Sauveur. Later we are told (ch. 41) that Mühler and Justine Marie are engaged.

Müllenberg, Amélia: one of Frances Henri's most turbulent pupils at Mlle Reuter's school in *The Professor*. See ch. 15.

Murgatroyd, Frederick: one of the mill-hands or overseers at Hollow's Mill (ch. 2), and a suitor of Sarah, the maid at the Hollow (ch. 8), who prefers his "middling face" to that of Moses Barraclough (ch. 8). It is Murgatroyd who betrays Barraclough's part in the frame-breaking.

Murray, Charles: youngest child of the Murrays in *Agnes Grey*. His mother's favorite, he is characterized (ch. 7) as pettish, cowardly, and selfish, and an inveterate liar. He is very backward, but his mother wants him educated without any effort on his part.

Murray, John: elder son of the Murrays in *Agnes Grey*. A healthy, good-natured boy, but unruly and ill-educated. Agnes, in a rare admission, says he "might have been a decent lad" but for his defective education (ch. 7).

Murray, Matilda: younger daughter of the Murrays, around 14 when Agnes Grey arrives as governess. A hoydenish girl, mainly interested in horses, she is not ill-natured but thoughtless and careless of other's feelings.

Murray, Mr (no first name given): employer of Agnes Grey at Horton Lodge. He is characterized in ch. 7 as a roistering, fox-hunting squire figure but we subsequently hear very little more about him.

Murray, Mrs (no first name given): wife of the above. A handsome, dashing lady whose principal interest is in her own social life. She treats Agnes Grey casually, and is mainly concerned to acquire showy accomplishments for her daughters, whom she inculcates with her own worldly values.

Murray, Rosalie: elder daughter of the Murrays. Flirtatious, worldly, and superficial, she is the victim of the values prevalent in her family, and in chs. 22 and 23 we see the price she pays, in a loveless marriage. Though many biographers assume a near-identity between the Murrays and the Robinsons, Anne Brontë's second employers, it is worth noting that Rosalie marries for entirely worldly, mercenary motives, whereas Lydia Robinson made an imprudent marriage to an actor for love, or at any rate sexual attraction.

Musical Library, The: collection of piano pieces and transcriptions bought by or for Emily after she returned to Haworth from Brussels. Marks in the contents tables suggest she had a taste for the greatest composers available in the collection – Beethoven, Handel, Gluck, Haydn, and Mozart. Though there are transcriptions from, for example, Beethoven's symphonies, these are individual movements, not complete works.

"My Angria and the Angrians": chronicle by Charlotte, narrated by Lord Charles Wellesley, which begins with the exodus from Verdopolis to the new kingdom of Angria, and its capital Adrianopolis. After resisting the rush of young notables Lord Charles follows it on foot, and at this point there occurs the meeting with Patrick Benjamin Wiggins and his gross inflation of the importance of his home town of "Howard" and his denigration of his sisters ("I wasn't satisfied with being a sign-painter at Howard, as Charlotte and them things were with being sempstresses," EW, v. 2, pt 2, p. 250). Charlotte then introduces us to various of the new inhabitants of the Kingdom, suggests trouble in the marriage of Douro and Mary Henrietta, trouble which cannot be separated from the machinations of her father, Northangerland, and the piece ends with the death of Douro's former father-in-law the Duke of Badhi (Dr Hume) and the birth of twins to Douro, now King of Angria, and his Queen.

Branwell probably began what was to become his monumental narrative entitled "Angria and the Angrians" in May 1834; Charlotte's narrative "My Angria and the Angrians" was finished in October of the same year. It seems likely that the "My" in the title is of significance, and marks the beginnings if not of a split then of a partial separation between the two Angrian collaborators. Charlotte is announcing that she is interested in different characters to her brother, or at least in different aspects of their personalities or lives. Where he is concerned with war and politics she is concerned with love and intrigue. This distinction is very visible in their later writing, and takes its most extreme form when Branwell kills off Queen Mary Henrietta for political reasons and Charlotte revives her in a highly romantic narrative, "The Return of Zamorna." By extension it is possible that this title is also a declaration by its supposed narrator Lord Charles Wellesley that though his brother now reigns in

Angria and surrounds himself with statesmen and soldiers, his own interest is in these great men's wives, whose darling he is, and also in an assorted collection of artists, riff-raff and outcasts, in one of which category Patrick Benjamin Wiggins surely has his place.

See also Juvenilia: 3. The rise of Angria, 4. Angria redivivus

Myers, Alice: the least discussed of all the governesses in the Brontës' novels, she is brought in by Arthur Huntingdon apparently to teach his son, in reality as his paramour. The assumption that Alice is her first name is based on *The Tenant of Wildfell Hall*, ch. 47.

N

Nab Cottage: Hartley Coleridge's home from about 1840 to 1849, where the farming Richardsons took care of him as far as was possible. Branwell visited him there in May 1840, and Charlotte sent to him there chapters of "Ashworth" in December of the same year. The cottage was also known as The Knabbe, and is still standing.

Napoleon 1, Emperor of the French (1769–1821; reigned 1804–15): one of the childhood heroes of the Brontës, particularly Branwell. He is frequently mentioned in the juvenilia, as well as making occasional appearances. Branwell has him invading Angria with immense armies, and has detailed tallies of losses (see e.g., the narratives of the "War of Encroachment" and the "War of Aggression," WPBB, v. 1, pp. 365–446). He later contemplated a poem on the subject. Charlotte concerns herself with him much less, since her hero was his great opponent, and when she writes about him in Brussels (*"La Mort de Napoléon"*) she struggles with the subject, making strong points such as "Napoleon believed himself a whole nation in one body" (BE, p. 274) – but in the end retreating from the magnificent enigma to concern herself with Wellington. He lies behind the difficulties of the cloth trade in *Shirley*, and M. Paul Emmanuel in *Villette* is given some "imperial" characteristics which ally him to Napoleon, including "a shameless disregard of magnanimity" (ch. 30).

Nasmyth, Rev. (no first name given): marries Miss Temple in *Jane Eyre*. He is mentioned but not characterized.

National Gallery: the greatest British collection of art. It was founded in 1824, and moved from Pall Mall to its present position in Trafalgar Square in 1839. It was probably visited by Charlotte and Emily on their way to Brussels in 1842, and certainly by Charlotte and Anne on their brief visit to London in 1848. Charlotte went again on her London visit in late 1849. At that time it housed the Royal Academy as well as the great collection based on that of John Julius Angerstein, so it had many of the classical paintings that the Brontës had always wanted to see, as well as the more modern British painters whose works had been familiar, mainly through engravings, since their childhood. Soon the collection was to be increased by the notable directorship of Sir Charles Eastlake, helped by his wife, formerly Miss Rigby, *Jane Eyre*'s fiercest and most unfair critic.

National School, Haworth:

National School, Haworth: Patrick Brontë had a strong interest in establishing a school for the poor children of Haworth (the boys of the better-off parents were catered for, though none too effectively, by the Grammar School) which culminated in appeals in late 1843 to the National Society, which had the aim of establishing just such schools. In a series of letters – many of them only recently published in Dudley Green's (2005) edition of Patrick's letters – to the Rev. W. J. Kennedy, Secretary to the Society, Patrick pleaded his case most urgently and showed a considerable skill in the art of begging. The Society revealed a certain dilatoriness in carrying out its promises, so that Patrick had to keep them up to the mark in respect of the £50 a year they had promised for the schoolmaster, which seems to have been received in full in August 1844, eight months after the school's opening.

Soon after that opening he was reporting to Kennedy (19 Jan 1844) that they had nearly two hundred pupils, but in August he had to report that owing to the "ever busy, and meddling Methodists" who had opened a school of their own, the numbers were down to 150–60 (letters of 2 and 8 Aug 1844). Right from the beginning he was anxious to provide for both sexes: "Now, I very much want a Mistress, here, for the Girls," he wrote (9 Jan 1844), and he took advantage of the first schoolmaster Ebenezer Rand's desire to take a wife to squeeze more money out of the Society for her to teach in the school. All in all Patrick was justified in proclaiming the school "prosperous, and of vast importance" (26 Oct 1844). Owing to his failing eyesight he was forced to give up a great deal of the day-to-day school business to his curate Arthur Bell Nicholls, who taught religious knowledge there every day. The Rands left to go to a school near Staley Bridge in Cheshire, and were succeeded by Joseph Purnell.

Nelson, Horatio, Lord (1758–1805):

Nelson, Horatio, Lord (1758–1805): English naval hero, killed at the Battle of Trafalgar. Patrick changed the spelling of his name Prunty or Brunty to conform to the Dukedom of Bronte, conferred on Nelson in 1799 by the King of the Two Sicilies. He and his publishers used various means to convey that the name was pronounced with two syllables, not one. Nelson excited the Brontë children less than Wellington or Napoleon, probably because he was dead long before they were born. There are several mentions of him in the juvenilia, however, including from Branwell the information that Northangerland held Nelson in respect solely from his connection with Lady Hamilton ("Angria and the Angrians," WPBB, v. 3, p. 136). The adult Branwell found the diminutive and sickly lady-killer an appealing figure, and made three versions of a poem to him which Daphne du Maurier thought "quite easily his worst" (IWBB, ch. 10).

Nero: a merlin hawk acquired by the Brontë family in 1841 and apparently disposed of by Aunt Branwell along with the geese Adelaide and Victoria in 1842, while Charlotte and Emily were in Brussels. Mentioned in two diary papers (AB, 30 July 1841, EJB, 31 July 1845). In the latter Emily mentions that she "enquired on all hands and could hear nothing of him." He was no doubt named, as a bird of prey, after (reputedly) the most bloodthirsty and depraved Roman emperor, cited memorably in ch. 1 of *Jane Eyre*. In "Passing Events" a newspaper talks of Zamorna's actions as "of Nero-like brutality, ferocity, absurdity and filth" (FN, p. 74). The hawk was earlier thought, by a misreading, to have been called Hero.

Newby, Thomas Cautley (d. 1882): publisher of all three novels by Emily and Anne Brontë. The firm of Newby and Co. was then new, having been founded in 1843 in imitation of the methods of Henry Colburn, a somewhat dicey firm to model oneself on. Newby specialized in new authors, and expected them to contribute to the cost of their books' publication. Charlotte recorded after her sisters' deaths that they had paid £50 towards the cost of their first novels' publication, no part of that sum ever being returned, and that Newby printed 500 copies of *Tenant*, paying by agreement £25 on publication and the same sum when 250 copies had been sold (letter to WSW, 10 Sep 1850).

Trollope's first novel *The Macdermots of Ballycloran* was published by him, also in 1847. Newby, out of courtesy to Trollope's mother Fanny Trollope, did not take a subsidy for publishing it, but he delayed its appearance for 18 months and paid the author nothing: "I can with truth declare that I expected nothing. And I got nothing" (Trollope, *Autobiography*, ch. 4). After Fanny Trollope's death Newby published novels by an unknown author whom he called Frank Trollope, but with either "Trollope" or "F. Trollope" on the spine.

One of Newby's cleverest (and least honest) ploys was creating confusion about the authorship of works. Thus, when it did not sell, *The Macdermots* was attributed to Trollope's mother, and similarly a work by the estranged father of Julia Kavanagh was attributed to her. He was helped by authorship often running in families, he being the publisher, usually, of the less promising or popular members. With the three Bells his aim, in so far as he had any kind of master strategy, seems to have been to create total confusion as to who wrote what, and in addition to pin quotes from critics on to any book that it suited him to – as when on the flyleaf of *Tenant* he had a critic from the *Atlas* describe *Agnes Grey* as "a colossal performance" (in reality a paraphrase of a description of *Wuthering Heights*). All this was leading up to his attempt to persuade an American publisher that all the Bell novels were "the production of one writer" – a claim that led to Charlotte and Anne's notable visit to London in July 1848 (to MT, 4 Sep 1848).

Charlotte attempted during that year to influence her sisters against their "scamp" of a publisher, but her pressurizing of Emily at least had its usual effect: strengthening her resolve to act against her sister's wishes. At the time of the republication of *Wuthering Heights* and *Agnes Grey* together with some hitherto unpublished poems (1850), the books' new publisher George Smith made great efforts to secure for Charlotte what Newby still owed her dead sisters. This gave Charlotte more wry amusement than hope, but it did result in a check for £90 reaching her years later, in 1854.

The man whom John Sutherland calls "without doubt, the most notorious publisher of fiction in the Victorian period" (1988, p. 461) gave up his business in 1874, the firm ceasing to exist.

See also Colburn, Henry

Newgate Prison:

one of London's most notorious jails, dating back to the twelfth century. Outside it public executions took place, hence Branwell's reference in "And the Weary are at Rest" to "taking a last look on this weary world from the elevation of Newgate scaffold." The building Charlotte visited in 1853 was the last of several jails on this site, and dated from 1780. She tried to talk to a young girl "with an interesting face, and an expression of the deepest misery" (see CBL, v. 3, p. 109). The girl had killed her illegitimate baby. Warders stepped in and stopped the conversation. The jail was demolished in 1903.

Newman, Francis William (1805–97):

brother of Cardinal Newman, and author of *The Soul*, which Charlotte admired, calling it "daring . . . but it is pure and elevated" (possibly to James Taylor, 19 Dec 1849?). Mrs Gaskell shared her high opinion of the book.

Newman, John Henry, Cardinal (1801–90):

Catholic convert in 1845 and author of *The Dream of Gerontius* (1866), he was made a cardinal in 1879. Charlotte probably attended some of his 1850 series of lectures on "Certain Difficulties Felt by Anglicans in Submitting to the Catholic Church," since later that year she told Mrs Gaskell about them "in a very quiet concise graphic way" (ECG to C. Winkworth, 25 Aug 1850). Newman was a much loved figure in all his religious stances from evangelicalism to moderate Catholicism, and Charlotte spared him the barbs she directed at Cardinal Wiseman.

Newton and Robinson:

solicitors of York. They were the Robinsons' legal firm, and later acted for Lady Scott, formerly Mrs Robinson, when that lady mobilized the forces of the Establishment, including Sir James Stephens, to fight Mrs Gaskell's allegations against her in the *Life*. See articles by Edward Chitham and Tom Winnifrith (BST, v. 21, pts. 3 & 4, 1994). A collection of this firm's papers is in the Brontë Parsonage Museum.

New Zealand:

the country figured in the Brontë children's imaginative life even in the 1830s, before white immigration had seriously begun. In "My Angria and the Angrians" (1834) Patrick Benjamin Wiggins (a version of Branwell) imagines a tombstone for himself which, among other fantastic absurdities, names him as civilizer of Australia and founder of "the city of Wigginopolis in New Zealand" (EW, v. 2, pt 2, p. 251). Later the country loomed much larger, when Charlotte's friend Mary Taylor and her brother Waring went out among the very early settlers there. Mary was eventually joined by her cousin Ellen Taylor, and together they opened and ran a shop. Mary urged Ellen Nussey to join them there, claiming she could do several jobs that would be social death in England. It is to be hoped that a little of Mary's far-sighted vision for women in the new colony had some influence in its very early embrace of female suffrage (1893). She returned to England, however, in 1860.

Mary's adventurous decision to go to the colony doubtless inspired Anne's remarks about the immigrant to New Zealand who awakes to "find himself at Port Nelson ... with a world of waters between himself and all that knew him" (*Agnes Grey*, ch. 7). Rose Yorke in *Shirley* is naturally sent to "some region of the southern hemisphere" (v. 1, ch. 9).

Nicholl (no first name given): acquaintance of William Crimsworth in the town of X—, possibly a workmate or fellow lodger. Mentioned but not described in ch. 5 of *The Professor*.

Nicholls, Alan (d. 1890): third son of William and Margaret Nicholls. With the next son Arthur he was virtually adopted by their maternal uncle and aunt. He was one of the party that welcomed Arthur and his new bride Charlotte to Dublin (where he was manager of the Grand Canal) in July 1854. She described him as "a sagacious well-informed and courteous man" (to MW, 10 July 1854).

Nicholls, Rev. Arthur Bell (1819–1906): fourth son of William (d. 1849) and Margaret Nicholls (née Bell, d. 1830), small farmers in Co. Antrim in the north of Ireland. There is a resemblance here to Patrick's early years, but it ceases when he and his brother Alan were taken from the small farmstead where they were born (which is still standing) and into the family of his maternal uncle Alan Bell – an act of great generosity, granted Bell's own growing family. Bell and his wife Harriette lived at Cuba House, Banagher, Co. Offaly, where Bell was headmaster of the prestigious Royal High School. Arthur thenceforth grew up in surroundings of gentility, even of some state, and his uncle seems to have paid his way through Trinity College, Dublin, which he entered in 1836 and graduated from in 1844. It is possible that some spells of teaching, perhaps in his uncle's school where he had been a pupil, accounted for the length of his undergraduate stay at Trinity College. Certainly when he went to Haworth teaching was a prominent part of his duties there.

Though Charlotte registered his arrival in Haworth with a note of approval ("a respectable young man, reads well," to Mrs Rand, 26 May 1845?), most of the early references contain disapproval verging on dislike, either on her part or that of his parishioners: "A cold, far-away sort of civility" exists between her and him she tells Ellen Nussey (10 July 1846), and "his narrowness of mind always strikes me chiefly" (to EN, 15 Oct 1847?). He returned regularly for lengthy visits to Ireland, and Charlotte records that Haworth people, during his absence, "express a desire that he should not trouble himself to re-cross the channel" (to EN, 7 Oct 1847).

As the 1840s turned into the 1850s, and Charlotte faced life as the last of the Brontë children, the references become more favorable: he is "mild and uncontentious" at a tea-drinking (to EN, 28 July 1851?), and when she describes the maneuverings of the congregation of a tiny church in Filey "not more than thrice the length and breadth of our passage" her comment that "had Mr. Nicholls been there – he certainly would have laughed out" (to PB, 2 June 1852) suggests she felt a certain mental kinship with him. The momentous declaration of his love at the end of that year brought from Charlotte an admission that she had suspected an attachment for some time, judging this from his "constant looks – and strange, feverish restraint" (to EN, 15 Dec 1852). It is clear from the same letter that the vehement, tormented demeanor of her new suitor impressed her mind in Nicholls's favor. The contempt and cruelty with which Patrick treated him in the following months also did him no harm in Charlotte's eyes.

Her feelings continued sadly mixed until Nicholls left Haworth in May 1853. She confessed to Ellen Nussey that "I don't like that dark gloom of his" (4 Mar 1853), and there is pathos and uncertainty in her admission that "I do not know him well enough to be sure that there is truth and true affection . . . at the bottom of his chagrin" (6 Apr 1853). However, she records all signs of Haworth esteem and concern for Nicholls, and their last interview before he left the town mirrored his initial confession of love: he displayed an almost inarticulate strength of attachment, and Charlotte was moved by it. Over the summer of 1853 he became curate of Kirk Smeaton, near Pontefract, and by September, and perhaps as early as July, he was back visiting in the Haworth area. Charlotte was moved by his constancy and persistence, and by April 1854 he was her accepted suitor, with a summer marriage determined on. Charlotte still, unattractively, insisted on his lack of "talents, congenial tastes and thoughts," but was grateful for his "tender love" (to EN, 11 Apr 1854).

After a quiet wedding, at which Margaret Wooler gave the bride away in place of her father, Charlotte and Arthur (as he now was to her) set out for the honeymoon trip through North Wales to Ireland. In his native land Arthur showed to better effect than in Haworth, and Charlotte was impressed not only by the standing of his adoptive family but also by the strength of their affection and esteem for her husband. He too showed that her artistic and romantic side would be deferred to, if it could not be understood, notably at Kilkee, where Charlotte's usual strong emotion at the sight of the sea was accepted without demur.

After marriage the references to Arthur are uniformly warm, admiring (with the odd amused demurral), and grateful for the continuing strength of his affection and care for her. "[E]very day makes my own attachment to him stronger," she wrote to Margaret Wooler (15 Nov 1854), and "he *is* 'my dear boy' certainly, dearer now than he was six months ago" (to EN, 26 Dec 1854). There is the occasional insistence of Arthur that she perform the duties of what was in all but name the incumbent's wife: he insists that certain things be done "and it generally seems the right thing – only I sometimes wish that I could have written the letter as well" (to MW, 22 Aug 1854). However, there is no real evidence, only insinuations written after Charlotte's death, that he would have interfered with her career as a novelist. For the brief period of their marriage Charlotte was probably more interested in absorbing the exciting and pleasurable experiences of the married state. In the months of her last illness she paid tribute to his tender nursing, and wrote: "No kinder better husband than mine it seems to me can there be in the world" (to L. Wheelwright, 15 Feb 1855). She gave concrete expression to her gratitude in her will, which annulled the cautious provisions of the marriage settlement. His great and lasting grief at her death, and his loyalty in defending her memory, for example over her picture of Cowan Bridge School, is undeniable.

In the six years he lived with Patrick after Charlotte's death the two men shook down to a reasonable working relationship. On many religious matters they were wide apart in their attitudes (e.g., on dissenters and Puseyism), and their way of doing homage to the Brontë both held dear was very different: Patrick welcomed the tributes paid by admirers, Nicholls jealously guarded the privacy of himself and his late wife and repelled them. He acquiesced reluctantly in the commissioning of the memoir from Mrs Gaskell (probably neither man contemplated a biography on the scale that actually resulted), but stood out against christening babies "Brontë" (there he had to be circumvented). But by and large he remained devoted to his father-in-law and fulfilled the duty (as he fulfilled all duties) that he had promised Charlotte on their marriage.

When Patrick died in 1861 it seemed to many a foregone conclusion that Nicholls would succeed him, but the Haworth trustees, traditional enemies to foregone conclusions, had other thoughts, and the perpetual curacy went to the Rev. John Wade, later known in Haworth as "envious Wade," from his hostility to Brontë-worship. If they rejected Arthur, therefore, because of his distaste for the lucrative tourist trade then growing around the Brontë name and novels, they fell from the frying pan into the fire. Arthur returned to Ireland, and never afterwards sought clerical preferment. Perhaps his experience in Haworth had sickened him with the Church. Certainly his cast of mind, always putting duty and his brand of morality above personal relationships, had not always been appreciated there. It is pleasant that one relationship, that with Martha Brown (who, Charlotte had said earlier "hates him," to EN, 6 Apr 1853), survived his move back home: indeed she accompanied him, and spent long periods with him and his wife in her remaining years.

For Arthur married again. His second wife, Mary Bell, was one of his cousins with whom he had been brought up – almost a younger sister. She accepted, it is said, that Charlotte was the great love of his life, and she joined him in revering the woman she had met on the honeymoon trip. Arthur became a farmer "in a very small way: we have two cows, a heifer and a calf" (ABN to a clerical friend, 5 Nov 1861, quoted in Cochrane, 1999, p. 111). The latter part of the nineteenth century, a time of agricultural depression when, in Lady Bracknell's words, "land has ceased to be either a profit or a pleasure," was not a time to increase one's fortune by it. Arthur at Hill House, Banagher, drifted towards poverty. This cannot be the only reason why he sold Brontë letters and juvenilia, along with copyrights, to Clement Shorter, acting for the forger T. J. Wise, for the amount he received was way below their value. Perhaps, like Ellen Nussey, he was deceived by a mendacious promise that, after he had used them, they would be given to the British Museum or the Victoria and Albert. They were in fact sold. His note to Shorter, on a collection of letters, "Don't let Mr Wise appropriate them" was in vain. Arthur's widow, in very straightened circumstances, sold Brontë memorabilia and manuscripts in sales in 1907 and 1914.

Arthur had died in 1906. His coffin rested under Charlotte's portrait by Richmond before its burial in Banagher churchyard. He was nearly 88, and his life had spanned five reigns – not something many people whose maturity was spent under Queen Victoria could say.

See also Bell, Alan; Bell, Harriette; Bell, Mary; Sowden, Rev. Sutcliffe

Nicholls, Margaret, née Bell: mother of Arthur Bell Nicholls. She died in 1830 (see article by Betty O'Sullivan, BS, v. 31, pt 1, March 2006).

Nicholson, Thomas Watson: landlord of the Old Cock Inn in Halifax, who dunned Branwell for money he owed in the last months of his life. He threatened a court summons, and if he went ahead with that, said Branwell, "I am RUINED." Branwell claimed he would request an advance from Dr Crosby at Thorp Green "which I am sure to obtain" (to J. B. Leyland, 17 June 1848?).

Noah o'Tim's: Moses Barroclough's supporter in the deputation that waits on Robert Moore in ch. 8 of *Shirley*.

"Noctes Ambrosianae": a series of conversation pieces that appeared throughout the 1820s in *Blackwood's Magazine*. They were written by John Wilson as "Christopher North" (more than half), James Hogg, and J. G. Lockhart among others, who appear thinly disguised as the conversationalists. The punning title refers to a real Edinburgh tavern, Ambrose's. Branwell was much taken with the knockabout intellectual humor of the series (he made particular mention of it in his letter to *Blackwood's* of 7 Dec 1836), and tried to reproduce the same atmosphere, with less promising materials, in the male drinking groups of Haworth, Bradford, and Halifax.

Noel, Baptist Wriothesley (1798–1873): popular evangelical preacher. He was the darling of the Williams family (cousins of Aunt Branwell) who visited Haworth in August 1840, and it was possibly through them that he recommended for Charlotte and Emily a school in Lille when they were having difficulty finding a suitable one in Brussels. Fortunately the Lille plan fell through when the Pensionnat Heger was recommended. Noel's popularity was established within the Anglican Church, but he validated his first name (a family one) when he was baptized into the Baptist Church in August 1849.

North American Review: periodical that published in October 1848 Edwin Whipple's harsh review of the first four Bell novels, the most severe judgment of any thus far in their careers. Charlotte read this to Emily in the last weeks of her life, and aroused some amusement with the *NAR*'s descriptions of Ellis as "dogged," "brutal," and "morose" (to WSW, 22 Nov 1848). Whipple said that *Tenant* contained "conversations such as we hoped never to see printed in English." The *Review* had close Unitarian connections, but this did not prevent its being highly critical of Gaskell's *Life*, feeling

that a biography written while major players in the life in question were still alive could only injure their "rights and susceptibilities" (see Barker, 1994, p. 797). The review summed up the dilemmas both of Mrs Gaskell and also of the two men who commissioned her book.

Northangerland, Alexander Percy, Earl or Duke of, a. k. a. Rogue, Rouge, or Rougue, Lord Elrington or Ellrington: with Zamorna one

of the twin columns supporting the narrative structure of the Glasstown/Angrian saga. His father, Edward Percy, was in early life a high-handed, rack-renting landlord in Northumberland who became a gambler and swindler in Ireland, and finally took his aristocratic wife Lady Helen to live an aristocratic life in Africa, where his moral character did not improve. Alexander is a great mystery even to his mother, and to Captain John Bud his tutor, who writes his Life. His one redeeming feature is his great musical ability, which is a humanizing factor equivalent to Zamorna's gifts as a poet. Otherwise he is as choleric and tyrannical as his father, with whom he is perpetually warring. While still in his teens, and monstrously in debt, he marries Augusta de Segovia and is exiled to the Philosopher's Island, where he is a brilliant student but also a leader of student unrest, espousing the causes of atheism and republicanism. When he returns home he and Augusta, with plenty of authorial nods towards Macbeth and his lady, plan to murder Alexander's father. One "wild and stormy morning" the deed is done. Not for the first time Alexander is over-clever and he and Augusta try to double-cross his associates, a plan which leads to the death of Augusta.

His second wife, Maria Henrietta Wharton, is mother to three sons, another Edward, William, and Henry, and also to a daughter. The last-named is much loved, and later becomes Queen of Angria, while the sons are handed to the hit-man Sdeath to be murdered. In fact, in a rare example of mercy, he lets them live and grow up secretly to plague their father later on. After Maria's death Alexander's life becomes a muddle of political conspiracies and rebellions, alternating with unlikely career choices such as a cattle-drover and pirate. His life changes when he marries one of his piratical captives, Zenobia, Lady Elrington. She remains his wife throughout the rest of the saga, though she is physically more attracted to Zamorna, and though Alexander has a string of mistresses, notably Louisa Dance/Vernon, the mother of Caroline. After his marriage Alexander swiftly moves to the forefront of political life in Verdopolis and Angria.

His political principles remain fairly constant: he is a republican, which means he is in favor of a dictatorship with himself as absolute (but not royal) ruler. To attain this he enters into many political alliances, all of which he reneges on. In personality he is now magnetic when speaking or writing, but seen to be incapable of loyalty and generally unreliable. His alliances with Zamorna are matters of convenience, but they also implicitly acknowledge a soul-likeness, particularly in their common egotism and insistence on total control and immediate satisfaction of all desires. Briefly during the civil wars that blight Verdopolis and Angria he attains his ambition and dictatorship. The "blood red banner of Percy and Revolution" (WPBB, v. 2, p. 630) means, predictably, tyranny and slaughter for many of the inhabitants of Angria. In one of the last sections of "Angria and the Angrians" (WPBB, v. 3, p. 270) Zamorna years later rescues Northangerland from a raging mob by taking his arm and leaving his own party together with him and Zenobia. In Charlotte's later juvenilia, for example "Caroline Vernon," the two are still sparring, still morally reprehensible, but there is something of a going through the routine about it all, some recognition that they are talking man to man and despot to despot. However, it is Charlotte who revives him most convincingly, Anglicizes him, and presents him with great panache in the first chapters of "Ashworth."

Northangerland, it seems, took over Branwell's life, though his use of the name as a pseudonym is nothing more than a convenience in his later and published poetry, which generally deals with non-Angrian subjects. But he was clearly Branwell's favorite character in the saga, always being reinvented with delight and relish. What was the appeal? Perhaps first of all the complete amorality of the man, his flouting of every civilized code, his ruthlessness, his determination to stew in the mayhem he has masterminded. He is a Macbeth who never falls into "the sere, the yellow leaf," who always relishes the curses which follow his every public move. He has the appeal of someone who goes the whole hog to a young man who would dearly love to, but never in fact goes much of a hog at all.

North British Review: Scottish periodical that published in August 1849 a review of the first Bell novels, which Charlotte objected to because the reviewer first eulogized *Jane Eyre* and then declared that if it was the work of a woman "she must be a woman pretty nearly unsexed" – thus following in the path of the *Quarterly*'s reviewer. This periodical was consistently hostile to the novels of Emily and Anne, talking of "language too disgusting for the eye or the ear to tolerate" in *Wuthering Heights* and this led it to revise the early favorable opinions of *Jane Eyre*.

Northern Society for the Encouragement of the Fine Arts: society which
held a regular exhibition in early summer in their gallery in Albion Street, Leeds, at which Charlotte exhibited two pictures in 1834. Leyland gives an account of the Brontës' attendance there that year, but was clearly unaware that Charlotte was an exhibitor. Both Leyland's brother Joseph and William Robinson were regular contributors, and pictures by the best-known artists of the time could be seen there, including Turner, Raeburn, Landseer, and Sir Thomas Lawrence. Many of the local artists were of dubious merit, and the advertisement encouraging submissions stated: "If Copies, the Exhibitor must mention from whence copied; but copies from Prints can on no account be submitted" (*Leeds Intelligencer*, 2 Jan 1833). This last prohibition seems to have been flouted by Charlotte with her picture of Bolton Abbey. It is possible that the presence of the Brontës at the 1834 exhibition marked the beginning of the Brontës' association with William Robinson – possibly that with Leyland too. Disappointingly the *Leeds Intelligencer* found the 1834 exhibition "Certainly inferior to any that has preceded it in the Gallery of the Northern Society" (28 June 1834).

North Lees Hall: a gentry residence near Hathersage, home to the Eyre family.
Charlotte and Ellen Nussey visited the house two or three times (EN to Mary Gorham,

22 July 1845), and during one of these visits Charlotte must have seen the Apostles Cupboard now in the Parsonage Museum, and perhaps heard the story of the mistress of the house who had gone mad. There are many competing houses with claims to have suggested Thornfield in *Jane Eyre*, but North Lees' claim is a good one.

Norton Conyers: Jacobean manor house near Ripon, the home of the Graham family since 1624, with strong family traditions of a madwoman confined in the attic or a room on the top floor. The association with Charlotte originates with Ellen Nussey, who said she remembered Charlotte's description of the place and also her memories of the tradition. Charlotte's visit is conjectured to have taken place during her stay at Swarcliffe, while she was governess to the Sidgwick family. There is no mention of any such visit in Charlotte's extant letters, or in memories of her stay from the Sidgwick side. Sarah Fermi and Robin Greenwood, "*Jane Eyre* and the Greenwood family" (BST, v. 22, 1997) have suggested that the house was probably unoccupied in 1839, making a visit to the interior unlikely, though she could have seen the exterior, and heard the story of the mad ancestor of the Grahams.

Nowell, William: a young weaver from the Dewsbury area whose arrest and imprisonment in 1810 became a local *cause célèbre*. He was accused of having accepted the king's shilling (i.e., taken the usual small inducement to join the army) and then deserted. His enlistment was said to have taken place at a local fair, and the soldier who claimed to have recruited him was one James Thackray. There were many Dewsbury inhabitants ready to swear that Nowell was not at the fair, but they met with a dogged refusal to reopen the case from the Wakefield magistrate who had imprisoned him. Patrick and other prominent locals got publicity for the injustice, and recruited to their side national figures such as William Wilberforce and Lord Palmerston (with both of whom Patrick had had some dealings while at Cambridge). With their support, and with many new witnesses, Nowell's release was secured. An account was published in the *Leeds Mercury* of 15 December 1810 in the form of a letter signed "Sydney." This may or may not be a pseudonym of Patrick's (Barker, 1994, thinks not). The case was certainly an early example of Patrick's energy and effectiveness in a matter of social justice.

Noyer, Marie-Josephine: first wife of Constantin Heger, who, with her child, died after three years of marriage in the cholera epidemic of 1833. Her sister was married to M. Chapelle, who shared with M. Heger English lessons from Charlotte. Charlotte may refer to this first wife, and her husband's feelings for her, in the figure of Justine-Marie in *Villette*.

Nunnely, Lady (no first name given): widow of Sir Monckton Nunnely and mother of Sir Philip in *Shirley*. She is lightly characterized as a conventional, disapproving old woman with a stony eye (ch. 31).

Nunnely, Misses (no first names given): Sir Philip's sisters, conventional young ladies of great propriety, briefly sketched in ch. 31 of *Shirley*.

Nunnely, Sir Monckton: Sir Philip's father (*Shirley*, ch. 31).

Nunnely, Sir Philip: owner of Nunnely Priory and a suitor for Shirley in the later sections of *Shirley*. He is an amiable and well-intentioned young man of no great force of character, and any chance he might have had with her is ruined by his writing of feeble, facile verse.

Nussey: the name of the family Charlotte knew most intimately outside her own, though she had no strong liking or respect for any member of it apart from her greatest friend Ellen. The family was already without a head when she first got to know them in the early 1830s, Ellen's father John, a cloth manufacturer, having died in 1826. Ellen seems always to have been conscious of being socially Charlotte's superior, though it was not very easy to see in what that superiority consisted, and it was a precarious one, particularly for the women. There was a darker side to the men's lives too: her brother Joseph seems not to have prospered, and there was a vein of mental instability in the family, with her brother George confined in a private institution for many years, and her brother William committing suicide while in the grip of depression. A fuller account of the family can be found in Barbara Whitehead's (1993) *Charlotte Brontë and her "Dearest Nell."*

The members of the family who impinged most strongly on the Brontës have separate entries below.

Nussey, Ann (1795–1878): eldest sister of Ellen, and therefore "Miss Nussey." Charlotte quite early formed an unfavorable opinion of her, based on her snobbishness: "Fashion, Wealth, Standing in Society seem to be her sole Standards for measuring the worth of a character. Your Sister thinks she has given up the world but some of the most absurd notions of that world cling to her like a pestilence" (to EN, 30 Apr 1840). This is plain-talking indeed, and suggests that in private the two friends were quite unbuttoned about their respective families. Ann's better qualities were not forgotten, however, and she was sometimes consulted about housekeeping matters. Her experience in nursing a drunken and dissolute brother prompted a letter to her from Charlotte after Branwell's death which, in a guarded but moving way, acknowledges the similarities in their experience. Charlotte's irritation with her wells up again, however, when at 53 she was about to marry Robert Clapham, and seems to have had doubts as to whether his homely appearance would compromise her gentility: "Ann wants shaking to be put out about his appearance. What does it matter whether her husband dines in a dress-coat or a market-coat, provided there be worth, and honesty, and a clean shirt underneath?" (to EN, 23 Aug 1849?). Like many of the other female Nusseys, Ann enjoyed very poor health over a very long lifetime.

Nussey, Mrs Ellen (née Wade) (?1771–1857): mother of Charlotte's friend Ellen, who was her youngest child. Since she had Ellen when she was in her mid-forties, Charlotte only knew her as an elderly woman. Her references to Mrs Nussey in letters to her friend are always respectful, but contain few suggestions of anything approaching affection. She couples Ellen's mother with Ellen and her sisters in the feeling that the women of the family were used and exploited by the selfish and weaker males. Most of the references to her concern her health. Though it was continually bad she, like her eldest daughter, contrived to live with it for a long time. Charlotte was delighted (to EN, 25 Nov 1851) at her "so cleverly cheating the doctors" (or at least proving them wrong) by not dying.

Nussey, Ellen (1817–97):

Charlotte's best friend was a full year younger than her, and, in spite of her assumptions of social superiority, was never in any doubt about the greater intellectual power and daring of her friend. They first met when they were both in their early days at Roe Head School (January 1831), and though Charlotte later claimed that when they first met "I did not care for her" (to WSW, 3 Jan 1850), in fact the closeness was very quickly achieved and lasted, with one important interruption, for the rest of her life – and even, it may be said, beyond.

The first letter between them was written as a school exercise, and is a stiff affair (though possibly Charlotte's tongue is occasionally to be observed sliding into her cheek), but by the winter holiday of 1831–2 she was writing to Ellen in a more relaxed style, and when she left Roe Head after 18 months there, writing to Ellen clearly became a relaxation and relief from the "somewhat monotonous course" (to EN, 21 July 1832) of her Haworth existence. Visits to and from Ellen, and a shared family trip to Bolton Abbey, were more vivid interludes in this uneventful life, and Ellen's accounts of these are sharp and often moving. They are also well-written, a testimony to the lasting quality of the education received at Margaret Wooler's school. These visits were well spaced-out: Charlotte first visited Ellen at Rydings, the family home, in September–October 1832, and Ellen paid her first visit to Haworth in July 1833. Her description of the experience, published in *Scribner's Monthly* for May 1871, is the best, fullest, and most lifelike picture we have of the Brontë household in the years when the children were growing to maturity.

When Charlotte returned to Roe Head, this time as a teacher (1835–8), the relationship strengthened and deepened. This was a crisis period for Charlotte, and it is clear she hid her troubled state of mind from Anne (a pupil at the school) but poured her heart out to Ellen. The crisis was both religious and personal, but Ellen's characteristics and views played their part in it: Ellen's piety (many commentators prefer to use the word pietism, for Ellen seems to excite an iconoclasm in modern chroniclers of the Brontë story) became in Charlotte's eyes a sort of challenge, so that her faith by comparison seemed lukewarm and inadequate. "My Darling if I were like you I should have my face Zion-ward" she wrote (10 May 1836), and later: "I often plan the pleasant life which we might lead together, strengthening each other in that power of self-denial, that hallowed and glowing devotion, which the first Saints of God often attained to" (5 and 6 Dec 1836). Often the letters show a warmth of affection which sounds odd to modern ears, but was probably common enough among young people of the time, denied any easy outlet for strong feelings toward the opposite sex: "I have lavished the warmest affections of a very hot, tenacious heart upon you – if you grow cold – its over" (Oct/Nov 1836?) and "we are in danger of loving each other too well" (20 Feb 1837?). This jumble of feelings and desires probably sprang from her pessimistic sense that she was unlikely to be married, and was trapped in a sphere of work that she found not just unsatisfying but abhorrent. Ellen herself, though far from prosperous, did not have abject poverty staring her in the face.

After Charlotte left Roe Head and tried private governessing, Ellen came to her rescue – the first of several times – by proposing a holiday in or near Bridlington. These five weeks gave Charlotte a great deal to remember, not least the sight of the sea, but also a period of continued intimacy with her best friend. By now thoughts of men and marriage were in both their minds, and candidates for Ellen's mate included William Weightman, whom Charlotte satirically said Ellen "adores in her heart" (29 Sep 1840?), the clerical Mr Vincent who toyed with Ellen's affections over many years ("Mrs Vincent Does it sound well Nell? I think it does," 3 Jan 1841) and one of the Taylor men: Charlotte jokingly conjectured that Ellen's name would soon be Mrs J. Taylor, though "I can't for the life of me tell whether the initial J stands for John or Joe" (14 Jan 1843?).

How much Ellen guessed of the emotional turmoil of her friend's two years in Brussels we do not know. Certainly something of the truth must have been confided to her after Charlotte's return home: this is implied by Charlotte's confession to her (14 Oct 1846) that she returned for the second year in Brussels "against my conscience – prompted by what then seemed an irresistible impulse." However shocked Ellen may have been by Charlotte's spending a year in close proximity to a married man whom she realized she was in love with, her devotion to Charlotte did not falter. She came to be with her at the lowest point in her life, after Emily's death, and she accompanied her and Anne on what they all knew was a death journey. Her account of this, written for Mrs Gaskell from a rough sketch of the events (now in the King's School Canterbury), is moving and beautiful in its simplicity.

The fact that during these years Charlotte hid from her the fact of her authorship is accounted for by the insistence of Emily in particular on maintaining the agreed anonymity, but it still leaves a slightly unpleasant taste. Perhaps the shrill tone of Charlotte's denials sprang from feelings of guilt, since on a personal (not an artistic) level, Ellen was closer to her than her sisters were.

The years of Charlotte's loneliness saw both women facing up to spinsterhood, though the widowed Mr Vincent renewed his attentions to Ellen, and Charlotte never quite lost her early conviction that "you will be married before you are many years older" (to EN, 15 May 1840). The friendship, however, came under its one real cloud during the troubled courtship of Charlotte and Arthur Bell Nicholls. A late marriage by an apparently confirmed spinster had caused trouble in Ellen's own family, and it did so again – perhaps naturally – between these two long-standing best friends.

The terms of Ellen's objections to Charlotte's marriage are known, for she wrote to Mary Taylor in August 1853, when the rift was probably incubating if not yet open, and Mary quoted her words back at her, exasperatedly, in her return letter of 24 February–3 March 1854:

> You talk wonderful nonsense abt C. Brontë in yr letter. What do you mean about "bear-
> ing her position so long, & enduring to the end"? . . . If it's C's lot to be married shd n't

she bear that too? or does your strange morality mean that she shd refuse to ameliorate her lot when it is in her power . . . It is an outrageous exaction to expect her to give up her choice in a matter so important, & I think her to blame in having been hitherto so yielding that her friends can think of making such an impudent demand.

That Ellen had used such arguments to Charlotte herself seems likely, for Charlotte took Mary's line in a letter after a reconciliation had been effected: "Providence offers me this destiny. Doubtless then it is best for me" (to EN, 11 Apr 1854). Modern commentators invariably take Mary Taylor's side on this, and even impute a submerged jealousy to Ellen, but it was Ellen, not Mary, who knew Mr Nicholls, Ellen who had received letters from Charlotte expressing feelings close to dislike for him, as well as contempt for his mind. It was not surprising if she thought that Charlotte might, by clutching at a last straw, be preparing great unhappiness for herself.

Things were patched up, thanks in particular to a "kind mediating word" from Miss Wooler (to MW, 12 Apr 1854). From Spring 1854 onwards the old intimacy was resumed, and Charlotte displayed real hope that she could establish a friendship between her husband-to-be and her best friend, something which was never to happen.

After the wedding, at which Ellen was the bridesmaid, she was the recipient of letters expressing Charlotte's growing satisfaction at the step she had taken, and her personal happiness. Ellen stayed at the Parsonage in September, but that was the last she saw of Charlotte. In October Arthur made trouble about the letters between the two women, which Charlotte told Ellen, with some amusement, he thought were written "too freely" (20 Oct 1854?). Ellen promised in a note hedged with proviso, to destroy their correspondence, but fortunately did not do so. The first she heard about Charlotte's illness was from a letter that hinted at pregnancy ("Don't conjecture – dear Nell – for it is too soon yet," 19 Jan 1855). A few more notes from her sickbed close the long and fascinating correspondence. It was Arthur who communicated the by-then-expected news of Charlotte's death.

From that point on a large part of Ellen's life was devoted to preserving the memory of her dead friend. It was she herself, after she had read the *Sharpe's Magazine* article, full of errors and deriving ultimately from Mrs Gaskell, who suggested that lady as a suitable writer of a memoir of her friend and fellow-novelist. Ironically Nicholls soon after recommended Ellen to Mrs Gaskell as someone who had letters from Charlotte. Thereafter the collaboration was close, and Ellen became the principal source for the *Life* – not surprisingly, for she had abundant documentary evidence, where Patrick had only an old man's fallible memory.

The aims of Gaskell and Ellen were very similar: to have Charlotte recognized as a martyr to her duty, and as a Christian paragon. The letters were quoted extensively, and Ellen achieved a shy prominence as "E." Despite her involvement with the project and her liking for Mrs Gaskell, Ellen later conceived the idea that the *Life* had not done full justice to Charlotte's Christian virtues: she collaborated with other biographers such as Wemyss Reid, she tried to bring out a volume of Charlotte's letters (however, she owned the letters but not the copyright, which was Nicholls's), and most notably she wrote for the American *Scribner's Monthly* the "Reminiscences" which provide the most beautiful and vital picture of the young Brontës, their home lives, and their behavior at certain crucial moments of their brief lives. They are of incalculable value to the biographer.

Ellen perhaps never quite reconciled her middle-class reticence with a desire to be recognized as Charlotte's most intimate friend, but it is ungrateful to contrast unfavorably her communicativeness about her friends with Mary Taylor's refusal to talk about them at all. Her desire to make some money from the letters seems to have been largely due to calls on her charitable purse. She was swindled out of the letters by T. J. Wise (aided by Clement Shorter), but Ellen was only one of a large congregation of Wise victims in the literary world. In her last years she was muddled but well-meaning, and many of her best friends were people she had initially met through the Brontë connection. She died, aged 80, in Moor Lane House, Birstall, which still stands.

Nussey, George (1814–85): brother of Ellen. He seems to have been the dearest to her of all her brothers – partly from closeness in age, partly perhaps from his willingness to engage in her interests and her friendships. He is mentioned often in Charlotte's letters from Roe Head, and he was one of the Nussey party who explored Bolton Abbey and its environs with the Brontës. The onset of his mental illness in the early 1840s was particularly distressing to Ellen, and the fact that he had at this time a fiancée, Amelia Ringrose, cemented a friendship between these two. One element that added to the traumatic nature of this crisis was that George, in his delusions, turned against his family (as his aged mother was later to do when she was ill). This fact was often commented upon by Charlotte: "[h]is delusion is of the most painful kind for his relations – how strange that in his eye affection should be transformed into hatred – it is as if the mental vision were inverted" (to EN, 17 Nov 1846). He never regained his sanity, the engagement was abandoned, and he had to be cared for by outsiders for the rest of his life.

Nussey, Henry (1812–60): brother of Ellen, a clergyman of evangelical persuasion. His early progress in the Church was marred after a fall from a horse, and possibly by mental problems such as affected several of the Nusseys. In 1839 he proposed marriage to several young women of his acquaintance, including Charlotte Brontë. "I have no personal repugnance to the idea of a union with you," she wrote in her unenthusiastic reply, but she claimed to refuse him for altruistic reasons: "mine is not the sort of disposition calculated to form the happiness of a man like you" (to HN, 5 Mar 1839). When he was – or thought he was – engaged later in the same year, she wrote honoring him for "not hunting after wealth" (to HN, 28 Oct 1839), but when he actually got engaged she told Ellen "I am glad . . . to hear that Henry is really going to be married, and still more so to learn that his wife elect has a handsome fortune" (to EN, 14 Nov 1844). She and Ellen spent some time in Hathersage preparing the vicarage for him (he had been given the living by the Duke of Devonshire), but both girls took against his bride Emily Prescott, who seemed to Charlotte "cold and narrow." Her view of him, only half-concealed from Ellen by politeness, was amused but unimpressed: she included him in her general view of the Nussey men as displaying

"coldness and neglect" of their womenfolk (to EN, 10 July 1846), and when he claimed to want to work as a missionary she mocked the ambition, said the climates of places where missionaries were in demand would kill him within a year, and any-way "None of your family have much stamina" (to EN, late June 1843?). All in all Henry may have provided some hints for St. John Rivers, but he had none of the cold pas-sion, single-mindedness, and zeal of the man. He also seems to have been tactless and blundering in his dealings with people, even falling foul of the excellent Duke of Devonshire. From 1847 he and his wife apparently sought better health on the Continent, living mainly in Nice. However he died at Wootton, Warwickshire, on August 29, 1860 (*Leeds Intelligencer*, 8 Sep 1860).

Nussey, John (1793–1862): eldest brother of Ellen, and London general practitioner and apothecary. He was early successful under the aegis of his cousin (and eventual father-in-law) Richard Walker, and he was apothecary to George IV and his two successors, being in attendance (in the next room) during some of Queen Victoria's numerous confinements. Ellen made two long visits to him in 1834 and 1837, probably to help with the family rather than to sample the pleasures of London. The picture that emerges of him through Charlotte's letters (and we must remember that we have no documents in which the lesser Nusseys speak for themselves) is of a selfish, grasping man who fails to honor his family obligations and is especially neglectful of his mother and sisters. She sees him as of "the world" and "cold-blooded" (to EN, 10 and 17 Sep 1851), and she included his wife Mary in this judgment: "Madame her-self thought fitting to call, very stately in her carriage" she wrote to Ellen (28 Jan 1853) during her last visit to London, indicating confidence in a shared opinion. There is much comment on John in letters of mid-1849 when he proposed a financial arrange-ment whereby his sisters would will their property to him or his heirs and in return he would cancel debts they owed him ("offers to relinquish a present claim in your sisters' favour" is the phrase of Charlotte's that suggests this arrangement, rather than a compensating annuity). Charlotte found the proposal "worldly, but not inequitable" (to EN, 14 July 1849), but emphasized that Ellen's position was different from her sisters, since she was still of child-bearing age (32), and her interests should not be ignored in favor of her sisters', which were different. In general Charlotte saw in John and Mary Nussey the same faults, in heightened form, that she saw in all the Nussey men: she talks of "the crust of worldliness with which their hearts are too completely overgrown" (to EN, 31 Jan 1850?). Remarkably John Nussey was the only one of Ellen's siblings to have produced children.

Nussey, Joseph (1797–1846): second-eldest brother of Ellen, who for a time was engaged in the woolen industry. By the mid-1840s he was described by Charlotte (to EN, 31 July 1845) as a "burthen" on his mother – one that his brothers, particu-larly John, should have her relieved of. By the time of his death she talks openly of his sufferings being "taken as sufficient expiation for his errors" (to EN, soon after 3 June 1846). The deduction that he was dissolute seems correct, but whether this con-sisted simply of alcoholism or included other sins is unknown. Clearly Joseph was the Nusseys' Branwell – one more bond between Ellen and Charlotte.

Nussey, Joshua (1798–1871): third-eldest of the Nussey sons, who went into the Church and married in 1832 Anne Alexander, 10 years his senior. Though Ellen stayed with them several times, and took refuge at their Oundle vicarage after leaving the Upjohns, with whom she had contemplated going to live as a companion, she seems to have disliked both of them, and her best friends Mary Taylor and Charlotte joined her in disparaging them. "Is she a frog or a fish –?" asked Charlotte (to EN, 19 Jan 1847?), "She is certainly a specimen of some kind of cold-blooded animal." She returns to her (and Ellen's) distaste for the pair a week later, for it seems to be them she is talking about when she describes "the coldness, dreariness, and barrenness of these respected individuals' minds and hearts" (to EN, 28 Jan 1847?). Joshua's attainments and judgment were similarly disparaged by Mary Taylor.

Nussey, Mary (Mercy) (1801–86): sister of Ellen. She was for a time a member of the Moravian Single Sisters' House at Fairfield, where she was given the name Mercy. See Margaret Connor, "Clerical Connections" (BS, v. 28, p. 1, March 2003) for the Moravian sisterhood. Charlotte's early references to her are more affectionate than most of her references to the Nusseys, and at one point she seems to have aroused Ellen's jealousy by trying to start an independent correspondence with her. Later, however, the mentions of her conform to the norm by being tinged with exasperation: she distrusts her judgment, regrets that she rather than Ellen has most to do with George in his time of mental breakdown, and concludes that the trouble she causes others springs from "the wilfulness of a weak person" (to EN, 11 May 1850). This irritation leads her to her most extreme judgment: "I suppose that is her use – to test and try others like a fiery furnace" (to EN, 10 May 1851). She was the family fowl-keeper, taught in a small school, and was frequently ill. Juliet Barker presents as fact that the "forty-one years old" Mercy (she was actually 48) was "so jealous of her elder sister's good fortune that she threatened the happiness of the whole household" (Barker, 1994, p. 602). This is unfair, resting only on a conjecture of Charlotte that she had "some little sense of bitterness" that Ann rather than she was to be married (to EN, 13 Sep 1849?). Charlotte's comparison of Mercy with Ellen's puppy Flossy Junior, however, is telling: they both draw "very heavily on good-nature and forbearance" (to EN, 10 May 1851).

Nussey, Richard (1803–72): brother of Ellen, he helped to run the family firm, moving to Leeds when he married Elizabeth Charnock (1846) to live in her family home in Woodhouse Lane. Charlotte, who had met him on the Bolton Abbey excursion of 1833, describes him and his wife as "<u>very</u> vulgar in their mode of shewing their feelings" (to EN, 20 Sep 1851?). He inherited his father-in-law's mills in Leeds and, since the marriage was childless and his wife predeceased him, his sisters Ann, Mercy and Ellen benefited from his death.

Nussey, William (1807–38): unmarried brother of Ellen, who committed suicide while depressed. He had worked with his brother John in London, and threw himself in the Thames while oppressed by the sense of his own sinfulness. Both Anne and Charlotte had had their own religious crises at Roe Head in the years 1836–7.

O

Oak Apple Day: 29 May, a public holiday in Britain until 1859, it commemorated Prince Charles's escape by hiding in an oak tree from the forces of the Protector after the Battle of Worcester. A popular story about the young Brontës has them re-enacting this episode, using a cherry tree in the Parsonage garden, a favorite of their father's. Emily played the escaping prince, and broke one of the boughs. Branwell seems to refer to this incident when he mentions someone who "has been spoiling his Father's trees" ("Young Soult's Poems with Notes," WPBB, v. 1, p. 53). The episode is mentioned by Erskine Stuart and Ellis Chadwick (1914), though there are discrepancies in the two accounts.

Oakwell Hall, Birstall: believed to be a late sixteenth-century stone house, built on an earlier wooden one. Pevsner, however, doubts the date of 1583 on the porch. Early owners included the aggressively accumulative Batts (sixteenth and seventeenth centuries), but by the Brontës' time it was a girls' school. It is believed to be the original of Fieldhead in *Shirley*, and the resemblances are still striking today. Charlotte describes in 1851 having seen one of her old charges, Sarah Louise White of Rawdon, there "a few years ago" (to John White, 18 Sep 1851). The house, with its attractive garden, is open to the public.

Oakworth: village north-west of Haworth, which was part of Patrick's parish until 1845. J. C. Bradley (*Shirley*'s Mr Sweeting) was its curate 1843–5, and the *Leeds Intelligencer* commented in 1845 that "This new district abounds with good church feelings" (17 May), which presumably means Anglican feelings rather than dissenting ones.

Observer: a Sunday newspaper whose review of *Shirley* (after a largely favorable one of *Jane Eyre*) particularly aroused Charlotte's contempt. She spoke of its "shallow weakness" (to WSW, 9 Nov 1849?), and commented: "The praise of such critics mortifies more than their blame" (to James Taylor, 6 Nov 1849). The review was in fact favorable; what angered Charlotte was its superficiality.

O'Gall, Mrs Dionysius: imaginary employer of Jane Eyre, invented by Rochester when he is pretending that he will soon be married to Blanche Ingram and that he will find new employment for Jane.

Old Bell Chapel, Thornton: the church from which Patrick conducted his ministry in Thornton 1815–20. It was an early seventeenth-century building, by all accounts a mean and unattractive one (Leyland describes it as "narrow, contracted, and unsightly," v. 1, ch. 1). It was in poor repair when Patrick arrived, and characteristically he undertook a program of repairs. Early in his ministry he conducted there a thanksgiving service for the victory at Waterloo, and all his and Maria's children, except Maria the eldest, were baptized there. It produced for its incumbent, by Patrick's reckoning, around £127 a year. After the building and consecration of the Church of St James it first became a ruin, then the mere fragments of masonry that exist today.

Old Cock Inn, Halifax: pub at which Branwell Brontë drank a great deal on the slate. In the last years of his life he was frequently threatened with legal action by T. W. Nicholson, the landlord, over sums owing.
See also Halifax

Oliver, Bill: owner of a needle factory in the village of Morton in *Jane Eyre*. His father was a self-made man, but the family is clearly on the way up socially, and he lives in a "grand hall" in Morton Vale.

Oliver, Rosamond: daughter of the above in *Jane Eyre*. A beautiful heiress, she is loved by and loves St John Rivers, who puts his vocation as a missionary above his own feelings. Her character is analyzed in v. 3, ch. 6, but she exists in the book mainly as a beautiful presence. She is later said to be engaged to the well-connected Mr Granby.

Ostend packet: used by Patrick, Charlotte, and Emily for their journey to Brussels in February 1842, and again by Charlotte in January 1843 and on her return home in January 1844. On their return to England following the death of their aunt, Charlotte and Emily sailed from Antwerp. William Crimsworth in *The Professor* also sailed to Ostend, and in ch. 7 there is a detailed account of the journey by road from Ostend to Brussels.

Otway, Thomas (1652–85): Restoration dramatist who figures on a list (one of two such lists) of possible subjects for poetry, made by Branwell when he was at Luddenden Foot. Perhaps Otway's destitution and early death coincided with a premonition Branwell had about his own fate. Otway's *Venice Preserved* was still a popular play at the time, and it is possible that the heroine Belvidera's mad scene at the end of the play – fragmentary, disjointed, and pathetic – contributes something of its feel to Catherine's scene with Nelly in ch. 12 of *Wuthering Heights*.

Outhwaite, Frances (Fanny) (1796–1849):
daughter of Thomas, and great friend of Elizabeth Firth. She was a major participant in the tea-drinkings and other little festivities that marked the Brontës' association with the Firths during their Thornton years. She became joint godmother with Elizabeth to Anne Brontë just before the family left for Haworth. The two families remained in contact in later years, Patrick recording in letters of the 1830s to Elizabeth Franks (née Firth) that he had seen one of her children in the care of Miss Outhwaite (6 July 1835), and that he had visited Fanny when she broke her arm (13 June 1836). Charlotte thanked her, through Mrs Franks, for a shawl in 1831 (the first recorded time when she used the dieresis on the "e" in her name was in this letter of May 1831), and Miss Outhwaite seems to have tried to get Charlotte a governessing job just before she left for Brussels. Her legacy to Anne of two hundred pounds smoothed the last months of her life.

Outhwaite, John (1792–1868):
son of Thomas, and also a surgeon in Bradford. Clearly an energetic man, prominent in the medical, social, and financial affairs of his native town. He was a prime mover in the establishment and building of the Bradford Exchange, and was prominent in the running of the Bradford Infirmary. Praise for and testimonials to his work abounded (e.g., "we understand Dr Outhwaite has received a present of a whole deer for the occasion," *Leeds Intelligencer*, 7 Jan 1830). Elizabeth Franks went to him in her last illness and died at his home in Leeds Road. He was married late in life (at St Luke's, Chelsea), to Fanny Dobson of Leeds in 1846, and had a son in 1848.

Patrick seems to have maintained contact with him after leaving Thornton, probably consulting him on medical matters, since his copy of Graham's *Modern Domestic Medicine* contains mention of an eye ointment he had recommended. However, the relationship faltered in September 1844 when Patrick replied bitterly to a letter from him, mentioning their disparity in wealth and influence ("God . . . will judge You and [me], on the day of Doom, when we shall be more on a Level than we now are," a proud assertion that seems to prefigure Jane Eyre's "equal – as we are" to Rochester), and clearly repressing the inclination to be very rude to him. Possibly Outhwaite had written to him about rumors of his having taken to drink. Patrick marked the two letters "Dr O.te's Answer & My reply, to be retained – semper, Septr. 1844 B–."

Outhwaite, Thomas (d. 1823):
father of Fanny and John. He was part of the circle around the Firth family in Thornton, and his wife was twin sister to the step-mother of Elizabeth Firth. On his death he was described in the *Leeds Intelligencer* as "of Bradford, surgeon" (19 June 1823). His widow died in January 1829.

Oxenhope:
two miles south of Haworth, part of Patrick's parish until 1849. Joseph Grant was curate there from 1845, under Patrick, and incumbent after 1849. As befits

the original of Mr Donne in *Shirley* he was a very busy and efficient minister, being a leading figure in establishing the National School there (functioning until recently), building the new church, and even getting Oxenhope brought into the regular postal service. Arthur Bell Nicholls read one of the lessons at the consecration of the church, dedicated to St Mary the Virgin (Oct 1849).

Oxenhope National School: opened in 1846, this was a school which Patrick had been prominent in pushing for since 1841. Also among its founding fathers was the Oxenhope curate J. B. Grant (Mr Donne in *Shirley*). From 1847–9 the school was licensed to serve as a church, and the new church was consecrated in October 1849, with Grant as perpetual curate.

P

Padiham: now part of Burnley, then a nearby village, in which Gawthorpe Hall is situated. Sir James Kay-Shuttleworth offered Arthur Bell Nicholls the living of the nearby church, worth £200 a year, but the Bishop of Manchester insisted it go to a cleric from his diocese, and in any case there was no question of Charlotte or her husband leaving Haworth while her father was alive.

Paganini, Niccolò (1782–1840): violinist and composer, one of the great string virtuosi of all time. He visited England in 1831–2, earning prodigious sums from his appearances in London, and later touring the provinces, including Leeds and Halifax. It was doubtless these concerts, allied with stories of his Byronic excesses and his supposed pact with the devil, that ensured mentions of him in the juvenilia. Of Zamorna (whom Charlotte at this date could seldom allow to be bettered in anything), it was said that on the violin "He would have excelled Paganini had he concentrated his powers" ("A Day Abroad," EW, v. 2, pt 2, p. 111).

Paget, Henry William, First Marquis of Anglesey (1768–1854): Master General of the Ordnancy, addressed by Patrick in a letter of 4 July 1848. In it he suggested a device which, in naval warfare, might produce the destructive effect of both a ball and a shell, as well as having the capacity of "*horizontal* firing," thus being "extremely destructive to the enemy." The suggestion was taken seriously, but in August the Director General of Ordnance reported to the Master General that the object Patrick proposed "has long been fully accomplished," and that his suggested device was merely "a crude illustration of the early practice of Shell-firing."

"*Palais de la Mort, Le*": essays written by Charlotte and Emily in October 1842, following a theme ("*matière*") probably dictated to them by M. Heger. The subject matter derives from Jean-Pierre Florian's *Fables*, with some additions by M. Heger.

Both essays depict Death's attempt to choose a prime minister, with some promising candidates (Ambition, Fanaticism, War, etc) being finally rejected in favor of Intemperance (neither sister was inclined to change Florian's choice of the most indiscriminate destroyer, and Emily insists that Intemperance's influence descends from father to son). Charlotte's essay becomes rather sketchy and hurried at the climactic choice, but Emily gives Intemperance a longer speech in which to state her claims. In general Emily's is the more dramatic presentation, while Charlotte sets the scene in the palace with a more painterly eye. Lonoff (BE, 1996) writes convincingly of the relationship between the two pieces, and what they tell us about the two women's attitudes to the teaching process they were participating in.

Palladium: periodical based in Edinburgh in which Sydney Dobell published his intelligent appreciation of the early Bell novels, in particular his ground-breaking assessment of *Wuthering Heights*.

Palmerston, 3rd Viscount (Henry John Temple) (1784–1865): contemporary of Patrick's at St John's College, Cambridge, where he was one of three officers in the Volunteer Corps in which Patrick served. Ellis Chadwick (1914) is probably right to doubt whether there was anything that could be called a friendship between the peer and the young Irishman, but Patrick successfully enlisted his help in the case of William Nowell, when Palmerston was at the beginning of his long service as Secretary of State for War (1809–28). He was later a Foreign Secretary notable for his assertive and aggressive policies. He conducted his love life on similar principles.

Panache, Madame (no first name given): temporary history teacher at Mme Beck's school in *Villette*. She was a bête noire of M. Paul who disapproved of her plan of teaching and "pursued her vindictively" (ch. 30). Later, somewhat belatedly, when she fell on hard times he procured her a teaching post.

"*Papillon, Le*": one of Emily's essays written in Brussels and dated 11 August 1842. The writer meditates on the view that nature "exists on a principle of destruction" (BE, p. 176), each species preying on another, killing to exist. These reflections are rebuked by a beautiful butterfly, which becomes a symbol of a "new heaven and a new earth." The trajectory may have been felt by some to prefigure that of *Wuthering Heights*, progressing from violent hatreds and vengeances to a rich peace at the conclusion. The essay has been much commented on, perhaps for this reason.

Parent, Anne-Marie: aunt of Mme Heger, who fled to Brussels to be with her brother, Mme Heger's father, when the convent at Charleville in which she was a nun was broken up by the armies of the French Revolution. She set up a school in her brother's house, which on her death was taken over and moved to the Rue d'Isabelle by her niece.

Parker, Thomas (1787–1866): notable tenor of great fame in and around Yorkshire, who was a native of Haworth and frequently performed there. He was

probably the man who "for fifty years has had one of the finest tenor voices I ever heard" who is mentioned in an insertion to ch. 2 of Gaskell's *Life* (p. 434). He was painted by Branwell in December 1838. A benefit concert for him in Haworth church in 1846 was boycotted by Arthur Bell Nicholls (but not Patrick) on the grounds that he was a Baptist.

Parry, Captain William Edward (1790–1855): distinguished sailor who

led several expeditions to the Arctic regions (including one attempt to reach the North Pole from Spitzbergen), and thereby became a hero to the Brontë children. His boats were models of good fellowship and Christian practice, and the tedium of long periods away from home was alleviated for the men by dramas, ship-made magazines, and so forth. He was knighted in 1829 and made a rear-admiral in 1852. Emily named her soldier after him, after first calling him "Gravey," and he had a "land" to himself in the geography of Glasstown.

Parsonage, Haworth: the Parsonage was built in 1779, and was first occupied by

John Richardson, the then incumbent. The building as seen by the visitor today, and as reproduced in countless photographs and on souvenirs, is unhistorically substantial: the Wade Wing, built to accommodate Patrick's successor's large family, makes the house much more dominant of its vicinity and more commodious. The Parsonage the Brontës knew and lived in, as seen in early photographs and even in Mrs Gaskell's rather inaccurate sketch, is quite a small, unpretentious house, where everyone must have lived on top of each other and a variety of different activities would have been going on simultaneously. Emily could "see around me tombstones grey" (on two sides of the house, anyway) but she must also have been conscious of Sally Mosley "in the back Kitchin," and doubtless of the double privy out at the back as well. Anyone who valued privacy could well, as Patrick did, prefer to take his meals on his own.

The principal rooms of the house were Patrick's study, to the right of the front door, and the dining room, to the left (though both these rooms, at one time or another, seem to have been known as the parlor). Charlotte enlarged the dining room in 1850 by taking the wall shared with the hallway 18 inches toward the front door – thus disturbing the eighteenth-century symmetry of the hall. The room where the young Brontës chronicled the events of their imaginary kingdoms was therefore very small indeed, and perhaps for this reason Aunt Branwell kept to her room upstairs for much of the day.

Patrick conducted parish business in his study, but the more lowly parish officials often reported to the kitchen. This was behind the study, and had a back window. Modern attempts to recreate the atmosphere of the kitchen in the Parsonage Museum are set at nought by the lack of a window (the Wade wing prevents this), and by the "open plan" set-up, with the kitchen open to the hall. The Brontë kitchen was small, busy, and warm – and doubtless smelly too. Behind the dining room was a large store room which eventually became Mr Nicholls's study, and the entry to the commodious cellar.

Ellen Nussey reports these main rooms of the house to be lacking "drapery of any kind" (see CBL, v. 1, p. 599), including curtains, due to Patrick's fear of fire. She mentions the "pretty dove-coloured tint" of the painted interior walls, and, though she admits that some would have found the living area of the Parsonage "[s]cant and bare indeed," she suggests that there was diffused through the whole place something that she nearly calls elegance but settles on the word "refinement."

Upstairs the rooms had changing functions over the years. Patrick shifted to the bedroom presently known as his after his wife's death, and kept it (sharing with Branwell during his son's last years for safety's sake) until his death. The room presently known as Charlotte's was Aunt Branwell's during her lifetime (sharing it with Anne during the latter's childhood), but later probably had various inhabitants, depending who was resident in the Parsonage at the time. Charlotte and her husband shared it during their brief married life. The tiny room now called the children's study, illustrated in Emily's 1845 diary paper, seems impossibly small today, but its width was contracted by 18 inches when Charlotte made her major changes to the house: when it was in use it would have been practical and cozy.

At the top of the stairs the servants' room was used mainly by Tabitha, and was reached from an outside staircase. At some point the central position the servants occupied in the household was recognized by the room being given access from the landing. The room called Branwell's studio today may never have served as such, and was for most of the time a bedroom for some of the children. Like the kitchen it lost its outside window when the Wade Extension was built.

There can be no doubt of the central position of the Parsonage in the Brontë sisters' emotional lives. It is the subject of one of Emily's few personal poems ("A little while, a little while," written at Law Hill); a longing to be back there underpins all Anne's references to her governessing posts; and Charlotte, while she emphasizes to her personal friends how humble it is, and to her literary friends in London how remote it is, nevertheless always stresses how she is only totally at home there, and feels at her best and happiest there. It was there that all the women, but perhaps not Branwell, came closest to leading fulfilled lives.

The Wade wing, added in 1878, currently houses the library on the ground floor, together with the Bonnell Room for temporary exhibitions, and on the first floor the exhibition which traces the Brontë story for visitors. A further development was added to the rear of the Parsonage in the late 1950s, originally family accommodation for the manager of the Museum, now a shop and office accommodation. The attempt in the early 1990s to replace this with a large extension was unsuccessful. It was characterized by one of the heritage bodies called by Bradford Council to report on the plan as "a classic case of how to kill the character of the building which the visitors have come to see." This proposal, out of scale and out of style, was scuppered by Brontë Society members, who in successive years voted off the Society's Council members who had supported it.

Pascal, Blaise (1623–62):

French mathematician, theologian, and philosopher. M. Heger gave Charlotte the *Pensées* (on the necessity of leading a religious life) during her Brussels stay, and Charlotte later compared A. W. and J. C. Hare's *Guesses at*

Truth to Pascal, suggesting that Hare recalls Pascal "as the light of the sun recalls that of the Moon" (to WSW, 13 Sep 1849; she surely must have meant the reverse).

Pastoral Visitor, The: short-lived evangelical magazine published and edited by William Morgan. Three articles "On Conversion" signed PB appeared in the magazine, and followed three unsigned pieces on the same subject which Kate Lawson conjectures were by Morgan himself. According to Lock and Dixon (1979) the magazine also contained a sermon by Patrick, and a review by Morgan of his book *The Cottage in the Wood*, so there was a degree of mutual backscratching. Patrick's articles, with an introduction by Lawson, are in BST (v. 19, pt 6, 1988).

Patchett, Elizabeth (b. 1796): proprietress of Law Hill School, in Southowram near Halifax, where Emily taught for six months in 1838–9. The most information about her is to be found in Ellis Chadwick's *In the Footsteps of the Brontës*. She talked to ex-pupils and neighbors, and the consensus was that Miss Patchett was a beautiful woman, a fine horsewoman, and an extremely capable schoolmistress by the standards of her time. She also seems to have involved her pupils and their teachers in the busy cultural life of Halifax. She married the Rev. John Hope in December 1842, but according to Chadwick he died in the next year. She gave up the school on marriage, and information about her later life is sparse. However, a neighbor remembered her in her eighties visiting Law Hill, still spry: she "could nip about from room to room quite gaily" (Chadwick, 1914, p. 126).

Paternoster Row: narrow street immediately to the north of St Paul's Cathedral, where the Chapter Coffee House was to be found. It was primarily a street of bookshops and small publishers, and it was from there that Messrs Aylott and Jones launched copies of the *Poems* of the Bells on to an indifferent market.

Path, Louise: pupil at Mlle Reuter's school in *The Professor*, a happy and obliging girl, but with the usual habit of dissimulation and with the lack of principle which Charlotte ascribes to almost all the pupils. See ch. 12.

Patriotic Fund: established in Autumn 1854, in the early months of the Crimean War, in aid of "the widows and orphans of soldiers and mariners engaged in the war" (*Leeds Intelligencer*, 14 Oct 1854). Contributions and subscriptions were solicited from the general public. Patrick was active (using Charlotte and her husband as his amanuenses) in summoning people to a meeting in Haworth to raise a general subscription. The meeting was held on 16 December.

Paxton, Sir Joseph (1801–65): superintendent of the gardens at Chatsworth, the Derbyshire home of the Dukes of Devonshire, and architect of the Crystal Palace, described by Charlotte as "the Magician Paxton" (to L. Wheelwright, 12 Jan 1851). Patrick wrote to him in 1858 in some embarrassment after Haworth people had gone behind his back and approached the Duke of Devonshire for a contribution to new heating for the church and Sunday schools: "fifty pounds remain as a debt, but this may – and ought to be rais'd by the Inhabitants," he wrote sternly (16 Jan 1858). The Duke had visited Patrick the year before, and this may have been part of a general Haworth policy of capitalizing on famous and wealthy visitors.

Peace Congress: well-meaning but ineffectual anti-war organization which invited Charlotte to "appear on the platform" of their meeting at Exeter Hall on 30 October 1849 (to WSW, 1 Nov 1849). Charlotte was understandably bemused as to the reason (apart from indiscriminate toadyism) behind the invitation. The meeting was addressed by William Ewart MP, the father of public libraries in Great Britain.

Pearson, Mary (née Walton): the owner of a commonplace book in which Branwell drew sketches and copied poems when he stayed at her father's inn at Ovenden Cross near Halifax in 1846. Mary's interest in her guest is obvious from the number of solicited contributions, and Branwell was willing to reveal a great deal of himself, or the dramatized persona he presented to the world, to this young woman, who seems to have been around 20. The sketches include a Byronic picture of Alexander Percy, a gravestone with "I IMPLORE FOR REST" inscribed above a skull and crossbones, and a self-portrait. Mary Pearson later used the entries to point a moral for her son, describing Branwell as "an inveterate drunkard" whose "energies and talents were shipwrecked" and as one who was "of the earth, earthy" rather than one who relied on God (AOTB, p. 358).

Pearson, The Misses Ann, Kate, and Susan: daughters of a manufacturer in *Shirley*. Ann, the eldest, was believed in the area to be setting her cap at Robert Moore. Perhaps it was her lack of success that led her to describe him as a "sentimental noodle" (ch. 9).

Pearson, Mr (no first name given): Whinbury manufacturer who had been shot through the window of his own home in *Shirley*.

Peel, Sir Robert (1788–1850): the great Conservative statesman and Prime Minister. Peel figures prominently in the juvenilia, most notably in "Tales of the Islanders" (v. 2, ch. 1) when real life intrudes into the African saga and the passing of the Catholic Emancipation bill in both houses of Parliament is described. Peel, with whose name the Act is associated, was earlier a pronounced opponent of the measure.

The young Brontës' feelings towards Peel were ambiguous (as were those of the young Queen Victoria, who had to be taught to admire him by Prince Albert). Possibly they saw him as a rival to Wellington, to whom he acted as second-in-command in the Tory party. Charlotte depicts him "whispering and wheedling in the Duke's ear" ("Tales of the Islanders," v. 3, ch. 1, EW, v. 1, p. 141) and later commented that "One's heart does not warm to him so much, because he has not a very sincere look" ("The Moores," ch. 2). Patrick's views were similarly mixed: he talks of him as "the truest and greatest statesman" (*Leeds Intelligencer*, 27 May 1843), but is almost contemptuous of his pusillanimous reforms of the Criminal Law, saying that they "have done little more than condensing and simplifying what before was often perplexed and unintelligible" (*Leeds Mercury*, 10 Jan 1829), and describing his bill on forgery as "nearly an entire blank" (*Leeds Intelligencer*, 6 May 1830).

See also Pelham, Sir Robert Weever

Pélagie, Mlle (no first name given): teacher at Mlle Reuter's school in *The Professor*. Described in ch. 12 as totally and in every respect ordinary.

Pelet, François: director of the boys' school at which William Crimsworth teaches in Brussels in *The Professor*. Crimsworth's first impressions of him are misleading: he finds him melancholy and mild, and wonders if he is stern enough to be a schoolmaster. This view is changed, partly by the man's treatment of his Flemish ushers. As the story proceeds, Pelet is seen as sarcastic, devious, the complete politician who rules by guile, and is the perfect complement to Zoraïde Reuter. In matters of sexual morality Crimsworth suspects a Continental laxity and cynicism, which is confirmed by the encounter with Mlle Reuter in her garden, which he overhears in ch. 12. Analyses of Pelet's character, of which Crimsworth shows a developing understanding, occur in, for example, chs. 7, 8, 13, and 20. He marries Mlle Reuter, but it is mentioned at the end of the book that "their domestic harmony is not the finest in the world". Their schools, however, prosper.

Pelet, Mme (no first name given): the mother of M. Pelet, and his housekeeper. Talkative, meager and yellow in appearance, she is both good-natured and open in her manners, with a frank enjoyment of the good things of life. The scene in ch. 8 of *The Professor* between herself, Mme Reuter, and William Crimsworth is one of the best things in the book.

Pelham, Sir Robert Weever (Bart.): important subsidiary character in the juvenile chronicles, largely based on the public image of Sir Robert Peel. Resemblances include the name and baronetcy, the name of his fine new house, Tamworth Hall (Peel's constituency was Tamworth, and he was shortly to produce the Tamworth Manifesto of 1835, which formed the foundation stone of modern Conservatism) and above all the picture of the man, which conforms to all the more superficial impressions of Sir Robert. On his introduction (in Branwell's "The Politics of Verdopolis") he is described as having "cool clear judgment," the reverse side of which is "cold cautious calculation," and "a strange, sinister expression and a deceitful smile" (WPBB, v. 1, p. 346). Peel's awkward and cold demeanor in personal and political relationships, universally commented on by friends and foes alike including the young Queen Victoria, is brilliantly caught by Branwell, and a later party thrown by Douro allows the women of Glasstown to comment satirically on him: "He's as smooth as oil and as hollow as a gun barrel" (WPBB, v. 1, p. 361). The character of Pelham, characterized more subtly than most of the Angrian figures, allowed the elder Brontë children

to express their very partisan feelings about what they saw as Peel's treachery toward Wellington at the time of the Catholic Emancipation Bill.

Peninsular War (1807–14): war against Napoleon in the Iberian Peninsular, called by the Emperor himself his "Spanish ulcer." He provoked it by declaring war on Portugal and then jettisoning his unreliable ally the King of Spain, installing in his place as puppet king his own brother Joseph. The war was conducted by an alliance of Wellington and the peoples and armies of the peninsular, and it tied up French troops until the invasion of Russia, Napoleon's second major unwise move. After the victory at Vitoria Wellington advanced on the frontier with France, and later crossed it. The war was the making of his reputation as a military commander and strategist, probably the reason it figures strongly in the Brontë children's personal mythology.

The war itself and its consequences are narrated briefly in Branwell's "History of the Young Men," ch. 6, where it is antedated by some 25 years to fit in with Glasstown history. Later the war, and in particular its effects on trade after the Orders in Council led to a trade war with the USA, was the most important background event in *Shirley*, with characters arguing about Wellington's merits and demerits, on the one hand "the most humdrum of common-place martinets," and on the other "the soul of England" (ch. 3).

Penistone Moor: the lands to the back of Haworth Parsonage, stretching west towards Lancashire. The name is used in *Wuthering Heights*.

Pensionnat Heger: the school in Brussels where Charlotte and Emily studied and taught, the former in 1842–3, the latter for the first year only. The school was an early nineteenth-century building, on a site closely associated with the Infanta Isabella, daughter of Philip II of Spain, and Regent of the Low Countries, part of the Spanish king's dominions. Zoë Parent had moved to the Rue d'Isabelle in 1830, with the school she had taken over from her aunt Anne-Marie, the former nun. Six years later she married Constantin Heger as his second wife, and he was one of several visiting masters at the school.

Charlotte (to EN, May 1842) refers to the Pensionnat as "a large school," which compared to Roe Head it certainly was, since she says it comprised 12 boarders and 40 day pupils. In July, mystifyingly, she tells Ellen that the school contained "nearly ninety pupils (boarders & day-pupils included)." The feature of the school that was most to her taste (and possibly, eventually, to Emily's as well) was the individual tuition given them by M. Heger, which gave rise to the series of *devoirs* which are a fascinating addition to the corpus of Brontë writings. Least to Charlotte's taste was the "*lecture pieuse*" each evening, but this the Brontë sisters did not attend, being Protestant, so her knowledge of it must have been partial, perhaps overheard.

The location and layout of the Pensionnat is best studied in Eric Ruijssenaar's (2000) *Charlotte Brontë's Promised Land*, and indeed in the largely accurate descriptions of it in *The Professor* and *Villette*. She stressed in many letters that it was a well-run institution, though she does complain (a Haworth woman!) of cold – no fires as late as mid-October. Gradually she came to have a view of the school (which received its latest and finest form in *Villette*) in which the efficiency of the operation is a result of a coldness of heart and an all-embracing system of spying which had at its center Mme Heger herself. Much of this was probably a sort of personal mythology springing from her suppressed passion for M. Heger, and it is contradicted or severely modified by the accounts of the Heger children and later pupils. That a degree of quiet information-gathering was necessary in any institution which needed to keep up a spotless reputation should have been obvious to Charlotte, and the relationship between the older pupils and any of the male teachers was a matter of prime concern. The fact that the principal male teacher was the husband of the *directrice* was no doubt comforting to parents, but it made any rumor or scandal concerning him more dangerous and difficult to counter.

Charlotte's attitude to the school's pupils was of a piece with her attitude to Belgians generally: she loathed and despised them. She found them duplicitous, lethargic, and in the grip of a superstitious religion. Her expression of these views, to modern ears, oversteps the boundary between chauvinism and racism. The fact that Constantin Heger was a devout Catholic and had strong patriotic feelings only made him stand out in her eyes as a swan among sparrows. Though Emily had an affectionate relationship with a fellow-student, Louise de Bassompierre, Charlotte had none. Her claim in a letter to one of her former pupils, Victoire Dubois, that "I loved my pupils" (18 May 1844) is contradicted by all the evidence; however, she clearly suppressed her feelings sufficiently for her pupils to feel affection as well as respect for her, as the packet of letters from her pupils in the First Class which she received in 1844 testifies.

The school remained open until 1894, when it amalgamated with a school in the Avenue Louise. The Pensionnat in the Rue d'Isabelle was demolished in 1910–11.

Pentonville Prison: a model prison, mainly for those awaiting transportation, who were taught a trade. It was only 10 years old when it was visited by Charlotte during her last visit to London (Jan–Feb 1853), and it was run on the "silent system," with very strict regulations.

Penzance: Cornish birthplace of the Brontës' mother and aunt, Maria and Elizabeth Branwell. Its climate suited invalids, and it was a lively trading center and fishing port. The Branwells were important merchants and property-owners in the town. Their home was both central and imposing, suggestive of an extensive social life. Ellen Nussey says that Aunt Branwell "talked a great deal of her younger days, the gaities of her native town, Penzance in Cornwall, the soft warm climate &c ... the social life of her younger days she appeared to recall with regret" (EN, in CBL, v. 1, p. 597).

Percy, William, Edward, and Mary Henrietta: in the Angrian chronicles, the children of the Earl of Northangerland. The two boys (and another boy, Henry, murdered in youth) are handed over to Sdeath by their father with orders to kill them.

No reason is advanced for this, but conceivably Northangerland is attempting to ensure that they do not treat him as he treated his own father. Sdeath lets them live, and Edward, a thrusting, ruthless and unpleasant man, pushes his way onward and upward as an industrialist in Glasstown. He employs his younger brother William, but there is a long history of his mistreating him: William bitterly chronicles in "The Duke of Zamorna" his brother's "savage, hard, calculating barbarity" and his being overwhelmed by the elder boy's "strength and bulk." This points forward very clearly to the physical mistreatment of William Crimsworth and Willie Ellin by their elder brothers. Edward, through cunning and determination, contrives to push his way into the country's political elite, helped by his rescue of the Duke of Fidena from the Verdopolitan mob. William moves more quietly ahead, is prominent in the pursuit of the traitor Henry Hastings, and falls in love with Henry's sister Elizabeth. There are some hints that in the future William will exact vengeance on his brother for his treatment in boyhood.

Mary Percy is Northangerland's only acknowledged child, and is pursued and married by Zamorna when his second wife Marian Hume begins to fade. Mary is beautiful and lovable but inclined to play on her aristocratic birthright and naturally jealous when she becomes, as was inevitable, only one of the women in Zamorna's life. With time she becomes a political pawn whom her husband can use in his battles with her father. When Zamorna is exiled in the Civil War Mary wastes away, lonely and apparently deserted, at which point Branwell kills her off: "is she alone in the cold earth on this dreary night" Charlotte asks in her "Roe Head Journal"? Back home she dismisses the account of her death as mere rumor, brings back Zamorna and reunites the pair. But the continuing inability to trust to her husband's fidelity takes its toll on Mary Henrietta: the "bright and heavenly sharer of Zamorna's crown" ("Angria and the Angrians") at her coronation later becomes a "haughty jealous little Duchess" ("Mina Laury"), someone rather on the margins of Zamorna's life.

See also "Ashworth"; *The Professor*; "Willie Ellin"; "The Wool is Rising"

petition to the General Board of Health: the Board and its secretary Henry Austin were petitioned twice in 1849 by Patrick and other Haworth notables concerning the deplorable sanitary conditions in the town, and the need for a reliable fresh water supply. Further letters were written when the Board's response was dilatory, and Patrick's concern grew with the passing of time, particularly as support for the measure among Haworth notables began to crumble when they understood the financial implications. A reservoir, small but welcome, was not completed until 1858.

pets of the Brontës: the early pets are mainly known to us through pictures, and through Emily and Anne's diary papers. They include Grasper (described in AOTB as an Irish terrier); Rainbow, Diamond, Snowflake (species unknown), and a pheasant called Jasper – possibly these were all wild birds who were fed regularly. Later the family acquired Keeper, the most famous and characterful of the Brontë pets (his fictional equivalent, Tartar in *Shirley*, is described in ch. 11 as "of a breed between mastiff and bull-dog"); Nero (often called Hero), a hawk, lost while Emily and Charlotte were in Brussels; Black Tom and Tiger (d. 1844), both cats; two geese, Victoria and Adelaide; and a cage bird, Little Dick, mentioned in Anne's diary paper for 1845. Last of the major pets was Flossy, brought by Anne from Thorp Green in 1843 and painted by both her and Emily. Flossy sired a puppy, given to Ellen Nussey. In his last years Patrick acquired dogs called Cato and Plato. Charlotte's comparative indifference to animals is evidenced by the lack of references to them in her early letters. In her last lonely years she was touched by the dogs' display of affection, especially on her returns home.

See also Flossy; Flossy Junior; Hero; Grasper; Keeper, Plato; Rainbow; Snowflake; Tiger; Tom; Victoria

"Phenomenon, The; or An Account in Verse of the Extraordinary Disruption of a Bog, Which Took place in the Moors of Haworth on the 12th day of September, 1824": pamphlet by Patrick on the bursting of the Crow Hill bog. His sermon on the subject is simplified for younger readers, and a verse treatment of the same subject is added. The pamphlet (which misdates the eruption by 10 days), was intended for children "as a Reward Book for the higher classes in Sunday Schools" (*Leeds Intelligencer*, 13 Jan 1825).

Phillips, George Searle (1815–89): journalist and writer, publishing under the name "January Searle." After contributing and editing several newspapers and periodicals in England and the USA, including the *Leeds Times*, he became insane in 1873 and was confined in the asylum of Trenton, NJ. He wrote an early hostile review of *Jane Eyre* which Charlotte read. Later, in 1872, he claimed to have known Branwell, talked to him about his sisters, and heard complaints about how he was treated at home. Some skepticism about this claim has been voiced, since he reported Branwell as saying that many strangers had been attracted to Haworth by Charlotte's fame. Charlotte claimed that Branwell knew nothing of his sisters' publishing ventures, and so far as we know literary tourism to Haworth only started after Branwell's death with the publication of *Shirley* – both these assumptions, however, could be wrong. Leyland accepted Searle's claim to have become acquainted with Branwell in Bradford and agreed with his assessment of his "true elevation of character and gentleness of disposition" (Leyland, v. 1, ch. 10, p. 166). The fact of Leyland's acceptance of him as part of the artistic Bradford circle suggests that this was not a delusion of approaching madness.

phrenology: a popular pseudo-science in the nineteenth century that meant a great deal to the Brontës, particularly Charlotte. The notion that the brain had separate areas for different moral and psychological characteristics, and that the development or otherwise of these areas could be traced on the skull, was originated by the German Franz Joseph Gall (1758–1828) and popularized by his follower Johann Spurzheim (1776–1832), who lectured in Britain and gained a follower in George Combe (1788–1858), who popularized Gall's notions in *Essays on Phrenology* (1819). The notions

of "bumps of" and "organs of" appear over and over in Charlotte's novels and juvenilia, for example "What good can your bumps of ideality, comparison, self-esteem, conscientiousness, do you here?" (*The Professor*, ch. 3), or "Really your organs of wonder and credulity are easily excited" (*Jane Eyre*, v. 2, ch. 3). Mary Taylor told Mrs Gaskell that "Charlotte said she could get on with any one who had a bump at the top of their heads," meaning that they were conscientious (ECG, *Life*, ch. 7). In December 1842 there was a lecture in Haworth on the subject by J. Townend, a local man, but by then the Brontës were well up in the subject.

   The Brontës were not alone in their interest, though when Dickens wrote, toward the end of his life, about a "gallant officer's organ of destructiveness" (*Uncommercial Traveller*, "Poor Mercantile Jack") he may have had his tongue in his cheek, but many intelligent Victorians who considered themselves au fait with scientific thought were taken in – George Eliot and Harriet Martineau were obvious examples. To many Victorians phrenology could make them aware of their inborn strengths and weaknesses, and allow them to compensate for the latter. Gradually the theories of Gall were discredited, and by mid-twentieth-century they were no more than material for a music-hall act.

phthisis: a term used for pulmonary tuberculosis, and more loosely for wasting diseases and lung complaints such as asthma. It was put as the sole cause of death on Charlotte's death certificate.

Pierrot, Madame (no first name given): French teacher at Lowood School in *Jane Eyre*. She is characterized only as "not a bad sort of person" (ch. 5).

Pighills, Jeremiah: mill-hand at Moore's mill in *Shirley*, said by Martin Yorke to be a suitor for the hand of Sarah, the maid at the Hollow (ch. 33). The name was and is a Haworth one, but today it is often spelt Pickles.

Pillar Group: the only known portrait of the sisters together still in existence, painted by Branwell around 1834 (i.e., before most of his known portraits executed during his attempt to make portraiture his profession). It is now in the National Portrait Gallery. It was seen by Mrs Gaskell, who described it in a letter to a friend as "a rough, common-looking oil-painting," with Charlotte "a little, rather prim-looking girl of eighteen" and the other two "with cropped hair, and sad, dreamy-looking eyes" (Gaskell, *Letters,* ed. Chapple and Pollard, p. 249). Branwell was originally part of the group but painted himself out, thus making the "pillar" of the picture's nickname. Most commentators agreed on the excellence of the likenesses, despite the crudeness of Branwell's artistic techniques. This portrait, along with the Gun Group, which he largely destroyed, was taken to Ireland by Arthur Bell Nicholls and lay forgotten, or kept deliberately secret, in the top of a wardrobe. It was discovered in 1914 by a servant of Mr Nicholls's second wife, much to her surprise. The postcard of the picture is one of the best sellers at the National Portrait Gallery.

Pillule, Dr (no first name given): Mme Beck's family doctor in *Villette*. He is replaced by Graham Bretton first as family doctor, later as doctor to the young ladies at the school as well.

Plato: dog purchased by Patrick in 1855 from Mr Summerscale, the Haworth teacher, from whom he also purchased Cato, a dog "greatly admired" by Charlotte (PB's account book). He paid £3 for each of them, Plato being the offspring of a dog owned by the Busfeild Ferrands of Bingley. Plato went with Arthur Bell Nicholls to Ireland in 1861, and died in 1866. He was a cross Newfoundland/water-spaniel.

Plummer, Thomas (d. 1839): curate of Keighley, and headmaster of the Free Grammar School there. His daughter Margaret was an older contemporary of the Brontë girls at Cowan Bridge School. He officiated in place of Patrick at Haworth in June–July 1830. He is often named as teaching the Brontë children art, but this seems to be a mistake: he had a son of the same name who, according to the 1851 census, lived in Keighley and was by profession a portrait painter. This may be how the confusion arose.

Plymouth Grove: a street in Manchester. Number 42 (now 84) was the home of Mrs Gaskell and her family from June 1850. Charlotte paid a brief visit here after her London stay in late June 1851, then came again in April 1853 and May 1854. It was a roomy and handsome eighteenth-century house, then well away from the industrial part of Manchester. On her first visit Charlotte said that "in this hot weather, the windows were kept open – a whispering of leaves and perfume of flowers always pervaded the rooms" (to GS, 1 July 1851). The International Society of the University of Manchester used it for some years, and it fell into disrepair. Its future seems far from assured.

***Poems* by Currer, Ellis, and Acton Bell (1846):** The story of Charlotte's discovery of a manuscript book of poems by Emily, her attempts to persuade her to publish them, and Emily's ultimate agreement to a pseudonymous volume of poems by all three sisters, was first told in Charlotte's "Biographical Notice of Ellis and Acton Bell" (1850). Once Emily's participation was assured the business of selection, titling, punctuation, and removing vestiges of Gondal and Angria began. Probably the volume was intended as a preliminary toe in publishing waters, with the three novels they were writing as the follow-up. By January 1846 Charlotte was approaching a publisher, Aylott and Jones of Paternoster Row, probably on the advice of the publishers of *Chambers's Edinburgh Journal*. The authors-to-be then selected their pseudonyms, all gender-neutral first names before Bell (the assertion by Barker, 1994, that Charlotte agreed to the pseudonyms reluctantly at the insistence of Emily and Anne is unproven), and negotiations proceeded, ending with the sisters paying out over £40 of their small store of money to see their poems in print. The little book was published in May, and sank like a stone. It has become one of the best-known stories about the sisters. The collection of poems which the three put together to make a slim volume was as follows, in the order in which they were printed in the Aylott and Jones volume:

Of these poems "Song" (p. 43) is "The linnet in the rocky dells," "Stanzas" (p. 59) is "Oh, weep not, love," "Stanzas" (p. 126) is "If thou be in a lonely place," "Stanzas to —" (p. 138) is "Well, some may hate," "The Student's Serenade" is wrongly printed in the Index as "The Student's Life," and "Stanzas" (p. 148) is "I'll not weep that thou art going to leave me." The contents list in the 1846 and 1848 editions is unreliable.

In the selection Charlotte has 19 poems, Emily and Anne each 21. This does not mean that Charlotte bowed to the superior poetic gifts of her sisters. In fact page-wise Charlotte's take up more than the poems of her two sisters combined. Several of them are narratives, or dramatic situational poems. At least in range and ambition Charlotte puts her best foot forward in her selection. Whether her preponderance helped the collection as a whole is another matter. Doubtless it failed to find buyers because the authors were unknown and, as a consequence, their work was not widely reviewed, especially in the sort of journal that sells copies. However, to give more than half the volume over to the least talented poet of the family was a questionable decision (perhaps based on Emily's reluctance to publish many of her poems, possibly because she regarded many of them as still in the process of creation). Anne's poems, simple but often melodious, yet seem monotonous because so many pieces in the same vein were chosen: adolescent moping, not strong enough to be called melancholy, is the dominant theme, with occasionally a whinging edge. Emily's poems are much more varied, and she starts well (with "The Philosopher" and "Remembrance" in the early pages) and ends well, with "The Old Stoic." Between there is a plethora of poems with unrealized personifications of the "Pleasure still will lead to wrong,/ And helpless Reason warn in vain" kind – a tendency not unknown in Anne and Charlotte too. Certainly the modern reader can imagine a more appealing and impressive selection, but it was not the modern reader who was being aimed at.

The sisters' refusal to throw a lifeline to Branwell by asking him to contribute is notable. Juliet Barker is surely right that Branwell was not as ignorant of his sisters' publishing ventures as Charlotte made out. Branwell was at least a published poet, though the local Yorkshire newspapers that had printed his verses did not have the sort of prestige that would have added much to sales figures. In the end, the sisters knew him best, and were able to judge whether he was in a fit state to put a small collection of his poems into publishable shape. They decided to use *their* money to publish *their* poetry: a selfish decision possibly, but surely an understandable one.

The quality of the reviews of these unknown gentleman poets was, not surprisingly, unimpressive. Sidney Dobell in the *Athenaeum* certainly picked out Emily as the poet of the family, speaking of "an inspiration, which may yet find an audience in the outer world." However, both *The Critic* and the *Dublin University Magazine* wrote the sort of commendatory review that yet leaves the reader unconvinced that the critic's reading of the volume has been more than perfunctory, if that. It sold only two copies, and by the summer of 1847 it was being sent as a gift to various prominent writers and critics, including Lockhart, Tennyson, and probably Dickens. When the volume was reissued in 1848 there was more critical reaction, this time *The Critic* singling out Emily, *Tait's Edinburgh Magazine* sneering that if there were indeed three engaged on "this thin book, they must be marvellously alike," and the *Literary Gazette* singling out Charlotte as "the most indifferent at verse", but not, they imply, by much. Sales of the reissue were slow, and it was still in print at the time of Gaskell's *Life* (1857).

See also Aylott and Jones; poetry, Anne's; poetry, Branwell's; poetry, Charlotte's; poetry, Emily's

poetry, Anne's: Anne's first dated poem, like Emily's, is from 1836, and she went on writing poetry, again like Emily, until a few months before her death. However, Anne wrote much more poetry in her last years than Emily did, and her later verse represents new and ambitious directions for her, while Emily wrote only two versions of a bloodthirsty Gondal poem. Though she wrote less poetry than her sister, Anne's extant verse is, almost all of it, finished, accomplished, and shows a technique that she was always refining with delicate, meticulous taste.

Right from the start (which means presumably when she wrote poems that she thought worth keeping) she proclaims herself, in a series of Gondal poems, a poet who has her aims clear in her mind, though many traces of an essentially adolescent lifeview can be discerned. Edward Chitham sees most of these Gondal poems as heavily influenced by Emily (*Poems of Anne Brontë*, pp. 167–8) but it is worth underlining that Gondal was the creation of both sisters in partnership, and that Anne had an obduracy of her own that was to make her whole poetic output very different in style and subject matter from that of her probably overbearing elder sister. Even when she most recalls Emily's work, there is also a personality of her own and a sureness of touch that can take the breath away:

> I have passed over thy own mountains dear,
> Thy northern mountains – and they still are free,
> Still lonely, wild, majestic, bleak and drear,
> And stern and lovely, as they used to be
>
> (EC, p. 63)

Gondal presents Anne with a range of subject matter, but she comes back, again and again, both before and (more surprisingly) after her governessing years, to dungeons and solitary prisoners. It may be that these enabled Anne to express some of the frustrations she felt at home, feelings she attributed to Agnes Grey in her first novel: "brought up in the strictest seclusion . . . we never even went to school . . . no society in the neighbourhood . . . a vague and secret wish to see a little more of the world" (ch. 1). These frustrations may well have been aroused afresh when she returned from Thorp Green, where at least there had been company, local travel, and holidays, an occupation with duties and possibilities.

Nevertheless the trials of a governess are what engages Anne most urgently as soon as she takes up her posts. Even the bluebell, a flower with a "fine and subtle spirit," arouses despair in Anne at being forced to spend "a thankless life" in the midst of "heartless crowds" (EC, p. 74). Within days of writing this she is penning her most depressive poem, the first of two "Lines Written at Thorp Green." The poem clearly expresses Anne's unhappiness with her position ("My life is very lonely,/ My days pass heavily," EC, p. 75), but they also may refer to her separation from William Weightman (or indeed someone else she had come to love). By then Weightman had been in Haworth for a year. The "Lines" begin a series of poems which have as their subject, or as a background preoccupation, a figure that is similar to the image we have of Weightman from Charlotte's letters: "O beautiful, and full of grace," "I will not mourn thee, lovely one . . . That angel smile," CEC, pp. 76 and 87). Though the Thorp Green poems are not as a rule among her best, perhaps because of the cares and distractions of her job, there are signs of a deepening preoccupation with religion, in particular with universal salvation (in "A Word to the Calvinists") and the consolations of nature. One of the best of these poems, "Lines Composed in a Wood on a Windy Day," depicts her escape through the exhilarating experience of the wind, and it acts as a sort of counterpart to Emily's "High Waving Heather." But it must be said that the total impression given by too many of the other poems of this period is of one who is determined to persevere with an experience that is too alien and unpleasant for her young and timid nature to bear. High on the list of preoccupations that contributed to her misery was Branwell's probable affair with her employer Mrs Robinson.

In June 1845 Anne left her situation for good. It seemed as if matters at Haworth would return to pre-adult days, with all the children at home, and all of them writing. Emily and Anne had an excursion to York, during which they "played" Gondal characters. Anne commented that "The Gondals are not yet in first rate playing condition" (1845 diary paper, see CBL, v. 1, p. 410), a phrase that has been made to bear more weight than it probably should. Anne wrote Gondal poems in the years that followed, and there is no reason to think she had been forced to do that. However, before long it became clear to her, if we read her poetry aright, that things were not as they had been before. Apart from Branwell being frequently drunk it emerged that Anne and Emily had grown apart in thought and feelings. This was not surprising, when Anne's periods at home since 1839, apart from holidays, amounted to a few months between her two situations. Now Anne displays a strong sense of Emily's spiritual arrogance, which probably took pleasure in ridiculing her younger sister's more conventional faith. In Anne's ambitious poem "The Three Guides" (1847) the second guide, one of two that are rejected before Anne chooses Faith, is the Spirit of Pride, whose tone and harsh satirical manner completely alienate Anne: "I abhor thy scoffing tongue" (EC, p. 148). And she illustrates this in the Spirit's arrogant ranting: "Cling to the earth, poor grovelling worm,/ 'Tis not for thee to soar/ Against the fury of the storm" (EC, p. 147). And there is sheer contempt in the Spirit's language when it advises the poet that for her "'Tis best the beaten path to keep,/ The ancient faith to hold,/ To pasture with thy fellow sheep,/ And lie within the fold" (EC, p. 146). The picture of this "explorer" of spiritual states and mysteries who is drunk with her own daring could have taken its cue from Emily's own words in "Plead for Me" published the year before, in which she asks "Why I have persevered to shun/ The common paths that others run" (*Complete Poems*, ed. Gezari, p. 22).

This concern with a breach with Emily surfaces again in "Self-Communion," another long poem started in 1847 and finished the next year. It is an intricate work, both freer and more confident than most of Anne's earlier poetry, and its introspection and its conspectus of her own spiritual development allies her intellectually and spiritually with Wordsworth. The section on the relationship with Emily, less vivid and dramatic than the Pride verses in "The Three Guides," concentrates on the pain caused when what Anne held most dear was "slighted, questioned, or despised," and concludes that what was once one root had become two trees that could only mingle at "leaf and bough" level, that is, at levels that Anne would consider comparatively trivial (EC, p. 157). These two ambitious poems suggest that Anne was losing her innate modesty of aim and was on the verge of a great advance.

There remain the hymn-based poem of 1848 "Believe not those who say" and the painful poem of January 1849: "A dreadful darkness closes in." In this last we hear of the devastating effect on Anne of the news that she had advanced tuberculosis and could not live long. It was not to be expected that she would go anything but gentle into that good night, but the impact of the news on her, the weariness and bewilderment of her initial response and the reluctance with which she accepted God's will are searing in their honesty. Even in this last memorial to her piety we have the insistence on doing good, on work to improve the world: just like an Agnes Grey who had not lost her illusions, she wants to "toil amid the labouring throng/ With purpose pure and high" (EC, p. 163). It was one of the aims that lay behind almost everything she wrote, in prose or verse.

poetry, Branwell's:

"Branwell was the second best poet in the Brontë family" writes Tom Winnifrith in his edition of Branwell's poems (1983), and his view echoes, and has been echoed by, many other Brontë critics. It is not entirely clear what such a judgment bases itself on. One would be hard put to assemble a handful of his poems that are complete entities, hit their target, and say something interesting or illuminating. For example, the poem "Sir Henry Tunstall," which Winifred Gerin (1961) calls "the climax of Branwell's poetic achievement," one with "exceptional literary merit," is an account of the return home of Sir Henry, who has spent many years in India climbing his way up the military career ladder, to a family group not unlike Branwell's base at the Parsonage. The message of the poem is that he has changed, his experiences have destroyed the loving and carefree boy who left home, just as those he has left have been changed even by their event-free existence. Not a terribly original observation, but one that he might have carried off if the poem had comprised a page or two. But Branwell spreads it out to 15 pages, with instance upon instance of change, including mention of his "trusty dog – poor Rover! – where art thou?" of his father's "grey locks" and both his parents' failure to recognize in this "war worn warrior" the son they had nurtured. The material is spread so thin, the repetition so monstrous and unvarying in the responses it tries to evoke, that the reader is left screaming at the monotony of it all. This combines with fake antiquarian diction ("Say, thou no longer wert a guileless child") and with constant thumping inversions to gain a rhyme ("They fancied, when they knew me home returning,/ That all my soul to meet with them was yearning"). It all smacks of a poetaster, not a poet.

Perhaps Branwell's greatest problem was his inability to bring his own life and nature into any kind of focus. On the one hand there is the persona of his adopted pseudonym Northangerland, the amoral rebel figure. On the other hand is the grown-up child, mourning the loss of innocence. Not surprisingly several of his more successful poems are short, many in an adaptation of the sonnet form which forces him into concision and a sharper focus. The poem inspired by Landseer's "The Shepherd's Chief Mourner" contrasts in typical Brontë fashion the real grief and sense of abandonment of the sheepdog with the insincerities of human grief. However, it fails to clinch the point in its final lines, which are feeble. "On Peaceful Death and Painful Life" is similarly concise and centered on a simple contrast (allied to Branwell's frequent subject of the decay of childish innocence) between those who are fortunate enough to die early, and those who are victims to a living death because their "life departs, before his death has come." Perhaps the most interesting of his longer poems is the one centering on Nelson, which he eventually called "The Triumph of Mind Over Body". Though there is some of Branwell's usual flaccid language, tired with overuse, and also some of the conventional patriotic sentiments the subject naturally gave rise to (he talks of Nelson as someone "The memory of whose life still cheers old England on," and of his life "so gladly given, to free/ Her thousand happy homes from slavery"), there is also a struggling with language to find a genuine echo for Nelson's daring and distinction. Branwell well conveys the inspirational nature of Nelson's "feeble form" which performed such heroic acts. He revels in the infant tourist industry that makes his cabin a mecca, and he looks forward to his own death, asking for a fraction of Nelson's courage and persistency. The poem does not deserve du Maurier's scorn.

One of the few poems in which Branwell genuinely struggles to understand his own nature and fate is "Penmaenmawr," probably written in late 1845, but harking back to his Liverpool excursion with John Brown earlier in the year. Here the contemplation of the grim fortress of nature, mighty but without feeling or memory, brings him as always back to himself, but not with the usual self-pity – instead becoming a prayer leading to an (unfulfilled) resolution to "arise o'er mortal care;/ All evils bear, yet never know despair." It is one of the few poems which seem to exist as a unity, to have a structure that matches its material. It was the product of a mood which unfortunately was a fleeting one.

Branwell's poems were published most frequently in the *Halifax Guardian*, so that he was recognized as one of "their" poets – and it was a newspaper that prided itself on printing poetry by local writers who composed verse especially for it. He was beginning, in other words, to make a local reputation. One doubts if, for Branwell, this would ever have been enough.

poetry, Charlotte's: one mystery about Charlotte's poetic output is her own attitude towards it. She certainly, after the unsuccessful publication of *Poems* in 1846, tended to refer to her part of it disparagingly: to both Mrs Gaskell and Miss Alexander she called them "juvenile productions," and to the latter she confessed "they now appear to me very crude" (letter, 18 Mar 1850). Yet though her reaction when she surreptitiously read Emily's poems was an instant admiration and feeling that they should be published, the resulting volume contained an excess of Charlotte's poetry – as much as the other two's put together. A related mystery was why Charlotte hardly took the opportunity to condense the poems and to sharpen their focus. Sometimes the verbiage is so turgid, the points they make so imperfectly formulated in her mind, that it seems that the impulse behind the poem is simply the need to write, and then to go on writing.

There are some exceptions, some modest successes. Everyone's favorite Charlotte poem, which is in fact only a small part of a long one, are the three or four verses starting "We wove a web in childhood," which have charm and a controlled nostalgia. Among the poems she actually published, "Pilate's Wife's Dream" catches the interest with its unusual subject matter and its economical picture of the frozen Roman governor, sadistic yet cowardly, and the terrible marriage the two find themselves in. "Mementoes" starts with the cozy subject of memories stored away, but changes gear to focus on another dysfunctional family which it depicts and analyzes with some success.

There is also an interest in some of the poems that seem to touch on subjects treated more fully in the novels. "The Missionary" in particular seems to prefigure the St John Rivers section of *Jane Eyre*, and there are some points of comparison between "Gilbert" and the career of Mr Rochester, though the fact that the first is a cold-hearted, secretive schemer and the latter a warm-hearted and warm-blooded man makes the feel of their stories very different. The poems of her own that Charlotte inserted into her novels, where they act as speed bumps in the reader's progress, rarely add anything to the more detailed and subtle treatment of the same themes in the prose parts of the novels.

But the points of interest in Charlotte's collected poems are sadly outweighed by the almost unreadable: the endless wallowing in misery in "Frances," the simple-minded sensationalism of "Apostasy," and the sheer pointlessness of so many of the others suggest the thought that these overlong doses of dead poetic language inevitably disinclined the reader to take seriously the much superior poems that nestled between

Charlotte's efforts. All in all the main reason for reading her poetry in the future, as in the past, is likely to lie in what they tell us about Charlotte's life and nature, and what sidelights they cast on aspects of her novels. The first – biographical – interest has its obvious dangers. Most of her poems have a dramatic situation as their starting-point, however mistily presented that situation is (e.g., "Preference"). In addition the most obviously personal poems are often the weakest, as for example the two poems on her sisters' deaths. The preoccupations that surface in both the novels and the verse are always more involvingly treated in prose, are understood with a much more subtle intelligence. She is an interesting example of the writer of a poetic prose who, unlike Hardy or D. H. Lawrence, did not manage to be equally powerful in pure poetry. There are, indeed, times when, so bad is the verse, we seem to be close to the world of Patience Strong:

> We'll not let its [i.e. the world's] follies grieve us,
> We'll just take them as they come;
> And then every day will leave us
> A merry laugh for home.
>
> ("Parting," PCB, p. 61)

poetry, Emily's: the earliest extant poems by Emily date from mid-1836, and already in that year she was writing fully achieved verse, for example in "High Waving Heather." There is a steady flow of poems until early 1846, and thereafter a puzzling gap, filled only by one long Gondal poem ("Why ask to know the date – the clime?") later that year, and a revision of its opening lines in 1848. Within this span of time there are intensely creative periods – the Law Hill months, for example, and the period 1843–4, when she was first alone in the Parsonage with her father, then had the companionship of the desolate Charlotte. On the other hand there are comparatively infertile periods, such as the one mentioned, and the Brussels year, when Emily worked "like a horse" (Charlotte to EN, May 1842) and presumably had little time for poetry.

In February 1844 Emily began transcribing the poems she thought worth preserving into two notebooks, one for Gondal poems, the other for non-Gondal ones. This latter, the Honresfeld notebook, is often referred to as containing "personal" poems, but there is an element of dramatization, of adopting a voice, in many or most of them, and the personal or confessional note is comparatively rare.

A further element of selection came about when the 1846 volume of poems by all three sisters was prepared for publication. Here the matter of how the poems might appeal to a wider reading public entered into consideration for the first time. Some poems may have been selected because they were thought (wrongly, as it turned out, at least on their initial publication) to have the potential for general popularity. Of the 21 poems by Emily published in that volume there are one or two puzzling choices, granted the quality of some of the poems that were not selected.

The early poems of Emily are virtually unpunctuated, and punctuation was always very light until the question of publication arose. This causes few problems in the reading (the Penguin and the OUP editions of the petry are the closest to the manuscript in punctuation), partly because many of the poems are simple in sentiment, partly because they are dramatic and designed to be read aloud (certainly the best of them read well and easily).

There have been various reconstructions of the Gondal story, in the absence (odd, in view of the preservation of so many scraps of verse) of the prose narratives. All involve a great deal of faith and imagination, since narrative poems are few and elsewhere the "story" indications are very slight. Critics today tend to be skeptical as to whether the narrative framework can be usefully reconstructed.

In general critics have found the Gondal poems inferior to the non-Gondal ones, but it is important that the distinction is not made too clear-cut, because that impedes our appreciation of them. One of her greatest poems, the one beginning "Cold in the earth," was published in 1846 as "Remembrance" with all traces of Gondal removed. It can be read as a searing account of the loss of a loved one. For the one remaining, existence can only become tolerable again through a process of self-discipline and avoidance of the indulgence of wallowing in memory: "Then did I learn how existence could be cherished,/ Strengthened and fed without the aid of joy" as Emily puts it. The poem builds on the simplest of words and formulations, which by repetition and slight variation it invests with a terrible emotional force. The "surface simplicity and intensity of emotional effect" which Shostakovich found in Britten's music exactly describes what most readers find in this poem.

And yet. . . . The Gondal notebook version is headed "R Alcona to J Brenzaida." Julius Brenzaida, we can be fairly sure, is Gondal's equivalent of Zamorna, with added diabolism and a penchant for treachery and blood. Like Zamorna he is not even faithful to his principal lover, Rosina Alcona. The love depicted here, therefore, puts us in mind of Charlotte's Mina Laury and her love for Zamorna, which involves a total self-abnegation, a commitment to the loved one that is mindless and destructive of all pride and self-respect. This puts a less romantic slant on Rosina's blissless and despairing life after her lover's death. And if we turn to the 1846 version, improved but also more general, we find that this interpretation is still present in that text. The love so eloquently described is in its nature destructive, and whether the lover had died or survived he had swallowed up the writer rather than enriched her life and nature. And, as if the Gondal/Angrian connection were not enough, we may remember that in March 1845, when the first version of the poem was written, Emily had been living with Charlotte in her shattered emotional state for 15 months, since her return from Brussels.

Similarly with poems from the non-Gondal book. Many of them are self-announced as coming from one or more advocates for points of view: "The Old Stoic" is one such, and the mystical, almost Blakean "The Philosopher" is another. "No Coward Soul," always taken as Emily's credo, can be read just as easily as a dramatization of a belief, which makes the vainglorious boast of the first line more acceptable – not a defiant, macho proclamation but a generalized rendering of a state of mind. This leads more acceptably to the wonderful lines which epitomize such a speaker's bold confidence: the vision of the spirit that "Pervades and broods above,/ Changes, sustains, dissolves, creates and rears."

It is worth insisting that, just as the "personal" poems can be in fact miniature dramatic monologues, the Gondal poems can suddenly transcend the cardboard-cutout

Ruritania of their background and become intensely felt and utterly convincing. "The Prisoner" is the best-known example of this. In it the commonplace figure of the beautiful captive with the fair curls that sweep to the stone floor becomes a mystic who can escape her dismal surrounding to an exalted spiritual state where no tyranny can touch her. Emily, alas, never found a way of setting these wonderful verses into a convincing context. But while many of the early Gondal poems are marred by pasteboard conflicts and second-hand emotions, they may still rise to memorable encounters such as the beautiful but satanic young man (or woman?) sheltering in the shepherd's hut in "And now the house-dog stretched once more," or embrace an inspiration perfect in itself and transcending its context, as in "The linnet in the rocky dells."

What is undeniable is that in the last few years of her life Emily was writing verse of great richness, power, and variety. Undoubtedly Emily is *there* in the Gondal poems as well as in the non-Gondal ones, but where, when, and in what form she is there could be argued over indefinitely. The writer who took such elaborate pains in *Wuthering Heights* to keep herself out of her narrative was unlikely to signal plainly her appearance *in propria persona* in her poetry.

Stylistically the best poems are notable for their simplicity of language, and Emily often gains a powerful intensification of the emotional level by repetition of quite ordinary words or syntactical formulations ("Cold in the Earth" gives splendid examples of these characteristics). The fact that Emily was the natural poet of the family does not mean that she did not, by hard work and trial and error, refine her effects, extend her range, eradicate her early crudenesses. But the clanking melodramatics remained with her to the end, reminding us that she was only 30 when she died.

See also Gondal

poetry and miscellaneous writings of Patrick Brontë:

Patrick Brontë was one of the poets covered in W. C. Newsam's *The Poets of Yorkshire* (1845), where he was given five lines and an extract from the poem "Happy Cottagers." The only critical judgment is that his poems present "pious sentiments in a plain garb." With the "pious sentiments" one could not quarrel: there are few poems without a didactic intention that at some point is brought out into the open. He is often, after all, writing with young people in mind. The garb is not so "plain," though, as Mr Newsam suggests. Patrick writes in varied meters, which he keeps good control of; he writes confidently and often elegantly; there are few signs of desperate measures to secure rhymes – he has, in short, facility, which not all of his children had. It must be said that few of his poems remain in the mind of the modern reader, who distrusts poetry with an obvious moral purpose, and his messages are often trite: "the advantage of poverty," about which his wife wrote an article, is one of his constant themes, the beauty of a Christian family life is another. He writes at length on the temptations of the rich, the insincerities and greed of modern social life, the central need of all Christians to study the Bible for themselves. He is inclined to tell the well-brought-up lady that she is "but a breathing mass of clay,/ Fast ripening for the grave" (*Brontëana*, 1898, p. 44). He is hot against novels and plays, which he equates with pollution, and when he writes a poem on his wife's birthday his obvious contentment does not stop the poem being rather dull.

His first tale, *The Cottage in the Wood* (1815), tells the story of one of Patrick's Christian families who apparently rescue a young freethinker and debauchee through Christian homilies, only to find him first attempting to seduce their saintly daughter Mary, then offering her marriage. The second offer is rejected as heatedly as the first: Mary quotes St Paul – "Be not unequally yoked together with unbelievers" – which looks back to Patrick's use of the passage in a letter on the failure of his relationship with Mary Burder (LPB, p. 24). To his suggestion that with marriage she would probably bring him round to her way of thinking she replies that "some rash women" have gone into marriage with this aim, "but, for one that has had reason to rejoice at it, a thousand have had cause for sorrow" (*Brontëana*, pp. 111–12), which looks forward to Helen Huntingdon. Needless to say this *Pamela*-like plot ends in marriage, a loving and useful life, and above all a Christian death.

His last published work of any length, *The Maid of Killarney* (1818), shows him trying to get beyond the didactic, to make his moral theme part of a short novel that talks of contemporary issues and eternal dilemmas (what he in the subtitle calls "some cursory remarks on Religion and Politics"). So often is the action, such as it is, interrupted by discussions that one is reminded of some of Bernard Shaw's "talkathon" plays – *Getting Married*, for example. For a work of this sort to succeed the talk has to be good, and it must be said that Patrick's is only of variable interest. He can, through his characters, be forceful on such topics as the folly of enforcing capital punishment for a whole range of crimes. On the other hand he can put forward the silliest generalizations on the nature of Irish, Scottish, and English people, or the difference between men and women. The poor, deserving or undeserving, are wheeled out to praise the wonderful comfort of Bible-reading or to demonstrate their unreasonable demands (tobacco!) and ingratitude. As usual novels get a passing kick, and in the end the stock character Albion gets the stock character Flora as his bride and they disappear from the reader's mind as if they had never been.

Patrick never again published in book form, but he did publish much else during his children's period of growing up: pamphlets, sermons, letters to local newspapers. Particularly notable are the moving sermon on William Weightman's death, his letters on the new Poor Law Act of 1834 and on capital punishment, and also his misguided but forceful writings on the Crow Hill bog burst. But perhaps the greatest influence of his writings on his children was the fact that they could find them on shelves in the Parsonage together with the writings of internationally known figures such as Scott or Byron. He thus made the idea of publishing a living possibility for them.

"Politics of Verdopolis, The": one of the liveliest and most approachable of Branwell's early chronicles, written in the autumn of 1833. The main foci of the manuscript concern Rogue's relationship with his young and beautiful daughter Mary, and the democratic politics in the Glasstown Confederacy. An unexpected dissolution of Parliament spurs Rogue on to fashion a Liberal Party to contest the ensuing elections. Among his candidates are Quashia and Sir Robert Pelham, a new character, who

falls in love with Mary Percy. As was to be expected, Rogue's coalition of forces relies on bribery, bullying and false promises, and eventually crumbles when Rogue's promise of his daughter's hand to Quashia is broken. The chronicle ends with a vivid party scene in which Mary Percy is introduced to Glasstown society. The political disputes and intrigues of this story owe much to the wrangling and maneuvering around the Great Reform Bill of 1832, and Branwell's involvement in them at a local level.

See also Pelham; Percy; Quashia

Ponden House: today popularly known as Ponden Hall, in the time of the Brontës the home, near Stanbury, of the Heaton family. Old Ponden Hall, recently rebuilt from ruins, was a small seventeenth-century house, built close to the Ponden House proper. This larger house is probably partly Elizabethan, built on to over the centuries so that in the nineteenth century it was a gentleman's residence-cum-farm. A magnificent dresser from the house is currently in East Riddlesden Hall, near Keighley. Ponden's extensive library was dispersed when the family died out in the late nineteenth century. Scholars today tend to discount the notion that the Brontë children had the freedom of this library, because its strength was eighteenth-century works. However, though this was by no means their favorite literary period, the Brontës show a solid acquaintanceship with major works of the period through quotation and allusion.

The idea that Ponden House was Thrushcross Grange in *Wuthering Heights* does not bear close scrutiny: it did not have the Grange's fine and extensive park, it was a much more modest residence, and few of the architectural details correspond. However, some aspects, such as the library and its geographical relation to the Heights (i.e., Top Withens) may have provided germs for Emily's imaginary houses and landscapes, and it is interesting that at the end of the book Hareton becomes its master, since his name is an anagram of R. Heaton, the name of Ponden's master until his death in 1846, and of his eldest son, also Robert.

See also Heaton family

Ponden Kirk: an impressive, jutting expanse of gritstone about five miles from Haworth, dissected by a narrow tunnel. This is the "Peniston Crag" of *Wuthering Heights*, with its "fairy cave."

Pool, Rev. Robinson: one of Thornton's dissenting ministers during Patrick's time there. He wrote to Patrick after the publication of Mrs Gaskell's *Life*. "I can fancy, almost," wrote Patrick in his reply, "that we are still at Thornton, good neighbours, and kind, and Sincere friends, and happy with our wives and children" (18 Mar 1858).

Poole, Grace: nurse and attendant for Mrs Rochester. She is an asylum attendant, hard of face, generally capable except when she has taken too much to drink. Many of the things that are attributed to Grace in the early part of the book emanate in fact from Bertha Rochester, for example the mirthless laugh.

Poor Law Amendment Act (1834): the act, masterminded by the Benthamites, which established workhouses throughout Britain and abolished "outdoor relief" of poverty. The heartlessness of the new system was attacked in such novels as *Oliver Twist* (1837–9) and Mrs Trollope's *Jessie Phillips* (1842). In February 1837 Patrick chaired a meeting in Haworth so large it eventually had to take place in the open, calling for the Act to be repealed. Two months later he wrote a powerful letter to the *Leeds Intelligencer* pleading that the Act could not be tinkered with but must be repealed: "It is a monster of iniquity, a horrid and cruel deformity" he wrote, and followed Dickens in his indignation at the starvation diet prescribed for paupers: "*We will not live* on their water gruel, and on their two ounces of cheese, and their fourteen ounces of bread per day" he imagined them saying. He also trenchantly quoted from the Old Testament which exhorts people "to open our hearts to relieve" the poor.

Workhouses were finally abolished in 1947.

Pope, Alexander (1688–1744): Augustan poet whom Charlotte notoriously did not admire. However, there is quite frequent quotation from him in the Brontës' juvenile and mature works, from a range of sources including *The Dunciad*, the "Epistle to Dr Arbuthnot," and the *Essay on Man*, quoted twice in *Tenant*. The children seem to have been acquainted with both Pope and Dryden's translations from the classics, which doubtless enabled the girls to share Branwell's classics-orientated education.

Poplawska, Rosa: governess to the Kay-Shuttleworth children, of German-Polish extraction. Charlotte liked her greatly, thought her on the whole well-treated, but wearing "the usual pale, despondent look of her class" (to EN, 19 Mar 1850). The feeling was clearly returned, for on her second visit Miss Poplawska "was almost as pleased to see me as if we had been related" (to EN, 2 Sep 1850). In 1853–4 the Kay-Shuttleworth marriage broke down, and until Lady Kay-Shuttleworth died Poplawska was her constant companion in what was apparently a search for health. Margaret Smith emphasizes her "religious fervour" which matched her mistress's own, but the couple's eldest son Ughtred speaks of the "almost hypnotic influence" Poplawska exercised, which he attributed to "a love of power, [and] a hatred of my father" (Frank Smith, *Life of Sir James Kay-Shuttleworth*, 1923, p. 333). It is noteworthy that Lady Kay-Shuttleworth resisted even visits from her husband, insisting that her doctors assure him that any such would endanger her life, suggesting an extreme physical aversion.

"*Portrait: Le Roi Harold avant la Bataille de Hastings*": one of Emily's most powerful essays for M. Heger, attempting a great deal of concentrated psychological investigation of kinghood and heroism. It was written in June 1842, like the following essay by Charlotte.

See also Harold

"*Portrait: Pierre l'Ermite*": essay by Charlotte of June 1842, giving an enthusiastic and uncritical account of the man who launched the First Crusade: "his ardour was that of the soul, its flame was pure and it rose up to heaven" (BE, p. 118).

Postlethwaite family: employers of Branwell Brontë in Broughton-in-Furness Jan–June 1840. The father, Robert (1786–1859), was a magistrate with some landholdings and expectations of a substantial increase in them. He was described by Branwell as "of a right hearty and generous disposition" (to John Brown, 13 Mar 1840). He had advertised in the *Leeds Intelligencer* for a tutor twice in August 1837, and in substance repeated the advertisement three times in December–January 1839–40. Whether or not the earlier advertisement resulted in an appointment, this does not suggest that employment in such a remote area was a popular prospect. The advertisement stressed "the Classics, with the strictest attention to Grammar." Branwell may have felt that the situation, on the edge of the Lake District, had both poetic and practical possibilities. Once there his letter to John Brown of 13 March 1840 does not suggest that he took his duties over-seriously, but this may be an extension of his general boastings of drinking and sexual exploits. There are Postlethwaite family traditions that he was dismissed, either for drunkenness or for a lackadaisical approach to his charges' education, but evidence is lacking. He was home by late June.

His employer's wife Agnes he described in the same letter as "a quiet, silent, and amiable woman," and his charges were "two fine, spirited lads." Of these John (1828–86) was to enter the Church, and as a High Churchman prospered for some years. After his appointment as Bishop of New Westminster, British Columbia, came to nothing he seems to have effectively given up his calling and lived off his property, first in Broughton, then Cambridge. William (1829–1908) succeeded to the property (the Oaks, Millom) which his father had inherited in 1844 from his uncle. Unusually for a landowner with a family he left the country in 1872 for New Zealand, where he became a member of the House of Representatives, and then left that country for California. Perhaps some of Branwell's restless, unsatisfiable spirit had got into him.

"Preface *A Word to the 'Quarterly'*" see "Word to the 'Quarterly.'"

Prescott, Emily (?1812–1907): wife of Henry Nussey. He had collected a sheaf of refusals over several years, but when in 1844 he met with an acceptance it was from a woman with a "handsome fortune" (CB to EN, 14 Nov 1844). Emily was the daughter of a gentleman of Hampshire origins, and a citizen of Everton, whence she was married, with Ellen as bridesmaid. The latter's first impressions were favorable: "She is very pious but very agreeably so and quite free from all affectation" (EN to Mary Gorham, 6 Aug 1845). These impressions proved false. "I could not live with one so cold and narrow," Charlotte was soon writing, though she adds, unflatteringly for Ellen's brother, "still I think she is just the person for Henry – she will obtain influence over him and keep it" (to EN, 8 Sep 1845). Emily seems to have tried to make Ellen pay for her own washing while she remained with them at Hathersage after their return from their honeymoon, suggesting she was the sort of rich person who is bent on holding on to what she has. She and Henry did not remain long at Hathersage. He seems to have got on the wrong side of people in his new parish, including the Duke of Devonshire. Henry ceased to be a practicing clergyman (like many others in the Brontë story), and he and his wife lived for a time in the South of France. She died in Nice

in 1907. The notion that they were unhappy in their marriage and separated seems to be untrue.

Procter, Anne Benson (née Skepper) (1799–1888): wife of Bryan Waller Procter, known by his pseudonym of Barry Cornwall. She was related to the hated Sidgwick family, and was introduced to Charlotte when she was invited to come after the dinner party Thackeray gave (12 June 1850). With her was her daughter Adelaide Anne Proctor (1825–64), the poet, who wrote for *Household Words* and was the author of "A Lost Chord," later much loved, and later still much ridiculed, when set to music by Sullivan as "The Lost Chord" (as if it was some kind of musical Grail). Her conversion to Catholicism was commented on by Charlotte in a letter to Mrs Gaskell, who was a family friend of the Procters (6 Aug 1851). It was Anne, the mother, who described the evening spent with Charlotte as "one of the dullest evenings she had ever spent in her life" (Anne Thackeray Ritchie, *Chapters from Some Memoirs*, 1894, ch. 5).

Professor, The: written in the mid-1840s, rejected by many publishers including three times by Smith Elder, published posthumously in 1857 with minor changes made by Arthur Bell Nicholls and Patrick Brontë.

The novel opens with a letter sent by William Crimsworth to an Eton friend, though he insists that theirs was not a public school friendship of the "Pylades and Orestes" kind. The letter covers the relationship between Crimsworth and his mother's family, who have taken responsibility for him reluctantly and have no idea what to do with him when his education is finished. They offer him preferment in the Church and marriage to one of his six female cousins "all of whom I greatly dislike" (ch. 1). He rejects both offers, and casts off his aristocratic connection to throw in his lot with his mill-owning brother Edward. The letter ends with the brothers' first encounter as adults, and we are told the friend never received and therefore never answered the letter. The narrative then becomes a matter between Crimsworth and the reader.

If aristocratic patronage was not to his liking, preferment within his closer family proves even less so. Fraternal hostility had figured prominently in the juvenilia and continued to do so in this novel, *Wuthering Heights*, and the unfinished "Ashworth" and "Willie Ellin." From the first encounter Edward Crimsworth loathes William, regarding him with "gratuitous menace in his eye" (ch. 1). He engages him as a clerk on a normal commercial basis, insisting there be no "humbug" or "nonsense" (ch. 2) about family ties. The relationship can only deteriorate, and it ends with Edward taking a whip to his brother – a scene which is repeated in "Willie Ellin," but this is the more extraordinary example, as the younger brother is here an adult, and in genteel employment with his brother. The only lasting thing about Crimsworth's stay in the town of X— is his relationship – joshing, ironic, but ultimately affectionate – with the radical mill-owner Yorke Hunsden, who provides him with a letter of introduction to an influential man in Brussels, who finds for him an opening in one of the Belgian capital's boys' schools.

If Edward Crimsworth provided an example of naked power exercised in its most irrational and tyrannical way, William is faced with a much more subtle challenge in Brussels. His first impression of M. Pelet, the principal of the boys' school, is a tribute to the man's capacity for deception: Crimsworth finds him "melancholy," "*fine et spirituelle*," not stern or resolute enough to be a teacher (ch. 7). In reality he is a Machiavellian manipulator of those around him, a crafty politician – and one matched by Mlle Reuter, principal of the girls' school next door where William gains occasional employment. The maneuvers of these two schemers occupies the middle section of the book, and Crimsworth finds his own withdrawn and unexcitable nature a useful tool to counter their threats to his independence and integrity.

Mlle Reuter's interest in Crimsworth goes well beyond the pedagogical, and it is fortunate that at the same time as she tries to entrap him in an amorous web Crimsworth falls (inevitably coolly) in love. Frances Henri is the most generally admired element in the book: she is poor, friendless, but full of charm and independence of judgment. She marries a desire to learn and a respect for her teacher with a determination to make her own decisions – attitudes that mark all Charlotte's central female pupils. The love does not proceed without checks and impediments, but eventually the two schemers are outsmarted and find themselves caught in a marriage of convenience, while William and Frances are reunited, after a brief parting, in the Protestant Cemetery and then proceed at a stately pace towards matrimony. It does not suit Charlotte in this "plain and homely" narrative (Preface) that it should end with wedding bells. We have instead a long chapter about their marriage, their school, their son Victor and the principles behind his upbringing, their continuing relationship with Yorke Hunsden. Most readers would probably prefer the traditional wedding bells because Charlotte was not yet a confident enough writer to kick over a well-worn tradition.

The Professor was published in June 1857, three months after Mrs Gaskell's *Life*. If there had been a contest between the two for public interest the result would have been a foregone conclusion: the *Life* had all the qualities that *The Professor* was found to lack – pathos, signal virtue, tragedy, conflict. The reviewers were on the whole uncertain how to treat *The Professor*. The revelations of the *Life* prevented the sort of Mrs Grundyish condemnations sometimes lavished on the earlier books. On the other hand the improvised halo bestowed on Charlotte in the *Life* conflicted with the matter and tone of her first written novel: never was there a less committed warrior for truth and purity than William Crimsworth, and it was impossible not to find him somewhat contaminated by the "moral leprosy" (*Morning Post*) of the foreigners who surrounded him. All in all it was a mystery, and reviewers preferred to concern themselves with the meaty scandals caused by the *Life*. Even modern readers have been slow to search for the original and profound narrative that lies behind a few eccentricities and unwise narrative ploys. *The Professor*'s time is still to come.

Protestant Cemetery, Brussels: in fact only a slip of land making up part

of the larger cemetery, with "beautiful vistas of farther lines of hills, of intervening valleys, of farms and villas" (Theodore Wolfe, reprinted in Ruijssenaar, 2000, pp. 61–6). It was situated about three miles from Brussels, beyond the Porte de Louvain. Martha Taylor was buried here in October 1842, and her sister Mary went there with

Charlotte and Emily on the 30th of that month, Charlotte going again in September 1843. It figures in *The Professor* as the scene of Crimsworth's finding of Frances Henri after separation, and it is the subject of a rather intrusive passage in *Shirley* (ch. 9) where the fate of Jessy Yorke (based on Martha) is prefigured: "Here is the place; green sod and a grey marble headstone – Jessy sleeps below."

Pryce, Rev. David (1811–40): graduate of Trinity College, Dublin, and the curate of Christ Church, Colne, in Lancashire. On the basis of a brief visit to Haworth Parsonage, though one that involved "Hibernian flattery" (to EN, 4 Aug 1839), he proposed to Charlotte and was refused. Less than six months later he was dead of a ruptured blood-vessel. Charlotte described him as a "strong athletic-looking man," and she felt "shocked and saddened" by his death (to EN, 24 Jan 1840). In the earlier letter she revealed some of her feelings about Irish men: he was "witty – lively, ardent – clever too – but deficient in the dignity & discretion of an Englishman." The *Leeds Intelligencer* described him as a "benevolent friend" to the poor and one of the Church's "most active and faithful servants."

Pryor, Mrs Agnes: governess and companion to Shirley Keeldar, who turns out to be the mother of Caroline Helstone. She is a stately, conventional, conservative lady, who yet turns out to be very unsure of herself in emergencies, being unable to trust her own judgment. Perhaps this is just as well, as she gave away Caroline as a baby fearing that her prettiness was a sign of perversity. She had been a governess (her maiden name, oddly, was Agnes Grey) who fell in love with the handsome but dissolute James Helstone. After further unhappy experiences as governess with the Hardmans she is comparatively happy and at peace with Shirley. Her character and the motivation of her actions have been almost universally considered by readers and critics as unconvincing.

Punch: humorous magazine founded in 1841, and in the 1840s closely associated with W. M. Thackeray. There is no evidence that the Brontës took it, but Charlotte quoted its popularization of the word "snobbishness" (to EN, 28 Dec 1846), and alludes to two of its series in letters to George Smith in early 1850, suggesting she may have had access to it at that date.

Purcell, Henry (1658–95): Purcell's reputation as the greatest English composer was never wholly lost in the succeeding two centuries, though his stage works were forgotten. His anthems were admired, though heavily altered, and his ground basses were appreciated (Emily played one). Charlotte mentions "a delicious air" in "A Day Abroad," but Branwell is slightly more specific. He mentions "a noble piece" with a "plaintive melody" in "The Wool is Rising," and he singles out "those anthems that speak to us" by Purcell and other British composers in "And the Weary are at Rest".

Purnell, Joseph: the successor to Mr Rand as the Haworth school teacher. Charlotte says in a letter to Rand that he is "much liked" and the school does "extremely well" under him (22 Jan 1846).

Puseyism: movement in the Church of England associated with Edward Bouverie
Pusey (1800–82). Its tendency was High Church, emphasizing its place in the apos-
tolic succession, and encouraging ceremonial in church services. As such it was anath-
ema to the Brontës, Charlotte in particular, who distrusted anything that smacked
of (and could often lead to) Roman Catholicism. Charlotte considered "the extremes
of high & low Churchism foolish" (to EN, July 1842?), but Patrick went further, speaking of the movement's "subtle poison": "I thoroughly detest it both root and branch
... I only see in it, 'Satan transformed into the appearance of an angel of light'" (to
A. P. Irwine, 15 Apr 1851). The description of Mr Hatfield's religious convictions in
Agnes Grey, ch. 10 is a clear critique of Puseyism – see the paragraph beginning: "His
favourite subjects were Church discipline, rites and ceremonies, apostolical succession,
the duty of reverence and obedience to the clergy."

Q

Quarterly Review: periodical of impeccably Tory and established Church credentials, founded to counterbalance the *Edinburgh Review*. The fact that the *Quarterly* was prominent in the backlash to *Jane Eyre*, following the early admiring reviews, is ironic, since its editor John Lockhart was one of the book's most enthusiastic admirers. His reviewer, however, Elizabeth Rigby, focused on the novel's "murmuring against the comforts of the rich and against the privations of the poor," and identified the spirit behind the book as similar to that which animated Chartism in Britain and had "overthrown authority and violated every code human and divine abroad" (she was writing at the end of the year of revolutions, 1848). Ironically again, she aroused an awareness that *Jane Eyre* was a revolutionary book, and where her editor could only see Jane as "rather a brazen Miss" (*Life and Letters of John Gibson Lockhart*, 1897), Miss Rigby sees her as a heathen spirit, instinct with the sin of pride. She thus led the way from seeing the book as an original treatment of the rags to riches story to one that understood its ground-breaking force in its treatment of women and their role.

Quashia Quamina: in the Angrian chronicles, son of King Sai-Too-Too Quamina and adopted son of the Duke of Wellington (this based on an actual instance of the real Duke taking responsibility for the young son of a defeated Indian potentate). Quashia grows up with the Wellesley boys, but there is a strong mutual hatred between Arthur and him based on a "thrashing" (probably a fight) he inflicts on the Duke's eldest son. As he grows up he identifies more and more with his Ashantee heritage, and enmity between him and Arthur festers. Before long he is leading uprisings and full-scale rebellions against the white intruders, and Douro is talking about exterminating the whole tribe of Ashantees.

There is a dichotomy between descriptions of Quashia and statements about his nature. On the one hand he is "of lofty stature and noble deportment and an eye like a young Eagle" (WPBB, v. 1, p. 340). On the other hand his disposition is "bold, irritable, active daring and at the same time deeply treacherous" (CB's "The Green Dwarf," where the fullest treatment is given of his development, EW, v. 2, pt 1, pp. 178–9). In 1834, in the futuristic "Leaf from an Unopened Volume" (EW, v. 2, pt 1, p. 326) Charlotte goes so far as to describe him as "a man in whose person all the virtues of savage life were so nobly united." The Ashantees are often described as brave, but they are also "incarnate fiends" and "disgusting demons," and all the habitual taunts of nineteenth-century colonialism are lavished on them. The nadir of Quashia in the juvenilia is Branwell's description of Angrian troops entering the sacked town of Dongola and finding flayed and scalped corpses in hundreds hung up around the town (WPBB, v. 2, pp. 302–3). From then on in Branwell's prose writings Quashia becomes, oddly enough, a figure of rude fun – boasting, blaspheming, and almost invariable drunk. For all his hideous acts – for example the slaughter of Zamorna's eldest son Ernest (WPBB, v. 2, p. 603) – he is no longer a dangerous figure.

In Charlotte's writings contemporary with this, on the other hand, there is a change in Quashia but a more subtle one. In February 1836 the 19-year-old woman recorded in her Roe Head diary a vision of Angria as it was in those war-torn days. First she remembers Zamorna's queen in former days "imperially robed and decked with pearls, every waft of her garments as she moved diffusing perfume." But now the fortunes of war have brought a new occupant to the "silken couch": "a swart and sinewy Moor, intoxicated to ferocious insensibility, had stretched his athletic limbs" there, "his broad chest heaving wildly as the breath issued in snorts from his distended nostrils," and he is seen "savagely exulting . . . in the bower of Zamorna's lady!" (*Tales of Angria*, ed. Glen, p. 449). It is very much a late-adolescent fantasy, composed of delicious fear and sexual excitement. It was the sort of thing that had Home Secretaries in the 1920s reaching for a banning order. Perhaps this diary vision frightened Charlotte herself. By the time she wrote "Caroline Vernon" Quashia, in his letter soliciting Caroline's hand in marriage, had reverted to the hectoring black man with lumpish humor (Gerin is right that this resembled Branwell's letters of the period) and barefaced cheek in his exorbitant demands. Perhaps the vision of him was something that could not be developed even in semi-private writings, and certainly not in published fiction of the time. But could this view of Quashia have influenced Emily in her creation of Heathcliff?

Queen Anne's Bounty: fund founded in that Queen's reign for the relief of poor clergymen. Patrick appealed to it on several occasions to build a parsonage in Hartshead and to supplement his salaries in Thornton and Haworth.

Queen of Labassecour: seen by Lucy Snowe at the royal concert in ch. 20 of *Villette*. She is described as "mild, thoughtful, graceful," though the Bourbon ancestry of the actual Belgian queen (Louise, daughter of Louis Philippe, King of the French) is hinted at when her profile reminds Lucy of "remembered effigies" which showed characters that were "feeble, or sensual, or cunning."

Queen's College: the genesis of the present college within London University was in the work of the Governesses' Benevolent Institution, and it provided an education

for W. S. Williams's daughter Mary Louisa: "it is a step towards independency," Charlotte wrote to him, "and one great curse of a single female life is its dependency" (3 July 1849).

Queen's Hotel, Bridge Street, Bradford: the landlord William Oddy made this a place of resort for all those engaged in the visual arts in the area.

Quillinan, Edward (1791–1851): poet, widower of Wordsworth's daughter Dorothy (Dora). Charlotte and Harriet Martineau dined at his house, along with the Arnolds, in December 1850, eight months after Wordsworth's death. His daughter Jemima showed Mrs Gaskell Branwell's letter of January 1837 to Wordsworth, which the poet treated with contempt (*Further Letters of Mrs Gaskell*, 2000, pp. 159–60).

R

Rachel (no surname given): Helen Huntingdon's servant in *The Tenant of Wildfell Hall*. One of several loyal, tenacious, rather forbidding female servants in the Brontës' works.

Rachel, Mme (real name Élisa Félix) (1820–58): French classical actress, the daughter of Alsatian-Jewish traveling peddlers. Her talent was discovered when she was singing in the streets as a young girl, and nurtured in drama school in Paris. She revolutionized acting styles in classical drama, rather as Callas did in opera in the twentieth century, and was responsible for reviving many seventeenth-century French plays, particularly those of Corneille. Her most famous roles were Phèdre (Racine), Camille in *Horace* (Corneille), and Adrienne Lecouvreur, written for her by Scribe and Legouvé. Charlotte Brontë saw her in London in June 1851 in the last two of these roles, being particularly struck by her Camille, comparing her acting to bullfighting and Roman gladiatorial contests: "It is scarcely human nature that she shews you; it is something wilder and worse; the feelings and fury of a fiend" (to James Taylor, 15 Nov 1851). In all Charlotte's descriptions words such as "fiend," "devil," and "Beelzebub" recur. Rachel's private life was scandalous, and was chronicled with lip-licking relish by the European press: the *Leeds Intelligencer*, for example, noting her withdrawal from the role of Cleopatra, said her "success was becoming more questionable every day," as if an immaculate private life was essential for success in that role (*Leeds Intelligencer*, 8 Jan 1848). Her health was as fragile as her morals, and she died of consumption which commentators traced back to her deprived childhood. Charlotte depicted her in *Villette* under the name Vashti.

Racine, Jean Baptiste (1639–99): French dramatist and poet. The classical tragedies which are his claim to greatness were called "cold" and "stilted" in Branwell's essay on Bewick, and Caroline Helstone can only read them with "a degree of languor

... partaking rather of apathy than sobriety" (the words of Hortense Moore in *Shirley*, ch. 5). Shirley, however, has nearly ruined Louis Moore's copy of Racine during her schooldays, and begs him (ch. 27) to recite Athalie's dream foreseeing her own downfall in *Athalie*. It would seem that the Brontës' distaste for classical tragedy and poetry had been modified in Charlotte's case, probably through M. Heger's enthusiastic teaching.

Radcliffe, Mrs Ann (1764–1823): nowadays the best-known of the "Gothic" novelists, with *The Mysteries of Udolpho* still having a certain currency. Caroline Helstone probably speaks for Charlotte when she talks of *The Italian* opening "with such promise, – such foreboding of a most strange tale to be unfolded" but ending in "disappointment, vanity, and vexation of spirit" (*Shirley*, ch. 23). The reason for this disappointment may be because Mrs Radcliffe's skill in devising intriguing and sensational plots was not matched by any great psychological insight into character.

Rainbow: one of the pets fed by Emily on 24 November 1834, as recorded in the diary note of her and Anne. Generally assumed to be a dove, but it could be anything.

Rambler: periodical, at that time just commencing publication, which published unfavorable reviews of *Jane Eyre* and *Tenant*. It was, according to Margaret Smith, Liberal Catholic in tendency (CBL, v. 2, p. 120), and is not to be confused with Dr Johnson's periodical of the same name. It was one of the main brandishers of the word "coarse" in connection with the Brontës, and explained the charge by citing the books' tendency to "relapse into that class of ideas, expressions, and circumstances, which is most connected with the grosser and more animal portion of our nature." It believed the novels were "palpably the work of one hand," but was on surer ground in guessing that the hand was that of a Yorkshirewoman.

Ramsbotham, Rev. J. Hodgson: son-in-law of Samuel Redhead. In 1857 he wrote to Mrs Gaskell and the *Leeds Intelligencer* to correct Gaskell's account of Redhead's reception in Haworth in 1819. Gaskell didn't "see any great difference" (ECG to EN, 6 June 1857) between her coverage of the riotous three Sundays and Ramsbotham's account, which certainly makes it clear that the Haworth congregation's behavior was riotous and insulting. The main difference was his denial of Gaskell's story of a man riding on a donkey into church, and that of the drunken chimney-sweeper who attempted to embrace Redhead while he conducted the service. Barker (1994) accepts Ramsbotham's version, based on Redhead's diary, as entirely true, but one can lie to one's diary and omit embarrassing episodes. Politicians who have tomatoes thrown at them always play down the incidents as trivial – it is a natural impulse.

See also Redhead, Samuel

Ramsden, Mrs (no first name given): presumably the wife of Timothy, and one of the organizers of the hated "Jew's basket" in *Shirley*.

Ramsden, Timothy: the corn-factor of Briarfield in *Shirley*. A "stout, puffy" gentleman who is encountered at the school-feast in ch. 17.

Rand, Ebenezer and Sarah Ann Mary Elizabeth, née Bacon: master of the Haworth National School 1843–5, and his wife, also a teacher. Patrick had been petitioning the National Society for a master for some time, and was pleased with their choice of Mr Rand: he "does exceedingly well" (to W. J. Kennedy, 9 Jan 1844). He was in his early twenties, and had been trained at the Society's school. He was keen to marry, and had fixed on a woman who could help him in his teaching. This plan succeeded well, and Patrick insisted that Sarah must be properly paid for her labors. A son, Ebenezer Bacon Rand, was born to them in Haworth; he later went to Cambridge and entered the Church. Mrs Rand's mother was living with them in Haworth, and seems to have become a permanent fixture in the family. The couple were apparently liked and successful, but their stay in Haworth was short, perhaps due to the "unceasing opposition" mentioned by Charlotte in a letter to Mrs Rand (26 May 1845) after their move to a similar position at Dukinfield, near Staley Bridge, Manchester. Intermittent contact was kept up by letter, and in 1859 Patrick wrote to Ebenezer in Ipswich, congratulating him on regaining his sight. The Rev. John Rand, to whom Patrick sent a fragment of Charlotte's handwriting in 1860, was probably not related, and was most likely one of the Bradford Rands referred to in one of Maria's letters to Patrick (23 Sep 1812).

Ranger, William: inspector sent by the General Board of Health in 1852 to investigate the dispute in Haworth concerning improvements in the water supply, which many Haworth residents resented having to contribute to. Ranger had made similar investigations in other Yorkshire towns such as Shipley and Ripon. He recommended that the rate qualification for election to the Committee of Health be raised from £5 to £10. This was quite contrary to Patrick's wishes, and he protested, according to Lock and Dixon (1979), that there were only 10 houses of that ratable value in Haworth, five of them inns.

Raphael (Raffaello Sanzio) (1483–1520): great Renaissance painter, listed in 1829 as one of those whose work Charlotte wished to see, and mentioned in "The Swiss Artist Continued" in the December 1829 issue of "Blackwood's Young Men's Magazine." Charlotte in the mid-1830s made a copy of the central figure in Raphael's "Madonna of the Fish." In the latest surviving *devoir* that Charlotte wrote for M. Heger, her poor painter, writing to a great Lord, claimed that "As for natural genius, neither Titian nor Raphael nor Michelangelo would have known how to give me that which comes from God alone" – a familiar Romantic exaltation of innate, God-given qualities over ones learnt, and therefore possibly foreign to the learner's personal genius.

Rawdon: now a suburb of Leeds, but only a few miles from Bradford. When Charlotte went there, to become governess to the White children, it was a prosperous area with substantial houses built by the merchants and industrialists of the two nearby

Plate 36: Roe Head School, sketched by Anne Brontë. Anne stayed as a pupil at Roe Head for two and a half years, the longest of any Brontë girl.

Plate 37: Rydings. Home of the Nussey family when Charlotte first knew them, Rydings contributed some elements to Rochester's home Thornfield in *Jane Eyre*.

Plate 38: St Michael's and All Angels, as it appeared in the Brontës' time. The body of the church, all but the tower, was demolished in the 1870s.

Plate 39: George Smith was Charlotte's publisher, young, handsome and an unfailing support to this new and radically different author.

Plate 40: Stonegappe, near Lothersdale, in North Yorkshire. Home of the Sidgwick family, where Charlotte was briefly governess in 1839.

Plate 41: Mary Taylor, friend of Charlotte Brontë from her first days at Roe Head School, photographed in later life.

Plate 42: The Brontë birthplace at Thornton, near Bradford, was the place of birth of all the young Brontës who grew to adulthood.

Plate 43: Thorp Green. Anne was governess to the Robinson girls at Thorp Green from May 1840 to June 1845. Branwell was tutor to the son from January 1843 to July 1845. He probably lodged in the "Monks' House," seen in this sketch by him.

Plate 44: Upperwood House, home of the White family, in Rawdon, near Leeds and Bradford. Charlotte was governess to the White children through most of 1841.

Plate 45: The Reverend William Weightman was curate in Haworth (1839–42), and was a fount of gaiety and high spirits to the younger members of the Brontë family. The sketch is by Charlotte.

Plate 46: William Smith Williams was "reader" at Smith, Elder and Charlotte's most faithful correspondent in literary London.

Plate 47: The Reverend William Carus Wilson, the founding spirit behind the Clergy Daughters' School at Cowan Bridge.

Plate 48: Zamorna, by Charlotte. Portrait by Charlotte of her own hero in the Angrian saga, Arthur Adrian Wellesley, Marquis of Douro, King of Angria.

Plate 49: Zamorna, by Branwell. A more villainous version of Zamorna, from Branwell, who endows him with some of the characteristics of his hero Northangerland.

Plate 50: Zenobia, Marchioness Ellrington, by Charlotte. In depicting Northangerland's wife, Charlotte takes some of the features of a real-life scandalous woman, the Countess of Blessington.

towns, with fine views from its healthy high ground, and with many beautiful walks, some of which (e.g., that to Calverley) remain.

Rawfolds Mill: mill near Hartshead which was attacked by the Luddites in April

1812, when Patrick had been minister there for about a year. There had already been other mills attacked in the area, and Rawfolds was defended. The assault was defeated in quite a short time, and two of the Luddites were killed. This attack was probably the basis of stories that Patrick told his children: these and other facts possibly learnt at Roe Head formed the raw material for the attack on the mill in ch. 4 of "Something about Arthur" (1833), and contributed to *Shirley*, in her research for which Charlotte also consulted the files of the *Leeds Mercury* newspaper.

Redhead, Rev. Samuel (1778–1845): clergyman who in 1819 accepted the

perpetual curacy at Haworth from the Vicar of Bradford, who had not obtained the consent of the Haworth trustees, as was customary and probably a legal requirement. His subsequent three attempts to officiate at Sunday services and other duties caused violent scenes in the town: the unconsulted inhabitants protested against the new incumbent by a mass exodus from church, by chasing him out of town, "pursued," as Redhead himself wrote, "more like wild beasts than human beings," and various ridiculous escapades that Redhead's son-in-law claimed never happened but which seem quite possible as specimens of rural humor. After threats from the Archbishop of York had had no effect, he resigned on 15 November. Three years later he was presented with the living of Calverley, between Leeds and Shipley, and remained there, much loved and respected, for the rest of his life. He preached at Haworth in 1844, when he was received by the congregation with all the good humor of victors.

See also Ramsbotham, Rev. J. Hodgson

Red House: substantial house in the Gomersal district of Dewsbury, built in 1660

and thereafter the home of the Taylor family until 1920. The name presumably comes from the fact that it is a brick building, then unusual in this district. During Charlotte's several visits to the house it was standing as model for Briarmains in *Shirley*, home of the Yorke family. The early visits were notable particularly for bringing Charlotte the acquaintance of Joshua Taylor, perhaps the first cultured radical thinker she had known. One would guess from the portrait of the Yorkes in *Shirley* that what made the house special to Charlotte was the experience of a lively, passionate, political, argumentative family, but this is contradicted by Mary Taylor's reaction to the book: "You make us all talk much as I think we shd. have done if we'd ventured to speak at all" (to CB, 13 Aug 1850). Many features of the house are reproduced in the novel, including the stained glass windows in the dining room: "I have not seen the matted hall & painted parlour windows so plain these 5 years" wrote Mary in the same letter.

The house is now a museum to the Taylor family and the cloth trade, open all year. It, and the buildings in the grounds, have undergone extensive renovation and restoration in the last 15 years, and the coach house has been transformed into an exhibition area.

Redman, Joseph (1796–1862): parish clerk in Haworth. Patrick appointed him and Joseph Whitehead to share the position of clerk "owing to the hardness of the times, and very nearly an equality of merit" (to Mrs Taylor, 12 Apr 1826). They officiated on alternate months and shared the Easter collection which was the clerk's due. Redman was to be prominent in Haworth parish affairs for several decades: he was an enthusiastic Freemason, he was named as "architect" of the new peal of bells installed in 1846, and he witnessed Patrick's will. On a more human level, in May 1853 he tried to help Arthur Bell Nicholls recover when he broke down trying to administer communion to Charlotte on Whit Monday. His daughter Martha worked occasionally at the Parsonage, as additional help for Tabby and Martha Brown.

Reed (grandfather of Jane Eyre): mentioned in v. 1 ch. 3 as having cut Jane's mother off without a shilling for marrying a poor clergyman against his wishes.

Reed, Eliza: cousin of Jane Eyre. She grows up to be selfish, strong-minded, and without passions except for a bloodless kind of order. She converts to Roman Catholicism and enters a convent.

Reed, Georgiana: cousin of Jane Eyre, and one of Charlotte's spoilt, mindless beauties. When Jane returns to Gateshead for the death of her aunt she finds her an overblown, disappointed young woman whose only interest is an advantageous match. This she finally attains, when she marries a "wealthy worn-out man of fashion" (v. 2, ch. 7).

Reed, Jane: maiden name of Jane Eyre's mother. Her marriage to a poor clergyman led to her being cut off by her family, though her brother took care of the child Jane when she and her husband died of typhus.

Reed, John: the spoilt, unhealthy bully who makes the young life of Jane Eyre a misery. The apple of his mother's eye, he grows up to be a debauched gambler, and to tyrannize over his mother. He was thought to have committed suicide.

Reed, Mr (no first name given): uncle of Jane Eyre, dead husband of Sarah. It was his charitable instinct that ensured a home for Jane, though the promise he exacted from his wife to care for her meant it was a far from comfortable or loving one.

Reed, Mrs Sarah (née Gibson): the hostile and unloving aunt of Jane Eyre. Her foolish spoiling of her own children, especially her son, is matched by her equally foolish victimization of the niece she has sworn to care for. Her essentially shallow nature is suggested by the notable victory the child Jane scores over her (v. 1, ch. 4), where it is the child who makes all the moral judgments. On her deathbed she confesses to Jane that she gave her uncle to believe she was dead. Her death is hastened by the worries occasioned by her son's debauched career and death.

Reform Bill: measure of electoral reform passed by Lord Grey's government in 1832. Cautious and partial though it was, it divided the nation and pointed the way for successive, more radical reforms until full adult suffrage was achieved in 1928. The bill became law only after a series of narrow triumphs and serious setbacks. Patrick supported the bill, but felt impelled to write an apologetic letter to Elizabeth Franks, to be communicated to other old Bradford friends, explaining that he was in favor of "temperate reform" to avoid "insurrectionary movements" (28 Apr 1831). His children did not follow him in this (as they had when he had joined the Tories' *volte face* over Catholic Emancipation): Charlotte wrote to Branwell of "the extreme pleasure I felt at the news of the Reform-bill's being thrown out by the House of Lords" (17 May 1832). There is no evidence that this divide was regarded as a serious problem in the Brontë household.

"Return of Zamorna, The" the Angrian manuscript in which Charlotte rejects the death of Mary Wellesley, Douros's wife, which so upset her when Branwell announced his intention to kill her while Charlotte was away at school. Like most writers, even Dickens, who brings back characters from the dead, she ties herself into narrative knots to bring it about, without really rendering it credible. The resurrection is only one part of what is a larger account of the change in Zamorna's fortunes. It serves its purpose of resurrecting Mary but, as with Sherlock Holmes, many readers will feel that she was never quite the same after being brought back to life: she is even more marginal in her husband's life than she was at the time of her "death."

Reuter, Mme (no first name given): the mother of Zoraïde Reuter, and the housekeeper of her establishment: fat, rubicund, and jolly, she reminds Crimsworth of a farmer's wife. Of an earlier, earthier generation than her daughter, she regrets the "old heads" that young people of the younger generation have. She and Mme Pelet form a comic duo that contrasts with the sober tone of most of *The Professor*.

Reuter, Zoraïde: directress of the girls' school adjacent to M. Pelet's, where William Crimsworth teaches part-time in *The Professor*. As with Pelet, his first impressions of her turn out to be misleading. He judges her (ch. 9) serene, fresh, and with a bloom in her cheek that "was like the bloom on a good apple, which is as sound at the core as it is red on the rind." He soon realizes that she aspires to "the power of the politician" (ch. 10), that she rules her establishment and her life by finding the weak points of those around her and using them to gain ascendancy. The most favorable analysis of her character is in ch. 12. Later in the book she is seen as scheming, untrustworthy, and insatiable for power. Similarly in sexual matters she uses her attractions to assert power, and her sensuality is seen as perverse and corrupt. Her attempts to attract Crimsworth are rendered null almost as soon as they begin by his overhearing her conversation with Pelet in the garden (ch. 12). Thereafter she becomes a character with comic overtones – a study of thwarted sexuality and of devious, unworthy, manipulations. Her marriage to Pelet is a matter of business as much as love, and succeeds better on the former level than the latter. There are obvious points of comparison with Mme Beck in *Villette*, and with Charlotte's view of Mme Heger.

Revue des deux Mondes, La: prestigious French journal which reviewed *Jane Eyre* and *Shirley* in 1848 and 1849, reviews which delighted Charlotte, though the first came at one of the darkest periods of her life. She wrote to W. S. Williams: "The Notice in the 'Revue des deux Mondes' is one of the most able – the most acceptable to the author of any that has yet appeared" (16 Nov 1848). The reviewer was Eugène Forçade. The *Revue* was at that date nearly 20 years old, and had established a reputation for dealing with both political and literary matters with authority and imagination. It numbered among its contributors figures of great interest to Charlotte, including George Sand, Balzac, and Victor Hugo.

Richard (no surname given): coachman to Arthur and Helen Huntingdon at Grassdale Manor in *The Tenant of Wildfell Hall*.

Richardson (no first name given): vicar in a neighboring parish to Agnes Grey's home. Marries Mary Grey. He is described as comfortably off, in his mid-thirties and amiable, but he never appears in his own person.

Richardson, Samuel (1689–1761): novelist, author of one of the most famous books of the eighteenth century, *Pamela*. References to this novel, as well as *Clarissa* and especially *Sir Charles Grandison* are to be found in Charlotte's writings, but usually cloaked in an irony which makes her true attitude to his fiction difficult to discern. To Hartley Coleridge she suggested that Richardson wrote like an old woman, and in the unpublished "Word to the 'Quarterly'" (BST, v. 16, pt 85, 1975) she takes up Miss Rigby's suggestion that the author of *Jane Eyre* must have "long forfeited the society of her own sex" by saying that "the idiot (inspired or otherwise) Sam. Richardson" could have borne such a doom better than Currer Bell – a reference to the popular picture of Richardson in his later years as surrounded by a coterie of admiring women for whom he acted as some kind of moral guru. It is a fair guess that Charlotte found the plot-line of *Pamela* ridiculous, and it was brave of her to refer to the novel in chapter 1 of *Jane Eyre*, since there is a distinct resemblance between Pamela's situation (subject to sexual advances from her master) and that of Jane in Rochester's household.

Richmond, George (1809–96): artist and Royal Academician. The son and father of painters, he had been taught by Fuseli and influenced by Blake, but in a decided career change in the 1830s he became a portrait painter, typically in chalks, to the fashionable and artistic worlds, often presiding over four sittings a day. While staying with the Smiths in 1850 Charlotte sat to him three times, and the resulting picture was generally liked, except by Tabby. Being something of a conveyer-belt portraitist, Richmond produced images that bore a family likeness to each other, and while being subtly flattering, did not probe deeply. His picture was for years the only authentic likeness of Charlotte done from life, and was much reproduced. The National Portrait Gallery reports that its condition is now poor, and it is not generally on display.

Patrick found the portrait less than flattering, but thought the expression "wonderfully good and life-like" (CB to EN, 1 Aug 1850). Ellen Nussey, commenting on Mr Nicholls's refusal to let the portrait be copied for the *Life*, remarked rather mystifyingly: "there would always have been regret for its painful expression to be perpetuated" (to ECG, July 1856). Mrs Gaskell herself in the *Life* described it as "an admirable likeness" (v. 2, ch. 6), but seemed to agree later with Mary Taylor that it was "too much flattered" (ECG to GS, 17 Mar 1858). George Richmond's memories of the sittings, as reported by his son John, are not to be trusted.

Rigby, Elizabeth (Lady Eastlake) (1809–93): writer and journalist. Her

father was a physician of Lancashire origins, practicing in Norwich, and the author of some medical works. He had the distinction of fathering short-lived quadruplets at the age of 70. His daughter published her first short piece in *Fraser's Magazine* at the age of 21, and became a highly valued contributor to that magazine and to the *Quarterly Review*, being particularly famous for her contributions on art. She married Charles Lock Eastlake, a vapid painter, in 1849, and he turned out to be a notable administrator in the arts world, both as President of the Royal Academy (the Queen and Prince Albert lobbied for him, and she promptly knighted him), and at the same time a brilliant director of the National Gallery from 1855 to his death 10 years later. His wife's best writing tells of her travels with him throughout Western Europe in search of pictures for the national collection. *The Letters and Journals of Lady Eastlake* (1895) give a fair picture of her and her artistic tastes, which are enthusiastic and quirky: she doesn't care for Michaelangelo or his "Etruscan extravagance of muscle and action," but she pays tribute to his "fine personal character." Turner, on the other hand, she pays frequent tribute to as an artist, but she predictably shudders at his domestic arrangements (the "hag of a woman" he lives with, the "penury and meanness" of his house and its furnishings), and she calls him "pertinacious and stupid."

Her perverse judgments of *Jane Eyre* and its author can be seen as springing from her obvious prejudices: she is obsessed with gentility and breeding, and she is a sucker for duchesses ("it was something to be walked off one's legs by two Duchesses!") and leading lights of the Tory party. In literature her judgment is much less sure than in art: Wordsworth, for example, is "commonplace in thought and barren in word," and she feels that the "false principles" that Ruskin lays down in *Modern Painters* could be easily refuted. She has other prejudices usual for the time: "The Napaulese Princes were there, but I have no taste for savages." She was a notable mid-Victorian woman of letters, but not someone one would have wanted to meet (unless one was a duchess).

See also Lockhart, John Gibson; *Quarterly Review*

Rile, Dr (no first name given): medical practitioner in *Shirley*, described as
a "humbug."

Ringrose, Amelia (?1818–60):

friend of Charlotte, first through correspondence, later through personal contacts – perhaps rather more than Charlotte would have chosen. Amelia seems to have become engaged to George Nussey in the first part of 1845, but quite soon the onset of his mental illness put the engagement in doubt. Charlotte's early descriptions of Amelia's letters first to Ellen, later to herself as well, are approving, using words like "affectionate and sincere" (4 Nov 1845), "sensible" (13 June 1845), and "goodness and candour" (29 June 1847). She is conscious, however, of a "touch of phlegm" (13 June 1845) in her make-up, and a lack of any out-of-the-ordinary mental attainments. More irritation enters the letters as Amelia, despairing of George ever regaining his sanity, began to accept the advances of Joe Taylor, who repelled Charlotte by his coldness and self-regard. When the pair married Charlotte was surprised by the closeness and affection of the union, but soon irritated by their overwhelming absorption in their delicate daughter Tim – the constant watchfulness for alarming symptoms, the hypochondria on her behalf that caused them to break off their Scottish excursion with Charlotte (August 1853) almost before it had begun. Even Amelia's expressions of happiness are described as "a vacillating unsteady rapture" (to EN, 11 May 1852), and Charlotte claims seldom to have seen anyone "more unconsciously thoroughly and often weakly egotistic" (to EN, 9 Sep 1852). In this Charlotte seems to share her disgust and lack of sympathy with other of Amelia's acquaintances: when Amelia claimed to Margaret Wooler that little Tim had a forgiving disposition the former schoolteacher exploded in irritation: "Children don't forgive, they forget" (MW to EN, 10 Aug 1854). Joe became ill in 1854, and the self-absorption of the little trio became complete. It was decimated soon after Charlotte's death, Joe dying in 1857, little Tim in 1858, and Amelia herself probably in 1860.

Ringrose family:

Amelia Ringrose's father, Christopher Leake Ringrose, was a trader in hides, corn, and other agricultural products, with strong commercial links with the Netherlands, where the family had lived before returning to the Hull area. His wife was Mary Ann, née Boyes. Our impression of the two parents comes mainly from Amelia's letters, or reports of them, and perhaps partly from the Taylor family. Christopher seems to have been authoritarian and selfishly unwilling to part from his eldest daughter, who no doubt took over many of the duties of her invalid mother (she died in 1850). Neither parent seems to have felt much affection for their children, and self-absorption seems a family trait. Charlotte's trajectory of interest in Amelia's sister Rosy (Margaret Rosita) follows a similar pattern to her interest in Amelia. She is predisposed to her by her style of writing to Ellen, and after apparently meeting her she speaks of her "face – so pretty – modest – *sensitive* – *that* was the peculiar charm in my eyes" (to EN, 27 July 1849?). Her enthusiasm for the young woman recalls her occasional special interest in certain small children: "I should be tempted to make a pet of that Rosy – to spoil her" (to EN, 13 Sep 1849?). But it is a pattern in Charlotte's encounters with people that she is often misled by first impressions. After Rosy's marriage to John Dugdale she sees a hardness behind the charm, and refers to one of her letters as a "wretched heartless, flimsy, unsisterly scrawl" (to EN, 12 Apr 1851). By then she seems to have a confirmed distaste for the whole family.

Ripon: City in North Yorkshire. When Patrick went to Haworth in 1820 it was in the Archdiocese of York, but it became part of the new diocese of Ripon in 1836. William Weightman was ordained in Ripon in 1840, and Arthur Bell Nicholls was appointed to his curacy at Haworth by the Bishop of Ripon, Dr Longley, who was to visit Haworth in March 1853, at the height of the problems over Nicholls's declaration of love for Charlotte. Branwell may well have visited the town, perhaps from Thorp Green: in a poem, conjecturally written in 1844, he talks of "Ripon's holy fane/Like Yorks drew heaven toward our earth again" (WPBB, v. 3, p. 402, "Oer Graftons Hill . . .").

Rivers, Diana: one of the sisters outside whose home Jane Eyre collapses after her flight from Rochester. She turns out, by a plot turn that rather stretches the conventions of fictional coincidence, to be a cousin of Jane's, and Jane shares her fortune with the three remaining members of the Rivers family, who have come down in the world.

Rivers, Mary: the other of St John Rivers' sisters. Diana and Mary are sometimes said to be portraits of Emily and Anne Brontë, but though there is the odd suggestive glimpse of a family at work and study together, the "portraits" are without savor or individuality.

Rivers, Mr (no first name given): father of St John Rivers and his sisters, owner of Marsh End or Moor House, and a man of long-established family who died of a stroke three weeks before Jane Eyre collapses exhausted on the doorstep of the bereaved Rivers children.

Rivers, St John Eyre: the last of the triple character-pillars on which *Jane Eyre* is based. Rivers is a clergyman of good family, stern, charitable, just. He has a mission in life, which soon comes to seem like a monomania: the spreading of the Christian religion in the East. To fulfill this aim he ignores and suppresses his own emotional inclinations towards Rosamond Oliver. As he tries to persuade Jane, whom he does not love but whom he regards as a suitable wife for a missionary, to marry him, the reader's doubts about him increase: his spiritual mission seems tainted by a taste for power, and he seems to use both his eloquence and his religion in a sort of high-minded bullying. Jane is in no doubt that a loveless marriage to him would kill her, and she desperately resists the perverted emotional toils he tries to entrap her with until the call from Rochester enables her to break away. How far the unfavorable view of Rivers's character which modern and feminist critics take would be endorsed by Charlotte's conscious mind is open to doubt: it is notable, and odd, that the novel ends with what sounds like a ringing endorsement of him and his work as a missionary.

Some of the circumstances of Rivers's quest for Jane's hand in marriage may have been suggested by Henry Nussey's business-like proposal of marriage to Charlotte (she was one of a series to whom he made proposals that were not accepted). It seems unlikely that there was any stronger connection between the fictional and the living character.

Roakes, Mr (no first name given): mill-owner mentioned in *Shirley* as having been hard hit by the Orders in Council.

Roberson, Rev. Hammond (1757–1841): clergyman active over a long period in the Dewsbury area, where he was one of Patrick's predecessors at Hartshead church. He was the original of the Rev. Helstone in *Shirley*, though Charlotte claimed to have seen him only once. She would certainly have heard of him though, both from her father and from all her contacts in "the *Shirley* country." He was a man of the unyielding Right, with none of Patrick's pragmatism and little of his human sympathy. He hated change, he was adamant against Luddism and all forms of workers' combination, and he believed the social, religious, and political establishment to be ordained by God and not susceptible of improvement. He was a rigid, stern, and merciless man, with the sort of generosity that was financial (endowing churches, for example) rather than a sign of any human warmth. He was active in his support of William Cartwright and in defense of Rawfolds Mill. He was, inevitably, the most controversial churchman in the area. The Rev. Heald, himself a character in *Shirley*, said that Charlotte had got her ideas of the character through "an unfavourable medium, and does not understand the full value of one of the most admirable characters I ever knew" (W. M. Heald to EN, 8 Jan 1850). Patrick, according to Ellen, talked of the man's "unflinching courage and dauntless self-reliance," which certainly comes through in Helstone, but he also said "the ignorant and prejudiced population around misunderstood and misrepresented his worthiest deeds" (EN, "Reminiscences," in CBL, v. 1, p. 595). Mary Taylor, not surprisingly, would have nothing of that: he was one of the "black-coated and Tory savages that kept the people down," one who would walk in blood rather than have the existing state of things altered (MT to ECG, 30 July 1857).

Robert (no surname given): one of the stable employees at Horton Lodge whose company is agreeable to the horsy Matilda Murray.

Robinson, Rev. Edmund (1800–46): country gentleman with extensive estates around Thorp Green, not far from York. His more impressive family connections included one with Lord Goderich, briefly and lachrymosely one of George IV's prime ministers (he wept copiously on resigning his position, and the king offered him his own handkerchief). He took a third-class degree from Balliol, and entered holy orders – why is not clear, since he confined his activities to officiating at family occasions such as baptisms. He married in 1824 Lydia Gisborne, and it was their children who were taught first by Anne alone (from 1840), and then by Anne and Branwell (from 1843).

It is difficult to get an impression of the man unless we rely on *Agnes Grey* or on Branwell's letters to John Brown and other male friends – about equally dangerous. What seems clear is that it was not a happy household, or a well-run one. When Anne had been a part of it for a little over a year she recorded her "dislike" of the situation in her 1841 birthday note, and Emily at the same time refers to her as "exiled and harassed." Four years later she recorded that she had only just "escaped" from the place and how "wretched" she would have been if she had known she would spend five years in a situation where she would have "very unpleasant and undreamt of experience of human nature" (birthday note, 31 July 1845). This rings true. On the other hand Branwell's account of his employer shrinking from "the bare idea of my being able to write anything," and being ill on hearing that Macaulay had sent him a complimentary letter (to Leyland, 25 Nov 1845) may just be a way of inflating fairly meager literary achievements. Similarly Branwell's mention of Robinson's conduct towards Lydia may be designed to excuse his own relations with his employer's wife. What seems clear is that he was a man of uncertain temper, perhaps due to increasing ill health, and was therefore part of a tense, even rebellious, family group. He was the least interesting side of the triangle that (perhaps) developed in the years 1843–5, and one should take with pinches of salt his wife's reference to him as "My Angel Edmund" (Robinson papers, BPM).

Robinson, Edmund (1831–69):

son of the above and Lydia Robinson. He was tutored by Anne, but from the age of 12 was taken over by Branwell, presumably engaged on Anne's recommendation, or possibly after a successful visit to Thorp Green to see her. Edmund's parents do seem to have taken an oddly casual approach to the education of their only son and heir. This could be because they recognized his severe intellectual limitations, though more conscientious parents might have thought this called for added caution. After his father's death he was sent away to the care of a Somerset clergyman, again surprising, though possibly part of Lydia's disburdening process in preparation for her second marriage. This clergyman, Theophilous Williams, wrote when Edmund was 18 that "his moral conduct has been exemplary," and that his "very inferior" mental acquirements were not his fault – perhaps a criticism of his family, as well as of Branwell. He died in a boating accident soon after he had sold Thorp Green. His will included his sister Lydia and her two sons, suggesting that the family rift, which was never complete, had been healed.

Robinson, Elizabeth Lydia (1826–82):

second daughter of Edmund and Lydia, and one of Anne Brontë's pupils at Thorp Green. We learn nothing about her directly until Anne left her post there. Elizabeth and her sister Mary apparently corresponded with their former governess until their father's death, then ceased communicating for six months (possibly following a maternal prohibition), then renewed the relationship, amazing the Parsonage by "the continued frequency and constancy of their correspondence" (CB to EN, 28 Jan 1848). In the early letters they spoke with affection of their mother, but when she had sole charge of them this changed: they "complain of their Mother's proceedings" (to EN, 28 Jan 1848) and accuse her of being "only anxious to get them husbands of any kind that they may be off her hands" (to EN, 18 Aug 1848). When they visited the Parsonage Charlotte was on the whole agreeably surprised, though she doubted whether either would ever be much respected. Elizabeth was threatened with an action for breach of promise by a Mr Milnes, but weathered the scandal to marry in 1851 a Derbyshire ironmaster, William Jessop. Much of her brother Edmund's estate went to her and her children.

Robinson, Lydia (née Gisborne, later Lady Scott) (1799–1859):

the crucial and most ambiguous figure in the Thorp Green triangle. She was born into a *bien pensant* evangelical family with wide clerical/literary ramifications. Her father at the time of her marriage (1824) was a prebendary of Durham Cathedral, an ally of William Wilberforce, and a published writer. The marriage followed the usual Victorian pattern of frequent childbearing, though the son and heir was long in appearing. At some or several points in the first 20 years Mrs Robinson may have taken lovers: Mrs Gaskell states on the authority of members of Lydia's own family that Branwell "was not the first, nor the last" (to GS, 29 Dec 1856). The arrival of Branwell as her son's tutor in 1843 was, if this gossip was true, calculated to set a spark to the tinder-box: with his charm, his literary interests, and his many (if mostly trivial) talents he was just the type calculated to appeal to her, if only as a casual diversion. By May he was writing to John Brown "my mistress is DAMNABLY TOO FOND OF ME," and soliciting advice as to whether he should "go on to extremities, which she evidently desires." By November of the same year he talks of the "AGONY" involved in the relationship and, rather oddly, sends Brown a "lock of *her* hair, wch has lain at night on his breast – wd to God it could do so *legally*!" (Barker, 1994, pp. 459, 461). The letters also reveal that he thought she was only around 37, instead of 43.

These letters, or partial transcripts of them by Monckton Milnes, were one of the exciting finds of Juliet Barker, published in *The Brontës* (1994). At the time many reviewers (but not Dr Barker) claimed that they were "proof" that Branwell was having a full-blown affair with Mrs Robinson. They are nothing of the kind. They are proof that Branwell wanted his drinking cronies in Haworth to believe that he was. Whether he was or not the letters reflect badly on Branwell himself, and they leave the question very much where it was, particularly in view of Branwell's other communications with his male friends, full of boasting about things that men's groups consider "manly" – drink, sex, and so forth. Nor do the poems he wrote while at Thorp Green constitute any kind of evidence.

In July 1845 Branwell, in Haworth, received a letter from Edmund Robinson dismissing him, characterizing his conduct as "bad beyond expression" and ordering him never to communicate with any member of the Robinson family again. There was talk later about the pair being found together in the boat house, but this does not square easily with Edmund's apparent continuing trust in his wife. Conjectures have also been made that Branwell's transgression was with one of the daughters, with the son in his charge, or consisted of forging signatures on documents for his own financial gain. There is virtually no evidence for any of these suggestions, and the possibilities can sensibly be limited to an adulterous affair between Branwell and Mrs Robinson, to something less than that but with a genuine love on Branwell's side at least, or to an affair which existed mainly in Branwell's imagination.

On balance the first possibility seems to be the most likely: the fact that Mrs Robinson subsidized Branwell after his dismissal, sent her coachman (of all people) to feed him lies about her dead husband's will and her own distracted state (she really coped with widowhood very coolly), and above all the fact that a full-blown affair was accepted as a fact in the Parsonage, where Anne, who was a spectator throughout, would surely have cast doubt on Branwell's version if she had felt any. Lydia's conduct after Edmund's death was ruthless: her behavior to her daughters changed – she was now only anxious to get them married and off her hands – and she fixed on her next husband, Sir Edward Dolman Scott, Bart., even though his wife, an invalid, was still alive. These acts, though not evidence, do not square easily with a picture of a woman wronged.

Two months after Lady Scott's death in August 1848, Lydia married her widower. It has been suggested that the dying wife somehow "entrusted" her husband to Lydia, but there is no evidence for this. Lydia had always been part of "quite a worldly set," according to Ellis Chadwick, who spoke to people who knew them (1914, p. 176), and now she had Sir Edward's house in London from which she could launch herself into metropolitan life with some style. Nemesis was at hand, however, in the person of Mrs Gaskell. Without naming her, the *Life* nevertheless made it inevitable that she would be identified as the seducer of a much younger man, tutor to her own son, and as one who had then made an advantageous second marriage and become part of London society. Attempts were made to mobilize the Establishment in Lady Scott's favor, with apparent success: the offending paragraphs were withdrawn and apologized for. Mud, however, sticks, and in this case much of it seems to have been deserved. Lady Scott, now, since 1851, a widow for the second time, was already ill, and died two years after the publication of the *Life*.

Robinson, Lydia (b. 1825):

eldest daughter of the Robinson family. Unlike her equivalent in *Agnes Grey*, Rosalie Murray, she made a match not of material self-interest but of love, marrying Henry Roxby, an actor she had met at Scarborough – "A bad job" according to the Ouseburn diarist George Whitehead. Soon after their 1845 elopement she and her husband visited Thorp Green for a couple of days, and were apparently fairly well received. Thereafter they more or less disappear: she seems to have been subsidized by her family, lived in Manchester, and had two sons who were left substantial sums (£6,000 each) in their uncle Edmund's will, while Lydia herself received an annuity. Whether she and her husband were happy is not recorded.

Robinson, Mary (1828–87):

youngest daughter of the Robinsons, and apparently the favorite pupil of Anne Brontë their governess. The continuation of contact between teacher and pupils is discussed in the entry for her sister Elizabeth. Much of the concern of Anne was that both girls were being propelled into marriage by their mother, and that neither loved, or even much cared for, the men chosen: "Not one spark of love does either of them profess for her future husband" wrote Charlotte (to EN, 28 July 1848), who also referred to their marriages as sacrifices. She later described Mrs Clapham as infuriating the Keighley gentry by her "assumption of superiority" (to EN, 23 Nov 1848), though when she met her she was more favorably impressed. When Henry Clapham died after seven years of marriage, Mary married Rev. George Pocock, vicar of Pentrich in Derbyshire.

Robinson, William (1799–1839):

portrait painter from Leeds who, after a few years in London, during which he studied under Sir Thomas Lawrence and attracted some notable sitters, returned to live in Leeds. He taught Branwell painting (our authority, Leyland, is vague on the period, but it was probably 1834–5), and warm relations were established with the Parsonage family: there is a delightful letter from Patrick thanking him for sending him a picture of one of his (Robinson's) children. Branwell, however, remained hardly better than an amateur at painting, being deficient even in the matter of mixing his paints. When Robinson died various Yorkshire notables banded together to aid his destitute widow, so popular and admired was he.

Robson, Mr (no first name given): brother of Mrs Bloomfield in *Agnes Grey*.

He is a complacent, supercilious man who encourages Tom Bloomfield in his cruelty to animals and plays a part in the painful scene with the nestlings (ch. 5).

Rochemorte, M. (no first name given): one of the college professors who

are brought by M. Paul to "examine" Lucy Snowe in ch. 35 of *Villette*. They are described as "two fine, braided, moustachioed, sneering personages."

Rochester, Bertha Antoinetta: wife of Mr Rochester in *Jane Eyre*. His marriage

to her was engineered by his father, for cynical financial reasons. Her family wished for the marriage because he was "of a good race" (v. 3, ch. 1). The courtship was organized as a sort of parade of her beauty and accomplishments, but he was denied any close acquaintanceship that might have revealed her real nature. Later he discovers her coarseness and triviality, her violent temper, soon degenerating into a nature "at once intemperate and unchaste" (v. 3, ch. 1). When she is declared insane Rochester decides to conceal her existence and conveys her to Thornfield, where she becomes the hideous, destructive presence that gives the novel its thrilling popular appeal and place in the Gothic fictional tradition.

The idea that Bertha Mason's perspective on the marriage might have been very different from her husband's has not escaped modern critics, and it is the impulse behind a modern classic – Jean Rhys's *Wide Sargasso Sea* (1966).

Rochester, Damer de and Elizabeth: ancestors of Mr Rochester, the former

slain at the battle of Marston Moor. Their tomb looms over Jane Eyre and Rochester during their aborted marriage at Hay Church.

Rochester, Edward Fairfax: employer and eventual husband of Jane Eyre.

Though Mr Rochester has some of the traits of the Byronic hero (saturnine looks, emotional wound in the past) and has spawned innumerable romantic heroes in later (and cheaper) fiction, he needs to be looked at carefully for he is a totally individual creation. His looks and figure were not at the time conventionally attractive, though they helped to change tastes: he was heavily muscular in build, and so strongly featured as often to be described as "ugly." His conversation is often ironic and teasing, alternating with brutal frankness. It is only rarely that the passion that lurks beneath the surface bursts out, and it is the more effective for that. His emotional wound springs from a loveless family background and a marriage of passion that he almost immediately realized was a dreadful and humiliating mistake. There are elements of self-pity in his view of himself (as there are in Heathcliff's), and this enables him to rearrange his moral world to justify himself in various dealings that would otherwise be regarded as suspect: to attempt some kind of union with Jane when she knew the facts of his past would be one thing; what he actually attempted was something much less courageous, and it was no wonder that in the weeks leading up to the marriage Jane felt at times like the slave of a sultan. The crippled Rochester who eventually marries the strong and independent Jane is much more on an equality with her: earlier she could not have said "All my confidence is bestowed on him; all his confidence is devoted to me" (v. 3, ch. 12). In short a complex, changeable, fascinating character, and far from the handsome sticks of conventional romantic fiction.

Rochester, Mr (no first name given): father of Rowland and Edward. A scheming, avaricious man who schemes to marry his second son into the wealthy planter family of the Masons of Jamaica.

Rochester, Rowland: elder brother of Edward Fairfax Rochester. The whole family fortune was destined for him, and he seems to have conspired with his father to trap his brother into the disastrous but financially desirable marriage with Bertha Mason. He predeceased his father.

Roe Head journal: series of six fragments written while Charlotte was a teacher at Roe Head, 1836–7. They shift obsessively between her life as a teacher and the glorious intensity of the Angrian visions which she can indulge in only in occasional free time or while the girls are working by themselves. They are sometimes hysterical and self-pitying, and are full of contempt for the "dolts" she teaches – these are the passages frequently quoted by biographers. The six fragments are usually known by their first words.

1. "Well here I am at Roe Head" starts in the schoolroom but shifts to a magnificent palace where Zamorna's wife awaits him while he is away at the war. The picture is superseded by another, as the palace apparently falls to Zamorna's enemies, and the ottoman the Duchess had sat lonely on is now occupied by "a swart and sinewy Moor" (Quashia, in transition from a near-comic villain figure to one of Byronic sexual appeal with violent overtones). As the fragment climaxes with "his broad chest heaving wildly as the breath issued in snorts from his distended nostrils" Miss Wooler interrupts the reverie: "'A very stormy night, my dear' said she."
2. "Now, as I have a little bit of time" is a short vignette of Angria on a hot, sunny day, with peace newly declared, and Zamorna "young, but war-worn" at Hawkscliffe, his country seat.
3. "All this day I have been in a dream" is a strong impression of the struggle in Charlotte's mind between the real world of Roe Head and the insidious world of her imagination. School has already become a place of "wretched bondage," her pupils "these fat-headed oafs." But between the grind of teaching her mind

goes backwards and forwards to Angria, in particular to Dr Brandon (Charlotte seems already to understand the romantic appeal of a doctor), a woman who seems to be his wife, and a young woman called Lucy for whom Charlotte meditated an important role in future Angrian events. At the end of the fragment, as her pupils invade her privacy, she feels a heavy weight on her, "as if some large animal had flung itself across me." The fragment is dated 14 October 1836.

4. "I am just going to write because I cannot help it" is the fragment in which Charlotte, who clearly has heard from Branwell, wonders whether he has killed the Duchess of Zamorna. The wind reminds her of home – it sweeps "over our house[,] down the churchyard and round the old church." She realizes that it is only "the dream" that sustains her in her hated teaching post, filling "a little of the craving vacancy."

5. "My compliments to the weather" begins with Charlotte "calling up spirits" in a brief Angrian scene, only to be interrupted by school business. Again she expresses her gratitude for "reverie," and says how much the power of her imagination means to her. Then she conjures up an aristocratic Angrian reception, with a Lady Amelia at the center of it. Interest shifts to Jane Moore ("as clearly before me as Anne's quiet image sitting at her lessons on the opposite side of the table"), tells of her ambitious nature (she scorns "any offer that does not comprise a coronet" – rather a Daisy Ashford touch), then falls with her into a meditation concerning the corpse of "her oldest sister who died when she was a child." This is the longest of the fragments.

6. "About a week since I got a letter from Branwell" tells of an enclosure in the letter which includes a supposed letter from Northangerland to his daughter, Zamorna's wife. "I lived on its contents for days." Christine Alexander dates this letter around October 1837 (EW, p. 279), making it probably the latest of the fragments.

Though well short of depicting a mind at the end of its tether, the so-called Journal does suggest a mental crisis, a loathing of teaching and children, and a tendency to retreat into an imaginary world which is increasing rather than fading as she grew to adulthood.

Roe Head School: attended by Charlotte from January 1831 to June 1832. The school was probably recommended to Patrick by his friends the Atkinsons. It was fairly new, having apparently opened in 1830 though it had been advertised as early as January 1827 in the *Leeds Intelligencer*: "The Misses Wooler respectfully announce that their Establishment for the Education of Young Ladies at Roe Head, Mirfield, will be opened on Monday the 29th inst." Presumably difficulties arose in the negotiations for a lease on the property. The school was small in numbers (no more than 10 girls for most of its existence), and the house large and gracious, much of the space being taken up, presumably, with living accommodation for the Wooler sisters. It was an institution well run and led, and Charlotte was happy there, where her unusual talents were cherished and admired. The subjects taught in what was probably a fairly fluid syllabus included, apart from the basic syllabus ensuring literacy and numeracy:

geography, history, and French, as well as the "accomplishments" of drawing and music. Compare this with Trollope at Harrow: "I have no recollection of other tuition except that in the dead languages." Though the teaching at Roe Head may have been traditional and unexciting, it was thorough, and enabled Charlotte to teach her sisters when she got home. It is worth noting that of the tiny number of pupils there at the time, three – Charlotte, Mary Taylor, and Ellen Nussey – turned out to be remarkable women in one way or another.

Though Charlotte's education was found to be defective when she arrived (her ignorance of geography is puzzling, since she and Branwell used real regions as a basis for their imaginary kingdoms) she soon caught up and became the prize-winning student of her year. Her inability to play games (her poor eyesight prevented her from seeing the ball) was compensated for by her story-telling ability, which left her fellow pupils enthralled and sometimes terrified.

Her second period at the school, as a teacher (1835–8), was much less happy. Though initially modestly hopeful – "since I must enter a situation 'my lines have fallen in pleasant places'" (to EN, 2 July 1835) – she found that one of the few professions open to a woman, teaching, was distasteful to her: the routine, the pupils, the loss of her imaginative life sent her into a depression, and this coincided with, or caused, a religious crisis and guilt feelings about her own suppressed sexual longings. The company of first Emily and then Anne did not help, as she was unwilling to single them out from the other pupils. The shift of the school to Dewsbury Moor was if anything an aggravation of the problem, and after one near-resignation in May 1838 she finally severed the professional connection with Margaret Wooler in December 1838. Miss Wooler withdrew from the leadership of the school and for a time it was run by her sister Eliza. It closed in 1841.

See also Nussey, Ellen; Roe Head Journal; Taylor, Martha; Taylor, Mary

Rogers, Hannah: one of Nancy Brown's neighbors in *Agnes Grey*, one who Mr Weston's precepts help her to keep on good terms with.

Rogers, Samuel (1763–1855): minor poet, by profession a banker, who became more famous for his select "breakfasts" than his verse. Charlotte was invited to one of these (three guests was Rogers's maximum) in June 1851, and told Ellen that the occasion "proved a most calm refined and intellectual treat" (24 June 1851). To Patrick she wrote more bluntly that she was glad she had paid the ancient poet the visit "after it was over" (26 June 1851).

Rogue *see* Northangerland

Rollin, Charles (1661–1741): French ancient historian, sympathizer with the Jansenist movement persecuted in his native country. His *Histoire ancienne*, published in 1730, was in the Parsonage library, and was recommended by Charlotte in her letter of advice to Ellen on what she should read (4 July 1834).

Rooker, Rev. James Yates: curate at Hathersage during Henry Nussey's time as vicar. He and his sister were much in Charlotte and Ellen's minds during their stay there: though the sister seems to have been unexceptionable, the curate was judged to be intrusive, too interested in money, and below par socially. Ellen seems to have caused offense when she advised her brother and his new wife not to ignore this "vain and purse proud curate" (EN to Mary Gorham, 29 Dec 1845).

Ross, Sir John (1777–1856) and Sir James Clark (1800–62): uncle and nephew, both naval men and explorers. Sir John led expeditions in search of the North-West passage, one with his nephew James and William Parry. Sir James led an expedition to Antarctica. Both men were knighted, both became rear-admirals, both led unsuccessful expeditions to find the lost explorer Sir James Franklin. One or other, or both, were the models after whom Anne named "her" soldier in the "Young Men's Play," with a Ross's Land following as a consequence.

Rossini, Gioacchino (1792–1868): Italian composer, mainly of operas. When Anne and Charlotte were taken to *The Barber of Seville* at the old Covent Garden, soon to burn down, Charlotte merely remarked later to Mary Taylor that it was "very brilliant though I fancy there are things I should like better" (4 Sep 1848). Possibly she found the eighteenth-century flippancy and cynicism of the piece distasteful. Rossini was only occasionally, and almost against his nature, a nineteenth-century man. Branwell had already commented dismissively (and rather oddly) on "being bewildered for an hour with the hurry of an overture from Rossini" ("Thomas Bewick" in WPBB, v. 3, p. 398).

Rouse Mill: corn mill which provided the basis for the Wooler family's prosperity, and a home as well. The business was taken over, after the death of Margaret Wooler's father, by her brothers James and John (1838).

Rouse, Mrs (no first name given): parishioner of Briarfield in *Shirley*, and one of the contributors to the Jew's basket.

Rousseau, Jean-Jacques (1712–78): French philosopher, educationalist, novelist, and confessional autobiographer. Charlotte's reactions to his work were mixed, but distaste seems to predominate: she says he writes like an old woman, that characters of his order are "unnatural, unhealthy, repulsive" (*Shirley*, ch. 12 – the longest discussion of the man and his work) and she talks in *Villette* of a "French, Rousseau-like sentimentalizing" (ch. 34).

Roxby, Henry: actor with whom Lydia, the eldest Robinson daughter, eloped to Gretna Green in October 1845. Roxby was a younger member of a theatrical family that owned or leased theatres throughout the North of England (Scarborough, Sunderland, Manchester, etc.), so that the marriage, though undoubtedly a social misalliance, may have been less of a financial step-down than is usually assumed.

Royal Academy of Arts: art institution in London. There exists a draft letter from Branwell to the Academy's secretary asking when and where he could present his drawings, with the aim of trying for a place as a student there. The date of the draft is probably 1835. There is no evidence that any such letter was ever sent, or if it was that it was replied to. The likelihood is that Branwell's journey to London, during which his courage failed him and he did not present himself at the Academy, is a myth – a myth that was given renewed currency by Winifred Gerin in ch. 9 of her *Branwell Brontë* (1961), which is mainly based on part of Branwell's "Angria and the Angrians." Charlotte and Anne visited the Royal Academy exhibition in the National Gallery in 1848, and Charlotte alone visited the 1850 exhibition, when, loyal as usual to childhood predilections, she particularly praised Landseer's portrait of the aged Wellington revisiting Waterloo, and John Martin's picture of "The Last Man," based on a poem by Thomas Campbell.

The Royal Academy was founded by George III, with Joshua Reynolds as its first president. In the 1840s it still had a high reputation, but later in the century it began to be ridiculed for its artistic conservatism.

Royal Hotel, Kendal *see* Kendal

Royal Italian Opera Company: company founded by Benjamin Lumley and Frederick Gye to perform opera at Covent Garden, its first season being in 1847. It was this company that Charlotte and Anne saw performing Rossini's *Barber* in 1848, and which Charlotte saw again in 1850.

Royal Literary Fund Society: fund for aiding published authors in financial difficulties. In 1850 tickets were obtained for Charlotte to go to the annual dinner of this Society (as an observer, to listen to the speeches, since only men were allowed actually to eat), but her visit to London was put off and she was forced to miss it. "I don't think all London can afford another sight to me so interesting," she told Ellen (11 May 1850), because Thackeray and Dickens, she said, were always among the guests. This was not true. Dickens generally avoided the dinners, and though he was active in the Society he had grave doubts about it, particularly the lavish banquets and the attendant self-congratulation. He also pinpointed the swallowing up of its funds in management while promising writers could only obtain pittances as grants. He led a movement for the reform of the Society in 1855.

Royal Northern Society for the Encouragement of the Fine Arts
see Northern Society for the Encouragement of the Fine Arts

Royal School, Banagher: where Arthur Bell Nicholls was brought up from the age of seven in the family of Dr Alan Bell, his maternal uncle. The school was part of Cuba Court, where the large family lived, and where Charlotte stayed for a week on her honeymoon.

Rubens, Sir Peter Paul (1577–1640): Dutch painter, one of those whom Charlotte included in the list of artists whose work she wished to see. This did not prevent her making the usual jokes in both her novels set in Brussels on "the army of his fat women" (*Villette*, ch. 23, *The Professor*, ch. 24).

Ruddock, Mr (1814–60): medical man of Keighley. He attended Charlotte in 1851–2, prescribing mercury, which affected her badly. Though at the time she made light of this she lost patience with him, particularly when he intruded himself on her when she returned from Brookroyd in February 1852, hoping to have seen the last of him: "He seems to stick like a leech" (to EN, 16 Feb 1852). He also attended Patrick in the same year.

Rue d'Isabelle: the Brussels street in which the Pensionnat Heger was situated, named after the popular Infanta Isabella, daughter of Philip II of Spain, and governor of the Spanish Low Counties. An imposing staircase led up from the street to the statue of General Belliard in the splendid Rue Royale, and from the top of this staircase one looked down on the chimneys of the Rue d'Isabelle houses. In a letter to Emily (2 Sep 1843) Charlotte depicts herself in the long vacation taking walks beyond the city walls of Brussels, but also "threading the streets in the neighbourhood of the Rue D'Isabelle," reluctant to return to the loneliness of the Pensionnat. These streets were destroyed by the manic rebuilding fever of Leopold II in the early years of the twentieth century.

See also Pensionnat Heger

Rural Minstrel, The: Patrick's second volume of verse, published soon after his marriage in 1813, and containing among other pieces "Kirkstall Abbey," "Winter," and "Lines to a Lady on her Birthday" addressed to Maria. The publisher was P. K. Holden of Halifax.

Ruskin, John (1819–1900): essayist, art critic, and social thinker. His main writings on art coincided with Charlotte's period of fame, when she was receiving parcels of books from Smith, Elder, and she discovered Ruskin with delight. She particularly enjoyed picturing the personality behind the writing: she liked his "devout, serious admiration" (to WSW, 31 July 1848) and she rejoiced in thinking how much his "fanatical reverence for Art" (to GS, 7 Jan 1851) would annoy the utilitarians, with whom Ruskin was to struggle heroically after Charlotte's death. Her delight in Ruskin's writings was one shared by Mrs Gaskell, who found the man himself " 'nice': simple and noble" (ECG to C. E. Norton, 9 Mar 1859). Perhaps the best tribute to Ruskin's powers as a writer on art is Charlotte's "Hitherto I have only had instinct to guide me in judging of art; I feel now as if I had been walking blindfold – this book seems to give me eyes" (to WSW, 31 July 1848).

Russell, Lord John, later first Earl Russell (1792–1878): one of Britain's less-remembered prime ministers. Though involved in many reforming measures of lasting importance he was pugnacious and unwise in personal relationships. Charlotte predictably approved of his bellicose reaction to the Pope's establishment of Catholic sees in Great Britain, calling him "a spirited sensible little man for writing" a pamphlet on the subject (to WSW, 9 Nov 1850). In her meditation on pictures of contemporary politicians in "The Moores" she expresses her liking for him: "little ugly soul. There are lines of feeling as well as of care in his physiognomy" (*Unfinished Novels*, 1993, p. 81).

Ruth (no surname given): servant to the young Miss Marchmont in *Villette* (ch. 4).

Ryde, Colonel (no first name given): commander of the barracks in *Shirley*, who sends soldiers to aid Robert Moore when Hollow's Mill is attacked (ch. 19).

Ryde, Mrs?: nurse who helped Charlotte look after her father after his cataract operation in Manchester. She was paid 15 shillings a week and received her board in addition. Charlotte was uneasy with her: she was "too obsequious" and probably not to be trusted (to EN, 26 Aug 1846).

Rydings: Ellen Nussey's home in Birstall in the early years of her friendship with Charlotte. Her family's association with the house and estate went back to the early eighteenth century. Richard Walker, Ellen's great-uncle, had modernized the facade and much of the interior of the house, leaving it with battlements which were to return to Charlotte's mind when she created Thornfield in *Jane Eyre*. Charlotte visited the Nusseys there in 1832 and 1835. Ellen and the rest of the family still at home moved to Brookroyd in 1836.

Ryott, Dr William Hall: medical man from Thirsk who was consulted by Edmund Robinson and on several occasions spent the night at Thorp Green. According to evidence handed down in his family, and given by his granddaughter to Winifred Gerin, he saw enough of the situation in the family to be sure that Mrs Robinson, and not Branwell, was to blame.

S

Sadler, Michael (1780–1835): Tory MP with an interest in social reform. He was responsible in 1831 for a bill to reduce the hours of children in factories, and worked for the poor agricultural workers in both Britain and Ireland. Chosen by Anne as her "character" in the Islanders play.

St Andrews: the parish church of Keighley. Patrick preached in the old building ("Divine Service for the Missionary Cause both morning and afternoon," letter to Stephen Taylor, 21 July 1819), and was close to its rector Theodore Dury. The foundation stone for the new church was laid in February 1846. It was consecrated in 1848, and is now one of the few buildings in Keighley that the Brontës would have known, though it is generally closed to visitors.

St Clair, Lady Harriet Elizabeth (d. 1867): daughter of the Earl of Rosslyn, who wrote to Charlotte to get more definite information than is provided in *Villette* on the fate of M. Paul Emanuel. Charlotte's reply left the matter "pretty much where it was" since she didn't want to "spoil [the ladies'] sport" (to WSW, 23 Mar 1853).

St George's House: Patrick's lodgings in Wethersfield, a gracious eighteenth-century house. It was owned by Miss Mildred Davy, aunt of Mary Burder, Patrick's first known and identifiable love. It is still standing.

St Gudule: fine cathedral church in Brussels, where Charlotte had an "odd whim" (to EJB, 2 Sep 1843) to go to confession during the terrible long vacation of 1843. Eric Ruijssenaars (2003) suggests that the confession in *Villette* is transposed to another church. The building is officially dedicated to St Michel and Ste Gudule.

St John's College, Cambridge: the college which Patrick entered in October 1802 and graduated from in April 1806. It was the largest Cambridge college, and rich enough to support undergraduates who otherwise could not have enjoyed a university education. It was also the college of Thomas Tighe and other members of his family, which doubtless helped secure Patrick a place. Patrick lived "very genteelly," according to his fellow-sizar Henry Kirke White, on his sizarship – a sort of scholarship – and various other grants, as well as donations from sponsors, one of whom was William Wilberforce. Patrick's evangelical inclinations were nourished by the college, and another side, the fascination with all things military, was boosted when the college contributed to the local militia formed to combat possible invasion by Napoleon. Patrick was justifiably proud of his excellent record at the college, and the college could be proud of their sponsorship of him and other promising students. It seems likely that Patrick had hopes of the influential connections he made there that were never to be realized.

See also Tighe, Thomas

St Mary Magdalene, Broughton-in-Furness: church sketched by Branwell in 1840, one of the few drawings of buildings by Branwell that survives. The church, down in the valley from the small town where Branwell was tutoring the Postlethwaite boys, was greatly altered later in the century.

St Mary's, Scarborough: Anne Brontë was buried in the churchyard here (30 May 1849), the funeral service having taken place at Christ Church, Vernon Road, since demolished. St Mary's could not be used for the service since it was undergoing extensive renovation (it reopened July 1850). The main mistake on Anne's gravestone (her age being given as 28 instead of 29) has never been corrected, and the stone is today suffering from erosion.

St Michael's and All Angels, Hathersage: church used by Charlotte, for worship and inspiration, during her visit to the village in July 1845. The vicarage abutting the churchyard was being prepared by Ellen Nussey to receive her newly married brother Henry, new also to the incumbency. The church has a tomb and brass memorials to the fifteenth-century Eyre family, and was at the time oddly arranged: the vicarage pew was upstairs, and doubled as a vestry, so that clergy and sexton robed there, much to Ellen's amusement. There were extensive renovations to the church in the 1850s, after Henry Nussey's rather fraught incumbency was terminated.

St Michael's and All Angels, Haworth: the church where the Brontës worshiped and which their father dominated for 40 years. It was built by Patrick's famed predecessor William Grimshaw, but it was always unworthy of its site and purpose. It was too small – mean of proportion, and inconvenient, with central pillars and high enclosed family pews. The large congregations, brought there by Grimshaw's oratory or fear of his horsewhip, had to be accommodated in galleries which excluded light, adding gloom to the building's disadvantages. The space was dominated by a three-tier pulpit, with the parish clerk at the lowest level, the minister on the second level,

and the minister or visiting preacher addressing the congregation from the highest level. It was the sermon alone that really attracted the Haworth worshipers. Ellen Nussey noted with typical perspicacity in such matters, that when it began "a rustic untaught intelligence gleamed in their faces," as well as "in some a daring doubting questioning look" (EN, "Reminiscences," CBL, v. 1, p. 600). Patrick Brontë's early sermons are said to have lasted an hour, later ones a half hour, always extempore.

In many ways Patrick Brontë transformed this unprepossessing structure into a typical Victorian church. The *Leeds Intelligencer* noted in 1853 that "Haworth has been celebrated for vocalists and music . . . for upwards of a century" (2 April) and this trend was accelerated by the installation of a new organ in 1834, replacing the usual church "orchestra" whose passing was lamented by Hardy in *Under the Greenwood Tree*. Henceforth the first acquaintance of many of the local people with fine music would be performances of Handel or Haydn with organ accompaniment in their parish church. In 1846 a new peal of six bells was hung, and in the succeeding years change-ringing became so frequent as to amount, to modern ears, almost to a public nuisance. But central to Patrick's ministry were not *things* but intangibles such as fine preaching, education, and for his parishioners a tender concern where that was appropriate (as in the letter to Eliza Brown on the death of her daughter, 10 June 1859) or a tactful interest that stopped well short of interference with their personal lives: "he minds his own business, and ne'er troubles himself with ours" was one Haworth inhabitant's description (ECG, *Life*, v. 1, ch. 3), putting the least flattering interpretation on it in a typically Yorkshire way.

The financial basis for Patrick's long perpetual curacy was not tithes but "the rent of Freehold Estates, which I like much better," as Patrick put it in a letter to Mrs Burder (21 April 1823). Later he came to see that his dependence financially on trustees with "almost unlimited" powers, with the most influential of them being dissenters, was a situation of great delicacy. Patrick's natural religious tolerance of evangelical dissent from strict Anglican beliefs played an important part in keeping the peace in this rather unnatural situation.

The churchyard, hideously overfull, played its part in spreading disease to the adjacent parsonage and down the hill throughout the village. Patrick was in the forefront of the fight for a clean water supply and a new burial place. However, Barker makes the point that "Bradford and Keighley had had similar mortality rates to Haworth's in the past: Haworth was simply late in tackling the problem" (1994, pp. 851–2). The obstinate and narrow self-interest of the Haworth mill-owners was always a mighty obstacle to the efforts of the parish's more far-sighted inhabitants.

Grimshaw's church was replaced, all but the tower, by the present building in the late 1870s. Though jealousy of the Brontë name and fame was attributed to the Rev. Wade, the prime mover in the rebuilding, the deficiencies of the old structure certainly played its part in getting agreement to the change in the parish.

St Oswald, Guiseley: the scene, in December 1812, of the double wedding of Patrick and Maria Branwell and William Morgan and Jane Fennell, each clergyman officiating at the other's wedding. The church has been much altered and extended since.

The transcript of the entry in the church register of these marriages in Lock and Dixon (1979) is remarkably defective.

St Paul (ca. AD 3–ca. 64): Pharisee from Tarsus (in present-day Turkey), a notable persecutor of Christians, who was converted to that religion on the road to Damascus and was thereafter a proselytizer, mainly among the Gentiles. Tradition has it that he was executed in Nero's Rome. St Paul's Epistles are much admired by evangelicals, among them Patrick, who spoke of them as having no equal "for colloquial elegance and force of argument" ("The Signs of the Times"). Women have tended to admire him less, due to his determined support of patriarchy. Charlotte gives Shirley some skeptical remarks concerning Paul's words of advice to women (1 *Timothy*, 2: 9–15) that they should "learn in silence with all subjection" and not "usurp authority over the man, but . . . be in silence." Joe Scott's determinedly male endorsement of such opinions unites Shirley and Caroline in opposition (*Shirley*, ch. 18).

St Paul's Cathedral: the closeness of Wren's great building to the Chapter Coffee House, where Charlotte stayed with both Emily and Anne, fixed it in her mind as symbolic of London, particularly its "great bell" with its "deep, deliberate tones, so full charged with colossal phlegm and force" (*The Professor*, ch. 7). The cathedral and its bell also feature in *Villette* chs. 5 and 6.

St Peter's, Colchester: church where Patrick stood in for the vicar for three weeks in 1807. It had a strong evangelical tradition.

St Peter's, Hartshead: church serving the communities of Hartshead and Clifton, where Patrick became minister in 1811. The church was of a good size, but in poor repair, and of no architectural pretensions. Patrick's ambition to get a parsonage built was not realized during his time there. Those years were high points in the activities of the Luddites, and Patrick experienced the hopeless fury of the rioters, put out of work by the new machines. His later accounts of this time contributed to *Shirley*. He exchanged the living with Thomas Atkinson, taking up his living in Thornton, near Bradford, in 1815.

Saint-Pierre, Bernadin De (1737–1814): French author, a follower of Rousseau, whose idealism, coupled with a quarrelsome nature, led to a fragmented and unsatisfactory early career, later to be sweetened by the favor of Napoleon. His *Paul et Virginie* (1787), the heroine of which was shipwrecked at the novel's end, like M. Paul Emanuel, was an international success. His complete works were given to Charlotte by M. Heger.

St Pierre, Zélie: a Parisienne, one of the senior mistresses in Mme Beck's school in *Villette*. She is much disliked by Lucy Snowe, being described as "prodigal and profligate" (ch. 14) and totally lacking in principle. She keeps splendid order in class, is an excellent organizer, but otherwise she is described in repellent terms. Almost

certainly based on Mlle Blanche, a teacher at the Hegers' school, described by Charlotte in a letter to Emily (29 May 1843) as "heartless, insincere and vindictive," and a spy of Mme Heger's. The same letter says that when she is in a fury *"elle n'a pas de lèvres"*; Mlle St Pierre is described as having "lips like a thread."

St Simeon Stylites: fifth-century saint who reputedly spent 36 years of his life on a pillar – "lifted up terrible on his wild column in the wilderness" (*Shirley*, ch. 22). Emily copied an engraving of him by S. Williams in 1833. Tennyson's well-known poem on the subject was published in 1842.

St Stephen's, Walbrook, London: fine Wren church attended by Charlotte and Anne, accompanied by W. S. Williams, in July 1848.

St Wilfrid's, Calverley: village church between Leeds and Shipley, where Maria Branwell worshiped in September 1812 and heard Mr Watman preach "a very excellent sermon" (letter to Patrick Brontë, 5 Sep 1812): "He displayed the character of our Saviour in a most affecting and amiable light" she commented. The church is within easy walking distance of Woodhouse Grove School, and seems to have been the church which Charlotte's employers the Whites attended, since they are buried in the churchyard. Charlotte may thus very well have heard and known Rev. Samuel Redhead, Patrick's predecessor at Haworth, ignominiously treated by the Haworth congregation. He was vicar of the church from 1822–45.

See also Redhead, Rev. Samuel

Salle de la Grande Harmonie: concert hall opened in Brussels in 1842 and attended by Charlotte on 10 December 1843 (and perhaps at other times). The program on that known occasion consisted mainly of short and light pieces, but the concert was attended by the King and Queen of the Belgians and their son the Duke of Brabant (later the infamous Leopold II), and was followed by a lottery. It is clearly the basis for ch. 20 of *Villette*, "The Concert." The notion of Ellis Chadwick (1914, p. 430) that the concert hall in *Villette* is really the ballroom at Devonshire House – which it is far from certain Charlotte ever saw – has not been generally accepted.

Sally (no surname given): maid to Agnes Grey's family.

Salon: a Brussels art exhibition of contemporary paintings held every three years of which Charlotte saw the fifth in 1842, describing it in *Villette*, ch. 19. The picture she calls "Cleopatra" was *"Une Almée"* by a painter called De Biefve, and Charlotte's four panels on *"La Vie d'une Femme"* were in fact a triptych by the Irish-born painter Fanny Geefs (see Ruijssenars, 2003, p. 40). Contemporary comment agreed with Charlotte that the standard of the artists' submissions that year was very low.

Sam (no surname given): footman at Thornfield, who figures during the house-party and the visit of the "gypsy" in *Jane Eyre*.

samplers: samplers exist embroidered by Maria and Elizabeth Branwell, by Maria and Elizabeth Brontë, and two each by the three Brontë girls to survive into adulthood. The earliest consist mainly of alphabets, numbers, and simple quotations from the Bible. The later ones consist of longer biblical quotations. The fact that Emily's is the neatest, the best-sewn, and best-organized may seem surprising, but she appears to have welcomed domestic tasks, perhaps because they could be combined with creative thinking. Though in her earlier one she reversed the U and V, the later one proves that the apparent illiteracy of the diary notes was due to carelessness, scorn for mere accuracy, or was a sort of camouflage – something that became endemic to her as a writer.

Sand, George (1804–76): pseudonym of French novelist less read than read about, by reason of her adventurous and varied private life. Born Amandine-Aurore-Lucile Dupin, she was married for nine years to Baron Dudevant, which seems to have put her against marriage. Among her lovers were numbered Alfred de Musset and Frederic Chopin. Charlotte probably encountered her first among French books loaned to her by the Taylors, and was later lent some of her books, along with others by Balzac, by G. H. Lewes. She expressed a strong preference for Sand's, noting her "grasp of mind," sagacity, and profundity (to G. H. Lewes, 12 Jan 1848). Along with her admiration there was a sense of Sand as a "[f]antastic, fanatical, unpractical enthusiast" (to G. H. Lewes, 17 Oct 1850), and Charlotte speaks in another letter to Lewes of her "strange extravagance" (12 Jan 1848). Mary Taylor also admired greatly her novel *Consuelo*.

Sara, Lady (no surname given): a "proud" but "not in the least insolent" young woman who is Ginevra Fanshawe's companion at the concert in *Villette* (ch. 20).

Sarah (no surname given): housemaid at Mrs Reed's, in *Jane Eyre*, and friend of Bessie: the pair exchange ghost stories after Jane's "fit" in the red-room. Perhaps by an oversight, she has the same first name as her mistress.

Sarah (no surname given): the servant at Hollow's cottage in *Shirley*. Her life is a continual skirmish with her mistress Hortense Moore, in which she by no means always comes off worst. The subjects are food, cooking, customs, and above all men-friends.

Sarah (no surname given): maidservant to the Millward family in *The Tenant of Wildfell Hall* (see ch. 47).

Sargent, Rev. John: member of the Wilberforce circle (he was married to Wilberforce's cousin, and his daughter married his son Samuel). He was solicited by Henry Martyn to contribute to Patrick's living expenses while an undergraduate at St John's.

Saunders, Rev. Moses: minister of the Hall Green Baptist Church, opposite what is now the Old Hall, at the bottom of Main Street, Haworth. This was one of two Baptist churches in Haworth, both still functioning. Patrick worked with him in the causes of temperance and improving sanitary conditions, but they clashed on the subjects of Church rates and the proper age for baptism. Patrick's pamphlet on this last was a rambling, discursive piece of polemic which hardly deserved to see print. It was followed by Saunders' "Baptism Without Controversy" – obviously a vain hope.

Sauveur, Justine Marie: M. Paul's godchild and ward in *Villette*. She is introduced somewhat misleadingly in ch. 31 (Lucy feels a "disagreeable anticipatory sensation" at the sight of her), but only enters the drama later, during the carnival chapter, where Lucy sees a girl, beautiful, "well-nourished, fair, and fat of flesh" (ch. 39) whom she fears M. Paul is in love with. The situation is explained at the very end of the novel: she is a loved ward *only*, and is engaged to Heinrich Mühler.

Scarborough: seaside resort much patronized by the better-off Northern families, having good hotels and lodgings. It was well known to both Anne and Branwell from holidays they spent there with the Robinson family, and to Charlotte from Anne's death and burial there. The Robinson family stayed in Wood's lodgings, prestigious places with superb sea views of South Bay. Anne makes good use of her acquaintance with the town in the final chapters of *Agnes Grey*. Her love of it is clearly attested by her choice of it as the place to spend her last days, and by her care to ensure that Charlotte and Ellen experienced the aspects that made her so fond of it. After her funeral, however, Charlotte found the place "too gay" (to WSW, 13 June 1849) and removed to Filey to recover from her third bereavement in nine months. She returned to the area in late May–June 1852, but she made her base Filey again, and only traveled to Scarborough to visit Anne's grave, where she discovered five mistakes on the gravestone.

See also St Mary's

Scatcherd, Miss: teacher of history and grammar at Lowood School in *Jane Eyre*. An ill-tempered, unjust woman who beats Helen Burns and hangs a placard with the word "Slattern" around her forehead. She represents the system at Lowood at its harshest, though Helen herself excuses her as being only "neat, punctual and particular" (ch. 6).

Schiller, Johann Christoph Friedrich Von (1759–1805): son of an army surgeon, and himself one briefly, who became one of Europe's most popular and controversial dramatists and poets. Part of the movement fathered by Rousseau, his early writing was in the *Sturm und Drang* (storm and stress) mode, but his later plays, often historical in nature if unhistorical in detail, are works of remarkable scope and force. His writings, with their strong scenes of confrontation, are of particular appeal to musicians – Schubert, Verdi, Donizetti and others set poems or plays of his to music. Charlotte translated several of his poems during her second year in Brussels, and he is mentioned in three of the novels: Hunsden has him on his shelves in *The Professor*; Jane Eyre reads him while at Morton; and Lucy Snowe and Paulina read his ballads, Lucy referring later to his poem "*Das Verschleierte Bild zu Sais*."

Scoresby, Rev. William (1789–1857): like his father an arctic navigator and explorer, with a strong scientific bent. After serving with his father he commanded his own ships very efficiently. He attended Edinburgh University, and after ordination became chaplain at the mariners' church in Liverpool. He became vicar of Bradford in 1839, and was immediately in demand as a lecturer, not just on arctic subjects but on socialism, magnetism, and "that unhappy country" America (*Leeds Intelligencer*, 16 Nov 1844), which he frequently visited. His voice, the same newspaper commented, was "not powerful, but his enunciation was very distinct" (27 July 1839). He seems to have run a very tight ship in Bradford, and was soon at odds with some clergy and the dissenting population on the ticklish subject of Church rates. He also wrote Patrick a peremptory letter insisting on graduates from Oxford or Cambridge as teachers at the free Grammar School – being very much in favor of "superior masters" (4 Jan 1844). Patrick was not averse to authoritarian rule when his own views did not run counter to it, and offered Scoresby warm support when he was in trouble in 1845. By then he was in resigning mood, which he threatened on and off for some years, finally going in 1847.

The young Brontës had had a childhood fascination with arctic exploration, but Scoresby makes no appearance in their extant letters. After his Bradford years, however, Scoresby seems to have enjoyed talking about his West Yorkshire experiences and acquaintances: the Rev. Joseph (or John?) Abbott wrote to Charlotte (22 Feb 1851, CBL, v. 2, pp. 576–8) recalling a conversation with Scoresby in Canada a year or two earlier in which he was told the "sad and melancholy" tale of his old friends from his Yorkshire days at Woodhouse Grove School. So it may be that Juliet Barker is unfair to Mrs Gaskell, as she sometimes is, when she describes her as pumping Dr Scoresby for tales of Haworth and its people, including the Redhead fiasco. He may have needed no pumping.

Scott, Sir Edward Dolman, Baronet (?1793–1851): second baronet and second husband of Lydia Robinson. He was rich, of good reputation, a former MP, and when Lydia and her family went to stay with him after the death of Edmund Robinson he was married to her cousin Catherine, née Bateman, daughter of Lydia's aunt Temperance Bateman, née Gisborne. If her daughters' letters to Anne (or Charlotte's account of them) are to be believed Lydia set her sights on her host while his ailing wife was still alive: at one point Lydia wrote to her agent that she was "greatly mortified at the illness of Lady Scott which has deranged all our holiday plans" (Gerin, 1961, p. 276) – surely independent confirmation of her insensitivity and heartlessness. She married Sir Edward three months after Catherine's death (8 Nov 1848), and honeymooned on his yacht in the Mediterranean. He died three years later, leaving her even better provided for than before, and ready to pursue her fashionable life – "kept afloat by her reputed wealth" as the first edition of Gaskell's *Life* had it.

Scott, Henry: son of Joe, who works at Hollow's Mill in *Shirley*.

Scott, Joe: overseer at Hollow's Mill in *Shirley*. Described as phlegmatic, calm, and reasonable, he is yet a doughty fighter, both physically and in words. He particularly enjoys defending (and indeed exalting) Yorkshire and its people, and he indulges in hard-hitting arguments with Shirley about women – on which subject he quotes St Paul, and bitterly resents the fact that his master's mill is owned by Shirley and is thus "in a manner, under petticoat government" (ch. 18).

Scott, Sir Walter, Baronet (1771–1832): the favorite novelist and poet of

the young Brontës, as he was of many of their contemporaries throughout Europe and America. His life, with his financial imprudence played down and his heroic acts of literary over-exertion idealized, fascinated them, and led Branwell to include him among the eminent men he meditated poems on. As befits children their admiration was wholesale rather than discriminating, and quotes from Scott and references to his work continue throughout their writing lives. These include references to the poems (*Marmion* rather than the Napoleonic wars pinpoints the era of Jane Eyre's adulthood), the novels we admire today (*Old Mortality* and *The Heart of Midlothian*, for example) and those we certainly do not (*Kenilworth*, described by Sutherland in *The Life of Walter Scott*, 1995, p. 247, as having "no more artistic durability than a 1953 Coronation mug," or *The Monastery*). Charlotte's condescension when Ellen Nussey voices her loathing of the villainous figure of Varney in *Kenilworth* may, however, suggest the birth of a degree of discrimination. Though her enthusiasm for Scott was often expressed in her adulthood, one does not get the impression that he was often reread, or was felt as a motivating or inspirational force in her writing of fiction. Many of the parallels between the Brontës' works and minor Scott (e.g., the influence of *The Black Dwarf* on *Wuthering Heights*) seem little more than the lodging of details in the younger writer's mind, and they emphasize the creative gulf between the two works. Study of Scott's part in the Brontës' fictional world perhaps awaits the coming of a critic equally saturated in Scott's output and the Brontës'.

Scott's Monument: monumental sculpture in East Prince's Street Gardens in

Edinburgh, including among other things a statue of Sir Walter and his dog, which struck a particular chord in Charlotte's breast when she visited Scotland with George Smith and his sister. "You [Londoners] have nothing like Scott's Monument" she wrote to W. S. Williams (20 July 1850).

Sdeath, Robert Patrick (a.k.a. S'death and King): a malevolent, evil, red-

haired character introduced by Branwell in "The Pirate" (1833). He is basically a hired hit-man, first for Edward Percy Sr. and later his son Northangerland. His one great advantage in his life of crime is that he cannot be killed. His one act of compassion (if that is what it is) was to disobey his master when he was ordered to murder Rogue's newborn sons. His last appearance is in Charlotte's "Ashworth" as Robert King (1841).

Seacombe, Hon. John: a younger son, maternal uncle of William Crimsworth

in *The Professor*. It is when he is standing as a candidate for Parliament for a Northern constituency that the Seacombes are blackmailed into taking responsibility for William's education at Eton. One of his daughters is proposed for William as a possible bride (ch. 1).

Seacombe, the Misses: the six daughters of the Hon. John in *The Professor*, one of whom is proposed as a bride for William Crimsworth, and "all of whom I greatly dislike." The only one who is individualized is Sarah, who is described as a "large and well-modelled statue" (ch. 1).

Severn, Julia: pupil at Lowood School in *Jane Eyre* whose curled red hair, though it is natural, rouses the particular wrath of Mr Brocklehurst: "we are not to conform to nature" (ch. 7).

Shaen, Emily, née Winkworth (1822–87) and William (1822–87):
close friends of the Gaskell family. They married with very little to support them. Charlotte was extremely interested in the marriage, and the accommodations both partners had to make in their reduced circumstances. Though she had never met Emily Charlotte asked her to find her lodgings for a planned visit to London in November 1853, but the visit never took place, perhaps due to the emotional shock of learning that George Smith was engaged to be married. William Shaen acted as the Gaskells' solicitor during the furore over the *Life* and its allegations against Mrs Robinson, by then Lady Scott.

Shakespeare, William (1564–1616):
the works and words of Shakespeare entered the Brontës' writings and lives from an early age. Quotes from him pepper the juvenilia and mature writings as insistently as do quotes from the Bible which they heard every day at home and in church. In the very year that Charlotte was encouraging Ellen Nussey to read Shakespeare but "Omit the Comedies" (4 July 1834) we find a quote from *Measure for Measure* embedded in "A Leaf from an Unopened Volume." *A Midsummer Night's Dream* is a favorite source for quotation from as early as "The Adventures of Ernest Alembert" (1830). Not surprisingly, however, the principal well they drew from for allusion was the tragedies – most notably *Hamlet*, *Macbeth*, and *Othello*. By the time they wrote their novels reference to phrases and situations in Shakespeare was second nature to them. Having such strong ideas about the plays and how they should be performed probably worked against Macready when Charlotte finally saw professional performances of the plays. But perhaps Shakespeare's most vital and integral effect on a Brontë work was on *Wuthering Heights*. Since that novel gained its classic status Shakespeare has always been one of the (few) points of comparison for critics of the novel: it matches his greatest plays for daring, both structural and intellectual. *King Lear* is the play most often used, perhaps because of the heath, the madness, or because it is explicitly referred to in ch. 2. If we take it that Heathcliff is partly of black origin, or at least divided from his adoptive family by his race (as we surely must from the description in ch. 1), then *Othello* provides an obvious germ for the situation, and some further parallels in details of the plot. Above all, Emily possessed to a large degree what Keats identified particularly in Shakespeare and called "negative capability" – that is, the ability of some authors to lose themselves totally in one of their characters or observed things – such as a sparrow, so that "I take part in his existence and pick about the Gravel" (Keats to Benjamin Bailey, 22 Nov 1817). One consequence of this is the ability to remain, like a living person, in "uncertainties,

Mysteries, doubts" (to George and Thomas Keats, 21 Dec 1817), and not use characters, as more dogmatic and ideological writers did, to project a point of view.

Sharp, Jack (d. 1790s): the builder of Law Hill, and an obvious source for the character of Heathcliff. His story is told in full in Gerin's *Emily Brontë* (1974) and Juliet Barker (1994) accepts the probable connection though she relegates it to a footnote. Sharp was adopted by his uncle John Walker of Waterclough or Walterclough Hall, to be trained in the wool business. Cunning, greedy, and violent, he soon became indispensable, displacing Walker's own son John, who was indisposed to engage in trade, then forcing John Walker himself out of the area. Tyrannical and spendthrift in his prosperity, he was displaced from the Hall when John Walker the younger married. Sharp built Law Hill and carried on as before, degrading his younger male relatives and teetering on the edge of bankruptcy, finally to be ruined by the American War of Independence. His story is to be found in the diaries of Caroline Walker, daughter of the younger John.

Sharpe's London Magazine: journal which consistently gave shocked reviews to the Brontë novels. It followed the general pattern in expressing revulsion at the "coarse and disgusting" language of *Tenant* and also objected to Anne's espousal of the doctrine of universal salvation. Even the comparatively sedate *Shirley* caused the reviewer to ape Lady Rigby and suggest that its author was "such that her sex disowns her." After Charlotte's death it published an article which Dickens had declined with distaste: it recycled extreme and sensational stories about the Brontë family, and the usual fictions about Patrick's behavior as husband and father. The article derived from letters written by Mrs Gaskell when she first met Charlotte, and its publication led, ironically, to her being asked to write the *Life*.

Shelley, Percy Bysshe (1792–1822): poet believed by Edward Chitham (1987) to be an important factor in Emily's creative life and thought. That the atheistic poet's works had made some headway in Haworth Parsonage is proved in a draft version of part of "Caroline Vernon," in which there is an attributed quote from Shelley ("wild-eyed charioteers," from *Prometheus Unbound*, II, iv, 132). There are other echoes in the poetry, in *The Professor* ch. 6, and even a possible source for one of *Wuthering Heights*'s best known lines in *Epipsychidion*: "I am not thine: I am a part of *thee*" (ll. 51–2). This was first noted by Ellis Chadwick.

Sherburn Tombs: tombs and other relics of the Sherburn family in the church at Great Mytton, one of the "interesting relics of antiquity" seen by Charlotte on her first visit to Gawthorpe Hall in March 1850 (to Laetitia Wheelwright, 25 Mar 1850).

Sheridan, Richard Brinsley (1751–1816): comic dramatist whom Charlotte knew from Moore's *Life* and from his plays (she quotes from *The Rivals* and *The Critic*). She was damning rather than praising him when she described him as clever: "scamps often are" (Mary Taylor to ECG, 18 Jan 1856 – see Stevens, 1972, p. 162).

Shibden Hall: fine manor house, now a museum, in Southowram, near Halifax. In the short period when Emily was teaching at Law Hill it was owned by the adventurous and unorthodox Anne Lister, whose relationship with Ann Walker shocked or titillated the neighborhood. Jill Liddington's full account of this relationship (BST, v. 26, pt 1, April 2001) suggests that its basis was financial as much as passionate. The identification of Shibden Hall with Thrushcross Grange is controversial – cautiously supported by Edward Chitham (1987), dismissed as beyond belief by Juliet Barker (1994). Fiction is fiction – one has to remember when dealing with all such identifications that they spring from rather than follow reality: writers are free to make what changes suit them or their plots. It does seem likely that the geographical relationship between High Sunderland Hall and Shibden Hall remained in Emily's mind from her time in the area. The most detailed treatment of topographical issues is to be found in Everard Flintoff's "The Geography of *Wuthering Heights*" in the *Durham University Journal* for 1986 (reprinted in BS, v. 31, pt 1, March 2006). Identifications of this sort are an enticing and endless game, particularly when, as in this case, the internal and external appearance of the building in the book are not described in detail.

Shielders (no first name given): curate, presumably at Gimmerton, who for a time teaches the elder Catherine, but who complains that the children are later let fall into "absolute heathenism" (*Wuthering Heights*, v. 1, ch. 6).

Shirley **(published October 1849):** Charlotte's second published novel begins with a serio-comic row about nothing among the curates of what she calls the Whinbury area of West Yorkshire, and continues with an all too real conflict between master and men at Hollow's Mill, where the Irish curate Malone is sent to assist its defense. The year is 1811, Orders in Council, restricting trade in Europe, have caused great distress in the industrial parts of Britain, and the new machines which have reduced the number of "hands" in factories and mills have increased the distress. The workers have banded together under the name Luddites, determined to protect their jobs by smashing machinery.

The initial confrontation between the mill's owner, Robert Moore, and the insurgents results in a victory for the former. Moore is a half-Belgian immigrant to England who is falling in love with Caroline Helstone. She is the ward of her uncle, the worldly and rabidly Tory clergyman Matthewson Helstone, who treats her (as he had treated his wife) with patronizing neglect. She comes regularly to Hollow's cottage, the mill's living quarters, to take French lessons from Moore's sister Hortense, and she has fallen in love with Moore, though she is often unhappy at what he does to protect his commercial interests. The novel seems set to become a study in personal relationships within a larger social context (cf. ECG's *North and South*). However, quite early on in the book Charlotte seems to acknowledge her deficiencies as a chronicler of the lives of the millworkers. When in ch. 5 the children laboring at Hollow's Mill have a brief break for breakfast Charlotte's comment is the fatuous "Let us hope they have enough to eat: it would be a pity were it otherwise." This does not signal the end of a concern with working-class conditions, but the balance of the book does tip sharply towards the personal and against the social.

When the Rev. Helstone decides that Moore is a "Jacobin" and that Caroline must sever her connection with him she acquiesces: she has already sensed a growing coldness as Moore realizes that marriage to her would be of no worldly use to him. Her position then is lonely and quite lacking in mental stimulus until the arrival in the neighborhood of Shirley Keeldar, the young owner of Fieldhead (Shirley was not then a girl's name, but a "masculine family cognomen," ch. 11). Shirley is a temperamental, assertive personality but one of great charm, and she complements Caroline's natural passivity. She is in her turn complemented by her companion Mrs Pryor, a formal, conservative lady with some very bad experiences of governessing in the past. From now on much of the interest in the book lies in Shirley's attempts to change the neighborhood, energize its women, and do something for its starving working population. The story at this point seems to become a series of scenes rather than a plot. The best of the scenes is perhaps chapter 15, "Mr Donne's Exodus," in which the most rebarbative of the curates is shown the door by Shirley. However, Robert Moore carries a fragile strand of plot line by recognizing Shirley as a potential financial savior and making her an unwise proposal of marriage. Her scorn convinces him of the unwisdom of a purely mercenary marriage. His perilous financial position, however, is underlined by a further attack on Hollow's Mill, which is again repulsed, with captives taken.

Meanwhile Caroline has fallen ill, and is nursed back to health by Mrs Pryor, who turns out to be her mother. This is the most criticized plot element in the novel, and especially the reasons why she has never made herself known to her child: "I let you go as a babe, because you were pretty, and I feared your loveliness; deeming it the stamp of perversity" (ch. 24, "The Valley of the Shadow of Death," the chapter Charlotte wrote soon after the last of the three deaths of 1848–9).

Shirley meanwhile has been busy with an unwelcome family visit, and subjected to pressure to marry and terminate the unnatural situation of being a female of power and influence. Along with her relatives the Sympsons has come their son's tutor Louis Moore, brother of Robert, whose strong feelings for Shirley seem to be returned. The political situation in the district is still polarized, with Rev. Helstone's reactionary position being challenged by the radical Yorke family (based on the Taylors), whose verve, energy, and sheer contradictoriness is well conveyed. Robert is brought closer to Yorke's political position by his experiences in Birmingham and London, during the prosecution of the rioters at Hollow's Mill. Ironically, as he confesses to his changed perspectives, he is shot by a Luddite, and is taken, wounded, to Yorke's home Briarmains. Shirley has earlier also faced death, when she is bitten by a dog she believes to be rabid. The two experiences act as catalysts for declarations of love, and the fortunes of the two pairs of lovers are aided by a change in the political situation: the Orders of Council are repealed, Wellington begins in Spain the military campaign that was to lead to Napoleon's defeat, and the popular threat to Britain's political status quo begins to falter. Difficulties and barriers are lifted, a double marriage is celebrated in Briarfield church, and Caroline is promised "Such a Sunday-school" as part of her future happiness.

The novel has a rich cast of characters, not all of them well attached to the plot of the novel. Among these is Mr McCarthey, based on Arthur Bell Nicholls, who is a mere character-sketch in the last chapter, and seems to be Charlotte's atonement for her picture of the other curates, as Dickens's Mr Riah in *Our Mutual Friend* is his atonement to Jews for Fagin.

Reviewers who preferred *Shirley* to *Jane Eyre* were thin on the ground at the time of its publication, and the qualities they chose to justify their preference were things not likely to bring in a mass audience: womanliness, "fine impartiality," refinement, and purity. Its unlikeness to *Jane Eyre* was often emphasized, particularly its lack of passion and excitement, and allied to that complaint is the sense of the novel's lack of unity, which Lewes attributed to Charlotte's inability to make up her mind as to what she wanted to do. Clearly the time for a novel as "unromantic as Monday Morning" (ch. 1) was not yet come, and though the novel in our time has had many distinguished admirers (Asa Briggs, A. Norman Jeffares, Terry Eagleton), it remains a "special case" among Brontë novels in general estimation.

Shorter, Clement (1857–1926): journalist who restarted the boom in Brontë biography with his *Charlotte Brontë and Her Circle* (1896) and later works, which used Ellen Nussey's store of letters – misused, she would have said, when letters and books that she had lent Shorter and Wise turned out to have been sold: "I have been shamefully treated by the greed and grab of these two men they have cheated and deceived me over and over again" she wrote at the end of her life (Whitehead, 1993, p. 252).

Sidgwick, John Benson (1800–72): head of the family at Stonegappe, where Charlotte was briefly employed as a governess in the summer of 1839. As usual it was the male of the household Charlotte entered who gained her approval: he was "a hundred times better" than his wife, with "a far kinder heart." Out walking with his children and his dog he spoke "unaffectedly" (Charlotte was very quick in scenting affection) to the people he met and seemed to her the model of a "frank, wealthy Conservative gentleman" (to EJB, 8 June 1839).

Sidgwick, Sarah Hannah (1803–87): wife of the above, daughter of a wealthy Keighley manufacturer John Greenwood, and sister-in-law of Rev. Theodore Dury. It was she who, in Charlotte's eyes, was the monster who made her months at Stonegappe and Swarcliffe among the unhappiest in her life. She felt ignored ("she does not intend to know me") and exploited, having loaded upon her a great "burden of sewing . . . I never in my whole life had my time so fully taken up" (to EJB, 8 June 1839). In addition Mrs Sidgwick never supported her governess's authority with the children. The latter (Margaret, William, Mathilda, and John) were "pampered spoilt & turbulent" (to EN, 30 June 1839) and "little devils incarnate" (to EN, 21 Mar 1841?). Though allowance must be made for the fact that the late 1830s was a time of great mental stress for Charlotte, it is difficult to see how her account of the household could be simply the result of an over-heated, grievance-seeking frame of mind, or how the

Sidgwicks could be truthfully described as "extraordinarily benevolent people, much beloved" who "would not willingly have given pain to anyone connected with them" (their relative A. C. Benson in his *Life of Edward White Benson*, 1899). Her time with them became for Charlotte a recurring nightmare, referred to over and over and bitterly rehearsed again for W. S. Williams in two letters of May and July 1848. Much of Jane Eyre's experience with Rochester's house-party probably has its origins in Charlotte's months with the Sidgwicks.

"*Siège d'Oudenarde, Le*": essays by Charlotte and Emily for M. Heger, based on Belgian history, and probably written early in the year 1842. The defender of Oudenarde, in Brabant, is forced to choose between betraying his country or having his two sons killed before his eyes. He chooses the latter, but the besiegers repent and the cavalry arrive. The essays proceed in very similar fashion, one no doubt laid down by Heger. Both emphasize the role of women in the besieged town, but while Charlotte has them participating equally in the defense, Emily takes the opportunity to condemn their "degrading privilege" of usually being "a heavy burden in any situation of action and danger."

"Signs of the Times": a pamphlet written by Patrick in 1835 meditating on the political situation of Britain in the years following the Reform Bill, and pleading for the reform, rather than the disestablishment, of his beloved Church of England.

Silas, Père: the Catholic priest to whom Lucy Snowe confesses in *Villette*. He is a man of feeling and kindness, of "a true benevolence" (ch. 34), but he has traces of Jesuitical cunning, and allows himself to be involved in family plots to prevent M. Paul marrying Lucy Snowe.

Silverdale: pleasant spot near Morecambe, where the Rev. Carus Wilson had a home. Charlotte and Emily, along with many other Cowan Bridge girls, were sent there during the typhus epidemic, but were fetched home almost at once by Patrick. By coincidence Mrs Gaskell wrote part of the *Life* there.

Simeon, Rev. Charles (1759–1836): one of the foremost of the evangelical clergymen in England. He was Fellow of King's College, Cambridge, where he was also vicar of Holy Trinity. Patrick knew him there, and was very interested in borrowing from Ellen Nussey his life by William Carus in 1848. Carus, along with William Carus Wilson, supported Simeon in many of his enterprises, and Simeon was a subscriber to the Clergy Daughters' School. He was one of the founders of the Church Missionary Society, which Patrick supported, and very active in societies promoting the conversion of Jews to Christianity.

Sinclair, Rev. John: vicar of Kensington and secretary to the National Society, with whom Patrick corresponded on the subject of grants towards Haworth's National School. He was succeeded by the Rev. M. J. Kennedy.

Sir Charles Grandison: novel by Samuel Richardson (1753–4). The eponymous hero, a pattern of virtue, is mentioned in Charlotte's letter which accompanied the chapters of "Ashworth" which she sent to Hartley Coleridge, and in the first chapter of that unfinished novel. Sir Charles was much admired in the eighteenth century, but ridiculed for the cardboard nature of his virtue in the nineteenth. The tone of Charlotte's references, here and in *The Professor* (ch. 24), suggest Charlotte took a typical nineteenth-century view of the book, which has not regained favor in our own times, unlike *Clarissa* and *Pamela*.

Sladen Beck: favorite walking place of the Brontës, which would take them to a convergence of springs which they named romantically the "Meeting of the Waters." Here, in Ellen Nussey's words, "nothing appearing in view but miles and miles of heather . . . a fresh breeze wafted on us its exhilarating influence, we laughed and made mirth of each other . . ." (EN, "Reminiscences," in CBL, v. 1, p. 598).

Sloane, Edward: a Halifax friend of Branwell who backed up William Dearden's assertion that Branwell was the author of *Wuthering Heights*. He claimed that Branwell had read him the book "portion by portion," so that when he read the published work he "was able to anticipate the characters and incidents to be disclosed" (Leyland, v. 2, p. 188). These assertions are generally discounted.

Smith (no first name given): acquaintance of William Crimsworth in the town of X—, possibly a workmate or fellow lodger. Mentioned but not described in ch. 5 of *The Professor*.

Smith, Charlotte (1748–1806): poet and novelist. Her novel *Ethelinde* is referred to by Charlotte in the draft of her letter to Hartley Coleridge (where she calls it by mistaken association *Evelina*) and in the actual letter, both times without a great deal of respect. One plot strand in the novel, however, may have lodged in her mind: it concerned a woman loved by a man who is married already to a deranged wife.

Smith, Elder & Co.: London bookselling and publishing firm started by George Smith Sr in 1816. The firm soon developed a thriving sideline supplying goods to India, and it remained willing to diversify, even when its main business became publishing. Smith and his young family lived "over the shop" in Fenchurch Street and 65 Cornhill, and not until 1841 did the Smiths move to a proper home. By then the younger George was already a member of the firm, and he took over during his father's last illness and death (1846).

The firm's early publishing ventures had included excursions into the innocuous field of fashionable annuals (their *Friendship's Offering* had been used by the young Brontës for copying pictures from), but also some scientific works and records of scientific exploration, including Darwin's. The younger George's tastes were eclectic: he published Ruskin's *Modern Painters* (much appreciated by Charlotte when it appeared in one of the parcels of books Cornhill dispatched to her), and also R. H.

Horne's contentious *New Spirit of the Age*. If Smith's own taste was not impeccable, he had the true leader's ability to select good seconds-in-command: he spotted in W. S. Williams "a most agreeable and most intelligent man," and invited him to join the firm as "general manager of the publishing department." He was rewarded when Williams was the first to read *Jane Eyre* (following his sympathetic rejection of *The Professor*) and immediately recognized its potential. After this first striking success in fiction the firm became one of the foremost novel publishers of the Victorian age.

Smith, Elizabeth G. née Murray (1797–1878): mother of George Smith,

Charlotte's publisher. Charlotte first met her when she and Anne were taken to dinner at the Smith home on the second day of their visit to London. The keeping up of the sisters' anonymity led to a degree of puzzlement on the part of the Smith ladies, and "awkward constraint" on the part of the sisters. The Smith family consisted of Eliza, George, Sarah, Alexander, and Isabella. Charlotte recorded the family likeness: "all dark-eyed – dark-haired and . . . clear & pale faces" (to MT, 4 Sep 1848). Dark hair and eyes were always a plus with Charlotte. Mrs Smith at this date (1848) had been a widow for two years.

The relationship between the two women became much warmer during Charlotte's 1849 visit to London, when she stayed with the Smiths, and was shown, at George's insistence, every attention. Her verdict on Mrs Smith was: "rather a stern woman – but she has sense and discrimination," and her chaperonage was quite comfortable to Charlotte, who half-realized she was not the only one being chaperoned: "I liked the surveillance – both when it kept guard over me amongst many or only with her cherished and valued Son" (to EN, 19 Dec 1849). From then on she and her son were modeling for Mrs Breton and Graham in *Villette*. When proposals came up that could have led to a closer relationship between the reclusive author and her son Mrs Smith was instinctively against them, but could be persuaded by George, as for example with the trip to Scotland: "his mother is master of the house – but he is master of his mother" Charlotte noted (to EN, 21 June 1850). The happiness of the 1850 stay was never to be quite repeated, however. Charlotte presumably at some stage got the notion that a marriage to George was a possibility, but that his mother would work, perhaps was working, against it. Or perhaps Mrs Smith was merely victim of the curse over all the important women in households that Charlotte entered, perhaps a consequence of a mild form of persecution complex. At any rate by December 1852 (by which time the last volume of *Villette* had been sent to her publishers) she was writing to Ellen, who presumably knew most about her relationships with the Smiths: "there is a note from Mrs. S – very kind – I almost wish I could still look on that kindness just as I used to do: it was very pleasant to me once" (to EN, 9 Dec 1852?). The relationship ended with an embarrassed sputter of notes, and one who had come as close as anyone to being a mother-figure to Charlotte was cast into outer darkness.

Smith, George (1824–1901): one of the great Victorian publishers, whose lists

at one time or another included most of the notable writers of the day, apart from Dickens. The firm of Smith, Elder had been founded by his father in 1816, but he had begun to take charge at the onset of his father's fatal illness in 1844. The firm's doomed attempt to promote G. P. R. James as a potential best-seller was an embarrassment behind him when his reader handed on enthusiastically the manuscript of *Jane Eyre* in the autumn of 1847. From then on he managed Charlotte's literary and financial affairs with commitment, tact and, after the meeting of July 1848, personal warmth. From the early days of the relationship Charlotte realized that the favors worked both ways, and that she was Smith, Elder's first big success in the league of major publishers: "it would chagrin me" Charlotte wrote to Smith about the third edition of *Jane Eyre*, which she had feared might hang fire, "to think that any work of 'Currer Bell's' acted as a drag on your progress; my wish is to serve a contrary purpose..." (7 Nov 1848). A year later she could tell Ellen "I am proud to be one of his props" (19 Dec 1849). Her early descriptions of him focus on his appearance: "a distinguished, handsome fellow" (to MT, 4 Sep 1848) she calls him, and "elegant, handsome ... pleasant" (ibid). Most of the prepossessing young men that had hitherto come Charlotte's way had inevitably had a clerical tinge to them, or been fatally associated with hated employers. Even on first acquaintance with George, however, she had emphasized that beneath the gloss there was "a firm, intelligent man of business" (ibid) – one, moreover, who even as late as September 1849 had to be told that her first name was Charlotte, not Caroline.

Tracing the growth of their intimacy is difficult: we have one side of their correspondence, the more overt side of the relationship. We have very little from Smith himself, and no outsider's view that might have caught the giveaway signs that something more than a publisher–author closeness was growing up. Charlotte, when she meets him, is always quick to chronicle changes in his appearance: he is fatter, more careworn (Smith, Elder was the victim of a massive scheme of peculation by one of its principal employees, suggesting that the regime of George Sr had been too lax). Charlotte's George was not only energetic, entertaining, and solicitous: the relationship flourished because he was sensitive to Charlotte's needs. In her loneliness and comparative inexperience she needed books, contacts with the literary world, help in managing her financial affairs – all these he offered.

But this was essentially, like that with Heger, an "impossible" relationship. In this case they were divided not by a marriage, but by age, by their various commitments, by his vigor and her reclusiveness and natural gloom. He belonged to the metropolitan great world, she to Haworth and her father. Her feelings of duty were innate, not just imposed by contemporary mores, and her love and need for her father was great, her link with the past. The relationship with George was one that could *be*, but could never *become*. So the letters joke, they flirt, they advance and retreat, but in essence his interest in her is based on natural kindness and business acumen, hers in him on an impossible dream. He was responsible for many happy hours (in Edinburgh, for example), and for many fraught ones (mainly springing from his desire to launch her on the London literary scene, which he eventually seems to have realized was a doomed ambition).

It was the firm's reception of *Villette*'s third volume that, more even than Smith's engagement, was the catalyst for the end. Silence was followed by a check, then a letter, but not one that illuminated the situation. Charlotte reported to Ellen that "something in the 3rd. vol. sticks confoundedly in his throat" (to EN, 9 Dec 1852?). This sounds like Smith's own language, but it does not sound as if his objections were purely literary ones – such as the transfer of interest from Dr John to M. Paul Emanuel, the usual reason given for his distaste for the later chapters. Charlotte's use of the relationship between his mother and himself all belonged to the first two volumes, and had aroused no anger. Alison Hoddinott, in "Charlotte Brontë and the 'Little Men'" (BST, v. 26, pt 2, 2001) provides a detailed and convincing case for thinking that George Smith saw Paul Emanuel's enforced departure to the West Indies on family business, separating him from Lucy Snowe, as a coded reference to James Taylor's mission to India on firm business, separating him from Charlotte.

Communication between Haworth and Cornhill now became fitful. In November 1853 Mrs Smith – the useful mother as always – wrote to Charlotte signifying George's forthcoming engagement. He had met at a ball and fallen in love with Elizabeth Blakeway, daughter of a wine merchant. Mrs Gaskell later described her as his "pretty, Paulina-like little wife" (ECG to EN, 9 July 1856), suggesting that Charlotte had noted the sort of woman his eyes followed. She was mortified at the news, and when the engagement was announced wrote a graceless two-line letter offering her "meed of congratulation" (10 Dec 1853), leaving no room for doubt it was a very small meed. All that remained were a frigid letter of business and a letter replying to his congratulations on her own engagement – slightly more conciliatory, apparently wanting to end communication (which as she said had "waxed very frail . . . I don't wish it otherwise," 25 Apr 1854) on a reasonably even keel. Thus ended the pleasantest relationship with a male that Charlotte ever had.

George Smith prospered as he deserved to. He published, either in *The Cornhill* or independently, writers such as Thackeray, Mrs Gaskell, Trollope, George Eliot (unfortunately *Romola* proving a lemon), Hardy, Stevenson, Conan Doyle, and many more. He was the energizing force behind the *Dictionary of National Biography* (1885–1900), whose usefulness, with supplements, lasted throughout the twentieth century. If there is a hint of self-satisfaction in his account of himself (his unpublished *Recollections of a Long and Busy Life*) it was nourished by his upbringing and justified by his achievements. A good flavor of the man can be gained from his account of his courtship ("I was as energetic about my marriage as I was about every serious incident in my life") and marriage ("the very next morning after our marriage down came a clerk with a bag full of letters by the Indian mail") published in Jennifer Glynn's *Prince of Publishers* (1986). He was a man who knew his own worth.

Smith, Rev. James William: Patrick's curate from March 1843 to October 1844, a graduate of Trinity College, Dublin. He was enthusiastically praised by Patrick as "my Able and faithful Clerical Coadjutor [who], in Godly zeal, and the genuine spirit of Christianity heartily joins with me, in all our Apostolical labours of love . . ." (to John Sinclair, 4 Aug 1843). His orotundity may have concealed doubts about Smith in his professional persona. Of the private man he harbored grave misgivings: when he observed Smith showing some interest in Ellen Nussey during a visit of hers to

Haworth he was very disturbed, because he had summed him up as fickle: "if he marries he will soon get tired of his wife – and consider her a burden" (CB to EN, 29 July 1844?). It did not help that Mr Smith had been heard wondering about Ellen's personal financial situation. Charlotte came to dislike him very much, seeing him as totally selfish. He moved to a curacy in Keighley, in which he was confirmed in 1846. However, he absconded to Canada in 1847, leaving behind unpaid debts and taking with him money intended for charitable purposes. Charlotte depicted him as Mr Malone in *Shirley*, with at the end news of his "premature and sudden vanishing" and hints of a disgraceful cause for it (*Shirley*, ch. 37). However, as late as 1902 the Rev. J. C. Bradley (Mr Sweeting in *Shirley*) defended him in the *Tatler*, and a nephew wrote to the journal of the man's "exemplary life."

Smith, John Stores (1828–92 or 93): literary child prodigy who fizzled out young. A product of Manchester Grammar School, his professional work was in industry and commerce mainly in Manchester, Halifax, and Chesterfield. He published the intriguing-sounding *Barnard, A Modern Romance* in 1846, *Mirabeau* two years later, and *Social Aspects* in 1850, at the grand old age of 22. Charlotte was sent *Mirabeau* from Smith, Elder, and wrote about it at length to W. S. Williams. Her complaint was that its subject's early profligacy was glossed over and excused – a familiar complaint from her which clearly springs from Branwell's self-indulgent life, and explains her dislike of many eighteenth-century novels. Not knowing that judgment had already been passed on it, Stores Smith sent *Mirabeau* to Charlotte in March 1850, following it up in July with *Social Aspects*. In return he received in September an invitation to dine at the Parsonage, of which, much later, he wrote an account (see Lemon, 1986). Though sometimes inaccurate (Patrick was not at that time blind) and generally over-heated by his conviction that the Brontës' lives were unrelieved tragedy ("Of all the sad, heart-broken looking dwellings I had passed through this looked the saddest") much of the account carries conviction, including his description of Charlotte's appearance, her noticing gaze at her visitor ("There was no boldness in the gaze, but an intense, direct, searching look"), and, in conversation, her strong dislike of the generality of London literary figures. He left, glad to shake off the "one overclouding nightmare" which in his view was the Brontës' life.

Smith, Miss (no first name given): sewing mistress at Lowood in *Jane Eyre*.

Smith, Mr (no first name given): the "draper, grocer, and tea-dealer" (ch. 1) in Agnes Grey's home village, who drives her to her first governessing post.

Smythe, George, later 7th Viscount Strangford (1818–57): visitor to the Parsonage in 1850, in a group from Harden Grange, William Busfeild Ferrand's estate. Smythe was a poet, a journalist, an admirer of Byron, and a member of the Young England group in the Tory party – extravagant, profligate, and unwise. He was also the only man, Disraeli said, who had never bored him. Two years later he fought the last duel on English soil, and died young of tuberculosis, marrying money on his

death bed. He is Coningsby in Disraeli's novel of that name, and Waldershare in his
Endymion. See Robert Blake's *Disraeli* (1967, pp. 168–70).

Snowdonia: mountain region in north Wales visited by Charlotte and Arthur
Bell Nicholls during the first stage of their honeymoon.

Snowe?, Charles: uncle of Lucy, mentioned in ch. 6 of *Villette.*

Snowe, Lucy: central character in *Villette.* Uniquely for a hero or heroine in a
nineteenth-century novel, we are told nothing at all about her parentage and almost
nothing about her upbringing. The implication (opening of ch. 4) is that she was brought
up by "kindred" and was unhappy with them. In this respect she resembles almost all
Charlotte's other central characters – William Crimsworth, Jane Eyre, and Caroline
Helstone. The consequence of this reticence on the part of Lucy as narrator, the leaving of a great gap in our knowledge of her, is that we feel her to have been loveless,
neglected, and that as a consequence she herself does not believe her "lines have fallen
in pleasant places," or are ever likely to. Even in the idyllic opening scenes at Bretton,
Lucy is "a good deal taken notice of" rather than loved by Mrs Bretton, her godmother.
When she goes abroad it seems as if she is fleeing to somewhere where it is natural
rather than unnatural for her to have no one to care for or about her.

Once she is in Labassecour, at Mme Beck's, we are told about her contentment with
a life of low expectations, with dull routine work and no intimate friends, but are made
aware subterraneously of her hunger for affection. She has fantasies about Ginevra
Fanshawe, and as soon as "Dr John" comes on the scene one is conscious of a yearning to be noticed by this handsome presence, this masculine yet kindly figure. Though
she indignantly denies that she is entertaining any false ideas about the warmth of
Graham Bretton's feelings for her, her desperate behavior over the lost letter from him,
her anguish when the post brings nothing from him, her feelings of neglect when the
Brettons forget about her, all testify to the power of her suppressed emotional needs,
as does her hysteria during the long vacation.

When the mutual attraction of Graham and Paulina becomes obvious it is natural
for Lucy to withdraw rather than compete: though painful, her withdrawal corresponds
to her own view of herself and her destiny. However, the reader also sees it as natural that her suppressed passionate nature should start to transfer her affections to
M. Paul Emanuel: the physically god-like, the favored-by-fate man is acknowledged to
have been a delusive dream. M. Paul is physically almost comic, though Lucy is
attracted by his energy, his quick passions. What attracts her primarily is the power
and complexity of his mind, the strength of his principles and his emotions. By the time
that Lucy actually stands up and fights Mme Beck for M. Paul (ch. 41) we have no
doubt that this is the passion of her life, and that she puts up a worthy fight for it.

The ending, in which the reader is allowed to hope M. Paul survives the storm at
sea while given the strongest hint that he does not, corresponds closely to the passage
about Lucy's home life at the beginning of ch. 4. It may owe more to Charlotte's view
of her own fate than to any true fictional need for Lucy to end the book still

unfulfilled. But Charlotte's view of the character is well known (she changed the name from Snowe to Frost and then back to Snowe, because "A *cold* name she must have," to WSW, 6 Nov 1852, on account of "an external coldness"), and though there is no question of Lucy being *emotionally* cold it may be that in giving Lucy a mutually acknowledged love Charlotte was going as far as she wanted in allocating happiness to her.

Snowe?, Wilmot: uncle of Lucy, mentioned in ch. 6 of *Villette*.

Snowflake: a creature described by Winifred Gerin (1969) as a cat and (1971) as a dove. All we in fact know is that it was a member of the animal kingdom fed by Emily on 24 November 1834, when she wrote her first diary note.

Society for Promoting Christianity Amongst the Jews *see* London Society for Promoting Christianity Amongst the Jews.

Society for the Propagation of the Gospel: society founded in 1701 to undertake missionary work. A. B. Nicholls applied to them to send him as a missionary to Australia. This was during a low point in his courtship of Charlotte (January 1853). He later (April 1853) cried off, pleading rheumatism.

Sophie (no surname given): the French maid engaged by Mr Rochester when he decided to bring Adèle to England. Jane Eyre speaks French to her, but her answers are so "vapid and confused" (ch. 12) that no close relationship develops.

Sophie, Mlle: one of Charlotte's fellow teachers at the Pensionnat Heger. It seems to be she who is described as a future "old maid" (to EN, May 1842) and perhaps also in *Villette* as "an honest woman, but a narrow thinker, a coarse feeler, and an egotist" (ch. 14). Her letter to Charlotte on her leaving Brussels (17 Dec 1843) speaks as much of herself as of Charlotte.

Southey, Rev. Charles Cuthbert (1819–88): eldest son of Robert Southey, and author of his *Life and Correspondence* (1849–50) in six volumes. He wrote to Charlotte in 1850 asking permission to include in that *Life* Southey's two letters to her of March 1837. Charlotte felt the letters "ought to be published," but asked for the omission of some sentences that quoted "somewhat silly" words of her own (to C. C. Southey, 26 Aug 1850). She also asked for her name to be suppressed, so she was referred to in the *Life* as a lady "now well known as a prose writer of no common powers."

Southey, Robert (1774–1843): one of the Lakeland group of Romantic poets, Poet Laureate from 1813. His shift away from idealistic radicalism to a conservative standpoint brought on him the contempt and ridicule of other literary figures such as Byron, who pilloried him in the masterly "Vision of Judgment" and other poems: "Oh, Southey! Southey! cease thy varied song!/ A bard may chant too often and too long" (*English Bards and Scotch Reviewers*). He was among the "first rate" poets Charlotte recommended to Ellen Nussey (4 July 1834), and when she wrote to him in late 1836 it was probably in the spirit of genuine admiration. Southey's words of admonition in reply are those of an elderly literary man confronted by a young enthusiast, but for the most part they are sensible: there was a real danger that Charlotte, in cultivating the "daydreams in which you habitually indulge" would unfit herself for ordinary life "without becoming fitted for anything else." However his warning that "Literature cannot be the business of a woman's life" (12 Mar 1837) was not only unprophetic (it was the business of many women in the second half of the nineteenth century), but blind to the realities of his time: Mrs Trollope, Mrs Gore, Mrs Norton were only three of several women (sometimes perforce, or by choice, the breadwinner of the family) who were already making a living from writing. Southey's wife died insane in the year he wrote to Charlotte. He was remarried in 1839 to the poetess Catherine Anne Bowles, but his own brain was failing, and his last years were spent as a mental invalid. He is the most forgotten of once highly regarded poets, but his story of "The Three Bears" still has a general currency.

Southowram: the area in which Law Hill, where Emily taught, is situated, as well as Shibden Hall and the now demolished High Sunderland Hall. There is a fairly general acceptance that the area contributed to *Wuthering Heights*, though no general agreement as to which features of the area contributed to which features in the novel.

Sowden, Rev. George (1822–99): brother of Sutcliffe. His gentle "Recollections of the Brontës" in the *Hebden Bridge Parochial Magazine* were little noticed until reprinted by the Angria Press in 2005.

Sowden, Rev. Sutcliffe (1816–61): Arthur Bell Nicholls's best friend in Yorkshire, and someone who had known Branwell in his Sowerby Bridge/Luddenden days. At the time of Nicholls's dispute with Patrick over his suit for Charlotte, Sowden offered support, hospitality, and – when Nicholls applied to become a missionary – glowing testimony to his virtues. He was rewarded by the joy of conducting his friend's wedding service. He stayed twice at the Parsonage during Arthur's brief married life, and the couple seem to have wondered whether a marriage was possible between him and Ellen Nussey. Charlotte apparently liked and respected him, though she deplored his and Arthur's dry-as-dust style of correspondence (to EN, 20 Oct 1854? and 31 Oct 1854). Plans for the living at Padiham to be offered to him when Arthur perforce refused it came to nothing: "I fear Mr S hardly produced a favourable impression" (on Sir James Kay-Shuttleworth) Charlotte wrote to Ellen (19 Jan 1955).

He conducted Charlotte's funeral service, was a mourner at Patrick's funeral, and two months later (8 Aug 1861) on a foul night fell into the canal in his parish at Hebden Bridge. Arthur, in an obituary, mourned one he regarded as "more of a relation than a friend," adding: "I have no relations whose loss I would deplore more sincerely" (*Halifax Guardian*, 10 Aug 1861).

See also Fennell, Rev. John

Sowdens: a stone building in Haworth dating from Stuart times, with "H. E. 1659" carved over the door. William Grimshaw lived there for 20 years, and it served as his parsonage. After his death, however, his drunken son took it over. By the Brontës' time it was a house with multiple tenancy of a fairly humble kind – mill-workers, hand-loom weavers, and so on. It was at one time considered the original of Wuthering Heights. It is still standing.

Sowerby Bridge: small town four miles south of Halifax. Branwell lived here for some months (Sept. 1840–April 1841) while working as the new railway line's assistant clerk in charge. It was during his time there that the present station was under construction. He consolidated his friendships with local writers and artists during this time, but there is no evidence of the sort of debauchery that he later descended to during his time at Luddenden Foot. He was promoted there with a greatly increased salary, and Charlotte and Emily were agreed that "it *looks* like getting on at any rate" (to EJB, 2 Apr 1841?).

Spectator: periodical founded in 1828, borrowing the old Addison/Steele title. It was radical in social and political outlook, which makes its reception of *Jane Eyre* the more surprising: it was critical of the "low tone of behaviour" in the conduct of the characters, and the relationship between Jane and Rochester was felt to be "hardly 'proper'." Charlotte feared that other reviewers would take their cue from this one: "The way to detraction has been pointed out and will probably be pursued" (to Smith, Elder, 13 Nov 1847). The condemnatory tone of comment was continued in reviews of the other Bell books, until with *Villette* there was a change of tone, or reviewer. The perceptive critic noted the absence of plot as it was then understood, the "morbid feeling" in the narrative, showing "the hunger of the heart which cannot obtain its daily bread, and will not make believe that a stone is bread."

Stael, Anne Louise Germaine, née Necker (1766–1817): daughter of Louis XVI's first minister at the time of the Revolution, she was a writer, conductor of brilliant salons, and frequently a victim of France's instability, exiling herself during the Reign of Terror and being exiled by Napoleon later. Her brilliant talents, particularly as a conversationalist, appealed to the young Charlotte, who refers to her at least twice in the juvenilia ("Albion and Marina" and "A Peep into a Picture Book") and then much later in *Villette*, where M. Paul is said to have been capable of exiling "fifty Madame de Staels, if they had annoyed, offended, out-rivalled, or opposed him" (ch. 30).

Stanbury: village about a mile from Haworth. Patrick and A. B. Nicholls were active in getting built there a school which doubled as a church. It opened in 1848 and is still standing and in use.

Stanningley Hall: home of Mr and Mrs Maxwell in *Tenant of Wildfell Hall*. They have brought Helen up since the death of her mother, and it is here that part of Arthur

Huntingdon's courtship of her takes place. Her uncle's death occurs shortly after her husband's which is convenient because if it had occurred earlier the Hall, which is willed to her, would have become her husband's property. She goes to live there with her aunt after her husband's death, and it is here Gilbert Markham at length finds her and proposes to her. Anne is cagy about the whereabouts of the place, resorting to dashes to disguise the county it is in and the nearest town. She similarly declines to describe it in detail.

Steighton, Timothy: clerk to Edward Crimsworth in the town of X— in *The Professor*. A Methodist, and also an "ingrained rascal," he is a sly, heavy man who acts as spy for Edward Crimsworth on his brother's activities. Steighton is a survival (as are Edward and William Crimsworth in their relations with each other) from the early writings of Charlotte and Branwell.

Stonegappe: substantial eighteenth-century house outside Lothersdale, near Skipton. It was one of the homes of the Sidgwick family, with whom Charlotte in 1839 accepted a temporary position as governess. It was an imposing house: when advertised for sale in 1846 it had, as well as the ground floor rooms and servants' quarters "14 excellent bed rooms," stables, barn, and spacious gardens, "Pleasure grounds, and Plantation" (*Leeds Intelligencer*, 6 June 1846). Charlotte readily admitted that every prospect around the house pleased: "pleasant woods, winding white paths, green lawns" (to EJB, 8 June 1839). She was here from May to June, when the family left for Swarcliffe. The house is still standing, but recently much altered internally.

Story, Robert (1795–1860): poet of peasant birth in Northumbria. Leyland numbers him among Branwell's Bradford circle of writers – a "little band of literati" among whom "he delighted . . . to spend his evenings" (v. 2 ch. 5, see also v. 1, chs. 12 & 13). He was, like Branwell, a poet staunchly committed to the Conservative cause. The *Leeds Intelligencer* regularly plugged the poems of this "Conservative bard" as they called him, and his pen was very fecund. In 1843 Peel's government awarded him a post in the audit office, and he moved to London and an apartment in Somerset House. Thereafter disaster struck, with at least four of his children dying in the years 1846–52 – a human tragedy comparable to that in the Brontë family.

Stowe, Harriet Beecher (1811–96): author of *Uncle Tom's Cabin* (1852). Charlotte was extremely interested in the book and its author, feeling in it genuine experience and anger. She felt that "the iron of slavery" had entered into Stowe's heart "from childhood upwards long before she ever thought of writing books," and that therefore "her work is sincere and not got up" (to GS, 30 Oct 1852). She may be contrasting this genuine and well-informed opposition to slavery with the more superficial reactions of, for example, Dickens and Mrs Trollope. Mrs Gaskell recorded (*Life*, v. 2, ch. 13) that Mrs Stowe's "small and slight" appearance confirmed some theory of Charlotte's.

Sue, Eugène (1804–57): French novelist whose books, often melodramatic and sentimental, were for a time extremely successful (Yorke Hunsden is said to have his books on his shelves in *The Professor* ch. 4), but palled as Sue's proletariat-worship went out of fashion. Into his story "Mary Lawson" an inset story was inserted in the English version, and this story, "Kitty Bell, the Orphan," probably not by Sue, was a blatant plagiarism of *Jane Eyre*. Charlotte was alerted to this by an anonymous correspondent, K. T., and an interesting exchange of letters followed in which Charlotte tried to gauge the "ordinary reader's" reaction to *Shirley*, to try to account for its tepid reception.

Suffolk Exhibition: scholarship founded by a Duchess of Suffolk to aid poor students of St John's. This was won by Patrick jointly with another student in 1803, and it paid him a small amount until 1807.

Sugden, Daniel (?1793–1846): landlord of the Talbot Inn, Halifax, and a man of "extensive and varied musical knowledge" (*Leeds Intelligencer*, 7 Nov 1846). His position in the Talbot seems to have been taken over by his wife Mary, whose "most kind and motherly" treatment of Branwell during a "temporary illness" was gratefully acknowledged by him (to J. B. Leyland, 9 Jan 1848?).

Sugden family of Eastwood House, Keighley: rich and benevolently inclined family, heirs of the mill-owner William Sugden, who died in 1834. His son William was unmarried, and when Charlotte talks of "the Sugdens" she means primarily the younger William and his unmarried sister Sarah. The Sugdens were "very kind" to Mrs Collins, and "the circumstance is greatly to their credit" wrote Charlotte to Ellen (4 Apr 1847?) when Mrs Collins returned to the Keighley area. Sarah was "quite smitten" with William Weightman (to EN, 14 July 1840), and later proved an easy touch for £5 for the slippery Rev. Smith. Charlotte's approval of a mill-owning family is rare enough to be remarked on.

Sugden, Mr (no first name given): a constable who assists in the arrest of Moses Barraclough (*Shirley*, ch. 8).

Summerscale, William: teacher at Haworth National School and organist who assisted Patrick's campaign for a clean water supply, and sold Patrick his last two dogs, Plato and Cato.

Sumner, Mr (no first name given): a teacher in Mark Yorke's grammar school in *Shirley*.

Sunday school, Haworth: the present Sunday school building was opened in 1832, and over the years Charlotte, Anne, and Branwell taught there. Patrick particularly prized the work of the school, having taught many years earlier in Yorkshire's first Sunday school in Dewsbury. He referred to it usually as the Church National Sunday School, since as a National School it functioned on weekdays as well. Literacy as well as Bible study was a prime aim of the school, and as well as a schoolmaster and mistress the curates were expected to take their share of classes. Charlotte was the most conscientious of the Brontës as a teacher, and in *Shirley* gives a spirited account of a feast day for the Sunday scholars. In Haworth this was usually held on Whit Monday, with a procession, speeches, "tea, spice cakes, buns etc" (*Leeds Intelligencer*, 5 June 1847). After Charlotte and A. B. Nicholls returned from their honeymoon they gave a party for Sunday school pupils, teachers, and other helpers – five hundred in all.

Sunday Times: newspaper which gave *Jane Eyre* one of its most unfavorable early reviews. It found the interview between the "morose and savage" Rochester and his wife too disgusting to quote, and, like other reviewers, attributed to Currer Bell a conscious desire to shock, never satisfied until he had "passed the outworks of conventional reserve" (5 Dec 1847).

Sunderland, Abraham Stansfield: Keighley organist who taught the piano at the Parsonage from 1833. He participated in the inauguration of a new organ in Haworth church (May 1834), and was immediately used as a character in the Angrian saga: Patrick Benjamin Wiggins narrates the story of how the "fine and full new horgan was hoppened in Howard Church" in a way that casts ridicule both on himself (Branwell) and Mr Sudbury Figgs (Sunderland) (CB, "My Angria and the Angrians"). After his death his widow sold a collection of 123 "oil paintings and engravings," including works by Reynolds, Kaufman, Teniers, Hogarth, Blake, and Stubbs (*Leeds Intelligencer*, 22 Sep 1855).

Supplehough, Mr (no first name given): preacher at an "opposition shop," presumably a Methodist chapel, in *Shirley*.

"*Sur la Mort de Napoléon*": an essay by Charlotte (31 May 1843), a copy of which was given Mrs Gaskell by Heger in a form considerably altered by himself. The subject interested Charlotte greatly, but she allowed herself to be diverted by her King Charles's head, the Duke of Wellington: as Sue Lonoff says, "as soon as the hand of Wellington emerges, the body of the Corsican recedes" (BE, p. 307).

Surenne's New French Manual (1840): used by Patrick to compile his own notebook of useful French phrases for his trip to Brussels, using various headings (food, drink, numerals, days and months, etc), and useful short questions and sentences such as "*S'il vous plait montrez moi le privy.*"

Suzette: (no surname given): teacher of French extraction at Mlle Reuter's school in *The Professor*, one of two described as totally ordinary and commonplace (see ch. 12).

Swaine family: the families of Joseph Swaine and his half-brother Edward, of Brier Hall, Gomersal. The Nussey family were friends of theirs, but in 1845 Ellen was clearly afraid that the Swaines intended to do injury to the Nusseys – this at the time of the onset of George Nussey's madness, though this may be coincidental. In a letter of 7 October 1845 Charlotte speculates what the various members of the Nussey family could do to earn a living, which thought leads straight into a question of whether "these Swaines are really acting a false & dishonest part." In December she regrets that "so selfish and mean a set" as the Swaines "have it in their power to annoy you." She fears they will use that power, and hopes that their ability to injure Ellen's mother is limited (to EN, 30 Dec 1845?). All this is something of a mystery, and in fact relations between the Swaines and Nusseys seem to have remained friendly. Another mystery is why Charlotte should have expressed the view, on hearing rumors that Joseph's youngest daughter Catherine was to be married, that her doing so would be "an unwise and even a wrong thing" (to EN, 18 Aug 1851).

Swarcliffe House: near Harrogate, and one of the residences of John Greenwood of Keighley, father of Mrs Sarah Sidgwick. The Sidgwicks and their temporary governess went in June 1839 to be part of a house party, to the governess's great discomfiture: "imagine the miseries of a reserved wretch like me – thrown at once into the midst of a large Family – proud as peacocks & wealthy as Jews – at a time when they were particularly gay . . ." (to EN, 30 June 1839). This discomfiture probably produced the house party scenes in *Jane Eyre*. Charlotte admitted that the surrounding scenery was beautiful. The house was enlarged in the 1850s.

Sweeny, Mrs (no first name given): Mme Beck's nursery governess in *Villette*, replaced in ch. 8 by Lucy Snowe. She is a coarse, untrustworthy Irish woman who drinks.

Sweeting, Mr David: curate of Nunnely in *Shirley*. He is the most amiable of the three curates, but a mother's boy and a drawing-room pet of the parish ladies. Like many small men he is devoted to large ladies, and he finishes the book married to "the weightiest woman in Yorkshire" – formerly Dora Sykes. Charlotte's note that they "lived long and happily together" certainly became true of the original of the character, the Rev. James Chesterton Bradley, curate of Oakworth, who died in 1913 at the age of 95. Like Sweeting he played the flute and this fixed the identification in the minds of local people.

Swinburne, Algernon Charles (1837–1909): poet, dramatist, and critic. During a low point in the Brontës' reputation he wrote enthusiastically and discriminatingly about both Charlotte and Emily – on the first in *A Note on Charlotte Brontë* (1877) and on the second in a review of Mary Robinson's biography (*Athenaeum*, 16 June 1883). The second volume of the Shakespeare Head *Lives, Friendships and Correspondence* also has an interesting letter on the question of Emily's subject matter, which so horrified the Victorians. Swinburne's predilection for the wilder shores of sexuality does lead him to see brutality and perversion as a rural norm, but his views are an interesting corrective, and his enthusiasm refreshing.

Sykes (no first name given): mill hand at Hollow's Mill, not to be confused with the wool merchant's family, in *Shirley*.

Sykes family: Christopher Sykes is a wool merchant in *Shirley*, in partnership with Pearson. He is a stout, handsome man, but described as "soft" (ch. 5) and "feeble of physiognomy" (ch. 8). In his main appearance in the novel (ch. 8) his conduct is craven, until given some stiffening by alcohol. His wife is a "tall bilious gentlewoman," much given to piety and cultivating the clergy. Dora, the most prominent of the daughters is described in ch. 7 as "vast, ponderous: seen from behind, she had the air of a very stout lady of forty," but it is also said that she had "a good face, and no unkindly character." Being large she is admired by the tiny curate Sweeting, to whom she is given at the end of the book, when they are described as "beloved by their parishioners."

Of the other sisters Hannah is described in ch. 7 as "conceited, dashing, pushing." Like her sisters she pretends devoutness, and seems to spend much time ministering to clergymen and sampling preachers. Harriet is a "high and cold" beauty, and Mary is a "well-looked, well-meant, and, on the whole, well-dispositioned girl," though there is a complacency about her and her sisters that, if Charlotte Brontë is to be believed, was shared by "all (or almost all)" English country ladies (*Shirley*, ch. 7). The young ladies have a brother John, who only rates a mention.

Sylvie (no surname given): pupil at Mlle Reuter's school, and one of the few for whom Crimsworth has any words of praise. She is mentioned as "the ugliest and most attentive" of his students in ch. 10 of *The Professor*, and is analyzed at greater length in ch. 12, where her gentleness and intelligence are said to be nullified by her total subservience to her religion, which is of course Catholicism. She is apparently a "future religieuse," and her soul had been blighted by "Romish wizard-craft."

Sympson, Gertrude and Isabella: cousins of Shirley Keeldar. Together they are described as "two pattern young ladies, in pattern attire, with pattern deportment" (ch. 22). The descriptions of most of the young ladies in *Shirley* suggests how tedious Charlotte Brontë found the majority of her female contemporaries. They are described most fully in ch. 26.

Sympson, Harry: the lame, sickly, but sensitive and sympathetic son of the Sympson family. He is a pathetic but lovable boy, and his boyish love for Shirley is delicately handled. His character is displayed most fully in ch. 26 of *Shirley*.

Sympson, Mr (no first name given): uncle of Shirley Keeldar. Described in ch. 26 as "a man of spotless respectability, worrying temper, pious principles and worldly views." He reveals himself later (ch. 31) to be a blustering but ineffectual tyrant, with very poor judgment.

Sympson, Mrs (no first name given): wife of the above. A very good woman, patient, kind, and well-bred, she is nevertheless a woman of narrow views – her mental horizons consist of prejudices and bigotry, and she regards her son as "a new Samuel," and his oddities "a mark of election" (ch. 26).

T

Taylor, Mrs Anne (1781–1856): mother of Mary, disliked by Charlotte and apparently by nearly everyone she came in contact with. She is depicted as Mrs Yorke in *Shirley* – autocratic, narrow-minded, repressing every sign of joy, originality, and vigor in those around her. After her husband's death her children fled the Red House, except Joshua, who with his family stuck with her until 1845, when he left her in sole occupancy of the family home for the rest of her life – years in which she probably fulfilled Charlotte's prophecy that "her unhappy disposition is preparing for her a most desolate old age" (to EN, 20 Nov 1845).

The nature of her relationship with her energetic and free-thinking husband is a mystery. Charlotte speaks of her having "made her spouse give up his pre-matrimonial friends & kin" (to EN, 3 or 10 Aug 1851?), a piece of subservience on his part that seems quite out of character both with his real-life character and his depiction as Mr Yorke. In *Shirley* Charlotte suggested that Yorke's "shadowy side found sympathy and affinity in . . . his wife's uniformly overcast nature" (ch. 9). This seems an unsatisfactory explanation for the real-life situation. It seems likely that Joshua left to his wife the early upbringing of the children, hence Mary's declaration that they never "ventured to speak at all" (MT to CB, 13 Aug 1850). Joshua perhaps relied on their native originality emerging with adolescence. It was not a formula that made for a united or happy family.

Taylor, Ellen (1826–51): cousin of the Red House Taylors, daughter of William and Margaret (née Mossman) Taylor, both of whom died in the 1830s. A maternal uncle, G. R. Mossman, cared for her for some time, and another uncle, Abraham Dixon, took an interest. Plans to send her to the Heger school in Brussels were abortive, and in 1849 she and her brother William Henry sailed for New Zealand, where their cousins Mary and Waring Taylor had been established for some years. By then she was probably already tubercular, but Mary had great joy in the early days of their companionship and partnership. They established and ran a shop, each alternating housework and shopwork week by week. Letters, sometimes joint ones, speak of their happiness together: they sketch on Sundays, hoping to send a batch home, though they "seldom succeed in making the slightest resemblance to the thing we sit down to" (MT to CB, 5 Apr 1850); they go out more, because Ellen is a more welcome guest than Mary alone was; they talk about how much profit will secure an "independence" and enable them to return home. The shop was a modest success, aided by gifts from Mary's brothers John and Joe. But all the time there is the undercurrent of Ellen's ill-health. "I fear hers will not be a long life" wrote Charlotte, experienced in short female lives (to EN, 6 Jan 1852). Before long she was informing Ellen Nussey of her death, her mind still running on her own losses: "the death-bed was just the same – breath failing etc" (4 May 1852).

Taylor, Emily Martha ("Tim") (1851–8): daughter of Joe Taylor and Amelia Taylor, née Ringrose.

Her parents' unremitting care for and worry over this child caused Charlotte to say feelingly "I should not like to be in its socks" (to EN, 23 Mar 1852) and Patrick to remark with grim humor that "if that child dies – its parents ought to be tried for infanticide" (to EN, 22 Apr 1852). Charlotte's frequent references to Tim and her upbringing (she was one of very few babies in her immediate circle) may indicate that she worried about her own lack of maternal feelings. The child followed her father to an early grave, suggesting that not all the fuss was hypochondriacal.

Taylor, George (1801–65): son of Stephen,

a Stanbury resident and Haworth church trustee, and part of the Brontë family's small social circle in the area. He lived in the Manor House (which is still standing), was an executor of Aunt Branwell's will, and was a recipient of one of Charlotte's wedding cards. His wife died, with a baby daughter, in July 1842.

Taylor, James (?1817–74): employee of Smith, Elder and Co.,

in charge of a small army of clerks. He was one of the enthusiastic early readers of *Jane Eyre*, and also one of the first critics of the opening chapters of *Shirley*. He collected the completed manuscript of that novel from the Parsonage in September 1849, and from then on Charlotte, who the previous month had had to ask "Did I see Mr. Taylor when I was in London?" (to WSW, 24 Aug 1849), had ample opportunities to form an impression of him. Superficially he seemed to conform to the pattern of masterful men Charlotte was drawn to, but with him there was a strong degree of antipathy from the beginning: she compared him to her creation Mr Helstone, "rigid, despotic and self-willed," with a "determined, dreadful nose in the midd[l]e of his face which . . . cuts into my soul like iron" (to EN, 5 Dec 1849?). This strong physical reaction if anything intensified. During their last meeting in April 1851, before his departure for India, she speaks of her veins running ice when he came near, and of growing "rigid – stiffening with a strange mixture of apprehension and anger" (to EN, 9 Apr 1851). It was during this meeting that Mr Taylor either proposed or perhaps attempted to come to some more vague agreement with Charlotte.

Granted the strength of her aversion to his presence it is odd that Charlotte seems not to have dismissed the possibility of marriage out of hand. That aversion was increased by the conviction that he was not a gentleman: "I could not find one gleam – I could not see one passing glimpse of true good-breeding" (to EN, 23 Apr 1851). Oddly she almost never mentions his principles, which might have been expected to weigh heavily. But with all this against him, it is odd to find Charlotte finding his departure leaving a "blank" in her life, and waiting anxiously for possible mail, as in the years after her return from Brussels.

Charlotte felt that there was "a certain mystery" (to EN, 4/5 Apr 1851) about Smith, Elder's packing off of Mr Taylor to India, something more personal than the need to rescue a failing subsidiary firm. This has been convincingly investigated by Alison Hoddinott (BST, v. 26, pt. 2, 2001) to explain why George Smith reacted so strongly against the third volume of *Villette*: she suggests that the plan of a little group of new characters in the novel to separate Paul Emanuel and Lucy by persuading him to go to the West Indies for a few years mirrors Smith's plan (for whatever motives, benevolent or mercenary) to separate the irritable and iron-willed employee from one of the firm's most profitable novelists. In both novel and real life the conspirators were successful, but there was a residue of resentment in both publisher and author.

The enterprise Taylor went out to direct in Bombay (Smith, Taylor & Co) was not a success, and he returned to Britain in 1856. However, he went back to Bombay in 1863, where he edited a newspaper and a review, became secretary to the Bombay Chamber of Commerce and registrar of the city's university. He died in 1874 after an apparently trivial accident in the billiard room of the Bombay Club. He married a widow, Annie Ritter, in 1862, but the marriage was not a success. There is no reason to believe a marriage to Charlotte would have been any more of one.

Taylor, John (1813–1901):
elder brother of Mary. He aroused Charlotte's contempt by being changeable in some attentions he paid to Ellen Nussey. She calls him "capricious" (to EN, 20 Jan 1851?), "a strange enigma" (to EN, 12 Apr 1851) and under provocation, "a noodle" (to EN, 10 May 1851). He had been, however, generous to Mary in New Zealand, both lending and giving her money with which she bought cattle: "I should be ill off, but that Joe & John have given me the money which at first they lent me" (MT to CB, 5 Apr 1850). He seems to have been similarly generous when she returned home. He himself emigrated to New Zealand in the 1870s, and Mary left him an annuity in her will, perhaps fearing his lack of drive and fixed purpose would incommode him for life in a pioneer environment. He never married.

Taylor, Joseph (Joe) (?1816–57):
brother of Mary Taylor, whom he helped and supported during her early years in New Zealand. He was the male Taylor who most fascinated Charlotte, as a human study in himself, and perhaps because she realized she had not exhausted his possibilities in the character of Martin Yorke in *Shirley*. He was talented, mercurial, and often generous. He was also aggressive, self-obsessed, and inconsiderate. Charlotte speaks of his "organ of combativeness and contradiction" (to EN, 1 July 1852), but could at times admire his devotion and "great

kindness" to his wife and to the child to which they both showed "unbounded indulgence" (to MW, 30 Aug 1853). She spoke most admiringly of the young Joe – "worthy of being liked and admired also" (to EN, late June 1843?) – but as his puppyish self-regard and heedlessness took hold of him she lost patience with him entirely. Joe for his part managed to call at the Parsonage surprisingly often, not from any romantic interest in Charlotte, so perhaps because he valued her judgment, wanted to impress her, or eventually because she was a "celebrity" to be cultivated. She, for her part, thought well enough of him to make him a trustee of her wedding settlement.

It was in the years after Brussels that Charlotte was most critical of him, particularly his heartlessness and chronic inclination to flirt with vulnerable single women. She felt that the world of commerce had changed him, and wondered to hear him talk of marriage from a purely worldly and monetary point of view. Inevitably, when his roving eye finally settled on Amelia Ringrose, Charlotte was apprehensive. In a series of long analyses of his character she spoke to Ellen of it being "imbued with selfishness and with a sort of *unmanly* absence of true value for the woman whose hand he seeks" (31 Jan 1850?), and pitied Amelia as being caught between a "coarse father and cold, unloving suitor" (7 Feb 1850). When finally they married she hoped for the best, and it turned out to be a much more loving relationship than she expected, and her exasperation shifted focus to the pair's besotted upbringing of their daughter. She often talked about Joe's own ill-health as if it was hypochondriacal, though Joan Bellamy's suggestion (2002, p. 58) that his long sickness and death in 1857 were probably the result of his work as an industrial chemist carries conviction.

All in all he had provided Charlotte with one of her most complex characters for study, and her interest in him never waned. Though she tried in her analyses to do justice to his bouts of generosity and good-feeling, the sense of coldness predominated. A story which she told Mrs Gaskell, presumably about the Joe Taylor family, emphasized that coldness: the father shows the little girl a dead bird he has trapped to prove that children have no false sentimentality about natural creatures. It is a distasteful and disturbing picture (ECG to John Forster, 8–14 May 1854?).

Taylor, Joshua (known as Joshua II) (1766–1840): father of Mary.

His family had been involved in the cloth trade for many generations. He himself was of a type new and fascinating to Charlotte when she visited the family: he was a manufacturer who could talk broad Yorkshire when it suited him, where others might be fearful of compromising their "gentry" status, but who was a traveled man, a first-rate French speaker, and one who kept abreast of artistic and intellectual trends in Britain and (especially) on the Continent. So a figure who was radical (in the early nineteenth-century sense), a republican, and a man of wide culture invaded Charlotte's Tory, provincially limited mind, to exhilarating effect. She found the whole family much more stimulating than the Nusseys, and Joshua contributed to various families in the juvenilia, as well as eventually to Mr De Capell in "Ashworth," York Hunsden in *The Professor*, and Mr Yorke in *Shirley*. When Charlotte knew Joshua he had been a declared bankrupt since 1826. He was determined to repay in full the losses of "my suffering creditors" (*Leeds Intelligencer*, 16 Feb 1826), and they in their turn realized it was better for the cloth-manufacturing concern, with its lucrative government contracts for army uniform cloth, to continue. Initially five shillings in the pound was paid, but three years after Joshua II's death the creditors had been paid off in full.

It was due to Joshua as much as to Mary that Charlotte found the "society of the Taylors . . . one of the most rousing pleasures I have ever known" (to EN, 15 Apr 1839); he challenged her prejudices and preconceptions, often displayed human frailties and oddities, but was a man instinct with a confidence in human potential.

Taylor, Joshua (known as Joshua III) (1812–80):

son of the above. He inherited leadership of the family business on his father's death, and the Red House on his mother's (he and his family had tried to live with his widowed mother, but the experiment had predictably failed). His wife was a Moravian, and the family was active in that church. He seems to have run the business competently, employing a large workforce, but his nature was moody, jealous, and changeable (Charlotte's unattractive and menacing picture of him as Matthew Yorke in *Shirley* seems to have been generally accepted), and he is never mentioned by his sister Mary. At the end of his life he became a victim of grasping spiritualists.

Taylor Martha (1819–42):

the ebullient and charming youngest daughter of the Taylors, often described by Charlotte in adjectives connoting childish qualities, though in fact she was only her junior by three years. She knew Martha at home, and then at Roe Head, and words like "chatter," "clatter," and "vivacity" cling to her accounts of her, as well as references to her "constant flow of good-humour" (to EN, 9 June 1838). This was during the visit Mary and Martha made to the Parsonage, a notable milestone in the relationship between the families. Even when Charlotte complains of her, there is a good-humored toleration behind the words: "you have a peculiar fashion of your own of reporting a saying or a doing and Martha has a still more peculiar fashion of re-reporting it" (to EN, 17 Mar 1840). The close relationship continued in Brussels where she and Mary were pupils at the Château de Kockleberg (more expensive than the Pensionnat Heger). Taylors, Dixons, and Brontës enjoyed frequent meetings, marred only by Emily's noncommunication. Martha's end came quickly – so much so that Charlotte heard of it too late to visit the deathbed. The cause of her death was almost certainly cholera – the idea that she might have died in childbirth rests more on speculation than documentation, and the haste of her burial and lack of information on the death certificate were probably a vain attempt to protect the school from gossip about cholera, about which there was still a large amount of ignorance. Mary nursed her sister in her last illness, though *Shirley*, presumably for pathetic effect, makes Martha's equivalent Jessy Yorke end "alone in a foreign country" and "cold, coffined, solitary" (*Shirley*, chs. 9 and 23).

Taylor, Mary (1817–93):

daughter of Joshua Taylor II, a school friend of Charlotte's at Roe Head who remained her friend for life: to her other lifelong school friend, Ellen Nussey, Charlotte wrote: "I have in fact two friends you & her staunch

& true" (20 Jan 1842). Mary Taylor's account of their schooldays together enlivens Gaskell's *Life* (ch. 2), particularly the visual impression Charlotte made on her ("a little old woman, so short-sighted that she always appeared to be seeking something") and her reaction to Charlotte's account of the games and compulsive writing of herself and her siblings ("I told her sometimes they were like growing potatoes in a cellar"). However, her memory that Charlotte spoke with a strong Irish accent has been questioned.

The friendship between Charlotte and Mary flourished after they left Roe Head, and there were frequent references to letters passing between them – letters almost all now lost, since they were not kept. When Charlotte went to teach at Roe Head the intimacy with the whole family could be resumed. Mary and Martha stayed at the Parsonage in June 1838, and Mary alone in June 1840 and December 1844. On one of these first two occasions, if Charlotte's observation was correct, Mary began to conceive a romantic interest in Branwell, whose attitude to her changed immediately to contempt – an interesting sidelight on both characters.

Charlotte's admiration for Mary as a free spirit was a little tempered by conduct in her friend that overstepped boundaries that she herself would have observed: teaching in Germany was brave and commendable and "if her pupils had been girls it would be all well – the fact of their being <u>boys</u> or rather young men is the stumbling block" (to EN, late June 1843?); later, when she left for New Zealand, Charlotte felt her letters displayed "a certain tendency to flightiness – it is not safe, it is not wise" (to EN, 18 Sep 1845). Such comments are less criticism than they are recognition of a different sort of soul to her own.

The company of Mary and Martha in Brussels was of inestimable value to Charlotte, if not Emily, and in the midst of both families' distress at Martha's death Charlotte could comment on Mary's devoted nursing of her: "more than a Mother – more than a Sister watching – nursing – cherishing her – so tenderly, so unweariedly" (to EN, 10 Nov 1842). It is as if she was relieved to know Mary could fill conventional female roles. But already there was talk of New Zealand, where her brother Waring had gone before her, and Charlotte decided she had done right to set out on this unconventional course which she calls a "path for adventure and exertion" (to EN, 2 Apr 1845). From then on communication was regular but more infrequent, with a four-month time gap between sending and receiving letters. But, if slow, the mail service seems to have been reliable, and from summer 1848 onwards Mary was reading the Brontë novels, finding *Shirley* ideologically unsound on working women, and *Wuthering Heights* a "strange thing" (MT to CB, 6–24 July 1848). Her accounts of her life in New Zealand went to Charlotte or Ellen Nussey indiscriminately – they were at this point a threesome, and letters would always be sent on.

Mary's early years in New Zealand were spent sensibly getting her bearings, teaching (including piano) when that was called for, lodging with Waring among others. With her cousin Ellen she started a shop, getting into a regular and adventurous routine for acquiring stock, and before long successfully running a useful amenity in a small pioneer town, which was all Wellington was. This was clearly Mary's happiest time, with Ellen the perfect companion, and doing work which she would not have been able to do at home – something that delighted her. She also acquired cattle and farmed in a small way. Both women were clear they were earning a living in New Zealand in order to provide them with a competence to live on when they returned home – an odd preference in Mary, to leave a place where women had unusual opportunities for a life of leisure in a country where they were much more restricted in scope. Perhaps she had already marked out a future for herself as a feminist propagandist. She coped as she had to with Ellen's death, buying out her share of the shop, and she wrote to Mrs Gaskell to contribute her recollections of Charlotte to the *Life* – something she probably later regretted. She sailed for home in 1859.

Thereafter she lived the life of a single lady in the community in which she grew up, being fairly gregarious with members of her own sex (which did not include Ellen Nussey, who she felt was trading in the Brontë connection), and gaining a reputation for eccentricity or daring, depending on the observer's point of view. There is no sign of her regretting being unmarried, and she had pleasure from her relationship with Grace Hirst, a young woman who was a sort of daughter to her. She lived in High Royd, owned by her brother Joshua, and she was looked after by successive sisters from Switzerland, a country and people she loved. The sisters were said to be slapdash servants but they were welcome companions, and Mary's closeness to them seems to have aroused jealousy in her small circle.

Her journalism – a series of articles in the *Victoria Magazine* for women – was forthright, sometimes pungent, and ably argued. The articles extended over 11 years, 1866–77, and were collected as *The First Duty of Women*. They give a vivid picture of the level on which feminist and anti-feminist argument was conducted at the time: the condescension and ridicule of the opposition were countered by Mary's logic, impassioned rhetoric, and an ability to turn hostile arguments on their head. Toward the end of her life, when she felt she had said her piece through journalism, she completed her long-promised novel *Miss Miles*, exploring various fates and possibilities for women. But by 1893 its day was long past.

Mary had earlier referred to herself as "obstinately lazy" (MT to CB, 13 Aug 1850), and later complained to Ellen that while there was always plenty to do in Wellington, it was "never anything that I really felt was worth the labour of doing" (8 Jan 1857). This may account for a life that seems to lack focus and definition, one in which the early daring and originality seem to peter out into propagandizing that bears little relation to the facts of her own life, though certainly she shared the lack of a voice and the legal disabilities which all British women of the time labored under. She was Charlotte's most original friend, but it was Charlotte, not Mary, who could gather together the contradictory emotions and impulses of her nature into a convincing life-view.

Taylor, Stephen (1772–1831): one of the trustees of Haworth Church, and one of those most involved in the complex and rather disgraceful disputes that preceded Patrick's acceptance of the incumbency. He was a strong supporter of Patrick, but Patrick demurred at being invited to preach at St Michael's during the negotiations, as if it were some kind of contest in eloquence: "my aim has been, and I trust, always will

be, to preach Christ and not myself" (PB to Stephen Taylor, 21 July 1819). The Taylors of Manor House, Stanbury, were one of the few families to whom Patrick felt close in the Haworth area, and this closeness continued after Stephen's death, when his sons George, Robert, and John remained involved in church affairs. The Brontë children seem to have "visited" with the widow of Stephen, and invited her and members of her family back to the Parsonage for tea-drinking.

Taylor, William Henry, known as Henry (1828–99): brother of Ellen, he emigrated to New Zealand with her in 1849. He soon went off to Sydney to buy sheep and remained incommunicado for five months, to his sister's annoyance. He inherited his sister's share in the Taylors' Wellington shop, and was bought out by Mary. His rather unsatisfactory life left few traces, and he died in a home at Wanganui, North of Wellington, on the west coast of North Island in 1899, when his former occupation was said to be "carter."

Taylor, William Waring, known as Waring (1819–1903?): youngest brother of Mary. He emigrated to New Zealand in 1842, and was thus there to welcome Mary in 1846, and help her to acclimatize and set up a business. He himself was a "general merchant," and he seems to have settled well into the newly established community. Mary records him as enjoying "good trade & fair health" (to CB, 5 Apr 1850). He married Mary Knox, whose uncle Robert Knox, a well-known anatomist, was revealed at the trial of Burke and Hare to have made use of their services, and he was progenitor of a New Zealand Taylor clan – he had 11 children in all. Later in life things turned less genial and prosperous, with a bankruptcy and imprisonment for embezzlement. Charlotte had described him as a "weak vessel" (to EN, 13 Sep 1846) whom Mary would have to strengthen, though in fact they seem to have been mutually supportive. By the time he validated Charlotte's judgment Mary had long been settled back in Yorkshire.

Teale, Thomas Pridgin (1800–67): surgeon of Leeds. As one of the most respected practitioners in the area he was called in to examine Anne (with the new stethoscope, Charlotte insisted in her letters) shortly after Emily's death. He could hold out little hope, beyond a possible "truce and even an arrest" of the disease, forbidding, according to Charlotte "the excitement of travelling" until the truce had been brought about (to GS, 22 Jan 1849). Both Anne and Patrick, however, stressed that he believed travel to a better climate would "hardly ever fail of success . . . if the remedy were taken in *time*" (AB to EN, 5 Apr 1849, with a note to the same effect by Patrick). It was after Mr Teale's visit that Patrick came in to Anne, drew her to him, and simply said "My *dear* little Anne" (EN quoted in BST, v. 8, pt 42, 1932). Charlotte always spoke well of Mr Teale, and urged her father to consult him when he had bronchitis. Arthur Bell Nicholls did consult him shortly before his marriage, but Mr Teale could only discover "an over-excited mind" (CB to EN, 27 May 1854).

Teale, like several others associated with the Brontës, was similarly unfortunate in his family life, losing at least five sons and two daughters in his own lifetime.

Temple, Miss Maria: the superintendent of Lowood School in *Jane Eyre*. She is depicted through Jane's eyes as a sort of ladylike saint – a realistic depiction of a schoolgirl's crush. She is contrasted with the unreasoning harshness of Miss Scatcherd, but also with Mr Brocklehurst: she is a woman of kindness, principle, and understanding of children, where he is none of these things. It is her marriage to a clergyman and removal from the school that precipitates Jane's decision to leave and find "a new servitude" as a governess in a private family.

The identity of the original Miss Temple was a matter of controversy and muddle in 1857, when Arthur Bell Nicholls was defending his late wife's picture of Cowan Bridge School as Lowood. A letter was produced then and later from a lady said to be the original of Miss Temple who was married to a clergyman and a head of a college in the United States. This was accepted by Wroot (1935), one of the few instances of his being at fault. In fact Brett Harrison (in BST, v. 16, pt 85, 1975) shows that Ann Evans, superintendent of Cowan Bridge School, married in 1826 the Reverend James Connor, late Rector of Knossington, near Melton Mowbray. Mrs Connor died in February 1857, and therefore could not have responded to Mrs Gaskell's identification of Cowan Bridge and Lowood.

Less certain is the identity of the lady in America who did, but it seems that she was a Mrs Hill, and that she may be identical with the "Miss Andrews" who was said to be the original of Miss Scatcherd – an obviously tainted source for the testimonial to the excellent running of Cowan Bridge School.

See also Evans, Anne; Andrews, Anna

Tenant of Wildfell Hall, The **(published in June 1848):** Anne's second novel takes the form of a ridiculously long letter from Gilbert Markham to his brother-in-law Jack Halford, who takes no part in the action of the book. The setting is a rural community not too far from the sea, and it seems likely that Anne had the vicinity of Scarborough in mind. To this close-knit but small-minded circle comes Helen Graham, the tenant of the title, arousing interest generally as a newcomer with a young child, and interest of a more personal nature in the narrator, Gilbert Markham, a young farmer. The gossips of Lindenhope focus on the mysterious background of Helen, and are scandalized by her strong opinions, freely expressed: even decided views on the upbringing of children mark her out from other country matrons and characterize her as a quiet but determined rebel.

The progress of Markham's interest in her presents her with a dilemma, and the reader registers that her off-putting behavior is often assumed and reluctant, brought about by her ambiguous position. Quite soon we realize that she is in hiding, that Mr Lawrence, a local squire, is privy to her secret, and that she is unwilling to trust it to anyone else. We also register that she is anxious to earn her keep with her painting, an attempt at independence that similarly makes her a marked person. The ambiguous position of Frederick Lawrence, the owner of Wildfell Hall, is one of the main complicating factors in the relationship between Gilbert and Helen, and Gilbert's misunderstanding of the situation (Lawrence is in fact Helen's brother) leads to a violent confrontation in which Gilbert takes a whip to his erstwhile friend, a physical encounter that carries less conviction than the mental and psychological cruelties later in the book. This violent episode leads to Mrs Graham's decision to explain her situation to Gilbert by entrusting her diary to him. The preliminary matter takes up much of volume 1 in the original edition. The diary then follows for all of volume 2 and half of volume 3. The matter with which it deals is the marriage of Helen Graham.

The diary starts with the lead-up to her marriage to Arthur Huntingdon. The model for this marriage was probably the disastrous marriage of Lord and Lady Byron, as it was commonly understood at the time. Helen had been brought up by her aunt, a good woman, but one with a joyless, inward-looking religion. Helen sees the rake Huntingdon as a challenge to her more active and positive faith, and she makes no bones about intending to reform her husband-to-be. The reader, from the start, has doubts about his promises to reform. After an initial happy few months the marriage begins its inevitable decline into unhappiness. Huntingdon strays into bouts of drunkenness and infidelity which are followed by promises of reform. Soon he hardly even bothers to give these promises any conviction. He surrounds himself with a drunken crew of associates, of whom the most dangerous is Walter Hargrave, who is plausible and attractive. When a son, Arthur, is born to the unhappy couple the father soon becomes jealous of Helen's absorption in him and uses him – and the "manly" habits he can be initiated into – as a means of tormenting his wife. Soon he has a woman in the house who doubles the roles of governess to the boy and mistress to the father. Helen succeeds in her second attempt to flee the marital home, Grassdale Manor, and with the help of her brother and maid settles into Wildfell Hall. Here the journal ends.

In the last part of the novel Helen returns to Grassdale to nurse her dying and unwelcoming husband and to do her best to reclaim his soul. Here the doctrine of universal salvation, which has been Helen's creed throughout the book, becomes painfully relevant. When Huntingdon dies and Helen, who has inherited her uncle's estate, becomes trustee of the Grassdale estate for her son, Gilbert Markham goes through some crises of principle before he can propose to the rich widow. The book ends with their marriage.

The Tenant has been slow to make its way into readers' affections, but in the twenty-first century it is advancing steadily. Perhaps it would have gained more admirers if, instead of pushing a theological viewpoint, it had made as its central message the appalling lack of rights – particularly rights to property and to the children – that married women suffered in nineteenth-century Britain. The novel has not been helped by most texts until recently being defective: the cheap edition of 1854 was followed in almost all reprints, which among other changes and omissions deprived the novel of ch. 1 (and thus most of its epistolary structure), and also most of ch. 28. The Penguin edition of 1979, edited by G. D. Hargreaves, pioneered a return to the first edition text.

It was inevitable that a novel with debauchery as its central subject would meet with opposition at that time, and there was certainly an outcry against Anne for her honesty and outspokenness. Her Preface to the Second Edition is notable for its simple declaration of her aim ("I wished to tell the truth") and her stirring refusal to be judged by different standards from those that would be used for a male author: "All novels are or should be written for both men and women to read. . . ." It is a fine and firm declaration of faith.

Tennyson, Alfred, later Lord (1809–92): poet born to a Lincolnshire clerical family, whose early volumes, like Keats's, were met with widespread ridicule, but who from the 1840s onwards began to be seen as the spokesman for "Victorian" feelings and ideas. He was made Poet Laureate in 1850, and a baron in 1884. Though Charlotte, according to Mrs Gaskell, "can not bear" him (to C. Froude, 25 Aug 1850?), and found *In Memoriam* cumulatively monotonous and dubiously sincere, Emily admired him, and Charlotte and Anne brought from London for her a copy of *The Princess*, at that time one of his most admired poems. Charlotte sent him a copy of the unsold *Poems* of 1846.

Thackeray, Anne Isabella, later Lady Ritchie (1837–1919): elder daughter of W. M. Thackeray, who later became a novelist (*Old Kensington*, 1873, is probably her best-known work) and a memoirist of famous contemporaries. She and her sister Harriet (Minnie, later and briefly Mrs Leslie Stephen) were allowed to meet Charlotte on the evening of her disastrous dinner at Thackeray's, noticing her "grave and stern" demeanor, but also her "kindling eyes of interest" when the great man's conversation pleased her (CBL, v. 2, p. 754). Ritchie herself was later described as Mrs Hilberry in Virginia Woolf's *Night and Day*, with "large blue eyes, at once sagacious and innocent."

Thackeray, William Makepeace (1811–63): novelist and humorous writer. How Charlotte came to read *Vanity Fair* in its monthly numbers we do not know – probably on loan from the Nusseys or the Taylors (she always took care to keep Ellen fully informed about her relations and encounters with him). Thackeray (who engaged governesses for his daughters with a keener eye for their gentility than their qualities as educators) was sent an early copy of *Jane Eyre*, and when he reacted with enthusiasm Charlotte received the news with all the gratitude and incredulity of a new author tiptoeing towards the Pantheon: "There are moments when I can hardly credit that anything I have done should be found worthy to give even transitory pleasure to such men as Mr. Thackeray" (to WSW, 11 Dec 1847). The letter in which Thackeray said he had been "exceedingly moved and pleased" by the book also said "The plot of the story is one with wh. I am familiar" (WMT to WSW, 23 Oct 1847), probably an allusion to his own marital circumstances: like Rochester he was indissolubly married to a woman who had lost her reason. This allusion passed Charlotte by, and her dedication of the second edition to Thackeray caused him and her considerable embarrassment (which surely Smith or Williams could have stepped in to spare her). Her allusion to him in the Preface to that edition as "the first social regenerator of the day" may be regarded as one of the first shots in the Dickens–Thackeray rivalry: *Vanity Fair* had, when she wrote it, only reached the 12th of 18 numbers.

The serio-comic story of the personal relationship between the two great novelists after their first meeting in December 1849 has at its heart Charlotte's early confusion between the man and the writer: "He seems terribly in earnest in his war against the falsehood and follies of 'the World'," she wrote in her early enthusiasm (to WSW, 11 Dec 1847). She found on acquaintanceship that this was far from the truth: he was of the world, worldly. She wrote scathingly of the "admiring Duchesses and Countesses" at his lectures, and said he was "sold to the Great Ladies" (to EN, 2 June 1851 and to Amelia Ringrose, 11 June 1851). She found that the man she had compared to the Old Testament prophets (he "speaks truth as deep, with a power as prophet-like and as vital" – Preface to 2nd ed. of *Jane Eyre*) also could speak with the most abominable cynicism, so that his conversation was "too perverse to be pleasant" (to MW, 14 Feb 1850). So all-embracing was his skepticism about human motivation that there was a danger that his satire would have no positives – like Pooh Bah's list of victims, on which anybody could be put because none of them would be missed.

This pair, as physically ill-matched (six foot plus and five foot minus) as they were mentally incompatible, had several notable encounters during Charlotte's visits to London. At the dinner party which was their first meeting Thackeray made an illusion to Rochester and his cigars which could have brought her authorhood out into the open. When in May 1851 she attended one of his lectures on the English humorists he introduced her to his mother (a notably straight-laced lady) as "Jane Eyre." Worst of all was the invitation to dine at Thackeray's with a collection of other women writers: what little social gift Charlotte had withered and died, and the evening became a nightmare of embarrassment from which the host escaped to his club – a piece of discourtesy and cowardice which can only have increased Charlotte's distrust of his morals and manners.

Inevitably she began to see that the brilliant promise of *Vanity Fair* was not fulfilled in the author's subsequent works. Even in the novels that still have some currency, *Pendennis* and *Henry Esmond*, the narrative sweep which was the glory of *Vanity Fair* was weakened, and the garrulity and easy cynicism had strengthened its hold. Charlotte had already decided that he wrote with Mephistopheles on one hand and the Angel Raphael on the other, with the former the dominant influence (to WSW, 10 Jan 1850). When she read the complete *Esmond* she burst out in irritation at the common description of Thackeray as the "second writer of his day," and her irritation sprang from her knowledge that the judgment was true: "He need not be the second. God made him second to no man." And the trouble was that "Mr. Thackeray is easy and indolent and very seldom cares to do his best" (to GS, 14 Feb 1852). On the whole posterity has endorsed this verdict.

It seems likely that the greatest pleasure Charlotte got from her encounters with Thackeray were in the private meetings, when they ranged over literary matters, and when she told him bluntly what she thought of his strengths and weaknesses. It may be that Thackeray enjoyed these sessions less than she did. However he always had a sort of tenderness for her, even if it was sometimes expressed condescendingly, as in his analysis that she was "a little bit of a creature without a penny worth of good looks" who only wanted "some Tomkins or another to love her," but "no Tomkins will come" (WMT to Lucy Baxter, 11 Mar 1853). Six years after her death he published the fragment known as "Emma" in his *Cornhill Magazine*, with a fine appreciation.

See also Brookfield

Thackray, James: soldier who falsely claimed to have enlisted William Nowell of Dewsbury in 1810. His claim was vigorously fought by Patrick and other local notables, was found to be false, and resulted in Thackray's being sentenced to seven years' transportation.

Thiers, Adolphe (1797–1877): French statesman. He made his name as a democrat in the 1820s as Charles X's rule drifted towards autocracy, modifying the old definition of constitutional monarchy from "The King Reigns but does not govern" to the more specific "The King reigns and the people govern themselves." He took office several times under Louis Philippe, conducting at times a flamboyant but ineffective foreign policy. This "dwarf of genius" (Maurois) was probably at his best and most useful to his country after the fiasco of Napoleon III's war against Germany in 1870. Charlotte had read his historical writings, including the unreliable *History of the French Revolution*, but she imagined them as having been dictated by "the Shade of Bonaparte" (to WSW, 28 Feb 1848). She predicted in the same letter, accurately, that the French would be "glad of him by and by. Can they set aside entirely anything so clever, so subtle, so accomplished, so aspiring, in a word, so thoroughly French, as he is?" Daring, unprincipled, immoral, Thiers was the complete politician, and he outlived most of the people he served or opposed in his tempestuous era.

Thom, Dr David: minister of the Scotch church in Liverpool and author of *Dialogues on Universal Salvation* (1838) and other theological works. He wrote to Anne in 1848 to express his pleasure in finding the doctrine of universal salvation expounded and welcomed either in *Tenant* or the reissued *Poems*. Anne's "gratified" reply is dated 30 December 1848.

Thomas (no surname given): clerk to the Rev. Helstone in *Shirley*, mentioned in ch. 19. Possibly he is also the "Tom" of ch. 2, who comes with Helstone to Hollow's Mill, and is described as his "aid-de-camp" (*sic*).

Thomas (no surname given): servant to Miss Marchmont in *Villette*.

Thomas (no surname given): servant of Mr and Mrs Maxwell in Staningley in *The Tenant of Wildfell Hall*.

Thomas, Enoch: landlord of the Black Bull (referred to as the "Devil's Thumb" in a Branwell letter of 13 Mar 1840) who suffered from melancholia and alcoholism, and died in March 1848. His mental trouble, which may have been connected to the Beaver forgery trial, was described by Patrick as a "very severe and great affliction" in a letter of 29 February 1844 to George Taylor, whom he asked to throw a tea party to divert Thomas's mind. This does not seem to have worked a cure.

Thompson, J. H. (1808–90): one of Branwell's artistic circle in Bradford, both a friend and a helper, apparently putting finishing touches to some of his commissioned portraits. They had both been pupils of William Robinson, and at some point Thompson painted (probably not from life) the portrait of Charlotte now owned by the Parsonage Museum. After he left Bradford Branwell relied on Thompson to clear up some of his unfinished or unsettled business, notably Mrs Kirby's complaints about the portrait he painted of her – one of Branwell's liveliest and sharpest works, perhaps enjoying the benefit of some touches of Thompson.

Thompson, William ("Bendigo") (1811–89): British bare-knuckle pugilist, whose epic fights with Benjamin Caunt became legendary. Caunt defeated Bendigo in 1838, but lost to him on a return bout in 1845 that lasted 93 rounds. This latter fight was commemorated by Branwell in a drawing a day after the fight, with the legend "alas! poor Caunt!" underneath. The bodies of the fighters are blacked in, and Caunt wears chains, giving the sketch an anti-slavery appearance. Bendigo's was a life crowded with incident both in and out of the ring: in 1853 the *Leeds Intelligencer* recorded him jumping half-naked from a house in Nottingham and running through the town to the police office, where he smashed the window-panes ("This soon aroused the attention of the police") and was eventually strapped, handcuffed, and taken to a lunatic asylum (25 June 1853). He later became an evangelical minister. The gold-rush town in Australia is named after him.

Thomson, James (1700–48): poet remembered today, if at all, for his *The Seasons*. He was recommended among the "first-rate" poets when Charlotte compiled her reading list for Ellen on 4 July 1834, and he is quoted in *Agnes Grey* (twice) and in *Jane Eyre*.

Thornfield Hall: the manor in which Mr Rochester lives, and in which most events in the central section of *Jane Eyre* are played out. The house is three stories high, though Jane seldom visits the top one (where normally the servants would sleep) until the climactic revelations after the aborted wedding. Jane's initial description of the house concentrates on small areas of snugness (Mrs Fairfax's parlor, her own bedroom) within a rather forbidding stately house with a "very chill and vault-like air" (but then Jane, as she says, was "little accustomed to grandeur" – v. 1, ch. 11). She finds embroideries by long-dead fingers on the third floor, but in general we encounter few relics of earlier members of the Rochester family in the house – perhaps banished by Edward, who had no pleasant memories of his immediate family. From the outside the house is battlemented, like Ellen Nussey's home Rydings, and rooks contribute to the Gothic atmosphere. When Jane returns to answer the supernatural summons of Mr Rochester she finds the house a blackened shell, and when she marries Rochester there seems to be no question of rebuilding it, with its memories of childish unhappiness and madness.

See also North Lees Hall; Norton Conyers; Rydings

Thornton: village about four miles from Bradford (of which it is now a suburb) and six from Haworth. Patrick became minister here in 1815, and all his children who survived to adulthood were born here. It was a poor area, which brought its minister, Patrick estimated, no more than £127 a year. He made good friends there, however, and became part of a little circle of like-minded Christians, Tory in politics, evangelical in religion. The birthplace in Market Street is now open to the public in the summer months, and Kipping House, home of the Brontës' best friends the Firths, still stands, though the Old Bell Chapel, where Patrick officiated, is no more than ruined masonry. The Bradford Council has not dealt sensitively with this area.

See also Pool, Rev. Robinson

Thorp Green Hall: substantial manor house near Little Ouseburn, six miles from Boroughbridge, where Anne went as governess to the Robinson family in 1840, and Branwell followed her as tutor to Edmund, the one son, in 1843. The family had lived there for nearly 50 years, and the Rev. Edmund Robinson seems to have been a country gentleman in his tastes and pursuits. The estate was large and beautiful, and the possibilities for field sports were abundant. The house burnt down early in the twentieth century, but the rooms and their proportions can be found in the advertisements when the house was let after the departure of the Robinsons (*Leeds Intelligencer*, 21 Aug 1847 and 8 Dec 1855). Also part of the estate was the Monks' House, where Branwell apparently lodged. This building still stands. The rebuilt Thorp Underwood Hall is now a girls' school, Queen Ethelberga's.

Thrushcross Grange: home of the Linton family in *Wuthering Heights*, later acquired by Heathcliff through sharp practice. The house is nowhere described in detail, but through impressionistic reports and incidental information we experience it as a commodious and elegant house in an extensive park (Wuthering Heights is four miles from the Grange itself, but two miles from the park's limit). Heathcliff describes the children's first view of the interior breathlessly: "a splendid place carpeted with crimson . . . a pure white ceiling bordered by gold, a shower of glass-drops hanging in silver chains from the centre, and shimmering with little soft tapers" (v. 1, ch. 6). Elegant chandeliers would be a rarity in Yorkshire, and our impression of the house is that it is one with a large staff and with rooms beyond the normal needs: a study for the master of the house, her own parlor for the lady, separate staff and kitchen area and so on. Though the Lintons are not titled (Charlotte and Emily largely shun titles) they are substantial gentry. Wuthering Heights is the second house in the (admittedly sparsely populated) neighborhood, but the social step down is considerable, and it is remarkable that the Lintons before their deaths seem to foster the relationship between Edgar and Catherine. Though David Cecil sees the house as the embodiment of "calm" in the novel (*Early Victorian Novelists*, Collins/Fontana reprint, 1964, p. 130), our first sight of it involves quarrelling children and a savage dog, and considerable violence occurs there in the course of the novel.

See also Ponden House; Shibden Hall

Tiger: Parsonage cat, depicted by Emily in the watercolor "Keeper, Flossy and Tiger" (whereabouts currently unknown) and mentioned in Charlotte's nostalgic picture of the Parsonage kitchen written from Brussels, in which Tiger is imagined as "jumping about the dish and carving-knife" while waiting for "the best pieces of the leg of mutton" (to EJB, 1 Oct 1843). Died March 1844.

Tighe, Rev. Thomas (d. 1821): Rector of Drumgooland and patron of the young Patrick Brunty. He was of a landed family, but he lived simply and was an admirer of John Wesley, to whom his family had played host. He appointed Patrick as the teacher in Drumballyroney school and as tutor to his own sons. He may have taught him classics and helped him to gain admission to his old college, St John's, Cambridge.

Times, The: newspaper which strongly criticized *Shirley*, to Charlotte's distress (Mrs Smith saw "tears stealing down the face and dropping on the lap," ECG *Life*, v. 2, ch. 4). The paper is often said to have reviewed *Jane Eyre*, but their favorable remarks about that book (or on the first two volumes only) are prefaced to the review of *Shirley*, which they saw as far inferior – all on a level with the last volume of the previous novel. *The Times* critic was one of those who dined at the Smiths' on Charlotte's 1849 visit to London – she called him one of the "literary Rhadamanthi" (to L. Wheelwright, 17 Dec 1849) and noted satirically how much "grander, more pompous, dashing, shewy" the critics were compared to the authors she had met (to MW, 14 Feb 1850).

On at least one occasion *The Times* gave Patrick a degree of attention unusual for an obscure provincial clergyman. They published a very full report of his speech against the Poor Law to a large crowd outside the Sunday School (February 1837). They also, less surprisingly, showed interest in him in his last years when his dead daughters were famous.

Titterington, James (?1815–52): worsted manufacturer, of Midgley, near Luddenden. Branwell, in the notebook kept during his time in Luddendenfoot, records quarrelling and then wrestling with him, but later becoming friends (18 Aug 1841).

Tom: Parsonage cat who preceded Tiger. His death is recorded in Charlotte's letter to Ellen Nussey of 1 July 1841, and in the diary note of Anne in the same month: "We have got . . . a sweet little cat and lost it." Ellen recorded that, so gentle was the treatment it received, it "seemed to have lost cat's nature and subsided into luxurious amiability and contentment" (EN "Reminiscences," in CBL, v. 1, p. 600).

Top Withens: small farm on Haworth moors, now a ruin, reputed to be the original of "Wuthering Heights." The situation of the place is well suited to the identification, but the farm itself is a standard moorland farm, and quite unthinkable as the home of the second family in the neighborhood and the place described in the opening chapters of the novel. The identification was made by Ellen Nussey for E. W. Wimperis, engaged on the first illustrated edition of the Brontë novels, and it resulted in a striking engraving and numberless tourist pilgrimages.

Towns[h]end, Charles *see* Wellesley, Lord Charles

Tranby Lodge: home of the Ringrose family at Hessle, near Hull. It was, according to Charlotte, a "somewhat ungenial home" for Amelia (to EN, 28 Jan 1848), and she was always pleased when Amelia could escape from it to Brookroyd or elsewhere.

Trevelyan, Lady: probably Hannah, Thomas Babington Macaulay's sister, married to Sir Charles Trevelyan. He was an Indian and British civil servant, Assistant Secretary to the British Treasury 1840–59. While Mrs Gaskell was staying with the Trevelyans, Lady Trevelyan confirmed reports of a cousin of Mrs Robinson about her moral character: she had been "a bad heartless woman for long and long," and one whose own relations had "been obliged to drop her acquaintance" (ECG to GS, 29 Dec 1856). The Gisbornes (Mrs Robinson's family), the Babingtons, and the Macaulays were closely intermarried (see T. Winnifrith, "Mrs Robinson and her Cousins," BST, v. 24, pt 2, Oct 1999), and confirmation from two relatives of the woman of her nature, of which she had already had a similar account from Charlotte, decided Gaskell to attack her in the *Life* under a thin disguise.

Trinette (no surname given): nurse to the Beck children in *Villette*.

Trinity College, Dublin: alma mater of Arthur Bell Nicholls, whose fees were paid by his uncle. It was visited by Charlotte and her new husband in July 1854.

Trista, Juanna: pupil at Mlle Reuter's school, and subject of one of the most disagreeable portraits in a not very agreeable gallery. She is described (ch. 12 of *The Professor*) in mainly phrenological terms, and then characterized by the "swinish tumult" she orchestrates in class. Like many of Charlotte's bêtes noires on the Continent she is described as of mixed race (Flemish and Catalonian) and she rejoices in the prospect of joining her father on the island where he is a merchant (presumably the West Indies) where she is excited by the prospect of having slaves.

Trollope, Frances (née Milton) (1779–1863): novelist and travel writer. Charlotte declined to meet her and other novelists in 1849, probably to protect her anonymity. She had expressed her scorn of Trollope's *Michael Armstrong* while writing *Shirley*: it was a "ridiculous mess," and had taught her not to meddle with things she could not personally inspect (to WSW, 28 Jan 1848). Mrs Trollope did in fact do research on the working and living conditions of factory workers, and the pictures of the nightmare conditions in mills are forceful and a terrible indictment of laissez-faire. She had seen for herself as far as she was allowed to, and made good use of what she saw. The novel is spoilt, as often with Mrs Trollope, by the plot, which is indeed a "mess." Frances Trollope was the mother of Anthony and Thomas Adolphus.

Tunstall Church (St John the Baptist): church where the girls of the Clergy Daughters' School worshiped every Sunday, which in *Jane Eyre* is given the name

Brocklebridge Church, to emphasize the connection with the Brocklehurst family. Rev. Carus Wilson was vicar of Tunstall Church at the time of the Brontës' residence at the school.

Turner, Miss (no first name given): an English teacher at Mme Beck's school in *Villette* who has been dismissed because the girls rebelled against her. Described by Mme Beck as "weak and wavering" (ch. 8), her fate is an example for Lucy Snowe when she comes to teach.

Turner, Joseph Mallord William (1775–1851): great English painter, whose reputation reached the young Brontës, and whose paintings the mature Charlotte was able to see on her visits to London. She loved Ruskin's wholeheartedness in his admiration of Turner ("he eulogises, he reverences him," to WSW, 31 July 1848), and tried to follow him in this. The watercolors she saw "were indeed a treat," but the recent, revolutionary studies of light were "strange things – things that baffle description" (to MW, 14 Feb 1850).

Tyndale, Lord (no first name given): maternal uncle of William Crimsworth in *The Professor*. The living of Seacombe-cum-Scaife, which is in his gift, is offered to William when he leaves Eton.

U

Ulverston: small town in present-day Cumbria, nine miles from Broughton-in-Furness, where Mr Postlethwaite banked. Branwell visited there with him regularly, and reported himself as "drinking tea and talking scandal with old ladies" (to John Brown, 13 Mar 1840).

universal salvation: a doctrine that held that any punishment after death was purely temporary, and that all souls would be recipients of God's mercy. The doctrine is associated particularly with Anne, who alluded to it insistently in *Tenant* (see in particular ch. 20 and ch. 49), and also in her verse, where she expresses the hope that "even the wicked shall at last . . . / To light and life arise" ("A Word to the Calvinists"). Anne probably discussed the doctrine during her illness at Roe Head with James La Trobe, and her most explicit declaration of support for it was in a letter to the Rev. David Thom, written soon after Emily's death, where she talks of having cherished the doctrine "with a trembling hope at first," and how it later became "a source of true delight to me to find the same views . . . advocated by benevolent and thoughtful minds" (30 Dec 1848). Interest in the doctrine was not confined to Anne, however: Charlotte strongly supported it in a letter to Margaret Wooler (14 Feb 1850), and it has been suggested that Patrick accepted it (though Winnifrith, 1973, provides cogent evidence to the contrary). What does seem likely is that the idea formed the basis for discussion in the Parsonage during the growing-up years of the children.

Upjohn, Rev. Francis (1787–1874) and Sarah (1792–1881): a couple living at Gorleston, near Yarmouth, in Upjohn House, Francis having ceased to be an active clergyman. A reference to "affectionate remembrance" (to EN, 31 Oct 1852) suggests that Mrs Upjohn knew, or perhaps even was related to, the Nusseys. In 1852 they proposed to Ellen that she come and live with them either as some kind of companion/housekeeper, or as an unofficially adopted daughter, on an "all found" basis, and that something would be left to her in their wills. Both Charlotte and Patrick advised caution, and Charlotte put her finger on one of the problems with the arrangement: "I wish the 'future advantage' were more defined" (to EN, 5 Nov 1852?). Charlotte's initial impression of Sarah, formed from a letter, was of "a warm-hearted good-natured woman" with "a sort of vivacity of temperament and feeling" (to EN, 31 Oct 1852). As so often, Charlotte had to revise her opinion. Both Francis and Sarah were invalids, and Sarah's problems with servants were endemic, and probably indicative of her own character, marked as it was by indecision, procrastination, and what Charlotte called "fluctuations" (22 Mar 1853). It is typical of her that when Ellen eventually arrived at Gorleston in May 1853 for a month's visit, Mrs Upjohn was away from home. The stay was abandoned after a fortnight, and Ellen took refuge with her brother Joshua in Oundle. Charlotte wrote (13 June 1853?) to Ellen commiserating with her on having had "a hard time of it and some rough experience," and adding "I wish much to talk with you about these strange, unhappy people at G[orleston]." To cap it all, the house was said to be haunted.

Mary Taylor's opinion of what she called the Upjohns' "impudent proposal" was predictable and trenchant, and her letter ended "Don't go and live with Mrs Clergyman" (to EN, 21 July 1853) Joan Stevens (1972) gives a full account of the Upjohns and the whole affair. The fact that the Upjohns both lived to a ripe old age suggests that Ellen's hasty exit from Gorleston was a lucky escape.

Upperwood House: home of the White family, where Charlotte was governess in 1841. The house was situated up the hill from Woodhouse Grove School, where her parents first met. Photographs show the house to have been modest by comparison with other houses where Charlotte and Anne acted as governess. It was replaced later in the century by Ashdown, a much more imposing building which today is the preparatory division of Woodhouse Grove, and is called Brontë House.

V

Valpy, Richard (1754–1836): author of *Delectus Sententiarum et Historiarum*, a teaching aid bought by Anne in November 1843, probably to coach Edmund Robinson in Latin. Angeline Goreau (ed. *Agnes Grey*, Penguin 1988) states that Anne's notes reveal "a knowledge of the language beyond that of most governesses of the time," for girls were rarely taught Latin. Her purchases during her years with the Robinsons (e.g., a German dictionary and reader) prove she was determined to use her time there for self-education, as well as that of others.

Vandam (no first name given): one of two Flemish ushers at M. Pelet's school in *The Professor*, both heavy and soulless, both treated tyrannically by him (see ch. 11).

Vandenhuten, Jean Baptiste: Flemish pupil at M. Pelet's in *The Professor*, a large and ponderous youth. Crimsworth rescues him from drowning, and his father is brought in rather maladroitly as a deus ex machina to help Crimsworth when he leaves Pelet's school.

Vandenhuten, Mme (no first name given): mother of Jean Baptiste, mentioned in ch. 21 of *The Professor*, where the implication is that she is a fond, somewhat foolish mother.

Vandenhuten, Victor: father of Jean Baptiste. Described as quiet, kind, and sincere, though not excitable. He helps Crimsworth to a job as principal English teacher at a college in Brussels. Warmly approved of, he is, perhaps for this reason, made Dutch rather than Flemish.

Vanderhuten, Jules: moon-faced, stupid, and complacent pupil of William Crimsworth's at M. Pelet's school in *The Professor* (see ch. 7).

Vanderkelkov, Louise: the pupil at Mme Beck's school whose part in the play at Mme Beck's fête (ch. 14) is played by Lucy Snowe when she falls ill, or is claimed to have done so by her "ridiculous mother."

Van Dyck, Sir Anthony (1599–1641): included by Charlotte in a "list of painters whose works I wish to see" (1829), and mentioned in the same year in the story "The Swiss Artist" in "Blackwood's Young Men's Magazine" ("the living portraits of a Vandyke"). A "splendid painting" by him plays its part in the early courtship of Helen Graham by Huntingdon (*Tenant*, v. 1, ch. 17).

He was one of the great portraitists, whose mature work was mainly done in England.

Varens, Adèle: Jane Eyre's pupil at Thornfield Hall, putative illegitimate daughter of Mr Rochester, though he denied it, and took care of her out of affection for her. A charming, coquettish, empty-headed child, whose mind runs on presents and clothes – the usual caricature Frenchwoman, in fact, rendered in a childish miniature.

Varens, Céline: Adèle's mother, and one of Rochester's former mistresses. She is a flattering and false dancer and courtesan, avaricious and shallow. Rochester's cool account of his affair to Adèle's governess (v. 1, ch. 15) is one of the most surprising things in the book even today, and in its time was one of the most shocking.

Varney, Richard: the villain in Scott's novel *Kenilworth*. In a letter of 1 January 1833 to Ellen Nussey Charlotte contrives to condescend to the "characteristic and naïve" expression of Ellen's detestation of Varney's villainy, while showing her own more sophisticated way of talking about character in fiction: "in the delineation of his dark and profoundly artful mind Scott exhibits a wonderful knowledge of human nature as well as surprising skill in embodying his perceptions so as to enable others to become participators in that knowledge."

Vashti: actress whose performance Lucy Snowe witnesses in ch. 23 (which is named after her) of *Villette*. So startling and harrowing is her performance in a play that is not named that Charlotte can only describe its effect in a series of paradoxes: it was "a marvellous sight: a mighty revelation," and at the same time "a spectacle low, horrible, immoral." She thus is given something of the force of a fallen angel. Charlotte notes that in her private life the actress was "not good," and describes her as "a spirit out of Tophet" (a place of destruction).

The chapter is undoubtedly based on the actress Rachel, whom she saw in *Adrienne Lecouvreur* and as Camille in Corneille's *Les Trois Horaces*. She describes the disturbing effect her acting had on her in a series of letters June–November 1851, in one of which (15 Nov 1851) she uses the bullfight image which she also uses in *Villette*. To Ellen Nussey she wrote (24 June 1851): "she made me shudder to the marrow of my bones: in her some fiend has certainly taken up an incarnate home."

Vashti, in the Old Testament book of Esther, refused the commands of her husband, King Ahasuerus, to display her beauty to the guests at his feast. She was banished, and the king decreed "that every man should bear rule in his own house." The significance of Charlotte's choice of name is unclear.

Verdopolis/Verreopolis: *see* Glasstown

Vere, Lord Edwin: a suitor of Georgiana Reed in *Jane Eyre*. Georgiana accuses her sister of spying on her from jealousy and then ruining her prospects with Lord Edwin. This was presumably during Georgiana's season in London when, according to Rochester, she "was much admired for her beauty" (v. 2, ch. 6).

Vicomte (no first or surname given): lover of Céline Varens in *Jane Eyre*. He is preferred to Rochester by Céline, is described as "brainless and vicious" (v. 1, ch. 15), and fights a duel with Rochester in which he is shot in the arm.

Victoria: a goose. See Adelaide.

Victoria, Queen (1819–1901): the accession of the 18-year-old princess was noted in Emily and Anne's 1837 diary paper. Her childhood, surrounded by "wicked" uncles and an ambitious and sexually unwise mother, must surely have fascinated all the young Brontës, echoing their own fevered royal chronicles. The christening of a goose after her is a more ambiguous, but probably loving, tribute. When Charlotte, alone in Brussels, wrote to Emily an account of the Queen's state visit to Belgium she knew she had a receptive audience. She depicts a plump, plain, but (in modern newspaper parlance) fun-loving figure: "The Belgians . . . said she enlivened the sombre court" (1 Oct 1843). When she described Thackeray's deferment to his "Duchesses and Marchionesses" who wanted to go to the races because the Queen would be there, or to a royal "Fancy Ball" (to PB, 7 & 14 June 1851) the tone is more ambiguous: she clearly despised his toadyism. The Queen repaid her interest, finding *Jane Eyre* "intensely interesting" but "melancholy" when she read it with Albert in 1858. She reread it after his death in 1880.

Victoria Theatre: formerly called the Royal Coburg, its foundation-stone was laid by Princess Charlotte's husband Leopold of Saxe-Coburg (later King of the Belgians) in 1816. It was renamed in honor of the Princess Victoria, later becoming popularly known as the Old Vic, dispensing Shakespeare and opera in English, most famously under Lilian Baylis, on the South Bank in London, and becoming the home of the National Theatre in its early years. When it performed a dramatic version of *Jane Eyre* in the first months of 1848 it was at one of its low points: W. S. Williams's account of the theatre was so graphic that Charlotte described it as "*loathsome*." Of the play itself, she anticipated that it would be "woefully exaggerated and painfully vulgarised," and this seems to have been realized by the event: "You must try now to forget entirely what you saw" (to WSW, 5 & 15 Feb 1848).

Villette: Charlotte's last novel was published in late January 1853, having been deferred in order not to coincide with the publication of Mrs Gaskell's *Ruth*. It opens

in the home of Mrs Bretton in the town of Bretton, where the heroine Lucy Snowe
is staying for a visit. The coincidence of surname and place seem to suggest a long-
standing stability and permanence which was not to bless either Lucy or the Brettons
in later life. The visit to Mrs Bretton and her son is enlivened by another visitor, Paulina
Home, a child of great charm who forms an immediate bond with Graham Bretton.
The delightfulness of these first three chapters is in fact a false start. When Lucy returns
home a stormy period begins. From the hints she gives, the reader conjectures she is
nominally taken care of by relatives who are indifferent or positively hostile – thus
ranging Lucy along with Jane Eyre, William Crimsworth, and Caroline Helstone. At
any rate she suffers what she describes as a shipwreck, and becomes the companion
of a difficult woman, Miss Marchmont, whose life has been saddened and soured by
the death of her fiancé. Her death in turn leaves Lucy shaken and poor ("the posses-
sor . . . of fifteen pounds," ch. 5) but eager to sample life outside the sickroom. She
decides on the Continent, and almost sleepwalks to Villette, the capital of Labassecour
(Brussels, capital of Belgium).

On the boat over she becomes acquainted with Ginevra Fanshawe, an empty-headed
and selfish beauty on her way to school in Villette. Lucy obtains employment there,
and it remains the setting for the rest of the novel. Mme Beck's Pensionnat de
Demoiselles is an excellent school, run on generous principles: "easy, liberal, salutary,
and rational" (ch. 8). However, Mme Beck herself rules absolutely, and does so on a
system of spying by which she gains a complete knowledge of her teachers and pupils,
and can when necessary set one off against another. She is also ruthless in getting
rid of unsatisfactory or rebellious elements. She soon promotes Lucy from a domestic role to a teaching one, and Lucy finds satisfaction in the work, though she finds
her pupils almost uniformly antipathetic, and makes generalizations (as Charlotte did)
of a monstrous kind about "Labassecourians."

In her early weeks as a teacher there are several figures at or around the school who
arouse Lucy's interest: Mme Beck herself, with her political skills and her mixture of
insincerity and brutal honesty; M. Paul, her literature teacher – despotic, dramatic,
changeable. She is also much taken with Ginevra Fanshawe, whose superficiality she
recognizes, but whose charm and beauty come to obsess the plain Lucy. "Dr John,"
one of the doctors attending the school, a young man whose physical attractiveness
is balanced by strong and generous principles, also attracts her, and his unwise love
for Ginevra gives her great pain, especially as Ginevra is engaged in an intrigue with
the vapid De Hamal.

The texture of the novel is enriched in these central chapters by a variety of
expedients, one of which, the ghostly nun (who turns out to be De Hamal in drag)
has been generally disliked as giving an inappropriately Gothic feel to the humdrum
pensionnat. Much more successful are Lucy's engagement with cultural or adventurous events: acting in a school play, visiting an art exhibition, attending a play and a
concert, even attempting to make a confession in a Catholic church. All these show
Lucy's mind expanding, her understanding deepening as, probably, Charlotte felt
herself growing intellectually in Brussels. The confession leads to her reunion with
the Brettons, mother and son, the latter of whom turns out to be Dr John. The
relationship between Lucy and him deepens, helped by longed-for letters from him,

and he comes to realize the fatuity behind the beauty of Ginevra. However, with the return of Paulina Home into the story – inevitably under a new name, Paulina de Bassompierre – Lucy realizes that she has been nourishing hopes that can never come to fruition: Graham and Paulina are "natures elect, harmonious and benign" (ch. 37), beings quite remote from angst-ridden, divided, and contradictory natures such as Lucy's.

The interest of the novel now switches to M. Paul Emanuel, where it was always destined to go. Still more important than any plays or concerts in Lucy's personal growth has been the teaching of M. Paul, and the mutual delight they took in the teaching experience – he because he has a pupil who is capable of expanding intellectually and spiritually, unlike the majority of his pupils. Again, and as with most of Lucy's experiences in Villette, Mme Beck plays a malign role. M. Paul is her cousin, has remained faithful to an early love, and is a lynchpin in family relationships. For this reason the course of their love cannot run smoothly. Mme Walravens, another malign figure, and one comparable to the first Mrs Rochester, also plays a part in trying to separate M. Paul and Lucy, and Lucy's apprehension culminates in a hallucinatory scene in the park during a national celebration, where she jumps to the conclusion that M. Paul is to marry his ward Justine Marie. The next day, however, M. Paul worsts Mme Beck in their only real confrontation in the book. He then takes Lucy to show her a school he has set up for her, and which she will open and run while he is away restoring the prosperity of Mme Walraven's estate in Guadaloupe. The novel ends with a storm at sea as he returns to Europe. The reader, at Patrick Brontë's prompting, is allowed to believe that M. Paul arrives safely back in Villette, but Charlotte's original intention had been that he would be said unequivocally to have drowned at sea. Just as Lucy Snowe, originally Frost, had to have a cold name, so she would also have to have a lonely future.

The reception of the book was predominantly admiring, and there was a general feeling that it was a great advance on *Shirley*; the circumstances under which that book had been written were generally known since the publication of the "Memoirs" of her sisters, and the tone of the critical notices was notably softer than those for the earlier books. Among the admirers, Lewes hit the mark on the particular nature of the novel: "Hers is the passionate heart to feel, and the powerful brain to give that feeling shape" (*The Leader*, 12 Feb 1853). *The Spectator* notice rings true on Lucy's brave honesty when it talks of "the heart which cannot obtain its daily bread, and will not make believe that a stone is bread" (12 Feb 1853). The opinions of individuals varied as greatly as always with Charlotte's novels at this time: see the entries on Matthew Arnold and George Eliot. Perhaps the comparative lack of large and exciting incidents accounts for the varied opinions. Certainly it was slow to find its merited place, though today it is generally ranked as one of the three great Brontë novels.

Vincent, Rev. Osman Parke (d. 1885):

clergyman who proposed marriage to Ellen Nussey in 1841. The suit had been proceeding uncertainly since the spring of 1840, and Charlotte for one lost patience with the man: why, she wondered, did he not speak to Ellen herself, instead of "writing sentimental and love-sick letters to *Henry*" (to EN, 20 Nov 1840). She asked in the same letter "is he a knave a humbug, a hypocrite a ninny or noodle?" but concluded in a later letter to Ellen that he was "an ass" (3 Jan 1841). After Ellen's refusal of him in October/November 1841 we hear precious little about him until a contemptuous reference to "Mr V's precious note" (to EN, 26 Nov 1849). He had in the meanwhile married Elizabeth Hale Budd, daughter of an Essex rector, in May 1844 (*Leeds Intelligencer*, 1 June 1844). Possibly she had died, and he was trying to reopen lines of communication to Ellen in the hope that she had changed her mind. He seems to have been the eternal curate, and only got a living of his own in 1872.

Vining, Mr (no first name given): former tutor of Lord Ingram in *Jane Eyre* – described by Blanche as "whey-faced" (v. 2, ch. 2), and daring to fall in love with the girl's governess Miss Wilson. The young Ingrams used their discovery of this to get rid of both of them.

Violet or The Danseuse: a novel of theatrical life and social *mores*, published in 1836 and highly praised by Thackeray (see CBL, v. 2, p. 319 for a full account of the subject matter). Returning the novel to George Smith on Boxing Day 1849 Charlotte had clearly found her Christmas reading "far from pleasing," though it showed "a strange insight into the darker nooks of human nature." The novel was published anonymously.

Virginie (no surname given): one of the rebellious pupils at Mme Beck's school who try to disrupt Lucy Snowe's first lesson in ch. 8 of *Villette*.

Voltaire, François Marie Arouet De (1694–1778): French writer, dramatist, and philosopher, who added "de Voltaire" to his baptismal name. The first book of his much worked upon epic poem on Henri IV and religious tolerance, the *Henriade*, was translated by Charlotte in (surprisingly) August 1830. She shows her knowledge of *Candide* by a reference in *Villette* (ch. 34), but most of the references to him in Brontë writings seem derogatory, for example Lord Macara Lofty's "Voltaire's sneers & insinuations" in "Passing Events" (FN, p. 51), or Branwell's references in his *Halifax Guardian* article "Thomas Bewick" to the "servilely imitated" epics of, among others, Voltaire.

volunteer corps: Cambridge University's volunteer corps was separate from the town's force, and included Patrick Brontë and the future war minister Lord Palmerston. It was formed to meet the threat from the new Emperor Napoleon, and was mainly active in 1804.

Vyner, Mrs: character in G. H. Lewes's *Rose, Blanche and Violet*, criticized by Charlotte as being the product of real-life hatred and, unlike Becky Sharp, a portrait of unshaded villainy without human qualities: "She is a fiend" (to WSW, 1 May 1848). Charlotte avoids this artistic trap in her two portraits of Mme Heger.

W

Wade, Rev. John (?1833–1901): Patrick's successor as perpetual curate, later rector, of Haworth. He had a large family, and built the Wade Wing, which now houses the Library, Bonnell Room, and exhibition room of the Parsonage Museum. He also demolished Grimshaw's church, all but the tower, and built the present one. He was often referred to as "envious Wade" because of his supposed jealousy of his predecessor and his family. Quite possibly he found the burgeoning Brontë tourist industry, with its insatiable curiosity veiled by idolatry, inimical to his work as the village's minister.

Walker, Amelia (?1818–92): schoolfellow of Charlotte's at Roe Head, where already her affectations were remarked on. The connection was resumed when, visiting Mrs Franks at her Huddersfield vicarage in 1836, Charlotte and Anne found members of the Walker family waiting to greet them. The Walkers were a rich Huddersfield family, and they insisted that the two Brontës visit them for the day at Lascelles Hall. This visit went much better than Charlotte expected, but it prompted a long, vividly dramatized picture of Amelia, her affectations and absurdities (to EN, 7 July 1836?), suggesting that Charlotte was thinking of making use of her in an Angrian context. She very reluctantly paid her a longer visit in January 1839. Amelia reappeared in Charlotte's life in 1851. The Walkers were now living in their other home in Torquay after a stay on the Continent, which was perhaps for financial reasons, perhaps for health ones (Amelia's desire to keep their return secret suggests the former). She was by then something of a hypochondriac, but one who didn't let her supposed illnesses interfere with a busy round of genteel social engagements. Charlotte's old suspicion and dislike immediately returned. She is said to be one of the originals of Ginevra Fanshawe in *Villette*.

Walravens, Magloire: grandmother of M. Paul's dead fiancée Justine Marie, who had opposed the match when M. Paul's father failed financially. When she herself met with financial reverses M. Paul came to her aid. She is described in terms from fairy tales or Gothic romance: hunchbacked, dwarfish, her eyes are "malign, unfriendly" and she is covered in jewels – "adorned like a barbarian queen" (ch. 34). She reappears in the carnival scene, but essentially she is in the book as part of Mme Beck's scheme to convince Lucy that M. Paul is beyond her reach.

Walton, Mr (first name unknown): porter at Luddenden Foot station, who defrauded the railway company of some £11. Branwell, his manager, was held responsible, and dismissed.

Walton, Agnes (b. 1820): one of the main objects of William Weightman's affections. She was from Crackenthorpe, near his home town of Appleby, and it was assumed he was intending to marry her, though he flirted with other women, including possibly Anne Brontë. Agnes Walton married a well-to-do farmer, John Horn.

Warner, Warner Howard: Angrian landowner with "property worth the enormous sum of *290000£ a year*!!!" (WPBB, v. 2, p. 382). He is also a sort of local chieftain, with around 12,000 armed men under his control. He is, surprisingly, small, delicately made and soft of voice, and Charlotte in particular has characters referring to him as a "semi-hermaphrodite" (EW, v. 2, pt 1, p. 14) and "womanish in outward form" (ibid, p. 28). This characterization tapers off as Warner proves to be firm in his principles and loyal in his conduct. His enormous wealth makes him one of Zamorna's main and most valued supporters in the civil wars, and he eventually becomes Prime Minister of Angria. He is one of the few consistently honorable men in the Glasstown/Angrian saga.

Warren (no first name given): servant of the Brettons who meets Mr Home's coach in ch. 1 of *Villette*.

Warren, Samuel (1807–77): physician, lawyer, and novelist, one *Blackwood's* contributor that Charlotte didn't care for. His most successful novel, *Ten Thousand a Year*, deals with a draper's assistant, with the Thackerayan name of Tittlebat Titmouse, who inherits a fortune after shady work by lawyers. Much snobbish humor and farcical incident result. "I never liked Warren," Charlotte wrote to Ellen Nussey (8 Dec 1851).

Watsons (no first names given): passengers on "The Vivid" in ch. 6 of *Villette*. They are much appreciated by the stewardess for the value of their tips. They turn out to have "the confidence of conscious wealth in their bearing." The women are youthful and beautiful, the men are "of low stature, plain, fat, and vulgar." Lucy is shocked to find the oldest of the men is newly married to one of the young women.

Watts, Isaac (1674–1748): Nonconformist clergyman whose hymns became staple fare in all British denominations. References to his hymns are frequent throughout the juvenilia and occur in *Shirley* and *Tenant*. Charlotte owned his *Doctrine of the Passions* and Anne received his *The Improvement of the Mind* as a good conduct prize while at Roe Head. His stirring imaginative hymns such as "O God, our help in ages past" and "There is a land of pure delight" clearly spoke directly to the young Brontës, and perhaps influenced their poetry.

See also Wesley

Weekly Chronicle: reviewed *Jane Eyre* with enormous enthusiasm, calling it "true and interesting beyond any other work that has appeared for many years." Charlotte was disconcerted, however, by their hints that the novel could have been written by Mrs Marsh, author of *Emilia Wyndham*, whose novels Charlotte had never read.

Weightman, Rev. William (1814–42): Patrick's curate in Haworth 1839–42.

He was born in Appleby, the son of a brewer, and at Durham University studied for a Licentiate in Theology, which he attained shortly before being made a deacon and taking the curacy in Haworth. He was ordained a year later in the summer of 1840.

He burst on the Haworth scene like a ray of sunshine. He was handsome, engaging, and fun, and the lives of all those at the Parsonage were enriched by his energy and enthusiasm. One gets the impression from Charlotte's letters of a young man giving a performance – perhaps as the archetypal inconstant lover from some eighteenth-century comedy. From the start and throughout he professed devotion to the girl he left at home, Agnes Walton, but quite soon we learn of the girl he treated badly in Swansea, then the girls he had on a string in Keighley – Caroline Dury, the vicar's daughter, and Sarah Sugden, rich and generous with money. His relationship with the daughters of his own vicar was flirtatious, confidential, as if he aimed to entertain them with stories of perpetual lovemaking, if not with the actual thing. He sent them valentines, took them to lectures he was giving in Keighley, even saw to it that they involved themselves in such matters as the Church rates controversy.

Since his indiscriminate hints of being smitten also involved Ellen Nussey, Charlotte spent much time warning her that he was fickle, that what he seemed to promise to one girl he promised to plenty of others besides. She herself was delighted with him, painted his portrait, and also one – presumably under his close direction – of Agnes Walton. Though she found much to criticize about his conduct in Haworth and around, that early glow never entirely faded. She could write quite benevolently about his parody-lover attentions to Anne – "sighing softly – & looking out of the corners of his eyes to win her attention" adding "they are a picture" (to EN, 20 Jan 1842). In her fascination with this vivid performance, she largely ignored his actual work as a clergyman. This was brought home to her when she heard that her favorite Sunday school scholar Susan Bland was ill and thought to be dying. She found that Weightman had been before her to visit the girl, and had sent her port wine. Susan's mother said he was "always good-natured to poor folks," having "a deal of feeling and kind-heartedness about him" (to EN, 29 Sep 1840?). This devotion to duty among the poor never left him, and he sickened of cholera after visiting others similarly and fatally afflicted. He was nursed by Branwell, not the least affected of those in the Parsonage. He was celebrated and then mourned in at least one poem by Anne, if we accept Edward Chitham's persuasive arguments (1991, ch. 6). For the three years of his curacy he had transformed Haworth into a hotbed of gossip, conjecture, flirtation, and fun. Whether or not he aroused love he certainly aroused interest, admiration, and amusement, and was not soon forgotten.

Wellesley, Lord Charles a.k.a. Charles Towns[h]end: younger brother of Zamorna. In the early juvenilia they are a devoted pair, united in adventures and escapades. Charles's unlikeness to his brother soon hardens into irreverence and antagonism, however, so they become the first of the "hostile brothers" in Charlotte's writings. Throughout the early years of the saga there is an odd dichotomy in the presentation of Charles between, on the one hand, his supposed age (10 in "Visits in Verreopolis," EW, v. 1, p. 295) and the mothering of him by many of the fine ladies in Verdopolis, and on the other hand the tone of his commentaries on life there – world-weary, satirical, delighting in showing up pretension and bombast. It is probably best to think of him as a precocious late-teenager.

With this mind-set he inevitably becomes a journalist: he takes little or no part in the major actions of the saga, never has a major love affair (an almost unheard of abstention in Verdopolis) and spends his time jeering at and manipulating the major players. The word "elfish" clings to him in the early stories, but later he becomes something slightly more serious: a precursor of the modern journalist, with his own byline, one whose personality becomes part of the story and the commentary.

From "Passing Events" (1836) onwards he changes his name to Charles Townshend. Possibly the reason for this is that his brother is teetering on the verge of defeat in the civil war and is a hate-figure in both Verdopolis and Angria. This interpretation is strengthened by the fact that the new name seems to coincide with a disguise which he calls "the thorough alteration that had taken place in my own person" so that even members of his own family do not recognize him (FN, p. 53). His new identity also gives him greater freedom to comment on the glittering aristocratic scene which has always had a great fascination for him.

In "Stancliffe's Hotel," written two years after "Passing Events," when the new personality has had time to establish itself, Charles Townsend sums himself up for his readers: "I'm a neat figure, a competent scholar, a popular author, a gentleman and a man of the world" (*The Times* T2 Supplement, 14 Mar 2003, p. 17). One might add a performing flea and a fictional pioneer of a new form of journalism – a rather ugly form at that.

Wellington: Shropshire town in which Patrick served as curate for most of 1809. The area was more industrial than any he had previously known, and provided opportunities for clergymen of an evangelical bent such as himself. He made many friends and acquaintances there, such as William Morgan and John Fennell, and was introduced into the circle of Mary Fletcher, widow of the saintly John. It is fair to say that, though brief, Patrick's time there set the tone and direction of his Christian belief and activities for the rest of his life.

See also Fletcher, Rev. John

Wellington, Duke of (Lord Arthur Wellesley) (1769–1852):

conqueror of Napoleon at Waterloo, subsequently Tory politician. Charlotte chose him as "her" character when the juvenilia sagas were first begun, and he became a character (often a deus ex machina) in the early stories. Her hero worship was doubtless in imitation of her father's: he praises the Duke fulsomely in *The Maid of Killarney* and in letters and other published writings: he is "the most famous, and the greatest of living heroes" ("A Brief Treatise on . . . Baptism"), "the greatest man in the world" (PB to *Leeds Intelligencer*, 27 May 1843), and when he criticizes the actions of the churchwardens in the Bradford area he remarks, somewhat comically, that "this plan of campaigning . . . was not that adopted by Alexander, Caesar, Buonaparte, and Wellington" (PB to *Bradford Observer*, 3 Feb 1842).

Wellington's political career was less than glorious, involving at least as many retreats from entrenched positions as it did victories, but the father, and his eldest daughter and son, never ceased to admire and sing his praises. Seeing him in the flesh at the Chapel Royal, St James's, Charlotte called him "a real grand old man" (to EN, 12 June 1850), and she was moved by Landseer's imaginative picture of him on the field of Waterloo, as she was later by the portrait George Smith sent for her father (which Tabby, perceptively, maintained was a portrait of Patrick Brontë). In her writings every opportunity was taken to pay tribute to him, often in disputes in which the contrary view is put by one person, who is worsted by the Duke's admirer (*The Professor*, ch. 24, *Shirley*, ch. 3, and elsewhere: setting the novel during the Spanish campaign gave her ample opportunity for triumphal partisanship).

The closest any member of the family came to real contact with the Duke was when Patrick wrote to him, as well as to the Master General of the Ordnance, concerning the design and construction of muskets. From the Iron Duke he received a gruff and dismissive reply, written in the third person. He pointed out that he currently held no political office and considered it "his duty to refrain from interfering in the details of duties over which he has no controul." He ended magisterially: "Much Time would be saved if others . . . would follow the Duke's example; and avoid to interfere in matters over which they have no Controul" (LPB, p. 361). The great man, obviously, was not strong in delicacy or human feelings. He would surely have been surprised to learn how large he loomed in the imaginative life of the obscure Yorkshire parsonage and even more surprised that his not very satisfactory sons loomed larger still.

See also Juvenilia, 1. The "Young Men's" play; Juvenilia, 2. War and peace

Wellington, New Zealand:

settlement colonized on the North Island from 1840 onwards. When Mary Taylor arrived in 1845 it had under 3,000 inhabitants, with a thousand or so more in the country around. By the early 1850s the population had doubled, an important factor in Mary's success as a shopkeeper. She owned a house in the town, which she let, and the shop and living quarters which photographs show to be a large undertaking for a fledgling community. The shop was on the corner of

Cuba and Dixon Street, and Cuba Street (the first colonizing ship was the *Cuba*) remains an important thoroughfare today.

See also Taylor, Ellen; Taylor, John; Taylor, William Henry; Taylor, William Waring

Wesley, John (1703–91): charismatic and tireless leader of the Methodist

movement within the Church of England. On his extensive journeys around Britain, focusing particularly on neglected groups such as the industrial working class, he invigorated Protestant Christianity from the inside. He visited Haworth many times, on one occasion exclaiming in his journal: "What has God wrought in the midst of these rough mountains!" He also visited the north of Ireland several times, so Patrick's inclination towards Methodism could have sprung from personal experience of its leader. With his brother Charles (1701–88) he enlivened the act of worship by placing great emphasis on hymn-singing, often to familiar tunes. Enthusiastic Methodist hymn-singing is several times mentioned in the Brontës' writings, often with satirical intent.

Westbourne Place No. 4: George Smith's home during Charlotte and Anne's 1848

visit to London, in the Bayswater/Paddington area. It was then a highly respectable residence, but during Smith's lifetime part of it became a hairdresser's: "you may . . . have your hair cut, curled, singed, and shampooed in the little room in which I read the manuscript of 'Jane Eyre'" (GS, quoted in Barker 1994, p. 939, n. 60). Charlotte and Anne dined there on 9 July 1848, and Charlotte stayed there on her 1849 visit to London.

West-End Hotel, Kilkee, Co. Clare: unpretentious inn with a pretentious name

that Charlotte laughed at when she and Nicholls stayed there on their honeymoon. The splendor of the scenery compensated her for "indoor short-comings" (to Catherine Wooler, 18 July 1854).

Westminster Review: Benthamite review founded by James Mill which was

from 1851 edited by John Chapman, assisted (or perhaps directed) by George Eliot. *Jane Eyre* was very favorably reviewed for it by Lewes, who later reviewed *Villette* admiringly, along with Gaskell's *Ruth*. Charlotte was very interested in an article on the enfranchisement of women in the July 1851 issue, which was by Harriet Taylor, companion and by then wife of John Stuart Mill (who Charlotte believed was the author). She praised its logical treatment and the trenchant tone of many passages, but lamented its omission of such possibilities as "self-sacrificing love and disinterested devotion" in the world (to ECG, 20 Sep 1851).

Weston, Edward: curate of Horton, later vicar of F— and husband of Agnes Grey.

He is clearly Anne's ideal clergyman: attentive and considerate to the poor, uncowed by the gentry, and an animal lover. Particular stress is laid on his simple, forceful style in preaching, and his eagerness to read scriptures with suffering parishioners. The character is hardly vivid, and if, as Gerin (1959, ch. 12) asserts, he is based on William

Weightman, Anne has omitted most of the qualities that endeared him to the Brontës, as well as those that irritated them. We are told on the last page that the marriage produced three children: Edward, Agnes, and Mary.

Wethersfield: sizeable village near Braintree in Essex. Patrick's first curacy was here (October 1806 to January 1809) and for much of each year he deputized for an absentee vicar, Joseph Jowett, a Cambridge professor. Though he was ill-paid, Wethersfield was an attractive and demanding first post, and Patrick spoke of it with affectionate nostalgia – though this was when he was trying to renew his relationship with Mary Burder, his landlady's niece. Nonconformity was strong in the village, which was a wealthy one, and both factors could have brought about the broken engagement between the two: her family was well-off, and Congregationalist.

Wharton, Miss (no first name given): daughter of one of Frances Henri's employers, whose wedding lace Frances repairs (*The Professor*, ch. 21).

Wharton, Mr (no first name given): a college friend of St John Rivers who marries Mary Rivers at the end of *Jane Eyre*.

Wharton, Mrs (no first name given): Frances Henri's employer, who helps her to get a job in the "first English school at Brussels" (*The Professor*, ch. 21).

Wheelhouse, Dr John Bateman (1819–52?): Haworth doctor who attended Branwell and Anne in their last months. Emily refused to see him, but he signed her death certificate. He married the widow of Enoch Thomas, a dipsomaniac publican, and they lived in her house in West Lane. Branwell wrote a vituperative piece of doggerel about him – one of his last poems, the insults strained and silly. It has been suggested that Wheelhouse had angered Branwell by forbidding him alcohol.

Wheelwright family: an English doctor, his wife and daughters, who made the acquaintance of Charlotte and Emily in Brussels in 1842. The reasons for their sojourn there are unclear, though perhaps the large family of daughters (five) and the cost of educating them is the answer. It was the girls' presence among the small contingent of English pupils at the Pensionnat Heger that began the relationship. Their parents Thomas (1786–1861) and Elizabeth (d. 1882) were clearly regarded affectionately by Charlotte, but they were not individualized in her letters. They were subsumed into the generalized happy, energetic, slightly philistine air exuded by the younger members of the family. The three youngest girls, Frances (1831–1913), Sarah Ann (1834–1900), and Julia (1835–42) are remembered for having been taught piano by Emily Brontë in recreation time, so that she did not lose any of her lessons. These were sessions from which the young girls sometimes emerged in tears. Julia died in Brussels, and it may be that the "primitive and wholly inadequate" (Frances's words) sanitation at the Pensionnat was to blame (CBL, v. 1, p. 301). Emily (1829–88), as well as being a strong Christian, was a fine pianist, but this was not due to Emily Brontë, for she never taught her.

The pupil at the Pensionnat who was closest to Charlotte was naturally the eldest, Laetitia Elizabeth (1828–1911), who seems to have resumed contact with Charlotte in 1848, and was responsible for Charlotte's renewed interest in her family, and visits from the famous author when she was in London. Charlotte had a pleasant picture in her mind of the family – "healthy and merry" with "blooming looks and unflagging vivacity" (to Laetitia Wheelwright, 25 Mar 50). The family was thus, for Charlotte, people whom it was pleasant to be with, and a relief from the strain of the more famous men and women she would meet at the Smiths'. They were the subject of one of Charlotte's rather frequent condescending remarks about her nonintellectual friends: "they are of the class, perfectly worthy but in no sort remarkable – to whom I should feel it quite superfluous to introduce Currer Bell; I know they would not understand the author" (to GS, 19 Nov 1849).

Some of the sisters lived to a great age, and spoke to Shorter and Mrs Chadwick, giving the latter many good stories, such as the one (from Frances) that describes Charlotte being attracted to Laetitia when she saw her standing on a stool watching the misbehavior of the Belgian schoolgirls with an expression of contempt and disdain ("It was so English," Charlotte said.)

Whipp, Mrs (no first name given): landlady of David Sweeting in *Shirley*, mentioned in ch. 1.

Whipp, Fanny (1832–66?): niece of Mrs Hudson, with whom Charlotte and Ellen Nussey stayed in Autumn 1839 on their visit to the East Coast. Charlotte later mentioned "romps with little Fanchon" as among her pleasant memories of that stay (to EN, 24 Oct 1839), and the girl is often cited as a possible model for the young Paulina in *Villette*. Fanny inherited two pictures by Charlotte: an uncharacteristic view of Easton House with foreground figures, presumably the Hudsons, and a portrait of Mrs Hudson. Both vanished for a long while, but the second has recently reappeared.

White, Henry Kirke (1785–1806): poet and hymn-writer, remembered today chiefly for the latter (e.g., "Oft in danger, oft in woe"). Byron described him as having "a great deal of cant, which in him was sincere" but also "poesy and genius" (to Robert Charles Dallas, 21 Aug 1811). Like Patrick he was from a humble background, and obtained a sizarship (scholarship) at St John's, Cambridge. He wrote admiringly of Patrick's ability to manage "very genteelly" on an income even smaller than his own. His poetry was admired by Southey. He was said to have died from overwork.

White family: Charlotte was governess to the family of John White (1790–1860?) of Upperwood House, Rawdon, between Leeds and Bradford, from March until Christmas, 1841. After an initially favorable impression of John and his wife Jane (née Robson, 1800–78?), her feelings about them followed a familiar pattern in Charlotte's life, with strong preference for the male of the household: "I like Mr White extremely," she wrote to Ellen Nussey (21 Mar 1841), but she objected to Mrs White's demands on her sewing powers and to her uncertain temper, which involved sudden changes from "the most

familiar terms of equality" to "coarse unladylike" anger (to EN, 4 May 1841?). As usual with Charlotte she began to sniff out lack of gentility: "Well can I believe that Mrs W. has been an exciseman's daughter," she wrote in the same letter, and even Mr White was not exempt from this strong, somewhat ridiculous, attempt to assert a social superiority: "I am convinced also that Mr W's extraction is very low" (ibid).

Gradually, however, she got the children under control, and this improved a relationship that never plumbed the depths of that with the Sidgwicks. Jasper Levens (1834–65?), Sarah Louise (b. 1832?), and the baby Arthur Robson (b. 1840?) were "over-indulged" when she arrived (to EN, 21 Mar 1841?), but by August she could write to Ellen that they were under "*decent* control" (7 Aug 1841). She bought the two eldest books, and was interested later in life to meet Sarah Louise at Oakwell Hall, though the girl had forgotten her (to John White, 18 Sep 1851). By the later months of Charlotte's term as governess she was on good terms with both her employers, and was pleased to be able to consult them concerning her plans to finish her education on the Continent. Patrick wrote to the family while Charlotte and Emily were in Brussels – a letter which assumed the family's agreement with his own Tory politics, mentioned the second Mrs Fennell, and noted that "My daughter, has always spoken well of you, and Mrs White, and your Family" (to John White, 22 Sep 1842). The Whites returned the good opinion, genuinely regretting that they had promised Sarah Louise as a pupil to the Cockhill sisters at Oakwell Hall. Newspaper reports of John White praise him for his piety, hard work, and generosity – "his well-known open heartedness" as the *Intelligencer* puts it (9 May 1857). John White and his family are commemorated by a memorial in Calverley churchyard and a stained-glass window in Rawdon church.

Whitehead, Joseph *see* Redman, Joseph

White Lion, Haworth: one of the main hotels in the village. According to Lock and Dixon, perhaps relying on local tradition, Patrick used to address the Conservative Club at meetings there. It is still flourishing as the Old White Lion.

White Lion, Heptonstall: one of several inns in the Hebden Bridge area patronized by Branwell during his time at Luddenden Foot. It is still standing.

Whiteside, Rev. J. W.: clergyman who conducted Anne's funeral service at Christ Church, Scarborough, before her burial in the churchyard of St Mary's. Appropriately he was a popular local lecturer to mechanics' institutes on literary subjects such as Dr Johnson and Cowper.

Wide Sargasso Sea: novel by Jean Rhys (1966) with Antoinette (Bertha) Cosway Mason as its central character. It is often described as the story of Mr Rochester's first marriage told from his wife's point of view, but in fact most of the long second part of the novel is told by Rochester himself. It is best regarded as an imaginative offshoot of *Jane Eyre* rather than an alternative version of the same events. The novel revived Jean Rhys's reputation, but she never wrote another.

Wilberforce, William (1759–1833): English politician and evangelical philanthropist, leader in the long fight to abolish the slave trade at home and abroad. He was a benefactor to poor evangelically inclined clergymen and ordinands, contributing to Patrick's upkeep while he was at St John's. Later he helped him to obtain justice in the William Nowell affair. Whether he and Patrick met during the latter's Cambridge years is not known, but they could have been brought together later, for example during Wilberforce's stay with Dury, the vicar of Keighley, in July 1827.

Wildfell Hall: an Elizabethan mansion, built of stone, with aggressive-looking cannon-ball decorations and an overgrown and decaying garden. Here Helen Huntingdon takes refuge when she escapes from her husband, living in a few rooms renovated for her by her unacknowledged brother Frederick Lawrence for use in her emergency. The garden is described in detail – once an ambitious creation, and fitting a house of some pretensions, though in poor land. Now it is a tangle of weeds and dying vegetation, mirroring the state of Helen "Graham"'s mind and fortunes: her ambitions for her marriage and the reform of her husband in tatters, her income dependent on the sale of her pictures, and both it and the guardianship of her son dependent on evading the unjust laws of the country. The house itself makes less impression, as Anne is much less interested in place than her sisters, but the visits there of Gilbert Markham and other neighbors illustrate that, *pace* Sherlock Holmes, things that would go unmarked in a large town become, dangerously, the topic of constant interest and comment in a rural district.

Wildman, Abraham (1803–70): Keighley mill worker who supported Patrick in his campaign against the new Poor Law in the 1830s. He was a popular poet, and his sympathies are clear from the titles of such poems as "The Factory Child's Complaint" and "The Negro's Dream." Like many in the area he and his wife suffered frequent losses of young children.

Williams family (John): in July/August 1840 the Parsonage had an overnight visit from a cousin of Maria and Elizabeth Branwell, John Branwell Williams, with his wife and daughter. As usual Charlotte preferred the man of the family, whom she praised in familiar terms: "a frank, sagacious kind of man – very tall and vigorous with a keen active look" (to EN, 14 Aug 1840?). His wife she thought pretentious – "much more noise than work" – and their daughter Eliza was full of "Low-Church" talk which contrasted comically with her "round rosy face and tall, bouncing figure" (ibid). They had been on an extended visit to John Fennell, who was near death.

Williams family (W. S.): though Charlotte met the wife and children of her editor infrequently, and had an oddly antipathetic reaction to most of them, she was perforce involved vicariously with many of them when W. S. Williams consulted or confided in her his family affairs. The letter in which she tries to find words for her unfavorable impression (to EN, 12 June 1850) is not very revealing: she juxtaposes the family's "ease and grace" and "natural gentility" at a ball given by the Smiths with the painful impression they made on her when she called on them at home. She was bewildered that, with nothing she could point to to criticize or censure, she nevertheless felt "inclined to shrink" (ibid) from all except the father and the eldest daughter, Margaret Ellen (1827–81). This last married a painter, Lowes Cato Dickinson, and became the mother of Goldsworthy Lowes Dickinson, writer on philosophical and classical subjects. Two of his other daughters were musical: Fanny (b. 1829?) who became a music teacher, being temperamentally unfitted for public performance, and Ann Catherine (known as Anna, 1845–1924) who became a distinguished professional singer and later teacher at the Royal College of Music (see her entry in *Grove Dictionary of Music and Musicians*, 5th edn) However, she was very young when Charlotte met the family. Anna commented that all her family had voices, in this resembling their friends and near-neighbors the family of Leigh Hunt (see *Bleak House*, ch. 43 where the Skimpoles are modeled on the Hunts). Charlotte was particularly concerned with the daughters whose future might lie in the governessing trade – Fanny and Louisa (Mary Louisa, b. 1833?). Her letter to W. S. Williams of 3 July 1849 is admirably balanced and sensible (granted her hatred of the job) about Louisa's chances of success, cataloguing her advantages ("pleasing exterior (that is always an advantage – children like it –) good sense, obliging disposition," etc) but adding that it is fortunate she has "no prominent master talent to make her miserable by its cravings for exercise by its mutiny under restraint." There is less talk in the letters about the boys, but Charlotte rather reluctantly wrote a letter of introduction to Mrs Gaskell for Frank (William Francis, b. 1831?), who seems to have pleased that lady, and who shortly afterwards emigrated to Australia.

All in all the impression given by the children of W. S. Williams is of a close, happy, and talented group, likely to do well either at a national or a familial level. It seems probable that the reason for Charlotte's doubts lies with their mother (Margaret Eliza, née Hills), and in the nature of things her antipathy was unlikely to surface in her letters to Williams. Before her apprehension of the painful effect that most of the family had on her, her mentions of Mrs Williams, her illnesses, a family bereavement, and so forth, are kind but cool. Afterwards they are confined to casual remembrances, with a note (20 Sep 1850) to the effect that these, when not expressed, are to be understood. Clearly Charlotte shrank from too frequent hypocritical courtesies.

Lacking any specific cause for Charlotte's antipathies, one is driven to the view that she expressed as an almost psychic reaction (such as one of her characters might have) what was her usual reaction when faced with a new family: a preference for the male.

Williams, William Smith (1800–1875):

the "reader" (effectively editor) at Smith, Elder who discovered *Jane Eyre*. Though he later regarded his forced residence in London as resembling, in Charlotte's words, that of a "caged bird" (to WSW, early Sep 1848?), he was in fact born there, and was early apprenticed to the publishing firm of Taylor and Hessey. John Taylor, the head of the firm, was keen to nurture and publish young talent, and he had taken on the young Keats and encouraged him through the trauma of being publicly ridiculed by J. G. Lockhart ("if I die, you must ruin Lockhart," the dying Keats told him). The young Williams was probably among those who said goodbye to the poet in his publishers' office when he set off for Italy on 17 September 1820. The good publishing habits learnt at Taylor and Hessey stayed with Williams during his long drudgery as book-keeper to Hullmandel and Walter, lithographers, and emerged shining when he was rescued from it by George Smith: his nurturing of "Currer Bell" was very like Taylor's nurturing of Keats, and involved much of the same bolstering of a young author's confidence. Williams's friendship with a forward-thinking, rather raffish group (Leigh and Thornton Hunt, Lewes etc) placed him among people to whom *Jane Eyre* was likely to appeal: when even Mrs Gaskell hemmed and hawed about the book, Williams could sense its underpinning of energy and rage, and foresee its wildfire success.

Charlotte, at the beginning of the correspondence, was afraid that he was over-optimistic about the book's prospects, but when he was proved right by reviews and sales he established himself in her mind as reliable and a fine judge. She loved his letters, and made no bones about the pleasure they gave her: "they seem to introduce such light and life to the torpid retirement where we lie like dormice" she wrote (to WSW, 21 Dec 1847). Quite soon Williams and Smith began sending her (and her "brothers") books, and these play a large part in her correspondence with them. Though there was no clear division, she tended to write to Smith about fiction and its authors, with Thackeray looming very large, and to Williams to discuss the nonfiction he sent to her, and the ideas it engendered – Ruskin and Turner, the life of Southey by his son, Humboldt's letters, Goethe (but never, alas, Keats) – and also affairs of the day such as the overthrow of the French monarchy. It seems likely that Williams saw himself as an educator, remedying the narrowness and false gentility of female education at the time, and opening the mind of his greatest literary discovery to the ideas current among educated minds of the time. More study needs to be undertaken of Charlotte's development under the course of reading he provided her with. This ad hoc education only ceased when the relationship between author and publisher became strained at the time of *Villette* (see entry on James Taylor). The saddest of her letters is that in which she bids him not to send any more books: "These courtesies must cease some day – and I would rather give them up than wear them out" (to WSW, 6 Dec 1853). It was the end of a process that had given her long and lively pleasure, and emotional stimulation when it was most needed: being in regular touch with Williams had surely been a major factor in getting her through the dark days of 1848–50.

On a personal level she liked him, admired his taste and discrimination, but found in him none of the force and fire that was possessed by all the men she felt any attraction to. She mentions his "little faults and foibles" (to EN, 2 June 1851), and in general found his mind too theoretical for her taste: he "lives too much in abstractions" (to MT, 4 Sep 1848) and he regarded the world too hopefully, like Emerson – "the world is not yet fit to receive what you and Emerson say" (to WSW, 18 Oct 1848?). She probably detected in him the frustrated writer, one who, even in his congenial work for Smith, Elder, would have preferred to plow his own furrow rather than guide and smooth someone else's. However, the one letter we have of his from the correspondence, on the death of Emily, and presumably kept by Charlotte for that reason, though intelligent in its analysis of the nature of loss and grief, nevertheless has an orotundity of language, a preference for the abstract rather than the vivid word, which suggests an earlier age and does not bespeak the born writer.

Williamson (no first name given): female servant at the Murrays in *Agnes Grey*.

"Willie Ellin": tentative starts of a new novel by Charlotte, written in spring 1853. The material is another reworking of the early chapters of *The Professor*, with relationships that go back to the juvenilia (the warring brothers, one overbearing and sadistic, the other passive and intellectual). Charlotte makes two abortive attempts to begin, the first apparently narrated by the younger brother Willie, the second by something that seems to be "the spirit of the house" which is here called Ellin Balcony. The third attempt is told by an omniscient narrator and has Willie, aged 10, taking refuge in Ellin Balcony from the physically abusive brother, who soon appears shouting threats and demanding Willie be given up to his tender mercies. He is accompanied by a Jewish businessman with "a certain command about him, but it was unmixed with any propensity to oppress." He rescues the boy and insists on Edward, the elder brother, desisting from plans to punish him. He may in the long term have been intended as Willie's savior, but as soon as he is out of the way Willie is whipped in a highly sadistic scene. The fragment ends with his being comforted by a servant girl.

It is possible that this fragment was intended to lead on to the same material as "Emma" was to deal with. However the appearance of Willie Ellin in the latter fragment proves nothing, as Charlotte was extremely uninventive in her use of names.

Wilmot, Annabella (later Lady Lowborough): character in *The Tenant of Wildfell Hall*. She is flirtatious, bold, and unscrupulous, and marries Lowborough for his title and family seat. Though he is besotted by her she soon starts deceiving him with Arthur Huntingdon, with whom for some time she has a regular affair. After she has separated from her husband she is said (ch. 50) to have eloped with another man to the Continent and eventually sunk into "debt, disgrace and misery."

Wilmot, Mr (no first name given): suitor of Helen Huntingdon in *The Tenant of Wildfell Hall* (see ch. 16), described by her as a "worthless old reprobate." He is uncle to Annabella Wilmot.

Wilson, Miss (no first name given): governess to the Ingram children, described in *Jane Eyre* as a "poor sickly thing" (v. 2, ch. 2).
See also Vining, Mr

Wilson, Sir Broadley: one of the "old codgers" at Rosalie Murray's coming out ball in *Agnes Grey* (ch. 9).

Wilson, Jane: minor character in *The Tenant of Wildfell Hall*, whose character is analyzed in ch. 1, where she is credited with a good-looking and elegant exterior which hides an ambition and grasping heart. She insinuates herself into the heart of Frederick Lawrence, and it is only after a warning from Gilbert Markham that he sees through her. Later (ch. 48) she is described as remaining single, and living "in a kind of closefisted, cold, uncomfortable gentility."

Wilson, John ("Christopher North") (1785–1854): one of the most
frequent and admired contributors to *Blackwood's Magazine*. Though he was party to Lockhart's attack on the "Cockney school" of British poets, he was friendly with many of the great Romantic poets (he lived for some years in the Lake District) and an admirer of their works, though his prevailing spirit of contradiction and controversy led him to attack them now and then, to prove his independence. His most popular work was the "Noctes Ambrosianae" (he wrote 39 of the 70 dialogues which appeared in *Blackwood's* under this title). Branwell was aware when he wrote to the magazine on 7 December 1835 that Wilson had been for some years in effect editor, but he was doubtless sincere in talking about the "poetry of language" and the "divine flights in that visionary region of imagination" of Wilson's contributions to the magazine. Branwell's letters were considered as the products of a madman, and were not answered. Wilson was elected, through political jobbery, to the Professorship of Moral Philosophy at Edinburgh University, proving notably inadequate even by the standards of the time. His literary reputation has not lasted well, but his humor and his literary tastes were vital in the self-education of the young Brontës.

Wilson, Mary Ann: a favorite schoolfellow of Jane Eyre at Lowood, described as
shrewd, witty, and original. Jane turns to her during Helen Burns's illness.

Wilson, Mrs (no first name given): mother of Jane, Richard, and Robert Wilson
in *The Tenant of Wildfell Hall*, a widow and a "narrow-minded, tattling old gossip" (ch. 1).

Wilson, Mr (no first name given): an English teacher whose failure to arrive
precipitates Lucy Snowe into teaching the "second division" class in *Villette* (ch. 8).

Wilson, Richard: brother of Jane in *The Tenant of Wildfell Hall*. He is a scholarly,
gentle man whose gradual notice of Mary Millward and eventual marriage to her is noticed in several passages of quiet charm. He eventually succeeds his father-in-law as Vicar of Lindenhope.

Wilson, Robert: brother of Jane and Richard, described in ch. 1 of *The Tenant
of Wildfell Hall* as a "rough countrified farmer." His sister, in her frigid gentility, tries to ignore his existence.

Wilson, Rev William Carus (1791–1859): wealthy clergyman, ordained in
1816 (after having earlier been refused ordination because of "Calvinist" tendencies), the founder of the Clergy Daughters' School, situated first at Cowan Bridge, later at

Casterton (and still there as Casterton School). He was, in many of his aspects, the original of Mr Brocklehurst in *Jane Eyre*. The school undoubtedly answered to a great need, both educating and where possible finding posts as teachers or governesses for the daughters of clergymen. Wilson was clearly sharp-eyed and intelligent in identifying spheres for action, as in his later concern for British and foreign soldiers, and for the education of servants. His wealth, and the tenacity of his character, meant that he was generally to be found when evangelical causes were being promoted in the North of England. The outlines of a case for him can be found in Wroot's *Persons and Places* (1935), where an obituary of him by the then Bishop of Rochester speaks of him as "the father of the cheap religious literature of the day" and its "blessed results," and sums up his character as "remarkable for energy and a moral courage that was sometimes sublime, a most singular forgetfulness of self, and the deepest humility." The reason we are surprised by this is attributable to Charlotte's Brontë's great novel.

There are many grounds for thinking that Charlotte accurately portrayed at least aspects of his character and practice. The portrait of the school and its patron was widely recognized on the novel's first publication. Charlotte herself joyfully records seeing a clergyman reading the novel, naming the school and the originals of Brocklehurst and Miss Temple, and saying the former "deserved the chastisement he had got" (to WSW, 4 Jan 1848). Carus Wilson's own writings for children, with their emphasis on death, often by means such as hanging (with illustrations), usually for some trivial fault and followed by eternal damnation, speak strongly of a perverted religion. A fairly minor point in the picture of Brocklehurst, his interference in all matters of the running of the school, including matters best left to the staff, is confirmed by a letter in Wroot, in which Wilson complacently remarks that "It was often said of me that I had eyes in every part of me," and congratulates himself on the "apparently little, but really important matters" that he would take up, calling this "one of the chief services I rendered to the school" (Wroot, 1935, p. 43).

That Charlotte saw with the eye of childhood, and with the passionate vision that was always part of her nature, is not to be denied. But a caricature such as she produced may often see more clearly certain dominant aspects that a balanced portrayal may refine away. Dorothea Beale's testimony as to the atmosphere at the Clergy Daughters' School tells strongly against him too. There is good evidence that his religion was hell-obsessed, and that he believed children should be frightened into piety and bullied into conformity. In spite of the Bishop of Rochester one wouldn't bet too heavily on his humility either. Though he was not a teacher, Brocklehurst ranks high among fictional characters seen, and seen through, from a school desk.

See also Beale, Dorothea

Wilson, Dr William James (d. 1855): notable Manchester surgeon, specialist in eye diseases. When Charlotte and Emily went on a "pilgrimage" to "search out an operator" (to EN, 9 Aug 1846) on their nearly blind father, Wilson was the man they found, and since he could only tell if the cataract was ready for removal by seeing Patrick in person, Charlotte soon returned with her father. The cataract was

"ripe" and the operation was successful. Wilson was helpful, recommending lodgings, and his fee was very reasonable. Charlotte only complained that he gave them little information beyond generalized assurances. He was by birth a Leeds man, and his obituary in the *Intelligencer* claimed that "he knew not what professional jealousy was," and that he was "Vir integer, scelerisque purus" (an upright man, and free from wickedness).

Wimperis, Edmund Morison (1835–1900): wood-engraver and printer, who in 1872 was commissioned to illustrate the first collected edition of the Brontë novels with engravings based on the localities said to have inspired their settings. He was aided in his quest by Ellen Nussey. The *Dictionary of National Biography* is sniffy about his work, calling his watercolors "neat and finished, but somewhat characterless and old-fashioned in technique." It also points to his lack of success with figures, a point borne out by his illustrations, where houses and landscapes predominate and figures are rare and secondary. There is a fine moorland scene by him in the Leeds City Art Gallery collection.

Winkworth, Catherine (1827–78) and Susannah (1820–84): sisters, daughters of a Manchester silk manufacturer, and friends and correspondents of Mrs Gaskell. They had lived and studied in Dresden, and specialized in translation, Catherine of hymns, both together of the lives of the historian Niebuhr and the publishers Perthes. Mrs Gaskell thought, or pretended to think, that Susannah was setting her cap at her husband William, and asked another friend "*Can't* you marry her to Mr Forster; then I *cd* die in peace feeling that my husband was in safety" (Gaskell, *Letters*, 1966, p. 190). Charlotte met the sisters in spring 1853, when they sang Scottish ballads for her, and again in 1854 when Catherine had a long, not entirely serious talk to her about marriage. Charlotte was touched when she received a letter from Catherine on her honeymoon. The pair were among the most intellectual women whom Charlotte made the acquaintance of.

Winterbotham, Rev. John: Baptist minister of the West Lane Baptist Chapel, who co-operated with Patrick in many of his projects in the village, but was his vitriolic opponent on such topics as Church rates and the establishment of the Church of England. Patrick's put-downs of him in the two Leeds newspapers were lordly, but perhaps as likely to win him sympathizers as they were to do him harm: "His education has not been liberal, nor his opportunities for the expansion of his mind favourable. . . . when he can write as a scholar, and feel as a Christian and a gentleman, I may hold a literary controversy with him, but not till then" (PB to *Leeds Intelligencer*, 8 Feb 1834). He later resigned his post and took up a living in Canada.

Wise, Thomas James (1859–1937): the Brontës do not figure largely in accounts of the career of Thomas J Wise, probably because he is interesting as a forger, rather than as a dodgy dealer in things literary, and it is in the latter capacity that he figures in the Brontë story. Wise acquired the large Brontë holdings of Ellen Nussey and Arthur

Bell Nicholls by various means, and distributed them through the world, often bound together in indefensible ways designed with a view to profit rather than on any other more scholarly principles. Ellen soon bitterly regretted her connection, through Shorter, with Wise, but there is no evidence that Nicholls felt anything but a vague distrust of him, and he kept up his connection with Shorter, whom he clearly liked.

Wise used literary societies, then something of a vogue, to make contacts with scholars and potential customers. He was involved in Brontë Society matters almost from the first, and fed many of his false stories of how he acquired manuscripts through the Society, of which he became President, briefly, in 1926. The Wise and Symington edition of the Brontë letters was being put together, with help from the much more expert C. W. Hatfield, in the 1930s, and some of its deficiencies may have sprung from the fact that exactly at this time Wise was being exposed for the frauds he had perpetrated on the literary world of Britain, in particular a fake edition of E. B. Browning's *Sonnets from the Portuguese*. He was a crook and a bully, and he died in disgrace.

Wiseman, Cardinal Nicholas Patrick Stephen (1802–65): Archbishop of Westminster from 1850, when he was also made a Cardinal. Charlotte went to hear him speak to the St Vincent de Paul Society, and her account in a letter to Patrick is vitriolic, if extremely vivid: "He came swimming into the room smiling, simpering, and bowing like a fat old lady . . . The Cardinal spoke in a smooth whining manner, just like a canting Methodist preacher" and so on (to PB, 17 June 1851), including a rather unwise comparison between his figure and that of Patrick's friend William Morgan. Jan Jedrzejewski makes the case that Charlotte's presentation of Catholics and Catholicism in the novels is more nuanced than is generally believed, and even in real life her prejudice did not prevent her taking a balanced view of many Catholics past and present (BST, v. 25, pt 2, Oct 2000). Wiseman, however, she could not stomach.

Wood, Alice: the young orphan girl, "teachable and handy" (v. 3, ch. 5) and chosen by Rosamond Oliver, who is Jane Eyre's servant in the schoolhouse in Morton.

Wood families: Haworth had a number of notable people called Wood, of whom the best-known to the young Brontës were the following: (1) William Wood, the carpenter who made furniture and coffins for the family, and frames for the young Brontës' pictures, being paid by them in drawings. (2) His wife Sarah, who left a vivid picture of Emily "scribblin' away on bits o' paper" in the kitchen while waiting for the bread to bake or the kettle to boil. She was an occasional helper at the Parsonage. (3) Susannah, Tabby Aykroyd's sister, with whom she went to live in 1839, returning to the Parsonage probably in the first half of 1843.

Wood, James (1760–1839): one of Patrick's tutors at St John's College, Cambridge, allotted to him on 1 October 1802, the day he was entered on the register. He specialized in mathematics, and later became Master of the College from 1815 until his death, and Vice-Chancellor of the University. Since he was born into a Lancashire weaving family and was, like Patrick, supported by a college scholarship, he is a prime

example of St John's success in discovering men of humble origins with an aptitude for academia.

Wood, Mark: a consumptive laborer in Horton in *Agnes Grey*, also known (presumably by a mistake of Anne's) as "Jem" (ch. 11). Treatment of this dying man is a sort of touchstone, like that of Nancy Brown. The testimonies of him and his wife to the goodness and patience of Mr Weston predispose Agnes Grey in his favor.

Wood, Mr: the clergyman who would have married Jane Eyre and Rochester in Hay Church if the ceremony had not been interrupted (v. 2, ch. 11).

Woodhouse Grove School: school at Apperley Bridge, between Leeds and Bradford, founded in 1812. Its first headmaster was John Fennell, Patrick's friend from Wellington days, and when he asked Patrick to be the external examiner in "Classical Learning" he set in train the events that united his friend with his niece by marriage, Maria Branwell.

The school, for the sons of the Methodist clergy, was housed in a substantial house of the previous century. Maria had come to help her aunt with the domestic side of the operation. The early years of the school (like those of the Clergy Daughters' School, which it strongly resembled) were rocky. One has an impression of physical cold, dubious hygiene, poor food, and, after Fennell's departure, sheer physical cruelty. Fennell himself, judging by his account of the boys begging for an hour more of prayer in addition to their already unconscionably long allotment of time for it, seems to have been a naive and impractical man. As the Methodists began the process of making a clear break with the Anglican Church, Fennell, preferring to remain an Anglican, became unacceptable as head and was ousted.

The school still stands, operates successfully, and still has the kernel of the Georgian house Patrick and Maria knew, as well as the barn and stables of the old establishment.

Wooler family: of the large collection of Margaret Wooler's siblings the one with whom Charlotte had most to do was probably the sister she called Catherine, Katherine Harriet (1796–1884). Charlotte thought that, unlike Mme Heger, who possessed a similar degree of cultivation, she was "soured" by spinsterhood (to EN, May 1842) and she criticized the falsity and verbiage of one of her letters to Ellen as "palaver" (to EN, 1 Sep 1851). Eliza (b. 1808), though much younger than Katherine, took over the running of the school, now at Dewsbury Moor, but did not make a go of it. Charlotte tried to procure pupils for her, but in vain. For Marianne (1802–43) see Allbutt, Marianne. Susan (1800–72) like Marianne was married, and the company of her and her husband, the Rev. Edward Nicoll Carter, was welcome to Charlotte at Stonegappe. Carter was curate-in-charge at Lothersdale, and Charlotte came to have "quite a regard" for the family, though she takes care to add: "At home I should not care for them, but here they are friends" (to EJB, 8 June 1839). They were a relief from the Sidgwicks, obviously, but Charlotte is usually careful to make clear her lack of enthusiasm when talking about the lesser Woolers. She felt some sympathy for Thomas (1803–95) who suffered from lack of self-confidence and hypochondria, and who seems to have emigrated to America – an odd choice. Dr William Moore Wooler (1795–1873) was a doctor, but he was enabled to retire early, possibly due to the comfortable wealth of the family. His first wife was a sister of the Rev. Thomas Allbutt, but she died after only five years of marriage, in 1832. He married Anne Medley in 1845. In his retirement he dabbled in writing. He contacted Charlotte in 1853, wishing to consult the famous author on his own prospects as a writer, but she gave him a "dissuasive" reply and was amused that he assumed she was progressive in her ideas, presumably like himself (to MW, 13 Apr 1853). He had already published *The Physical Causes of Moral Sadness* (1840), and went on to give the world five hundred pages on *The Physiology of Education*. How much he lost on these works is unknown.

Wooler, Margaret (1792–1885): the headmistress at Roe Head, where Charlotte was first a pupil and later a teacher. She was the daughter of a prosperous maltster and part of a large family with strong and lasting bonds. Charlotte's time as pupil at the school was unusually happy: there was a small core of other pupils, among whom she found two lifelong friends, and Miss Wooler was cultivated, something of a linguist, and presented an attractive front to her pupils, with her beautiful voice and her story-telling abilities, exercised especially during the evening, when she would walk up and down the large rooms of the house with favored pupils around her to converse with. The syllabus of the school seems conventional, but it was broader than that of most good boys' schools of the time, where classics dominated. Margaret Wooler seems to have been not the flamboyant, personality-impressing kind of teacher, but genuinely one of those for whom "education is a leading out" (Muriel Spark, *The Prime of Miss Jean Brodie*, 1961, where Miss Brodie is a poor example of her principle). Her personality was retiring, quietly impressive, and her moral judgment was something that Charlotte would always want to take into consideration.

Later on the relationship went through some bad patches, notably when Charlotte was teaching at Roe Head and was herself going through crises both religious and personal. She felt a lack of sympathy in Miss Wooler, began to find her commonplace and conventional, and she quarreled with her over Anne's illness. Later still Charlotte would have no truck with her old headmistress's doubts about *Jane Eyre*, taking offense particularly at her "earnest assurance that in spite of all I had gone and done in the writing line – I still retained a place in her esteem" (to EN, 16 Feb 1850?). She wrote back a tart response which put her in her place: "I have ever observed that it is to the coarse-minded alone – 'Jane Eyre' is coarse," claiming this to be a quote from another woman (to MW, 14 Feb 1850).

The relationship survived. Soon Charlotte was claiming that Miss Wooler improved with time, like good wine and she paid visits to the Parsonage, where she was much liked. She advised Charlotte during her troubled courtship by Mr Nicholls, and gave her away at her wedding when Patrick changed his mind about doing it. Charlotte visited her at Hornsea and worried that she was too solitary (though this could have been a cherished luxury for one from a large, close family who had also kept a school). Patrick described her to Mrs Gaskell as "a clever, decent and motherly woman"

(20 June 1855), and her nephew Thomas Clifford Allbutt described her more vividly as "a keen-witted, ironical, and very independent Yorkshire woman." If her personal characteristics do not emerge very sharply from Charlotte's letters, it is probably because she was so well-known to her main correspondent that her character needed no elaboration between them.

She lived to a great age, and helped not only Charlotte's first biographer, but also her second, Wemyss Reid, with their books.

"Wool is Rising, The": substantial manuscript written by Branwell in May–June 1834. The story is often referred to by biographers and critics because it contains a first attempt at the "hostile brothers" theme that comes into "Ashworth," *The Professor*, and "Willie Ellin." It here occupies a minor place, mainly in chs 3 and 5, and is a pale foretaste of the hatred and violence the subject had accrued by the time Charlotte's first novel was written. Edward Percy, the elder brother, has the principal place in this story. He is a chip off the Northangerland block, steaming with arrogance, acquisitiveness, and aggression. The story ends with Edward's marriage to Princess Maria of Sneaky's Land. William Percy plays little part in it.

The importance of "The Wool is Rising" is just as much its crucial position in the story of the Brontës' African kingdom, at the point where interest switches from Glasstown to Angria. We begin with the parliamentary debates by which Zamorna, after his victories in the War of Encroachment, lays claim to "the provinces of Angria, Calabar and Northangerland, and Gordon, to be yielded up to me unconditionally and immediately" (early draft, WPBB, v. 2, p. 20). In ch. 6 we have a sketch of Angria and its population, the latter not unlike the popular idea of Yorkshiremen: "Bold, rough, hardy Old Glasstowners, stern and unsophisticated in their character, ardent and warlike in temperament, and proud and independent in principle." (WPBB, v. 2, p. 66). By the time the story ends Zamorna has collected round him the nucleus of an Angrian government, enjoys the adoration of the populace of Angria and Glasstown as a whole, and is becoming bloated with the arrogance of power. One minor joy in the story is Branwell's picture of himself as a put-upon color grinder in the studio of De Lisle, the artist. The Brontë family may have begun its connection with the painter William Robinson about this time.

Woolven, ?Thomas: railwayman who is said by Leyland to have seen Branwell and been impressed by him at Tom Spring's Castle Tavern in Holborn. But on the whole the balance of probability is against Branwell having made a London visit, so the evidence is unconvincing (though invention was not in Leyland's line as a rule). Again, he is said to have been employed on the Manchester–Leeds railway project, and even to have worked with Branwell at Luddenden Foot. Barker (1994) is skeptical about this, but a Woolven does surface later in an interesting context. A Thomas Woolven absconded from his post with the Oxford and Worcester railway, having cashed £221 6s 4d in checks, and taking with him, probably to Liverpool, his wife, children, and furniture (*Leeds Intelligencer*, 12 May 1860). The name is not a common one, so it seems possible that this could be the man.

"Word to the 'Quarterly', A": Charlotte wrote this intended Preface to *Shirley* as a reply to Elizabeth Rigby's review of *Jane Eyre* and other novels in the *Quarterly*. The "word" aroused alarm and opposition both in W. S. Williams and George Smith and, under protest, Charlotte withdrew it but declined to replace it with another preface. Her publishers were surely right: the heavy chaffing of the reply was the last way to protest against the reactionary opinions and random insinuations of Rigby's long piece. Charlotte's only sharply made point came too late, in a note at the end of the "letter": "just turn out and be a governess yourself for a couple of years: the experiment would do you good: a little irksome toil – a little unpitied suffering – two years of uncheered solitude might perhaps teach you that to be callous, harsh and unsympathizing is not to be firm, superior and magnanimous" (CBL, v. 2, pp. 244–5). Where the aim of all the rest of the reply shows uncertainty of aim, this postscript hit the target.

Wordsworth, William (1770–1850): the greatest English poet of the Brontës' time, admired, quoted by them, and his influence digested. His aim to simplify poetic language to bring it closer to "language really used by men" surely affected Emily's practice of using simple language and investing it with great emotional force (e.g., in "Cold in the Earth"). Branwell wrote him a very unwise letter, calling him a "divinity of the mind" and using abuse of other poets of the time ("there is not a *writing* poet worth a sixpence") to suggest, rather ludicrously, that "the field must be open if a better man can step forward" (to WW, 10 Jan 1837). Wordsworth kept the letter but did not reply, being disgusted by it. Perhaps the best tribute to Wordsworth and his effect on the minds of Victorian writers is in *The Professor*, ch. 25, where Charlotte uses Wordsworth and his "deep, serene and sober mind" to in a sense "Anglicize" Frances Henri.

Wright, Martha (1792–1883): Haworth woman who nursed Maria Brontë during her last illness in 1821. She was dismissed by Patrick, and this dismissal had long-lasting consequences when she talked to Mrs Gaskell, who was searching for material for the *Life*. Wright got her own back on Patrick by telling her stories which suggested eccentricity or worse, including cutting up a too showy dress of Maria's (while she was on her deathbed?), burning the children's shoes, and so on. The story that he denied them meat in their diet was particularly damaging to him, suggesting as it did to the Victorian mind that he thus weakened their constitutions. At this time Wright was living in Burnley, and was introduced to Mrs Gaskell through Lady Kay-Shuttleworth. She later returned to Haworth, living, like so many of those known to the short-lived Brontë children, to a ripe old age. See Ann Dinsdale, "Mrs Brontë's Nurse" (BS, v. 30, pt 2, Nov. 2005).

Wuthering Heights: published December 1847, it was reprinted with amendments by Charlotte in 1850. It is the latter text that was used for almost all reprints until the Penguin English Library edition of 1965, edited by David Daiches. Emily's story of two generations of the Earnshaw and Linton families begins close to its end: Mr

Lockwood, the new tenant of the Linton home of Thrushcross Grange, walks across the moors to see his landlord Heathcliff at Wuthering Heights. He records Heathcliff's swarthy complexion and his air of being the social superior of the average Yorkshire farmer. Lockwood sees himself as being a misanthrope, after an unsuccessful love affair, but next day he returns to the Heights, braving a reception that is positively hostile. He makes a series of mistakes about the inhabitants of the farm and their way of life that borders on the comic, and then is forced by snow to beg a room for the night, where he has a dream about an endless sermon on minutely differentiated sins, and then a visitation from the ghost of Catherine Earnshaw/Linton, a fragment of whose diary he had read before going to sleep. When he returns to the Grange and falls sick his housekeeper, Ellen (Nelly) Dean, tells him the story of Heathcliff and Catherine.

Heathcliff arrives at the Heights in 1771 as a cuckoo in the nest, having been literally picked up as a waif and stray (why is never entered into) by Mr Earnshaw while on a visit to Liverpool. Discord is the immediate result: he arouses the jealousy of the only son Hindley by his closeness both to Mr Earnshaw and to the daughter of the house Catherine. The two young people develop a bond which is closer than any family or sexual bond, and which is summed up by Cathy's declaration "Nelly, I *am* Heathcliff." When Hindley succeeds to the property he reduces Heathcliff to the level of farm laborer and treats him brutally. This only strengthens the bond.

However, on their wanderings together on the moor Cathy is attacked outside Thrushcross Grange by the Lintons' dog, and has to convalesce there, arousing the admiration of the son of the house, Edgar. The Lintons are the first family in the neighborhood, and Catherine is in a sense seduced by their greater wealth and status. When she returns to the Heights she sees marriage to Heathcliff as impossible, something which would "degrade" her. When he overhears her telling Nelly this, Heathcliff disappears from the area, and the story, for three years, and when he returns Cathy has been in a loving but tame marriage with Edgar Linton for six months.

The returned Heathcliff has bettered himself socially and financially, and has changed psychologically: his dignified manner is belied by the "half-civilised ferocity" that lurks behind "eyes full of black fire" (ch. 10). He entangles the drunken widower Hindley in gambling debts, wins the heart of Edgar's sister Isabella, in spite of hardly masking his contempt for her, and regains Cathy's affection while at the same time stirring up a latent scorn for her mild husband. She is pregnant, and the affair proceeds, becoming increasingly passionate, until she temporarily loses her reason and dies giving birth to the young Cathy. Heathcliff meanwhile has married Isabella and driven her off through ill-treatment. She is already pregnant and has a son, Linton Heathcliff, whom she brings up in the south of England. The story is to be resolved through this second generation.

Twelve years pass and Isabella dies. Her son, weak and vicious, is brought to Yorkshire by Edgar, and stays at the Grange just long enough to arouse the young Catherine's interest. Heathcliff then claims him through his undoubted rights as a father (something Anne deals with more centrally in *Tenant of Wildfell Hall*). As Edgar moves towards death Heathcliff matures his plans. The younger Cathy, her father's heir, is virtually kidnapped and married off to the repellent Linton. On Edgar's death

Thrushcross Grange is inherited by her, but passes by right to her husband. All the young people including Hindley's son Hareton, are now in Heathcliff's power. When Linton approaches death Heathcliff does not even bother to summon a doctor. He is now in the Lintons' former position of first gentleman of the neighborhood, and the largest landowner to boot.

The story now having reached the point at which we entered it in ch. 1, it shifts forwards nine months. Casually, almost by accident, Lockwood returns to the neighborhood, and hears from Nelly Dean the events of the intervening period. At the height of his power, when his "revenge" is attainable, Heathcliff's iron grip loosens. He is unmanned by the burgeoning love of Hareton (whom he has tried to degrade as Hindley degraded him) and the younger Cathy. He sees in them a mirror of his early love for Cathy's mother, and hers for him. He cannot eat or rest, anxious only for a reunion with her spirit. When he does die, with a look of exultation on his face, he is buried beside Catherine and Edgar. Lockwood visits the Heights, overhears a charming scene between the two young lovers, who are about to move to the Grange, then walks to the three graves on the moors, where he senses, or imagines, a conclusion of peace and harmony to the extraordinary events of the novel.

The book shocked many of its first readers, though several critics showed an appreciation of its power and originality and the grandeur of its conception. Many of the early encomia came from poets – Sydney Dobell, Matthew Arnold (who echoed its haunting conclusion in his poem "Haworth Churchyard"), and Swinburne.

Wuthering Heights: in the novel which bears its name Wuthering Heights is a
farmhouse set just below the summit of high moorlands. Externally it has a stone doorway, elaborately carved, a garden with straggling bushes, windows that are narrow and deep-set, and extensive farm buildings serving a variety of purposes. Internally the main room, known as "the house," stretches up to the roof, its "entire anatomy" lying bare except where a wooden frame laden with joints of meat conceal it. This large, high room is furnished with a dresser laden with pewter dishes, and commonplace furniture such as high-backed chairs and a table. The furniture, we may note, is "nothing extraordinary" and might be owned by any Northern farmer, whereas the house itself is decidedly above average in its pretensions.

This large room is the center of farm and family life. Further into the ground floor of the house, this part three stories high, there is a kitchen, at least one other room, and beneath them cellars. Above, reached by a probably outdoor staircase or an indoor ladder, there are three or four bedrooms on the first floor, with storage and more bedrooms (for the servants, and for Heathcliff and Hareton when they are reduced to laborer status). In many ways this house conforms to the main characteristics of "the Halifax house," which Pevsner calls "the houses of moderate size but swagger detail" which abounded in the Halifax area and the West Riding generally (Pevsner, *Yorkshire: the West Riding* in the Buildings of England series, p. 38).

But what seems clear on investigation is that Emily's farm is not based on any one house that we know about: Top Withens is much too modest, but its geographical position is comparable; High Sunderland Hall is too grand, but it contributes its sculptured gate (imperfectly remembered by Emily, or altered for her own purposes); Sowdens contributes its initials and date (the former spelt out as Hareton Earnshaw), and so on. When they reread the novel readers steeped in Brontë biography will notice details that ally the house to the Parsonage: the outside staircase, the straggling fruit bushes, the cellar for drink, the barn with windows. Emily saw, we may conjecture, many of the houses that Pevsner mentions as "Halifax houses," including Oakwell and East Riddlesden halls. Wuthering Heights is more modest than these, but it has its grand entrance (the "swagger detail" that Pevsner mentions), its main room resembles a banqueting hall, with suggestions of generations of warm hospitality, and it has outbuildings that emphasize that this is, after all, a prosperous farm, with a multitude of activities going on. If we take this house in conjunction with Thrushcross Grange we can understand Everard Flintoff, the best writer on the subject, when he suggests that "It is as though the whole landscape of Yorkshire has . . . been miniaturised" and that the landscape and the houses on it are "brought together within a small compass to form a microcosm of England, or perhaps Yorkshire, as a whole" ("The Geography of Wuthering Heights," reprinted in BS, v. 31, pt 1, 2006).

Wynn, Mr (no first name given): one of the Briarfield magistrates in *Shirley*.

Wynn, Sam: a solid, heavy young man, who has designs on Shirley's hand and her fortune. He tries to make clumsy advances during the Sunday school feast (ch. 17), and later his father proposes "in form" for him – a proposal favored by Mr Sympson. The young man has in any case no chance, but his character is most searchingly revealed by the episode in which his "bruised and beaten" pointer Phoebe bites Shirley, which leads her to fear she might die of hydrophobia. Thus cruelty to animals is added to the other charges (profligacy, coarseness, vulgarity) which Shirley details in ch. 27.

Wynn, The Misses (no first names given): two daughters of Mr Wynn, one fair and one dark, who have been mentioned as possible wives for Robert Moore (ch. 2).

Y

York: a favorite place of the Brontës, due to Anne and Branwell's visits during their time at Thorp Green. Mrs Robinson subscribed to a circulating library there, and it seems likely that during their time of favor in the household they visited the city frequently with the family. Anne bought books and music there, and Branwell established a connection with Henry Bellaby, who ran the library and bookshop and published the *Yorkshire Gazette*, which printed Branwell's poems. No doubt during those visits Anne conceived her great love of the Minster, which led, after her resignation from Thorp Green, to a short expedition she and Emily paid to York in June–July 1845 – "our first long journey by ourselves together" as Emily rather touchingly calls it. Later Charlotte, Ellen Nussey, and Anne broke their journey there on the way to Anne's chosen dying-place of Scarborough. Charlotte in her cash-book identifies things to be bought there as "Bonnet. Corsets, Stockings black silk. Dress. Gloves. Ribbon for neck" but commented in a letter to Ellen what a "dreary mockery" talk of such purchases seemed (12 & 14 May 1849?). Anne's pleasure at seeing the Minster again is movingly recorded by Ellen.

York was also visited by Patrick for the York Assizes, where the Beaver forgery case was tried in March 1843, and where Branwell would have been taken to jail if his debts had not been settled in 1846. To some it was synonymous with institutions for the insane such as housed George Nussey for many years. As early as 1812 Maria wrote to Patrick "Mr Fennell said you were certainly *mazed*, and talked of sending you to York etc" (18 Sep 1812).

York and North Midland Railway Company: one of the most prized lines of George Hudson, the railway pioneer and financier, known as the "railway king." The line was invested in by Aunt Branwell at the height of the railways boom. When the sisters inherited their legacies from her, Emily on their behalf continued with the investment, "reading every paragraph & every advertisement in the news-papers that related to rail-roads" (CB to MW, 23 Apr 1845). Charlotte was nervous, with reason, when the boom showed signs of having peaked, but this particular line for a time resisted the downward trend. The year 1849 was crucial in Hudson's enterprising if fraudulent career, and it is then that Charlotte started expressing serious doubts and realizing the extent of her likely losses on "one of Mr. Hudson's pet lines" which "had the full benefit of his peculiar management – or *mis*-management" (to GS, 27 Sep 1849). The shares were sold in 1853. One result of Hudson's dominance of the early development of rail was his favoring York over the more logical central Northern town of Leeds, resulting in a distortion which had repercussions that can be seen to this day.

Yorke, Hester: wife of Hiram Yorke in *Shirley*. She is a large, gloomy, censorious woman who goes around enveloped in "the sort of voluntary, exemplary cloud and burden people ever carry who deem it their duty to be gloomy" (ch. 9). She is suspicious of very nearly the whole world, and holds that her own views and ways of doing things are the only sensible and respectable views and ways, and that variations from them show moral backsliding – an attitude she shares with Hortense Moore, one person she manages to get along with. Her temper makes for unhappy relations with her own children.

The model for this character is agreed to be Ann, wife of Joshua Taylor, mother of Charlotte's friend Mary Taylor.

Yorke, Hiram: manufacturer in *Shirley*. A forthright, opinionated, yet compassionate man who, in spite of a nature that does not easily brook opposition, manages his relations with his workers much better than most of his fellow mill-owners. He is a cultivated and well-read man who has traveled on the Continent and acquired works of art. His speech varies between broad Yorkshire, which he prefers, and standard English. His political views are radical and idiosyncratic, which makes him something of an outsider in Briarfield. Though he is generally presented as an original, a man of singular uprightness and insight, he is not above counseling Robert Moore to marry Shirley (ch. 9) – an incident which may have led to Mary Taylor's judgment that, as a portrait of her father, Mr Yorke was "not honest enough. It was from my father I learnt not to marry for money nor to tolerate any one who did . . ." (to CB, 13 Aug 1850). Though Yorke and his family are introduced to the reader at great length (chs 4 & 9) they have singularly little to do as the story progresses, and almost no influence on its development.

The picture of Hiram Yorke is agreed to be based in Joshua Taylor, Mary Taylor's father.

Yorke, Jessy: younger daughter of the Yorkes, a girl of "piquant face, engaging prattle, and winning ways" (ch. 9). Charlotte Brontë breaks into the story even as she introduces Jessy to talk of the foreign grave that was the lot of the original of Jessy, Martha Taylor.

Yorke, Mark: second son of Hiram Yorke in *Shirley* – a "bonnie-looking boy," but with a dry and cutting way of giving his opinions and a joyless attitude to life. Charlotte

Brontë says of him that "His body is now fourteen years of age, but his soul is already thirty" (ch. 9).

He was based on Mary Taylor's brother John, whose nephew Edward commented, in annotating *Shirley*, that Charlotte Brontë's likeness was "A very fair description," adding: "Very phlegmatic as I knew him."

Yorke, Martin: youngest son of Hiram Yorke in *Shirley*. He is not handsome, but he will "make himself handsome" (ch. 9). He is a bright, original boy, and the one who is not afraid of his own feelings. He is given an important role in the maneuverings at the end of the novel around the sickbed of Robert Moore (chs. 32–5).

Martin was based on Mary Taylor's brother Joe, the one Charlotte Brontë knew best. Her feelings for him and his wife veered between wary affection and exasperation.

Yorke, Matthew: the eldest son of Hiram Yorke in *Shirley*. The description of him in ch. 9 emphasizes his dangerous, volcanic nature, the care his parents take to propitiate him, the "sinister" side to him that seems to prefigure the emergence of a tyrant. Charlotte Brontë compares him to "an Italian stiletto in a sheath of British workmanship." He plays little part in the action, perhaps because Charlotte Brontë had least to do with Joshua Taylor III, Mary's eldest brother on whom the portrait is based.

Yorke, Rose: elder daughter of Hiram Yorke, and 12 at the start of *Shirley*. She is a still, stubborn girl whose life is in her mind, "thick-sown with the germs of ideas her mother never knew" (ch. 9). Though Rose does not play an important part in the story, she is prominent in ch. 23.

Rose is based on Charlotte's friend Mary Taylor. "What a little lump of perfection you've made me!" she commented (letter of 13 Aug 1850).

Yorkshire Gazette: newspaper edited by James Lancelot Foster, in which Branwell published five poems in 1845. Only two of these ("The Emigrant" I & II) were recent compositions.

See also York

Yorkshire Penny Bank: founded in 1859, with Patrick as the first president of the Haworth branch. It took over the premises of the Haworth Mechanics' Institute in 1894, and the first Brontë Museum was located on its first floor from 1895 to 1928.

Young Street, Kensington: no. 13 was the home of Thackeray in 1850, when he invited Charlotte to what turned out to be a disastrous dinner party with literary notables on 12 June of that year.

Z

Z—, M. (no first name given): a Parisian academician who attends the de Bassompierres' party in ch. 27 of *Villette*. He is a courtly man who draws out Paulina's best qualities in conversation.

Zamorna, Duke of, a.k.a. Marquis of Douro, King of Angria, Arthur Augustus Adrian Wellesley: the young Douro of the early parts of the Glasstown saga is a supremely beautiful youth with every talent (especially poetry) and every virtue – a creature, in short, about as close to real life as Lord Peter Wimsey. As Charlotte realizes the limitations of this sort of figure she sees him more and more through the cynically reductive eyes of Lord Charles Wellesley, his brother, who has become an all-purpose literary man and jobbing journalist. We gradually see another side to this paragon of a brother, in particular his tendency toward absolutism in politics and war: "I cannot submit to act an under part in any enterprise" he tells Ned Laury (EW, v. 2, pt 1, p. 26) and in "Arthuriana" he declares he could not "*follow him,* [Ellrington] even to heaven" (EW, v. 2, pt 1, p. 259). When we come to see his married life with Marian Hume we see a similar principle at work in the family, and in "The Secret" (EW, v. 2, pt 1, p. 276) he tells his wife "I ought to reign paramount." These tendencies are underlined in "A Leaf from an Unopened Volume" in which Charlotte sets her story in the future (1858) but foresees events still later than that, when the Emperor Adrian's eldest son and successor was, with his wife, to descend by the "path of blood and mourning . . . to their untimely grave," in his case after decapitation by a "remorseless regicide" (EW, v. 2, pt 1, p. 359). The kinship of the Wellesley dynasty to the French Bourbons and Zamorna's to the Sun King need no further underlining.

The sexual side of the Emperor's self-confessed mastery develops with Charlotte's own growing understanding of sexual politics. His absolutist tendency makes itself felt in the need for total obedience and an almost religious adoration. This he gets from

Mina Laury, who understands and accepts the consequences for herself but does not consider the consequences for him: that unquestioning worship feeds and fuels the need for it in him, making him totally amoral and obsessed with his own self-image as a glorious creature above ordinary moral codes.

His wives Marian Hume and Mary Percy also center their lives around his smiles and frowns but, unlike Mina, they cannot accept that they share their husband with other women. This results in many of the traditional scrapes of the unfaithful husband, so that Zamorna is from time to time reduced to a comic figure, desperately lying and improvising his way out of trouble, for example when his wife arrives at Mina Laury's country hideaway. After Zamorna's return from exile Charlotte has grasped that her earlier treatment of him sprang from an adolescent moral obliquity, and by the time of "Caroline Vernon" and her child-like determination to become Zamorna's mistress (a determination he goes along with) he is being treated with a wry cynicism, almost as a pathological case. We are by then a long way from Charlotte's apostrophe in an "interesting but chaotic" poem of January 1836 in which she tries to explain what the Angrian saga has meant to her: "Shake hands, Zamorna! God or man" (see PCB, pp. 295, 410). Zamorna has grown middle-aged, but he has not grown up. He can be seen for what he is: not quite a tin-pot dictator, not quite squalid, but headed in those directions – very definitely man rather than god.

See also Juvenilia; "Mina Laury"; "Caroline Vernon"

Zenobia, Countess of Northangerland a.k.a. Countess of Ellrington, Lady Zenobia Ellrington: long-term third wife of Northangerland. In Branwell's "The Pirate" she, along with her father and brothers, is captured by Rogue in his pirate-king persona. She is so attracted to him that she marries him and becomes one of the means by which he re-enters Verdopolitan polite society. Zenobia is immensely learned, especially in classical languages, and she runs the principal *salon* in Glasstown/Verdopolis. She is also passionate and willful, and loves simultaneously Northangerland and Zamorna, a particularly dangerous balancing act. For much of the time she sits around looking sexy and intellectual, but in the course of the saga she develops as a determined, vivid character, frequently enraged or upbraiding her husband, or scheming with or against him. However, she is given little to do that takes forward any story line: she just conspires and gains accretions of embonpoint. In later sections of the saga she is separated from her husband by the failure of his monstrous ambitions, and his being in hiding or on the run. However, the reconciliation scene between them is notably well-handled, with the ageing Northangerland apparently (or perhaps feigning to be) near to death and coming back to his natural mate. She admits, "It's because you're what you are that I've loved you" (WPBB, v. 3, p. 166). She is usually described as raven-haired, stately, "high and haughty" and "freezingly exclusive" (WPBB, v. 1, p. 252). Captain Bud's description of her "in her usual attire of a crimson robe and black plumes" (EW, v. 1, p. 306) suggests the well-known portrait by Lawrence of George IV's queen Caroline.

See also Northangerland

Zéphyrine, Mlle (no first name given): one of three teachers at Mlle Reuter's school who are of French extraction. She is described in ch. 12 of *The Professor* as more distinguished in appearance than the other two, but a coquette, and "perfidious, mercenary, and dry-hearted."

Zillah (no surname given): housekeeper at Wuthering Heights during much of Heathcliff's tenure as master. A narrower, less sympathetic woman than Nelly Dean, she has moments of compassion and good will, but they cannot be relied on.

Zoological Gardens: the secretary of the Society sent Charlotte a ticket of admission to the Society's gardens (now the London Zoo) in Regent's Park, and Charlotte wrote to her father (4 June 1850) with a detailed account of what she had seen, including "strange ducks and water-fowl which seem very happy and comfortable" and "some great Ceylon toads not much smaller than Flossy."

Bibliography

Primary Sources

Brontë, Anne: *Agnes Grey*, ed. Angeline Goreau. London, Penguin, 1988.

Brontë, Anne: *Agnes Grey*, ed. Robert Inglesfield and Hilda Marsden. Oxford, Oxford University Press, 1988.

Brontë, Anne: *The Poems of Anne Brontë: A new text and commentary*, ed. Edward Chitham. London, Macmillan, 1979.

Brontë, Anne: *The Tenant of Wildfell Hall*, ed. G. D. Hargreaves. Harmondsworth, UK, Penguin, 1979.

Brontë, Anne: *The Tenant of Wildfell Hall*, ed. Herbert Rosengarten. Oxford, Clarendon Press, 1992.

Brontë, Branwell: *The Hand of the Arch-Sinner: Two Angrian chronicles*, ed. Robert G. Collins. Oxford, Clarendon Press, 1993.

Brontë, Branwell: *The Poems of Patrick Branwell Brontë*, ed. Tom Winnifrith. Oxford, Basil Blackwell, 1983.

Brontë, Branwell: *The Works of Patrick Branwell Brontë*, 3 volumes, ed. Victor A. Neufeldt. New York, Garland, 1997, 1999.

Brontë, Charlotte: *Ashworth: An unfinished novel by Charlotte Brontë*, ed. Melodie Monahan. *Studies in Philology*, vol. LXXX, no. 4, 1983.

Brontë, Charlotte: *An Edition of the Early Writings of Charlotte Brontë*, ed. Christine Alexander, v. l The Glass Town Saga 1826–1832. Oxford, Blackwell, 1987.

Brontë, Charlotte: *An Edition of the Early Writings of Charlotte Brontë*, ed. Christine Alexander, v. 2 The Rise of Angria 1833–1835. Part 1: 1833–1834; Part 2: 1834–35. Oxford, Blackwell, 1991.

Brontë, Charlotte: *Five Novelettes: Passing Events, Julia, Mina Laury, Captain Henry Hastings, Caroline Vernon,* transcribed from the original manuscripts and ed. Winifred Gerin. London, Folio Press, 1971.

Brontë, Charlotte: *Jane Eyre*, ed. and intro. Margaret Smith. London, Oxford University Press, 1976.

Brontë, Charlotte: *Juvenilia, 1829–1835*, ed. Juliet Barker. London, Penguin, 1996.

Brontë, Charlotte: *The Letters of Charlotte Brontë: With a selection of letters by family and friends*, ed. Margaret Smith, v. 1 1829–1847; v. 2 1848–51, v. 3 1852–55. Oxford, Clarendon Press, 1995, 2000, 2004.

Brontë, Charlotte: *The Poems of Charlotte Brontë: A new annotated and enlarged edition of the Shakespeare Head Brontë*, ed. Tom Winnifrith. Oxford, Blackwell, 1984.

Brontë, Charlotte: *The Professor*, ed. Heather Glen. London, Penguin, 1989.

Brontë Charlotte: *The Professor*, ed. Margaret Smith and Herbert Rosengarten. Oxford, Oxford University Press, 1987.

Brontë, Charlotte: *Shirley*, ed. Andrew and Judith Hook. Harmondsworth, UK, Penguin, 1974.

Brontë, Charlotte: *Shirley*, ed. Herbert Rosengarten and Margaret Smith, Oxford, Oxford University Press, 1979.

Brontë, Charlotte: *Tales of Angria*, ed. Heather Glen. London, Penguin, 2006.

Brontë, Charlotte: *Unfinished Novels*. Stroud, UK, Alan Sutton Pocket Classics, 1993.

Brontë, Charlotte: *Villette*, ed. Mark Lilly. Harmondsworth, UK, Penguin, 1979.

Brontë, Charlotte and Emily: *The Belgian Essays*, ed. and trans. Sue Lonoff, New Haven, CT, Yale University Press, 1996.

Brontë, Emily: *The Complete Poems*, ed. Janet Gezari. London, Penguin Classics, 1992.

Brontë, Emily: *The Complete Poems of Emily Brontë*, ed. and intro. Philip Henderson. London, Folio Society, 1951.

Brontë, Emily: *The Poems of Emily Brontë*, ed. Derek Roper with Edward Chitham. Oxford, Clarendon Press, 1995.

Brontë, Emily: *Wuthering Heights*, ed. Ian Jack. Oxford, Oxford University Press, 1991.

Brontë, Patrick: *Brontëana: The Rev. Patrick Brontë, A. B., His collected works and life*, ed. J. Horsfall Turner. Bingley, UK, T. Harrison, 1898.

Brontë, Patrick: *The Letters of the Reverend Patrick Brontë*, ed. Dudley Green. Stroud, UK, Nonsuch, 2005.

Gaskell, Elizabeth: *Further Letters of Mrs Gaskell*, ed. John Chapple and Alan Shelston. Manchester, Manchester University Press, 2000.

Gaskell, Elizabeth: *The Letters of Mrs Gaskell.* ed. J. A. V. Chapple and Arthur Pollard. Manchester, Manchester University Press, 1966.

Nicholls, Arthur Bell: *Dear Martha: The letters of Arthur Bell Nicholls to Martha Brown*, ed. Geoffrey Palmer. Haworth, Brontë Society, 2004.

Wise, Thomas J. and Symington, John A. (eds.): *The Brontës, Their Lives, Friendships and Correspondence*. Oxford, Blackwell, 1933, 4 vols. Reprinted in two vols. 1980. Part of the Shakespeare Head Brontë.

Secondary Sources

Alexander, Christine: *A Bibliography of the Manuscripts of Charlotte Brontë*. Haworth, The Brontë Society, 1982.

Alexander, Christine: *The Early Writings of Charlotte Brontë*. Oxford, Blackwell, 1983.

Alexander, Christine and Sellers, Jane: *The Art of the Brontës*. Cambridge, UK, Cambridge University Press, 1995.

Alexander, Christine and Smith, Margaret: *The Oxford Companion to the Brontës*. Oxford, Oxford University Press 2003.

Allott, Miriam: *Charlotte Brontë: Jane Eyre and Villette*. Casebook Series. London, Macmillan, 1973.

Barker, Juliet: *The Brontës*. London, Weidenfeld & Nicolson, 1994.

Barnard, Robert: *Emily Brontë*. London, British Library, 2000.

Bellamy, Joan: *"More Precious than Rubies": Mary Taylor: friend of Charlotte Brontë, strong-minded woman*. Beverley, UK: Highgate Publications, 2002.

Chadwick, Ellis H.: *In the Footsteps of the Brontës*. London, Pitman, 1914.

Chitham, Edward: *The Birth of Wuthering Heights*. Basingstoke, UK, Palgrave, 1998.

Chitham, Edward: *A Brontë Family Chronology*. Basingstoke, UK, Palgrave Macmillan, 2003.

Chitham, Edward: *The Brontës' Irish Background*. London, Macmillan, 1986.

Chitham, Edward: *A Life of Anne Brontë*. Oxford, Blackwell, 1991.

Chitham, Edward: *A Life of Emily Brontë*. Oxford, Blackwell, 1987.

Chitham, Edward and Winnifrith, Tom: *Brontë Facts and Brontë Problems*. London, Macmillan, 1983.

Cochrane, Margaret and Robert: *My Dear Boy: The life of Arthur Bell Nicholls, B. A., husband of Charlotte Brontë*. Beverley, UK: Highgate Publications, 1999.

Davies, Stevie: *Emily Brontë: Heretic*. London, The Women's Press, 1994.

Delafield, E. M. (ed.): *The Brontës: Their lives recorded by their contemporaries*. London, Hogarth Press, 1935.

Dinsdale, Ann and White, Kathryn: *Family and Friends: The Brontës' social circle*. Haworth, The Brontë Society, 1994.

Du Maurier, Daphne: *The Infernal World of Branwell Brontë*. Harmondsworth, UK, Penguin, 1960.

Emsley, Kenneth: *Historic Haworth Today*, Bradford, UK, City of Bradford Arts, Museums & Libraries Division, 1995.

Ferrett, Mabel: *The Taylors of the Red House*. Huddersfield, UK, Kirklees Leisure Services, 1987.

Fraser, Rebecca: *Charlotte Brontë*. London, Methuen, 1988.

Gaskell, Elizabeth: *The Life of Charlotte Brontë*. London, Smith, Elder, 1857.

Gerin, Winifred: *Anne Brontë*. London, Allen Lane, 1959.

Gerin, Winifred: *Branwell Brontë*. London, Nelson, 1961.

Gerin, Winifred: *Charlotte Brontë: The evolution of genius*. London, Oxford University Press, 1969.

Gerin, Winifred: *Emily Brontë: A biography*. Oxford, Clarendon Press, 1971.

Glen, Heather (ed.): *The Cambridge Companion to the Brontës*. Cambridge, UK, Cambridge University Press, 2002.

Gordon, Lyndall: *Charlotte Brontë: A passionate life*. London, Chatto & Windus, 1994.

Hanson, Lawrence and K. M.: *The Four Brontës*. London, Oxford University Press, 1949.

Hewish, John: *Emily Brontë*. London, Macmillan, 1969.

Hopkins, Annette B.: *The Father of the Brontës*. Baltimore, MD, The Johns Hopkins University Press, 1953.

Johnson, Edgar: *Charles Dickens*, 2 vols. London, Gollancz, 1953.

Kellett, Jocelyn: *Haworth Parsonage*. Haworth, The Brontë Society, 1977.

Lemon, Charles (ed.): *Classics of Brontë Scholarship*. Haworth, The Brontë Society, 1999.

Lemon, Charles (ed.): *Early Visitors to Haworth*. Haworth, The Brontë Society, 1996.

Leyland, Francis A.: *The Brontë Family: With special reference to Patrick Branwell Brontë*, 2 vols. London, Hurst & Blackett, 1886.

Lock, John and Dixon, Canon W. T.: *A Man of Sorrow: The life. letters and times of the Rev. Patrick Brontë. 1777–1861*. London, Ian Hodgkins, 1979.

MacKay, Angus M.: *The Brontës. Fact and fiction*. London, Service & Paton, 1897.

Martineau, Harriet: *Selected Letters*, ed. Valerie Sanders. Oxford, Clarendon Press, 1990.

Miller, Mrs F. Fenwick: *Harriet Martineau*. London, W. H. Allen, 1884.

Miller, Lucasta: *The Brontë Myth*. London, Cape, 2001.

Neufeldt, Victor (ed.): *Bibliography of the Manuscripts of Patrick Branwell Brontë*. New York & London, Garland, 1993.

Newsam, William Cartwright: *The Poets of Yorkshire* (completed by John Holland). London, Groombridge and Sons, 1845.

O'Neill, Jane: *The World of the Brontës*. London, Carlton Books, 1997.

Pendered, Mary L.: *John Martin, Painter*. London, Hurst & Blackett, 1923.

Petit, Jean-Pierre: *Emily Brontë. A Critical Anthology*. Harmondsworth, UK, Penguin, 1973.

Ratchford, Fanny E: *The Brontës' Web of Childhood*. London, Oxford University Press, 1941.

Raymond, Ernest: *In the Steps of the Brontës*. London, Rich & Cowan repr., 1952.

Ruijssenaars, Eric: *Charlotte Brontë's Promised Land*. Haworth, The Brontë Society, 2000.

Ruijssenaars, Eric: *The Pensionnat Revisited*. Leiden, Dutch Archives, 2003.

Reid, T. Wemyss: *Charlotte Brontë. A monograph*. London, Macmillan, 1877.

Robinson, A. Mary F.: *Emily Brontë*, 2nd edn. London, W. H. Allen, 1889.

Sanger, C. P.: *The Structure of Wuthering Heights. Hogarth Essays 19*, London, Hogarth Press, 1926.

Selleck, R. J. W.: *James Kay-Shuttleworth: Journey of an Outsider*. Ilford, UK, The Woburn Press, 1994.

Shorter, Clement: *The Brontës and their Circle*. London, Dent, 1896.

Smurthwaite, John: *The Life of John Alexander Symington, Bibliographer and Librarian. 1887–1961: A bookman's rise and fall*. Lewiston, NY, Edwin Mellen Press, 1995.

Spark, Muriel and Stanford, Derek: *Emily Brontë*. London, Peter Owen, 1953.

Steed, Michael: *A Brontë Diary*. Clapham, UK, Dalesmans Books, 1990.

Stell, Christopher: *An Inventory of Nonconformist Chapels and Meeting Houses in the North of England*. London, HMSO, 1994.

Stevens, Joan (ed.): *Mary Taylor: Friend of Charlotte Brontë*. Dunedin, Auckland University Press, 1972.

Sutherland, John: *The Longman Companion to Victorian Fiction*, Harlow, UK, Longman, 1988.

Turner, J. Horsfall: *Halifax Books and Authors*, Brighouse, UK, privately printed, 1906.

Wallace, Robert K.: *Emily Brontë and Beethoven*. Athens, University of Georgia Press, 1986.

White, W. H.: *Directory and Topography of the Borough of Leeds and the whole of the West Riding of Yorkshire*. Sheffield, 1842.

Whitehead, Barbara: *Charlotte Brontë and her "Dearest Nell": The story of a friendship*. Otley, UK, Smith Settle, 1993.

Wilks, Brian: *The Brontës*. London, Hamlyn, 1975.

Wilks, Brian: *Charlotte in Love: The courtship and marriage of Charlotte Bronte*. London, Michael O'Mara, 1998.

Winnifrith, Tom: *The Brontës and their Background: Romance and reality*. New York, Barnes & Noble, 1973.

Wright, Dr William: *The Brontës in Ireland*, 2nd edn. London, Hodder & Stoughton, 1893.

Wroot, Herbert E.: *Persons and Places: Sources of Charlotte Brontë's novels*, Shipley, UK, The Caxton Press, 1935 (Brontë Society Publications, Supplementary pt. no. 4 of vol. 8).